Technical Change and Economic Theory

AOMU

Economics

D0543914

This book has been edited and compiled by MERIT and is issued as IFIAS research series number 6.

Other books in the IFIAS research series are:

Hallsworth, E. (1987)
The Anatomy, Physiology and Psychology of Erosion
John Wiley, Chichester

Koudstaal, R. (1987)
Water Quality Management Plan, North Sea: Framework for Analysis
Balkema, Rotterdam

Dekker, L., Bower, B. and R. Koudstaal (1987)
Management of Toxic Chemicals in an International Setting: A Case Study of Cadmium in the North Sea
Balkema, Rotterdam

Kristensen, T. and J. Paludan (1988)
The Earth's Fragile Systems: Perspectives on Global Change
Westview Press, Boulder

Stren, R. and R. White (1988)
Urban Reform in African Cities: Managing Rapid Urban Growth
Westview Press, Boulder

Maastricht Economic
Research Institute on
Innovation and Technology

The International
Federation of Institutes
for Advanced Study

Technical Change and Economic Theory

Edited by

Giovanni Dosi
Christopher Freeman
Richard Nelson
Gerald Silverberg
Luc Soete

Pinter Publishers, London and New York

© The contributors, 1988

First published in Great Britain in 1988,
Reprinted in 1990 by
Pinter Publishers Limited
25 Floral Street, London WC2E 9DS

British Library Cataloguing in Publication Data

A CIP catalogue record for this book is available from the British Library

ISBN 0 86187 949 X (Hardback)
ISBN 0 86187 894 9 (Paperback)

Library of Congress Cataloging-in-Publication Data

Technical change and economic theory/edited by G. Dosi . . . [et al.].
p.   cm.
   Bibliography: p.
   Includes index.
   ISBN 0-86187-949-X
   ISBN 0-86187-894-9
   1. Technological innovations—Economic aspects. 2. Economics.
I. Dosi, Giovanni, 1953–
HC70.T4T4 1988
338'.06—dc19   88-17844
                                                                                   CIP

Typeset by Florencetype Ltd, Kewstoke, Avon; and Unicus, Horsham
Printed by: SRP, Exeter

Contents

Preface

This book emerged out of the growing dissatisfaction felt by a number of economists and non-economists alike with the way technical change has been and continues to be treated in mainstream economics. Each one of us, in his own way, had been involved in critical assessments of the way orthodox economic theory deals with 'change'. Each one of us had come to the conclusion that any analysis of change which ignored the fundamental role and special character of technical change, even in the very short run, could not be valid. The time seemed ripe to bring together in a coherent framework a number of authors working in related directions to formulate a systematic critique of orthodox economic theory and to sketch out the common elements of a first, alternative theory on the role of technical change in microeconomic behaviour, processes of structural change and macroeconomic transformation of the economic system. This book presents such a first attempt.

This ambitious aim received a major boost when the International Federation of Institutes for Advanced Study (IFIAS) decided to support our proposal within the framework of their project 'Rethinking Economic Theory'. With the support of Henryk Kierzkowski, the proposal was given further shape and the list of contributors enlarged. We are particularly grateful to him for his early involvement and support. The active support of IFIAS during the whole project is gratefully acknowledged. With IFIAS, we wish to express appreciation for financial support to the Salen and Wallenberg Foundations, Stockholm, to the Rockefeller Brothers Fund, New York, to the MacArthur Foundation, Chicago and to the Exxon Educational Foundation, New York. Financial support in the final phases of the project was also provided by the newly created Maastricht Economic Research Institute on Innovation and Technology (MERIT) and a grant from the Dutch Ministry of Economic Affairs.

The writing of this book itself was a long undertaking, as a glance at its length and the number of contributors and editors will confirm. The project began with an informal meeting of potential authors in Venice in March 1986. First drafts of most of the final contributions were discussed by the authors at a workshop in Lewes, England, in October 1986. We are very grateful to the Science Policy Research Unit of the University of Sussex, and in particular to Linda Gardiner for her organisational support. In May 1987 a second conference was organised in Maastricht, where a somewhat enlarged circle of authors presented revised versions of their contributions. The final painstaking process of editing the various chapters also took place in Maastricht, thanks to the organisational support of MERIT.

We are grateful to the participants at these various meetings for their comments, advice and criticism. In particular, we would like to thank Tibor Barna, Luigi Pasinetti, Keith Pavitt, Christopher Saunders and Nick von Tunzelmann for their willingness to contribute from outside the immediate circle of authors to the formative process leading to this book.

Last but not least, we wish to express our gratitude and admiration to Wilma Coenegrachts who typed, edited, converted, re-edited and re-converted with infatigable good spirits these 650 pages.

The Editors,
Maastricht, 7 March 1988

Part I Introduction

1 Introduction*

Christopher Freeman
Science Policy Research Unit, University of Sussex, Brighton and
MERIT, State University of Limburg, Maastricht

Main objectives and epistemological considerations

When Jewkes, Sawers and Stillerman (1956) wrote their classic (though still controversial) study, *The Sources of Invention*, they commented on the neglect of technical change by most of the economics profession and suggested three reasons for this neglect. First, they suggested that economists were generally ignorant of science and technology and felt unprepared to venture into this unknown territory. Secondly, there were very few statistics to guide them. Finally, ever since the Great Depression of the 1930s they had been mainly preoccupied with problems of cyclical fluctuations in the economy and of the unemployment associated with these fluctuations. They were simply too busy with other things to pay much attention to technical change.

In this book we attempt to show that the first two problems can be at least partially overcome and indeed Jewkes and his colleagues already demonstrated this in their own work. What is of extraordinary interest here is the third explanation given by Jewkes *et al*. It is particularly revealing because, quite unconsciously, they show that even some of those economists who were prepared to make a considerable effort to do theoretical and empirical work in the area of technical change regarded this as something totally separate from the study of cyclical fluctuations in the economy.

We have only to turn to Schumpeter's (1939) *Business Cycles* to see the gulf which separates his work from this view. For Schumpeter, as for us, technical innovation is not a separate phenomenon, but is on the contrary a crucial factor in the explanation of business cycles and the dynamics of economic growth generally (Chapter 3).

This book is an exploration of a new approach to economic theory, capable of incorporating technical and institutional change into the mainstream of economic analysis and policy-making, rather than treating it as part of the rag-bag of 'residual' or 'exogenous' factors. This leads us not just to a critique of mainstream economic theory, but also to an attempt at an alternative formulation of some of the main issues. It is not more than a first attempt but the somewhat ambitious aim is to analyse in depth the role

* I am grateful to my co-authors for helpful suggestions and particularly to Giovanni Dosi and Norman Clark.

of technological change in relation to microeconomic behaviour, adjustment processes and macroeconomic patterns of transformation of the economic system.

We suggest some possible explanations and interpretive hypotheses, which we shall attempt to show fit the historical evidence rather better than mainstream neo-classical theory. We can summarise the main features of our approach as follows:

(a) Technical change is a fundamental force in shaping the patterns of transformation of the economy.
(b) There are some mechanisms of *dynamic adjustment* which are radically different in nature from those allocative mechanisms postulated by traditional theory.
(c) These mechanisms have to do both with technical change and institutional change or the lack of it. As regards the former, we suggest it is both disequilibrating—and a source of *order* for the directions of change and the 'dynamic adjustment processes', as new technologies diffuse through the national and international economies. Paradoxically, despite its fluctuations and crises the world is actually more stable and better ordered than could be deduced from prevailing economic theory.
(d) The socio-institutional framework always influences and may sometimes facilitate and sometimes retard processes of technical and structural change, coordination and dynamic adjustment. Such acceleration and retardation effects relate not simply to market 'imperfections', but to the nature of the markets themselves, and to the behaviour of agents (that is, institutions are an inseparable part of the way the markets work).

These propositions are hardly surprising for a non-economist or for those economists acquainted with Schumpeter. Neither would they be denied by most neo-classical economists. However, whilst nominally accepting the importance of technical and institutional change, mainstream theory and most modelling have in practice divorced economics from these crucially important processes of change, relegating them to the status of 'residual factors' or 'exogenous shocks' even though they were at one time subsumed within the general framework of classical 'political economy'. The various 'growth accounting' exercises, even after allowing for an entire Kamasutra of variables, generally remain with a big unexplained 'residual' (e.g. Denison, 1962) and fail to deal with the complementarities and interactions of these variables (Nelson, 1981). In general they are only a pale shadow of the growth theories of classical economics. For the classical economists it was quite natural to discuss technical and institutional change as an integral part of a general theory of economic growth and development.

In this introductory chapter we first of all raise some fundamental epistemological issues which are briefly discussed. We then consider

Schumpeter's heroic attempt to provide an alternative theory of economic development and why in our view it was not enough. Finally we outline the structure of the book and the way in which we propose to tackle our difficult and challenging objective.

Some basic epistemological issues

All of those contributing to this book have been actively involved in empirical research on technical innovation and institutional change in many different countries. The results of this empirical research are presented in the book. They cannot be easily reconciled with some of the central assumptions of equilibrium theory and mainstream economics. All of us have come to feel that the main weakness of this theory has been inadequate attention to social learning processes, particularly technological accumulation and the institutions affecting these processes.

In its anxiety to be the 'theoretical physics of social sciences' and to achieve logical elegance and mathematical formalisation, neo-classical economics elaborated and refined quantitative equilibrium analysis and mathematical models, which, although useful as a modelling exercise on highly restrictive assumptions, neglected some of the crucial elements involved in the long-term behaviour of the system. They therefore appeared to non-economists and to other social scientists to be concerned with the endless elaboration and refinement of assumptions which lacked both realism in relation to certain fundamental features of the system's behaviour and rigorous falsifiability of the predictions derived from the models.

It is of course far from easy to remedy these weaknesses and one of the main reasons that the mainstream neo-classical paradigm continues to exert such enormous influence, despite its acknowledged flaws, is the apparent lack of any satisfactory alternative which could offer anything approaching the same power and rigour.

However, the difficulty of developing an alternative and more satisfactory theory should not deter efforts in this direction for anyone who is convinced that the mainstream theory is increasingly in conflict with much empirical evidence. We certainly do not claim to have developed a completely satisfactory alternative to the dominant theory, only to have taken a number of steps in the direction which all of us must ultimately take if we are to develop such a theory and appropriate models. We are encouraged in this effort not only by a great deal of work which has already been done both by 'heretics' such as Schumpeter and by those working within the neo-classical tradition, but also by parallel developments within other branches of the social and natural sciences.

It would of course be as dangerous for economic theory simply to adopt wholesale the concepts and methodology of biology as of physics. However, *all* the natural and social sciences face certain methodological problems in modelling the evolution of complex systems once the terrain of Newtonian reductionism is left behind.

This attempt of course raises the most fundamental epistemological issues (these are discussed more fully in Sections II and III). Our approach has much in common with that of the classical political economists, as well as with the more recent tradition of the institutional and 'evolutionary' economists. In the words of Wilbur and Harrison (1978), it is 'holistic, systemic and evolutionary' (p. 71): *holistic* in the sense both that the whole shows behaviour which cannot be deduced merely by aggregating that of its constituent parts *and* that the parts themselves cannot be individually understood separately from the relationships they maintain with each other to make up the whole; *systemic* and *evolutionary* in the sense that the socio-economic system under investigation is conceived of as always in a state of flux and qualitative change, as its constituent elements alter their behaviour in relationship to each other and to the extra-systemic environment. In this work we have of course built on the pioneering contribution of Nelson and Winter (1982) in their evolutionary theory of economic change.

A satisfactory theory should certainly be one which conforms more closely to the available empirical evidence; it should also (like the other social sciences) take more account of the emergence of qualitatively new features of the system's behaviour and of the capacity of human agents to falsify predictions based on past experience. Greater humility is important as well as greater realism. The vitally important contribution of economists to policy debates and formation will not be diminished if it is more modest in its claims.

Many of the problems with the prevailing neo-classical orthodoxy have of course been raised by those working within the paradigm itself. Most of the criticisms raised in this book are familiar to its leading practitioners and indeed for many years some of them have felt the same uneasiness as we ourselves have felt with this framework. For example, Hahn (1987), in an interesting paper on 'Information Dynamics and Equilibrium', takes up the problem of imperfect information—'. . .agents cannot act on information which they do not have'—and more general problems of dynamic theory. He concludes:

Current economic theory by and large avoids dynamics at least non-equilibrium dynamics. This has the virtue that it allows orderly argument and conclusion. *But this order is bought at too high a price. Moreover even then it is not quite as satisfactory as was once thought* [my italics, CF]. Once it was recognised that we must study sequence economies it also became urgent to include expectations in the description of the agent. To avoid some of the difficulties we have been through rational expectations were simply postulated . . . Even so, it was soon found that this postulate is mostly insufficient to yield determinate equilibria . . .
This has led us to suggest that dynamics should be viewed as a learning process both about demand conditions and the strategies of near competitors. Once again, when an equilibrium is defined relatively to such processes it seems that they are

indeterminate unless history—that is information—is explicitly modelled and known. The path of history is the outcome of individual decisions and in turn helps to fix the latter. This is really the main message: the information available to agents at any time is determined by the particular path followed. The economy could have followed a different path and generated quite different information. There is something essentially historical in a proper definition of equilibrium and of course in the dynamics itself.

This conclusion, with its emphasis on the importance of history and of learning processes, closely resembles some of the conclusions of Sections III and IV of our own book.

But even though some of the main contributors to General Equilibrium Theory are well aware of difficulties with the neo-classical approach (Hahn, 1984; Solow, 1985), many economists nevertheless believe that it is epistemologically progressive and can be extended and strengthened. They have generally preferred to attempt to handle their problems within the framework of the paradigm rather than make a radical break with it. This type of situation is familiar to historians of scientific thought. It is reminiscent of the story told by Nelson (1981) of the drunkard who looked for his key under the street lamp because it was the only clear spot although he knew he had lost it somewhere else. Despite its logical elegance and the extreme sophistication of many contemporary developments, its failure to address some of the crucial problems of technical and institutional change and its lack of historical perspective weaken its claims to represent a satisfactory theory of economic growth.

Why Schumpeter is not enough

Most economists, when they *do* consider technical change and the long-term dynamics of the system, turn to Schumpeter, and it is true that almost alone among major twentieth-century economists Joseph Schumpeter *did* attempt to place technical change at the heart of his system and did also address problems of social and institutional change. His work is certainly one of the major points of departure for this book.

Among the positive merits of Schumpeter's work were his consistent emphasis on innovation as the main source of dynamism in capitalist development, his sense of historical perspective, his recognition of the importance of the conceptual distinctions between invention, innovation and diffusion of innovations, and his recognition of the vital importance of the links between organisational, managerial, social and technical innovations. This led him, like other great economists (such as Smith, Mill and Marx), to a unified theory of the disparate social sciences and a general theory of global development.

However, he was only partially successful in his endeavour. He made rather poor use of economic statistics and, as he himself was at pains to emphasise, he only made the first attempt to open up some of the major problems. He paid little attention to peripheral areas or what would now be called the 'Third World'. Although he certainly stressed the role of technological competition, he did not really extend his analysis to the case of international trade, or international diffusion of technology. He never formalised his models, which may well have helped the richness of his theory but did not help the exploration of the coherence and consequences of his propositions.

Some economists, such as Almarin Phillips (1971), have distinguished 'two Schumpeters'—the young pre-war economist before the First World War emphasising the role of the entrepreneur and the small innovative enterprise, and the 'mature' Schumpeter stressing the advantages of the big monopolistic firm and the bureaucratised process of technical change. These differences may of course be partly explained by the way the world was changing during Schumpeter's lifetime and illustrate the great importance of studying qualitative change within the system. But by the same token, more than thirty years after Schumpeter's death, we must take account of the enormous changes in the world economy and in our knowledge about the process of technical change and economic development. Although he pioneered the study of the relationship between technological revolutions and long cycles of economic development, he did not really develop any satisfactory theory of depressions. Moreover, he had very little to say about government policies for industry, technology and science, or the relationship between universities, government institutions and industrial research and development.

Finally, on more theoretical grounds, it is hard to reconcile Schumpeter's view of innovation, economic dynamism, and partial monopolistic appropriation of technological advances with his other view that equilibrium could still be defined in Walrasian terms. In this respect, the task of analysing the relationship between the dynamic forces of the economic system (i.e. what makes it change) and its equilibrating mechanisms (what keeps it together) is still largely unfulfilled.

For all these reasons and others, although a constructive critique of Schumpeter is the starting point for much of our work, we have tried to go well beyond Schumpeter in many respects, and especially in our treatment of international development issues, international trade (Part VI), the dynamics of the science and technology system, the taxonomy of technical change, government policies for science and technology (Parts IV and V), and generally the role of institutions in regulating the macroeconomic system (Part II).

Structure of the book

This book has been written by a large group of authors from a dozen different countries. It has been a difficult undertaking and the editorial group has had major problems of coordination and integration. We felt that the gains from the pluralistic involvement of this wide group out-weighed the possible loss of that degree of coherence which can be achieved in a single-author book. Nevertheless, it is a complex book to read. For that reason we have provided brief editorial introductions to each of the six sections which follow. Here we outline the main themes of the book as a whole.

The chapters in Part II are intended to illustrate our basic ideas about technical and institutional change in relation to the long-term dynamic behaviour of the economic system, which have been briefly touched upon in this introduction.

This is followed in Part III with four chapters which return to some of the main problems of economic theory in attempting to formalise and model the behaviour of the system. Parts IV and V are concerned with the sources of invention and innovation in contemporary, industrialised, capitalist societies and the effectiveness of strategies and policies designed to promote technical innovation. Part IV deals with these problems at the level of the firm; Part V at the national level. The chapters in these sections are intended to provide a reasonably up-to-date account of the way in which the process of technical change actually takes place in advanced industrialised economies today. They are followed in Part VI by five chapters which take up the international dimensions and discuss inter-national trade, differences in growth rates, the problems of under-development and 'catching up' in world technology and the role of multinational enterprises in the international diffusion of technology. Finally, in Part VII we take up some of the problems of formal modelling of this complex process of innovation, diffusion of innovations and economic growth.

It is evident from this brief summary that our book is by no means comprehensive and leaves many big gaps in our analysis. For example, we do not address such fundamental problems as the change in patterns of consumer behaviour associated with waves of new technology (Pasinetti, 1981) or the theory of consumption more generally. Nor do we address the role of armaments and military policies in shaping technology and the behaviour of the economic system; nor even the issues of monetary and fiscal policy and the theory of money and banking. This is not because we think these issues are unimportant; on the contrary, all of us recognise that they are fundamental for any satisfactory general theory of economics. It is because we preferred to make a more limited contribution based upon our own special areas of competence. We do not claim to have developed a new General Theory, only to have shown the direction in which we must go to develop such a theory and to have taken a few steps down that road.

We hope also that those who work in the current mainstream of econ-omic theory and policy-making will still find something of value to their own work and will make some response to our challenge, whether within the existing paradigm or by striking out in new directions. But above all we hope that our book will serve to stimulate a new generation of researchers and students to tackle the many problems which remain for economics to regain its credibility as a discipline and to make a more valuable contribution to policy formation. For this reason we conclude the book with a brief 'policy-orientated research agenda' (Part VIII).

References

Denison, E. (1962), *The Sources of Economic Growth in the United States and the Alternatives Before Us*, London, Allen and Unwin.

Hahn, F. (1984), *Equilibrium and Macroeconomics*, Oxford, Basil Blackwell.

——— (1987), 'Information Dynamics and Equilibrium', paper to Conference of Scottish Economists, mimeo.

Jewkes, J., Sawers, D., and Stillerman, J. (1956), *The Sources of Invention*, London, Macmillan.

McCloskey, Donald N. (1985), *The Rhetoric of Economics*, Madison, University of Wisconsin Press.

Nelson, R. R. (1981), 'Research on Productivity Growth and Productivity Differences: Dead Ends and New Departures', *Journal of Economic Literature*.

Nelson, R. R. and Winter, S. G. (1982), *An Evolutionary Theory of Economic Change*, Cambridge, Mass., The Belknap Press of Harvard University Press.

Pasinetti, L. (1981), *Structural Change and Economic Growth: A Theoretical Essay on the Dynamics of the Wealth of Nations*, Cambridge, Cambridge University Press.

Phillips, A. (1971), *Technology and Market Structure*, Lexington, Mass., Lexington Books.

Schumpeter, J. A. (1939), *Business Cycles: A Theoretical, Historical and Statistical Analysis of the Capitalist Process*, New York, McGraw-Hill.

Solow, R.M. (1985), "Economic History and Economics", American Economic Review, Papers and Proceedings, vol. 75, no. 2, May 1985, pp. 328–331.

Wilbur, C. K. and Harrison, R. S. (1978), 'The methodological basis of institutional economics', *Journal of Economic Issues*, vol. XII, no. 1, pp. 68–89.

Part II Evolution, technology and institutions: a wider framework for economic analysis

Preface to Part II

Christopher Freeman
Science Policy Research Unit, University of Sussex, Brighton and MERIT, State University of Limburg, Maastricht

The introductory chapter has outlined the general structure of the book as a whole. But because of the size and complexity of the subject, we shall introduce each section of the book with a brief preface, indicating the scope of the subsequent chapters in that section and drawing out some of the main points which are essential for the flow of ideas in the book as a whole.

In this section Dosi and Orsenigo first introduce the general problem of accounting for the relatively ordered patterns of growth which have been a feature of industrialised capitalist economies for quite long periods—as in the quarter century after the Second World War. They reject the orthodox explanation of this 'dynamic stability' for reasons which have been touched on in the introduction and will be developed at greater length in Part III ('How well does established theory work?'). They are concerned with the inherent uncertainty associated with technical innovation and argue forcefully against any theory which assumes 'hyper-rationality' on the part of representative agents.

How then to account for dynamic stability? They suggest that the problem should be approached in two ways: on the one hand, by studying and understanding the regularities and patterns in the process of technical change itself; and, on the other hand, by recognising the role of institutions (including markets but not *only* markets) in regulating and stabilising the behaviour of the system. These two aspects of long-term dynamic stability are taken up in the two following chapters by Freeman and Perez (Chapter 3) and Boyer (Chapter 4).

Dosi and Orsenigo point out that despite the great diversity in the sources and consequences of technical change, it is not a purely random process. There *are* regularities in the pattern of technical change which have been analysed in empirical studies and which may account in part for the relatively stable patterns of growth. In particular they point to the existence of 'technological trajectories' and 'technological paradigms' which offer opportunities for profitable, innovative investment and growth of new markets over relatively long periods along rather well-defined paths of development and diffusion.

The notion of 'paradigms' and 'paradigm change' is at the heart of the chapter by Freeman and Perez on business cycles and investment behaviour. They observe that Keynes himself and representative neo-Keynesians, such as Samuelson, did not believe in the capacity of the self-adjusting market mechanism to equilibrate investment behaviour, and that a 'climate of confidence', 'animal spirits' and state intervention had to be invoked to achieve a sustained, full employment growth path. Then they examine the influence of technical change in generating a 'climate of confidence' which might sustain expansionary waves of investment, when business only 'pretends to itself' that it believes in the 'rational' *ex ante* calculations of future return on investment.

The Freeman–Perez chapter suggests that some new technologies, after a prolonged period of incubation and crystallisation, offer such a wide range of opportunities for new markets and profitable new investment that, when social and institutional conditions are favourable, entre-preneurs have sufficient confidence to embark on a prolonged wave of expansionary investment. They point out that Keynes himself once acknowledged the validity of this Schumpeterian explanation of major investment booms.

Their analysis is based on the idea of a 'techno-economic paradigm' first advanced by Carlota Perez. This differs from similar ideas advanced by Kuhn, Dosi and others in two ways. Most importantly her concept is one of a '*meta*-paradigm' — a dominant technological style whose 'common sense' and rules of thumb affect the entire economy. It thus corresponds most closely to Nelson and Winter's concept of a 'generalised natural trajectory' or 'technological regime' which dominates engineering and management decisions for several decades.

Secondly, its powerful influence throughout the system derives from a combination of technical *and* economic advantages (hence the expression 'techno-economic' paradigm). This point is an important one since it means that her concept recognises from the outset the influence of the economic selection environment in shaping and crystallising the new technology within the wide realm of the technically feasible. A 'techno-economic paradigm' is a cluster of interrelated technical, organisational and managerial innovations, whose advantages are to be found not only in a new range of products and systems, but most of all in the dynamics of the relative cost structure of all possible inputs to production. In each new paradigm a particular input or set of inputs may be described as the 'key factor' in that paradigm characterised by falling relative costs and universal availability. The contemporary change of paradigm may be seen as a shift from a technology based primarily on cheap inputs of energy to one predominantly based on cheap inputs of information derived from advances in microelectronic and telecommunication technology.

The Freeman–Perez conceptualisation has much in common with Schumpeter's theory of long cycles. It differs from that theory, however, in several ways. In the first place the notion of change of techno-economic paradigm is wider than Schumpeter's key radical innovations introduced at intervals of forty to sixty years. It recognises the pervasive effects of a change of technological style not just in a few motive branches of the economy but throughout the system. The process of structural change associated with the transition from one paradigm to another affects all industries and services.

Secondly, Perez has offered a more convincing explanation of the periods of deeper depression, which in Schumpeter's model were a pathological phenomenon, but in her model represent periods of 'mismatch' when the established social and institutional framework no longer corresponds to the potential of a new techno-economic paradigm. Structural crises of adjustment are thus periods of experiment and search and of political debate and conflict leading ultimately to a new mode of regulation for the system.

Clearly there are important points of correspondence between the Freeman–Perez model of the role of institutions and that of the French 'regulation' school described in Chapter 4. In this chapter Robert Boyer provides a lucid synthesis of the ideas developed over more than a decade by this group of French economists. (Because this literature is rather scattered and is still inadequately known outside France this chapter also includes a full bibliography of the school's publications.)

In their view it is institutions which provide the 'glue' which holds the system together and enables accumulation to proceed in a relatively ordered manner for quite long periods. Each particular 'regime of regulation' is designed to control and stabilise a particular phase of capitalist growth, differing in important respects from the preceding phase.

They define a 'mode of regulation' as

any set of rules and individual and collective behaviours which have the three following properties:

— to bring into compatibility possibly conflicting decentralised decisions without the necessity for individuals or even institutions to bear in mind the logic of the whole system;
— to control and conduct the prevailing accumulation mode;
— to reproduce the basic social relationships through a system of institutional forms historically determined.

They concentrate their analysis on the institutional forms governing five key features of the mode of regulation: monetary and credit relationships, the wage–labour nexus, the type of competition, the forms of state intervention, and the 'forms of adhesion' to the international regime. They show that all these institutional forms differ considerably between the regimes of early and mature 'competitive regulation' in the nineteenth century and 'monopolistic regulation' in the twentieth century. Their analysis of the 'monopolistic' (or 'Fordist') mode of regulation in the period since the Second World War is particularly well developed and they are able to use it as a basis for formal modelling of the economic system, as illustrated in the second chapter contributed by Robert Boyer to this book (Chapter 7).

To the reader it may appear that the ideas of Perez and of the French Regulation school are sufficiently complementary to offer scope for an original synthesis. The French regulation school, although acknow-ledging the importance of technical change, have paid relatively little attention to it, whilst Freeman–Perez have not developed so far their analysis of institutional forms or of aggregated formal models of the economy. Both chapters contain tables with suggestive tentative sketches of the historic succession of modes of regulation or paradigm change. But both point to the need for much historical research to flesh out these first approximations.

As Boyer points out in his chapter, historians have too often been reluctant to challenge the prevalent schools in economic theory, whether neo-classical or Marxist, whilst economists have too often tried to impose their theoretical preconceptions in all periods of history (as in the extreme example of 'Robinson Crusoe' theorising). A historical perspective is crucial for any research programme which seeks to understand technical and institutional change, but it must be one which recognises the impor-tance of *qualitative* change in the system.

This conclusion emerges with particular force from the final chapter in Part II by Peter Allen (Chapter 5). He puts the current debate about economic theory in a far wider context, affecting epistemological problems in all the natural and social sciences. This perspective is healthy for economists, since one of the problems, increasingly recognised in the profession, is the need for reintegrating economic theory with the other social sciences, as was considered quite normal by the classical economists. The chapters which have just been discussed and (from an entirely diffe-rent direction) the work of the 'New Institutional Economics' school are both indications of this need to reconstitute 'Political Economy' with a full recognition of the role of institutions and institutional change. A bridge to the physical sciences in the understanding of technical change is no less important.

Allen points out that all branches of science have been limited in their thinking and ambitions by the prolonged domination of a Newtonian mechanistic perspective, which hinders the analysis of *qualitative* change and evolutionary development. He points to new developments in physics, chemistry and biology, as well as the social sciences which are stimulat-ing the analysis and formal modelling of systems undergoing qualitative change:

The real message of the new concepts in science is that change and disequilibria are probably more natural than equilibrium and stasis. Those who can adapt and learn will survive. And this will depend on their 'creativity'.

The ideas advanced by Peter Allen in this chapter on 'self-organising evolutionary systems' are of the greatest importance for the subsequent parts of the book dealing with established theory (Part III), the behaviour of firms (Part IV), national systems of innovation (Part V), and formal modelling (Part VII).

2 Coordination and transformation: an overview of structures, behaviours and change in evolutionary environments*

Giovanni Dosi
Faculty of Statistics, University of Rome, Rome and SPRU, University of Sussex, Brighton

Luigi Orsenigo
Bocconi University, Milan, and
SPRU, University of Sussex, Brighton

Introduction

One of the common themes of all contributions to this book is *change*: change not only in the techniques of production and the characteristics of the product but also in the behaviours leading to new discoveries and their economic exploitation; in the general structure of economies and their performance—whether assessed in terms of employment, or income, international competitiveness, productivity, etc.; and, finally, in the mechanisms and institutions through which economies and societies coordinate the economic efforts of their agents, produce change and govern them. Of course, there are micro and macro dimensions to these processes of change. Individuals and/or organisations deviate from the 'normal way' of doing things; adjust to 'external' (environmental) changes; respond in 'creative', new and sometimes unexpected ways to competitive or conflictual challenges; or explore what they believe to be (rightly or wrongly) unexploited opportunities. In turn, individual and organisational behaviours, to different degrees and through different processes, are *selected*, penalised or rewarded. They are selected *ex ante* on the basis of the cognitive structures, 'visions of the world' and competences of individuals, and of the prevailing norms of organisations. They are also selected *ex post*. In contemporary mixed economies, market competition and other forms of more discretionary selection (such as choices by governments, financial institutions, etc.) sort out the behaviours, products, techniques, and organisational forms which—on some economic and/or institutional criteria—are 'preferred'.

---

* Comments on related papers, on which this work is partly based, by R. Nelson, S. Winter and the participants of the Lewes and Maastricht meetings that led to this book, have been helpful to the present draft.

Finally, the processes of exploration, development, selection and diffusion of new technologies, new 'ways of doing things', organisational structures and institutions, and market interactions, may well often be beyond the control or even the imagination of individual actors.

Of course, processes of change are continuously intertwined with processes of allocation of resources and coordination among agents, which in contemporary mixed economies occur to a good extent via the markets. In fact, the relationship between market signals and market organisation, growth and technical change has long been recognised as one of the central issues in economic analysis. This was one of the major analytical tasks of classical economists, from A. Smith to Ricardo and Marx, who tried to account for the determinants and regularities in the dynamics of industrial economies (the 'laws of transformation . . .') and explain the patterns of allocation and the related coordination of economic activities. The latter appear to produce relatively ordered and efficient outcomes from the multiplicity of decisions by individual agents. One must recognise that the classical economists have not been entirely successful in this task, in that they partly failed to establish a satisfactory link between the properties of price-based allocative mechanisms (with the related competitive process) and the dynamic patterns of growth of the economic system.

Facing the double function of decentralised markets as instruments of allocation of resources and as instruments for the transmission of impulses to change (Kaldor, 1984, 1972), classical economists often considered the second one as by far the most important, without feeling any need to analyse the functional relationship between the two. Fundamental dynamic properties such as the relationship between expansion of markets, division of labour, and productivity growth in Smith, or the 'increasing organic composition of capital' in Marx, are examples of a class of propositions argued on the grounds of the *irreversible transformations* originated by processes of what we could call 'dynamic competition'. Moreover, their neglect of explicit microfoundations was justified on the grounds of what we may term a 'holistic' or 'macroinstitutional' assumption about behaviour: it seemed obvious to them that, for example, given an opportunity, capitalists were ready to seize it, or that their 'institutional' function was to invest and accumulate the surplus.

Conversely, neo-classical economists focused on the problem of allocation of given resources within a context of fixed and freely available technologies. In the neo-classical world the function of the market is only the allocative one: change must be treated either parametrically or reduced to an allocative decision. Correspondingly, the organising principle of the system is the 'economic rationality' of individual agents, taken to be an invariable procedure of maximisation of some known objective function.

The relationship between allocative processes, economic behaviours, innovation and economic change was at the heart of Schumpeter's analysis. Schumpeter stressed the dichotomous role of markets and tried to reconcile them in an uneasy compromise between, first, statics and equilibrium

—to which Walrasian processes were supposed to apply—and, second, dynamics—with the domain of entrepreneurship, disequilibrium and qualitative change of the economic system.

In our view, the contributions to this book should be read in this light: how can we understand *change, coordination and relative dynamic order in environments* characterised by *discovery, learning, selection, evolution and complexity?* Certainly, these contributions do not tell the entire story of these processes. However, several of them can be considered as attempts to tackle, with varying degrees of generality, parts of a big analytical puzzle wherein technological and institutional changes are 'disequilibrating' factors producing non-stationarity in the environment, but, at the same time, emerge in ways which are often rather 'patterned' and—except for major discontinuities—do not yield fundamental breaks in the process of coordination among a multitude of economic agents.

This chapter is meant to suggest a broad interpretation of, and a set of conjectures about the linkages between innovative behaviour, market processes and institutions. In some instances, the argument is backed by references to specific contributions in the economic literature. In other instances it is somewhat more speculative.

Overall, in this essay we try to highlight a broad research programme and some research results on how economic coordination and relative dynamic order may go together, in contemporary economies continuously characterised by technological and institutional change.

Order and change: some preliminary remarks on technology, technical change and the theory of production

Technical change occurs all the time, often endogenously produced within industry by profit-motivated agents who try to appropriate the economic benefits of their innovative success. The institutions that organise production and sales vary, too, both over time and across sectors, ranging from many small producers selling in competitive markets, to oligopolistic firms which can behave strategically in relation to their environment and their future. Technological and institutional change and the varying innovative success of the different agents are part of a continuously changing environment.

We shall ask: are there some mechanisms and processes which can maintain the system on a self-sustained path, however defined?

Let us first consider the characteristics of change—and in particular technical change—as they emerge from the empirical literature. One of us has surveyed them in other works (Dosi, 1986 and Dosi's chapter in this book on the features of innovation). There we conclude that general features of technical progress are (i) sector-specific degrees of appropriability and levels of opportunity of technological advance; (ii) partial tacitness of technological knowledge; (iii) variety in the knowledge-base of and search procedures for innovation; (iv) uncertainty; (v) irreversibility of technological advances (i.e. unequivocal dominance of new processes and products over old ones, irrespective of relative prices); (vi) endogeneity of market structures associated with the dynamics of innovation; (vii) permanent existence of asymmetrics and variety between firms (and countries) in their innovative capabilities, input efficiencies, product technologies, and behavioural and strategic rules.

Under such circumstances, we suggest, a first element which accounts for the emergence of relatively ordered patterns of change stems from the very nature of the *learning process* underlying technological advances. As discussed at greater length elsewhere (Dosi, 1984 and Dosi's chapter in this book), technologies develop along relatively ordered paths shaped by the technical properties, the problem-solving heuristics and the cumulative expertise embodied in *technological paradigms*. Each 'paradigm' entails a definition of the relevant problems that must be tackled, the tasks to be fulfilled, a pattern of inquiry, the material technology to be used, and the types of basic artifacts to be developed and improved. A *technological trajectory* (Nelson and Winter, 1977; Sahal, 1981; Dosi, 1982a; Gordon and Munson, 1981; Saviotti and Metcalfe, 1984) is then the activity of technological progress along the economic and technological trade-offs defined by a paradigm.

In this view, technology is not a free good, but involves specific, often idiosyncratic, partly appropriable knowledge which is accumulated over time through equally specific learning processes, whose directions partly depend on firm-specific knowledge and on the technologies already in use. This view also implies a *theory of production* whose main features are, in the short term, diversity of (relatively fixed) coefficients between firms, and, in the longer run, relatively ordered patterns of accumulation of firm-specific competences (Winter, 1982) and of the development/diffusion of unequivocally superior techniques and products. Relatedly, the local and irreversible nature of technological advances is likely to induce the emergence of strong non-convexities (see Arthur's chapter and Atkinson and Stiglitz, 1969; David, 1975, 1986; Arthur, 1985).

As Arthur (1985) and David (1986) show, cumulative localised and irreversible forms of technical progress yield (i) non-predictability of equilibria; (ii) inflexibility (random walks having absorbing barriers); (iii) non-ergodicity (the past is not 'forgotten' and strong hysteresis effects emerge); and (iv) potential inefficiency (a particular equilibrium or, dynamically, a particular path might be inferior in terms of some welfare measure but the system may still be 'locked' in to it).

Against this background, consider the relationship between market signals and technical change. Technological paradigms and technological trajectories bind to rather narrow limits any process in inter-factoral substitution based on a *given* state-of-the-art of technology, induced by changes in relative prices. However, they provide at the same time relatively ordered 'avenues' of technical progress. With positive technological opportunities, the economic agents tend to react to (or anticipate) changes in relative prices and demand conditions by searching for new techniques and new products *within* the *boundaries* defined by the nature of each technological paradigm (Nelson and Winter, 1982; Dosi, Pavitt and Soete, 1988). These new techniques and new products, in turn, are likely to be or become superior to the old ones irrespective of relative prices (immediately, as in the case of several microelectronics-based innovations, Soete and Dosi, 1983, or after some learning time as in agricultural machinery, David, 1975). In other words, if they had existed before, they would also have been adopted at the 'old' relative prices. Using a biological metaphor, technological paradigms provide a *relatively coherent source of mutations*, while at the same time constraining the adaptability of the system to optimal allocations for *given* technologies. Conversely, in environments with relatively high technological opportunities and paradigm-bound changes, markets tend to perform as rather powerful stimuli to change, even where they are relatively poorer optimal allocators of given amounts of resources.

Innovation, uncertainty and economic behaviour

Due to the specific characteristics of the innovation process (discussed in Freeman, 1982; Nelson and Winter, 1982; and Dosi, 1986, and Dosi's chapter in this book) one should expect to find innovative environments showing both an *information gap* (i.e. information is necessarily imperfect) and a *competence gap* of every agent (in that the capability of efficiently processing the available information is heavily constrained by the complexity of the causal links characterising the environments to which the information refers).[1] Limits on available information and on the capability of efficiently processing it obviously entail uncertainty in the formation of the expectations on which economic agents base their decisions: the existence of a permanent gap between the 'competence' of the agents and the 'difficulty in selecting the most preferred alternatives' (which is at the core of the very existence of uncertainty) is such that the restriction on the number of allowed alternatives (i.e. the 'routinisation' of behaviour) may well increase 'the chance of "correctly" selecting the action at the right time relative to the chance of "mistakenly" selecting it at the wrong time' (Heiner, 1983, p. 565).

Moreover, one is likely to find another—and even stronger — source of uncertainty which rests on the impossibility of mapping preferences, states-of-the-world, actions and outcomes, even for a notional agent with *infinite* computing capability of all the information that the present can deliver about the future. The nature of this strong uncertainty is twofold. First, the set of outcomes of different courses of action is often unknown (Nelson and Winter, 1982) and might not even be enumerable (which is the *theoretical* condition of computability, let alone the *practical* computability of empirical agents: see Lewis, 1985, 1986.) Almost by definition, trying to do a new thing involves the impossibility of knowing what the new thing will look like, what its economic properties will be, what is the best way of doing it and even what are the feasible ways of achieving the result, if any. Second, the states-of-the-world are at least partly endogenous in that, for example, the future technological advances and the related pay-offs depend in complex and often unpredictable ways on present allocative decisions of a relatively high number of non-collusive agents.

Both phenomena involve *uninsurable* and *unmeasurable* uncertainty (in the sense of Knight, 1965, and Schackle, 1961). Markets may well work efficiently, deliver all the information that they can, and even discount contingencies for future states-of-the-world to which probabilities can notionally be attached (although empirically these markets rarely exist). What markets *cannot* do is to deliver information about or discount the possibility of future states-of-the-world whose occurrence is, to different degrees, the unintentional result of present decisions taken by *heterogeneous agents* characterised by different competences, beliefs and expectations. Whenever these circumstances apply, one may reasonably doubt whether economic agents apply maximisation procedures in their decision-making (e.g. in their allocations to research activities, the directions of search, the choice of products to be developed, etc.), and even whether it is efficient *to try* to do so in environments characterised by environmental complexity, uncertainty and potential surprise. A unique 'rational' behaviour may be hard to define, not only in terms of the information set and computational capabilities of individual agents, but even for a notional external observer who is not God (and thus cannot read in the hearts and minds of the agents) but still knows all the information that markets deliver and also knows that all agents have self-seeking goals; what is 'right' or 'wrong' for any one agent may still depend on uncertain behaviours of all other agents in ways that can hardly be represented in simply game-theoretic frameworks (more on this point is in Winter, 1971; Nelson and Winter, 1982; and Dosi, Orsenigo and Silverberg, 1986).

This is not to say that the agents do not try to be forward-looking and behave strategically in the knowledge that their actions influence the world.[2] However, what acquires a major importance in the description of decisions and behaviours is the actual priors they hold (that is, their actual set of beliefs and *Weltanschauungen*), their problem-solving rules, their specific knowledge, the ways they change them in *non-stationary* systems, and the nature of the environmental selection amongst different classes of agents who hold different beliefs (thus behaving differently even under identical information and incentives from the environment). Putting it another way, in order to discriminate among a very large set of conceivable games, strategies and (possible) equilibria, which the analyst can devise to describe innovative environments, one must introduce also the knowledge of the *actual rules and institutions* governing decisions, learning and adjustment processes.

Uncertainty necessarily implies institutions, in two senses. First, one requires *behaviour-shaping* institutions (which may well be just endogenous developments of organisations, rules, beliefs and *Gestalten* or may also involve external organisations, laws, etc.). Second, uncertainty—even in the weaker form of *imperfect information*—requires institutions to organise the interactions and the coordination between agents who (a) at best have an approximate knowledge of the possible states-of-the-world and of the possible outcomes of their own actions, and (b) operate in an environment where interactions necessarily produce externalities and unintentional outcomes.

Both the technological and institutional knowledge of *how and what people learn, what are their beliefs and how they change* occupy, in the approach suggested here, a role theoretically analogous to maximising rationality in neo-classical models: they are factors of *behavioural order* which contribute to explain coordination and consistency in uncertain, complex and changing environments.

Institutions, firms and performance

Let us suggest two—complementary—definitions of institutions. A first, more conventional one comprises non-market, non-profit organisations (governments, public agencies, universities, etc.). Their importance in the generation and diffusion of technological innovations is surveyed in Freeman (1982) and Dosi (1986) and discussed analytically in Freeman's and Nelson's chapters in this book. A second, broader definition—nearer to what one finds in sociology—comprises all forms of organisations, conventions and repeated and established behaviours which are not directly mediated through the market.

What has just been said about behaviour in complex and non-stationary environments implies that one might not be able to deduce behaviour, with any reasonable approximation, solely from knowledge of market-delivered information and the self-seeking goal of the agents. In turn, this implies that the institutions which shape 'visions of the world', behavioural conventions, perceptions of opportunities, and interactions between the agents are an important ingredient in the explanation of what the agents actually do, e.g. how much they invest in innovation, what kind of technical progress they expect in the future, what appropriability mechanisms they try to build, how much they cooperate, and to what extent they compete with each other. In this respect, compare, for example, Schumpeter's 'heroic' innovators of the *Theory of Economic Development* with the 'routinised' innovations of *Capitalism, Socialism, Democracy*. These archetypes can be interpreted to represent different institutional patterns which govern different innovative behaviours, even for the same latent opportunities of technical progress.

Institutions, in the broader definition, matter because the 'architecture' of the system affects performance for the same set of underlying incentives. This is so in simple cases of imperfect information (Stiglitz, 1985; Sah and Stiglitz, 1985; Herriott, Levinthal and March, 1985) and institutions matter even in the simplest 'rational expectations' world (Frydman, 1982). *A fortiori*, this applies to all innovative environments which present those strong forms of uncertainty described earlier. Moreover, in general, market processes themselves cannot be adequately understood without reference to the institutions which shape behaviour and adjustment mechanisms (cf. Akerlof, 1984; Okun, 1981).

In fact, even the 'economic agents' which we generally represent as the decision-makers are as such theoretical constructs. What one typically observes are complex institutions—modern corporations—organised around rules, hierarchies and various mechanisms of behaviour of selection and performance assessment (for detailed and conceptually diverse discussions, see Simon, 1957; Cyert and March, 1963; Nelson and Winter, 1982; Marris and Mueller, 1980; Williamson, 1975, 1985; Kay, 1984; Teece, 1982b; and Kay's, Pelikan's, Teece's and Freeman's chapters in this book). There is an important theoretical point here. If richer institutional knowledge is required in order to narrow down the wide set of possible dynamics of any innovative environment consistent with some set of latent technological opportunities, market-delivered information and profit goals, then economic theory faces the task of achieving robust 'stylisations' of different types of firms, the ways they emerge and the influence that these different organisational forms have on firms' behaviour and performance. Relatedly, any theory of the firm must also be a theory of how competences are organised and decisions are taken, and how organisational hierarchies relate to the knowledge base of technological advances (for developments along these lines, see Teece's and Kay's chapters and Nelson, 1981, 1987; Teece, 1982a, 1986; Kay, 1979, 1984; Pavitt, 1984b). In this perspective, the nature of business firms certainly relates to (i) the procedures for coordination, control, and monitoring of the performance of individual members; (ii) an incentive structure; (iii) criteria and procedures for resource allocation; (iv) a (related) information-processing network; but also, at least equally important, to (v) procedures for problem-solving, learning, and storing/reproducing specific competences. The *internal organisation, boundaries and performances* of firms always reveal, we suggest, various combinations *and tensions* between these basic functions (the general issue is discussed in Dosi, Rumelt, Teece and Winter, 1988; see also Aoki, 1986).

Market processes, evolution and performance

We have been discussing so far some technological and institutional properties of non-stationary environments which tend to provide coherence to patterns of change and 'order' behaviour, despite high degrees of uncertainty and problem-solving complexity. These properties, related to the nature of learning and of specific institutional set-ups, operate *ex ante* with respect to market interactions. However, the economic feasibility and success of any one behaviour of economic agents is often ultimately determined by market processes, so that no *a priori* consistency of plans is guaranteed. Thus, one should also investigate the coordinating properties of market mechanisms under non-stationary conditions.

The interaction between institutions which govern innovative activities and market-based patterns of change remains a major theoretical challenge. An understanding of the pattern of change is basic to the understanding of the nature of particular economic institutions (this is increasingly recognised also within the neo-classical tradition: see Arrow and Honkapohja, 1985, p. 22). The converse is also true—the nature of economic institutions contributes to shaping the rates and directions of change. Thus, how does one disentangle the process? How can one model change in economic environments where innovation—with the characteristics outlined earlier—features predominantly?

Whatever specific theoretical representation is chosen, we suggest that these environments present characteristics that are (a) *evolutionary* in the sense that change proceeds also by means of slow or fast, but never instantaneous processes of selection amongst heterogeneous agents who actually compete, make mistakes and (unlike biological evolution) learn over time; (b) *irreversible*, so that past history structures present available options and selection mechanisms; (c) *self-organising* in the sense that the 'order' in the evolution of the system is the *largely unintentional* outcome of the coupled dynamics between technological progress (innovation, learning, etc.), strictly economic activities (investment, pricing, financing, competition for market shares), and the institutions governing decisions and expectations.[3]

Relatedly, a major theoretical challenge concerns the existence and properties of 'equilibrium', however defined, in evolutionary environments with the features briefly described earlier. How can we characterise 'order' in this context? What are the equivalents in an evolutionary environment of the 'existence and stability properties' of more standard equilibrium models?

As introductory remarks, let us suggest two partly complementary definitions. As a first *behavioural* or subjective definition of 'equilibrium', take that notional state of the economy which 'generates messages which do not cause agents to change the theories which they hold or the policies which they pursue' (Hahn, 1984, p. 59). In the framework of this discussion, this 'subjective' definition of an evolutionary equilibrium corresponds to a set of *'structurally' stable strategies*, i.e. the strategies that heterogeneous agents continue to pursue in non-stationary environments which, in turn, fulfil the objectives of these strategies[4].

However, the message-spaces and the action-spaces corresponding to these structurally stable strategies are rather different from those of a Walrasian world of the Arrow–Debreu–Hahn kind in three senses. First, the 'theories' are also about technological developments, market trends, fundamental rules of interaction—in a word, they also embody fundamental and commonly shared *Gestalten* and beliefs about future technological and market contingencies for which there is no forward market and which are indeed the partly endogenous outcome of expectations and individual strategies. Thus, particular sets of 'theories' and beliefs perform in evolutionary equilibria a role vaguely similar to contingency markets in the Walrasian world, in that they provide for the *relative consistency* of expectations of individual agents over time.

Second, the message-space has a much higher dimensionality than in a Walrasian world. However, *theories* and *institutions* simplify it, in the sense that (a) only particular kinds of information trigger attention and behavioural change (cf. also Heiner's contribution to this project). Structurally stable strategies are also likely to embody higher-level rules of selection in the message-space. (Think for example of the computer industry and the complexity of the messages it delivers. It is plausible that several, especially small, firms have a 'theory' that says something like the following: look primarily at IBM, wait six months to see if a new product succeeds, then produce an IBM-clone at lower cost and do not bother with the rest unless major technological or market revolutions occur). These strategies embody problem-solving rules which are sufficiently general and 'redundant' to cope with computational complexity and environmental non-stationarity (Dosi and Egidi, 1987).

Third, the 'policies' also involve (i) rules on 'how much I should adjust prices and quantities and how much I should innovate', on 'innovation versus imitation', on what direction to innovate in, etc.; (ii) beliefs on the origins and effects of change; and (iii) relatively abstract and general strategies on how to cope with and/or *generate* environmental non-stationarity.

Fourth, there might be more than one strategy which is 'stable' over time, without any unequivocal possibility of ranking this as 'better' or 'worse', as compared to others.

In some respects, the 'subjective' definition of a Walrasian equilibrium is a special case of a 'behavioural' one whenever (a) the latter collapses to one specific 'theory' (everyone believes that the world works more or less in a Walrasian way), (b) the world and the theories about it are such as to allow strict separability between some sort of 'short term' about which the agents hold stationary and 'Walrasian' beliefs and a 'longer term' where different (possibly more 'Schumpeterian') beliefs apply.

A second definition of 'evolutionary equilibrium' relates to the *selection mechanisms* at work in the system and the sequence of attractors that they entail. Let us suggest the following definitions. A series of 'evolutionary equilibria' is that path of evolution of the system whereby (a) technical progress proceeds along any one technological trajectory (as defined earlier and discussed in Dosi's chapter); (b) the distribution of firms according to their organizational characeristics and technological asymmetries (that is, their technological lags and leads) is stable; and (c) the distributions of the performance variables (prices, profit rates, productivities, etc.) of the firms in an industry is also stable. Obviously, a steady-state growth is a very special case of an evolutionary path. However, evolutionary equilibria are also, for example, those situations suggested by Nelson (1985) is which two groups of 'innovative' and 'imitative' firms coexist characterised by identical profitabilities and a stable technological lag between 'imitators' and 'innovators'. More generally, evolutionary/self-organisation-type models are likely to generate evolutionary equilibria, in the definition adopted here, for relatively stable combinations of technological *opportunity*, *appropriability* of innovation and *strategic rules* of behaviour.

It is our conjecture that, for established technological paradigms and for given institutions, there exist one or more sequences of evolutionary equilibria (i.e. one or more evolutionary paths) which are stable in the sense that they correspond to the series of attractors which lead the evolution of the system. Actual economic systems may well never be on any sequence of 'evolutionary equilibria'. However, given sufficient stability in technological paradigms and institutional conditions, an evolutionary path, we conjecture, is likely to lead to a relatively stable evolution of the system. For example, it is plausible that any profit for an innovating firm in excess of that level allowed by technological asymmetries *vis-à-vis* imitators will be eroded by mechanisms of both 'stationary adjustment' (i.e. changes in prices and quantities produced by other firms, etc.) and 'Schumpeterian adjustments' (more firms will try to join the 'innovating group', etc.).

A fundamental point, however, is that *in general*, the series of attractors defined by an evolutionary path are *behaviour-dependent* and *path-dependent*. That is to say, it is the very process of approaching any one 'attractor' which may well change the value of the attractor itself: the process of 'getting there', and the ways one tries to get there, influences the 'centre of gravity' itself. Putting it another way, any evolutionary equilibrium implies forces which keep the industry together and forces which keep it moving. However, the two cannot be rigorously separated. Take, for example, that process by which the industry adjusts to, say, 'excess profits' of some innovators. Most likely one will see an expansion of the quantities produced by the other firms and, *ceteris paribus*, a price reduction (this is a 'stationary adjustment'). This same process, however, also implies a change in the average conditions of production of the industry, in average R & D propensity (both due to the change in the distribution of output between innovative and imitative firms), varying 'spill-over' of technical knowledge from 'leading' to 'backward' firms, changes in the average rate of change of production costs, and, ultimately, changes in the 'evolutionary attractor'.

In general, the stability of an evolutionary path, we suggest, is likely to rest upon those technological conditions of opportunity, appropriability and cumulativeness characteristic of each technological paradigm and on the permanence of the institutions governing behaviours and expectation formation.

Conversely, the transition between different evolutionary paths is driven by changes in technological paradigms, forms of organisation, market structures, etc. — often anticipated by relatively small 'deviant behaviours' which, under certain micro and/or macro conditions, become autocatalytic, progressively amplify and may end up being dominant.

An obvious, but extremely difficult, question comes immediately to mind, namely, what is the relationship between the 'subjective' and the 'selective' definitions of 'evolutionary equilibria'? So far, we do not have any robust answer. It seems plausible that a set of evolutionary stable behaviours entails a corresponding 'selective equilibrium' (otherwise people, sooner or later, would change their 'theories' and their 'policies'). However, the converse is not necessarily true: a sequence of selective equilibria could be stable, for example, even at the price of a high rate of mortality of firms, and/or a very high volatility of market shares, productivity, profits (and thus, plausibly, changes in 'visions' and 'policies') of individual firms.

Finally, note that in evolutionary environments, 'theories' and 'policies', on the one hand, and selection mechanisms, on the other, are by no means independent: the selection environment for any one agent is determined by what all others think and do. The endogeneity of selection processes ranges between 'hyperselection' (and thus self-fulfilling prophecy of one or a group of agents) and total counter-intentionality ('if everyone else thinks and behaves like me, my behaviour will be selected out'). The endogeneity of selection rules is, of course, an essential characteristic of *behaviour-dependent* and *path-dependent* evolutionary paths. (More on this and on why these processes cannot generally be reduced to simple game-theoretic concepts is in Silverberg's chapter.)

How does coordination occur and what are the performance characteristics of evolutionary environments? The analysis of these properties is still at a very early stage and here we shall simply suggest some conjectures.

Take, for example, the short-term performance analysis of industries and markets, which is one of the traditional concerns of industrial economics. In another work (Dosi, 1984a) it has been argued that the permanent existence of *asymmetries between firms*, in terms of production costs and product technologies, represents a sort of *factor of order* which (i) limits the set of feasible strategies regarding price/quantity adjustments available in the short term to each firm; and (ii) tends to order them hierarchically (so that, for example, price leadership, under certain conditions, stems from technological leadership). In other words, existence of inter-firm asymmetries reduces the typical indeterminacy of oligopolistic games by introducing hierarchies between the players and asymmetric constraints on their feasible strategies. Technological and organisational asymmetries between firms are likely to be, to a *first approximation*, predictors of short-term performance (in terms of prices, profit rates, etc.). They have a role analogous to those entry- and mobility-barriers upon which the more 'structuralist' tradition in industrial economics has focused (see Bain, 1956; Steindl, 1976; Downie, 1958; Sylos Labini, 1967; moreover on mobility barriers, see Caves and Porter, 1977, 1978). In fact, economies of scale and product differentiation can be considered a sub-set of the asymmetries which tend to arise in innovative environments as a result of learning curves, lead times, cumulativeness in innovative capabilities and internalisation of complementary technologies. Therefore, the proximate determinants of short-term performance are factors directly related to the nature of each technological paradigm (such as the scope for economies of scale, the specific technological opportunities, the degrees of cumulativeness of each technology, etc.) and to the institutions which organise innovative activities (and thus the regimes of appropriability, degrees of corporate internalisation of technological capabilities, established business practices of cooperation versus competition, etc.).

In general, whatever the precise nature of the coordination process, evolutionary environments permanently show an intrinsic tension between a selective pressure toward a 'better' allocation of resources, on the one hand, and the inevitable (indeed, necessary) generation of mistakes, unsuccessful trials, 'wasteful' and partly duplicative processes of search, on the other (Nelson, 1981, and Nelson's chapter in this book). Let us now discuss these properties.

Change and dynamic stability: learning and selection

In standard models coordination among plans and actions of individual agents—and thus the theoretical possibility of economic 'order'—rests on the interaction between a simple behavioural assumption (maximisation) and some sort of scarcity constraint.

Conversely, the 'core' heuristics of the approach suggested here depends on the interaction between exploitable opportunities, present in non-stationary environments, which are too complex and too volatile to be fully mastered or understood by individual agents, and institutions which, to different degrees, simplify and govern behaviour and interactions. As a consequence, 'order in change' is generated by varying combinations of (a) *learning*, (b) *selection mechanisms*, and (c) *institutional structures*.

Figure 2.1 presents an extremely simplified illustration of such an 'evolutionary engine'. In the evolutionary process, asymmetries and diversity among agents are both a functional condition and a necessary outcome of innovation (Eliasson, 1986; Gibbons and Metcalfe, 1986;

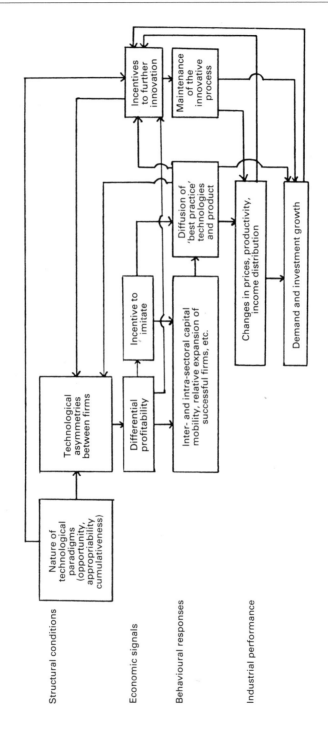

Figure 2.1   Change and dynamic stability: a microeconomic illustration

Nelson and Winter, 1982; Iwai, 1981; Dosi, Orsenigo and Silverberg, 1986). These Schumpeterian features of the system imply continuous 'disequilibrium' features and the dominance of dynamic processes over 'static' allocative mechanisms:[5] technical change is an asymmetry-creating process. Its precondition and outcome are varying degrees of appropriability of the innovation and differential profitabilities. This very process, however, provides both the incentive and the need for other firms to imitate and/or undertake further innovation. While innovation and diversity guarantee dynamism, imitation and market selection of the most successful agents prevent the system from departing too much from 'static' allocative efficiency. The net outcome is a relatively ordered pattern of change in the structure of the system (in terms of rates of innovation, productivity growth, market structures, profit margins, etc.).

The balance between learning and selection involved in each evolutionary process varies with technologies, countries, institutions and historical periods. Moreover, learning is not only (not even primarily) a sort of Bayesian process through which people try to estimate the 'true' coefficients of the world. More basically, people and organisations 'learn' by cumulatively improving on their technological capabilities, by building 'theories' and trying to develop robust rules on 'how to live' in environments where tomorrow never looks quite like yesterday. In other words learning has less to do with computational capabilities and information availability than with Piaget-type development of cognitive structures.

Different combinations of learning modes, selection processes and institutions, of course, yield significantly different environments with different performances and different evolutionary paths. Let us call each group of similar combinations an *evolutionary regime*. Interestingly, these 'regimes', we suggest, closely correspond to what in an important stream of French literature, pioneered by Aglietta (1982), Boyer and Mistral (1983), Coriat (1983), and Lipietz (1984), have called regimes of 'regulation' (*régulation* in French, which Boyer and Mistral translate as 'socioeconomic tuning': see Boyer's chapters in this book). Each regime is defined by reference to 'the whole set of institutions, private behaviour and actual functioning of the various markets which channel the long-term dynamics and determine the cyclical properties of the economy during an historical period for a given society' (Boyer and Mistral, 1984, p. 9). We suggest that each 'regime of regulation' represents the aggregate morphology of particular evolutionary/self-organisation processes. Or, to say it the other way round: particular self-organisation processes are the *microfoundation* of particular forms of organisation of the major markets (commodity, labour, financial markets), yielding, under certain conditions, relatively regular patterns of macroeconomic growth and transformation.

The evolving structure of the economy and the patterns of regulation of the system

An important intermediate link—at a level which some writers call 'meso-economic'—between microeconomic behaviours and strictly macroeconmic phenomena are industrail and technological interdependencies between sectors. The standard way of representing the commodity-related aspect of these interdependencies is via input/output analysis. Input/output relations organise the relationship between *industrial* performance variables, the level at which direct interaction between the agents essentially takes place, and the aggregate patterns of investment, demand, employment, etc.[6] Theoretically distinguishable from, although strongly overlapping with input/output flows, one must also consider inter-sectoral technologoical interdependencies, partly made of reciprocal stimuli, bottlenecks, information flows, spillovers of tehnological knowledge, etc.[7] Finally, industries are, to different degrees, behaviourally related via processes of vertical and horizontal integration.[8]

The fundamental aspect of these patterns of interrelation is that they are *heterogeneous and hierarchical*: the sources of technical change are not equally distributed across sectors but depend essentially on technology-specific opportunities.[9] The patterns of production and use of innovation vary as well as sectoral characteristics;[10] there are some sectors which are a fundamental source of technological advances and others that are essentially adopters. Groups of sectors also cluster around internal paterns of interrelation which are stronger than with the rest of the system. Impulses delivered to one particular point of the system may have an aggregate impact, either in terms of overall productivity or demand-generation effects, greater than those delivered at another point.[11] The French tradition of industrial economics tried to capture this aspect of a relatively ordered and hierarchical structure through the concept of *filière*, that is, a cluster of sectors which are connected by strong technological and behavioural input/output interlinkages. The crucial point for the present discussion is that vertically integrated sectors and filières provide a *differentiated and relatively ordered structure of diffusion, transmission and amplification of microeconomic impulses* and *dynamic feedbacks, whose intensity and direction depends on the overall structure of the system and the position of each element in it.*[12] Of course, the input/output structure of an economy at any point in time (or, for that matter, any structural description) is a 'picture' of its functional features (e.g. in terms of aggregate demand, inter-sectoral effects of technical change, etc.). It also shows the kinds of consistency conditions—e.g. between rates of sectoral investment and growth, between income distribution, propensity to invest and inter-sectoral distribution of demand—which must be fulfilled in order to keep the economy on a certain dynamic path. It does not show the *causes* and the *processes* of evolution of the economy. To understand them one must look at 'disequilibrium' behaviours (see the chapters by Allen and

Silverberg). Conversely, if one wants to understand the aggregate ('macro') order which appears in certain historical circumstances, one must look at the institutional and technological structures which constrain and shape the underlying ('micro') evolutionary process.

Indeed, one *does* observe significant aggregate relationships which hold with relatively stable coefficients over certain historical periods while varying from one period to the next. Examples are the relationship between wage growth, on the one hand, and price changes, productivity growth and rates of unemployment, on the other; the link between income and investment (i.e. 'the multiplier'); the relationship between labour productivity growth and output growth ('the Verdoorn–Kaldor law') and some others. These 'stylised facts' are also the main macro relationships in the Keynesian and post-Keynesian traditions. However, their *microfoundation*, we suggest, is to be found in specific classes of evolutionary processes. Moreover, our general conjecture is that the stability of their coefficients and functional form derives from the stability of the fundamental characteristics of the technologies, institutions and market processes which shape them.

At a very general level, let us heroically differentiate three fundamental 'sub-systems': (i) the *technological regime*; (ii) the *'economic machine* (with its inner feedbacks and adjustment mechanisms, related to relative prices, input/output flows, demand generation, investment, etc.); and (iii) the *institutional conditions* (including forms of regulation, prevailing behaviour, forms of organisation of economic activities, political conditions, etc.). We may then describe a *smooth configuration* as one where there are high levels of homeorhesis between these three fundamental 'sub-systems'. Conversely, a low level of homeorhesis is associated with structural *mismatchings* between them. Here, we suggest, is the link between the evolutionary/self-organisation approach to microeconomics, illustrated in this book by Silverberg, Allen, Arthur and Metcalfe, and the macroeconomic interpretations put forward here by Freeman, Perez and Boyer. *What underlies the 'Keynesian machine' linking investment, effective demand and income growth are micro (evolutionary) processes, which in turn are shaped and constrained by the specific characteristics of technologies and institutions.* Thus multiplier/accelerator coefficients will be affected by the amount of 'autonomous' ('Schumpeterian') investment which various technologies trigger. The prevailing 'modes of regulation', in the sense used above, will affect income distribution, the sensitivity of wages to unemployment rates and productivity growth, the propensity to invest and social consumption patterns. The nature of technological paradigms will influence the scope for static and dynamic economies of scale, etc.

Historically, one observes that periods of 'smooth configurations', characterised by efficient macroeconomic adjustment, high rates of growth, etc., are followed by other periods of mismatching, instability, low growth, etc. The substantive hypotheses we want to suggest are (i) there are *critical thresholds* for the variables and coefficients within which a distinguishable configuration is viable and (ii) it is the very process of growth within a configuration which may lead the system toward its critical thresholds.

The second hypothesis is clearly the stronger one and also more difficult to prove. It is somewhat akin to the Marxian–Schumpeterian view that 'it is success which contains the seeds of its own undoing'. Let us divide the argument into three parts, focusing on the institutional, technological and economic levels.

As regards the socio-institutional level, it may well be that there is a long-term unsustainability of high growth and near-full-employment *cum* social stability. The thesis of the long-term incompatibility of capitalism with full employment has been argued in the Marxian tradition by Kalecki (1943) and recently reappraised by Salvati (1983). It is impossible to discuss it here at length. Suffice to say that it may well be that in societies structurally characterised by conflict over income distribution and the conditions of labour, near-full-employment conditions are likely to generate a progressive relaxation of the discipline exerted by market mechanisms upon individual behaviour and induce rising collective expectations (about income and about power) at a rate higher than that at which the system can 'deliver the goods'.

With respect to technology, it is likely—as we argue at greater length in Dosi (1983)—that: (i) the pattern of 'normal' technological progress along the trajectories defined by the prevailing technological paradigm involve non-linear trends in mechanisation/automation of production with a higher rate in the phase of 'maturity' of each paradigm; (ii) the just-mentioned tendency may be accelerated by that part of technical progress which is endogenous to market-inducement mechanisms (cf. the preceding discussion of the impact of growth and relative prices on technical change); (iii) the rate of expansion of demand for new commodities is likely to slow down above a certain level, due to the nature of the prevailing baskets of consumption; (iv) for all the above reasons, the net balance in the dual nature of technical change may progressively shift in favour of its input-saving effect as compared to the demand-creating one.

Finally, as regards the 'economic machine', it should be clear from the foregoing discussion that (i) it does not necessarily embody mechanisms of self-adjustment; (ii) these mechanisms, when they exist, are *bounded* and *limited* in scope; (iii) even more important, rational-expectations models notwithstanding, 'the economic machine' may be a *myopic machine* characterised by high 'holistic effects', self-fulfilling expectations, irreversibilities and positive feedbacks which can guarantee both self-sustained 'vicious' and 'virtuous' circles.

These considerations, taken together, highlight the plausibility of the proposition about 'success which contains the seeds of its own undoing'. The microeconomic (evolutionary) counterpart of this proposition is that certain kinds of 'fluctuations' and 'non-average' behaviour which emerge within a relatively stable structure (stable in terms of basic technologies, institutions, rules of interaction and expectation formation, etc.), slowly or suddenly, with or without exogenous shocks, become self-reinforcing and destabilise the structure itself (they produce 'qualitative', 'morphological' changes).

One must stress that these fundamental properties of the system such as, first, (limited) homeorhesis, and second, endogenously generated discontinuities and critical thresholds, *do not* depend on rigidities, frictions, etc., in any meaningful sense. The argument so far, for example, implies that the price system *works well* and delivers *all the information it can*. If anything, the system may well reach its 'critical thresholds' *faster* if the microeconomic allocative mechanisms work, since it moves faster toward the exploitation of the technological and consumption possibilities.

In a sense, the great historical discontinuities are also periods of *search* for new consistency conditions and forms of regulation defining new 'smooth configurations' between new technological paradigms, patterns of accumulation, and forms of organisation of the major markets, baskets of consumption, and labour relations. The process of discovery/exploration/ development of new technological paradigms during one 'epoch' can be seen from the point of view of the whole society as a slack activity which increases the *number of possible worlds* (i.e. possible configurations) which could be notionally attained in the future. The process of transition and search obviously has a microeconomic dimension, which—as regards technical change in a narrow sense—also involves the emergence and growth of new industries, the slow (or traumatic) adaptation of existing ones, often the emergence and growth of new firms embodying somewhat different 'rationalities', the adoption of new productive techniques, and experimentation with new labour processes.

There is, however, a 'system dimension' of this search process which is crucial as well: the fact that the environmental requirements and processes of selections of microeconomic 'mutations' in one part of the system are likely to depend upon the state and evolution of other *unrelated* parts of it. By way of an illustration, think, for example, of the slow development of the 'consistency condition' involved in the relationship between the mechanisation of American agriculture, the development of the 'technological trajectories' in agricultural machinery, the structure of American land-ownership, and the trends in the relative prices of machines to labour (cf. David, 1975). Or, more recently, think of the socio-institutional requirements notionally demanded by an electronics-related period of high growth, e.g. in terms of work and leisure patterns ('the electronics home', etc.), organisation of the labour process, required infrastructure, etc.

Conclusions

In this highly exploratory discussion, we have tried to investigate the role that both technological change and various kinds of institutions play in the stability and transformation of modern economic systems.

Clearly, the explicit consideration of the properties of technology and technical change introduces irreversible dynamic features, complex interdependencies and uncertainty which have consequences somewhat similar to, but far more pervasive than those entailed by indivisibilities, increasing returns and imperfect information in general equilibrium models. In these conditions, it comes certainly as no surprise that the mechanisms conventionally thought of as ensuring stability of the system—simple market processes of the Walrasian type—cannot guarantee the emergence of stable and ordered patterns of change. Conversely, we suggested that the 'principles of order' are to be looked for precisely in those mechanisms and dynamic feedbacks which in stationary neo-classical worlds would most likely yield disequilibrium and instability. Non-stationarity, nonconvexities, the absence of a unique principle of rationality defining the behaviour of each agent, behaviour-guiding institutions and unintentional interrelations all contribute to generate paths of dynamic evolution of the economic system. Clearly, the nature of 'order' is in this context radically different from the conventional notion of equilibrium.

At the micro level it refers to the characteristics of learning processes and the properties of a sort of 'Evolutionary Hand'. Like the competitive 'Invisible Hand', it entails a competitive process which relates prices to costs of production and moves resources from low-return to high-return employments. However, the classic 'Invisible Hand', under the conditions of rather fast technical change, increasing returns, environmental complexity, etc., is quite crippled and too weak to keep the system in some sort of order while it grows and changes. Conversely, the 'Evolutionary Hand' also selects and orders the diversity always generated by technological and institutional change. Moreover, it is more powerful because it is not entirely invisible, but is forged within visible (indeed often dominant) technologies and institutions: it not only selects *ex post*, it also teaches and guides *ex ante*.

The emergence of 'order' is contingent on the formation of specific forms of institutional organisation governing the relationship between economic agents, of which markets are an important—but by no means unique— element. The dynamic coherence (homeorhesis) of economic systems in conditions of technical change, we conjecture, is the outcome of particular 'architectures' or forms of 'regulation' which define the functioning and the scope of markets in relation to the specific properties of technological paradigms, the prevailing forms of behaviour and expectation formation of agents, the structure of the interdependencies of the system, and, finally, to nature and interests of the institutions which plan an active role in the economy.

Notes

1. In addition to the classic contributions by Simon, 1955, 1957, see Heiner, 1983, 1985, and Heiner's contribution to this book.
2. In fact, as argued in Dosi and Egidi (1987), powerful problem-solving routines (that is, 'abstract' and robust decision rules which apply to entire classes of, often ill-structured, problems) are the general procedures through which 'intelligent' agents deal with environmental ('substantive') uncertainty and the (related) *procedural* uncertainty stemming from problem-solving complexity.
3. These features of evolutionary environments are discussed and formalised in Nelson and Winter, 1982; Iwai, 1981; Eliasson, 1984, 1986; Arthur, 1985; Silverberg, 1987; Dosi, Orsenigo and Silverberg, 1986; Gibbons and Metcalfe, 1986; in this book see the chapters by Allen, Arthur, Metcalfe and Silverberg.
4. Note that these 'stable strategies', which entail specific sets of problem-solving routines of different generality, may or may not correspond to 'evolutionary stable strategies' in the sense currently understood in 'evolutionary games'. See also Silverberg's chapter.
5. An implication is that 'a system—any system, economic or other—that at *every* given point in time fully utilizes its possibilities to the best advantage may yet in the long run be inferior to a system that does so at *no* given point in time, because the latter's failure to do so may be a condition for the level or speed of long-run performance' (Schumpeter, 1943, p. 83, quoted also in Elster, 1983). The point is discussed at greater length in Dosi (1988).
6. In this respect, Pasinetti's concept of vertically integrated sectors is an important theoretical device capable of tracing down the dual nature of technical change (in terms of demand creation and input efficiencies) to all direct and indirect consequences. Cf. Pasinetti (1981).
7. For an historical analysis, cf. Rosenberg (1976) and (1982). For an analysis of the inter-sectoral flows of innovation, cf. Pavitt (1984a) and Scherer (1982).
8. Cf. Teece (1982).
9. For a taxonomy of the patterns of production, use and sector of origin of innovation, see Pavitt (1984a).
10. ibid.
11. On the case of the differentiated productivity effects, cf. Strassman (1959).
12. See Toledano (1978), Perroux (1973), Montfort (1983), Jacquemin and Rainelli (1984), Gazon (1979), Lesage (1984).

References

Aglietta, M. (1982), *Regulation et Crise du Capitalisme*, 2nd ed., Paris, Calmann-Levy.

Akerlof, G.A. (1984), *An Economic Theorist's Book of Tales*, Cambridge, Cambridge University Press.

Aoki, M. (1986), 'Horizontal vs. vertical information structure of the firm', *American Economic Review*, vol. 76, no. 5, pp. 971–83.

Arcangeli, F., David, P. and Dosi, G. (eds) (1988), *The Diffusion of Innovation*, Oxford, Oxford University Press, forthcoming.

Arrow, K. and Honkapohja, J. (eds) (1985), *Frontiers of Economics*, Oxford, Basil Blackwell.

Arthur, W.B. (1985), *Competing Techniques and Lock-in by Historical Events: The Dynamics of Allocation Under Increasing Returns*, Stanford, Stanford University, CEPR.

Atkinson, A. and Stiglitz, J. (1969), 'A new view of technological change', *Economic Journal*, vol 79, pp. 573–578.

Bain, J.S. (1956), *Barriers to New Competition*, Harvard, Harvard University Press.

Boyer, R. and Mistral, J. (1983), *Accumulation, Inflation, Crises*, 2nd edn., Paris, Press Universitaire de France.

(1984), *The Present Crisis: From an Historical Interpretation to a Prospective Outlook*, Paris, CEPREMAP.

Caves, R.E. and Porter, M.E. (1977), 'From entry barriers to mobility barriers; conjectural decisions and continued deterrence to new competition', *Quarterly Journal of Economics*, vol 91, pp. 241–262.

—— (1978), 'Market structure, oligopoly and stability of market shares', *Journal of Industrial Economics* vol 26 pp. 289–313.

Coriat, B. (1983), *La Robotique*, Paris, La Découverte/Maspero.

Cyert, R.M. and March, J.G. (1963), *A Behavioural Theory of the Firm*, Englewood Cliffs, NJ, Prentice Hall.

David, P. (1975), *Technical Choice, Innovation and Economic Growth*, Cambridge, Cambridge University Press.

—— (1986), *Narrow Windows, Blind Giants and Angry Orphans: The Dynamics of Systems Rivalries and Dilemmas of Technology Policy*, Stanford, Stanford University, CEPR, Working Paper no. 10; paper presented at the Conference on Innovation Diffusion, Venice, 17–22 March 1986, forthcoming in Arcangeli *et al.* (1988).

Dosi, G. (1982a), 'Technological paradigms and technological trajectories: a suggested interpretation of the determinants and directions of technical change', *Research Policy*, vol 11, pp. 147–162.

—— (1982b), *On engines, thermostats, bicycles and tandems, or, moving some steps towards economic dynamics*, Brighton, SPRU, University of Sussex, mimeo.

—— (1983), 'Technological paradigms and technological trajectories: the determinants and directions of technical change and the transformation of the economy', in C. Freeman (1983).

—— (1986), *The Microeconomic Sources and Effects of Innovation. An Assessment of Recent Findings*, Brighton, SPRU, University of Sussex, DRC Discussion Papers.

—— (1988), 'Institutions and markets in a dynamic world', in *The Manchester School*, forthcoming.

Dosi, G. and Egidi, M. (1987), *Substantive and Procedural Uncertainty: An Exploration of Economic Behaviours in Complex and Changing Environments*, SPRU, Brighton, University of Sussex, DRC Discussion Paper; presented at the Conference on Flexible Automation and New Work Modes, Paris, 2–4 April 1987.

Dosi, G., Orsenigo, L. and Silverberg, G. (1986), *Innovation, Diversity and Diffusion: A Self-organisation model*, Brighton, SPRU, University of Sussex; paper presented at the Conference on Innovation Diffusion, Venice, 17–22 March 1986 forthcoming in Arcangeli *et al.* (1988).

Dosi. G., Pavitt, K. and Soete, L. (1988), *The Economics of Technical Change and*

International Trade, Brighton, Wheatsheaf, forthcoming.

Dosi, G., Rumelt, D., Teece, D. and Winter, S. (1988), 'Toward a theory of corporate coherence', preliminary results have been presented at the conference on Technology and the Firm in an Historical Perspective, Terni, Italy, 14 October 1987.

Downie, J. (1958), *The Competitive Process*, London, Duckworth.

Eliasson, G. (1984), 'Microheterogeneity of firms and the stability of industrial growth', *Journal of Economic Behavior and Organisation*, vol 5, pp. 249–274.

—— (1986), *Innovative Change, Dynamic Market Allocation and Long-Term Stability of Economic Growth*, Stockholm, Industrial Institute for Economic and Social Research; delivered at the Conference on Innovation Diffusion, Venice, 17–22 March 1986; forthcoming in Arcangeli *et al.* (1988).

Elster, J. (1983), *Explaining Technical Change: A Case Study in the Philosophy of Science*, Cambridge, Cambridge University Press.

Freeman, C. (1982), *The Economics of Industrial Innovation*, 2nd edn., London, Frances Pinter (1st edn., Penguin, 1974).

—— (ed.) (1983), *Long Waves in the World Economy*, London, Butterworth (2nd edn, London, Frances Pinter, 1984).

Frydman, R. (1982), 'Towards an understanding of market processes', *American Economic Review*, vol 72, pp. 652–668.

Gazon, J. (1979), *Transmission de l'influence économique: une approche structurale*, Paris, Éd. Sirey.

Gibbons, M. and Metcalfe, J.S. (1986), *Technological Variety and the Process of Competition*, Manchester, University of Manchester; paper delivered at the Conference on Innovation Diffusion, Venice, 17–22 March 1986; forthcoming in Arcangeli *et al.* (1988).

Gordon, T.J. and Munson, T.R. (1981), *Research into Technology Output Measures*, Gladstonbury, Conn., The Future Group.

Hahn, F. (1984), *Equilibrium and Macroeconomics*, Oxford, Basil Blackwell.

Harris, D. (1982), Structural change and economic growth: a review article', *Contributions to Political Economy* vol 1, pp. 25–46.

Heiner, R. (1983), 'The origin of predictable behaviour', *American Economic Review* vol 83, pp. 560–595.

—— (1986), 'Uncertainty, signal-detection experiments and modelling behaviour', in R.N. Langlois (ed.) (1986), *Economics as a Process: Essays in the New Institutional Economics*, Cambridge, Cambridge University Press, pp. 59–115.

Herriott, S.R., Levinthal, D. and March, J.G. (1985), 'Learning from experience in organisations', *American Economic Review, Papers and Proceedings*.

Iwai, K. (1981), *Schumpeterian Dynamics: Part I: An Evolutionary Model of Innovation and Imitation*; *Part II: Technological Progress, Firm Growth and 'Economic Selection'*, New Haven, Yale University, Cowles Foundation Discussion Papers; reduced and revised versions are published in the *Journal of Economic Behavior and Organization*, 1984.

Jacquemin, A. and Rainelli, M. (1984), 'Filières de la nation et filières de l'enterprise', *Revue Économique*, vol 35, pp. 379–392.

Kaldor, N. (1972), 'The irrelevance of equilibrium economics', *Economic Journal*, vol 82, pp. 1237–1255.

—— (1984), 'Teorie dell'equilibrio e teoria della crescita', in *Equilibrio, Distribuzione e Crescita*, Torino, Einaudi, originally published in Spanish in *Cuad-*

ernos de Economica (1974).

Kalecki, M. (1943), 'Political aspects of full employment, *The Political Quarterly*, October.

Kay, N. (1979), *The Innovating Firm*, London, Macmillan.

—— (1984), *The Emergent Firm*, London, Macmillan.

Knight, F.H. (1965), *Risk, Uncertainty and Profit*, London, Harper.

Leijonhufvud, A. (1981), *Information and Coordination*, Oxford, Oxford University Press.

Lesage, A. (1984), *Définition structurale d'une filière de production*, Liège, CREDEL, Discussion Paper No. 8401.

Lewis, A.A. (1985), 'On effectively computable realizations of choice functions', *Mathematical Social Sciences*, vol. 10.

—— (1986), 'Structure and complexity: the use of recursion theory in the foundations of neoclassical mathematical economics and the theory of games', Ithaca, Cornell University, Dept. of Mathematics.

Lipietz, A. (1984), *Accumulation, crises et sortie de crise: quelques réflexions méthodologiques autour de la notion de régulation'*, Paris, CEPREMAP.

Marris, R. and Mueller, D.C. (1980), 'Corporation, competition and the invisible hand', *Journal of Economic Literature*, vol. 18, pp. 32–63.

Montfort, A. (1983), 'A la recherche des filières de production', *Économie et Statistiques*, vol. 183, no. 131, pp. 3–12.

Nelson, R. (1981), 'Assessing private enterprise', *Bell Journal of Economics*, vol. 12, pp. 93–111.

—— (1985), *Industry growth accounts and cost functions when techniques are proprietary*, New Haven, Yale University, mimeo.

—— (1987), 'Technology and the firm', presented at the Conference on Technology and the Firm in an Historical Perspective, Terni, Italy, 1–4 October 1987.

Nelson, R., and Winter, S. (1977), 'In search of a useful theory of innovations', *Research Policy*, vol. 6, pp. 36–77.

—— (1982), *An Evolutionary Theory of Economic Change*, Cambridge, Mass., The Belknap Press of Harvard University Press.

Okun, A.M. (1981), *Prices and Quantities*, Oxford, Basil Blackwell.

Pasinetti, L.L. (1981), *Structural Change and Economic Growth*, Cambridge, Cambridge University Press.

Pavitt, K. (1984a), 'Sectoral Patterns of technical change: towards a taxonomy and a theory', *Research Policy*, vol. 13, pp. 343–374.

—— (1984b), Technological innovation and strategic management, SPRU, University of Sussex, Brighton, mimeo.

Perez, C. (1983) Structural Change and the Assimilation of New Technologies in the Economic and Social System, *Futures*, vol. 15, pp. 357–375.

Perroux, F. (1973), 'L'effet d'entraînement: de l'analyse au repérage quantitiative', *Économie Appliquée* vol. 26, pp. 647–674.

Rosenberg, N. (1976), *Perspectives on Technology*, Cambridge, Cambridge University Press.

—— (1982), *Inside the Black Box*, Cambridge, Cambridge University Press.

Sah, R.K. and Stiglitz, J. (1985), 'Human fallibility and economic organisation', *American Economic Review, Papers and Proceedings*.

Sahal, D. (1981), *Patterns of Technological Innovation*, New York, Addison Wesley.

Salvati, M. (1983), 'Political business cycles and long waves in industrial relations: a note on Kalecki and Phelps-Brown', in Freeman (ed.) (1983).

Saviotti, P. and Metcalfe, J.S. (1984), 'A theoretical approach to the construction of technological output indicators', *Research Policy*, vol. 13, pp. 141–152.

Schackle, G.L. (1961), *Decision, Order and Time in Human Affairs*, Cambridge, Cambridge University Press.

Scherer, F.M. (1982), 'Inter-industry technology flows in the United States', *Research Policy*, vol. 11, pp. 227–246.

Schmookler, J. (1966), *Invention and Economic Growth*, Cambridge, Mass., Harvard University Press.

Schumpeter, J.A. (1943), *Capitalism, Socialism and Democracy*, New York, Harper & Row.

Silverberg, G. (1987), 'Technical progress, capital accumulation and effective demand: a self-organization model', in D. Batten et al. (eds), *Economic Evolution and Structural Adjustment*, Berlin, Heidelberg, New York, Tokyo, Springer Verlag.

Simon, H. (1955), 'A behavioral model of rational choice', *Quarterly Journal of Economics*, vol. 69, pp. 99–118.

—— (1957), *Administrative Behavior*, New York, Macmillan.

Soete, L. and Dosi, G. (1983), *Technology and Employment in the Electronics Industry*, London, Frances Pinter.

Stiglitz, J. (1985), 'Information and economic analysis: a perspective', *Economic Journal*, vol. 95, pp. 21–41.

Steindl, J. (1976), Maturity and Stagnation of American Capitalism, New York, Monthly Review Press, 2nd edition.

Strassman, W.P. (1959), 'Interrelated industries and the rate of technological change', *Review of Economic Studies*, vol. 27, pp. 16–22.

Sylos Labini, P. (1967), *Oligopoly and Technical Progress*, 2nd edn., Cambridge, Mass., Harvard University Press.

—— (1984), *Le Forze dello Sviluppo e del Declino*, Bari, Laterza.

Teece, D. (1982a), 'Toward an economic theory of the multi-product firm', *Journal of Economic Behaviour and Organisation*, vol. 3, pp. 39–64.

—— (1982b), *Some Efficiency Properties of the Modern Corporation: Theory and Evidence*, School of Business Administration, Berkeley, University of California.

—— (1986), 'Profiting from technological innovation', *Research Policy*, vol. 15, pp. 285–306.

Toledano, J. (1978), 'A propos des filières industrielles', *Revue d'Économie Industrielle*.

Waddington, S. (1969), *Toward a Theoretical Biology*, Vol. II, Edinburgh, Edinburgh University Press.

Williamson, O. (1975), *Markets and Hierarchies: Analysis and Anti-Trust Implications*, New York, Free Press.

—— (1985), *The Economic Institutions of Capitalism*, New York, Free Press.

Winter, S.G. (1971), 'Satisficing, selection and the innovating remnant', *Quarterly Journal of Economics*, vol. 85, pp. 237–261.

—— (1982), 'An Essay on the theory of production', in S.H. Hymans (ed.), *Economics and the World Around it*, Ann Arbor, University of Michigan Press.

3 Structural crises of adjustment, business cycles and investment behaviour

Christopher Freeman
Science Policy Research Unit, University of Sussex, Brighton and MERIT, State University of Limburg, Maastricht

Carlota Perez
UNIDO-Ministry of Industry, Caracas and Science Policy Research Unit, University of Sussex, Brighton.

Introduction

This chapter discusses the revival of interest in long-term fluctuations in the growth of the world economy and particularly in the Schumpeterian theory of business cycles. After reviewing the common ground in relation to investment behaviour and business cycles, it goes on to discuss the failure of Keynesian economics to come to terms with the influence of technical change. The central theme of the chapter is that certain types of technical change—defined as changes in 'techno-economic paradigm'—have such widespread consequences for all sectors of the economy that their diffusion is accompanied by a major structural crisis of adjustment, in which social and institutional changes are necessary to bring about a better 'match' between the new technology and the system of social management of the economy—or 'regime of regulation'. Once, however, such a good match is achieved a relatively stable pattern of long-term investment behaviour can emerge for two or three decades. This point is illustrated with respect to the rise of information technology. It is argued that this pervasive technology is likely to heighten still further the instability of the system before a new, more stable pattern of growth is attained.

The resurgence of interest in Schumpeter's ideas (e.g. Elliott, 1985) is associated with the slow-down in the growth of the world economy in the last decade. Whereas during the prolonged post-war boom of the 1950s and the 1960s there was some tendency to assume that the general adoption of Keynesian policies would prevent the recurrence of any depression comparable to that of the 1930s and would smooth out smaller fluctuations, this confidence was somewhat undermined by the deeper recessions of the 1970s and 1980s and the return of much higher levels of unemployment. Not surprisingly, this has led to renewed interest in long-cycle or long-wave theories, which make analogies between the 1930s and the 1980s. This chapter concentrates on the explanation of these deeper structural crises of adjustment, without making any assumptions about fixed periodicity or statistical regularity.

We start by looking at the common ground in the analysis of business cycles. We shall quote extensively from Samuelson for several reasons. First of all, he is probably the most authoritative neo-Keynesian economist, and one who commands respect throughout the profession. Secondly, business cycles have always been one of his central professional interests. Thirdly, as the author of the most widely read economics textbook in the Western World, he provides in the successive editions of this book a convenient synthesis of the changing state of the art (Samuelson and Nordhaus in the most recent and thorough revisions, i.e. the 12th edition).

Areas of agreement in business cycle theory

There are of course many different explanations of business cycles and many explanations for the exceptional severity of the 1930s depression and of the recessions of the 1970s and 1980s. But, as Samuelson has pointed out and most textbooks on the business cycle confirm, there *is* actually a measure of agreement on *some* of the central issues.

Most importantly there is virtually universal agreement that one of the main sources of cyclical fluctuations in the economy is the instability of investment. All empirical studies of business cycles show much greater fluctuations in the capital goods industries than in consumer products, as in the extreme example of the Great Depression of the 1930s, when GNP fell by 30 per cent in the United States but output of producers' durable equipment fell by 75 per cent.

Samuelson (1980) comments:

Ordinarily, consumption movements seem the *effect* rather than the *cause* of the business cycle. In contrast, there is reason to believe that the movements of *durable* goods represent key causes in a more fundamental sense. [p. 242]

The wording is slightly changed in the 1985 edition but the emphasis on investment remains and indeed virtually all schools of economic theory would accept the empirical evidence on the relative amplitude of fluctuations in different sectors of the economy. Moreover, they would also agree that there are certain aspects of investment in plant and equipment which make some fluctuations almost inevitable: 'postponability' on the one hand and competitive pressures to expand capacity on the other; the uneven development in the relative growth rate and capital intensity of various sectors of the economy; indivisibilities in many large investments ('lumpiness') and the 'accelerator' principle tending to amplify investment in upswings and diminish it in downswings. On a smaller scale some similar considerations apply to inventories and to consumer durables. These 'endogenous' factors are in themselves sufficient to account for fluctuations in the system.

However, Samuelson (1980) points out in his 'synthesis' that 'external' factors also play an important part:

> Most economists today believe in a combination of external and internal theories. To explain major cycles, they place crucial emphasis on fluctuations in *investment* or *capital* goods. Primary causes of these capricious and volatile investment fluctuations are found in such external factors as (1) technological innovation, (2) dynamic growth of population and of territory, and even in some economists' view, (3) fluctuations in business confidence and 'animal spirits'.
>
> With these external factors we must combine the internal factors that cause any initial change in investment to be *amplified* in a cumulative multiplied fashion—as people who are given work in the capital goods industries respend part of their new income on consumption goods, and as an air of optimism begins to pervade the business community, causing firms to go to the banks and the securities market for new credit accommodation.
>
> Also, it is necessary to point out that the general business situation definitely reacts in turn on investment. If high consumption sales make business owners optimistic, they are more likely to embark upon venturesome investment programmes. Inventions or scientific discoveries may occur independently of the business cycle, but their appreciable economic introduction will most certainly depend on business conditions.
>
> Therefore especially in the short run, investment is in part an *effect* as well as a cause of income movements. [p. 246]

As Samuelson points out, essentially similar logic applies, of course, in the reverse direction leading to the danger of a cumulative downward spiral. Temporary over-capacity as a result of bunching of investment, perceived lack of sufficient new markets, the saturation of some existing markets, major instabilities in the international economy, over-restrictive monetary policies, uncertainties about technology, protectionism and general lack of business confidence are among the many influences which may trigger or accelerate a vicious circle of declining investment and national income. All of them have been identified as important influences in the severe depression of the 1930s.

Thus far, then, is an area of general agreement about the causes of business cycles and the problems of 'virtuous' and 'vicious' spirals in economic activity. However, a gulf still remains between those economists who, despite what has been said above, still look to the self-regulating private market mechanism, the rate of interest, capital-labour substitution, and monetary policy as the main stabilising forces governing investment behaviour and consequently the fluctuations in the system as a whole, and those who, like Keynes and Samuelson, lack faith in this mechanism to sustain long-term stable growth. The central issue is the possibility of rational optimising behaviour at the micro level of the firm. It will be argued in Part IV of this book that this model of entrepreneurial behaviour is fundamentally flawed. This means that periods of stable growth depend more on a general climate of confidence, including widespread belief in the future potential benefits from technical change, than on an unbelievable set of assumptions about perfect information and accurate calculations on the future rate of return of a wide variety of investments with uncertain outcomes.

Keynes

It is often said that Keynes was deeply rooted in the neo-classical tradition of economics and this is no doubt true. Nevertheless, even in his earliest writings, it is possible to trace his awareness of these limitations of the self-regulating market mechanism. Moggridge (1976) points out that already in 1913 in his book on *Indian Currency and Finance* he insisted on ' . . . the essential fragility of the economic order which others took to be natural and automatic and emphasized the need for conscious management'.

This already foreshadowed his more general onslaught on *laissez-faire* in the 1920s:

The world is *not* so governed from above that private and social interest always coincide. It is *not* so managed here below that in practice they coincide. It is *not* a correct deduction from the Principles of economics that enlightened self-interest generally *is* enlightened; more often individuals seeking separately to promote their ends are too ignorant or too weak to attain even these.

In 1934 in one of his broadcasts on the BBC, he was even more explicit (quoted in Eatwell, 1982):

On the one side are those who believe that the existing economic system is, in the long run, a self-adjusting mechanism, though with creaks and groans and jerks and interrupted by the time lags, outside interference and mistakes . . . on the other side of the gulf are those who reject the idea that the existing economic system is, in any significant sense, self-adjusting . . . The strength of the self-adjusting school depends on its having behind it almost the whole body of organised economic thinking and doctrine of the last hundred years. This is a formidable power . . . For it lies behind the education and the habitual modes of thought, not only of economists, but of bankers and businessmen and civil servants and politicians of all parties . . . thus if the heretics on the other side of the gulf are to demolish the forces of 19th century orthodoxy . . . they must attack them in their citadel. No successful attack has yet been made . . . I range myself with the heretics.

This broadcast foreshadowed the publication of his *General Theory of Employment, Interest and Money*, which at least temporarily was indeed a fairly successful attack (Keynes, 1936) on the 'citadel', and which argued that ' . . . the duty of ordering the current volume of investment cannot safely be left in private hands' and advocated the 'socialisation of investment'. By this he meant, of course, not public ownership or socialism, but public responsibility for the overall level of investment and employment. He insisted that if private decisions to invest were inadequate to overcome a depression, then it was the responsibility of government to compensate for this deficiency. Interest rate policy probably would not be in itself a sufficient inducement to stimulate the necessary flow.

An inadequate level of private investment might arise from many causes; in a famous and often-quoted passage Keynes stressed the impossibility of purely rational calculations about the future rate of return from new investment and compared it with an expedition to the South Pole. He stressed the crucial importance of a climate of confidence and the role of 'animal spirits'. He pointed to the problem of excess capacity even in some industries which had grown rapidly in the previous boom and the problem of temporary saturation of particular markets. He stressed ironically the good fortune of Ancient Egypt in having pyramids and large-scale investment which did not 'stale with abundance' and of the Middle Ages in having cathedrals: 'Two pyramids, two Masses for the dead are twice as good as one, but not so two railways from London to York.'

From the time of the publication of the *General Theory*, orthodox economics mounted a counter-attack mainly on the issues of monetary policy, fiscal policy, and wage flexibility. However, there has been no comparable counter-attack on his theory of private investment behaviour. Indeed, Siegenthaler (1986), quoting Shackle's (1967) essay on 'Keynes' Ultimate Meaning', argues that this is Keynes' most lasting and fundamental contribution to economic theory.

According to Shackle:

Keynes' whole theory of unemployment is ultimately the simple statement that, rational expectation being unattainable, we substitute for it first one and then another kind of irrational expectation; and the shift from one arbitrary basis to another gives us from time to time a moment of truth, when our artificial confidence is for the time being dissolved, and we, as business men, are afraid to invest and so fail to provide enough demand to match our society's desire to produce.

Siegenthaler comments on this passage:

This interpretation of Keynes calls for interpretation itself, but at least three things are made very clear by Shackle. First, confidence enters the scene in a context in which rational expectations cannot be formed on the basis of adequate knowledge, so that confidence must be 'artificial'; subjective certainty which encourages an actor to invest is grounded not in a true model of economic reality, but in an arbitrary one for which sufficient evidence fails to be available; in very particular situations confidence gets dissolved and actors become aware of objective uncertainty, of their inability to know the future and it is only in those 'moments of truth' that subjective uncertainty governs the behaviour of the actor . . . Actors get confident not on the basis of adequate knowledge, not as a result of procedures leading to objectively superior forecasting methods, not as an outcome of individual optimising strategies of selecting and handling information . . . But they do get confident despite uncertainty . . . Confidence, albeit an artificial one, prevails except on rare occasions.

Solow (Klamer, 1984) has scornfully dismissed the attempt of the new school of 'rational expectations' to argue that actors, whether consumers, wage earners or entrepreneurs, can indeed form rational, long-term expectations about such future events as the impact of electronic technology on the economy. And indeed few would attempt to deny the force of Solow's argument or that of Keynes, with respect to major technical innovations.

Nevertheless, because of the crucial importance of technical change for investment behaviour, which is acknowledged by all schools of economic thought, it is essential to examine in more depth the question of the influence of technical change, on the state of confidence and vice versa. At certain times technical change appears to undermine confidence and stability, while at others it has the opposite effect. At the level of the individual innovative investment, the findings of empirical studies of investment and evaluation in R & D are clear-cut and virtually unanimous: they strongly support the view of Shackle and Schumpeter that investment in new products and processes has an element of true uncertainty: by definition the outcome cannot be known (Freeman, 1982, Chapter 7).

However, the analysis cannot be restricted to the level of the individual innovation or to counting innovations; the qualitative aspects and the systems interrelatedness of innovations must be taken into account. Under favourable conditions, the Schumpeterian bandwagons roll and business confidence improves, leading to an atmosphere of 'boom' in which, although there are still risks and uncertainties attached to all investment decisions, animal spirits rise. Such favourable conditions include complementarities between innovations and the emergence of an appropriate infrastructure as well as some degree of political stability and institutions which do not hinder too much the diffusion of new technologies. In these favourable circumstances the growth of new markets and the profitability of new investments appear to offer a fairly stable prospect of future growth, despite the uncertainties.

But there are also circumstances when technical change could have the opposite effect and could destabilise investment by undermining confidence in the future prospects for the growth of some firms, industries or economies. Moreover, as technologies and industries mature over a long period, diminishing returns and declining profitability may set in, leading to sluggish investment behaviour. If this is at all widespread it may take major social and political changes to restore confidence in the future growth of the system on the basis of new technologies. In the section on 'Diffusion of new techno-economic paradigms and institutional changes' we shall discuss the circumstances in which this can occur.

Here we wish only to make the point that in the early stages of radical technical innovation uncertainty prevails, so that Schumpeterian entrepreneurship and Keynesian animal spirits are necessary for the first steps. Once diffusion is under way, even though diffusion itself involves further innovation, the excitement generated by rapid growth of markets and/or exceptional profits of innovations may generate rising confidence and waves of imitation, provided the social and institutional framework and the infrastructure favour these developments.

Keynes himself once acknowledged the dominant influence of technical change on investment behaviour in his *Treatise on Money* (1930):

In the case of fixed capital, it is easy to understand why fluctuations should occur in the rate of investment. Entrepreneurs are induced to embark on the production of fixed capital or deterred from doing so by their expectations of the profit to be made. Apart from the many minor reasons why these should fluctuate in a changing world, Professor Schumpeter's explanation of the major movements may be unreservedly accepted . . .

It is only necessary to add to this that the pace at which the innovating entrepreneurs will be able to carry their projects into execution at a cost in interest which is not deterrent to them will depend on the degree of complaisance of those responsible for the banking system. Thus while the stimulus to a credit inflation comes from outside the banking system, it remains a monetary phenomenon in the sense that it only occurs if the monetary machine is allowed to respond to the stimulus. [Vol. 2, p. 86].

This passage is remarkable not only for its unequivocal acceptance of Schumpeter's explanation of the major surges of investment in capitalist societies but also its emphasis on the enabling role of monetary policy. It is all the more surprising that neither Keynes nor the Keynesians followed up this recognition of the crucial role of technical innovation. In fact, in the *General Theory* Keynes regressed to a position of neglect of technology when he introduced the largely artificial concept of a secular decline in the marginal efficiency of capital unrelated to the actual changes in techniques or in the capital stock. Schumpeter was therefore justified in one of the main points of his critique of the *General Theory*:

it limits applicability of this analysis to a few years at most — perhaps the duration of the '40 months cycle'—and in terms of phenomena, to the factors that *would* govern the greater or the smaller utilisation of an industrial apparatus *if* the latter remains unchanged. *All* the phenomena incident to the creation and change in this apparatus, that is to say the phenomena that dominate the capitalist process, are thus excluded from consideration. [1952, p. 282]

For the Keynesians it became a matter of relative indifference *which* were the new technologies and the fast-growing industries. We shall argue that it does matter very much *which* are the important new technological systems, because they are unique and their effects on private and public R & D and investment strategies, and the government policies, and institutional changes, which are required to advance them, may be very different. We shall argue that Keynesian analysis and policies were and are deficient with respect to long-term changes in technology, their effects on business confidence and structural change in the economy and the specifics of infrastructural investment. Almost all neo-Keynesian (and much other) macroeconomic analysis and modelling is restricted to purely *quantitative* aspects of investment and employment, whereas Schumpeter rightly insisted on the crucial importance of *qualitative* aspects.

Clearly, this criticism of Keynesian theory rests on a particular view of the relationship between technical change and business cycles which is usually associated with Schumpeter's long-wave theory. It sees the major booms, such as those of the 1950s and 1960s or the 1850s and 1860s as based on the diffusion of major new 'techno-economic paradigms' into the world economy and the deeper depressions as periods of structural adjustment, when the social and institutional framework is adapting to the rise of major new technologies.

Interestingly enough, even though Samuelson (1981) has dismissed the likelihood of another major depression, he did stress the probability of a prolonged downturn in the rate of economic growth:

It is my considered guess that the final quarter of the 20th century will fall far short of the third quarter in its achieved rate of economic progress. The dark horoscope of my old teacher Joseph Schumpeter may have particular relevance here.

Samuelson's reference to Schumpeter clearly implies that the major long-term fluctuations in economic development cannot be explained simply in terms of conventional short- and medium-term business-cycle theory but require an additional dimension of analysis. This involves the rise of new technologies, the rise and decline of entire industries, major infrastructural investments, changes in the international location of industry and technological leadership and other related structural changes, for example, in the skills and composition of the labour force and the management structure of enterprises.

A taxonomy of innovations

It has been argued that a weakness of most neo-classical and Keynesian theories of technical change and economic growth is that they fail to take account of the *specifics* of changing technology in each historical period.

One reason that economists do not attempt this daunting task is, of course, the sheer complexity of technical change. How can the thousands of inventions and innovations which are introduced every month and every year be reduced to some kind of pattern amenable to generalisation and analysis? In this section we shall suggest a taxonomy of innovation, based on empirical work at the Science Policy Research Unit. We shall distinguish between (1) Incremental innovation; (2) Radical innovation; (3) New technology systems; (4) Changes of techno-economic paradigms. (See also the introductory discussion on paradigms and trajectories in Chapter 2).

(i) *Incremental innovations*: These types of innovation occur more or less continuously in any industry or service activity although at differing rates in different industries and different countries, depending upon a combination of demand pressures, socio-cultural factors, technological opportunities and trajectories. They may often occur, not so much as the result of any deliberate research and development activity, but as the outcome of inventions and improvements suggested by engineers and other directly engaged in the production process, or as a result of initiatives and proposals by users ('learning by doing and 'learning by using'). Many empirical studies have confirmed their great importance in improving the efficiency in use of all factors of production, for example, Hollander's (1965) study of productivity gains in Du Pont rayon plants or Townsend's (1976) study of the Anderton shearer-loader in the British coal-mining industry. They are frequently associated with the scaling-up of plant and equipment and quality improvements to products and services for a variety of specific applications. Although their combined effect is extremely important in the growth of productivity, no single incremental innovation has dramatic effects, and they may sometimes pass unnoticed and unrecorded. However, their effects are apparent in the steady growth of productivity, which is reflected in input–output tables over time by changes in the coefficients for the existing array of products and services.

(ii) *Radical innovations*: These are discontinuous events and in recent times are usually the result of a deliberate research and development activity in enterprises and/or in university and government laboratories. There is no way in which nylon could have emerged from improving the production process in rayon plants or the woollen industry. Nor could nuclear power have emerged from incremental improvements to coal or oil-fired power stations. Radical innovations are unevenly distributed over sectors and over time, but our research did not support the view of Mensch (1975) that their appearance is concentrated particularly in periods of deep recessions in response to the collapse or decline of established markets (Freeman, Clark and Soete, 1982). But we would agree with Mensch that, whenever they may occur, they are important as the potential springboard for the growth of new markets, and for the surges of new investment associated with booms. They may often involve a combined product, process and organisational innovation. Over a period of decades radical innovations, such as nylon or 'the pill', may have fairly dramatic effects, i.e., they *do* bring about structural change but in terms of their aggregate economic impact they are relatively small and localised, unless a whole cluster of radical innovations are linked together in the rise of new industries and services, such as the synthetic materials industry or the semiconductor industry.

(iii) *Changes of 'technology system'*: These are far-reaching changes in technology, affecting several branches of the economy, as well as giving rise to entirely new sectors. They are based on a combination of radical and incremental innovations, together with *organisational* and *managerial* innovations affecting more than one or a few firms. Keirstead (1948), in his exposition of a Schumpeterian theory of economic development, introduced the concept of 'constellations' of innovaions, which were technically and economically interrelated. An obvious example is the cluster of synthetic materials innovations, petro-chemical innovations, machinery innovations in injection moulding and extrusion, and innumerable application innovations introduced in the 1920s, 1930s, 1940s and 1950s (Freeman, Clark and Soete, 1982).

(iv) *Changes in 'techno-economic paradigm' ('technological revolutions')*: Some changes in technology systems are so far-reaching in their effects that they have a major influence on the behaviour of the entire economy. A change of this kind carries with it many clusters of radical and incremental innovations, and may eventually embody a number of new technology systems. A vital characteristic of this fourth type of technical change is that it has *pervasive* effects throughout the economy, i.e. it not only leads to the emergence of a new range of products, services, systems and industries in its own right; it also affects directly or indirectly almost every other branch of the economy, i.e. it is a 'meta-paradigm'. We use the expression 'techno-economic' (Perez, 1983) rather than 'technological paradigm' (Dosi, 1982) because the changes involved go beyond engineering trajectories for specific product or process technologies and affect the input cost structure and conditions of production and distribution throughout the system. This fourth category corresponds to Nelson and Winter's concept of 'general natural trajectories' and, once established as the dominant influence on engineers, designers and managers, becomes a 'technological regime' for several decades. From this it is evident that we view Schumpeter's long cycles and 'creative gales of destruction' as a succession of 'techno-economic paradigms' associated with a characteristic institutional framework, which, however, only emerges after a painful process of structural change.

We now turn to an elaboration of the main characteristics of 'techno-economic' paradigms and their patterns of diffusion through long waves of economic development. As the following sections will attempt to show, a new techno-economic paradigm develops initially within the old, showing its decisive advantages during the 'downswing' phase of the previous Kondratiev cycle. However, it becomes established as a dominant technological regime only after a crisis of structural adjustment, involving deep social and institutional changes, as well as the replacement of the motive branches of the economy (Table 3.1).

'Key factor' inputs and change of techno-economic paradigm

As the last section has made clear, our conception of 'techno-economic paradigm' is much wider than 'clusters' of innovations or even of 'technology systems'. We are referring to a combination of interrelated product and process, technical, organisational and managerial innovations, embodying a quantum jump in potential productivity for all or most of the economy and opening up an unusually wide range of investment and profit opportunities. Such a paradigm change implies a unique new combination of decisive technical *and* economic advantages.

Clearly one major characteristic of the diffusion pattern of a new techno-economic paradigm is its spread from the initial industries or areas of application to a much wider range of industries and services and the economy as a whole (Table 3.1). By 'paradigm' change we mean precisely a radical transformation of the prevailing engineering and managerial *common sense* for best productivity and most profitable practice, which is applicable in almost any industry (i.e. we are talking about a 'meta-paradigm').

The organising principle of each successive paradigm and the justification for the expression 'techno-economic paradigm' is to be found not only in a new range of products and systems, but most of all in the dynamics of the relative *cost* structure of all possible inputs to production. In each new techno-economic paradigm, a particular input or set of inputs, which may be described as the 'key factor' of that paradigm, fulfils the following conditions:

(i)   Clearly perceived low and rapidly falling relative cost. As Rosenberg (1975) and other economists have pointed out, small changes in the relative input cost structure have little or no effect on the behaviour of engineers, designers and researchers. Only major and persistent changes have the power to transform the decision rules and 'common sense' procedures for engineers and managers (Perez, 1985; Freeman and Soete, 1987).

(ii) Apparently almost unlimited availability of supply over long periods. Temporary shortages may of course occur in a period of rapid buildup in demand for the new key factor, but the prospect must be clear that there are no major barriers to an enormous long-term increase in supply. This is an essential condition for the confidence to take major investment decisions which depend on this long-term availability.

(iii) Clear potential for the use or incorporation of the new key factor or factors in many products and processes throughout the economic system; either directly or (more commonly) through a set of related innovations, which both reduce the cost and change the quality of capital equipment, labour inputs, and other inputs to the system.

We would maintain that this combination of characteristics holds today for microelectronics and we discuss this further in the section below on the 'information technology paradigm'. It held until recently for oil, which underlay the post-war boom (the 'fourth Kondratiev' upswing). Before that, and more tentatively, we would suggest that the role of key factor was played by low-cost steel in the third Kondratiev wave, by low-cost and steam-powered transport in the 'Victorian' boom of the nineteenth century (Table 3.1, column 5—'Key factor industries. . .').

Clearly, every one of these inputs identified as 'key factors' existed (and was in use) long before the new paradigm developed. However, its full potential is only recognised and made capable of fulfilling the above conditions when the previous key factor and its related constellation of technologies give strong signals of diminishing returns and of approaching limits to their potential for further increasing productivity or for new profitable investment. (In quite different types of society and different historical circumstances, archaeologists have also recognised the crucial importance of 'key factors' in economic development in their classification of the 'Stone Age', 'Bronze Age' and 'Iron Age'.)

From a purely technical point of view, the explosive surge of interrelated innovations involved in a technological revolution could probably have occurred earlier and in a more gradual manner. But, there are strong economic and social factors at play that serve as prolonged containment first and as unleashing forces later. The massive externalities created to favour the diffusion and generalisation of the prevailing paradigm act as a powerful deterrent to change for a prolonged period (see Chapter 26 by Brian Arthur). It is only when productivity along the old trajectories shows persistent limits to growth and future profits are seriously threatened that the high risks and costs of trying the new technologies appear as clearly justified. And it is only after many of these trials have been obviously successful that further applications become easier and less risky investment choices.

The new key factor does not appear as an isolated input, but rather at the core of a rapidly growing system of technical, social and managerial innovations, some related to the production of the key factor itself and others to its utilisation. At first these innovations may appear (and may be in fact pursued) as a means for overcoming the specific bottlenecks of the old technologies, but the new key factor soon acquires its own dynamics and successive innovations take place through an intensive interactive process, spurred by the limits to growth which are increasingly apparent under the old paradigm (Table 3.1, column 7—'Limitations of previous techno-economic paradigm . . .'). In this way the most successful new technology systems gradually crystallise as a new 'ideal' type of production organisation which becomes the common sense of management and design, embodying new 'rules of thumb' and restoring confidence to investment decision-makers after a long period of hesitation.

Clearly, this approach differs radically from the dominant conceptualisation of changing factor costs in neo-classical economic theory, although it has points of contact, such as the persistent search for least-cost combinations of factor inputs to sustain or increase profitability. Most formulations of neo-classical theory put the main emphasis on varying combinations of labour and capital and on substitution between them, and implicitly or explicitly assume responsiveness even to small changes in

Table 3.1 A tentative sketch of some of the main characteristics of successive long waves (modes of growth)

1	2 Approx. periodisation Upswing Downswing	3 Description	4 Main 'carrier branches' and induced growth sectors infra-structure	5 Key factor industries offering abundant supply at descending price	6 Other sectors growing rapidly from small base	7 Limitations of previous techno-economic paradigm and ways in which new paradigm offers some solutions	8 Organisation of firms and forms of cooperation and competition
Number							
First	1770s & 1780s to 1830s & 1840s 'Industrial revolution' 'Hard times'	Early mechan- isation Kondratieff	Textiles Textile chemicals Textile machinery Iron-working and iron castings Water power Potteries Trunk canals Turnpike roads	Cotton Pig iron	Steam engines Machinery	Limitations of scale, process control and mechanisation in domestic 'putting out' system. Limitations of hand-operated tools and processes. Solutions offering prospects of greater productivity and profitability through mechanisation and factory organisation in leading industries.	Individual entrepreneurs and small firms (< 100 employees) competition. Partnership structure facilitates co-operation of technical innovators and financial managers. Local capital and individual wealth.
Second	1830s & 1840s to 1880s & 1890s Victorian prosperity	Steam power and railway Kondratieff	Steam engines Steamships Machine tools Iron Railway equipment	Coal Transport	Steel Electricity Gas Synthetic dyestuffs	Limitations of water power in terms of inflexibility of location, scale of production, reliability and range of	High noon of small-firm competition, but larger firms now employing thousands, rather than hundreds. As firms and

	'Great depression'	Railways World Shipping		applications, restricting further development of mechanisation and factory production to the economy as a whole. Largely overcome by steam engine and new transport system.	markets grow, limited liability and joint stock company permit new pattern of investment, risk-taking and ownership.
Third	1880s & 1890s to 1930s & 1940s 'Belle epoque' 'Great depression'	Electrical and heavy engineering Kondratieff	Electrical engineering Electrical machinery Cable and wire Heavy engineering Heavy armaments Steel ships Heavy chemicals Synthetic dyestuffs Electricity supply and distribution	Steel	Automobiles Aircraft Telecommunications Radio Aluminium Consumer durables Oil Plastics	Limitations of iron as an engineering material in terms of strength, durability, precision, etc., partly overcome by universal availability of cheap steel and of alloys. Limitations of inflexible belts, pulleys, etc., driven by one large steam engine overcome by unit and group drive for electrical machinery, overhead cranes, power tools permitting vastly improved layout and capital saving. Standardisation facilitating world-wide operations	Emergence of giant firms, cartels, trusts and mergers. Monopoly and oligopoly became typical. 'Regulation' or state ownership of 'natural' monopolies and 'public utilities'. Concentration of banking and 'finance-capital'. Emergence of specialised 'middle management' in large firms.

Table 3.1—*cont.*

1	2	3	4	5	6	7	8
Number	Approx. periodisation Upswing Downswing	Description	Main 'carrier branches' and induced growth sectors infra-structure	Key factor industries offering abundant supply at descending price	Other sectors growing rapidly from small base	Limitations of previous techno-economic paradigm and ways in which new paradigm offers some solutions	Organisation of firms and forms of cooperation and competition
Fourth	1930s & 1940s to 1980s & 1990s Golden age of growth and Keynesian full employment Crisis of structural adjustment	Fordist mass production Kondratieff	Automobiles Trucks Tractors Tanks Armaments for motorised warfare Aircraft Consumer durables Process plant Synthetic materials Petro-chemicals Highways Airports Airlines	Energy (especially oil)	Computers Radar NC machine tools Drugs Nuclear weapons and power Missiles Micro-electronics Software	Limitations of scale of batch production overcome by flow processes and assembly-line production techniques, full standardisation of components and materials and abundant cheap energy. New patterns of industrial location and urban development through speed and flexibility of automobile and air transport. Further cheapening of mass consumption products	Oligopolistic competition. Multinational corporations based on direct foreign investment and multi-plant locations. Competitive subcontracting on 'arms length' basis or vertical integration. Increasing concentration, divisionalisaton and hierarchical control. 'Techno-structure' in large corporations.

| Fifth* | 1980s & 1990s to ? | Information and communication Kondratieff | Computers
Electronic capital goods
Software
Tele-communications equipment
Optical fibres
Robotics
FMS
Ceramics
Data banks
Information services

Digital tele-communications network
Satellites | 'Chips' (micro-electronics) | Third generation' biotechnology products and processes
Space activities
Fine chemicals
SDI | Diseconomies of scale and inflexibility of dedicated assembly-line and process plant partly overcome by flexible manufacturing systems, 'networking' and 'economies of scope'. Limitations of energy intensity and materials intensity partly overcome by electronic control systems and components. Limitations of hierarchical departmentalisation overcome by 'systemation', 'networking' and integration of design, production and marketing. | 'Networks' of large and small firms based increasingly on computer networks and close co-operation in technology, quality control, training, investment planning and production planning ('just-in-time') etc. 'Keiretsu' and similar structures offering internal capital markets. |

*All columns dealing with the "fifth Kondratieff" are necessarily speculative

Table 3.1—*cont.*

9 Number	10 Techno-logical leaders	11 Other industrial and newly industrial-ising countries	12 Some features of national regimes of regulation	13 Aspects of the international regulatory regime	14 Main features of the national system of innovation	15 Some features of tertiary sector development	16 Representative innovative entrepreneurs engineers	17 Political economists and philosophers
First	Britain France Belgium	German states Nether-lands	Breakdown and dissolution of feudal and medieval monopolies, guilds, tolls, privileges and restrictions on trade, industry and competition. Repression of unions. Laissez-faire established as dominant principle.	Emergence of British supremacy in trade and international finance with the defeat of Napoleon.	Encouragement of science through National Academies, Royal Society, etc. Engineer and inventor-entrepreneurs and partnerships. Local scientific and engineering societies. Part-time training and on-the-job training. Reform and strengthening of national patent systems. Transfer of technology by migration of skilled workers. British Institution of Civil Engineers. Learning by doing, using and interacting	Rapid expansion of retail and wholesale trade in new urban centres. Very small state apparatus. Merchants as source of capital	Arkwright Boulton Wedgwood Owen Bramah Maudslay	Smith Say Owen
Second	Britain France Belgium Germany USA	Italy Nether-lands Switzerland Austria–Hungary	High noon of laissez-faire. 'Nightwatchman state' with minimal regulatory	'Pax Britannica'. British naval, financial and trade dominance.	Establishment of Institution of Mechanical Engineers and development of UK Mechanics' Institutes. More rapid development of professional education and	Rapid growth of domestic service for new middle class to largest service occupation. Continued rapid	Stephenson Whitworth Brunel Armstrong Whitney Singer	Ricardo List Marx

		functions except protection of property and legal framework for production and trade. Acceptance of craft unions. Early social legislation and pollution control.	International free trade. Gold standard.	training of engineers and skilled workers elsewhere in Europe. Growing specialisation. Internationalisation of patent system. Learning by doing, using and interacting	growth of transport and distribution. Universal postal and communication services. Growth of financial services	Marshall Pareto Lenin Veblen
Third	Germany USA Britain France Belgium Switzerland Netherlands	Italy Austria–Hungary Canada Sweden Denmark Japan Russia	Nationalist and imperialist state regulation or state ownership of basic infrastructure (public utilities). Arms race. Much social legislation. Rapid growth of state bureaucracy.	Imperialism and colonisation. 'Pax Britannica' comes to an end with First World War. Destabilisation of international financial and trade system leading to world crisis and Second World War.	'In-house' R and D departments established in German and US chemical and electrical engineering industries. Recruitment of university scientists and engineers and graduates of the new Technische Hochschulen and equivalent Institutes of Technology. National Standard Institutions and national laboratories. Universal elementary education. Learning by doing, using and interacting	Peak of domestic service industry. Rapid growth of state and local bureaucracies. Department stores and chain stores. Education, tourism and entertainment expanding rapidly. Corresponding take-off of white-collar employment pyramid. London as centre for major world commodity markets.	Siemens Carnegie Nobel Edison Krupp Bosch

Table 3.1—*cont.*

9 Number	10 Techno-logical leaders	11 Other industrial and newly industrial-ising countries	12 Some features of national regimes of regulation	13 Aspects of the international regulatory regime	14 Main features of the national system of innovation	15 Some features of tertiary sector development	16 Representative innovative entrepreneurs engineers	17 Political economists and philosophers
Fourth	USA Germany Other EEC Japan Sweden Switzer-land USSR Other EFTA Canada Australia	Other Eastern European Korea Brazil Mexico Venezuela Argentina China India Taiwan	'Welfare state' and 'warfare state'. Attempted state regulation of investment, growth and employment by Keynesian techniques. High levels of state expenditure and involvement. 'Social partnership' with unions after collapse of fascism. "Roll-back" of welfare state deregulation and privatisation during crisis of adjustment	'Pax Americana' US economic and military dominance. Decolonisa-tion. Arms race and cold war with USSR. US-dominated international financial and trade regime (GATT, IMF, World Bank) Destabilisation of Bretton Woods regime in 1970s	Spread of specialised R and D departments to most industries. Large-scale state involvement in military R and D through contracts and national laboratories. Increasing state involvement in civil science and technology. Rapid expansion of secondary and higher education and of industrial training. Transfer of technology through extensive licensing and know-how agreements and investment by multinational corporations. Learning by doing using and interacting.	Sharp decline of domestic service. Self-service fast food and growth of super-markets and hypermarkets, petrol service stations. Continued growth of state bureaucracy, armed forces and social services. Rapid growth of research and professions and financial services, packaged tourism and air travel on very large scale.	Sloan McNamara Ford Agnelli Nordhoff Matsushita	Keynes Schumpeter Kalecki

Fifth*		'Regulation' of strategic ICT infrastructure. 'Big Brother' or 'Big Sister' state. Deregulation and reregulation of national financial institutions and capital markets. Possible emergence of new-style participatory decentralised welfare state based on ICT and red–green alliance.	'Multi-polarity'. Regional blocs. Problems of developing appropriate international institutions capable of regulating global finance, capital, ICT and transnational companies.	Horizontal integration of R and D, design, production and process engineering and marketing. Integration of process design with multi-skill training. Computer networking and collaborative research. State support for generic technologies and university–industry collaboration. New types of proprietary regime for software and biotechnology. 'Factory as laboratory'.	Rapid growth of new information services, data banks and software industries. Integration of services and manufacturing in such industries as printing and publishing. Rapid growth of professional consultancy. New forms of craft production linked to distribution.	Kobayashi Uenohara Barron Benneton Noyce	Schumacher Aoki Bertalanffy
	Japan USA Germany Sweden Other EEC EFTA USSR and other Eastern European Taiwan Korea Canada Australia						
	Brazil Mexico Argentina Venezuela China India Indonesia Turkey Egypt Pakistan Nigeria Algeria Tunisia Other Latin American						

*All columns dealing with the "fifth Kondratieff" are necessarily speculative

Source: based on Freeman (1987)

these relative factor prices in either direction, i.e. 'reversibility'. Our approach stresses the system's response to *major* changes in the price of *new* inputs, and *new* technologies which exploit their potential to reduce costs of both labour and capital, as a result of new total factor input combinations and organisational–managerial innovations. Such major changes are the result of an active and prolonged search in response to perceived limits, not on the basis of perfect information but on the basis of trial and error, i.e. the historical learning process stressed by Hahn (see Chapter 1). Once the new technology is widely adopted, the change is generally irreversible (i.e. the principal actors became 'locked in' by the pervasive economic and technical advantages and complementarities; (see Chapter 26).

We have stressed the role of a key factor or factors in creating widening investment opportunities and creating the potential for big increases in productivity and profits. We turn now to consider the wider societal problems involved in the transition from one 'techno-economic paradigm' to another.

Diffusion of new techno-economic paradigms and institutional change

It is a clear implication of our mode of conceptualising successive 'techno-economic paradigms' that a new paradigm emerges in a world still dominated by an old paradigm and begins to demonstrate its comparative advantages at first only in one or a few sectors. The fastest-growing new sectors are thus *not* those which are the motive branches of an established, technological regime (Table 3.1, columns 5–'Main "carrier branches" and 6–'Other sectors growing rapidly'). There is no possibility of a new paradigm displacing an old one until it has first clearly demonstrated such advantages and until the supply of the new key factor or factors already satisfies the three conditions described above: falling costs, rapidly increasing supply, and pervasive applications. Thus a period of rapid growth in the supply of the key factor(s) occurs already *before* the new paradigm is established as the dominant one, and continues when it is the prevailing regime.

A new techno-economic paradigm emerges only gradually as a new 'ideal type' of productive organisation, to take full advantage of the key factor(s) which are becoming more and more visible in the relative cost structure. The new paradigm discloses the potential for a quantum jump in total factor productivity and opens up an unprecedented range of new investment opportunities. It is for these reasons that it brings about a radical shift in engineering and managerial 'common sense' and that it tends to diffuse as rapidly as conditions allow, replacing the investment pattern of the old paradigm.

The full constellation—once crystallised—goes far beyond the key factor(s) and beyond technical change itself. It brings with it a restructuring of the whole productive system.

Among other things as it crystallises, the new techno-economic paradigm involves:

(a) a new 'best-practice' form of organisation in the firm and at the plant level;
(b) a new skill profile in the labour force, affecting both quality and quantity of labour and corresponding patterns of income distribution;
(c) a new product mix in the sense that those products which make intensive use of the low-cost key factor will be the preferred choice for investment and will represent therefore a growing proportion of GNP;
(d) new trends in both radical and incremental innovation geared to substituting more intensive use of the new key factor(s) for other relatively high-cost elements;
(e) a new pattern in the location of investment both nationally and internationally as the change in the relative cost structure transforms comparative advantages;
(f) a particular wave of infra-structural investment designed to provide appropriate externalities throughout the system and facilitate the use of the new products and processes everywhere;
(g) a tendency for new innovator-entrepreneur-type small firms also to enter the new rapidly expanding branches of the economy and in some cases to initiate entirely new sectors of production;
(h) a tendency for large firms to concentrate, whether by growth or diversification, in those branches of the economy where the key factor is produced and most intensively used, which results in there being distinctly different branches acting as the engines of growth in each successive Kondratiev upswing;
(i) a new pattern of consumption of goods and services and new types of distribution and consumer behaviour.

From this it is evident that the period of transition—the downswing and depression of the long wave—is characterised by deep structural change in the economy and such changes require an equally profound transformation of the institutional and social framework. The onset of prolonged recessionary trends indicates the increasing degree of mismatch between the techno-economic sub-system and the old socio-institutional framework. It shows the need for a full-scale reaccommodation of social behaviour and institutions to suit the requirements and the potential of a shift which has already taken place to a considerable extent in some areas of the techno-economic sphere. This reaccommodation occurs as a result of a process of political search, experimentation and adaptation, but when it has been achieved, by a variety of social and political changes at the national and international level, the resulting good 'match' facilitates the upswing phase of the long wave. A climate of confidence for a surge of new investment is created through an appropriate combination of regulatory mechanisms which foster the full deployment of the new paradigm. Since the achievement of a 'good match' is a conflict-ridden process and proceeds very unevenly in differing national political and cultural contexts, this may exert a considerable influence on the changing pattern of international technological leadership and international patterns of diffusion (Table 3.1 and Chapter 23).

Schumpeter's (1939) theory of depression was rather narrowly 'economic' and strangely, for someone who was so much aware of social and organisational aspects of technical innovation, tended to ignore the institutional aspects of recovery policies. This was one of the main reasons for the relative neglect of his ideas compared with those of Keynes.

The information technology paradigm

The technological regime, which predominated in the post-war boom, was one based on low-cost oil and energy-intensive materials (especially petrochemicals and synthetics), and was led by giant oil, chemical, automobile and other mass durable goods producers. Its 'ideal' type of productive organisation at the plant level was the continuous-flow assembly-line turning out massive quantities of identical units. The 'ideal' type of firm was the 'corporation' with a separate and complex hierarchical managerial and administrative structure, including in-house R & D and operating in oligopolistic markets in which advertising and marketing activities played a major role. It required large numbers of middle-range skills in both the blue- and white-collar areas, leading to a characteristic pattern of occupations and income distribution. The massive expansion of the market for consumer durables was facilitated by this pattern, as well as by social changes and adaptation of the financial system, which permitted the growth of 'hire purchase' and other types of consumer credit. The paradigm required a vast infrastructural network of motorways, service stations, airports, oil and petrol distribution systems, which was promoted by public investment on a large scale already in the 1930s, but more massively in the post-war period. At various times in different countries both civil and military expenditures of governments played a very important part in stimulating aggregate demand, and a specific pattern of demand for automobiles, weapons, consumer durables, synthetic materials and petroleum products.

Today, with cheap microelectronics widely available, with prices expected to fall still further and with related new developments in computers and telecommunications, it is no longer 'common sense' to continue along the (now expensive) path of energy and materials-intensive inflexible mass production.

The 'ideal' information-intensive productive organisation now increasingly links design, management, production and marketing into one integrated system—a process which may be described as 'systemation' and which goes far beyond the earlier concepts of mechanisation and automation. Firms organised on this new basis, whether in the computer industry such as IBM, or in the clothing industry such as Benneton, can produce a flexible and rapidly changing mix of products and services. Growth tends increasingly to be led by the electronics and information sectors, taking advantage of the growing externalities provided by an all-encompassing telecommunications infrastructure, which will ultimately bring down to extremely low levels the costs of access to the system for both producers and users of information.

The skill profile associated with the new techno-economic paradigm appears to change from the concentration on middle-range craft and supervisory skills to increasingly high- and low-range qualifications, and from narrow specialisation to broader, multi-purpose basic skills for information handling. Diversity and flexibility at all levels substitute for homogeneity and dedicated systems.

The transformation of the profile of capital equipment is no less radical. Computers are increasingly associated with all types of productive equipment as in CNC machine tools, robotics, and process control instruments as well as with the design process through CAD, and with administrative functions through data processing systems, all linked by data transmission equipment. According to some estimates computer-based capital equipment already accounts for nearly half of all new fixed investment in plant and equipment in the United States.

The deep structural problems involved in this change of paradigm are now evident in all parts of the world. Among the manifestations are the acute and persistent shortage of the high-level skills associated with the new paradigm, even in countries with high levels of general unemployment, and the persistent surplus capacity in the older 'smokestack', energy-intensive industries such as steel, oil and petrochemicals.

As a result there is a growing search for new social and political solutions in such areas as flexible working time, shorter working hours, re-education and retraining systems, regional policies based on creating favourable conditions for information technology (rather than tax incentives to capital-intensive mass production industries), new financial systems, possible decentralisation of management and government, and access to data banks and networks at all levels and new telecommunication systems. But so far, these seem still to be partial and relatively minor changes. If the Keynesian revolution and the profound transformation of social institutions in the Second World War and its aftermath were required to unleash the fourth Kondratiev upswing, then social innovations on an equally significant scale are likely to be needed now. This applies especially to the international dimension of world economic development.

The structural crisis of the 1980s

From this brief summary of some of the characteristics of the new paradigm it will have become apparent that the widespread diffusion of the new technology throughout the economic system is not just a matter of incremental improvements, nor just a question of the extension of existing capacity in a few new industries. It involves a major upheaval in *all* sectors of the economy and changes in the skill profile and capital stock throughout the system. It is for this reason that periods like the 1930s and the 1980s cannot be treated in the same way as the minor recessions of the 1950s and 1960s.

The structural crisis involved in the transition from one technological regime to another increases the instability of investment behaviour for a number of reasons. The leading-edge industries of the new paradigm are growing so rapidly that they constantly tend to outstrip the supply of skilled labour. However, the headlong rush to increase capacity as bandwagons get rolling also leads to periodic crises of over-capacity, as there is no way in which the supply can precisely anticipate and match smoothly the growth of market demand (in Hahn's terminology, the 'true' demand function cannot be known). Moreover the technology is still changing so rapidly that successive generations of equipment and products rapidly become obsolete. The tempestuous growth of the chip industry and the computer industry in the 1970s and 1980s has also been marked by periodic, though short-lived, crises of over-supply (Ernst, 1983, 1987). There were similar problems with the leading-edge industries of the 1920s and the 1930s—automobiles, consumer durables and organic chemicals.

The problems in the other sectors of the economy are even more severe. Some industries which have previously been at the heart of the (now superseded) paradigms now experience much slower rates of growth or absolute decline. They may also have problems of over-capacity and rationalisation which are prolonged, as has been the case in some of the energy-intensive industries in the 1970s and 1980s, such as steel, petrochemicals and synthetic fibres. Similar problems were encountered by the railways and railway equipment industries as well as by coal and textiles in previous structural crises.

There are also severe problems in those manufacturing and service sectors which still have ample growth potential but are confronted with the need to change their production processes, their product mix, their management systems, their skill profiles and their marketing to accomplish the shift to an entirely new technological paradigm. This is a painful and difficult process of adjustment, involving, as we have seen, a kind of cultural revolution as well as the need for major re-equipment. These problems can be seen very clearly today in such industries as printing, vehicles and machine tools, as well as in services such as insurance, distribution and transport. They were equally apparent in many industrial sectors adapting in the 1920s and 1930s to the new energy-intensive mass and flow production systems which at that time represented the leading edge of the new techno-economic paradigm.

The depression of the 1930s was certainly one of extraordinary severity, especially in the leading industrialised countries—the United States and

Germany. Between 1929 and 1933 GNP fell by 30 per cent in the United States, industrial production by nearly 50 per cent, output of durable producers' equipment by 75 per cent and new construction by 85 per cent. It is hardly surprising that Keynesian economists, such as Samuelson (1980), discount the likelihood of the recurrence of such a catastrophe:

Although nothing is impossible in an inexact science like economics, the probability of a great depression—a prolonged cumulative chronic slump like that of the 1930s, 1890s or 1870s—has been reduced to a negligible figure. No one should pay an appreciable insurance premium to be protected against the risk of a total breakdown in our banking system and of massive unemployment in which 25 per cent of workers are jobless. The reason for the virtual disappearance of great depressions is the new attitude of the electorate . . . The electorate in a mixed economy insists that any political party which is in power—be it Republican or Democratic, the Tory or Labour Party—take the expansionary actions that can prevent lasting depressions. [p. 251]

This may be an over-optimistic view. Whilst not dissenting from Samuelson's description of economics as an inexact science, this chapter suggests that it is quite possible for the world economy to experience a depression, which, even if not so severe in all respects as that of the 1930s, could be more severe than the earlier recessions of the 1870s and the 1890s.

This somewhat pessimistic view is based on the observation that the main sources of instability which gave rise to the depression of the 1930s are also present today, albeit in a somewhat different form: the international debt situation, extreme imbalances in international payments, weakness in agricultural prices, instability in exchange rates, creeping protectionism, the absence of an adequate system of regulating the international economy and in particular the absence of an adequate international lender of last resort, disarray in the economics profession, and lack of long-term vision in policy-making. The present wave of technical change sweeping through the world economy is likely to exacerbate the problems of instability in investment, and of structural change at the national and international level and the associated disequilibria in the international economy.

It is notable that Samuelson's argument that severe depressions can be averted rests not on any faith in the self-regulating powers of the market, but unequivocally on the belief that *political* factors, principally the level of unemployment, will put pressure on governments to adopt expansionary policies, which are assumed to be available and applicable. We share with him and other Keynesians their scepticism that the rate of interest and monetary policy are in themselves sufficient to achieve an equilibrium growth path.

But for his argument to carry conviction it would be necessary not only for governments to adopt *national* policies to counteract tendencies toward depression, but also at least for the leading countries to act in a co-ordinated manner at the *international* level. Recent experience must cast some doubt on both these assumptions. It is no doubt true that the experience of recession and stagnation does induce a search for expansionary policies at the political level. But, as in the 1930s, this search may lead to nationalistic, protectionist and even militaristic policies as well as to neo-Keynesian policies and other as yet untried solutions. It may also be hindered by the extreme divergence of views from the economics profession on such questions as the feasibility and desirability of a return to fixed exchange rates.

The uneven and varied response of governments, firms and industries to the threats and opportunities posed by information technology tends to accentuate the uneven process of development. Typically in the past, major changes in techno-economic paradigm have been associated with shifts in the international division of labour and international technological leadership. Newcomers are sometimes more able to make the necessary social and institutional innovations than the more arthritic social structures of established leaders. Erstwhile leading countries such as the United Kingdom or the United States may become the victims of their own earlier success. On the other hand, countries lacking the necessary minimal educational, managerial, R & D and design capability may be even more seriously disadvantaged in international competition.

This means that changes of paradigm are likely to be associated with the temporary aggravation of instability problems in relation to the flow of international investment, trade and payments. The enormous Japanese trade surplus and the US trade deficit reflect not merely exchange rate problems, but also the more successful Japanese exploitation and application of IT outside the leading-edge industries, and the introduction of many institutional innovations facilitating this process (Chapter 23). The US economy leads in military applications of IT but lags in other areas. There is thus a major 'structural' component in the international trade imbalances, as there was in the 'technological gap' which the United States opened up between the 1920s and the 1950s (Freeman, 1987).

The same is even more true of the problems of Third World countries. A report of the Inter-American Development Bank has highlighted these critical problems confronting the world economy and has warned that the IMF measures to deal with the crisis have been short-term palliatives, not long-term solutions. Albert Fishlow (1985) points out that Latin America faces a burden of debt service repayments greater than the level of reparations that Germany found impossible after the First World War. Only a widespread recovery of productive investment and technical innovation in Latin America could sustain the growth needed to finance even a much lower level of debt repayment and interest payments. It is not without interest that Samuelson and Nordhaus in the 12th edition of *Economics* (1985) do introduce a sentence or two suggesting that 'default of major heavily indebted countries' could lead to a Great Depression.

The Third World countries are experiencing difficulties in developing the new information technology industries to sustain their competitive power, but the new technologies do actually offer some major advantages to them, provided they modify their trade, industrial and technology policies, as indicated in Chapter 21 by Perez and Soete.

However, these 'catching up' efforts of Third World countries also require some resolution of the basic structural problems confronting the entire world economy. This implies new measures to facilitate the international transfer of technology as well as a resolution of the debt problem. Thus the greatest problem of institutional adaptation lies in the sphere of international financial and economic institutions, to take account of these long-term structural adaptation difficulties. The development of new national and international 'regimes of regulation' is discussed in the following chapter by Boyer.

References

Dosi, G (1982), 'Technological paradigms and technological trajectories', *Research Policy*, vol. II, no. 3, June, pp. 147–162.

Eatwell, J. (1982), '*Whatever Happened to Britain?*', London, Duckworth.

Elliot, J.E. (1985), 'Schumpeter's theory of economic development and social change: exposition and assessment', *International Journal of Social Economics*, vol. 12, Parts 6 and 7, p. 6–33.

Ernst, D. (1983), 'The global race in microelectronics: innovation and corporate strategies in a period of crisis', MIT.

——— (1987), 'Programmable automation in the semiconductor industry: reflections on current diffusion patterns', GERTTD Conference on Automisation Programmable, Paris, 12–14 April 1987.

Freeman, C. (1987), *Technology Policy and Economic Performance: Lessons from Japan*, London, Pinter.

Freeman, C., Clark, J. and Soete, L.L.G. (1982), *Unemployment and Technical Innovation: A Study of Long Waves in Economic Development*, London, Frances Pinter.

Freeman, C. and Soete, L.L.G. (eds) (1987), *Technical Change and Full Employment*, Oxford, Blackwell.

Galbraith, J.K. (1961), *The Great Crash, 1929*, Harmondsworth, Pelican.

Hollander, S.G. (1965), *The Sources of Increased Efficiency: A Study of DuPont Rayon Plants*, Cambridge, Mass., MIT Press.

Jewkes, J., Sawers, D. and Stillerman, J. (1956), *The Sources of Invention*, London, Macmillan.

Keirstead, B.S. (1948), *The Theory of Economic Change*, Toronto, Macmillan.

Keynes, J.M. (1930), *A Treatise on Money*, vol. 2, London, Macmillan, p. 86.
(1936), General Theory of Employment, Interest and Money, New York, Harcourt-Brace.

Klamer, A. (1984) *The New Classical Macroeconomics*, Brighton, Wheatsheaf.

Kuznets, S. (1940), 'Schumpeter's business cycles', *American Economic Review*, vol. 30, no. 2, p. 257–71.

Mensch, G. (1975), *Das Technologische Patt: Innovationen Uberwinden die Depression*, Frankfurt, Umschau; English edn: *Stalemate in Technology: Innovations overcome Depression*, New York, Ballinger, (1979).

Moggridge, D.E. (1976), *Keynes*, London, Fontana.

Nelson, R.R. and Winter, S.G. (1977), 'In search of a useful theory of innovation', *Research Policy*, vol. 6, no. 1, pp. 36–76.

Perez, C. (1983), 'Structural change and the assimilation of new technologies in the economic and social system', *Futures*, vol. 15, no. 5, October, pp. 357–75.

—— (1985), 'Microelectronics, long waves and world structural change', *World Development*, vol. 13, no. 3, pp. 441–63.

—— (1986), 'The new technologies: an integrated view'; original Spanish in C. Ominami (ed.), *La Tercera Revolución Industrial*, Buenos Aires.

Rosenberg, N. (1975), *Perspectives on Technology*, Cambridge, Cambridge University Press.

Samuelson, P. (1980), *Economics*, 11th edn., New York, McGraw-Hill.

—— (1981), 'The world's economy at century's end', *Japan Economic Journal*, 10 March, p. 20.

Samuelson, P. and Nordhaus, W. (1985), *Economics*, 12th edn., New York, McGraw-Hill.

Shackle, G.L.S. (1967), 'To the *QJE* from Chapter 12 of the General Theory: Keynes' "Ultimate Meaning", in Shackle, G.L.S. (ed.), *The Years of High Theory: Invention and Tradition in Economic Thought 1926–1939*, Cambridge, Cambridge University Press. (Shackle refers to the article of J.M. Keynes on 'The general theory of employment' in the *QJE* (1937), February, pp. 209–23.)

Schumpeter, J.A. (1939), *Business Cycles: A Theoretical, Historical and Statistical Analysis of the Capitalist Process*, 2 vols, New York, McGraw-Hill.

—— (1952), *Ten Great Economists*, Allen & Unwin, London.

Siegenthaler, H. (1986), 'The state of confidence and economic behaviour in the 30s and 70s: theoretical framework—historical evidence', in I.T. Berend and K. Borchardt (eds) (1986), *The Impact of the Depression of the 1930s and its Relevance for the Contemporary World*, papers of Section 5 of the International Economic History Congress, Berne, pp. 409–37.

Soete, L. and Dosi, G. (1983), *Technology and Employment in the Electronics Industry*, London, Frances Pinter.

Townsend, J. (1976), *Innovations in Coal-Mining Machinery: The Anderton Shearer-Loader and the Role of the NCB and Supply Industry in its Development*, SPRU Occasional Paper No. 3.

4 Technical change and the theory of 'Régulation'

Robert Boyer

Centre National de la Recherche Scientifique et Ecole des Hautes Etudes en Sciences Sociales—
Ceatre d'Etudes Prospectives d'Economic Mathématique Appliquées à la Planification, Paris

Mixing technology with economics: a difficult task

The economist has many problems in dealing with technical change, for at least three interrelated reasons.

If technological systems are supposed to evolve smoothly and continuously in response to mainly *external factors* (such as advances in pure and applied science), their only effect would be to shift the long-run equilibrium path of the economy. This results in the usual method of injecting technological trends into a given macroeconomic model, and neglects any feedback from the economic side to the technological one. The really big problem is to combine economics with technology *in the very long run*, in the Marshallian sense, i.e. with industrial structures and labour both adapting to technological paradigms.

A second difficulty lies in the temptation to relapse into *technological determinism* according to which economic growth as well as most social institutions derive from purely technical matters. If this kind of statement was not made by Schumpeter himself, it turned out to be a salient feature of the present recovery of neo-Schumpeterian ideas. This is not so much surprising, since standard theory usually does not deal with *social forms of organization*, either supposing them to be given by history, or totally ignoring them. Hence a major challenge is to see if one can distinguish clearly between two dynamics—one concerning institutional forms, and the other the technological system—and then to investigate their *ex post* compatibility.

But the problem is made still more complex by another puzzling finding: neither innovations nor growth exhibit steady trends in the long run, since, on the contrary, the so-called *Kondratiev waves*—i.e. the succession of a long-lasting boom and then stagnation over a period of half a century—are once again considered as a true problem for economic historians. Theoreticians are mainly interested in equilibrium path growth models, and only a few of them have tried to formalize Kondratiev-style cycles. To my knowledge, very few successful examples are available on this last topic. Similarly, economists have a lot of problems in analysing why the same technological trajectory might have positive effects upon employment and stability during some periods, but negative ones during others (see Chapter 3). The traditional theories point to an invariant impact—usually positive in neo-classical models, negative in the pure Keynesian closed-economy framework—whereas the issue at stake is to understand *changing patterns through time.*

Clearly, many economists are now trying to cope with these problems, since numerous national or international projects have been launched, especially during the last decade. This chapter intends to suggest a tentative theoretical approach, the aims of which are precisely the same, even though initially at least the question of technological change was not at the forefront. This approach, called *'régulation'* in French, is not easily translated into English, since the English word 'regulation' is usually associated with the much narrower problem of regulation of the behaviour of public utilities, whilst the expression *'socio-economic tuning'* brings a connotation of a conscious and sophisticated adjustment mechanism. Actually the process of fitting production and social demand in a given set of structures and institutions is always an uneven, unbalanced and usually contradictory consequence of very partial rationalities and strategies, however integrated modern corporate economies may seem. For this reason we simply use the word 'régulation' in the French sense of the word. This approach is far from being a fully-fledged theory, but its interest is precisely its implications for these three puzzles.

Contrary to the usual approach in economics, the focus is not on short- or medium-term issues but on the *long run and structural change* in advanced capitalist countries. For example, the US and French economies have been studied over nearly two centuries. Over such a period technology, industrial structures, labour force composition and institutions cannot be assumed given or constant.

Similarly, technology cannot be dealt with in isolation from the rest of *the economic and social system.* The major question is, then, the coherence and compatibility of a given technical system with a pattern of accumulation, itself defined by a complex set of economic regularities and mechanisms affecting competition, demand, the labour market, credit and state intervention. The major finding is the following: there are several different modes of development and 'régulation' observed in history—there is no single universal mode.

Within each mode of development the very factors which account for a successful, long-lasting boom also explain the reversal of economic dynamics *from growth to crisis.* Once totally mature, a socio-technical system gives rise to new economic imbalances and social conflicts. Hence possible obstacles arise during the process of accumulation itself, leading to a major, i.e. a structural, crisis, characterized by quasi-stagnation and large instabilities. Therefore the same ongoing technical change—crudely measured by average productivity growth—might have negative effects upon employment, in complete opposition to the situation during periods of high and stable growth.

This chapter first presents the major concepts of the 'régulation' approach. Then a summary is given of the main findings on the relationship between technology and long-run economic dynamics.

A method for the analysis of structural change: the 'régulation' approach

Between economic history and theory

In fact, most of the problems previously stressed derive from very unsatisfactory links between two departments of the social sciences: economic and social history on the one hand, economic analysis on the other. Most *historians* are fond of assessing the validity of accounts of events, sources and data. When they do dare to propose and test causal mechanisms, they mainly refer to the state of the art of other social sciences, especially economics, but sociology and anthropology as well. The New Economic History is a clear example of such a strategy, which has led to very mixed controversies among scholars: sometimes interesting, often provocative but in other cases, quite dubious! If the French 'Annales' school is excluded, almost no historian challenges existing economic theories, whether neo-classical, Keynesian or even Marxian! Implicitly, at least, historical facts are supposed to fit into a given general theory, already available.

In contrast, the *economist* is rarely as modest. Whatever the precise contents of his theory, his aim is to derive general results from very basic principles and as few as possible (the principle of maximization for neo-classicists, the law of value for Marxists, and so on). While testing his models the economist is strongly induced to interpret any discrepancy as a purely casual phenomenon, more or less related to historical or sociological peculiarities, and thus without any theoretical importance. Just to give an example, most monetary histories are no more than stubborn attempts to prove the truth of one variant or another of the quantity theory of money. Even completely perverse evolutions of income velocity are interpreted as a minor phenomenon. Why bother with reality and history, since the basic theory is necessarily true according to first principles!

Paradoxically, such a caricature is not absent from many Marxist analyses: has not Marx said everything about the laws of capitalism in the long run? In a capitalist system production is undertaken solely in order to obtain a profit on commodities as exchange value, and not just to satisfy direct individual or social needs, i.e. according to their use value! Therefore there appears a tendency to make accumulation an end in itself, an absolute novelty with respect to all previous production modes. Labour itself becomes a commodity, but a very special one which brings a surplus value, the root of profit. Hence, a propensity exists to exploit more and more workers according to new production methods obtained by applying science and techniques to economic activity. Marx is thought to have proved a fundamental dynamic law of capitalism: its necessary collapse due to the famous tendency for the rate of profit to fall. Since this has not been the case until now, the followers of Marx stress the succession of transitory counterbalancing forces. When used indiscriminately, such a device can interpret any discrepancy, whatever the size of the gap between the prediction of the theory and observed historical events. Just to give an example, some Marxists in the 1960s contended that since the First World War productive forces have been continuously declining, and others that the unprecedented growth observed from 1945 to 1973 was the strongest evidence of the deepening of the structural crisis of the inter-war years!

From a methodological point of view such severe shortcomings derive largely from insufficient links between theory and empirical analysis on the one hand, and from purely deductive or inductive methods on the other. Would it not be surprising, for example, for physicists to wait until the basic concepts of mechanics (the notion of forces, weight, acceleration) had been completely elaborated before attacking the evolution of particular complex systems? In fact, the successful method has been to build a series of intermediate models which use the general laws of mechanics in order to analyse the exact composition of forces, and then to check if the expectations derived from the model fit the facts. *Mutatis mutandis*, the economist faces the same problem and should adopt a similar strategy: try to work out intermediate notions and models in order finally to organize an appropriate and careful comparison with observed facts.

In this respect, the 'régulation' approach is an attempt to elaborate a *continuum of concepts* from the more abstract ones (for example, that of production modes) to the observed regularities in the behaviour of economic agents (as part of the 'régulation' mechanisms). Some of these intermediate notions are accumulation regime, structural or institutional form, wage-labour nexus, and so on. They benefit from the conclusions of long-run historical studies and point in the direction of a new theoretical framework which would combine a critique of Marxian orthodoxy, and an extension of Kaleckian and Keynesian macroeconomic ideas, in order to rejuvenate a variant of earlier institutional or historical theory. Let us now present these different topics.

The notion of accumulation regime

The 'régulation' approach, progressively elaborated in France since the early 1970s, is basically built upon a critique of mechanical and catastrophic interpretations of Marx. The logic of accumulation is certainly central to capitalist economies. Of course, the spreading of the market relationship introduces into the system the possibility of crises, while all the conflicts based upon exploitation of workers and competition among capitalists make these crises more and more likely, at least during particular periods. But actual historical records suggest that the inherent contradictions of the system can be contained at least partially and for a time. Then minor crises are sufficient to promote a recovery within a cumulative growth pattern. Such episodes need not be characterized as pure accident but as possible *stable configurations of the economy*. This is the basic idea and the reason why the concept of *regime of accumulation* is so important.

In order to analyse the possibility of such a process in the long run, the economist has to find out what are the various technological, social and economic regularities which allows it. Let us mention five of them:

a pattern of *productive organization* within firms, defining the way wage-earners work with the means of production;

a *time horizon* for capital formation decisions, within which managers can use a given set of rules and criteria;

income shares between wages, profits and taxes, which reproduce the various social classes or groups;

a *volume and composition of effective demand* validating the trends in productive capacity;

a particular set of relationships between capitalist and *non-capitalist modes* of production.

Hence a regime of accumulation is defined by the whole set of regularities which allow a general and more or less consistent evolution for capital formation, i.e. which dampen and spread over time the imbalances which permanently arise from the process itself. The five features previously defined are sufficient to build either a macro model with two departments (producing respectively consumption and production goods) or an aggregated model, for simplicity's sake (final section, 'A research agenda'). Given the evolution of the technical coefficients, income shares, composition of demand, transfers to other social groups, and the time lags involved, it is possible to close the dynamic model (Boyer, 1975; Bertrand, 1983; Fagerberg, 1984).

Of course, the method is not brand new and has a long historical tradition. Nevertheless, this approach tries to overcome some major shortcomings of previous attempts. First, the game is not purely mathematical— the key parameters are chosen according to statistical and econometric studies as detailed as possible. Second, the technological determinants are combined with economic and social mechanisms, thus preventing capital from being reduced merely to a question of reproduction in a quasi-technical sense: for example, workers are not a special productive commodity but part of the social relationships defining their place in society. Third, the regime of accumulation is by no means the end of the analysis, since it seems to be a very abstract concept, largely unobserved by economic units. But then, why do capitalists, workers and other social groups behave in such a way as to substantiate this regime?

The importance of institutional forms

This notion of institutional forms illuminates the basis of social regularities which channel economic reproduction. Basically, a structural or institutional form denotes a codification of a main social relationship. Here again the idea is that the same invariant and abstract relationship might have very different realizations either for a given country over time or for different countries during the same period. In some sense, the 'régulation' approach tries to extend to organizational forms what technological theorists have done for *technological systems or paradigms*. Is it not clear that the characteristics of the first industrial revolution are not those of the present one? Similarly, all forms of labour organization, state intervention, monetary creation and so on are not at all equivalent as far as economic dynamics is concerned.

Monetary and credit relationships are essential in defining the mode of interaction between separate economic units. This abstract form can take several configurations according to the direction of causality between money and credit on the one hand and the degree of sophistication of national and international financial systems on the other. At first sight this form might seem quite removed from the question of technological change. But after all, Schumpeter in his *Theory of Economic Development* attributed credit to a major role in shifting resources from old industries and products to new ones. Furthermore, many contemporary analysts see some links between technological change (i.e. the mix between product and process innovations) and the tendency towards inflation or deflation, whether associated with a *Kondratiev* style of reasoning or not (Freeman, 1978, Mensch, 1978).

Historical studies do confirm significant changes in the forms of the monetary constraint. In the nineteenth century, under the so-called gold standard, inflows or outflows of currencies continually controlled the evolution of domestic credit. Hence a very typical business cycle resulted, associating bankruptcies with declining prices and production. In contrast, after the Second World War the volume of credit given by banks to firms and households became the key determinant of the money supply. External capital flows exerted only transitory constraints, usually overcome by a once-for-all devaluation in the late Bretton-Woods system. Therefore a cumulative expansion of credit money with permanent inflation became possible, at least until the 1970s. Consequently, one observes a very specific pattern of investment in industrial structures and of research and development.

The wage–labour nexus defines a second and a crucial institutional form, since it characterizes the relationship between capital and labour, management and employees. Broadly speaking, it involves all problems relating to work organization and the standard of living of wage-earners. A form of the wage–labour nexus is defined by a coherent system encompassing the following five components: the type of means of production and control over workers; the technical and social division of labour and its implications for skilling/deskilling; the degree of stability of the employment relation, measured, for example, by the speed of employment or work duration adjustments; the determinants of direct and social wages in relation to the functioning of labour market and state welfare services;

the standard of living of wage-earners in terms of the volume and origin of the commodities they consume.

Empirical investigations have revealed very different forms through history or across countries at a given period of time. To be brief, a *competitive wage–labour nexus* used to prevail in the last century: most of the consumption of the workers came from non-capitalist modes of production, and few collective organizations existed to oppose business strategies and market forces. Hence there was a high responsiveness of wages to employment fluctuations and no indexing. In contrast, since the First World War, collective bargaining and the emergence of the welfare state have introduced a new wage–labour nexus, called *Fordist*. In this system, wages are not only a cost but also a key determinant of consumption and hence effective demand. Implicitly, or by explicit agreement, nominal wages become indexed to consumer prices and to expected productivity gains, and thus have a very low sensitivity to unemployment. This point is of interest for technological change analysis, since the concept of Fordism closely relates mass production to mass consumption, therefore defining a new stage of capitalist development (see p. 84, for more details).

The *type of competition* is a third component introduced into the analysis. The concept of accumulation regime assumes completely homogeneous capital, whereas in fact many separate private units compete to get higher profits via production cost reductions and/or product differentiation. This competition expresses itself through various price mechanisms, which may have quite opposite effects upon the direction and intensity of technological change. It is necessary to make a clear distinction between purely static approaches (market power as a source of extra profits via oligopolistic pricing) and dynamic analyses (the issue is then whether more concentration spurs product and process innovation).

In this respect, historical analysis yields interesting results by contrasting at least two different types of competition. In the nineteenth century, even if financial concentration was not negligible, price variation was the only way to adjust for discrepancies between demand and productive capacity. The logic was very myopic and operated only *ex post*. The closure of plants, bankruptcies and redundancies were the usual way for providing a new equilibrium in the system. This is *traditional price competition*. From 1945 to the 1970s, the 'régulation' has been quite different. A much higher centralization of financial assets and concentration of markets led to *oligopolistic competition*. In this system, firms compete through advertising, and more generally through product differentiation, while prices are derived from a mark-up applied to average costs. Basically this is associated with a form of internal planning, in which firms try to expand capacity in step with expected demand. To the extent that real wage income increases with productivity (the Fordist wage–labour nexus), cumulative growth is then possible, with *ex post* adjustments only between minor discrepancies in growth rates rather than production levels themselves. This is the distinguishing feature of the Fordist development in contrast to that of the last century. Finally, the canvas has to be completed by examining two other components.

The mode of adhesion to the international regime plays a pre-eminent role when one passes from a purely abstract analysis to the study of a given national economy. This concept is defined by the set of rules and conventions which organize the exchange of commodities, the location of production units (via direct foreign investment) and the financing of external disequilibria. This conception is quite at odds with traditional discussions which contrast open to closed economy, free trade to protectionism, fixed to flexible exchange rate systems, etc. In fact, the 'régulation' approach is developing a series of intermediate concepts which relate the international growth regime (i.e. the division of economic space and their linkages) to the existence of strategic areas and, ultimately, to the opportunities and constraints imposed or offered to each nation by the world system (Mistral, 1986).

The issue is quite important as far as technical change is concerned. The advances in abstract knowledge as well as in applied technology are mainly defined at the international level, not separately in each country. Nevertheless, countries are not equally able to take advantage of these general opportunities and translate them into profitable production to be sold at home and abroad. Hence various countries occupy different places in the international regime of growth, due both to their mastering of new technology and to their access to world finance. This explains, for example, why the rate of growth in Japan is not equal to that of the United States, and why German and UK macroeconomic achievements differ. Similarly, the international regime may change in the long run, due to a combination of technological domination, financial intermediation and political hegemony. Historical evidence suggests that contrasted periods do alternate during the domination of the same country, be it the United Kingdom during the last century or the United States after the Second World War. Relative stability and cumulative growth take place when all the factors of domination are simultaneously mastered by the leading country, but large instabilities and slow growth or even stagnation occur when technological and economic hegemony, but not necessarily financial intermediation, are declining.

The forms of state intervention are the last institutional configuration. In some respects, this is related to the previous configuration, since it has always been an attribute of the state to organize the relations with the world economy. Basically, the state operates in a different way from pure market relationships: coercion by law replaces mutually profitable exchanges, whereby the power to tax is clearly at odds with the free exchange of commodities. Hence, contrary to an old Marxist view, the state does not necessarily originate in purely capitalist relations. Rather, it seems to express a nexus of linkages between social classes and groups, qualitatively through laws and regulation, quantitatively through public spending (André and Delorme, 1983).

The attraction of this concept is to allow very different patterns of state interventions. For a long period of time a *bounded state* prevailed, the role of which was mainly to enforce private contracts and laws about property and to guarantee internal and external security. Nevertheless, the economic role of this limited state was not nil, since it helped a great deal to preserve the existing social order. After the First World War (and still more the Second), all advanced capitalist countries have evolved towards an *interventionist and large state*. Its role is now crucial in organizing the production of public services, financing infrastructure and productive investment, and managing the social wage within the so-called welfare state. Of course, one should add the intervention in science and technology by means of education, the tax system, defence programmes, general regulation about technical norms, etc. Both qualitatively and quantitatively, these two types of state are not at all equivalent as far as economic dynamics and social reproduction are concerned.

Modes of regulation and crisis types

It is now necessary to pass from these limited and partial regularities involving numerous economic agents and their behaviour to the possibility of a consistent dynamic system. Standard economic theory uses the general concept of equilibrium and assumes that for a broad category of 'tatonnement' processes, the model converges towards a stable and unique equilibrium. Of course, in more sophisticated mathematical economic theory many equilibria can exist, but such a result is rarely related to any real world economic problems. In contrast, the 'régulation' approach stresses the possibility of *several modes* of adjusting production to demand, credit to money, income distribution to demand formation. More basically, each wage–labour nexus, firm organization and competition type, public institution and monetary rule may—or may not—induce a coherent adjustment process for the economy as a whole. This institutional and structural setting is not set against market mechanisms but rather may enable it to function efficiently. In this framework institutions and markets, state and private units, jointly determine economic and social dynamics.

The analysis is hence converging towards the notion of *mode of régulation*, a partial and modest alternative to the overwhelming tyranny of static equilibrium. Consequently, we use this expression to designate any set of rules and individual and collective behaviours which have the three following properties:

— they make possible conflicting *decentralized decisions* compatible without the necessity for individuals or even institutions to comprehend the logic of the whole system;
— they control and regulate the prevailing *accumulation mode*;
— they reproduce *basic social relationships* through a system of historically determined institutional forms.

The trick is now to show that this notion is not an empty box, but can be filled with several different examples of systems of regulation, that is precisely the aim of the next section (p. 77). Note, too, that technology is present in many places in this scheme, but integrated into industrial organization, the wage–labour relations, standard of consumption, etc. However, a final definition and typology first has to be presented.

The concept of 'régulation' has to be complemented by its twin, that of crisis. In common language, as well as in most economic theory, this notion has either a specific narrow meaning (the oil, debt, welfare state, Keynesian economic policy crisis) or none at all (except perhaps a lasting under-employment equilibrium or a breakdown in growth trends). Our approach attributes a very central place to it and proposes a clear distinction between two broad categories of crisis.

According to the first definition, *cyclical crises* are the usual feature of any stabilized mode of 'régulation'. Since the accumulation of capital drives economic dynamics, disequilibria frequently occur within the system as a result of the necessary lags between the demand and capacity effects of investment or the discrepancy between stocks and flows in financial decisions. Therefore, after a period of boom, the economy adjusts to the previous imbalances by a downwards movement of inventories, production, investment, employment, etc. This type of crisis is part of the system's self-equilibration, and does not destroy it. Thus it might be misleading to speak of a crisis, since this expression lends an image of catastrophe and drama to what is *the usual business cycle*.

Nevertheless, two qualifications have to be made. First, from cycle to cycle the various institutional forms and industrial structures change slowly, so that some drift in the 'régulation' mode occurs. Qualitatively, however, it remains the same, and the question of new institutions does not arise. Second, economic policy rules do not have to be changed to promote the recovery: without discretionary intervention by the state, growth can resume as soon as the previous disequilibria have been eliminated by the 'régulation' process.

A second and quite opposite definition deals with *structural crises*. We shall use this designation for any episode during which the very functioning of regulation comes into contradiction with existing institutional forms, which are then abandoned, destroyed or bypassed. In other words, the limits to the 'régulation' mode and regime of accumulation—the combination of which defines a *mode of development*—become obvious in every sphere of social and economic life. One is now well justified to speak about the existence of a crisis, since the system can no longer reproduce itself in the long run, at least on the same institutional and technological basis.

At least three criteria allow us to distinguish a cyclical crisis from a structural one. First, the social and economic conflicts are such that, within the given mode of 'régulation', no self-correcting mechanism for profits exist. Second, most—if not all—of the institutional forms are questioned by the spreading of the crisis from its local and seemingly accidental origin to the whole system. Third, the way out of the trouble is not attained by letting the economic mechanisms play out their role, since they are precisely at odds with each other. Thus strategic choices made by leading firms, unions and governments are necessary to promote a new mode of development. In other words, the system is no longer totally deterministic; rather, political and social choices have to play a role in shaping and restructuring the economy.

Such a distinction is not purely semantic. If the mild recessions of the 1960s belonged to the first category, the period which opened in the early 1970s is clearly of a different nature, more or less of the second category. The consequences as regards economic policy are far-reaching. This central conclusion of the 'régulation' approach will now be elaborated in detail.

The place of technology in long-run dynamics: the main results of the 'régulation' approach

Three 'régulation' modes: old, competitive, monopolist

A historical analysis of the French economy since the end of the eighteenth century gives many hints about such changes. In order to substantiate them, the method tries to combine various tools which are usually disconnected. This begins with a precise characterization of the institutional setting (using available syntheses and monographs by historians). The next step is to formulate a hypothesis about the logic of economic regularities associated with each institutional form. The third stage consists of statistical and econometric tests of the derived hypotheses in each area (price and wage formation, credit and money, etc.). Fourth, the components are synthesised in order to check the coherence and viability of the whole 'régulation' system. Finally, when possible, models are constructed in order to assess the exact properties of each mode of 'régulation'.

A very brief synthesis of such a study is given in Table 4.1 to give some idea of the method, which has been kept at a high level of generality in the preceding presentation. One significant piece of evidence is that, over two centuries, the cyclical pattern of the French economy has been changing rather drastically:

In the old 'régulation' ('régulation a l'ancienne'), the agricultural sector plays a dominant role, since modern capitalist industry is only emerging. This produces a unique cyclical pattern: every bad harvest leads to soaring prices of corn and more generally agricultural prices; hence peasants cannot buy industrial goods and the industrial sector is hit by the second round of the crisis; then workers are fired and the nominal wage is lowered, even if the general price level is climbing. The 'régulation' is by nature *stagflationnist*, since it associates unemployment with inflation (Figure 4.1).

Table 4.1 A brief summary of a historical study of French capitalism (the major institutional forms have experienced a transformation)

PERIODS / INSTITUTIONAL FORMS	1789	1848	1873	1896	1914 - 1918	1929	1939 - 1952	1967	1973	1980
WAGE LABOUR NEXUS										
· Work organization	Manufactures replace craftsmen	Work duration is extended but reaches crisis levels	Limitations of manual work rules	Early scientific Management	Massive use of taylorisation methods......	...implemented for civilian goods......		Fordism becomes dominant......	but hits some limits : the search for new forms	
						......but workers oppose to it				
· Lifestyle	Basically out of the capitalist sector	slight evolution in consumption norms		Slow insertion of wage earners in society		Social wage is recognized as a principle	Launching of a complete welfare system : Workers benefit from mass consumption			The slowing down shakes Welfare State : financial stability
COMPETITION										
· Concentration and centralisation	Large plants are emerging.....	...Tendency towards concentration	Finance capital is strengthening		Cooperation large firms/ State	Industrial cartels and financial holdings	Basis for national planning	Concentration of markets..... ......French holdings become international...		...a new balance between home and international strategy
· Price formation	Controled by guilds	Principle of free market	Prices clear the market	Early monopolistic pricing	State price controls	First example of mark-up pricing	State controls	· Administered prices, public control · medium term strategy in pricing decisions		...the return to more price competition
STATE										
· Budget and taxes	limited to general functions.	...even if regulations are important	Significant economic interventions (railways)	Small size GDP budget/	Unprecedented surge	Budgetary cuts......	New and high level for public spending /GDP	Slow growth......stabilization......growth of the size of State		tentative to curb down public regulations
· Money and credit	Metallic reserves limit money creation		Credit is checked by external balance and interest rate variations		The war is financed by paper money credit......	.....so is the postwar boom		Credit money has a more leading role......	periodic devaluations.....	tentative crisis monetary policy
						Return to gold standard			monetary controls	
INTERNATIONAL REGIME										
· Hegemonic country	England is the core of industrial revolution......		...and the banker of the world	...United States and Germany are challenging British hegemony	British dominance is reinforced	.....surge of US might	US are now hegemonic organize and stabilize the international regime......		...which is challenged by new competitors	underlying crisis of US leadership
· Cohesive forces	Exchange of manufactured goods versus primary commodities		The relative stability derives from the position of England		The loss of competitiveness	.....destabilizes the system	A new international order.....	OECD allows growth.....	...till the crisis of the Bretton Woods System	a very unstable system

Source: CEPREMAP–CORDES (1977).

In competitive 'régulation' ('régulation concurrentielle'), the pattern changes very significantly. Now the industrial sector imposes more and more its logic on to the whole system. The crisis derives from over-production in industry rather than from under-production. Even in agriculture social and economic relationships are transformed in such a way that more productivity is obtained. So during the nineteenth century the scarcity of food is replaced by abundance. Therefore the *modern industrial business cycles* emerge: the boom is slightly inflationary, the crisis deflationary. Most of the macroeconomic variables now behave pro-cyclically. The difference from the previous 'régulation' is therefore large and clear-cut (Figure 4.1).

In monopolist 'régulation' ('régulation monopoliste'), the distribution of income is significantly socialized through a series of compromises between capital and labour (Fordist wage formation along with inflation and productivity), between firms (mark-up pricing), between the state, citizens and capital (welfare state, pattern of public spending and tax system). Therefore the pure price adjustment mechanism bears only a minor part of the burden in adjusting social demand and production. To a larger extent, a complex set of institutions, conventions and rules constantly aims at developing effective demand at the same rate as production capacity, which in turn is partially linked to the intensity and direction of technical change via the accumulation process.

The economic dynamics are now fairly different: growth is faster since the increasing returns to scale associated with Fordist industries can be reaped via a steady demand evolution, easy to forecast. The business cycle becomes milder and milder and inflation does not stop even during recessions. Hence a *new stagflationist pattern* emerges, very characteristic of monopolistic 'régulation', if not toally unique in long-run history (recall the old 'régulation'). So the central approach stresses the specificities of modern economies, which bear little resemblance even to the inter-war period. The conclusion is further strengthened by an analysis of accumulation regimes.

Very constrasted modes of development

It turns out that the two last 'régulation' systems were associated with different accumulation regimes, and this is another reason for diverging patterns of crisis in 1929 and today (see below). More generally, since the middle of the last century, three major patterns of growth have been observed. In this characterization, the interplay between technology and economic and social factors is decisive.

Extensive accumulation exhibits a significant use of science and technology in production processes, but firms mainly try to apply existing knowledge

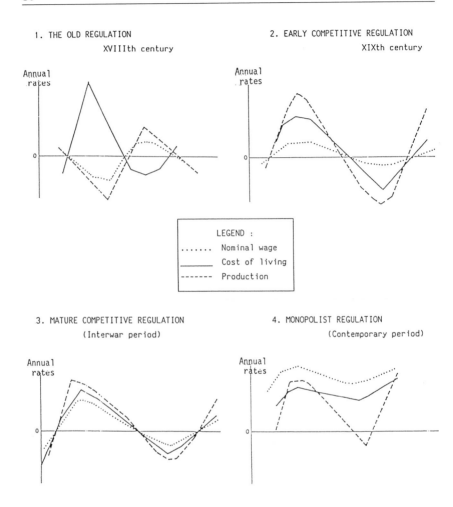

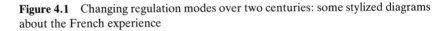

Figure 4.1   Changing regulation modes over two centuries: some stylized diagrams about the French experience

Source: Boyer (1978).

to their business and do not strive to improve them continuously. Similarly, the time horizon of firms is generally rather short, whereas the wage-earners in industry are mainly producers of commodities, and not so much consumers of them. Thus from 1895 to 1920, average productivity is quasi-stagnating, as are real wages, while growth is only obtained by a lengthening of working hours or by the hiring of more workers (Table 4.2). This quasi-stagnation may be related to numerous factors: lack of technological opportunities, limitations of the home and world markets, consequences of

Table 4.2   A brief statistical survey of development modes in France, 1856–1985
After the Second World War production norms and wage-earners consumption
norms run parallel.

A. Real wage and productivity in the long run

(average annual rates in per cent)

INDEXES PERIODS	Industrial Employment	Weekly Hours	Total Hours	Producti- vity per Employee	Real Wage	Accumulation Regime
1856-1870	- 1,0	- 0,8	- 1,8	2,4	1,4	Intensive
1870-1895	0,8	- 1,0	- 0,2	2,3	2,0	Intensive and its crisis
1895-1913	0,8	- 0,3	0,5	0,3	+ ε	Extensive
1913-1920	0,3	1,2	1,5	- 1,8	- 3,0	Extensive
1920-1930	1,2	- 2,8	- 1,6	5,8	2,2	Intensive without mass consumption
1930-1937	- 3,1	- 2.8	- 6,0	2,8	1,5	....and its crisis
1937-1949	1,0	0,9	1,9	- 0,3	- 0,5	Extensive
1949-1959	1,1	0,2	1,3	4,9	3,9	Intensive
1959-1973	0,8	- 0,4	0,4	4,8	4,1	...with mass con- sumption..
1973-1985	- 2,0	- 0,9	- 2,9	3,5	1,5	...and its crisis

Sources: CEPPREMAP–CORDES (1977): Insee vol II pp. 59–90 (1986).
Wage-labour is the dominant form of activity

B. The place of wage earners in the whole economy

(figures in percent)

SHARES OF	1913	1929	1938	1949	1959	1969	1979	1985
Wage earners in total labour force	57,9	60,4	56,6	61,8	69,4	78,4	83,8	84,4
Direct wage in household disposable income	38,3	43,2	43,1	41,4	46,7	47,3	47,1	44,5
Direct wage and social benefits in household disposable income	39,4	45,7	48,0	57,3	67,2	72,3	78,3	86,0
. Food in total consumption	47,7	47,7	44,7	47,9	39,7	28,4	20,4	19,3
. Industrial goods in total consump- tion	27,4	29,9	29,4	28,1	29,1	29,9	34,3	33,6

Computed on the basis of the following data: L.A. Vincent (1972) pp. 322–325;
A. Sauvy (1967) p. 496; INSEE (1986) vol. 3
From competitive to Fordist regulation of wages
C. Estimates for the relation $W = \varepsilon \cdot p + \theta_0 \cdot N + \theta_1$ with W: nominal wage;
p: consumer price; N: employment (annual wage rates); ( ): t of student.

	ε	θ_0	θ_1	R^2	D^W
1923-1938	0.47 (3.37)	1.49 (2.99)	3.1 (2.8)	0.81	1.82
1953-1969	0.59 (4.4)	0.91 (2.56)	4.65 (6.1)	0.66	1.64
1959-1977	0.96 (8.0)	0.39 (1.17)	4.44 (4.49)	0.81	1.64

Source: Basle, M., Bautier, P., Mazier, J., Vidal, J.F. 'Emploi, revenu salarial prix et profit'.
Economie et Prévision 1982.

competitive regulation upon the boldness of investment in brand new industries, ruinous impact of the war.

Intensive accumulation without mass consumption is a second ideal type. After the Second World War, industrial organization undergoes drastic transformations under the pressure of Scientific Management, and not only because the wrecked economies have to be rebuilt. Many new production processes are available, while some products cross the barrier of mass consumption. Along with authors like Braverman and Coriat, the 'régulation' approach insists upon the so-called Taylorian revolution. During the 1920s, productivity speeds up, more than usual after such an episode. But this period is relatively short and most of the positive effects are reversed after 1930 (Table 4.2). Basically, mass production is technically possible but cannot be sustained since the prevailing 'régulation' strongly moderates real wage increases, at the same time as wage-earners become a dominant fraction of the total labour force. It turns out that such intensive accumulation is highly contradictory (the profit rate is too high to permit an adequate effective demand) and unstable (look at inter-war production statistics). Therefore this is not a viable mode of development in the long run.

Intensive accumulation with mass consumption has been observed since the 1950s and defines a third configuration. Not only does scientific management continue to advance (diffusion of the assembly line as the key configuration of industrial organization) and new products are launched (radio and TV sets, electrical appliances for the home), but a *new social compromise* between capital and labour ensures that workers will benefit from economic and technological progress. Workers are now both *producers and consumers* of capitalist new goods. Similarly, wages are a cost but also a key determinant of consumption and hence aggregate demand (via an investment accelerator effect). The shift away from a purely competitive mechanism towards an administered 'régulation' of Fordist-Keynesian flavour facilitates such a move towards a new mode of development. In this respect, the period 1945–73 is without any historical precedent: stable and high growth, propelled by a simultaneous evolution of productivity and real wages (Table 4.2).

One sees clearly that this interpretation differs from the traditional long-wave interpretation 'à la Kondratiev'. Of course, each of the three accumulation regimes witness a long boom and then a period of decline, stagnation and crisis. But beneath these rough macroeconomic regularities, the underlying mechanisms and the factors explaining the downswing are quite different: exhaustion of the reserve army of wage-earners in extensive accumulation, lack of demand linked to the capacity dynamics in intensive accumulation, and adverse evolution of profit rates in intensive accumulation with mass consumption.

Technological change but no new wage–labour nexus: the inter-war crisis

To recapitulate the previous discussion, there is no doubt that technology and industrial organization play very important roles in long-run economic change. But the 'régulation' approach does not adopt a purely deterministic view of technological factors: everything depends on the compatibility with the basic institutional forms and the ability of the mode of 'régulation' to deal with the kind of disequilibria or conflicts that accompany accumulation. One can give no better evidence of this general proposition than the inter-war period.

Technological change but no new wage–labour nexus: the inter-war crisis

Many empirical studies converge towards the general conclusion that the technical system underwent a drastic change after the Second World War: dissemination of electrical power and new mechanical devices (for example, the assembly line), emerging new goods such as cars, home appliances, not to mention dwellings and buildings. The war had made mass production possible, first of weapons and products for the army but, later on, of civilian goods. Thus the same organizational system, called either Scientific Management or Taylorism, is extended to new branches when the economy has to be rebuilt after the war.

It is no accident that this period has been called the 'Roaring Twenties': lagged consumption has to be met while investment is rising to keep pace with modernization and demand. But the long-term viability of such an accumulation regime is not evident: one observes either over-accumulation and the appearance of adverse trends in profit rates, or a discrepancy between production capacity and demand. For some period of time, selling to small and medium bourgeoisie, peasants and foreign countries softens this imbalance. But as wage-earners now constitute the most significant part of the total labour force (remember the euthanasia of the *rentiers* due to inflation or debt repudiation), their consumption plays a key role in determining effective demand.

But after a while the system becomes increasingly troubled. In spite of some new features of collective bargaining (for example, regarding wage indexation), the regulation of the labour market remains basically competitive. The nominal wage is fairly sensitive to ups and downs in employment, whereas Taylorism generates very important productivity increases (see Table 4.2). Hence a very slow growth of the real unit wage results in spite of the boom of the 1920s. Then comes the 1929 crisis, resulting from the diverging trends between real wages and productivity, consumer demand and investment. The paradox can be summarized in one sentence: when wage formation is mainly competitive, a new industrial revolution leads to such a high profit rate that it cannot be sustained in the long run because of a lack of appropriate total demand (Figure 4.2).

Therefore a still more general conclusion can be proposed: *the effects*

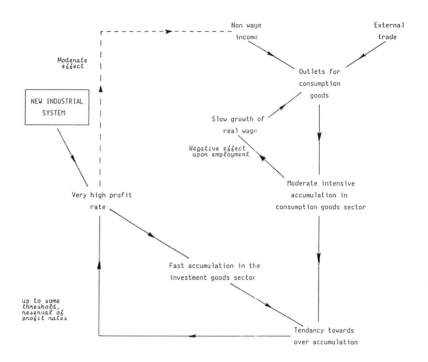

Figure 4.2   The vicious spiral of intensive accumulation without mass consumption

of any new technological system cannot be assessed independently of the existing or emerging mode of 'régulation'.

Compatibility between the technical system and the capital/labour compromise: the post Second-World War Fordist regime .

More or less the same technological basis is extended to new sectors after 1945. As a first approximation, the 1920s and the 1960s can be said to belong to the same technological paradigm. But, then, how do we explain why growth replaced stagnation as a long-run tendency, and that, contrary to contemporary fears, the collapse of 1929 did not repeat itself in the 1950s? The answer of the 'régulation' approach is simple enough: due to drastic social and political transformations, a new 'régulation' replaced the old one and made rapid technological change, quasi-full employment and sustained growth compatible.

The more drastic shift is in the wage–labour nexus. On the one hand, workers and unions accept capitalist modernization and do not oppose Scientific Management and Taylorist methods. On the other, managers agree to share productivity gains with wage-earners, so that the wage norm now permits employees to benefit from economic progress, regardless of sector, size of firm, location and skills. Thus, this new form of collective

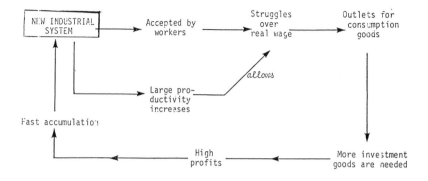

Figure 4.3 The virtuous spiral of monopolist growth

bargaining diffuses through the whole system and generates a *permanent improvement in consumption norms*. Since simultaneously investments are creating new modern capacity, the process now becomes self-sustaining. More demand for consumption goods induces investment opportunities in related sectors; hence outlets for equipment goods producers, who earn high profit. Thus a virtuous circle emerges in which the monopolist 'régulation' mode both stabilizes growth and promotes it (Figure 4.3).

According to this view, the major difference from the inter-war period lies in the *'régulation mode'* and not that much in the technological system. Of course, other institutional changes help in passing from one mode to another, or in some cases are made possible by the shift towards Fordist wage–labour relationships. *Oligopolistic competition* thus moderates possible struggles between firms by eliminating price cuts as the usual tool for obtaining market shares. Early US hegemony guarantees an international regime in which the various OECD countries can jointly grow without strong competitive pressure: when the state of business is good in the United States, everybody benefits from it. Finally, *Keynesian counter-cyclical policies* give the final touch to the Fordist regime: money and public spending are conceived as means for preventing departures from full employment or for reducing inflationary pressures.

Interestingly enough, this conclusion approaches the thinking of most of the specialists of technical progress: the success of Keynesian policy was based on a *coherent and dynamic technical system*. If the latter enters into crisis, so does the former. To risk a metaphor: Keynesian policies were the accelerator and the brake, not necessarily the engine of growth. Now a fourth result will be discussed.

The limits of Fordism as a social, economic and technical regime: the present crisis

Needless to say, this regime was very attractive for almost everybody: profit rates were kept at a high level, workers benefited from rising living standards and almost no risk of unemployment, and the state could extend public and welfare expenditures without any vocal dissent. The speeding up of growth could pay for such uses of income. But then how does this Eldorado come to an end? The answer is straightforward: the very development of the Fordist regime leads to new conflicts and imbalances which, up to some threshold, induce tendencies towards stagnation and/or stability. Three of these limits are now considered (Figure 4.4).

Fordism becomes counter-productive

From a technical point of view, the search for increasing returns to scale leads to larger and larger manufacturing plants, which produce a significant part of total output. It then becomes increasingly more difficult to balance the output of the assembly line with demand, both qualitatively (changes in models) and quantitatively (adaptation to short-run shocks). According to another arguement, Fordism is fairly efficient as regards labour and capital productivity when it replaces older systems, but it becomes harder and harder to get the same results when the issue is to deepen—and no longer to extend—the same organizational methods. Hence a possible decline in productivity growth rates sets in (in the United States during the mid-1960s) and/or in capital efficiency (in almost all OECD countries during the same period). But a third factor can also play a role: blue-collar workers revolt against Taylorist and Fordist methods through turnover, absenteeism, and a slacking of work intensity. In many cases they convert their protest into wage demands (recall May 1968 or autumn 1969). This leads to a possible profit squeeze to the extent that firms cannot pass on their cost increases because of strong external competition. Let us now examine two other limits.

From national complementarities to the struggle for external competitiveness

Fordism is just as much a socio-economic principle of organization as a technological one. Since the larger plants are usually more efficient, once national monopolies are set up, they tend to compete with one another at the world level. Thus, oligopolistic pricing, which has stabilised at home, turns into competitive pressures for external markets such that the previous price formation mechanism weakens or even breaks down. In a sense, if competition had led to monopoly, now monopoly turns back into competition! This change is far-reaching, since it destabilizes mark-up pricing and consequently the previous mechanisms governing wage forma-tion. National economies are no longer the boundaries within which

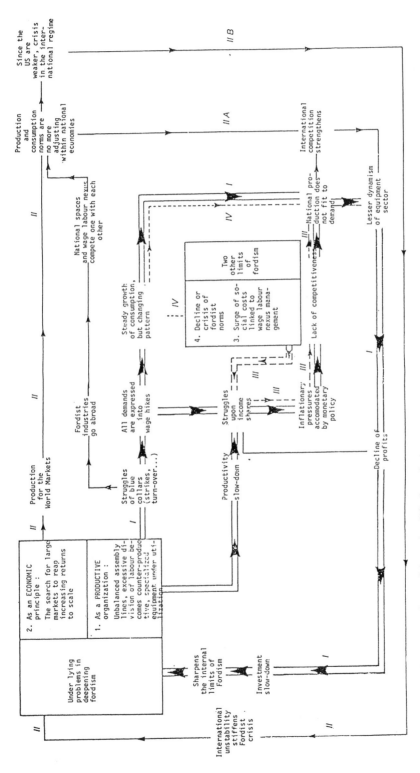

Figure 4.4 From growth to crisis: a simplified analysis

production and consumption norms jointly evolve. For example, a given firm or country benefits from high wages elsewhere but is hurt by wage increases which are faster than those of foreign competitors.

Simultaneously, the *erosion of US hegemony* introduces many destabilizing factors: unstable expectations about the value of the dollar when the fixed exchange rate system is replaced by a flexible one; lesser multiplier effects of US growth compared to other OECD countries; competitive struggles between Japan and the United States, and eventually Europe, over new products and technologies. In the 1980s, the emergence of a lasting and huge US external deficit on one side and of German and Japanese surpluses on the other triggers protectionist measures in spite of the free trade statements of most governments. Roughly speaking, the growth of one country is seen to take place at the expense of another; thus the search for competitiveness spreads all over the system and fuels stagnationist tendencies.

Let us emphasize that this very complex evolution is closely related to both technological (the mastering of new techniques and products) and socio-economic factors (the possibility of adjustment within the existing wage–labour nexus), not to mention financial and monetary determinants (position within financial intermediation and degree of autonomy of each national monetary policy).

The contradictory effects of Fordist wage formation: positive on demand, possibly negative on profits

Since the end of the 1960s and up to the early 1980s, advanced capitalist countries suffered from evils quite different from those of the inter-war period. A quasi-perfect indexation of nominal wages to consumer prices, jointly with oligopolistic pricing, generated a wage–price–profit spiral, which culminated after the two oil shocks in two-digit inflation. Hence pressures to reverse previously accommodating monetary policies increased in inverse proportion to the strength of each nation's productive system. Fordist collective bargaining sustained demand via a form of real wage rigidity, as previously described. This explains why the recessions initiated in 1973 or 1979 were not a repetition of the collapse observed between 1920 and 1932. Moreover, the speed of adjustment of employment was lower, in such a way that firms hoarded labour as a quasi-fixed factor; at least they did at the beginning of the present crisis!

But this process has an evident drawback: if the shock is mainly about a deterioration in the terms of trade, and if the national economy is a price-taker at the world level, then the profit rate is squeezed. Furthermore, the existing monopolistic 'régulation' is unable to recover its previous level, since that kind of perturbation never occurred in the past. Thus investment slackens, which leads to less capacity and lower productivity growth, since a slower embodiment of technical progress and diffusion of new production processes take place. So in contrast to the inter-war crisis, the *profit rate is now too low* compared to the growth in demand. The major structural crises repeat themselves but are not identical in their origin and form. The present crisis does not seem to be resolvable within the existing development mode. All its components, or at least a large part of them, have to evolve: the search for a new technical paradigm (post-Fordist, but for a more precise description see Chapter 27); the reorganization of the wage–labour nexus (short-term flexibility of wages and employment and/or adaptation to a 'new' New Deal); the basic principles guiding economic policy; and the negotiation of a new international regime in order to solve the debt problem as well as to moderate competitive struggles between large OECD countries.

Let us hope that these results are of some interest to students of technical change. Our leitmotiv is simple, even a little naïve; *the fate of any technological system cannot be disentangled from social (particularly the wage–labour nexus) and economic determinants (the evolution of the mode of development as a whole)*. But the reader may rightly consider this statement to be too general and demand more detailed hypotheses and analyses.

A research agenda

Some of these investigations of the role of technology in the 'régulation' approach were carried out during the last decade. A number of them are listed in section II of the references. Let us summarize briefly the main domains covered and present possible extensions of this line of analysis.

1. Confronting the basic hypotheses with the findings of science and technology research

As technology is not the only point of entry in the 'régulation' approach, more detailed analysis is needed to substantiate the succession of the three historical stages: extensive, intensive without and then with a mass consumption accumulation regime. It would be interesting to survey the existing literature and check if the features attributed to technology are confirmed. To give an example, Hounshell (1984) shows that Ford's original model of industrial organization was replaced by a more flexible one during the 1920s and 1930s. Contrary to a now common belief, the first crisis of the pure Fordist model takes place during the inter-war period. Thus the present one would be the second, so that product differentiation within mass consumption would not be totally new.

At a more conceptual level, it would be stimulating to compare this approach with the notions elaborated by SPRU to interpret the vast amount of case studies, sectoral and global analyses made over one or two decades. In particular, the concepts of technological system and technological paradigm (Dosi, 1982) display the same features as the 'régulation' approach for institutional forms. *A priori*, one could imagine a marriage of these two lines of analysis. The convergences are already very significant:

in a sense the mismatch between technology and institutions (Perez, 1983) is closely related to what has been said about structural crisis ('The place of technology in long-run dynamics' in this chapter).

2. Formalizing various accumulation regimes besides the Fordist one

A second agenda concerns macroeconomic theory. All the previous hypotheses have been kept fairly general, without any analysis of their coherence. For such a purpose, a minimum of formalization is called for, especially in order to check under which conditions a regime is structurally stable or runs into a major crisis. Prototypes of such models have already been proposed and even submitted to various econometric tests. For example, a cross-section and medium-term Kaldorian model seems to confirm the role of increasing returns in post-Second World War growth (Boyer and Petit, 1981b) and the breakdown of this model since the early or mid-1970s (Boyer and Ralle, 1986b). Similarly, the significance of the Fordist model for the US economy has been investigated by Caussat (1981).

Nevertheless, many points remain rather obscure and call for new analysis. First, a minimal and very simplified model of Fordism has to be agreed upon by the 'régulationists' themselves. The interested reader will find such an attempt in a recent paper (Boyer and Coriat, 1987), which in a sense synthethizes some previous work (Aglietta, 1974; Billaudot, 1976; Bertrand, 1978, 1983). Second, a more general approach has to address the extreme variablility across countries and historical periods of accumulation regimes and 'régulation' modes. Hence a vast research programme is called for, which ideally would combine different productivity regimes—linked, amongst other things, to the precise technological system—and various demand regimes associated with given mechanisms for income distribution and demand generation (see my Chapter 27 in this volume). More generally, theoreticians should work on *macroeconomics of technological change*.

3. Searching for the roots of the present crisis: what role does technology play?

The analysis, however, should not be restricted to the study of equilibrium growth paths, i.e. to self-stabilizing processes, as most macroeconomic theory does. We need to understand the causes of crises considered as periods of stagnation and/or large instabilities. As mentioned earlier, the very success of a 'régulation' mode might lead to a slow shift in structural parameters, such that the system becomes globally unstable. This might offer a possible explanation of this aspect of long waves and a way to analyse their underlying social and economic determinants. In this respect the 'régulation' approach converges with other recent analyses (Screpanti, 1986; Hanappi, 1986; Goodwin, 1986).

Furthermore, special attention should be devoted to the origins of the present crisis. Combining a theoretical Fordist model with some estimates of the key parameters would allow us to answer a difficult but central question: would the exhaustion of the technological system have led to another form of crisis, quite apart from the changes affecting the distribution of income and the dynamics of the world economy (Bertrand, 1983)? Similarly, are the so-called Fordist rigidities a major cause or only the unintended consequences of a crisis originating in economic and social factors? Subsequent work should check the validity of very preliminary work already available (Boyer and Coriat, 1987). A more confident answer should help to resolve the puzzle about the exact role of technology during the present crisis.

4. What could the next accumulation regime and technological system look like?

The previous analysis, if correct, has important consequences. One may no longer rely upon cyclical regularities (the Kondratiev waves) to assess the date and the conditions of a way out of the present disorder. The underlying complex process is of course dependent upon past conditions, but not totally, since social struggles, political choices, favourable (or dramatic) innovations, as well as chance, shape the final outcome. Therefore a major challenge for economic analysis is to discard the ambition to forecast the long-term future, but nevertheless attempt to assess the viability of a set of changes in institutional forms and technology.

Of course, this exercise in 'macroeconomic fiction' is tricky indeed, but seems worthwhile. It would allow us to discuss the long-run consequences of economic and social policies. The usual debates too frequently focus upon short- or medium-term issues. The first tentative steps in this direction seem promising, if not conclusive (Boyer and Coriat, 1987, and Chapter 27 of this book). These analyses provide two major hints. First, measures encouraging technological change and policies of market return seem to be rather contradictory as far as economic stability and the fight against mass unemployment are concerned. Second, contrary to a now widely held view, public and private cooperation might help a good deal in promoting a new growth regime.

References

I Basic references to the 'régulation' approach

Aglietta, M. (1974), *Accumulation et régulation du capitalisme en longue période: Exemple des États-Unis (1870–1970)*, Thèse Paris I, October.

—— (1976), *Régulation et crises du capitalisme*, Paris, Calmann-Levy, (2nd ed., 1982).

Aglietta, M. and Brender, A. (1984), *Les métamorphoses de la société salariale*, Paris, Calmann-Levy.

Aglietta, M. and Orlean, A. (1982), *La violence de la monnaie*, Paris, P.U.F.

André, C. and Delorme, R. (1983), *L'État et l'économie*, Paris, Seuil.

Basle, M., Mazier, J. and Vidal, J.F. (1982), 'Emploi, revenu salarial, prix et profit', *Economie et Prévision*.

Basle, M., Mazier, J.,Vidal, J.F. (1984), *Quand les crises durent. . .*, Paris, Economica.

Benassy, J.P., Boyer, R. et Gelpi. R.M. (1979), 'Régulation des économies capitalistes et inflation', *Revue Économique*, vol. 30, no. 3, May.

de Bernis, G. (Destanne) (1983), 'Une alternative à l'hypothèse de l'équilibre économique général: la régulation de l'économie capitaliste', dans 'Crise et Régulation', publication du GRREC, Grenoble, P.U.G.

Bertrand, H. (1978), 'Une nouvelle approche de la croissance française de l'après-guerre: l'analyse en sections productives', *Statistiques et Études Financières*, Série Orange, no. 35.

—— (1983), 'Accumulation, régulation, crise: un modèle sectionnel théorique et appliqué', *Revue Économique*, vol. 34, no. 6, March.

Billaudot, B. (1976), *L'accumulation intensive du capital*, Thèse Paris I.

Boyer, R. (1975), 'Modalités de la régulation d'économies capitalistes dans la longue période: quelques formalisations simples', mimeo, CEPREMAP, June.

—— (1978), 'Les salaires en longue période', *Économie et Statistique*, no. 103, pp. 99–118.

—— (1979), 'La crise actuelle: une mise en perspective historique. Quelques réflexions à partir d'une analyse du capitalisme français en longue période', *Critiques de l'Économie Politique*, no. 7/8, April–September, pp. 3–113.

—— (ed.) (1986a), *La flexibilité du travail en Europe*, Paris, La Découverte. English Translation, Oxford University Press, (1988).

—— (ed.) (1986b), *Capitalismes fin de siècle*, Paris, Presses Universitaires de France.

—— (1986c), *La théorie de la régulation: une analyse critique*, Paris, La Découverte. English Translation, Columbia Press, (1988).

Boyer, R. and Mistral, J. (1978), *Accumulation, inflation, crises*, Paris, P.U.F. (2nd ed., 1983).

CEPREMAP–CORDES (Benassy, J.P., Boyer, R., Gelpi, R.M., Lipietz, A., Mistral, J., Muñoz, J. et Ominami, C.) (1977), 'Approches de l'inflation: l'exemple français', Convention de recherche no 22, mimeo.

Coriat, B. (1978), *L'atelier et le chronomètre*, Paris, C. Bourgois.

Fagerberg, J. (1984), 'The "régulation school" and the classics: modes of accumulation and modes of regulation in a classical model of economic growth', Couverture Orange CEPREMAP, no. 8426, July.

GRREC (1983), *Crise et régulation*, Grenoble, P.U.G., DRUG.

Lipietz, A. (1979), *Crise et inflation, pourquoi?*, Paris, Maspéro.
—— (1983), *Le monde enchanté: de la valeur à l'envol inflationniste*, Paris, La Découverte/Maspéro.
Lorenzi, J.H., Pastré, O., Toledano, J. (1980), *La crise du XXè siècle*, Paris, Economica.
Mistral, J., 'Metamorphoses du systéme international' in Boyer, R. ed. (1986b).
Ominami, C. (1986), *Le Tiers Monde dans la crise*, Paris. La Découverte.

II Some investigations of the effects of technological change made at CEPREMAP

Boyer, R. and Coriat, B. (1987), 'Technical flexibility and macro stabilisation: some preliminary steps', mimeograph CEPREMAP, Conference on Innovation Diffusion, Venise, 17–21 March 1986, revised version.
Boyer, R. and Petit, P. (1981a), 'Employment and productivity in the EEC', *Cambridge Journal of Economics*, vol. 5, no. 1, March.
Boyer, R. and Petit, P. (1981b), 'Forecasting the impact of technical change on employment: methodological reflections and proposals for research', in Diettrich and Morley (eds), *Relations Between Technology Capital and Labour*, Commission of the European Communities, Eur. 8181 En Brussels, pp. 49–69.
—— (1981b), 'Progrès technique, croissance et emploi: un modèle d'inspiration Kaldorienne pour six industries européennes', *Revue Économique*, vol. 32, no. 6, November, pp. 1113–53.
—— (1984), 'Politiques industrielles et impact sur l'emploi: les pays européens face à la contrainte extérieure', *Revue d'Économie Industrielle*, no. 27, January.
Boyer, R. and Ralle, P. (1986a), 'Croissances nationales et contrainte extérieure avant et après 1973', *Économie et Société*, Cahiers de l'ISMEA, no P29, January.
—— (1986b), 'L'insertion internationale conditionne-t-elle les formes nationales d'emploi? Convergences ou différenciations des pays européens', *Économie et Société*, Cahiers de l'ISMEA, no. P29, January.
Caussat, L. (1981), 'Croissance, emploi, productivité dans l'industrie américaine (1899–1976)', mimeograph CEPREMAP, September.

III Other references

Cripps, F. and Tarling, R. (1973), 'Growth in advanced capitalist economies 1950–1970', Cambridge University Press Occasional Paper 40.
Dosi, G. (1982), 'Technological paradigms and technological trajectories: a suggested interpretation of the determinants and directions of technical change', *Research Policy*, vol. II, no. 3, June, pp. 147–62.
Freeman, C. (1978), 'Les cycles de Kondratieff, l'évolution technique et le chômage', OECD Experts Meeting, 7–11 March 1977, Paris.
Goodwin, R. (1986), 'Towards a theory of long waves', International Workshop, 'Technological and Social Factors in Long-Term Fluctuations', Certosa di Pontignano, Siena, December.
Hanappi, G. (1986), 'The stages of industrial capitalism', International Workshop, 'Technological and Social Factors in Long-Term Fluctuations', Certosa di Pontignano, Siena, December.

Hounshell, D.A. (1984), *From the American System to Mass Production, 1800–1932: The Development of Manufacturing Technology in the U.S.*, Baltimore, Md., Johns Hopkins University Press.

Insee (1986) 'Comptes de la Watron 1985', Collection L, no. 131–132.

Mensch, G. (1978), *Stalemate in Technology*, Cambridge, Mass., Ballinger.

Perez, C. (1983), 'Structural change and assimilation of new technologies in the economic and social systems', *Futures*, vol. 15, no. 5, October, pp. 357–75.

Sauvy, A., (1965) 'Histoire économique de la France', Volume 1, Fayard, Paris.

Screpanti, E. (1986), 'Some demographic and social processes and the problem of Kondratieff cycle periodicity', International Workshop, 'Technological and Social Factors in Long-Term Fluctuations', Certosa di Pontignano, Siena, December.

Vincent, L.A. 'La comptes nationales' in Sauvy, A. (1972) 'Histoire économique de la France', Volume 3. Fayard, Paris, pp. 309–343.

5 Evolution, innovation and economics

*Peter M. Allen**

International Ecotechnology Research Centre, Cranfield Institute of Technology, Cranfield

Introduction

Technical change and innovation are the subject of this book, and the forum of most of the discussion will be that of economic theory. But really, economic change is just one aspect of the more general question of evolution. The parallel has already been recognized by several authors who have argued convincingly for the idea that economies should be understood on the basis of the 'evolutionary paradigm', rather than that of the more traditional assumptions of equilibrium, or of deterministic mechanics.[1-4]

But this seems to be only the first step in the recognition of the fact that it is our lack of understanding of creative processes, adaptation and evolution itself which is the core of the problem. What we are really faced with is an evolving complex system, and the creation, acceptance, rejection, diffusion or suppression of 'innovations and technical changes' cannot be considered in terms of 'economics', separated from history, culture, social structure, the ecological system and so on. That we should have ever attempted to do so is a symptom of our past unwillingness to 'grasp the nettle' of the holistic, dynamic,'more than mechanical' nature of the real world.[5]

The very idea that areas of study can be hived off into separate domains in which 'closed' sciences can be constructed seems to be based only on organizational convenience, not on reality. Economics is only one aspect of a human system. Cultural habits and rituals, music, technology, beliefs, psychological and biological needs are others. Ultimately all 'economic' decisions must be based in this wider reality and will both reflect and affect these broader areas. Human values underlie 'prices', and either as individuals, or in measures of collective welfare, the monetary and the non-monetary must meet and interact. Any action will have effects on many different aspects, and these in turn will influence others, and so in a complex chain of responses which defy simply, intuitive evaluation.

It is not enough that we should try to understand economics in 'evolutionary' terms (though apparently this alone is considered dangerously radical by most economists), but rather that economics should be seen as

* The urban models cited in this paper were funded by contracts from the Department of Transportation, USA, the Province of North Holland and the Regional Government of Wallonie, Belgium. The work concerning fishery modelling was supported by the Global Learning Division of the United Nations University, Tokyo, and by Fisheries and Oceans, Canada.

just one aspect of evolving, complex systems. And if this is the case, then a proper understanding of innovation and technical change can only come from improved knowledge about the general problem.

What therefore is the science of evolution?

What basis does it offer for discussing the discovery and diffusion of improvement and adaptation and what 'laws' can possibly apply?

Newtonian clocks and Darwinian watches

Until recently, the only answer to such a question would have been that offered by theories of evolution based on the ideas of Charles Darwin.[6] But these ideas, although certainly correct as far as they go in biology, present evolution simply as the fruit of 'selective' forces acting on randomly occurring mutations. The theory is not really predictive, but instead is a plausible explanation of whatever is observed. If some animals are observed to behave in a certain way, then it must be because a mutant arose who did so, and whose innovation was advantageous. Because of this, the behaviour must have been selected for, and that it why we see it . . . While Darwin's theory represented a tremendous step forward for the biological sciences, its connection to physics was tenuous, and it was simply assumed that they applied to different, and separate, domains.

In Newtonian science, understanding of a system was to be obtained by identifying its 'parts' together with the causal connections between them. The resulting assemblage of mechanisms then constituted a 'model' of the system, and provided a tool for understanding observations and making predictions.

This idea reflected and confirmed the notion of the universe as a kind of giant 'clockwork' mechanism, conceived of and set in motion by God, and running according to immutable laws. Science was about discovering these 'laws of nature', and hence revealing the intricacy and power of the creator's work. And science succeeded in this quite brilliantly. Two basic situations were found. In the absence of friction (planetary motion, for example), the movement was unchecked, going on for ever. There was no 'net effect' from such movements, and there would be no way of telling whether a film of such events was being shown forwards or backwards. The movement was 'reversible'.

But with dissipative processes such as friction, any initial concerted motion would eventually be damped until the system reached thermo-dynamic equilibrium and all its initially high-grade energy had been dissipated into random, thermal motion. This was an irreversible, deterministic progression to equilibrium, and this final state could be predicted as the maximum of the appropriate thermodynamic potential. The image here is of a universe gradually 'winding down' as it uses its initial potential for creativity.

However, evolution in biology or the human sciences, and more specifically the understanding of the birth and diffusion of innovations in the modern world, is about creative forces. It does not concern so much the simple functioning of the existing system, although this is interesting. Instead, it is primarily concerned with how the system became what it is, and how it will evolve in the future. In other words, if the world is viewed as some kind of 'machine' made up of component parts which influence each other through causal connections, then instead of simply asking how it 'works', evolutionary theory is concerned with how it got to be as it is. It is fundamentally about the origins of qualitative change in things, and how the 'parts' of a system came into being, and are maintained.

The Newtonian paradigm was not about this. It was about mechanical systems either just running, or just running down. At best, existing structure was maintained, while usually it was eroded during the approach to equilibrium, as entropy increased. Any representation of 'creative processes' was entirely absent.

Despite this obvious shortcoming, the extraordinary success of Newtonian physics, and of thermodynamics, vindicated every day in calculations concerning industrial processes, made it a tempting theoretical framework to apply to *all* complex systems. Because of this, in fields such as economics, biology, ecology, anthropology, etc., theories appeared in which 'understanding' was based on assumptions of 'equilibrium' and a search for the 'appropriate' potential function which *governed* the evolution of these systems—utility, fitness, efficiency, etc.

But the real difference in approach between this Newtonian–Darwinian view and the new perspective today lies in whether we think of evolution as being over, or as still continuing. The key issue is centred on the passage between detailed microscopic complexity of the real world, which clearly can evolve, and any aggregate, macroscopic 'model' of this. In economics, the passage from micro to macroeconomics is 'achieved' by simply supposing that the system is always at economic equilibrium. In this way the particular actions of individuals and entrepreneurs are assumed to be such that equilibrium relationships always hold between macro variables. Two time-scales are supposed. A very short one, for the approach to price equilibrium where all markets clear, and a longer one which describes the displacement over time of this equilibrium as a result of changing 'parameters'. Change is then always exogenous to the model, being driven by imposed changes of the relevant parameters. In other words, this corresponds merely to a 'description' of change (and not an accurate one), mechanically impacting on a system of fixed structure, imposed changes in parameter values. Indeed, calibrating any such model becomes simply a task of finding changing values of parameters such that it reproduces the observed time variations of variables. And this amounts to a 'curve fitting' exercise with no real content. It explains only the economists' obsession with simultaneous equations, regressions and static curves, and denies the importance of history, of time delay, of anticipation, and indeed of consciousness.

The real sources of economic change are in the system. They are due to the creative actions of entrepreneurs and consumers. These are rooted in the perception of changes in technology, the distribution of available consumers, and changing tastes. To a physicist (or even an ex-physicist) causality relates the change that occurs at a particular moment to the state of the system as specified by the values of variables, for given parameters. So, for example, after a period of over-supply of some good, the quantity of the stock can only be 'explained' in historical terms, as the result of a previous period of over-zealous production. What cannot be done is to 'explain' the size of this stock in terms of the existing situation as given by the values of the other factors. This would only be possible at equilibrium when the over-supply had been 'corrected', and the perfect information of actors had been used to adjust prices, and through them supply and demand, so that all markets cleared. In reality, though, the actual behaviour of the system will in fact be described by the series of actions and changes which correspond to the state of previous over-supply. What will happen is described by differential equations relating to change to state, and not by simultaneous equations relating between themselves the values of different variables.

However, the equilibrium hypothesis is tenacious, mainly because it avoids all the real difficulties of life, and can lead to elegant theorems and lemmas, which are the very stuff of Ph.D.s, professorial appointments and honorary degrees. Despite the fact that it flies in the face of everyday experience, it has therefore been the foundation on which the whole edifice of economic theory has been built.[7]

Although in retrospect the acceptance and adoption of such an assumption may seem a little extraordinary, the underlying reason for its adoption was simple—there was no alternative. Microeconomics might discuss individuals' and firms' behaviour, Schumpeter[8] might base his thinking on entrepreneurs, and Simon[9] might show the importance of limited information and computation time, but somehow the illusion was still clung to that, whatever these details were, their 'sum' was necessarily controlled by the competitive forces underlying economic equilibrium, and even that this latter expressed some kind of 'optimal' use of resources, some 'maximum economic activity'.

The image that this presents is one of evolution as a 'blind watchmaker',[10] where the intricate machinery of the world is comparable to that of a watch, whose cogs and bearings are the fruit of the selection, in the past, of unspecified trials. Behind this is the idea of evolution as an optimizing 'force', which has led to the retention of the individuals and organizations we see because of their functional superiority. In this way, the classical theories of economics, of evolutionary biology and of anthropological interpretation have been permeated by the materialist ideas of the mechanical paradigm of classical physics. Carried deep within this is the idea of 'progress', of the rightful 'survival of the fittest', and of a natural 'justice' which must characterize the long-term evolution of a complex system.

However, equilibrium models based on these ideas have proved in practice to be quite unsatisfactory as a basis for decision-making. Despite an enormous investment in research into economic, ecological and social systems, these concepts have failed to provide satisfactory models, and our understanding of the evolution that we observe remains essentially based on 'experience'. The fundamental reason for this is that the basic paradigm—our whole way of thinking about such things—is wrong. The systems which we see around us are neither at nor on their way, necessarily, to thermodynamic equilibrium. The sunlight which is incident upon the earth makes sure that this is not the case. All living things have evolved in a situation of *non-equilibrium*! And for such systems evolution can lead to the emergence of structure and form, and to qualitative change even in relatively simple physical systems.

Self-organizing systems: the new evolutionary synthesis

The central question which arises is that in order even to think about reality, to invent words and concepts with which to discuss it, we are forced to reduce its complexity. We cannot think of the trillions of molecules, living cells, organisms, individuals and events that surround us, each in its own place and with its own history. We must first make a taxonomic classification, and we must also make a spatial aggregation. This is shown in Figure 5.1. On the left we represent the cloudy, confused complexity of the real world. Each part is special, each point unique. On the right is a 'model' of that reality, in terms of 'typical elements' of the system, where classifications and spatial aggregation have been carried out. But the point is that however good the choice of variables, parameters and interaction mechanisms may be, these only concern average behaviour. If we compare reality with the predictions of our model, then we shall necessarily find that variables and parameters 'fluctuate' around average values, and also that there is much greater microscopic diversity than that considered at the level of the macroscopic model.

By making the right taxonomic and spatial aggregations we can model present reality by such a system of boxes and arrows. But the description that results is necessarily probabilistic in character, reflecting the loss of precise information concerning all the details of the system. However, at this first level of reduction it does take into account therefore all possible sequences of events into the future, from the most to the least probable.

A solution of a very simple problem at such a level of description is discussed in the chapter by Brian Arthur, and other more complicated systems have been studies and solved in the physical sciences.[11] But in general most realistic systems would be somewhat too difficult to discuss at such a complex level of description, and this is one reason why such models

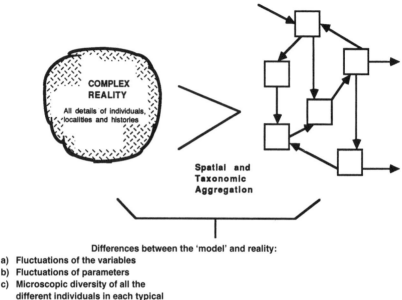

Figure 5.1   Modelling, and even thinking about a complex system, necessitates a simplification into categories, which constitute the system. We make a 'mechanical' replica of present reality. But evolution concerns change in this structure—new boxes and arrows

are not frequently discussed. The other reason is satisfactory for most people. They would immediately go on to ask, 'yes, I see that the evolution is probabilistic and contains all possible evolutions, including very improbable paths, but all I want to know for the moment, in this case, is what will most probably happen, what would happen on average!' By asking this question, we then can proceed to ignore all the non-average behaviour of the system, and find (or create) a satisfying (but misleading) single trajectory for the average behaviour of the system.

So if, in addition to our basic taxonomic and spatial aggregations, we assume that only average elements make up each category, and that only the most probable events actually occur, then our model reduces to a 'machine' which represents the system in terms of a set of differential equations governing its variables.

But such a 'machine' is only capable of 'functioning', not of evolving. It cannot restructure itself or insert new cogs and wheels, while reality can! And this is because of the differences between the left- and right-hand side of Figure 5.1, which must mean that the key to understanding evolution must lie in what has been taken out from complex reality in order to reduce it to the model on the right. Our programme of research must therefore be aimed at exploring how to put back these non-average effects that we have removed, and examining the evolutionary effects that these may have.

Clearly, therefore, evolution is due to two things: first, to the effects of non-average values—fluctuations—of variables and parameters, and, second, to changes introduced by the microscopic diversity which underlies the 'taxonomic' classification of the model. Let us consider these in turn.

Dissipative structures: the origins of complexity

The work of many authors on self-organization and synergetic phenomena has demonstrated the fact that for systems far from equilibrium, basic physical non-linearities can in fact amplify fluctuations of variables and lead to symmetry-breaking instabilities in which structure and organization appear or, if already present, evolve qualitatively.[12-14]

Let us briefly describe a simple example of convection in a fluid which is heated from below. Initially, for only weak temperature gradients heat passes through the fluid from the bottom to the top by thermal conduction alone. However, as the temperature at the lower surface is increased, at a critical value, something quite remarkable happens.

Suddenly, the fluid itself starts to move. Thermal energy is now transported 'bodily' by the fluid itself in a convection process. But the movement is not just some general, random drift which is uniform throughout the system. Instead a remarkable pattern of regular, hexagonal convection cells appear spontaneously in the fluid, which moves upwards in the centre of each cell, and downwards at the edges. This is shown in Figure 5.2.

In fact, as the temperature is further increased a whole series of successive patterns appear in the system until, finally, for very strong thermal gradients complete turbulence occurs and structure can no longer be observed.

The pattern which we observe, and which involves the coherent behaviour of trillions of molecules, is stable but does not necessarily express any particular 'optimality'. Does it give 'maximum' heat transfer between the upper and lower surfaces, for example? Is it the 'most efficient' flow pattern possible, minimizing dissipation as the thermal energy moves through the system? Or, on the contrary, is it the pattern of 'maximum dissipation', taking most 'out of' the heat source? The point is that, even for such a simple system, we cannot answer these questions.

And this is a fundamental point to which we shall return. In systems

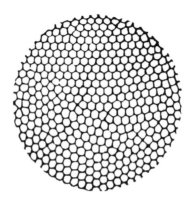

Figure 5.2 Beyond a well-defined critical temperature gradient, the Benard convection cells appear spontaneously

which evolved to thermodynamic equilibrium there was a potential function which governed the evolution of the system. Either the entropy or the free energy imposed a deterministic relaxation process towards a predetermined equilibrium state. And this was where physics got its powers of prediction from. But non-equilibrium systems achieve some kind of autonomy and freedom which means that they become 'creative', generating structure and complexity. The price which we pay for this, however, is a loss of 'predictability'. Many other examples of such behaviour now exist, and a chemical example is shown in Figure 5.3.

In reality, we find that the equations which describe the average evolution of the variables really only specify a tree of potential behaviours. This branching tree of potential structures is typical of non-linear dynamical systems, and is called a bifurcation tree (Figure 5.4). Different branches of solution differ from each other qualitatively. That is, they have distinctive characteristic symmetries, which means essentially that they have different forms. In such a vision, therefore, sudden large jumps and discontinuities can occur, even for systems subjected to slowly changing conditions, and the jump to a new branch may be accompanied by a structural reorganization of the system. In this way new mechanisms can appear spontaneously, and in a human system this may bring into focus new issues and problems, as well as new satisfactions and goals.

Here, at last, is the mathematics of creative processes, where traits and characteristics are not conserved, and where structural instability and evolution can find their legitimate expression.

And yet all of them may be generated by the same simple, unchanging scheme of average kinetics, providing that it is non-linear. Which pattern is actually observed in a particular experiment cannot be controlled from the

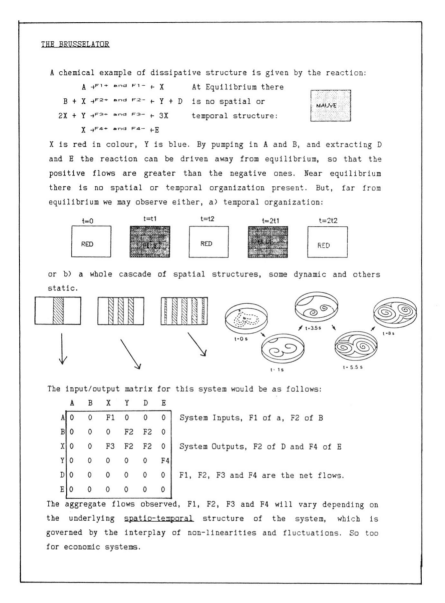

THE BRUSSELATOR

A chemical example of dissipative structure is given by the reaction:

A →F1+ and F1- + X   At Equilibrium there

B + X →F2+ and F2- + Y + D is no spatial or

2X + Y →F3+ and F3- + 3X   temporal structure:

X →F4+ and F4- +E

X is red in colour, Y is blue. By pumping in A and B, and extracting D and E the reaction can be driven away from equilibrium, so that the positive flows are greater than the negative ones. Near equilibrium there is no spatial or temporal organization present. But, far from equilibrium we may observe either, a) temporal organization:

t=0   t=t1   t=t2   t=2t1   t=2t2

RED   BLUE   RED   BLUE   RED

or b) a whole cascade of spatial structures, some dynamic and others static.

t-0 s   t-3.5 s   t-8 s   t- 1s   t- 5.5 s

The input/output matrix for this system would be as follows:

	A	B	X	Y	D	E
A	0	0	F1	0	0	0
B	0	0	0	F2	F2	0
X	0	0	F3	F2	F2	0
Y	0	0	0	0	0	F4
D	0	0	0	0	0	0
E	0	0	0	0	0	0

System Inputs, F1 of a, F2 of B

System Outputs, F2 of D and F4 of E

F1, F2, F3 and F4 are the net flows.

The aggregate flows observed, F1, F2, F3 and F4 will vary depending on the underlying spatio-temporal structure of the system, which is governed by the interplay of non-linearities and fluctuations. So too for economic systems.

Figure 5.3   An example of chemical self-organization

outside. While the external parameters can be fixed at the boundary, and may limit the actual choice, the fact remains that it is the system itself that 'decides' which of the possible patterns it will in fact adopt.

For any particular system, this 'choice' is made by the fluctuations which are present in the system. And this confirms the deduction made above that the key to evolutionary change lays in the differences between reality and its average representation. Because of fluctuations the real system is

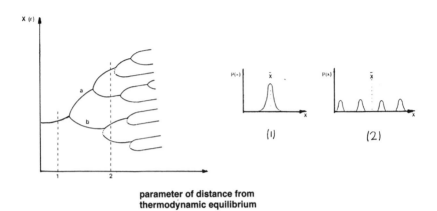

Figure 5.4 The stationary states which are possible for a dissipative structure are given by a 'bifurcation tree'

always in fact probing the *stability* of the particular situation and, depending on which fluctuation occurs at a critical moment, the system will move to one or another of the stable behaviours which are possible. The real world is therefore much more 'lively' than its mechanical representation in terms only of average events occurring for average types. Symmetry-breaking transitions can occur spontaneously and so truly 'new' structures can be created. In this fact lies the real source of innovation in the physical world.

However, in physics and chemistry the elements of the system are atoms or molecules, which are essentially identical and incapable of internal reorganization beyond that fixed by the chemical transformations. But in the living world, we must examine the possibility that the internal structure of the individuals or elemental objects themselves could evolve in time. Indeed, these elements could themselves be dissipative structures in competition for the energy and matter that they need to maintain and transcend themselves.

In this connection, then, it is the existence of microscopic diversity and modes of individual liberty that must be discussed.

Evolutionary drive: the role of noise and error-making in evolution

Studies concerning dissipative structures and the self-organization of systems have largely concentrated on the aspects discussed in the preceding section, while the possible effects of microscopic diversity have been relatively neglected. In some very recent work,[15] however, it has been shown that this too is of major importance.

The point in question here is that of attempting to understand the possible effects of 'putting back' the existence of real microscopic diversity into a model which has assumed populations made up only of average individuals. This assumption was made in order to obtain nice, deterministic differential equations governing the changing populations inhabiting the system. But the price paid was that evolutionary processes due to innovative acts and non-average performance were eliminated. If we wish to understand evolution, therefore, or to frame our strategies so as to take into account evolutionary processes, then we must try to put back into our model the mechanisms of mutation and innovation which create and maintain the real pattern of microscopic diversity. But can we put back what has been taken out?

The answer is no. Once we have 'averaged over' the detail, then there is no way that it can be recreated with certainty. This is the source of contention and confusion as to whether 'mutations' are random or not. In the absence of any information concerning the precise nature of the variability that may be present, then it may well be that an assumption of 'complete randomness' is the most reasonable one that could be made. Darwin himself adopts this point of view. But in fact there is a whole variety of possible hypotheses that could be made, which range from the completely random to a view in which the 'environment' completely determines which mutations occur. In problems of human and technological evolution one may favour an intermediate solution in which one views innovations as being 'channelled' somewhat by existing practices. However, the real issue is simply that having thrown away the really important detail which is involved, in order to build a mechanistic model of a system, then we can only try to guess the precise way in which non-average events may occur in the system. The first important step, however, is to study models which at least do include non-average behaviour, even if its exact nature in a particular case is uncertain.

In simple ecological models of competition we have examined the effects of 'error-making' in reproduction, which we have supposed to be due to the occurrence of some 'random mutations', or variablility. On average, however, we have assumed that random changes such as these would lead more often to less efficient individuals than to more efficient ones. In this way, the net effect is to introduce on average a negative drift into the performance parameters of a population, which is counteracted by a positive drift caused by the differential elimination of the less effective individuals. What our model shows explicitly, as we summarize in Figures

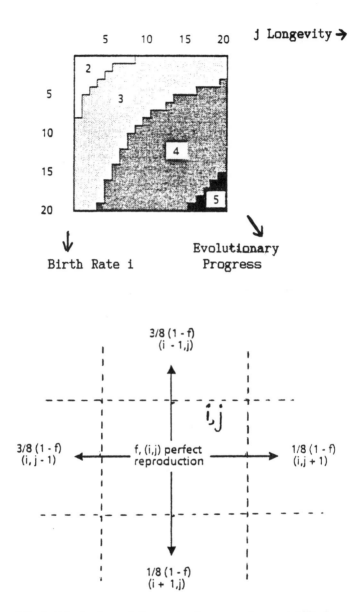

Figure 5.5 In this simple evolutionary landscape random variability in reproduction leads mostly to less efficient individuals, but also to some which are more efficient

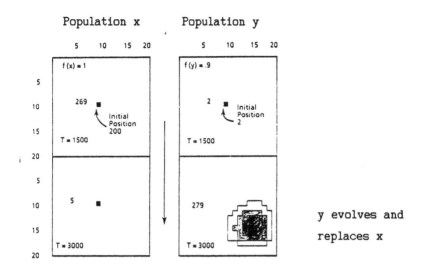

Figure 5.6 Evolution selects for the population with variability, even though at each instant it would be more efficient not to make 'errors'

5.5 and 5.6, is that in competition between a population with perfect reproduction and one with mutations and variability, evolution retains the latter rather than the former.

In an evolutionary landscape of hills and valleys representing levels of functional efficiency of different possible organisms, it is the error-maker who can move up a hill, eventually out-competing a perfectly reproducing rival. And this despite the fact that at each and every instant it would be better not to make errors, since the majority of these are loss-making.

This work shows that evolution does not lead to optimal behaviour, because evolution concerns not only 'efficient performance' but also the constant need for new discoveries. What is found is that variability at the microscopic level, individual diversity, is part of the evolutionary strategy of survivors, and this is precisely what mechanical 'systems' representations do not include. In other words, in the shifting landscape of a world in continuous evolution, the ability to climb is perhaps what counts, and what we see as a result of evolution are not species or firms with 'optimal behaviour' at each instant, but rather actors that can learn!

Because of this, at any moment, behaviour in the system itself will not be optimal, because of the existence of apparently random or highly eccentric behaviour, which at that time is meaningless and on average loss-making. However, in order to maintain adaptivity to the environment some stochastic, risk-taking behaviour is retained by evolution. In short, then, evolution is both driven by, and leads to, microscopic diversity and individual variability. Selection viewed at the 'macroscopic level' of averages cannot destroy the microscopic diversity. Indeed, it is just this diversity which drives evolution!

The fluctuations, mutations and apparently random movements which are naturally present in real complex systems constitute a sort of 'imaginative' and creative force which will explore around whatever exists at present. Selection or, rather, the dynamic mechanisms of the system operate on these attempts which will either regress or, on the contrary, will sweep the system off to some new state of organization.

We can liken this ecological problem to the situation of many small firms competing for a particular market. In some of these, the present state of technological know-how is translated into a very clear plan of production which is put into operation with little or no error. In others, however, the plan is less clear, and variations in production technique lead somewhat randomly to a product of variable aspect and costs. This process could also be carried out in the imagination of an innovator, and perhaps many ideas would be rejected without being realized materially. In this way, pre-existing ideas and concepts may well channel 'invention', and could even block a real breakthrough. Of course, most such initiatives will give rise to less satisfactory products, but a few of them will be improvements. The 'information' created by this random probing can be used by the discoverers to change their product. This would correspond to 'learning by doing' and obviously if production plans are too rigid, then no such discoveries will be made. What is really required is the right compromise between local 'experimentation' (resulting either from error, ignorance or research) and efficient production techniques.

Of course, it may be true that the exact 'pattern' of the innovative variability is not truly 'random', because there may be technological channelling of ideas and initiatives. This was information that was available perhaps in the more complete probabilistic description which took into account all possible sequences of events—with their appropriate probabilities. However, once the discussion is reduced to the average behaviour of a particular set of variables, corresponding to a given level of disaggregation, then we have eliminated precisely the information which, as regards evolutionary change, is the most vital.

Here we can see the paradox which surrounds the very notion of stability—it can only be defined in terms of an ability to return to a pre-existing state or trajectory when subject to a particular fluctuation. But if the fluctuations are simply the result of the 'non-average' behaviour of the system, then what we see is that the choice of variables and the level of disaggregation partly determine what is 'state' and what is 'fluctuation'. It therefore becomes very important to study the differences between observed and predicted values of the variables of the system. This may even be the real use of such models, since they may 'take out' what is the result of 'normal' or 'average' behaviour for a system and allow us to focus

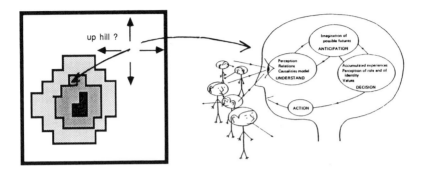

Figure 5.7   In human systems, behaviour is no longer shaped predominantly by natural selection. Instead it is affected by the perception of 'success' and imitative processes

on what is not! The behaviour of the system with respect to these fluctuations is then what may be decisive for the future evolution.

Returning to our example, we see that because in general each firm is in competition with others, technological and organizational changes will lead to responses and counter-measures, to an 'arms race', with no obvious end. Evolution, therefore, is a continuing process, and that is why selection favours individuals and firms which maintain the ability to adapt and learn new things.

In the biology of simple beings, genetic reproduction ensures that the 'information' about a successful strategy resulting from advantageous genetic variability can only be passed on to the descendants. But, of course, an entirely new phase of evolution is reached once information can be 'perceived' and imitative modes of behaviour are possible. The fulcrum of evolution passes from 'genetics' to 'perception–judgement–behaviour' (Figure 5.7). For higher animals, the diverse personalities and circumstances of individuals lead to experimentations which, when successful, can be imitated by others. For this, however a gradient of some measure of 'success' must be defined in the 'mind' of each individual concerned, and here selection will act upon diverse systems of value, leading to cultural evolution. Once again, if conformity is too strong, then the creativity of the system will decline.

Such a mechanism represents a much faster mode of evolution than that which required the physical elimination of the 'unfit'. But in this new, more rapid evolutionary mechanism the discovery of better strategies and the concealment or diffusion of this information become the key elements and evolution moves to a new focus. Given the complex complementarities (divisions of labour, family roles, complex loyalties) and competitivities of the human situation, as well as the existence of processes with long time-scales, we see that a very important element of evolution concerns what individuals decide to consider as being 'advantageous'. In a complex social system, any single 'cultural consensus' as to what goals are, if strictly adhered to, would greatly reduce the diversity of the system and make it more fragile and less capable of adaptation. Clearly, the corollary in human systems of the 'genetic diversity' underlying biological evolution is the existence of many different views and values. This will lead to diverse behaviours and explorations. Information creation and channelling will be key factors in obtaining the right compromise between a rigid 'mono-culture' of clear values and duties, and the chaos of totally disparate individuals with no consensus at all, unable to act together.

The concepts of innovation and the diffusion of technical change are profoundly rooted in these basic evolutionary issues, and in the next section we shall briefly discuss some practical applications of these ideas, in order to point the way that these new paths can be explored.

Generic studies

Science is about finding generic statements and widely applicable principles which can be used to understand particular systems, and this should be distinguished from simply making descriptive models in case studies. The models described below are based on mechanisms and processes which underlie appearances. They discuss global behaviour which results from microscopic processes, and recognize the 'cognitive' dimension that must be taken into account when considering human behaviour.

The first example which we shall briefly describe concerns the development of mathematical models of fisheries. This may seem to be a subject rather far removed from that of 'hi-tech' and 'Silicon Valley', but we shall see that it is an example which makes the basic issues and problems very clear. It is an 'archetypal' complex system, with many aspects: the physical behaviour of the ocean or coastal waters; the complexity of the marine ecosystem with its many levels and species in constant evolution; the behaviour (and technology) of fishermen deciding what and where to fish; the needs and directives of the processing industry which buys much of what is landed; the need for employment both in the fishing and processing industries; the demand from both local and foreign consumers and the competition with other foodstuffs in the international and domestic marketplace.

In several recent papers[16], [17] these applications have been described, Here we shall just briefly outline some of the main features.

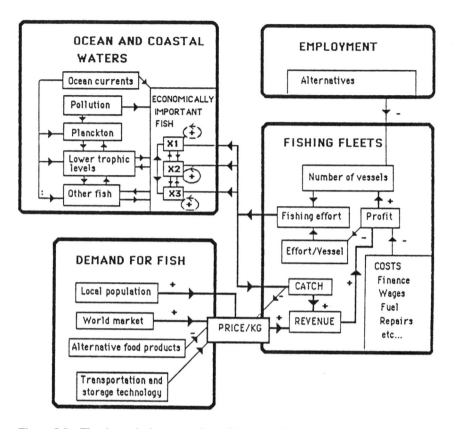

Figure 5.8 The dynamical system of our fishing model

The first and simplest consists of a dynamic model of a fishery corresponding to the scheme shown in Figure 5.8. Contrary to the customary management models, we have included the complexity of the fisherman's behaviour over time, and that of the market. Also, our model is dynamic and is based on the effects of mechanisms of growth and decline in fish populations, fishing fleets, fish prices and fish markets, whereas the models which are used at present assume that these are in equilibrium.

The first important result concerns the qualitative nature of the behaviour observed. If we run our 'mechanical model' of Figure 5.8 purely deterministically from some initial condition, it will tend to a steady equilibrium state. It may take some thirty years to get there, but there is an equilibrium. Previous management strategies are based on the relation between this equilibrium state and the fishing effort applied by the fleets. However, if we insert the reality of environmental fluctuations, which affect the yearly production of young fish, then the result is dramatic. The system amplifies these short-term, random events into large, long-term (seventeen years) cycles of 'boom' and 'bust'. This, in fact, agrees with

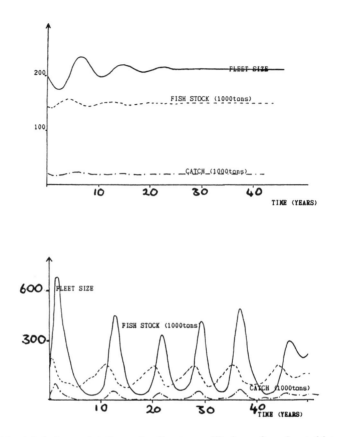

Figure 5.9 (a) A deterministic run leading to equilibrium after about thirty years; (b) the effects of yearly fluctuations is to introduce 'boom' and 'bust' cycles with a period of roughly seventeen years

reality for the Canadian fisheries which were the subject of our model. This bears out the points made by Figure 5.9, where an understanding of the qualitative state of the system cannot be obtained from the mechanical model. The effects of fluctuations must be considered.

Furthermore, if we add in the effects of microscopic diversity of behaviour on the part of fishermen, and the economic success that accrues to those with faster responses, and better technology, we see that in fact we can understand the long-term evolution of most fisheries, as they move from the stable exploitation of a large stock to the unstable, over-exploitation of a much reduced one (Figure 5.10).

Also, our model shows that there can exist two possible regimes of functioning of the fishery. The first is the relatively normal one of 'boom' and 'bust' cycles referred to above. The second occurs at some time during a system 'crash'. If the elasticity of demand is sufficiently low, the price of

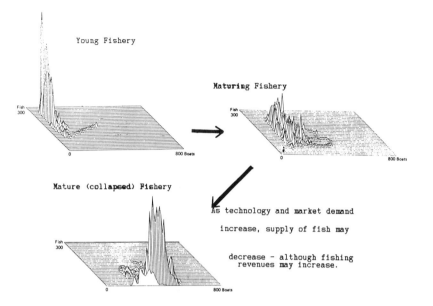

Figure 5.10   The long-term evolution of our model fishery shows how an initially under-exploited stock (a) becomes progressively less stable, until at some point, for large demand and greater fishing effort, it ceases to be a source of food

the rare fish caught rises dramatically, permitting fishermen to earn a living from the tiny stock. This means that they continue their efforts, and the stock remains small and prices high. The fish have become a 'luxury' product and the industry may well survive, but as a source of food the resources has largely disappeared. All of these results give a far greater understanding of the effects of different policies, and also of the different regimes possible (Figure 5.11).

In another, more detailed fishing model, however, we generate the spatial behaviour of the fishing fleets and the fish stocks and show how extraordinarily complex behaviour emerges. This model focuses on fishermen's behaviour, including the manner in which they make decisions about where, and what, to fish.

Our model has two sets of equations, one for the fish in each spatial zone, and the other for the boats. We shall focus briefly here on the latter. Interested readers should consult the original publications for more details. This set of equations describes how the numbers of boats of a given fleet, situated at a point, changes over time due to two terms: an economic 'selection', where revenue must exceed costs; and a term governing the movement of the boats to zones of high expected profit.

Now, for us, the important point is that these 'expected returns' can only be formulated in the light of information about the catches that are being made in the different zones. Therefore it requires both the presence of

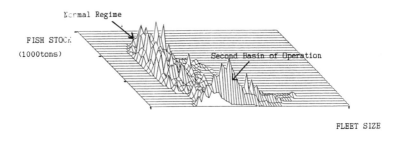

Figure 5.11   Two possible regimes of operation of a fishery. In one we have 'normal' cycles of 'bust' and 'boom', based on fish stock variability, and in the other the fish are a rare luxury of very high unit value

boats making catches in that zone, and the flow of information between those boats, and the boat that is considering where to fish. This gives rise to a positive feedback mechanism which will shape the spatial pattern of fishing effort. This pattern over time will in fact be 'explained' not according to an 'optimal' rationality, but instead according to history, accident and communication.

However, apart from this fairly obvious 'rational' term, there is the dependence of attractivity, and decision, on the personality and beliefs of the skippers. How carefully do they weigh the evidence? We can identify two extremes. At one limit, we have 'Stochasts'. They pay absolutely no attention to economic rationality and simply diffuse at random. At the other extreme, we have 'Cartesians'. These weigh absolutely precisely the information available, and move with probability 1 to the point with the greatest attractivity, even if this is only marginally better than elsewhere.

Obviously, fishermen fall somewhere between these two extremes, but nevertheless, the idea of 'stochasts' and 'cartesians' seems to capture a basic truth about people. In the Canadian fleets, as elsewhere, we find 'risk-takers', who make the discoveries of new fish aggregates, and the others, who are content to rely on the information generated by risk-takers.

What our model allows us to do is to explore the evolution of such a system, and we find that a population of 'cartesians' alone survives poorly on a small part of the system's potential, never exploring beyond this. However, although 'stochasts' can beat 'cartesians', they remain too dispersed to exploit their discoveries efficiently. A most efficient strategy for the fishing fleets as a whole is to have 'cartesians' who 'spy' on 'stochasts'.

We can show that providing, say, 1/10 of the information about catch gets through to them, they succeed in creaming off the good fishing areas discovered by the 'stochasts', and in making a good living. Of course, all kinds of complexities such as spying, lying, communicating in code, code-breaking, alliances, etc., can emerge, and this has been reported on else-where,[18] but these results are of fundamental importance in our discussion of evolution, and of economic innovation and enterprise.

The key point about these models is that they attempt to consider the globality of the processes taking place in a given region, and also the 'cognitive' aspects of the decision-making behaviour. They are really examples of a 'Regional Science', where the ecosystem and the economic, social and cultural realities and values are brought together in a unified framework. A similar initiative with a different emphasis underlies our work in developing evolutionary models of 'urban' systems.

In this work dynamic spatial models describing urban and regional evolution of socio-economic structure have been developed.[19–20] Vastly different spatial scales were modelled, from that of a city like Brussels,[21] to that of the entire continental United States,[22] and simple versions of these models have also been applied to some French cities.[23]

The models consist of sets of interacting equations, each of which represents the change occurring at a particular point in the different activities and populations located there.

Running the model over a long period generates the evolution of each employment sector and population in each spatial zone. In doing this it also generates the changing flows of commuters, raw materials, intermediate components, finished products, and services between the different sectors of the economy and different places. This evolution can then be compared with the actually observed, and the parameters which characterize the different activities adjusted until they produce an evolution which agrees with reality.

In each aggregate category—manufacturing, services, etc.—there will in fact be parts which are growing and others declining. Evolution results not from the 'average' behaviour shown in the input–output table, but from the relative growth and decline of small sub-sectors which make up the real 'microscopic' diversity of the system. The important point, then, is to identify the parts (sub-sectors, particular zones) which are growing, and to specify more accurately their particular 'input–output' matrices. In this way, we can focus on the 'growth system' in the economy, and facilitate the processes of technical change and innovation.

We can also examine the extent to which evolutionary processes are captured by a model such as ours. There are four basic kinds of evolution which can influence an urban or regional system: (a) the spatial diffusion of population and activities according to perceived opportunities; (b) changes resulting from technological progress, changing input and output requirements and costs; (c) entirely new activities resulting from some technological breakthrough; (d) changes in people's expectations and desired lifestyle.

Now, our model can in fact deal quite well with the first two of these. The system evolves through the perception of opportunities by the different actors. These may be due to earlier changes, to technological advance, demography, or to changing terms of trade. Our model makes the input–output table dynamic, but underlines the fact that what really matters for evolution is what is happening at the 'leading edge' of all this. It is in the growth of some sub-sectors, and the inductive loops of these that the future lies. The model therefore serves as a framework within which to identify and study these important, diffusing disequilibria.

The third and fourth types of evolution are not really in this model and it is difficult to see how they could be included in any precise way. Entirely new products cannot be anticipated easily, or they would not be new. Neither is it easy to say when and in what way people may modify their values and adopt new goals. What could be done, however, would be to explore the consequence of some possible change. If this were done, some estimate could be made of the 'advantages' for individuals making such a 'move', and from that it would be possible perhaps to estimate whether such a change was really very likely or not.

Conclusions

The fundamental point raised in this chapter is that discovery and innovation can only be achieved by going 'beyond' the present system. We require 'stochasts' who, for whatever reason, do not respond simply to the information which exists about the present returns on effort. The 'cartesians', on the other hand, are the backbone of the system. They represent 'normality', and also will be the ones who push any particular activity to its ultimate in excellence. The success of the overall system will be determined by the balanced existence of the two types, and the manner in which new information is channelled into the system. While the adaptive capacity of a system lies in its 'stochasts', the stability, and efficient performance resides with the 'cartesians'. A harmonious system must alllow 'discoveries' to recuperate their search costs, or risk losing them, and this will depend critically on the time of 'monopoly' allowed to them.

A period of expansion will follow a discovery, as the spread of information leads to increased demand, economies of scale and 'learning by doing'. However, after some time either the market begins to saturate, or the resource required starts to become rare. Either way, competition intensifies, and a period of 'rationalization' follows when investment is directed to making production more efficient, usually decreasing employment in the sector. Competition increases, and only the discovery of new activities and products, made perhaps by the displaced 'stochasts', can save the situation.

Usually, 'cartesians' will not listen to news of discoveries while things in the established areas are not in crisis. Hence, venture capital may well be lacking during a period of prosperity. When a crisis approaches, however, the first reaction is for 'cartesians' to try to do what they already do, better! The more they do this, the greater the crisis will be when it comes. When catastrophe finally does occur, then information concerning discoveries will be acted upon, by all those still in a position to act. New structure will emerge, new job definitions and new specialities will come into being, and start to fossilize, as they 'hill climb' up to apparently greater rationality and efficiency. And so our model suggests the existence of a 'long wave' or Kondratiev cycle, and offers a real possibility of its analysis.

This underlines the aim of this approach. It is not to predict the future. Instead, it is to offer an integrating framework into which existing knowledge can be put. With this, the future can be explored and better imagined. However, the real world is really much richer than any model, and therefore will always manage to evolve in ways that have not been included in the model. This is not a reason to abandon modelling, but rather the opposite! Without the model, we would not be able to 'order' the system to an extent sufficient to realize that something 'inexplicable' was occurring. With it, we can be aware of the emergence of some new mechanism or factor, and we can then search for the best manner in which to include it. That is to say that the model we have of a particular situation will probably always require modification because the real world is itself evolving.

The real message of the new concepts in science are that change and disequilibria are probably more 'natural' than equilibrium and stasis. Those who can adapt and learn will survive. And this will depend on their 'creativity'. For example, when we suppose that change is a response to perceived opportunities, then it is saying that the potential for growth and diversity of any region or city depends to an extent on the imagination of the people who live there. What openings for what activities do they perceive? This will depend on the finer details of their history, culture and social interactions. Generally speaking, microscopic diversity resulting from the mixing of cultures, conflicting doctrines and individual freedom will be an important ingredient in this response. In other words, technical change and economic evolution are related to factors such as originality, risk-taking and creativity in a population.

In human systems, the 'pay-off' of any particular behaviour will depend on what other individuals do. For example, an 'intelligent' move may only be deemed to be so if others keep behaving 'unintelligently'. And it may well be true that the real 'intelligence' of the system is precisely in having several different behaviours present. Once again, what we have stressed above is that evolution will select for variability, and this may well be interpreted by an observer (particularly a Newtonian) as corresponding necessarily to individuals with different systems of values, or degrees of intelligence! In reality, though, there may be an evolutionary explanation of the spectrum of behaviour, but not of each specific spectral line.

Furthermore, if we consider the whole system, with its many levels of interacting populations and interdependent mechanisms, then the progress made in one sector will set the standard for others, and once again the evolution of a population and its artefacts cannot be considered in isolation. Each living cell is part of an organism and cannot be understood alone. Similarly, each individual and artefact is part of a culture, and its behaviour can only be viewed correctly within the larger unit. Ultimately, each population is part of the ecosystem, and evolution acts on the global entity. Traditionally, science has accepted as 'explanation' of behaviour a description of the internal functioning of an object considered in isolation. Here, however, we see innovation and change as part of an evolving whole, and the explanation of history reflects the inherent unity of the living world.

Hopefully, the ideas discussed here can help to lay the foundations of a new synthesis in the human sciences. Creativity and change find a place together with structure and function in this new scientific paradigm. Although the reassuring feeling lent by 'determinism' has had to be sacrificed, in return we now have a unified view of the world which bridges the gap between the physical and the human sciences. And it is not true that this represents a final 'reduction' of human and social phenomena to the 'mechanical' dictates of physics! Instead, the latter has been 'elevated', and has had to abandon its immature search for absolute certainties. What we now see is a world of multiple facets and reflections, perceived in different ways, evolving through successive states of organization as a result of non-average events and individuals. Instead of being limited to approaching human systems from a descriptive or ideological standpoint, science now offers us a mathematical basis on which to understand how such complex systems came into being, and how they may evolve in the future. The next decade will see a rapid growth in research aimed at exploring this new and exciting path.

References

1. Nelson, R. and Winter, S. (1982), *An Evolutionary Theory of Economic Change*, Cambridge, Mass., Belknap Press of Harvard University.
2. Boulding, K.E. (1981), *Evolutionary Economics*, Beverly Hills, Cali., Sage Publications.
3. Silverberg, G. 'Modelling economic dynamics', this volume, Chapter 24.
4. Clark, N. and Juma, C. 'Evolutionary theories in economic thought: a systems approach', this volume, Chapter 9.
5. Rosen, R. (1985), 'Information and Complexity, in Ulanowicz and Platt, (eds), 'Ecosystem Theory for Biological Oceanography', *Canadian Bulletin of Fisheries and Aquatic Sciences*, vol. 213, Fisheries and Oceans, Ottawa, Canada.
6. Darwin, C. (1859), *The Origin of Species*, London, John Murray.
7. Bell, D. and Kristol, I. (1981), *The Crisis in Economic Theory*, New York, Basic Books.

8. Schumpeter, J. (1934) *The Theory of Economic Development*, Cambridge, Mass., Harvard University Press.
9. Simon, H. (1969), 'The architecture of complexity', in *Sciences of the Artificial*, Cambridge, MIT Press.
10. Dawkins, R. (1986), *The Blind Watchmaker*, Harlow, Longman.
11. Nicolis, G. and Prigogine I. (1977), *Self-Organization in Non-Equilibrium Systems*, New York, Wiley Interscience.
12. Prigogine I. and Stengers, I. (1985), *Order out of Chaos*, New York, Bantam Books.
13. Haken, H. (1977), *Synergetics: An Introduction*, Synergetics Series, vol. 1, Berlin, Springer Verlag.
14. Allen, P.M. (1986), 'Towards a new science of complex systems', in *The Praxis and Management of Compexity*, Tokyo, United Nations University Press.
15. Allen, P.M. and McGlade, J. (1987), 'Evolutionary drive: the effects of microscopic diversity, error-making and noise', in *Foundations of Physics*, vol. 17, no. 7, July pp. 723–38.
16. McGlade, J. and Allen, P.M. (1985), 'The fishery industry as a complex system,' in R.Mohn, (ed.) *Towards the Inclusion of Fishery Interactions in Management Advice*, *Canadian Technical Reports in Fisheries and Aquatic Sciences*, no. 1347.
17. —— (1986), 'Dynamics of discovery and exploitation: the case of the Scotian Shelf Fisheries', *Canadian Journal of Fisheries and Aquatic Sciences*, vol. 43.
18. —— (1987), 'Modelling complex human systems: a fisheries example', *European Journal of Operational Research*, July.
19. Allen, P.M. and Sanglier, M. (1978), 'Dynamic models of urban growth', *Journal of Social and Biological Structures*, no. 1, pp. 265–80; (1981), 'A dynamic model of a central place system II', *Geographical Analysis*, vol. 13, no. 2; 'Dynamic urban models: III—the effects of a trade barrier', *Journal of Social and Biological Structures*, vol. 4, no. 3.
20. —— (1981), 'Evolution, self-organization and decision-making', *Environment and Planning A*, vol. 13.
21. Allen, P.M., Engelen, G. and Sanglier, M. (1984), 'self-organizing dynamic models of human systems', in E.Frehland (ed.), *From Macroscopic to Microscopic Order*, Synergetics Series, vol. 22.,Berlin, Springer Verlag.
22. Allen, P.M. and Engelen, G. (1985), 'Modelling the spatial evolution of population and employment: the case of the USA', in *Lotka–Volterra Approach to Cooperation and Competition in Dynamic Systems*, vol. 23, Berlin, GDR, Akademie–Verlag.
23. Pumain, D., Saint Julien, Th. and Sanders, L. (1987), 'Applications of a dynamic model', *Geographical Analysis*, vol. 19.

Part III How well does established theory work

Preface to Part III

Giovanni Dosi
Faculty of Statistics, University of Rome and SPRU, University of Sussex, Brighton,

The perspective in which the contributions to this book are generally written is, to different degrees, heterodox as compared with the assumptions, the methods and even the style of most contemporary economic analysis, whether theoretical or applied. Surely, this requires some justification. After all, many of the issues discussed in this volume also have a history of analysis within the standard discipline. And several economists would also be prepared to argue that many other topics discussed here, which currently draw scattered or no attention at all, could be handled within the framework which I shall call, 'neo-classical'. Of course, 'heterodoxy' acquires much more significance, and in some circumstances is even epistemologically required, if one is able to show either that it grows out of the preceding scientific achievements, or that some more radical change in theories and methods is needed in order to account for certain classes of phenomena. The contributions to this section, in different ways, do a bit of both. The broad heading they come under is the question whether a 'neo-classical' approach can be applied to the interpretation of economic dynamics and, at the same time, give reasonable explanations of the processes of coordination among economic agents in non-centrally planned economies. There are different ways to attempt an answer to this question.

First, one can check the analytical power of the results which can be derived from a theory. The more 'unlikely' the properties or predictions that are generated, the more 'powerful' the theory. Karl Popper would say that the power of a theory depends on the notional states-of-the-world or interpretative conjectures that it *excludes*, so that, to give an example familiar to the profession, establishing that an equilibrium exists, is unique, stable and 'is this one' is a powerful theoretical result, while saying that any point in the relevant space can be an equilibrium is dangerously bordering on tautology.

A complementary way of assessing a theory is by checking the boundaries of the sets of empirical phenomena to which it can be presumed to apply, exploring the consequences of relaxing the most restrictive assumptions, and investigating the implicit hypotheses that it makes on the nature of the phenomena that it tries to explain. In the first three chapters of this section both routes are pursued, and the general conclusion that can be drawn, in my view, is that indeed there are extremely serious problems in the use of 'neo-classical' tool-boxes and models in the analysis of dynamic economies, or even economies that are not *stricto sensu* dynamic but still sufficiently complex.

For clarity, let me outline what I mean by a 'neo-classical theory'. In my view, the 'core' of the *strongest* version of the theory embodies the following hypotheses:

(i)   the behaviour of the agents can in general be characterized by substantive rationality (literal maximization of something or approximations to it), or, alternatively, market processes are such as to select the 'maximizers', whether they know it or not;

(ii)   the economic system is characterized, in the final instance, by some sort of scarcity;

(iii)   the nature of the states toward which the system converges are generally path-independent and behaviour-independent (so that history does not count very much);

(iv)   non-intentional and counter-intentional outcomes of interactions, and positive feedbacks (such as, for example, increasing returns) are, at the best, weak;

(v)   uncertainty, when it occurs, can be reduced to incomplete information whereby the agents can still behave 'rationally' by generating probabilities with which they make maximizing calculations;

(vi)   extra-economic institutions do not count in shaping economic conducts and performances;

(vii)   markets embody processes which make them converge to some sort of equilibrium;

(viii) technology essentially consists of freely available information (production possibility sets). This implies that

(ix)   the agents are identical (apart from their preferences and endowments).

Of course, only the purest neo-classicist would accept all these assumptions and beliefs as empirical generalizations. Probably the most resilient ones are (i) and (v), or 'rationality'. However, if the theory is robust and sufficiently 'progressive' in its interpretative power, it must also prove that at least some results obtained under the most restrictive circumstances can be 'carried over' to analytical set-ups in which some of the assumptions are relaxed. The arguments of the chapters that follow show that, in fact, this is *not* generally the case.

The Coricelli–Dosi chapter discusses the recent attempts to interpret macroeconomics in terms of equilibrium dynamics of an *implicit* General Equilibrium world. The 'New Classical Economics' has certainly been a brave epistemological gamble to explain macro regularities in the purest neo-classical fashion, without empirical '*ad hocs*', institutions, etc. However, the analytical results do not support the claim: one cannot derive, in general, determinate and 'orderly' properties of dynamic economies even under the most restrictive assumptions about the nature of production activities, using only given (and uniform) technologies, given preferences and also a 'rationality' principle. This is when the multitude of agents is 'compressed' into a single representative agent. Moreover, it can be shown that such a reduction is generally illegitimate if one wants to maintain a microeconomic foundation with many agents, diverse at least in their preferences.

Lippi tackles a similar problem from a different angle and, in his difficult but important chapter, shows that aggregating agents each of which behaves according to very simple and stable rules may indeed produce very complex macro dynamics.

This is a result that applies in general to macro phenomena, and is certainly disruptive for any neo-classical interpretation of macro patterns based on their 'backward projection' onto micro behaviours derived from maximizing decision rules; but it also represents a challenge to the more 'institutionalist' and 'evolutionist' approaches suggested elsewhere in this book. What kind of micro behaviours must (heterogeneous) agents present in order to yield relatively ordered macro regularities? Clearly, especially on the side of production activities, relative 'macro order' must be related to the selection processes discussed in other sections of the volume. However, it must also depend on behaviour-governing rules and institutions. In this respect, Heiner's chapter demonstrates the general plausibility as well as the *superior efficiency* of rule-governed behaviour compared to rigorous attempts to 'maximize' in all those circumstances in which the information-processing capability of the agents is—as is empirically plausible—significantly less than perfect. Remarkably, his proof also applies to those in fact rather simple environments in which 'rational behaviour' in the neo-classical sense is easily representable, equilibria notionally exist, technologies do not change, etc. In this sense, Heiner's chapter is also an important *negative* result about the domain of applicability of standard rationality assumptions and a powerful argument in support of the need for detailed observation-based analysis of behaviour and institutions, such as presented in other parts of the book.

There are, of course, many other domains of analysis on which the positive general conjectures, results and interpretations presented in this volume converge or overlap with the neo-classical approach. Some are mentioned in the chapters that follow and elsewhere in the book. Others have been neglected either for obvious reasons of space or because we considered them to be quite well known.

For example, careful *caveats* on the use of standard General Equilibrium Theory as a positive interpretation of empirical coordination processes have been made by its major contributors, such as Arrow and Hahn, who have also highlighted the theoretical limitations of the adjustment processes needed in such a framework to maintain some sort of economic order.

At least since the early 1970s (cf., for example, Spence) it has been established that even in models consistent with most neo-classical assumptions, initial conditions (and thus, implicitly, history) may count. The importance of history in economic processes has also been emphasized recently by Hahn. This acquires even greater validity if, as often done in the contemporary literature, one allows for various sorts of non-linearities.

Stiglitz (and several others) have intensively explored imperfect information set-ups. Even when agents are represented as maximizers and technology is equated to information, he shows that, in a variety of domains, institutions governing incentive- and information-structures are of paramount importance in determining system performance. A huge literature, based on the theory of industrial organization and game-theoretic analysis, hints implicitly or explicitly at the crucial role of mechanisms of expectation formation, initial conditions, organizational contexts, the nature of the technologies, etc. Moreover, Williamson has explored the implications of information-related and incentive-related market imperfections, producing a quite general theory of economic organization.

The implications that can be drawn from these scattered references, together with those discussed in more detail in this section are, in my view, abundantly sufficient to justify exploring the properties of environments where *none* of the above 'neo-classical propositions' apply—which, incidentally, I believe to be generally the case when the economy is a rather complex and changing structure involving changing technologies. But, if this is so, why hasn't the economic discipline made greater efforts in this direction?

The last chapter of this section by Clark and Juma starts from a similar point of view and asks why economics has not developed as a fully 'evolutionary' discipline. This chapter is an exercise in the history of economic ideas which tries to trace the influence on the economic tradition of some of the major intellectual currents of Western culture. They see these as originating in the natural sciences (Newton and Darwin) and now undergoing a rapid extension in theories of complex systems, disequilibrium dynamics, theoretical biology, etc.

6 Coordination and order in economic change and the interpretative power of economic theory

Fabrizio Coricelli
IRS, Milan, and University of Pennsylvania, Philadelphia

Giovanni Dosi
Faculty of Statistics, University of Rome, Rome and SPRU, University of Sussex, Brighton

'I . . . side with Heraclitus in arguing that you could not step twice into the same river, for new waters are ever flowing on to you'. It is the appearance of stability that is illusory; just look a little closer and wait a little longer. We Herclitus types find it difficult to understand what the Ecclesiastes types—who think that 'there is no new thing under the sun'—are talking about, what with the universe expanding, the continents drifting, the arms race racing and the kids growing up. The observed predictive performance of economic models also seems to us to be considerably more consonant with the Heraclitus view than with the alternative [Winter, 1986 p. 428]

Introduction

This chapter discusses the ability of economic theory to interpret dynamic economies, and in particular those undergoing technical change.

In chapter 2 as well as in the contributions to Part V of this book, arguments are presented for an evolutionary approach to economic analysis in which the process of coordination among agents is intertwined with the processes generating change of various sorts. Here we shall address the question of whether such an analysis of dynamic economies can also be undertaken by separating—on theoretical grounds—the *coordination problem* of an economy, typically represented as a stationary system, on the one hand, from the interpretation of *dynamic factors* on the other. That is, can we analyse the problems of static allocation on the safe assumption that they are dynamics-independent? Can we reduce problems of change to exogenously determined changes in the parameters of the general equilibrium model?

A good part of the economic discipline, especially in the post-war period, has essentially explored three theoretical perspectives. First, the General Equilibrium tradition focused upon the *theoretical possibility* of coordination between agents who are uniform in terms of decision procedures (maximization, etc.), but diverse with respect to initial endowments and tastes. The exploration of the existence, determinacy and stability of equilibria under more or less restrictive assumptions (e.g. completeness of contingency markets and information, convexity of production possibility sets, etc.) has been in many respects a fascinating attempt to assess the power of the 'Invisible Hand' in a highly stylized, stationary and perfectly competitive environment defined in terms of some 'fundamentals' of the economy (given technology, given individual preferences and a universal maximizing decision procedure for individual agents).[1]

The other two major analytical perspectives are more directly macroeconomic-based. One of these approaches—recently rather out of fashion—focuses upon 'stylized' aggregate regularities (e.g. the patterns of investment, consumption, etc.) and 'explains' them on the grounds of both the 'fundamentals' of the economy and *ad hoc* (in principle, empirically derived) assumptions about context-specific behaviour, adjustment lags, etc. So-called 'neo-Keynesians' basically share this methodology.

Finally, some current macroeconomic analysis (of which possibly the most fashionable is the so-called 'new classical macroeconomics') attempts to 'carry over' to macroeconomics an *implicit* Walrasian equilibrium microfoundation and somehow 'explain' macro variables solely on the basis of a maximizing principle of behaviour and the fundamentals of the economy.

The principle of rationality and the role of the market as coordination mechanism have been extended to the study of dynamic economies. This programme has mainly constructed models of equilibrium dynamics, i.e. models in which equilibrium holds at each point in time, while their (supposedly General Equilibrium) microfoundations are, so to speak, squeezed into single ('representative') agent formalizations.

Of course, theories do, and *must*, abstract and simplify. Indeed, one of the criteria on which the analytical power of various theories can be assessed is the simplicity and degree of generality of their abstractions. However, one must always ask questions such as: how robust are these abstractions? What are the domains of interpretative applicability of the models? For our purposes, the assessment of the analytical results and perspectives of the neo-classical research programme in relation to the understanding of coordination and change in market economies involves two major questions, namely (a) can a model based only on the 'fundamentals' (given technologies and tastes) and on a rationality principle for individual choice reveal to us some fundamental properties of economic processes which hold irrespective of the (history-bound) specification of, for example, particular behavioural rules, institutions, adjustment processes, etc.?; (b) can one incrementally build upon the basic static model and apply it to the analysis of environments characterized by technical change and, more generally, non-stationarity? For an affirmative answer to these questions and in particular to the latter, one should require that, at least under the highly simplified conditions generally assumed by these models, the theory should be able to (i) generate and explain 'order' at the macro level; (ii) handle micro diversity (otherwise one of the major distinctions between micro and macro would disappear); (iii) define an adjustment process leading to the equilibria studied by the models.

We shall argue that, in fact, the project of building dynamic models with economic content and descriptive power by relying solely on the basic principles of rationality and perfect competition through the market process has generally failed. In order to give economic content to equilibrium 'macro' models, we shall argue, one has to sacrifice, in fact, the decentralization of the decision-making processes of economic actors, which is obviously a fundamental premise of the theory.

Conversely, if one sticks to a 'decentralized' representation of diverse actors, it seems hardly possible to retain any robust analytical result on economic coordination whenever one introduces any sort of dynamics, or even relaxes the most demanding assumptions about the perfection of the markets and information sets (needless to say, any innovative environment is *necessarily* characterized by, for example, asymmetric information, non-perfectly competitive markets, etc.). Thus one goes back to a somewhat Schumpeterian dilemma, namely, can one find a sort of division of labour between General Equilibrium theory—meant to explain static allocative processes—and evolutionary theory—meant to deal with dynamic processes? Such a complementarity is implicit in the 'Classical Defence' of equilibrium models and of 'as if' assumptions on literally maximizing agents (see Friedman, 1953, and, for a critical discussion, Winter, 1986). This conjecture has been recently revived by Lucas (1986). According to this view the realm of economic theory (identified with General Equilibrium analysis) is that of steady states or, in any case, regular repetitive environments; adaptive processes, describing dynamic situations, are instead complex, irregular, disturbed by a vast number of factors specific to individual actors, industries, countries. Economic theory—it is claimed—cannot be concerned with these 'noisy' problems. It remains crucial, however, to show that from such a noise the regular stationary equilibria reflecting the rationality of behaviour and expectations of economic actors are selected.

However, we will show, first, that *general equilibrium models with stationary preferences and technologies and with rational expectations do not in general yield simple and regular outcomes. Second, we will show that in general, rational expectations equilibria are not the stationary state of dynamic processes arising from adaptive rules.*

In the sections that follow we shall discuss the attempt to 'explain' the levels and changes of macro variables on the basis of a direct transposition of micro behaviours (maximization) and the fundamentals of the economy We shall then explore the coordination power of the markets (or lack of it) implicit in neo-classical macro models, and the impossibility of deriving, in general, robust results on macro-order simply on the grounds of the rationality principle, endowments and given tastes. On the contrary, complex dynamics and unpredictability of equilibria may well emerge even in simple competitive models. Can neo-classical macro models (of the rational expectation kind) be considered the results of adaptive processes? The section 'Rational expectations equilibria and adaptive processes' will discuss why this is not generally the case. Thus one must investigate the characteristics of individual behaviours and of economic environments which account for a relative order in *both coordination and change*. We shall suggest that some of these characteristics can be found precisely amongst those factors underlying the main difficulties of neo-classical theory in dealing with economic dynamics. Indeed, several features that are sources of theoretical problems for the neo-classical view are instead the main ingredients of a positive theory: diversity, heterogeneity of agents, non-linearities, continuous change, and hence non-stationarities, the role of learning, beliefs, the importance of 'history' and of 'contexts' and, situation-specific behaviours, are all fundamental features of the evolutionary, self-organization approach to economic dynamics.

Aggregation, 'representative agents' and competitive mechanisms

According to a taxonomy proposed by Malinvaud (1981), any attempt to place macroeconomic analysis on a solid microeconomic footing should go through the following three phases: (i) the microeconomic study of agents' decisions and, in addition, the interaction among agents and thus the constraint on individual behaviour of other agents; (ii) the aggregation of behaviours, i.e. the study of the macroeconomic implications of micro-behaviours and the deduction from the micro choices of the laws of macro-economic behaviour; (iii) the comparison of the findings of the theory with empirical data.

It seems to us that the current fashion in macroeconomic theory relies upon the mere direct transposition to the macroeconomic level of the results obtained in the microeconomic analysis of the behaviour of a single agent ('the representative agent'). The phase of 'aggregation' is completely neglected and the study of micro interactions is carried out in a very peculiar way: in fact, as we shall see, very little is left of 'inter-actions'. This approach implies, in terms of empirical testing, that the observation of empirical macro data is assumed to be directly consistent with microbehaviours; in econometric language, macroparameters are taken to be nothing but the reproduction on a larger scale of micro-parameters.[2]

Of course, it is generally acknowledged that the mere knowledge of individual characteristics is of little help in predicting the outcome at the level of the whole system. The interaction among agents introduces a qualitative difference between micro and macro behaviours. In that version of neo-classical macroeconomics which calls itself 'new classical macroeconomics', the solution to this problem has to be found in model-ling this interaction in terms of competitive equilibria. According to Lucas, it is the hypothesis of competitive equilibrium which permits group behaviour to be predicted from knowledge of individual preferences and technology without the addition of any free parameters . . . It is possible, we know, to mimic aggregate outcome of this interaction fairly well in a competitive equilibrium way, in which wages and manhours [Lucas is indeed referring to a competitive equilibrium theory of employment] are generated by the interaction of 'representative' households and firms. [Lucas, 1981, pp. 289–90]

Through a competitive equilibrium model, it is argued, the micro–macro link will be transparent, the aggregate outcome being predicted with precision from the knowledge of individual preferences and technology. As a consequence, there is no need to add any *free parameters* (the famous 'ad hockeries') to the structure of the model based on optimizing behaviour of fully rational agents. This type of model is claimed to be capable of pinning down macroeconomic equilibria which are consistent with both empirical observations and results of Walrasian general equilibrium theory—in particular with welfare theorems.[3]

The central message of such a research programme is that under *laissez faire* a competitive economy, not disturbed by destabilizing policies and/or exogenous shocks, will settle on stationary macro equilibria, resembling static Walrasian equilibria. In this way, not only the normative implications of general equilibrium models would carry over to macroeconomic theory, but the Walrasian approach would acquire an extraordinary descriptive power. What is the theoretical validity of this claim?

First, let us consider the theoretical implications of developing macroeconomic models—as is currently done—on the basis of optimizing behaviours of representative agents. Most of the recent developments in macroeconomics rely upon the simple assumption that economic actors are identical. This assumption is also accompanied by the identification of a macro model with a system with only one good. For an approach which claims to have put macroeconomics on steady microeconomic foundations, these are certainly heroic assumptions. By reducing the set of individuals to a 'representative agent' it is implied that aggregate behaviours are just a transposition of micro behaviours: qualitatively they do not differ. In this way the problem of aggregation of individual behaviours is hidden under the rug. It is a sort of paradox that a 'microfounded' approach to microeconomics, instead of shedding light on the complex nature of the link between individual behaviours and aggregate outcomes, has created so-called macro models as oversimplifications of the general equilibrium system (in fact, a general equilibrium model with only one agent and one good!). Moreover the assumption of 'representative agents' appears to lead to theoretical problems[4].

The difficulties arising in the aggregation of individual behaviours have been recognized in the economic literature since the last century, in the partial equilibrium approach to both the theory of consumption and the theory of production.[5]

In a general equilibrium setting the work initiated by Sonnenschein and developed by Debreu and others points out the important result that

strong restrictions are needed in order to justify the hypothesis that a market demand function has the characteristics of a single-consumer demand function. Only in special cases can an economy be expected to act as an 'idealized consumer'. The utility tells us nothing about market demand unless it is augmented by additional requirements. [Shafer and Sonnenschein, 1982, p. 672][6]

As a consequence we cannot expect aggregate relations, which we have called macro relations (i.e. relations between aggregate variables), to reproduce on a larger scale micro relations. The link between micro and macro behaviour does not entail a simple enlargement of scale but a qualitative change of perspective. In the general competitive equilibrium framework the descriptive and predictive power of the results on individual behaviour for the aggregate outcome is extremely vague. In the textbook by Varian (1984), the Sonnenschein–Debreu theorem is interpreted as an indication that since the utility maximization hypothesis places no restrictions on aggregate demand behaviour and hence any continuous function satisfying Walras's law can be an excess demand function for some economy, practically *any* dynamical system on the price sphere can arise from a Walrasian general equilibrium model of economic behaviour.[7]

The analysis can be pushed further, and it can be shown that in general the price dynamics involved in the tatonnement story can give rise to a whole family of extremely complex and erratic dynamics (Saari, 1983). Even leaving aside the question of dynamics out of equilibria, it can be easily shown that asymmetries among individuals modify the dynamical representation of equilibria over time.[8]

Let us summarize the implications of the discussion so far. In many respects, the General Equilibrium tradition has undertaken the fascinating task of exploring the interdependencies of a decentralized economy through the axiomatization of 'selfish' individual motives and an extremely parsimonious use of ancillary hypotheses (on adjustment processes, institutions, etc.). Under the assumptions of the theory (which, one must admit, are quite restrictive, on information, competition, etc.), one has demonstrated the *possibility* (i.e. the logical consistency) *of coordination* via the 'Invisible Hand' of the market. This is, in the last resort, the meaning of the existence theorems. However, without further (and somewhat *ad hoc* or observation-based) restrictions, the results are not determinate enough to be, so to speak, 'carried over' to a synthetic macro representation which would hold irrespectively of any specific representation of the underlying characteristics of actual agents (in terms of tastes, distribution of endowments, etc.). These properties, together with the quite heavy restrictions that must be introduced in order to obtain stability and determinacy (local uniqueness) of equilibria in an explicit general equilibrium model highlight, in our view, the boundaries of the set of empirical economic phenomena which the neo-classical research programme, at least in its present form, can interpret. Certainly, the set does not include non-stationary environments, but neither does it include relatively orderly sequences of macro states. At the very least, the latter cannot be explained via a 'reduced form' neo-classical macro model without losing the 'inter-dependencies' of the market, the autonomy of the agents (in terms of beliefs and expectations) and/or the 'parsimoniousness' in auxiliary assumptions (and thus the generality of the models). We shall now discuss these latter issues.

Decentralization and the coordination power of the market mechanism

It may be enlightening to see how the assumption of homogeneity among individuals which underlies the concept of 'representative agents', extends to the characterization of the uniformity of expectations and beliefs.

We shall consider here 'rational expectations' models. In fact, if expectations are non-rational, aggregation problems become even more serious (e.g. for the purposes of a synthetic representative-agent stylization of macro phenomena, identical agents with different rules of expectation formation are different agents: aggregation necessarily involves situation-specific knowledge of the rules, their distribution among agents, etc.). Even in the 'rational' case, as Frydman and Phelps (1983) put it, 'an instantaneous transition to the new rational expectations equilibrium requires a perceived and actual unanimity of beliefs. Such consensus of perceptions cannot generally be achieved by individual agents acting alone in decentralized markets'. To circumvent the problem of forming expectations of other agents' expectations, the Rational Expectations school assumes that every agent forms his expectations on the basis of the equilibrium model and everyone expects that the other agents form their expectations in the same way. This apparently innocuous assumption is in fact very 'totalitarian' and also in marked contrast with the leitmotiv of the neo-classical theory of individual behaviour, whereby 'individual behaviour is not based on the collective consistency of plans, but on the assumption of individual rationality' (Frydman and Phelps, 1983). Assuming an *ex ante* consistency of plans either contradicts the fundamental task of neo-classical microeconomics aimed at demonstrating how market processes, *ex post*, make consistent the independent plans of agents based only on selfish considerations, or makes the theory plainly tautological in the sense that, in order to demonstrate the existence of coordination amongst agents, it assumes it *ex hypothesi*.

It is not far from the truth to say that the current neo-classical approach to the microfoundation of macroeconomics is based on a representation of the economy as a *centralized* system. The assumption of a 'representative agent' together with the rational expectations hypothesis (with homogeneity of expectations) is tantamount to an *ex ante* collective consistency of behaviours in which the market plays no role. In fact, most of the results of the 'new macroeconomics' pointing to the power of *laissez faire* in achieving desirable macroeconomic equilibria derive from an *a priori* exclusion of the analysis of the relationship—and potential conflict—between individual behaviour and aggregate outcomes in a decentralized economy.

Indeterminacy of equilibria: beliefs and behaviour-dependent equilibria

In order to have any 'positive' meaning, that is, in order to have some interpretative power, equilibria have to be at least *locally* unique. If an equilibrium is not locally unique it follows that there are several equilibria arbitrarily close to it. If this is the case it is impossible to carry out any exercise in comparative statics, and thus the dynamic analysis becomes meaningless (loosely speaking, one has a macro model that simply says that 'anything can happen'). For these reasons, a situation characterized by the absence of local uniqueness is usually defined as indeterminacy of equilibria.

The dynamic extensions of equilibrium models to macroeconomic analysis generally suffer from this indeterminacy.[9] As a consequence, preferences, endowments and technology alone may not suffice to determine the allocation of resources in a dynamic economy, even when perfectly competitive markets exist for all goods. In this context the possibility arises of a critical role for the *beliefs* of the agents as well as for an active government policy. Phenomena such as 'sunspot' equilibria or bubbles may be interpreted as a way of selecting particular equilibria from among the large number of competitive equilibria.[10] These equilibria are characterized by the fact that the allocation of resources depends on beliefs, i.e. on factors which are unrelated to the fundamentals of the economy, and that these beliefs will be confirmed by the equilibrium of the system; in other words, expectations of the agents are self-fulfilling. Note that this result is consistent with the assumption of 'rational expectations' and, unlike 'bubbles', it is also compatible with stability of the equilibria. The implication is that beliefs of agents not only are relevant in determining the equilibrium allocations, but also that—when they are stationary—there are no forces causing the system to move necessarily to equilibria reflecting only the fundamentals (as it is the case for 'bubbles' which, by their nature, will eventually explode). It should also be noted that the multiplicity of equilibria in the above sense in a decentralized economy implies the need for every single agent to form expectations not only about the realizations of economic variables, but also about the expectations of other agents. A decentralized economy is therefore caught in the vicious circle of an 'infinite regress' of forecasts about how others forecast the forecast of their forecast, etc., reminding us of the famous 'beauty contest' discussed by Keynes. Consequently, the power of the competitive economy to coordinate agents' behaviour, as described by these neo-classical macro models, in the absence of external intervention, appears to be very weak.

Beliefs matter in determining aggregate outcomes. Moreover, individual forecasting mistakes—or deviations from optimal 'rational' behaviour—matter, regardless of how small they are. Akerlof and Yellen (1985) show that individual behaviours which are only marginally non-maximizing induce a significant effect on macroeconomic outcomes. Small departures from perfectly 'rational' maximizing behaviour which result in only second-order losses to the individual, will nevertheless have first-order effects on real variables.

Complex dynamics and unpredictability in simple competitive models

Of course, the belief-dependency and behaviour-dependency of equilibria challenge the extreme (or 'pure') neo-classical research programme to provide an account of macroeconomic order without invoking empirically based assumptions about behaviour. They do not challenge, *per se*, the theoretical conjecture that neo-classical macroequilibria (no matter how belief-ridden) can provide a justification for the 'Invisible Hand' which pulls together and provides coherence to a dynamic economy. However, the idea that under *laissez faire* a competitive economy, unaffected by exogenous shocks and destabilizing policies, will settle on stationary equilibria resembling the Walrasian equilibrium, is radically challenged by a growing body of literature.[11] Simple economies—simple in that utility and production functions are 'regular'[12] and the economy is populated by 'representative agents'—in which the environment (technology, preferences, endowments) is *stationary* and *deterministic* show in many, far from special, circumstances an extremely complex dynamic behaviour.[13] The complexity of the dynamics is solely the result of the workings of the competitive mechanism, and is not due to friction and disturbances. It has been shown that the motion of the system may present forms of highly irregular dynamic behaviour which is called deterministic *chaos*.[14]

There are several definitions and properties of chaos which cannot be discussed here. One aspect is, however, of greatest interest to us, namely the fact that chaotic systems are extremely sensitive to initial conditions.[15] As a consequence, the behaviour of the model in the future cannot be predicted from a knowledge of its 'fundamentals', nor can it be predicted from a knowledge of its history. The system is thus characterized by a serious problem of unpredictability.[16] Of course, the result is devastating for the assumption of rational expectations, since it implies that the predictive possibilities of agents are necessarily extremely weak and imperfect even if the environment itself is deterministic. Moreover, the fact that in deterministic and very simple models, with stationary preferences and technologies, the 'rational' (perfectly optimizing) behaviour of agents who also have the gift of perfect foresight leads to such complex and erratic dynamics of the economy is a strikingly negative result. This throws serious doubts on its ability to interpret empirical macrodynamics which inevitably reflect the non-stationarity of technology, tastes, etc.. Finally, note that in these models erratic behaviour is an *equilibrium* phenomenon and not the movement of the system out of equilibrium: equilibrium is actually assumed *ex hypothesi*, while attempts to show how agents 'learn' how to get there have generally failed. We shall now turn to this issue.

Rational expectations equilibria and adaptive processes

There have recently been attempts to overcome the difficulties discussed in the two previous sections by suggesting that rational expectations equilibria can be seen as a steady state of adaptive processes. These are ostensibly an attempt to build a bridge between the neo-classical approach and some kind of evolutionary theory (Lucas, 1986). (Note that in this instance 'evolution' only hints at 'adaptation', since there is no 'selection': the economic consequences of 'mistakes' are ruled out.)

However, it can be shown that, in general, rational expectations equilibria *cannot* be seen as stationary states of adaptive processes. To put it differently, dynamic paths determined by adaptive rules do not generally converge to rational expectations equilibria (see Fuchs, 1979). Obviously, examples of models in which adaptive rules and learning processes lead to a convergence to rational expectations steady states may be easily formulated (see also Bray and Kreps, 1987). This convergence, however, is linked to particular structures of the system. A simple example may help in clarifying the point.

Let us take a system in which the rational expectations steady state is not an attractor of the rational expectations dynamics. If rationality of expectations is assumed even outside stationary states, hence assuming instantaneous learning (which is equivalent to neglecting the 'gradualism' of learning processes), the system will not converge to the rational expectations steady state. In this situation, by assuming that expectations outside steady states are formed in an adaptive fashion, the instability property of the steady state can be repaired: the rational expectations steady state becomes stable in the adaptive expectations dynamics. This case is shown in Figure 6.1, which is derived from a slight modification of Lucas's example (Lucas, 1986). Every point on the A-curve is an equilibrium for a given instant t. Any sequence of points $\{q(t)\}$ with $t=0, 1 \ldots \infty$, on the same curve is a rational expectations (or perfect foresight) dynamic equilibrium. Consequently, there is a continuum of dynamic equilibria, each of them indexed to a different initial condition $q(0)$, which the model cannot endogenously determine. We are thus back to the indeterminacy problem

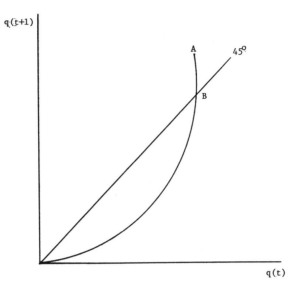

Figure 6.1

discussed earlier. Notice that there are two steady states, the origin and the point B. B is an unstable steady state, but it is the equilibrium point which reflects, so to speak, the 'predictions' of the theory. The locus of equilibrium points described by the curve A is obtained, for instance, from the dynamic solution of an overlapping generations model.[17]

The equilibrium dynamics of the system (see Note 17 for its derivation) is represented by the following equation: $q(t+1)=q(t)^2$. This is obtained by assuming perfect foresight, which allows us to substitute the actual realization to $Eq(t+1)$, that is, the expectation of $q(t+1)$. If we abandon this assumption in favour of an adaptive expectation function we obtain a different dynamic equation. For instance, if the expectation of $q(t+1)$ is based on a weighted average of current and past prices: $Eq(t+1) = q^a(t) q^{1-a}(t-1)$, with $0 < a < 1$, the dynamic equation of the system becomes $q^a(t) q^{1-a}(t-1) = q^2(t)$, which is equivalent to $q^{(1-a)/(2-a)}(t-1) = q(t)$. By propagating this equation one period ahead we obtain $q(t+1) = q^{(1-a)/(2-a)}(t)$. This equation gives rise to a curve which is a sort of mirror image of the A-curve, since $(1-a)/(2-a) < 1$. The new dynamics is illustrated in Figure 6.2.

The steady states are obviously the same as before; their dynamic properties are, however, inverted; the steady state B is now locally stable. For every initial condition $q(0)$ in $(0,1]$ the system will converge to B. All the dynamic paths reflect the *adaptive* expectation rule and they all converge to the rational expectations equilibrium B. It should be noted that the relation between adaptive processes and rational expectations equilibria

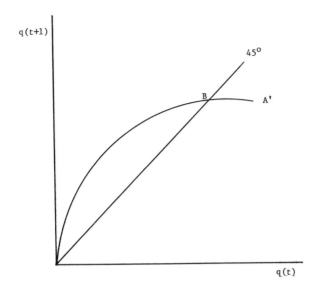

Figure 6.2

depends on the specific structure of the model considered. The same result could have been obtained by changing the functional form of the utility function. For example, with a utility function different from the one underlying the model just discussed we could have achieved a steady state stable in the rational expectations dynamics, but unstable in the adaptive rule dynamics (on these issues see also Grandmont and Laroque, 1986).[18] In such a case the rational expectations equilibrium cannot be seen as a steady state of adaptive processes. In fact the contrary would be true: in a sense, steady *adaptive* expectation dynamics would be the realization of a rational expectation process!

In general, the dynamic properties of the system are determined by the interplay between the structure of the system and the expectation function. However, the latter must be considered as a structural feature of the system: a change in the expectation function is in general indistinguishable from a change in utility or production functions. Borrowing a definition used by Azariadis (1983), a variation in the expectation function is 'observationally equivalent' to a change in preferences or technologies.

To summarize, once it is recognized that learning cannot be dismissed even in a rational expectations framework, it follows that one cannot dispose of a characterization of individual behaviour which is also 'situation-' or 'environment-specific'. However, inclusion of these factors into the theoretical picture makes the rational expectations assumption quite irrelevant: the rationality principle together with the nature of the fundamentals of the economy are *unable to determine the dynamic* processes of the economy, nor, in general, even the asymptotes of out-of-steady-states adaptive processes.

Finally, it is interesting to notice that problems of a somewhat similar nature also emerge in the stricter microeconomic domain whenever one goes beyond the analysis of the properties of equilibria and tries to model the (out-of-equilibrium) adjustment processes which could lead there. A recent, thorough and bold discussion can be found in Hahn (1987): 'whatever the form of learning that takes place on the grounds of the information that markets deliver, adjustment processes, *in general*, cannot be represented independently from history-specific and environment-specific conditions.'

Stabilizing, order-generating mechanisms and the power of macroeconomic theory

Most contemporary accounts of macroeconomics (and thus also of aggregate economic 'order') lead to a curious paradox. They generally start with an act of faith in both the 'Invisible Hand' and in the substantive capabilities of individual agents to process information and 'choose' correctly and freely—constrained only by their endowments—and end up with results that show a very crippled Hand, incapable of orderly coordination even in extremely simple environments. Moreover, note that these results are obtained despite an increasing attribution of rational competence and information processing power to individual agents.[19] Certainly, we believe, the attempt to 'explain' macroeconomics solely on the basis of some kind of 'hyper-rationality' of the agents (Winter, 1986) and the (pre-analytical) fundamentals of the economy (i.e. given technology and tastes) has failed.

There seem to be three ways out. First, one may, so to speak, 'stabilize the models' by working one's way 'backward', from the nature of the results one obtains to the restrictions one needs to impose in order to obtain the results one prefers. Just to give an example: the interpretation of the saddle-point properties of rational expectations macro models is quite instructive.[20] The structural model is characterized by a serious problem of instability: for every initial condition different from the one which puts the system on the unique convergent path, the system will diverge from the steady state. The heuristic strategy generally adopted to solve the problem is then to rule out, *a priori*, the instability of the solution, often justifying the choice on the ground that the world is not unstable. In the last instance one imposes stability to the solution (not to the model, which is highly unstable). One may forecast that, for example, the exploration of the conditions under which models generate chaos may lead towards a somewhat similar methodology: that is, use the results precisely to *assume away* these conditions. Frankly, it seems to us that this intellectual strategy is quite close to that scientific fallacy which epistemologists call '*explenans explenandum*': you assume your theory to be true and use your results to prove that it is true. Certainly, following this route no proper refutation is possible and economics becomes more akin to theology than empirical science.

The second strategy is to rediscover the *ad hocs*—auxiliary assumptions empirical character—plug them into a model which maintains a more or less strict neo-classical ascendancy (micro choices based on standard maximization, tatonnement assumptions about adjustments, etc.), and estimate econometrically using these auxiliary assumptions and 'free parameters' (e.g. expectation formation, etc.). This is, loosely speaking, that 'out-of-fashion' approach to macroeconomics mentioned in the introduction to this chapter, which the Rational Expectation school dismissed as theoretically unfounded.

However, there is a general point: in this kind of macroeconomic analysis, as well as in other domains, the results depend very little either on the 'core' behavioural model, based on individual rationality (in neo-classical sense) or on its implicit microeconomics, and very much on the auxiliary assumptions themselves (Simon, 1986), which, to repeat, are of an empirical nature, although generally introduced with the most casual empiricism.

The third approach is, broadly speaking, an 'evolutionary' and 'institutionalist' one. In a way, it starts with similar considerations, thus acknowledging that various institutions *structure* individual decision-making and collective coordination, but *explicitly* considers these institutions as an essential part of the interpretation of the (varying degrees of) order which one observes at the macro level.

An interesting example of the very simple micro 'rules' which order behaviour is shown by Heiner (1983 and Chapter 7 of this book). According to his view, the main source of unpredictability, and also of irregular, chaotic dynamics (see Heiner, 1986), is to be found in the assumption of perfect rational agents on which the conventional neo-classical approach rests. Introducing a form of 'imperfection' of agents, summarized by their 'competence gap' in correctly detecting environmental signals, he is able to show that previously unpredictable actions become regular and consistent with empirical observation of economic behaviour. Notably, Heiner's analysis applies to environments in which individuals *could* notionally be literal maximizers. As mentioned in Chapter 2 and analysed in Dosi and Egidi (1987), there is a wide class of (empirically very plausible) environments in which agents *cannot* adopt maximizing decision processes due to the environmental uncertainty associated with particular kinds of nonstationarity and/or the complexity of problem-solving tasks. Thus, rather general *rules* of behaviour inevitably emerge. Macro models, of course, should embody as their implicit or explicit microfoundations: (a) generalizations of these rules—whenever they are sufficiently stable—and (b) some theoretical propositions about how individual 'rules' aggregate and/or interact in order to produce the 'macro' (observed) patterns.

In a sense, macroeconomics neo-classical models attribute, at the same too much and too little freedom and power to individual agents: too much because their behaviour is totally unconstrained (apart, of course, from the endowed resources) in judging, computing, deciding; too little because, given their preferences, there is only one 'right' thing to do—all possible opportunities are exploited and it is hard to imagine how non-stationarity in technology, etc., can come about, except via some exogenous input.

Precisely the (observation-based) specification of 'structures', which encompass not only 'outside' institutions such as governments but also institutional aspects permeating individual behaviour, appears to be a promising way of avoiding the typical problems of unpredictability emerging from ahistorical, structure-free models. Social habits, routinized behaviour of firms, and contracts are a few examples of structures which delimit the context of individual behaviour and shape adjustment processes (see, for example, Okun, 1981; Kaldor, 1985).

In many respects, several 'positive' (that is interpretative rather than critical) chapters of this volume represent initial contributions to the understanding of these phenomena. Pushing it almost certainly beyond what the author intended, we place a central theoretical importance on the conjecture that 'There are collective norms . . . that are very important in social action. People just do not maximize on a selfish base every minute. In fact the system would not work if they did. *A consequence of that hypothesis would be the end of organized society as we know it*' (Arrow, 1987, p. 233, our italics). Certainly, continuing this quotation, we also agree that '. . . we do not have a good theory of how these norms come into existence' (ibid.). It remains a major inter-disciplinary challenge—to economists as well as organization theorists, sociologists, experimental psychologists, etc. However, we *do* have the *beginnings* of a theory of the *process* through which certain behaviours are selected and become dominant: combinations of learning and competitive selection contribute to these processes, as discussed at greater length in other chapters. Clearly, evolutionary/self-organization models focus precisely on these processes.

History, institutions and order in economic change: can they be explained within the neo-classical microeconomic framework?

One rather commonly held belief is that any alternative to the neo-classical research programme would have to be based on highly specific empirical observations and thus would not be very generalisable beyond its original context. Can the neo-classical approach avoid degenerating in this direction? Our foregoing assessment of the recent developments of neo-classical macro theory shows that it cannot. It is indeed recognized that without an explicit consideration of the specificity of economic behaviour depending on contexts, environments, initial conditions, of learning processes and, we could add, of institutions other than markets, equilibrium models have no economic content or descriptive power. Unfortunately, the lagging belief in the history-free interpretative power of the models sometimes only helps in justifying the most 'cavalier' attitude toward the specification of the structure of the model (for convenience we assume convexity, or infinitely lived agents, or homogenous of degree-one production functions, or risk-neutrality,' etc.), which in turn crucially affects the results.

Certainly, both neo-classically inspired models and that of 'alternative' (e.g. evolutionary/self-organization) models frequently entail a multiplicity of equilibria which may or may not be stable (the former) and a multiplicity of 'evolutionary attractors' and asymptotic states (the latter). What then is the difference in the analytical power between the two, and why should one choose the latter, given that the former derive from a longer established formal tradition.

The first point we want to make is that, equilibrium models *cum* rational agents are simpler, but at the price of a very low economic plausibility of the assumptions.

After all, apples tend to fall down from trees whatever their initial condition, shape, colour, etc. Indeed, it would not be so bad if a theory would allow more than one stationary state for the apples, provided that it specified under what circumstances it went towards either one, but it would certainly be devastating to have a theory that allowed the apples to go in almost any direction.

The story is different for evolutionary/self-organization approaches. There one specifies *economically meaningful processes*, behaviours, initial conditions—in principle, based on observation-related generalizations—and studies the dynamic paths of the system. These paths may often diverge, and there may be a number of asymptotic states (see, for example, Arthur's chapter in this volume). Such a theory would, of course, be highly redundant and unnecessarily cumbersome in all those cases of globally stable equilibria such as falling apples, but it appears to be the more necessary the more 'history matters' and the more the specific features of micro agents matter, too.

The second point is that an evolutionary/self-organization approach can deal more straightforwardly with various sorts of non-stationarities, while 'equilibrium' approaches, as we argued earlier, appear to be ill-suited to the task.

If one believes that a sequential, evolutionary and institutional representation is required in order to account for the values and changes in macrovariables, it is difficult to escape the implication that *its microfoundations, too,* must be in some sense 'evolutionary' and 'institutional', allowing for variety, learning, mistakes, selection and imitation. This, is, of course, one of the main points argued in this book, with particular reference to technology and technical change.

Some conclusions

At a very general level, one tends to observe broad regularities in the values and/or changes of macro variables such as, for example, relatively regular patterns of growth of output per head and capital per head; roughly cyclical, although irregular, movements of employment rates possibly around longer-term trends; relatively steady patterns of income distribution, etc. (for an extensive list of both long-term and cyclical 'stylized facts' drawing on Kaldor and Mitchell, see Simon, 1986). These empirical regularities plausibly hint at some underlying process governing both economic coordination amongst agents (otherwise no regularity whatsoever could be expected to appear) and economic change (for, otherwise, no regularity, however rough, would be likely in the time derivatives). Moreover, there appear to be 'micro' regularities, some of which are investigated in this book, which are related to typical patterns of behaviour of the agents (such as firms, but also recognizable aggregates, such as whole industries or even countries), technologies, the ways they cope or even themselves generate change, their internal structure, and the ways they interact with the external environment. Micro-observations of behavioural rules such as those discussed at length in this book, have, on the one hand, a strong flavour of 'idiosyncrasy', specificity to contexts, periods and institutions. On the other hand, there are phenomena related to quite general features of technologies, competitive environments and organizations, discussed at length in other chapters, which seem to hold, in different forms, across industries and across countries. Overall, the micro picture conveys an impression of marked inter-agent diversity and environmental non-stationarity. Ideally, one would like to find a unified or at least consistent theoretical link between 'macro' and 'micro' phenomena.

In fact, at the 'micro' (or, if one prefers, 'partial equilibrium') level there are two distinct views which compete for the theoretical representation of environments characterized by innovative phenomena. The first view draws quite closely on the way neo-classical economics handles choice, allocation and equilibria in stationary environments.

The other view (call it the evolutionary/self-organization approach), discussed at greater detail in the chapters by Dosi–Orsenigo, Allen, Arthur and Silverberg, takes in many respects an opposite stance and focuses on behavioural diversity, out-of-equilibrium processes, various sorts of externalities, environmental selection and unintentional outcomes of decentralized decision-making. In the former view, order in change comes from the fact that (i) in one and every period the system hits some scarcity constraint; (ii) the environment is 'transparent' enough for the agents to make 'rational' choices; and (iii) there are some processes which, although they have never been specified, ensure the *ex ante* consistency of individual strategies. Conversely, in the evolutionary/self-organization view, relatively ordered patterns of change come from (i) technological and institutional factors which form the basis of expectation formation and orient decision under general conditions of uncertainty and complexity; (ii) selection processes which limit (but do not eliminate) the variety of 'visions' and behaviours of the economic agents; and (iii) the continual generation of new sources of increased efficiency and new product markets.

It is our impression that there is a growing overlap between the stylized phenomena addressed by traditional economic theory—what we called the equilibrium/maximization approach and the emerging evolutionary/self-organization view. For example, within the former approach, various 'micro' and 'macro' models have demonstrated the relevance of beliefs in terms of attained equilibria; extensive form game models hint at the importance of institutions governing repeated behaviours; explicit accounts of market signalling even in simple set-ups highlight the role of initial conditions; theoretical accounts of externalities yield path-dependent models, etc.

This loose convergence in the underlying phenomena which the models address highlights both analytical complementaries and more radical differences in the frameworks underlying these models. Certainly, we agree with Hahn (1984, p. 140) that the study of asymptotic (equilibrium) states of evolutionary environments is also of theoretical importance. It helps in showing under what circumstances such states are actually the attractor of the evolutionary process. Here possibly rests one of the major complementaries between 'equilibrium' and explicitly 'evolutionary' analyses. However, as we have argued in this chapter, one of the few robust results that can be obtained by relaxing some of the most demanding assumptions of the 'unrestricted' equilibrium/maximization model is precisely the *lack of robustness* of its results (in terms of existence, determinacy, stability, and Pareto-optimality of its equilibria).

Conversely, the emerging evolutionary/self-organization approach takes as its 'building blocks' precisely what to neo-classical theory are 'extensions' or 'exceptions', such as externalities, increasing returns, non-stationarity, different and coexisting priors held by agents, complex strategic interactions without dominant strategies, and fundamental uncertainty. It might even be argued that the evolutionary/self-organization approach *predicates* its empirical adequacy on precisely these conditions.

Of course, one could assume that micro diversity, 'noise', mistakes, etc., cancel out in the aggregate by a sort of law of large numbers. Or one may assume that they simply represent empirical imperfections which nonetheless are in some sense 'ordered' by, or tend towards, a (theoretically) much simpler stationary state. Our position, however, is that detailed, observation-based analyses of behaviour, institutions and economic processes are *unavoidable* ingredients of both micro *and macro* theories of coordination and change, which—as the development of post-war economic theory shows—cannot be short-circuited by invoking a 'more general', history-free theory. This is also one of the *theoretical* justifications for many of the contributions to this book.

Notes

1. It might be worth recalling Arrow's view on the epistemological status of General Equilibrium analysis: 'I *do not* believe in the perfectly competitive view of the world, I think the general equilibrium theory is an imaginatively manipulative theory; one can get results out of it. It serves for many purposes as a good approximation for reasons that one does not fully understand. Therefore it is a useful tool for various micro problems. I think it is essential to remember the fact that in some industries there are increasing returns. But if you look at the economy, so to speak, in the gross these exceptions are very small. That is, all these exceptions are small on the scale of the economy. On the whole, what the existence problem has done was to force us to think a lot more rigorously about what it is. That may be the biggest benefit, rather than the existence theorem itself' (Arrow, 1987, pp. 197–8).

2. The following statement by Lucas describes very neatly the 'neo-classical' view of microfoundations: 'If we consider the question: How will a monkey that has not been fed for a day react to a banana tossed into its cage? I take it we have sufficient previously established knowledge about the behaviour of monkeys to make this prediction with some confidence. Now alter the question to: How will five monkeys that have not been fed for a day react to one banana thrown into their cage? This is an entirely different question' (Lucas, 1981, p. 289).

3. Obviously, the analysis of macroeconomic phenomena has forced a revision of the standard Arrow–Debreu model of general equilibrium; in order to deal with issues such as money, public debt, etc., the model has been modified and the main change has been that to make the general equilibrium model a truly dynamical model. An example of this extension, to which we will often refer in the sequel, is the overlapping generations model originally proposed by Samuelson (1958). This requires the issue of expectations to be tackled and the avenue taken has been that of assuming rational expectations, or perfect foresight in a deterministic world.

4. As far as welfare analysis is concerned, a very interesting work by Dow and Costa Werlang (1985) shows that welfare judgements based on the utility of the representative consumer are misleading. Indeed, they prove that it is possible 'that the representative consumer shows an increase in utility when, in fact, every consumer has been made worse off'.

5. See Antonelli (1886); Nataf (1953); Gorman (1953); Eisenberg (1961).

6. Recent contributions have tried to respond to the extremely negative implications of these results for neo-classical theory. It is interesting to note that the restrictions imposed either on the distribution of income (Hildenbrand) or on the shape of the distribution of preferences (Grandmont) 'cannot be deduced from the general hypothesis of individual rational behaviour alone' (Hildenbrand, 1986). They are indeed based on empirical facts. Obviously this avenue — although interesting for its empirical implications — is not a solution

to the weaknesses of the neo-classical view, based as it is upon a 'deductionist approach' which derives general results dependent only on primitive assumptions about the economy and not on *ad hoc* hypotheses justified in terms of empirical observations. Other attempts to solve the aggregation problem, such as the one by Grandmont (1985), are not applicable to general equilibrium models because they assume that income is independent of prices. Even after some qualifications indicated in recent works (see Balask, 1986), it is true that in a general equilibrium model, in order to satisfy the assumption of a 'representative agent', extremely strong restrictions have to be imposed.

7. Interestingly enough, if we consider a particular adjustment rule—of the form $p(i)=k(i)z(i)[p]$, with i denoting a particular good, p the price and z the excess demand—in order to obtain stability it is necessary to assume conditions ensuring that the aggregate excess demand function is a single consumer function; therefore, it is necessary to assume away differences among consumers or to impose strong restrictions on preferences and income distribution.

8. See Cass, Okono and Zilcha (1979).

9. See Woodford (1984); Kehoe and Levine (1983). This result is due to the fact that a dynamic economy such as the overlapping generations model can be seen as a general equilibrium system with an infinite number of agents and goods.

10. See Azariadis (1981); Cass and Shell (1983). It should be noted that sunspot equilibria arise even in economies in which equilibrium is unique (see Cass and Shell, ibid.).

11. That is, the utility function is continuous, differentiable, strictly quasi-concave, while the production function is continuous and homogeneous of degree one.

12. See, among others Grandmont (1985a); Benhabib and Nishimura (1985); Reichlin (1986).

13. We take just as an example the model by Pietra (1986). Deterministic chaos is obtained in an overlapping generations model with the following utility and production functions: utility function: $C(t+1) - (1/2) L^2(t)$, with $C(t+1)$ and $L(t)$ being respectively future consumption and current supply of labour. Production function (Leontief)): $Q(t+1) = \min \{L, K/\alpha\}$, with $\alpha < 1$.

14. Although often used in the economic literature (Benhabib and Day, 1981, 1982; and Day, 1982, 1983), the definition derived from the Li and Yorke (1975) paper, suggesting that the existence of a cycle of period 3 is a signal of chaotic behaviour, may be misleading, since there can be a stable cycle which can make the 'chaotic' set irrelevant (of Lebesgue measure 0). One can thus define chaos as the case in which all cycles are unstable (cf. Grandmont, 1984).

15. For a definition of sensitive dependence on initial conditions, see Collet and Eckmann (1980).

16. The attractor—i.e. the set where trajectories starting from different initial conditions asymptotically end up—peculiar to deterministic chaos has been denoted 'strange attractor'. The dimension of this attractor is smaller than the dimension of the system and is usually noninteger, making the attractors fractals.

17. For example, an overlapping generation model in which people live for two 'periods', consume when they are old and work in their youth—young people maximize the utility function $U(C,l) = C(t+1) - \frac{1}{2}l^2$, where C stands for consumption and l for labour. Technology is given by the trivial constant

return to scale production function $y(t)=l(t)$. The old receive from a central bank a fixed quantity of money, M, at the beginning of each period. The young solve the following maximization problem: max $U(.)$ subject to $p(t+1)C(t+1)=p(t)y(t)$. The first-order condition of this maximization yields the supply of output of the young at time t: $y(t) = p(t)/p(t+1)$. The old obviously try to get rid of all their monetary holdings. Real demand is thus $M/p(t)$. Equilibrium requires equality of demand and supply, or $M/p(t)=p(t)/p(t+1)$. Defining $m(t)=M/p(t)$, we can rewrite the equilibrium condition in terms of real balances, m: $m(t+1)=m^{(}t)$. Substituting q for m we obtain the equation in the text.

18. For instance, it has been shown that replacing rational expectations by an expectation function based on an explicit learning process does not generally stabilize the economy (Fuchs, 1979). As argued by Grandmont and Laroque (1986), 'one should be very cautious when interpreting the stability results one gets from dynamical rational expectation models in which times goes forward. Taking into account the agents learning behaviour on the transition path, as one should, may reverse the stability diagnosis' (p. 139).

19. One of the authors has discussed this issue in Dosi and Egidi (1987); recent and more classic references whose content we broadly share are Simon (1986) and Winter (1986); for a broad discussion see the special issue of the *Journal of Business* where the latter two references appear.

20. Recall that when a steady state is a saddle point its inset (the state of all points converging to it) has zero Lebesgue measure.

References

Akerlof, G. A. and Yellen, J. L. (1985), 'A near-rational model of the business cycle', *Quarterly Journal of Economics*, 100, pp. 803–38.

Antonelli, G. B. (1886), 'Sulla teoria matematica della economia politica', Pisa; English translation in J. S. Chipman *et al.* (eds.) (1971), *Preferences, Utility and Demand*, New York, Harcourt Brace Jovanovich.

Arrow, K. J. (1987), 'Oral history: an interview', in G. R. Feiwel (ed.), *Arrow and the Ascent of Modern Economic Theory*, New York, New York University Press.

Atkinson, A. and Stiglitz, J. (1969), 'A new view of technological change', *Economic Journal*, 79, pp. 573–8.

Azariadis, C. (1981), 'Self-fulfilling prophecies', *Journal of Economic Theory*, 25, pp. 380–96.

Azariadis, C. (1983), 'Intertemporal Macroeconomics: Lecture Notes', University of Pennsylvania, mimeo.

Balasko, Y. (1986), 'The class of aggregate excess demand functions', in W. Hildenbrand and A. Mas-Colell (eds.), *Contributions to Mathematical Economics*, New York, North Holland.

Benhabib, J. and Day, R. H. (1981), 'Rational choice and erratic behaviour', *Review of Economic Studies*, 4, pp. 37–55.

—— (1982), 'A characterization of erratic dynamics in the overlapping generations model', *Journal of Economic Dynamics and Control*, 48, pp. 459–72.

Benhabib, J. and Nishimura, K. (1985), 'Competitive equilibrium cycles', *Journal of Economic Theory*, 35, pp. 284–30.

Bray, M. and Kreps, D. M. (1987), 'Rational learning and rational expectations', in G. R. Feiwel (ed.), *Arrow and the Ascent of Modern Economic Theory*, New York, New York University Press.

Cass, D. and Shell, K. (1983), 'Do sunspots matter?', *Journal of Political Economy*, 91, pp. 193–227.

Cass, D., Okuno, M. and Zilcha, I. (1979), 'The role of money in supporting the Pareto optimality of competitive equilibrium in consumption-loan type models', *Journal of Economic Theory*, 20, pp. 41–80.

Collet, P. and Eckmann, J.P. (1980), *Iterated Maps on the Interval as Dynamic Systems*, Boston, Birkhauser.

Coricelli, F. (1987), 'Adaptive behaviour and rational expectations equilibria: some examples', Milan, Istituto per la Ricerca Sociale, mimeo.

Day, R. H. (1982), 'Irregular growth cycles', *American Economic Review*, 72, pp. 406–414.

—— (1983), 'The emergence of chaos from classical economic growth', *Quarterly Journal of Economics*, 98, pp. 201–212.

Dosi, G. and Egidi, M. (1987), 'Substantive and procedural uncertainty: an exploration on economic behaviour in complex and changing environments', Brighton, University of Sussex, SPRU, DRC Discussion Paper; presented at the Conference on Programmable Automation, Paris, 2–4 April 1987.

Dow, J. and Ribeiro da Costa Werlang, S. (1985), 'The consistency of welfare judgements with a representative consumer', Princeton University, Econometric Research Program Research Memorandum No. 318.

Eisenberg, B. (1961), 'Aggregation of utility functions', *Management Science*, 7, pp. 337–50.

Friedman, M. (1953), *Essays in Positive Economics*, Chicago, University of Chicago Press.

Frydman, R. and Phelps, E. S. (eds.) (1983), *Individual Forecasting and Aggregate Outcomes*, Cambridge, Cambridge University Press.

Fuchs, G. (1979), 'Is error learning behaviour stabilizing?', *Journal of Economic Theory*, 3, pp. 300–17.

Gorman, W. M. (1953), 'Community preference fields', *Econometrica*, 21, pp. 63–80.

Grandmont, J. M. (1984), 'Periodic and aperiodic behaviour in discrete one-dimensional dynamical systems', Stanford University, Economic Series Technical Report No. 446.

—— (1985a), 'On endogenous business cycles', *Econometrica*, 53, pp. 995–1046.

—— (1985b), 'Distributions of preferences and the "law of demand" ', mimeo.

Grandmont, J. M. and Laroque, G. (1986), 'Stability of cycles and expectations', *Journal of Economic Theory*, 40, pp. 138–51.

Hahn, F. (1984) *Equilibrium and Macroeconomics*, Oxford, Basil Blackwell.

Hahn, F. (1987), 'Information dynamics and equilibrium', presented at the Conference of Scottish Economists, mimeo.

Heiner, R. (1983), 'The Origin of predictable behavior', *American Economic Review, 83, pp. 560–95.*

—— (1986), 'The Origin of predictable dynamic behavior', Brigham Young University, mimeo.

Hildenbrand, W. (1986), 'Equilibrium analysis of large economies', Bonn University, Discussion Paper No. 72.

Kaldor, N. (1980), *The Role of Increasing Returns, Technical Progress and Cumulative Causation in the Theory of International Trade*, Paris, ISMEA.

—— (1985), *Economics without Equilibrium*, New York, Sharp.

Kehoe, T. J. and Levine, D. K. (1983), 'Indeterminacy of relative prices in overlapping generations models', MIT Working Paper No. 313.

Leijonhufvud, A. (1981), *Information and Coordination*, Oxford, Oxford University Press.

Li, T. and Yorke, J. A. (1975), 'Period three implies chaos', *American Mathematical Monthly*, 82, pp. 985–92.

Lucas, R. E. Jr (1981), *Studies in Business-Cycle Theory*, Cambridge, Mass., MIT Press.

—— (1986), 'Adaptive behaviour and economic theory', *Journal of Business*, 59, pp. 401–76.

Malinvaud, E. (1981), *Théorie macro-économique*, Paris, Dunod.

Nataf, A. (1953), 'Sur des questions d'agrégation en économétrie', Publications de l'Institut de Statistique de l'Université de Paris, 21, pp. 5–61.

Nelson, R. R. and Winter, S. (1982), *An Evolutionary Theory of Economic Change*, Cambridge, Mass., The Belknap Press of Harvard University Press.

Okun, A. M. (1981), *Prices and Quantities*, Oxford, Basil Blackwell.

Pietra, T. (1986), 'On the dynamic properties of an economy where production takes time: some examples of erratic and strange dynamics', University of Pennsylvania, mimeo.

Reichlin, P. (1986), 'Equilibrium cycles in an overlapping generations economy with production', *Journal of Economic Theory*, 40, pp. 89–102.

Saari, D. G. (1983), 'Dynamical systems and mathematical economics', in H. F. Sonnenschein (ed.), *Models of Economic Dynamics*, Berlin, Springer-Verlag.

Samuelson, P. (1958), 'An exact consumption-loan model of interest with and without the social contrivance of money', *Journal of Political Economy*, 66, pp. 467–82.

Shafer, W. and Sonnenschein, H. (1982), 'Market demand and excess demand functions', in K. J. Arrow and M. D. Intriligator (eds), *Handbook of Mathematical Economics*, vol. II, New York, North Holland.

Simon, H. A. (1986), 'Rationality in psychology and economics', *Journal of Business*, 59, pp. 209–24.

Varian, H. (1984), *Microeconomic Analysis*, 2nd ed., New York, Norton.

Winter, S. G. (1986), 'Adaptive behaviour and economic rationality: comments on Arrow and Lucas', *Journal of Business*, 59, pp. 427–34.

Woodford, M. (1984), 'Indeterminacy of equilibrium in the overlapping generations model: a survey', mimeo.

7 Imperfect decisions and routinized production: implications for evolutionary modeling and inertial technical change

Ronald A. Heiner

Department of Economics, Brigham Young University, Provo, Utah, USA

Introduction

Elswhere I introduced a theory of reliability to explain how imperfect information *and* imperfect ability to use information influence behavior (Heiner, 1983; 1985a,b; 1986; 1987a,b,d). The resulting analysis implies a close link between the scope of information agents can use reliably and the set of actions they can thereby benefit from choosing. In this chapter I briefly explore implications of this theory for understanding production methods and technical change within firms over time, and the need for explicit evolutionary modeling rather than postulating 'as if' optimization. In contrast with this approach, standard-choice theory assumes that agents use information perfectly, by always selecting actions that maximize expected utility based on observed information. Information may be costly to acquire, but there are no decision errors in using it once it has been observed. Suppose we relax this extreme assumption of no decision errors in responding to observed information. Instead, suppose agents' decision-making competence at using information is not necessarily sufficient always to respond optimally, no matter how difficult or complex their decision problems might be (separate from whether there are any costs of observing information in the first place).

Agents then face an additional dimension of uncertainty because there now exists a gap between their 'competence' at using information and the 'difficulty' of their decision problems (called a C–D gap). Standard-choice theory implicitly assumes that no C–D gap exists. Consequently, it has never investigated the behavioral implications of widening the gap; that is, of varying agents' decision-making competence *relative to* the difficulty of their decision problems. When this happens, agents become progressively worse at imitating optimal decision rules.

These issues are especially relevant to the major themes of this book. For example, the possibility of *non-linear* dynamic processes with bifurcation points between qualitatively different dynamic paths is discussed by Peter Allen (Chapter 5) and Gerald Silverberg (Chapter 24). Brian Arthur (Chapter 26) further discusses how such bifurcations can arise when the probability of adopting technical innovations is *path-dependent* on the history of previous adoptions. Similar themes are also developed by Dosi, Orsenigo and Coricelli (Chapters 2 and 6), namely, the intrinsic dynamic complexity of agents interacting in *non-stationary,* path-dependent environments.

All of these factors argue against the possibility of technical change proceeding in a dynamically simple and stable fashion (which could thereby be easily understood by agents within an economic system). To the contrary, technical change will typically display extremely complex and unstable patterns far beyond the competence of individual agents to design optimal strategies for when and how to adopt new technologies over time (so that a C–D gap for selecting dynamic strategies necessarily exists). Consequently, the modern theory of non-linear, path-dependent and non-stationary dynamics provides a basic explanation for why agents' decisions within a technologically evolving economy will be highly imperfect relative to that typically postulated by standard neo-classical investment and rational expectation models. Kenneth Arrow (1986) has recently voiced a similar theme about the weakness (even logical inconsistency) of rationality concepts in the presence of incomplete markets and imperfect competition.[1]

Moreover, even if we eliminate the sources of dynamic complexity noted above (i.e. no path-dependency, non-linearity, or non-stationarity is allowed), Marco Lippi shows (Chapter 8) that imperfect dynamic decisions can still arise from traditional macro models through the very process of *aggregating* individual micro-behaviors within a larger economy. In particular, he shows that static or quasi-static micro-behavior (with at most short lags of independent micro-variables, but no lags of dependent micro-variables) can aggregate to qualitatively more complicated macro-dynamic relationships (where dependent macro-variables now become noticeably lagged). Consequently, the macro-dynamic properties of an economy can be qualitatively *more* complex than the underlying micro-decision rules whose interaction gives rise to them.

This relationship means that trying to anticipate an economy's macro-behavior may require an understanding of relatively more complicated aggregate dynamic properties than needed to administer successfully the micro-decision rules which generate them. As a result, imperfect micro-agents may be unable reliably to affect macro-relationships by deviating from perhaps even simple routinized decisions (that is, the relatively more complicated macro-dynamics in part explains why micro-agents are only imperfectly reliable at deviating from simple micro-behaviors in ways that might successfully improve their performance). Lippi's analysis thus helps explain why the surrounding macro-environment within which individual agents interact is sufficiently complicated compared to their own behavior so as to require relatively simple micro-decision rules in order for them to compete successfully with each other.

In relation to the above introductory discussion, I wish to analyze the behavioral consequences of agents acting within a dynamic environment of sufficient complexity (through aggregation, path-dependency, non-linearity, non-stationarity, etc.) so that an unavoidable C–D gap exists in their decisions over time. To do so, I initially describe some key concepts and principles of reliability theory applied to production decisions within a firm. Three main topics are then discussed. First, I show how imperfect decisions lead to routinized behavior that is not optimally adjusted to all circumstances encountered by a firm. This is implied even if it is costless to adjust production methods to changing conditions. I then discuss why the analysis implies the need for explicit evolutionary modeling. Finally, I discuss how firms must inertially delay adjustment to new conditions in order to control errors in deciding when and how to appropriately use new technology. Here again, this is implied irrespective of whether there are any costs of physically adjusting production methods to new conditions or information.

Preliminary concepts and notation

Let S represent the set of possible *states* of the world and X represent a set of potentially observed *information* whose individual messages are imperfectly correlated with particular states. The set A denotes a firm's space of choosable *actions*, or *production methods*.

Individual consequences or outcomes result from different pairs of actions and states (a, s) taken from the Cartesian product $A \times S$. Let p denote a given probability distribution over outcomes (that is, a probability measure over $A \times S$), and the set of all such *outcome-distributions* is denoted P. Each particular outcome-distribution $p \in P$ in general depends on the likelihood of different states arising, the likelihood of receiving different messages conditional on given states occurring, and the likelihood of agents selecting particular actions in response to different messages. A distribution p can thus be conditioned on particular states occurring, messages received, or actions selected.

In particular, let $p_{A' \times S'} \in P$ be the outcome distribution p conditional on agents selecting an action from a set $A' \subset A$ when a state from the set $S' \subset S$ occurs (leaving unspecified what potential messages are observed when $s \in S'$ occurs). Similarly, let $p_{A' \times X'} \in P$ be the outcome distribution p conditional on agents selecting an action from $A' \subset A$ when a message from $X' \subset X$ is observed (leaving unspecified the occurrence of particular states which affect the likelihood of agents observing messages from X').[2]

Let $V(p)$ represent a value function which measures achieved performance associated with different outcome distributions $p \in P$; that is, the performance which arises from the statistical relationships between states occurring, messages being received, and agents responding to received messages. V might be a traditional expected utility function or one of the 'non-expected' utility functions of Chew, Machina, Fishburn, etc. (see Machina, 1983). In order to simplify notation, let $V(p_{K \times L}) = V(K, L)$ for any $K \times L$ contained in either $A \times S$ or $A \times X$. Thus, for example, $V(A', X')$ measures performance conditional on agents selecting an action from $A' \subset A$ when a message from $X' \subset X$ is observed; and similarly, $V(A', S')$ measures performance conditional on agents selecting an action from $A' \subset A$ when a state from $S' \subset S$ occurs.

Next, introduce the set β of correspondences from X into A. Each element $B \in \beta$ is interpreted as a decision rule or *behavior pattern* for selecting particular production methods in response to observed messages about output demand conditions, input costs, alternative production technologies, and so on. Particular behavior patterns are in general not optimal in selecting actions only when they maximize $V(\cdot)$ given observed information. Thus for a given $B \in \beta$ and $a \in A$, X_a^B represents those messages in X for which selecting action a is at least as preferred to actions chosen by B. That is, $X_a^B = \{x \in X \mid V(\{a\}, \{x\}) \geq V(\{a'\}, \{x\})$ for any $a' \in B(x)\}$. We can then interpret $\pi_a^B = p(X_a^B)$ as the probability of action a being a 'preferred deviation' from behavior B based on observed information. An optimal behavior pattern, denoted B^*, is one for which there does not exist any preferred deviations from it (i.e. $X_a^{B^*} = \phi$ for all $a \in A$). Consequently, there is zero probability of any preferred deviation from an optimal behavior pattern (i.e. $\pi_a^{B^*} = 0$ for all $a \in A$).[3]

A standard decision model would assume that firms always behave optimally and then investigate the implications of this assumption. Doing so implicitly assumes that firms will optimally deviate from any given behavior pattern $B \in \beta$ which is not itself fully optimal. Suppose instead we allow the possibility of decision errors in deciding when to deviate from a given 'status quo' behaviour pattern, so that a C–D gap exists as discussed in the introduction (due to intrinsically complex system dynamics through aggregation, non-linear relationships, path-dependency, non-stationarity, etc.). Firms will then *not* always deviate from a status quo behavior pattern when it is preferred to do so; and they may sometimes deviate when doing so is inferior to maintaining status quo behavior.

Thus, let $r_a^B = p(\text{selecting } a \in B(x) \mid X_a^B)$ be the probability of 'rightly' deviating away from $B(x)$ toward an action a when doing so is at least as preferred based on observed information. Similarly, let $w_a^B = p$ (selecting $a \in B(x) \mid X - X_a^B$) be the probability of 'wrongly' deviating away from $B(x)$ toward an action a when doing so is less preferred based on observed information.

The ratio $\rho_a^B = r_a^B / w_a^B$ then measures a firm's reliability at deviating from a given behavior pattern B by selecting action $a \in B(x)$ in response to observed messages $x \in X$. The special use of perfect decisions corresponds to $r_a^B \equiv 1$, $w_a^B \equiv 0$ (or $\rho_a^B \equiv \infty$) for all $B \in \beta$ and $a \in A$ (that is, perfect decisions are infinitely reliable at deviating in any way from any given behavior pattern).

On the other hand, imperfect decisions are only finitely reliable $(\rho_a^B < \infty)$ at deviating from a given behavior pattern. The objective is to generalize standard-choice theory by investigating the full range of possibilities permitted by $0 \leq r_a^B$, $w_a^B \leq 1$, instead of imposing the limiting assumption $r_a^B \equiv 1$, $w_a^B \equiv 0$.

To complete the necessary notation, define the net gain and loss due to deviating from a given behavior pattern when preferred messages for doing so are observed as compared to non-optimal ones. $V(B(x), X_a^B)$ is the performance achieved when the firm chooses according to $B(x)$ even though action a is the preferred choice given observed information. $V(\{a\}, X_a^B)$ is the performance achieved by selecting action a instead of from $B(x)$ when a is preferred given observed information. Thus, define $g_a^B = V(\{a\}, X_a^B) - V(B(x), X_a^B)$ as the net 'gain' in performance by deviating from behavior B toward action a when preferred messages for doing so are observed. Similarly, define $l_a^B = V(B(x), X - X_a^B) - V(\{a\}, X - X_a^B)$ as the net 'loss' by mistakenly deviating toward action a when non-preferred messages for doing so are observed.

Imperfect decisions and routinized behavior

The above concepts relate to those introduced in my 1983 paper on 'the origin of predictable behavior...'. That paper showed how imperfect agents may benefit from restricting the size and complexity of their decision space A. In this paper, I introduce a set of possible behavior patterns β and show that imperfect agents will not necessarily benefit from trying to deviate from a non-optimal behavior pattern $B \neq B^*$. However, the present formulation is more general in that a shift from a given non-optimal behavior pattern may not necessarily involve expanding the decision space A. Instead, it may involve a firm's attempt to decide more effectively over a fixed set of actions. In either case, the basic issue is whether imperfect agents will always benefit by shifting from a given decision rule $B \in \beta$ until B converges B^*.

Note that convergence to B^* is automatically implied for agents who are perfectly reliable at deviating from any given behavior $B \neq B^*$ (no matter how subtle or complex the deviations that may be required in order to shift B closer to B^*). On the other hand, if perfect decisions are no longer assumed, what then are the behavioral implications for firms composed of imperfect agents?

To answer this question, two assumptions about potential decision errors are introduced. The first assumption was mentioned earlier; namely, imperfect agents have *finite* reliability at deviating from non-optimal behavior patterns. That is,

A1

$$\rho_a^B < \infty \text{ for all } a \in A \text{ and } B \neq B^*.$$

Note, however, that decision errors would make no difference if the resulting losses became *arbitrarily small* compared to the gains from deviating when actually preferred to a given behavior pattern. Thus, for any potential action a, the loss l_a^B due to mistakenly deviating from an initial behavior pattern $B \in \beta$, is assumed to be at least some positive fraction of the gain g_a^B achieved by selecting action a when it is actually preferred to $B(x)$ based on the observed message $x \in X$. That is,

A2

$$\text{For some } K > 0, \ l_a^B / g_a^B \geq K \text{ for any } a \text{ and } B \neq B^*.$$

The necessity of routines over flexible optimizing: a general result

Let V^B denote the expected performance achieved by always choosing according to a given behavior pattern B. Similarly, let V_a^B denote the expected performance if agents can deviate from B toward action a whenever they so choose. Agents will thus benefit from the flexibility to deviate toward an action a if V_a^B exceeds V^B. The following theorem (developed in the Appendix) shows when this is the case.

Theorem 1 (reliability condition for improving on status quo behavior)

$$\text{For any } a \text{ and } B \neq B^*, \ V_a^B > V^B \text{ if and only if } \rho_a^B > T_a^B \tag{1}$$

where

$$\rho_a^B = \frac{r_a^B}{w_a^B} \quad \text{and} \quad T_a^B = \frac{l_a^B}{g_a^B} \cdot \frac{1 - \pi_a^B}{\pi_a^B} \tag{2}$$

T_a^B determines the *minimum* reliability or 'tolerance limit' (the minimum size of ρ_a^B) that must be satisfied before agents can benefit by sometimes deviating from behavior B toward action a. The inequality $\rho_a^B > T_a^B$ compares an agent's actual reliability ρ_a^B at so deviating with the minimum required reliability T_a^B. If ρ_a^B exceeds T_a^B, agents will benefit from allowing the flexibility to deviate toward action a; otherwise they will benefit from always choosing according to B.

Now apply Theorem 1 to an explicitly dynamic setting where different behavior patterns $B \in \beta$ may evolve, and consider the effect of moving toward an optimal pattern B^*. In particular, consider a sequence $B^v \in \beta$ such that $B^v \rightarrow B^*$. Since the latter implies $X_a^{B^v} \rightarrow X_a^{B^*}$ and since $X_a^{B^*} \equiv \phi$ by the definition of optimal behavior B^*, then $B^v \rightarrow B^*$ implies $\pi_a^{B^v} \rightarrow 0$ for all a (that is, the probability of any potential deviation being preferrred to status quo behavior B^v goes to zero as B^v gets closer and closer to fully optimal behavior B^*).

In addition, since $l_a^{B^v}/g_a^{B^v}$ is bounded above zero by Assumption A2, then $T_a^{B^v} = l_a^{B^v}/g_a^{B^v} \cdot (1 - \pi_a^{B^v})/\pi_a^{B^v}$ must approach infinity as $B^v \rightarrow B^*$ (since $(1 - \pi_a^{B^v})/\pi_a^{B^v}$ rises without limit as $\pi_a^{B^v} \rightarrow 0$). Consequently, Assumption A1 ($\rho_a^B < \infty$) implies the reliability condition $\rho_a^{B^v} > T_a^{B^v}$ *cannot hold* as $B^v \rightarrow B^*$ (so that trying to deviate from B^v will lower performance compared to not doing so). Thus, at some point *before* B^v converges to B^*, imperfect agents who try to deviate from B^v will have a selective disadvantage within a population of similar agents who always behave according to B^v.

Thus, as behavior approaches full optimality, imperfect agents will no longer benefit from trying to make preferred exceptions based on observed information, even though such exceptions still arise with positive probability $\pi_a^B > 0$. Or equivalently, as the preferred deviations to a given behavior pattern become sufficiently rare, imperfect agents will no longer benefit from trying to deviate from the behavior pattern. Instead, they will benefit from rules and procedures *adapted only to typical or recurrently observed messages.* Behavior adapted in this way (in order to satisfy $\rho_a^B > T_a^B$) constitutes *rule-governed* behavior.

Therefore, when imperfect decisions are combined with evolutionary stability, the generic result is rule-governed behavior; meaning behavior that approximates optimal choices only under typical or recurrently encountered information (so that $\pi_a^B > 0$ in general still holds). The above conclusion is similar to the idea of 'routines' used in Nelson and Winter's (1982) evolutionary models, and other related ideas such as 'satisfying' developed by Simon (1957, 1983). It is also consistent with various intuitive connotations of rule-governed behavior that have been applied to both humans and animals, such as habits, instincts, rules of thumb, cultural rituals, customs, norms and so on. All of these phrases collectively testify that some form of rigidity or inflexibility is a universal qualitative feature of behavior. The reliability condition $\rho_a^B > T_a^B$ enables this basic feature to be formally derived (from 'first principles') by generalizing standard-choice theory to incorporate explicitly the effects of decision errors on behavior.

The need for explicit evolutionary modeling

The inequality $\rho_a^B > T_a^B$ of Theorem 1 is a *diagnostic* condition which tells how performance will be affected by trying to deviate from a given behavior pattern. It does not assume agents are themselves competent to determine when or how it should be satisfied, nor that the very best or 'optimal' methods for satisfying it will necessarily evolve. However, we can still use the condition to analyze agents' behavior even if they have no special competence at applying it themselves, including inability to estimate the probability variables used in the condition (see Heiner, 1985a). (These questions are further discussed in Heiner, 1983, about selection processes sluggishly weeding out inferior performers, 1985a, about the 'tacit' nature of most evolved behavior mechanisms, and 1986, about the 'unintended' development of social institutions.)

In terms of the larger concerns of this book, a key, related conclusion should also be noted. It is simply that once imperfect decisions are considered, there is no longer any necessary feature in the formal analysis to guarantee that only appropriate (let alone 'optimal') decision practices will evolve. At best, conditions like $\rho_a^B > T_a$ can be used as a diagnostic tool to help determine whether deviating from given behavior patterns will be more or less likely to 'filter' through an evolutionary selection process. That is, satisfying or violating $\rho_a^B > T_a$ will respectively raise or lower the probability of survival. But this ('short-run') statistical effect does not guarantee that only 'optimal' behavior will eventually filter through a long sequence of selection trials. Only by combining diagnostic tools like $\rho_a^B > T_a$ with an explicitly formulated selection process can any precise results be obtained.

The latter conclusion is one of the most important implications of the reliability analysis presented above. Namely, *imperfect choice theory implies that evolutionary modeling must be added to any (diagnostic) analysis about the welfare effects of different behavior patterns.* Selection processes can no longer be assumed to generate behavior patterns 'as if' they were optimally chosen. In this regard, it is interesting that one of the major themes about understanding technical change emphasized in other chapters of this book (especially Parts II and VII) is the need for a theoretical framework that incorporates evolutionary processes as one of its essential features. Such a realization is intrinsically connected to analyzing imperfect choice (rather than excluding the possibility of imperfect decisions by hypothesis, as in neo-classical choice theory).

Adjustment costs and evolutionary stability

The above analysis made no mention about costs of physical switching between different decisions or production methods, and indeed remains valid even when such 'adjustment costs' are zero. On the other hand, the presence of adjustment costs is often given as a reason for routinized production methods within a firm. This is especially the case when changing methods requires investment in expensive capital equipment. A similar issue also arises in evolutionary biology, when behavioral rigidity is linked to constraints imposed by 'hardwired' neurological design, internal tissue structures, bodily morphology, and so on.

Suppose we agree that many production, institutional and biological features can impose significant costs of adjusting decisions. However, even granting this assumption, a more basic question still remains. Namely, *would such features evolve in the first place (or remain stable once introduced) if agents could perfectly handle any kind of decision flexibility no matter how subtle or complex their resulting behavior might become?*

In particular, suppose $\rho_a^B \equiv \infty$ for all a and B, but certain features of an agent (such as specialized capital equipment) make it prohibitively costly or even physically impossible to implement potential deviations from an initial status quo behavior pattern B^0. These features may thus deter the agent from deviating from B^0 despite their perfect reliability at doing so. Over the long run, however, such perfectly reliable agents would have a selective advantage in competition with similar agents from any change in their features enabling them more flexibly (or more cheaply) to deviate from any given routinized behavior pattern. This is implied no matter how particular 'adjustment cost lowering' features might be first introduced, even by pure random mutation or accident. Consequently, *any feature imposing high adjustment costs is evolutionarily unstable for perfectly reliable agents.*

On the other hand, the opposite conclusion applies to imperfect agents. The reason is that features creating high adjustment costs may help imperfect agents maintain routinized behavior patterns in the face of continual opportunities to deviate from them (yet trying to deviate would violate the reliability condition $\rho_a^B > T_a^B$). Consequently, certain 'adjustment cost *raising*' features may actually benefit imperfect agents. Thus, from an evolutionary perspective, high adjustment costs may themselves evolve to help imperfect agents regulate potential decision errors (instead of representing an independent reason for why agents typically behave according to routinized patterns).

Asymmetrically imperfect decisions

The general analysis presented above also allows another possibility that parallels a major development of neo-classical theory, namely, asymmetric information. That is, once standard theory dropped the assumption of perfect knowledge, the possibility that agents may have access to unequally or asymmetrically distributed imperfect information arose (instead of all agents having equally perfect information). Similarly, once one drops the assumption that all agents are equally perfect decision-makers, the possibility of unequally or asymmetrically imperfect decisions arises (even for the same person when making different types of decisions, or when deciding under different circumstances). A key example of this relevant to technical change is asymmetric competence across different agents within a business organization, including asymmetric competence at allocating individuals to particular jobs or management responsibilities. Some possibilities along these lines are discussed in Heiner (1987a). Asymmetric competence is also a key part of Pavel Pelikan's comparative institutional analysis in Chapter 18.

Inertially adjusting imperfect decisions and expectations

One of the major issues about technical change is how it develops within firms and spreads between a number of firms. New ideas and technology usually spread much slower than physically possible, even taking account of various adjustment costs of installing new equipment, compatibility of existing labor skills, and so on.

The relatively slow diffusion of industrial technology is part of a larger pattern where agents in general tend to sluggishly adjust away from their prior, 'status quo' decisions. These might refer to production output decisions as well as when and how much to adjust previously chosen output prices. Firms must also decide when and in what way to modify prior decisions about production methods.

Accordingly, this section applies the reliability condition $\rho_a^B > T_a^B$ within an explicitly dynamic setting in which agents must successively revise their decisions over time. It is shown that imperfect agents will not benefit from immediately adjusting their decisions to shifts in environmental parameters. Instead, they will benefit from no response for some positive interval of time after the environment shifts. In a production context, this means that firms will not immediately adopt new technology irrespective of whether there are any adjustment costs of doing so (i.e. even if it is costless to shift toward new production methods with no delay).

The analysis in part builds on work by Akerlof and Yellen (1985a,b) about what they call 'near rational' behavior (meaning non-optimal decisions that produce only 'second-order' losses compared to fully optimal adjustment). I thus begin with a short summary of their analysis.

Let an agent's objective function be $V(a, z)$, where a is a decision variable and z is a vector of decision parameters. The function $a^*(z)$ denotes the optimal selection of a which maximizes V for each given z. For simplicity, let us focus on a single z variable, denoted z, and write $a(z)$ only as a function of z, denoted $a(z)$; where the other z parameters are held fixed as z changes. Similarly, write $V(a, z)$ only as a function of z, denoted $V(a, z)$.

Suppose z initially equals z^0 and the agent has had sufficient time to learn the optimal decision $a^0 = a^*(z^0)$. Then let z start to shift from z^0 and compare two responses: (1) optimally adjusting according to $a^*(z)$; and (2) holding action a constant at a^0 as z starts to shift. Computing the net loss from not adjusting relative to optimal adjustment gives

$$\frac{\partial(a^*, z)}{\partial a} \cdot \frac{\partial a^*}{\partial z} + \frac{\partial V(a^*, z)}{\partial z} - \frac{\partial V(a^0, z)}{\partial z} \tag{3}$$

The first-order maximizing conditions imply $\partial V(a^*, z)/\partial a$ equals zero, so only the last two terms remain. The difference in these latter terms obviously goes to zero at the instant where z starts shifting from z^0 (because $a^*(z) \rightarrow a^0 = a^*(z^0)$ as $z \rightarrow z^0$). Hence, to a 'first-order' approximation, there are no net losses from not adjusting away from an initially optimal decision. (Consequently, any such losses must be 'second order' in magnitude.) This result might be used to explain why agents will not immediately adjust to shifts in z.

However, this conclusion is still not justified. To see why, consider a *completely arbitrary* response rule to shifts in z, denoted $a^?(z)$, and as before compute the net loss from adjusting according to $a^?$ instead of a^*. Calculations similar to (3) again imply that the first-order losses are zero. Consequently, zero first-order losses by itself gives no justification for singling out *any* particular type of response (such as not adjusting) as the assumed meaning of non-optimal behavior. On the other hand, delayed response to shifts in z can be derived with the reliability concepts developed earlier.

Delayed adjustment of imperfect decisions

The basic idea is that imperfectly reliable agents will not always adjust toward the new optimum level of contingent on z shifting. Let r equal the conditional probability of adjusting a in the right direction toward the new optimum when z shifts from z^0, and w equal the conditional probability of responding in the wrong direction away from the new optimum when z shifts from z^0. The reliability adjustment then equals the ratio $\rho = r/w$.

Note that for notational convenience the r, w, ρ variables are not superscripted with B as in the first three sections above. We are also not interested in any single selection of the a variable in response z, but rather in all those selections which adjust a from its initial value a^0 toward the new optimum $a^*(z)$; and similarly, all those selections of a that adjust it away from $a^*(z)$. To indicate this distinction, r, w, p are also not subscripted with the decision variable a as in the first three sections.

For an arbitrary response rule $a^?(z)$, let $a^w(z)$ represent the average or mean response to z conditional on adjusting in the wrong direction, and $a^r(z)$ represent the mean response to z conditional on adjusting in the right direction. The derivatives $da^w/dz = a^w_z$ and $da^r/dz = a^r_z$ then measure the mean rate of response to z conditional on adjusting in the wrong or right direction respectively.

Let ξ denote the length of time since z has shifted from z^0. The probability that time t is within ξ of t^0 is denoted $\pi(\xi) = p((t^0 \le t \le t^0 + \xi)$. The conditional response probabilities r and w may in general depend on ξ; because larger ξ provides more time to learn how best to react to shifts in z. They are thus written $r(\xi)$ and $w(\xi)$, so that $\rho(\xi) = r(\xi)/w(\xi)$.

Then let β represent the set of all *imperfect* response rules $a^?$, in that: (1) the probability of wrong responses $w(\xi)$ is positive (that is, $w(\xi) > 0$ for $\xi \ge 0$, so that $\rho(\xi) = r(\xi)/w(\xi) < \infty$ for $\xi \ge 0$); and (2) agents respond in the wrong direction at a rate that is at least some positive fraction of their responses toward the new optimum (that is, $-a^w_z/a^r_z \ge \lambda$ for some $\lambda > 0$). *Thus β contains any kind of imperfect response behavior that has a positive probability of wrong adjustments that are not arbitrarily small compared to correct adjustments.*

Next, introduce an explicit dynamic structure by writing z as a function of t, denoted $z = z(t)$, where $t = t^0 + \xi$. The net loss at time ξ beyond t^0 due to adjusting in the wrong direction from a^0 (where $a^0 = x^*(z^0)$ and $z^0 = z(t^0)$) is given by

$$l(\xi) = d[V(a^0, z(t^0 + \xi)) - V(a^w(z(t^0 + \xi)), z(t^2 + \xi))]/dt. \qquad (4a)$$

Similarly, the net gain at ξ beyond t^0 due to adjusting in the right direction from a^0 is given by

$$g(\xi) = d[V(a^r(z(t^0 + \xi)), z(t^0 + \xi)) - V(a^0, z(t^0 + \xi))]/dt. \qquad (4b)$$

Now consider whether agents will benefit from immediately adjusting according to some rule $a^? \in \beta$. The reliability condition of Theorem 1 can be used to answer this question. In the present dynamic context it amounts to determining whether the following inequality holds at the limit $\xi = 0$,

$$\frac{r(\xi)}{w(\xi)} = \rho(\xi) > T(\xi) = \frac{l(\xi)}{g(\xi)} \cdot \frac{1 - \pi(\xi)}{\pi(\xi)} \tag{5}$$

The 'first-order' results discussed just prior to this subsection imply that both $l(\xi)$ and $g(\xi)$ go to zero as ξ goes to zero. However, using l'Hospital's rule for the ratio of such limits and differentiating l and g with respect to ξ imply that the ratio of 'second-order' effects, $(\mathrm{d}l/\mathrm{d}\xi)/(\mathrm{d}g/\mathrm{d}\xi)$, converges to at least $- a_z^w/a_z^r$ (see the Appendix). Since $- a_z^w/a_z^r \geq \lambda > 0$ and $\pi(\xi) \to 0$ and $\xi \to 0$, then $T(\xi) \to \infty$ as $\xi \to 0$. This in turn implies inequality (5) cannot hold as ξ approaches zero so long as the adjustment reliability $\rho(\xi)$ is finite. We thus have the following result.

Theorem 2 (the necessity of delaying imperfect adjustment)

If $a^? \in \beta$ (where β is the set of adjustment rules satisfying conditions (1) and (2) above), when the adjustment-reliability condition (5) will be violated for all ξ below some positive time delay $\delta > 0$.

Theorem 2 implies that agents will not benefit from immediately responding according to any $a^? \in \beta$. More precisely, this means the probability of adjusting according to any $a^? \in \beta$ must drop to zero *before* ξ reaches zero in order to satisfy the adjustment reliability condition (5). Therefore, agents will in general never benefit from adjusting to new conditions immediately except at the limit where their reactions become perfectly reliable. Note also that Theorem 2 holds with no assumptions about the possibility of 'adjustment costs' (including information costs, transaction costs, etc.). It thus holds even in the limit where there are *zero* costs of adjusting faster to new conditions.

Application to diffusion models and evolutionary self-organization

I here briefly discuss how the preceding results relate to two analytical themes developed in other chapters on technical change and evolutionary competition (for example, Chapters 2 (Dosi and Orsenigo), 5 (Allen), 6 (Coricelli and Dosi), 24 (Silverberg), and 25 (Metcalfe)).

(1) Theorem 2 provides a theoretical underpinning for a key part of Metcalfe's model on diffusion. In particular, he introduces the parameters d and f as diffusion coefficients that reflect the rapidity with which users learn new technologies, or users' willingness to switch to new technologies or commodities. The diffusion parameters d and f are not themselves modeled, being instead exogenous to the model. Yet the resulting dynamic properties (especially tendencies toward inertially slowed diffusion) are largely driven by assumed variations in d and f. Theorem 2 explains why d and f are finite without having to assume *ad hoc* 'adjustment costs'. As noted above, imperfect decisions have intrinsically inertial dynamics even with zero costs of physically responding faster, or zero search costs of observing more information.

We can also further analyze when dynamic response errors are likely to increase or decrease, and thereby derive when the d and f coefficients will rise or fall (rather than having to assume exogenous shifts in order to explain different patterns of technological diffusion).

(2) Next consider the 'self-organization' models discussed by Silverberg in Chapter 24 (see also Dosi, Orsenigo and Silverberg, 1986; Silverberg, 1985). These models specify an explicit evolutionary process of competition between firms (that have the opportunity of enhancing their relative competitiveness by sooner or later, or rapidly or slowly adopting new technologies). In many cases there is no determinant 'optimal' dynamic equilibrium trajectory. Still, by using computer simulations it is clear that firms can 'mistakenly' adopt a new technology either too slowly or too rapidly, as well as too soon or too late in fact to raise (instead of lower) their rate of growth in profitability or relative market share compared to other firms. Indeed, the simulations suggest that the appropriate adoption time and rate of a new technology are affected by an extremely complex set of dynamic interrelationships. Consequently, it may be difficult for individual firms always to determine appropriately when and how fast to adopt a new technology.

We can thus use reliability variables to measure the probability of adopting a new technology at the 'right time' and at the 'right speed' instead of mistakenly adopting at the 'wrong time' (either too soon or too late to enhance the dynamic trend in their relative market share) or the 'wrong speed' (either faster or slower than needed to enhance relative competitiveness). The analysis of Theorem 2 can then be extended along the lines of Heiner (1987c) to model the behavioral effects required in order to control the incidence of these dynamic errors in both timing and speed of adoption. Here again, a generic tendency toward inertial diffusion is implied. It can also be shown that if the diffusion dynamics has a minimal degree of non-linearity, then the only way dynamic adjustment errors can be significantly reduced is for agents to slow their rate of adjustment so as to induce relatively more stable dynamic paths (in market share and profitability between firms) than would otherwise occur (see Heiner, 1987d).

Delayed revision of imperfect expectations

Up to now the variable a has been understood as a decision adjusted in response to a parameter from the vector z. However, the preceding analysis is consistent with other interpretations. For example, the variable a might not only refer to 'outward' behavior, but also to 'inward' subjective beliefs about probability or expectation variables. In a production context, moreover, expectations of future investment and technical conditions are important determinants of a firm's current plans either to maintain or alter its existing technology. Consequently, a tendency to delay forming new expectations could be a major additional factor causing firms to delay the introduction of new technology.

Let us consider a simplified illustration of the latter involving imperfect expectations. Suppose agents seek to maximize a quadratic utility function, $-\alpha(a-s)^2$, where $a-s$ is the difference between action a and a state variable s. However, they can only observe a noisy signal x which is normally distributed with mean s and variance σ^2. The state s also randomly varies according to a normal distribution with mean $\hat{s}$ and variance δ^2.

In this problem, maximizing expected (quadratic) utility requires the action a to be set equal to the agent's estimate of s, denoted e. The usual assumption is to assume expectations are perfect (i.e. 'rational expectations') in that e equals the optimal posterior Bayesian estimate of s, as given by $e^*(z) = (\delta^2 \hat{y} + \sigma^2 x)/(\delta^2 + \sigma^2)$; where $z = (s, x, \delta^2, \sigma^2)$. Suppose agents do set a equal to e (so that $a = e$ for each given subjective estimate e), but their expectations are not necessarily optimally related to z. Instead, their expectation of s is formed according to $e^?(z)$. where the question mark refers to an unspecified imperfection in adjusting expectations to shifts in the z variables (analogous to $a^?$ in the preceding section).

Mistaken expectations might arise because agents cannot perfectly detect shifts in the underlying $\hat{s}$, δ^2, σ^2 parameters (so that their beliefs about these parameters are not perfectly accurate), or because they are unable to combine them with the signal x according to Bayes' Rule. Whatever the reason for error, suppose $e^?(z)$ is imperfect in a similar manner to $a^?(z)$ discussed above. That is, there is a positive probability of adjusting e in the wrong direction (away from an initially optimal value $e^0 = e^*(z^0)$) at a rate that is not arbitrarily small compared to adjustments in the right direction. Let E be the set of all such imperfect expectation rules.

The assumptions (about quadratic utility, $\alpha(a-s)^2$; normally distributed s and x; and actions set equal to expected s, $a = e^?$) imply agents imperfectly maximize the following expected utility function (see Boyd and Richerson, 1986),

$$V(e(z), z) = -\alpha\left[\left(e^?(z) - \frac{\sigma^2 \hat{s} - \delta^2 x^2}{\sigma^2 + \delta^2}\right) + \delta^2\right]; \qquad (8)$$

where $z = (\hat{s}, x, \delta^2, \sigma^2)$ and $e^? \in E$.

We can then use Theorem 2 to imply that agents will always benefit from delaying adjustment (according to any expectation $e^? \in E$) for some positive ξ of time after shifts in the z variables. Thus, unless agents are perfectly reliable at forming expectations, they will never benefit from adjusting them immediately to new messages x, nor to shifts in either information parameters such as σ^2 or state parameters such as $\hat{s}$ and δ^2. Standard-decision theory avoids these results by postulating perfect or 'rational' expectations, so that $e = e^*(z)$ by hypothesis. Once this postulate is relaxed, a wider range of behavioral possibilities (such as a generic tendency to delay adjustment of subjective beliefs) opens up for analysis.[4]

Conclusion

I have argued that production methods within firms and technical change over time both systematically depend on how agents use information imperfectly, separate from whether their information is costly and imperfect. In order to do so, certain reliability principles were developed to analyze the effects of decision errors. These involved the probability of failing to select actions when they are superior to others based on observed information, and the probability of still selecting actions when they are inferior to others based on observed information. Depending on the relative incidence of these errors, agents may or may not benefit from trying to improve on any given behavior pattern by selectively deviating from it.

Imperfectly reliable agents will in general benefit from 'routinized' behavior governed by rules and procedures that prevent flexible response to all conditions encountered by a firm. Such behavioral routines are thereby adapted only to relatively likely and recurrent features of a firm's production environment. Nevertheless, the possibility of decision errors makes behavioral routines stable in an evolutionary setting despite the existence of numerous circumstances (that arise with positive probability) for which superior results can be achieved.

The analysis, however, does not guarantee that only appropriately structured routines will evolve; only that such routines will have a higher probability of surviving in competition with other firms. In order to complete the analysis one must explicitly model how raising or lowering the probability of survival (or altering relative profitability rates) will affect the likelihood of particular types of behavior 'filtering' through a long-run evolutionary process. That is, the principles of imperfect choice imply an intrinsic need for constructing evolutionary models.

Finally, imperfect decisions in the context of dynamic adjustment or adoption of new technologies were discussed. Imperfect agents will in general not benefit from trying immediately to adjust their prior production decisions to changing conditions or novel technology, even if there are little or no adjustment costs of doing so. Consequently, even with zero adjustment costs, the diffusion of new technology across firms will tend to be inertially delayed over time.

Taken together these implications provide a theoretical underpinning for the broader issue of 'evolutionary-modeling' in economics. First, instead of a uniform tendency toward the 'optimal solution' within a given environment, imperfect agents will in general benefit from displaying a (potentially wide) diversity of routinized behavior patterns. Second, such diverse yet routinized patterns will inertially adjust, thereby providing more time for selection processes to weed out relatively inferior behavior patterns. We thus have an explanation for the existence of micro-diversity within a larger system, and of behavioral inertia that gives selection processes time to work. Both of these are recognized as key features in understanding evolutionary systems. Finally, recall from Peter Allen's discussion (Chapter 5) that a system's resilience to external change often critically depends on the existence of micro-diversity within its internal structure combined with inertial features that preserve any existing micro-diversity until external conditions change.

Appendix

Proofs for Theorems 1 and 2 are here presented.

Let V_1, V_2, V_3, V_4 equal respectively $V(B(x), X_a^B)$, $V(B(x), X - X_a^B)$, $V(\{a\}, X_a^B)$, $V(\{a\}, X - X_a^B)$. The definitions of l_a^B, g_a^B then imply $l_a^B = V_2 - V_4$ and $g_a^B = V_3 - V_1$. In the special case of standard expected utility function, the linearity properties of V can be used to expand V^B and V_a^B as follows:

$$V_a^B = \pi_a^B [r_a^B V_3 + (1 - r_a^B) V_1] + (1 - \pi_a^B)[w_a^B V_4 + (1 - w_a^B) V_2]$$

$$V_a^B = \pi_a^B V_1 + (1 - \pi_a^B) V_2.$$

Then subtract these expressions and rearrange terms (also recalling the above definitions for g_a^B, l_a^B) to yield

$$V_a^B - V^B = \pi_a^B r_a^B g_a^B - (1 - \pi_a^B) w_a^B l_a^B \qquad (A1)$$

Hence, (A1) implies $V_a^B > V^B$ if and only if $r_a^B / w_a^B > l_a^B / g_a^B \cdot (1 - \pi_a^B) / \pi_a^B$, which is the desired result.

Heiner (1984) proves this result also holds for the recent 'non-expected' utility theories of Machina, Chew, Fishburn and others. The analysis remains valid with full generality of the probability measures which interrelate the sets A, X and S, as well as no restrictions on the size and topological structure of A, X and S.

It remains to prove Theorem 2 about delaying imperfect response to changing conditions. Recall the two properties that define the set of imperfect adjustment rules $a^? \in \beta$. They are stated in weaker versions than discussed in the main text, so as to hold only as ξ approaches zero. That is, $w(\xi)$ and $a_z^w(\xi)$, $a_z^r(\xi)$ are continuous functions for $\xi \geq 0$; where, (1) $w(0) > 0$, and (2) $-a_z^w(0)/a_z^r(0) \geq \lambda$ for some $\lambda > 0$.

Property (1) implies $\rho(\xi) = r(\xi)/w(\xi)$ becomes bounded as ξ approaches zero. Thus, condition (5) of the main text will be violated if $T(\xi)$ becomes *unbounded* as $\xi \to 0$. To show this, note that since $\pi(\xi) = p(t^0 \leq t \leq t^0 + \xi) \to 0$ as $\xi \to 0$, then $(1 - \pi(\xi))/\pi(\xi) \to \infty$ as $\xi \to 0$. Thus, $T(\xi) = l(\xi)/g(\xi) \cdot (1 - \pi(\xi))/\pi(\xi)$ is guaranteed if $l(\xi)/g(\xi)$ does not shrink to zero as $\xi \to 0$.

Before showing the latter, note that we have not ruled out the possibility of responding too rapidly toward the new optimum, so that $\partial a'/\partial z$ exceeds $\partial a^*/\partial z$. If the former derivative is sufficiently larger than the latter derivative, then $g(\xi)$ may become negative before ξ converges to zero. On the other hand, the loss $l(\xi)$ always remains positive from responses in the wrong direction for all $\xi > 0$ so that $l(\xi)/g(\xi) < 0$ if $g(\xi) < 0$.

This case represents an application of equation (A1) above where the corresponding l and g terms are positive and negative respectively, thereby guaranteeing that the net benefit from responding rather than delaying is negative regardless of how close $r(\xi)$ and $w(\xi)$ are to 1 and 0 respectively. This means sufficient *over*-reacting in the right direction can be detrimental even if agents never respond in the wrong direction (i.e. even if $w(\xi) = 0$). Thus a necessary condition to benefit from immediate reacting to shifts in z is that $l(\xi)/g(\xi)$ remain non-negative as $\xi \to 0$ (that is, $l(0)/g(0) < 0$ implies agents will not benefit from responding immediately according to $a^? \in \beta$). If this condition holds then, as noted above, we must still show that $l(0)/g(0)$ is strictly positive to guarantee that $T(0) = \infty$.

To answer these questions, begin by computing the formulas for (4a) and (4b) of the main text to obtain,

$$l(\xi) = \left\{ \frac{\partial V(a^0, z(t^0 + \xi))}{\partial z} - \frac{\partial V(a^w(z(t^0 + \xi)), z(t^0 + \xi))}{\partial a} \right.$$

$$\times \frac{\partial a^w(z(t^0 + \xi))}{\partial z} - \left. \frac{\partial V(a^w(z(t^0 + \xi)), z(t^0 + \xi))}{\partial z} \right\}$$

$$\times \frac{dz(t^0 + \xi)}{dt} \tag{A2}$$

$$g(\xi) = \left\{ \frac{\partial V(a^r(z(t^0 + \xi)), z(t^0 + \xi))}{\partial a} \cdot \frac{\partial a^r(z(t^0 + \xi))}{\partial z} \right.$$

$$+ \left. \frac{\partial V(a^r(z(t^0 + \xi)), z(t^0 + \xi))}{\partial z} - \frac{\partial V(a^0, z(t^0 + \xi))}{\partial z} \right\}$$

$$\times \frac{dz(t^0 + \xi)}{dt}. \tag{A3}$$

The common term $dz(t^0 + \xi)/dt$ can be cancelled from (A2) and (A3), so that $l(\xi)/g(\xi)$ equals the ratio of { }-bracketed terms, denoted $\bar{l}(\xi)$ and $\bar{g}(\xi)$ respectively. The discussion of the main text prior to the section on 'Inertially adjusting imperfect decisions and expectations' implies both $\bar{l}(\xi)$ and $\bar{g}(\xi)$ go to zero with ξ. Thus, differentiate these with respect to ξ to get the 'second-order' net losses and gains from reacting away or toward the new optimum,

$$
\frac{d\bar{l}(\xi)}{dt} = \left\{ \frac{\partial^2 V(a^0, z(t^0 + \xi))}{\partial z^2} - \frac{\partial^2 V(a^w(z(t^0 + \xi)), z(t^0 + \xi))}{\partial z^2} \right.
$$

$$
- \frac{\partial V(a^w(z(t^0 + \xi)), z(t^0 + \xi))}{\partial a} \cdot \frac{\partial^2 a^w(z(t^0 + \xi))}{\partial z^2}
$$

$$
- \frac{\partial a^w(z(t^0 + \xi))}{\partial z} \left[\frac{\partial^2 V(a^w(z(t^0 + \xi)), z(t^0 + \xi))}{\partial a^2} \right.
$$

$$
\left. \left. \times \frac{\partial a^w(z(t^0 + \xi))}{\partial z} + 2 \frac{\partial^2 V(a^w(z(t^0 + \xi)), z(t^0 + \xi))}{\partial a \, \partial z} \right] \right\}
$$

$$
\times \frac{dz(t^0 + \xi)}{dt} \tag{A4}
$$

$$
\frac{d\bar{g}(\xi)}{dt} = \left\{ \frac{\partial^2 V(a^r(z(t^0 + \xi)), z(t^0 + \xi))}{\partial z^2} - \frac{\partial^2 V(a^0, z(t^0 + \xi))}{\partial z^2} \right.
$$

$$
+ \frac{\partial V(a^r(z(t^0 + \xi)), z(t^0 + \xi))}{\partial a} \cdot \frac{\partial^2 a_z^r(t^0 + \xi)}{\partial z^2}
$$

$$
+ \frac{\partial a^r(z(t^0 + \xi))}{\partial z} \left[\frac{\partial^2 V(a^r(z(t^0 + \xi)), z(t^0 + \xi))}{\partial a^2} \right.
$$

$$
\left. \left. \times \frac{\partial a^r(z(t^0 + \xi))}{\partial z} + 2 \frac{\partial^2 V(a^r(z(t^0 + \xi)), z(t^0 + \xi))}{\partial a \, \partial z} \right] \right\}
$$

$$
\times \frac{dz(t^0 + \xi)}{dt}. \tag{A5}
$$

As before, the common multiplicative term $dz(t^0 + \xi)/dt$ can be cancelled from both (A4) and (A5). Recall also that responses in both the right and wrong directions begin from a^0, so that $a^r(z^0) = a^0 = a^w(z^0)$ for $z^0 = z(t^0)$. This implies the difference between the first two terms in the curly brackets of (A4) and (A5) both go to zero. It also implies $\partial V(a^0, z^0)/\partial a = 0$ so that the third term in both (A4) and (A5) goes to zero. Thus, the ratio of (A4) to (A5) reduces to the following expression at $\xi = 0$,

$$\frac{d\bar{l}(0)/dt}{d\bar{g}(0)/dt} = \frac{-\dfrac{\partial a^{w}(z^{0})}{\partial z}\left[\dfrac{\partial^{2} V(a^{0}, z^{0})}{\partial a^{2}} \cdot \dfrac{\partial a^{w}(z^{0})}{\partial z} + 2\dfrac{\partial^{2} V(a^{0}, z^{0})}{\partial a\, \partial z}\right]}{\dfrac{\partial a^{r}(z^{0})}{\partial z}\left[\dfrac{\partial^{2} V(a^{0}, z^{0})}{\partial a^{2}} \cdot \dfrac{\partial a^{r}(z^{0})}{\partial z} + 2\dfrac{\partial^{2} V(a^{0}, z^{0})}{\partial a\, \partial z}\right]}.$$
(A6)

To simplify the remaining calculations, let $u = \partial a^{w}(z^{0})/\partial z$, $v = \partial a^{r}(z^{0})/\partial z$, $A = \partial^{2} V(a^{0}, z^{0})/\partial a^{2}$, $B = \partial^{2} V(a^{0}, z^{0})/\partial a\, \partial z$. Expression (A6) then reduces to

$$\frac{d\bar{l}(0)/dt}{d\bar{g}(0)/dt} = \frac{-u(Au + 2B)}{v(Av + 2B)}.$$
(A6′)

Let $k = -u/v$, and recall that assumption (1) above implies $-u/v \geq \lambda$ for some $\lambda > 0$, so that $k > 0$ must hold. Then substitute $-kv = u$ in place of u in (A6′),

$$\frac{-(-kv)(-Akv + 2B)}{v(Av + 2B)} = k \cdot \frac{2B - kAv}{2B + Av}.$$
(A7)

At this point recall that the second-order conditions for maximizing $V(a, z)$ at $z = z^{0}$ imply $A < 0$, and in addition the optimum response derivative $v^{*} = \partial a^{*}(z^{0})/\partial z = -B/A$. That latter in turn implies $v^{*}B \geq 0$ (i.e., u^{*} and B must have the same sign). Since $\partial a^{r}(z^{0})/\partial z$ responds in the same direction as $\partial a^{*}(z^{0})\partial z$, then $vB > 0$ also holds (so v and B have the *same* sign).

Now consider two cases of $B \geq 0$ and $B < 0$. If $B \geq 0$ then $v \geq 0$, which in turn implies the *numerator* of (A7) is positive. If in addition $v > -2B/A$, then the *denominator* of (A7) is negative. Since $k > 0$, the latter implies (A7) is negative, which violates the necessary condition discussed prior to (A2) and (A3) above. On the other hand, if $v \leq -2B/A$, then the denominator of (A7) is nonnegative, so that (A7) is positive. This in turn implies $l(0)/g(0) > 0$ by l'Hospital's rule (which then implies $T(0) = \infty > \rho(0) = r(0)/w(0)$ as discussed prior to (A2) and (A3)).

The above results imply that (A7) ranges between $k > 0$ and $+\infty$ for $0 \leq v \leq -2B/A$ and between $-\infty$ and $-k^{2} < 0$ for $v > -2B/A$.

Finally, consider the last case of $B < 0$, which implies that $v < 0$ since v and B have the same sign. Similar argument to the case of $B \geq 0$ implies (A7) ranges between $k > 0$ and $+\infty$ for $-2B/A \leq v < 0$ and from $-\infty$ to $-k^{2} < 0$ for $v < -2B/A$.

Thus, regardless of the sign of B, either: (A7) is strictly negative (thus violating the necessary condition discussed prior to (A2) and (A3)); or (A7) is strictly positive (thus guaranteeing $T(0) = \infty$, so that $\rho(0) > T(0)$ is also violated). Hence, in all cases agents cannot benefit from responding according to any $a^{?} \in \beta$ for ξ sufficiently close to zero.

Notes

1. For example, Arrow's concluding remarks (1986, p. S397) include the following: 'The main implication of this extensive examination of the use of the rationality concept in economic analysis is the extremely severe strain on information-gathering and computing abilities…many of the customary defenses that economists used to argue…break down as soon as market power and incompleteness of markets are recognized…the combination of rationality, incomplete markets, and equilibrium in many cases leads to very weak conclusions, in the sense that there are whole continua of equilibria.'

2. For example, in the special case where A, S, X are finite sets, then for each $(a^0, s^0) \in A' \times S'$, we have

$$P_{A' \times S'}(a^0, s^0) = \sum_X \frac{p(a^0|x)p(x|s^0)p(s^0)}{p(A', S')};$$

where

$$p(A', S') = \sum_{A'} \sum_X \sum_{S'} p(a|x)p(x|s)p(s).$$

Similarly, for each $(a^0, s^0) \in A' \times S$, we have

$$P_{A' \times X'}(a^0, s^0) = \sum_{X'} \frac{p(a^0|x)p(x|s^0)p(s^0)}{p(A', X')};$$

where

$$p(A', X') = \sum_{A'} \sum_{X'} \sum_S p(a|x)p(x|s)p(s).$$

See Heiner (1984) for a precise discussion of the above when $p \in P$ are defined over algebras of both countable and noncountable sets A, S, X.

3. Note that it is not necessary that a fully optimal decision exist for each message $x \in X$. Indeed, no optimal strategy in general exists for certain dynamic evolutionary environments (as noted in Allen's and Silverberg's Chapters 5 and 24). The above concepts instead only require a ranking of whether it is preferred or not to deviate from a given behavior pattern $B(x)$ toward particular actions $a \notin B(x)$. We can thus apply the analysis to situations (such as competition between firms in dynamic game theory models) where optimality notions may not be fully determinant. This is briefly discussed in the section concerning inertial adjustment within dynamic evolutionary models.

4. This implication provides a theoretical rationale for distributed lag models of expectation adjustment often referred to as 'adaptive expectations' (see, for example, Cagan, 1956; Muth, 1960; Cooley and Prescott, 1973). Adaptive expectations have been criticized as seemingly 'ad hoc' or 'irrational' in not optimally adjusting to changes in the stochastic properties of an agent's environment (in favor of more recent 'rational expectations' models; see Lucas, 1981; Sargent, 1979). However, once the behavioral effects of imperfect expectations are explicitly modeled (instead of ruled out by hypothe-

sis), a generic tendency to delay expectation adjustment becomes systematically relevant. The opposite tendency toward immediately adjusting expectations applies only near the limit where agents become perfectly reliable at doing so.

The above analysis also accords with recent results by Smith, Suchanek and Williams (1986) concerning the behavior of prices and expectation formation in experimental spot asset markets. The rational expectations hypothesis introduced by Muth (REM) predicts well only after a sequence market periods where asset prices eventually converge to equilibrium patterns. However, the dynamic path leading to such convergence displays systematic adaptive expectation features, as indicated in the concluding sentence of their paper (1986, p. 36), '...the general conclusion [is] that the REM model of asset pricing is supported only as an *equilibrium concept* underlying an adaptive capital gains adjustment process' [emphasis original].

Finally, note that Lucas (1986) has recently suggested that adaptively adjusting expectations may be the essential factor in determining which rational expectation equilibria are dynamically stable.

References

Akerlof, G. A. and Yellen, J. L. (1985a), 'Can small deviations from rationality make significant differences to economic equilibria?' *American Economic Review*, vol. 75, September, pp. 708–20.

—— (1985b), 'A near rational model of the business cycle, with wage and price inertia', *Quarterly Journal of Economics*, C, pp. 823–38.

Arrow, Kenneth (1986), 'Rationality of self and others in an economic system', *Journal of Business*, vol. 59, no. 4, October.

Boyd, Robert and Richerson, Peter J. (1986), 'Rationality and tradition', *American Economic Review*.

Cagan, P. (1956), 'The monetary dynamics of hyperinflation', (pp. 23–117) in M. Friedman (ed.), *Studies in the Quantity Theory of Money*, Chicago, University of Chicago Press.

Cooley, Thomas F. and Prescott, Edward C. (1973), 'An adaptive regression model', *International Economic Review*, June, pp. 364–71.

Cyert, Richard and March, James G. (1959), 'A behavioral theory of organizational objectives', in D. Haire (ed.), *Modern Organization Theory*, New York, Wiley.

Dosi, Giovanni, Orsenigo, Luigi and Silverberg, Gerald (1986), 'Innovation, diversity and diffusion: a self-organization model', International Conference of Innovation Diffusion, Venice, Italy, March 1986.

Hayek, Friedrik (1945), 'The use of knowledge in society', *American Economic Review*, vol. 35, pp. 519–30.

Heiner, Ronald A. (1983), 'The origin of predictable behavior', *American Economic Review*, vol. 73, September.

—— (1984), 'On reinterpreting the foundations of risk and utility theory', The Institute for Advanced Study, August.

—— 1985a), 'Uncertainty, signal detection, and modeling behavior', in R. Langlois (ed.), *Economics as a Process: Essays in the New Institutional Economics*, New York, Cambridge University Press.

—— (1985b), 'Origin of predictable behavior: further modeling and applications', *American Economic Review*, May.

—— (1985c), 'Rational expectations when agents imperfectly use information', *Journal of Post-Keynesian Economics*, Fall–Winter.

—— (1986), 'Uncertainty and rule-governed behavior: on the evolution of legal precedent and rules', *Journal of Legal Studies*, June.

—— (1988), 'Imperfect decisions and organizations: toward a theory of internal structure', *Journal of Economic Behavior and Organization*. February 1988.

—— (1987b), 'The necessity of imperfect decisions', *Journal of Economic Behavior and Organization*.

—— (1987c), 'The necessity of delaying economic adjustment', forthcoming, *Journal of Economic Behavior and Organization*.

—— (1987d). 'The origin of predictable dynamic behavior', forthcoming *Journal of Economic Behavior and Organization*.

Kaen, Fred and Rosenman, Robert (1986), 'Predictable behavior in financial markets: some evidence in support of Heiner's hypothesis', *American Economic Review*, March.

Lucas, Robert E. (1981), 'Econometric policy evaluation: a critique', in R. L. Lucas (ed.), *Studies in Business Cycle Theory*, Cambridge, Mass., MIT Press.

—— (1986), 'Adaptive behavior and economic theory', *Journal of Business*, vol. 59, no. 4, October.

Machina, Mark (1983), 'The economic theory of individual behaviour toward risk: theory, evidence, and new directions', Center for Organizational Efficiency, Stanford University, no. 433, October.

Muth, J. F. (1961), 'Rational expectations and the theory of price movements', *Econometrica*, vol. 29, pp. 315–35.

Nelson, Richard and Winter, Sidney (1982), *An Evolutionary Theory of Economic Change*, Cambridge, Mass., The Belknap Press of Harvard University Press.

Sargent, Thomas (1979), *Macroeconomic Theory*, New York, Academic Press, pp. 112–25, 265.

Silverberg, Gerald (1985), 'Technical progress, capital accumulation, and effective demand: a self-organization model', Proceedings of the Fifth International Conference on Mathematical Modeling, July 1985, University of California at Berkeley.

Simon, Herbert (1957), *Administrative Behavior*, 2nd edn., New York, Macmillan.

—— (1983), *Reason in Human Affairs*, Stanford, Stanford University Press.

Smith, Vernan, Suchanek, Gerry L. and Williams, Arlington W. (1986), 'Bubbles, crashes, and endogenous expectations in experimental spot asset markets', *Econometrica*, June 1988, forthcoming.

8 On the dynamics of aggregate macroequations: from simple microbehaviors to complex macrorelationships

Marco Lippi
Dipartimento di Economia Politica, Università di Modena, Modena

Introduction

Hyperrational, hypercompetent economic agents have been the heart of most of macroeconomics and macroeconometrics in the last two decades. The menu of alternatives out of which they are assumed to be able to pick up the best one has been enlarged from familiar finite-dimensional spaces to temporal paths going from the current period to the most remote future, namely from t to infinity, while the expected magnitudes needed to evaluate the objective functions usually turn out from optimal processing of all the available information about the past.

Thus, for instance, demand for labor at time t, n_t, will be set along with the whole path n_{t+j}, j running from 0 to infinity, the path $\{n_{t+j}\}$ depending on the expected values, from $t+1$ to infinity, of, say, wage and output. Then, by eliminating such expected magnitudes according to some theory of the agents' expectations, one will obtain an equation between observables. Analogous procedures are applied to consumption as a function of income, demand for capital as a function of capital price, price as a function of cost, and so on.

The dynamic shape of the equation obtained depends both on the shape of the objective function and on the hypothesis on agents' expectations. Rational expectations, together with intertemporal objective functions containing terms accounting for the distance between current and desired level of the dependent variable as well as some kind of adjustment cost, yield a rich variety of dynamic equations between observables. One gets usually difference equations, that is equations containing the dependent lagged variable in addition to lagged values of the independent ones. Such dynamic equations have been extensively and quite successfully employed to fit actual aggregated macroeconomic time series.

The microeconomic foundations of macroeconomics briefly summarized above have been criticized from many points of view. It has been observed that the uncertainty faced by economic agents operating in a capitalist economy cannot be adequately represented in terms of a probability distribution based on observed frequencies. Moreover, according to an important theoretical approach, to which this book is strictly linked, agents' behaviors are better described by non-optimal, slowly changing routines, rather than a continuous process of choice within broad menus. As Nelson and Winter referring to firm behavior have put it:

As a first approximation…firms may be expected to behave in the future according to the routines they have employed in the past…it is quite inappropriate to conceive of firm behavior in terms of deliberate choice from a broad menu of alternatives that some external observer considers to be 'available' alternatives. The menu is not broad but narrow and idiosyncratic….[1]

In the present chapter we shall not deal directly with the behavioral issue. The problem we shall deal with is the correspondence between microbehaviors and observed relations linking macroeconomic time series. The question is whether we must consider the dynamic complexity of macroequations as evidence that the underlying microbehaviors are complex as well, or we can think that aggregate complexity can derive also, *by aggregation*, from dynamically simple microbehaviors. If the second alternative is shown to be possible, the way is open to challenge neo-classical macroeconomics by suggesting explanations of the available empirical evidence based on the above mentioned routinized microbehaviors.

Of course such an attempt can be undertaken only if we abandon a restrictive assumption upon which most of macroeconomics relies, namely the representative agent. Typically, macroeconomic models accept, as an 'explanation', or a 'microeconomic foundation' for a relationship among aggregate variables the behavior of a *single* maximizing agent, provided the equation derived from the maximization reproduces the main features of the given macroequation. We shall see that a significant difference between micro and macrodynamics emerges whenever one departs from the representative agent assumption with respect to two different aspects: first, there must be differences in the agents' behaviors; second, it is necessary that the independent variables corresponding to different agents do not have the same dynamic behavior, i.e. that different agents face different independent variables.

As for the first aspect — the existence of differences between agents' behaviors — even casual empiricism suggests this is the norm whenever the aggregates are so large as to include, for instance, different industries or different firms within one industry. However, also in the case where more homogeneous agents are aggregated, if one just allows for differences in tastes, available techniques, information-processing competence, on the one hand, and for changing environment, on the other hand, it will be easy to accept different behaviors. Indeed, even the constancy of such differences can be assumed only as a working hypothesis.

As for the second aspect — different agents face different independent variables — an important consequence of the representative agent must be pointed out. The representative agent who decides, say, aggregate consumption y_t, takes as independent variable the *aggregate* income x_t. This entails that the x_t variable, just because it is a result of aggregation over large numbers of agents and goods, does possess a dynamic regularity that could not be attributed to the variables actually faced by individual agents. Individual incomes, as well as individual prices, as well as many individual variables, have very often the aspect of fairly ugly jump processes, rather than the pleasant smoothness of the ARIMA models that have been successfully employed to approximate the dynamic behavior of macro-economic aggregates.

Now, it must be pointed out that the representation we choose for the individual independent variables does influence the way we theorize about individual behaviors. It is apparent that dynamically regular x_t's variables contribute to making it plausible rational expectations and intertemporal optimization extended to the remote future; while dynamically irregular x_t's may give support to simple routinized behaviors.

In conclusion, assuming the representative agent has two implications: first, behavior is uniform across agents; second, the dynamic features of aggregate variables are illicitly transferred to individual variables. Obviously, non-regular, non-uniform across agents, individual indepen-dent variables, upon which the agents base their decisions, are highly plausible features of the economic environments discussed in this book, characterized by various forms of technological and institutional change. However, we shall show, differences between micro and macroequations, emerge even if we simply assume that the x_t's are regular but different across agents while the microbehaviors are constant but different.[2] These assumptions, in spite of the little change they mean if compared with the representative agent practice, have proved useful to get interesting results. The dismissal of regularity and constancy of behaviors should lead to an even deeper understanding of the micro–macro issue.

Lastly, a reference to Ronald Heiner's work on routinized behavior (Heiner, 1983, and chapter 7 in the present volume) is necessary. Heiner is trying to show that

observed regularities of behavior can be fruitfully understood as 'behavioral' rules that arise because of uncertainty in distinguishing preferred from less preferred behavior. Such uncertainty requires behavior to be governed by mechanisms that restrict the flexibility to choose potential actions, or which produce a selective alertness to information that might prompt particular actions to be chosen. These mechanisms simplify behavior to less complex patterns, which are easier for an observer to recognize and predict. [Heiner, 1983, p. 561].

Now, what we are trying to show is that, as long as observations refer to the aggregates of macroeconomics, observed regularities can be understood by starting with microbehaviors that are much simpler than the observed regularities themselves. In particular, as we shall see, a dynamic regular relation between aggregated data can be consistent with static behaviors of the underlying agents.

As the content of the chapter is rather technical, an overview of prob-lems and results will be helpful both for the reader willing to come to grips with the technicalities and for the reader willing to have only a broad understanding of the results.

Let us consider the following example of a macroeconomic relationship, where y_t and x_t are assumed to be aggregate variables,

$$y_t - \alpha y_{t-1} = ax_t + bx_{t-1} + u_t, \tag{1}$$

in which u_t is a white noise. As stated above, the most usual explanation of equation (1) consists of the description of a single, intertemporally optimizing, representative agent: from the maximization of his objective function, whose arguments are current and expected values of specified variables, after having eliminated the expected variables on the basis of a theory of expectations, an equation reproducing the main dynamic features of (1) must result.[3]

Thus for equation (1) an explanation will be necessary for the presence of the lagged variable y_{t-1}. If $0 < \alpha < 1$, as usual, such an inertial feature is often attributed to an adjustment cost present in the objective function preventing the agent from immediately fixing the variable y_t at its desired level.

Our main analytical point consists in showing that if the representative agent is abandoned, that is if the aggregate nature of y_t and x_t is seriously taken into consideration, then the dynamic form of the relationship linking y_t and x_t can be dramatically different from the form of the corresponding microequations, the former being normally much more complicated. In particular, an equation like (1) can be explained by much simpler microbehaviors. For instance, assume that two agents follow this routine:

$$y_{it} = \Pi_i x_{it},$$

which is a static rule not containing any stochastic term. Assume further that the independent microvariables are generated by the following autoregressive processes:

$$x_{it} - \alpha_i x_{it-1} = v_{it}, \quad 0 < \alpha_i < 1,$$

where the v_{it} are orthogonal white-noise processes.[4] If $\Pi_1 \neq \Pi_2$, $\alpha_1 \neq \alpha_2$ then the relationship linking the aggregates $y_t = y_{1t} + y_{2t}$ and $x_t = x_{1t} + x_{2t}$ has the form (1).

The macroequations we have considered above, demand for labor, consumption as a function of income, price–cost, demand for capital, provide good examples of the aggregation problem we wish to deal with. In these instances: (a) both sides of the equation must be aggregated; (b) in the microequations linking the dependent microvariables to the independent ones different microparameters correspond, in general, to different agents; (c) moreover, the independent microvariables corresponding to different agents are generated by different stochastic processes. We shall show that when (a), (b), (c) occur, as in the case of the above two-agent example, the dynamics of the independent microvariables yields a complication of the macroequation dynamics. In particular, even though the microequations are simple routines such as

$$y_{it} = \Pi_i x_{it} + u_{it}, \quad y_{it} = \Pi_i x_{it-k_i} + u_{it}, \quad y_{it} = \Pi_i \sum_{s=0}^{m_i} x_{it-s} + u_{it},$$

where u_{it} is white-noise, the aggregate equation has the shape:

$$a(L) y_t = b(L) x_t + c(L) u_t,$$

where u_t is a white-noise process and, if we leave aside special negligible cases:

(1) the polynomials $a(L)$, $b(L)$, $c(L)$ are non-trivial, that is they are of positive degree;
(2) the shape of the aggregate equation is quite general: it is neither a rational distributed-lag model with a white-noise disturbance, that is $a(L) \neq c(L)$; nor a finite distributed-lag model with a ARMA disturbance, that is $a(L)$ is not a factor of $b(L)$;
(3) even though the explanatory microvariables are not Granger-caused by the dependent microvariables, the explanatory macrovariable is Granger-caused by the dependent macrovariable;
(4) the macroparameters depend not only on the parameters of the micro-equations but also on the parameters of the independent micro-processes; a phenomenon usually explained by rational expectations in recent literature may therefore be due to aggregation as well.

A short restatement of our central thesis will perhaps avoid possible misunderstandings. Within all of the models analyzed below the independent microvariables are generated by dynamic processes: the latter will be the main source of the dynamics of the macroequations. With the sole exceptions of the multiplier-accelerator model of Section 3, the question of the origin of the dynamics of the independent microvariables will not be explicitly examined in this paper: our main aim here is to show that aggregation causes a 'propagation' of the dynamics—which is *assumed* to affect the independent microvariables—to macrorelationships whose micro background is not necessarily dynamic, or is dynamic in a much simpler form. Thus we are not, obviously, denying the existence of dynamic behaviors in the economic system. We deny that the dynamics of an equation linking aggregate variables necessarily and adequately reflects the behavior of the agents underlying those variables.

The chapter is subdivided into the following sections. In Section 1 we shall set out the analytic problem. After a brief account of the simple case in which all agents face the same independent variable, we shall deal with the general case in which to different agents there correspond different, though co-stationary, independent variables. A general solution to the problem of determining the aggregate equation is given. In Section 2 we work out a computable case, namely that where there are only two different agents. In this case the macroparameters can be shown to be simple explicit functions of the microparameters. The above results, (1) to (4), are proved to hold. In Section 3 we analyze two simple prototypes: a price–cost equation, a consumption–income equation in the context of a multiplier-accelerator model. In Section 4 we outline the way the results obtained in Section 2 for the two-agent model can be generalized to the many-agent case. We also show that the dynamic shape of the aggregate equation, though complex in general, is quite unpredictable, not only in the case where the microequations are static but also when the microequations are dynamic. Lastly we briefly review the economeric literature on aggregation and dynamics. We shall argue that even in the few cases in which the problem is mentioned, the lack of analysis leads to understate the dynamics complications arising from aggregation.[5]

1. The problem in general

1.1 The same independent variable for all agents

Throughout Section 1 we shall refer to a consumption–income relationship. This is merely a convenient example in order to familiarize the reader with the problem.

We shall assume that consumers' behavior follows the microequations:

$$a_i(L)y_{it} = b_i(L)x_{it} + u_{it}, \tag{2}$$

where y_{it} and x_{it} are, respectively, consumption and income of the i-th agent, $a_i(L)$ and $b_i(L)$ are polynomials in the lag operator L, u_{it} is a white-noise orthogonal to x_{jt-k} and y_{jt-h}, for any j, k and $h > 0$; moreover, u_{it} and u_{jt} are orthogonal processes for $i \neq j$; lastly $a_i(0) = 1$.

Furthermore we assume that only the aggregate variables:

$$y_t = \sum x_{it}, \quad x_t = \sum x_{it},$$

are available. Under rather general assumptions on the x_{it} processes, partly specified below, it is possible to show that microequations (2) determine completely the *empirical macroequation*[6] or, as we shall also say, the *aggregate equation* linking y_t and x_t. Otherwise stated, there exist (finite) polynomials $a(L)$, $b(L)$, $c(L)$ and a white-noise u_t such that:

$$a(L)y_t = b(L)x_t + c(L)u_t, \tag{3}$$

where $a(0) = c(0) = 1$, u_t is orthogonal to y_{t-k} and x_{t-h}, $k > 0$, $h \geq 0$, $c(L)$ has no roots of modulus smaller than one. Moreover, $a(L)$, $b(L)$, $c(L)$ and u_t are unique.[7]

Equation (3) may be thought of as the factual counterpart for an investigator starting with a theory referred to a representative agent, deriving from that theory a dynamic relationship between y_t and x_t, and trying to specify, estimate and interpret such a relationship. As we shall see, aggregation tends to dynamize every relationship. Therefore, given the acceptance of the representative agent practice, the explanation of macro-equations will be strongly biased in favour of dynamic behaviors on the part of agents.

Before starting with the formal analysis we must point out that in the above definition of the empirical macroequation we implicitly supposed that, on the basis of the theory he is relying on, the investigator assumes as plausible that the relationship between y_t and x_t can be *identified* by the orthogonality of u_t to x_t (in addition to the usual orthogonality of u_t to the past of x_t and y_t; see the conditions below equation (3)). This is a simplifying hypothesis on the investigator's assumptions. We shall maintain it throughout this work, with the exception of the model in Section 3.2.

Let us start with the simplest case: we assume that there is no difference in the dynamic behaviors of the x_{it} variables: $x_{it} = r_i x_t$, $\Sigma r_i = 1$, i.e. individual incomes are constant fractions of national income. When such an assumption holds we can immediately write:

$$y_t = \left(\sum r_i \frac{b_i(L)}{a_i(L)} \right) x_t + \sum \frac{u_{it}}{a_i(L)}. \tag{4}$$

While no difficulty arises with y_t and x_t, obtaining the macroequation in the form (3) requires some effort owing to the second sum in (4). Since the solution of the problem may afford insight into more general issues we shall deal with it in some detail.

Assume for the sake of simplicity that the number of agents is 2 and that $a_i(L) = 1 - \alpha_i L$, $|\alpha_i| < 1$. Then the second sum in (4) equals:

$$\frac{(1 - \alpha_2 L) u_{1t} + (1 \alpha_1 L) u_{2t}}{(1 - \alpha_1 L)(1 - \alpha_2 L)}.$$

It is not difficult to show that there exists a scalar α and a white-noise u_t such that:

$$(1 - \alpha_1 L) u_t = (1 - \alpha_2 L) u_{1t} + (1 - \alpha_1 L) u_{2t}.^8$$

We note that once α is determined, for u_t we have:

$$u_t = u_{1t} + (\alpha - \alpha_2) u_{1t-1} + \alpha(\alpha - \alpha_2) u_{1t-2} + \alpha^2(\alpha - \alpha_2) u_{1t-3} + \cdots$$
$$+ u_{2t} + (\alpha - \alpha_1) u_{2t-1} + \alpha(\alpha - \alpha_1) u_{2t-2} + \alpha^2(\alpha - \alpha_1) u_{2t-3} + \cdots. \tag{5}$$

Starting from (5) it is easily seen that u_t is orthogonal to x_{t-k}, any k, and to y_{t-h}, $h > 0$.[9] Thus the empirical macroequation is:

$$(1 - \alpha_1 L)(1 - \alpha_2 L) y_t = [r_1 b_1(L)(1 - \alpha_2 L) + r_2 b_2(L)(1 - \alpha_1 L)] x_t$$
$$+ (1 - \alpha L) u_t. \tag{6}$$

First it must be pointed out that (6) is more complicated compared with the corresponding microequations (2). Secondly, going back to (5) we see that the disturbance term u_t, belonging to the aggregate equation, has no immediate economic meaning. As a matter of fact, far from being a sum of simultaneous microdisturbances, u_t is a highly artificial white-noise obtained by using the whole past of u_{1t} and u_{2t}, in addition to u_{1t} and u_{2t} themselves. Moreover, the parameters r_1 and r_2, which are not related to microbehaviors of agents but only to the independent microvariables, influence the parameters of the aggregate equation.

Notice lastly that apart from the last observation the same results obtain if the assumption $x_{it} = r_i x_t$ is replaced by $x_{it} = x_t$.

1.2 Dynamically different independent variables: a dynamic background

Let us now drop the extreme assumption $x_{it} = r_1 x_t$; i.e. let us suppose that the share of x_{it} in x_t is not constant. It is intuitively obvious that aggregation of microequations (2) requires the knowledge of the processes generating individual incomes. In other words, precise assumptions on the background of our consumption-income equation are necessary.

We shall base ourselves upon the so-called Slutsky–Frisch approach, that is, we shall assume that the economic system, or the part of it we are interested in, can be adequately represented by a system of linear stochastic difference equations:

$$A(L)z_t = B(L)\xi_t, \tag{7}$$

where z_t is a stochastic vector whose components are variables relative to individual agents, ξ_t is a white-noise vector, all roots of $\det(A(L))$ are of modulus greater than one. Obviously we are assuming that equations (2) are part of system (7) and therefore that the variables y_{it} and x_{it} are among the components of vector z_t.

The assumption on the roots of $\det(A(L))$ entails that there exist a stationary solution of (7). The latter is unique and can be written in the following way:

$$z_t = A(L)^{-1} B(L)\xi_t. \tag{8}$$

To this solution we shall always refer below.[10]

Before we go on working out expression (8) let us comment on the general assumptions, i.e. the representation of individual microvariables by system (7). This entails, as a consequence, the co-stationarity of the components of the vector z_t, the latter being variables referred to individual households or firms. Co-stationarity, in turn, means that the covariance structure of those components, both the cross-covariances $E(z_{it} z_{jt-k})$ and the covariances $E(z_{it} z_{it-k})$, are constant through time. This is, as we pointed out in the Introduction, a very unrealistic picture of individual variables and must be recognized as the main limit of the present work. However, a background like (7) makes the problem mathematically manageable while it does not appear to be unfair towards the point of view we are trying to criticize.

Moreover, we would argue that if a sizeable dynamic difference between micro and macroequations can be obtained within the co-stationarity assumption, it is likely that even more interesting results could be obtained in a more realistic framework, in which co-stationarity is a feature of aggregated, not of individual variables.[11]

As a further observation on system (7) we note that, in general, the parameters of the matrices $A(L)$ and $B(L)$ and the variance–covariance matrix of ξ_t are non-linear mixtures of behavioral parameters: suffice, by way of example, the case of behaviors based on expectations and the elimination of the latter.

1.3 A general formula for the aggregate equation

Vector stochastic stationary processes like (7) can be given a standard representation, the well-known Wold Representation (W.R. from now on):

$$z_t = M(L)\chi_t, \tag{9}$$

where χ_t is a white noise vector having the same dimension (number of components) as z_t (note that the dimensions of z_t and ξ_t can differ), $M(L)$ is a square matrix whose coefficients are rational functions of L, $\det(M(L))$ has no roots of modulus smaller than one, $M(0) = I$, the identity matrix.[12]

The difference between (8) and (9) lies in the fact that the former is still explicitly linked to the behavioral equations, whereas the latter is a standard representation summing up the correlation structure of the vector z_t. The examples in Section 3 will give some insight into the relationship between representations (8) and (9).

The last step necessary to obtain the aggregate equation consists in isolating the components y_{it} and x_{it} within z_t and aggregating. The resulting vector $(y_t\, x_t)$ is obviously a stationary vector. Moreover, considering its W.R.:

$$\begin{pmatrix} y_t \\ x_t \end{pmatrix} = D(L)\,\eta_t = \begin{pmatrix} d_{11}(L) & d_{12}(L) \\ d_{21}(L) & d_{22}(L) \end{pmatrix} \begin{pmatrix} \eta_{1t} \\ \eta_{2t} \end{pmatrix}, \tag{10}$$

where η_t is a white-noise two-dimensional vector, $\det(D(L))$ has no roots of modulus smaller than one, $D(0) = I$, we observe that the rationality of $M(L)$ entails that $d_{ij}(L)$ also are rational functions.[13]

Once (10) is obtained we need only some elementary algebra to get the aggregate equation. First multiply both sides of (10) by the adjoint of $D(L)$:

$$\begin{pmatrix} d_{22}(L) & -d_{12}(L) \\ -d_{21}(L) & d_{11}(L) \end{pmatrix} \begin{pmatrix} y_t \\ x_t \end{pmatrix} = \det(D(L)) \begin{pmatrix} \eta_{1t} \\ \eta_{2t} \end{pmatrix}.$$

Then multiply the second equation by a scalar K and subtract from the first:

$$(d_{22}(L) + Kd_{21}(L))y_t = (Kd_{11}(L) + d_{12}(L))x_t + \det(D(L))u_t, \tag{11}$$

where $u_t = \eta_{1t} - K\eta_{2t}$. For any K we find that u_t is orthogonal to y_{t-k} and x_{t-k} for $k > 0$, since η_{it} is orthogonal to the past of x_t and y_t, $i = 1, 2$. If we put

$$K = \frac{\text{cov}(\eta_{1t}, \eta_{2t})}{\text{var}(\eta_{2t})}$$

then u_t is also orthogonal to x_t.

The aggregate equation is got by eliminating denominators and common factors from the rational functions present in (11).

2. Two agents, exact microrelationships

2.1 Explicit formulas for the macroequation coefficients

Let us return to the process we described above starting from (7) and eventually reaching (11). It is impossible to model the coefficients of the latter as explicit functions of the parameters of (7) or of (9) without making some further assumptions. The following case, obtained thanks to drastic simplifications, appears to be both a convenient paradigm and a useful device to get some insight into the general model.

Let us write equations (2) again:

$$a_i(L)y_t = b_i(L)x_t + u_{it}.$$

We assume:

(a) $u_{it} = 0$ for any i, that is the microequations are exact;

(b) the agents are divided into two groups: to the members of each one corresponds the same ratio $b_i(L)/a_i(L)$; let us define: $\pi_1(L) = b_i(L)/a_i(L)$, i in the first group, $\pi_2(L) = b_i(L)/a_i(L)$, i in the second group.

(c) $\pi_1(L) - \pi_2(L)$ has no roots of modulus less than one. In particular, making $\Pi_i = \pi_i(0)$, we get $\Pi_1 \neq \Pi_2$. This assumption is there only for mathematical convenience.

First we aggregate the x_{it} within each group: for $i = 1, 2$, $X_{it} = \Sigma x_{jt}$, j varying within the i-th group. (Sometimes, as no confusion will arise, we shall avoid a proliferation of symbols and use x_{it} instead of X_{it} for $i = 1, 2$, as though the agents were actually two.)

Secondly, as the vector (X_{it}) is obtained by summing components of z_t, it also will have a rational W.R. (see Note 13):

$$\begin{pmatrix} X_{1t} \\ X_{2t} \end{pmatrix} = \begin{pmatrix} a_{11}(L) & a_{12}(L) \\ a_{21}(L) & a_{22}(L) \end{pmatrix} \begin{pmatrix} v_{1t} \\ v_{2t} \end{pmatrix}, \tag{12}$$

where $a_{ij}(L)$ are rational functions of L, $A(0) = I$, $A(L)$ has no roots of modulus less than one. We assume further that:

(d) the variance–covariance matrix of (v_{it}) is non-singular.

For the vector $(y_t \ x_t)$ we have:

$$\begin{pmatrix} y_t \\ x_t \end{pmatrix} = \begin{pmatrix} \pi_1(L) & \pi_2(L) \\ 1 & 1 \end{pmatrix} \begin{pmatrix} X_{1t} \\ X_{2t} \end{pmatrix}$$

$$= \begin{pmatrix} \pi_1(L) & \pi_2(L) \\ 1 & 1 \end{pmatrix} \begin{pmatrix} a_{11}(L) & a_{12}(L) \\ a_{12}(L) & a_{22}(L) \end{pmatrix} \begin{pmatrix} v_{1t} \\ v_{2t} \end{pmatrix}. \tag{13}$$

From (13) the W.R. of $(y_t \ x_t)$ can be obtained immediately:

$$\begin{pmatrix} y_t \\ x_t \end{pmatrix} = D(L)\,\eta_t, \tag{14}$$

where

$$D(L) = \begin{pmatrix} \pi_1(L) & \pi_2(L) \\ 1 & 1 \end{pmatrix} \begin{pmatrix} a_{11}(L) & a_{12}(L) \\ a_{21}(L) & a_{22}(L) \end{pmatrix} \begin{pmatrix} \Pi_1 & \Pi_2 \\ 1 & 1 \end{pmatrix}^{-1}$$

$$\eta_t = \begin{pmatrix} \Pi_1 & \Pi_2 \\ 1 & 1 \end{pmatrix} \begin{pmatrix} v_{1t} \\ v_{2t} \end{pmatrix}.$$

Applying (11) we obtain:

$$a(L)y_t = b(L)x_t + c(L)u_t,$$

where

$$a(L) = \frac{\Gamma_1(a_{12}(L) + a_{22}(L)) + \Gamma_2(a_{11}(L) + a_{21}(L))}{\Gamma}$$

$$b(L) = \frac{\begin{array}{c} \Gamma_1(\pi_1(L)a_{12}(L) + \pi_2(L)a_{22}(L)) \\ + \Gamma_2(\pi_1(L)a_{11}(L) + \pi_2(L)a_{21}(L)) \end{array}}{\Gamma}$$

$$c(L) = \frac{\pi_1(L) - \pi_2(L)}{\Gamma}\,(a_{11}(L)a_{22}(L) - a_{12}(L)a_{21}(L))$$

$$u_t = (\Pi_1 v_{1t} + \Pi_2 v_{2t}) - K(v_{1t} + v_{2t}) \tag{15}$$

$$K = \frac{\mathrm{cov}(\Pi_1 v_{1t} + \Pi_2 v_{2t}, v_{1t} + v_{2t})}{\mathrm{var}(v_{1t} + v_{2t})}$$

$$\Gamma = \Pi_1 - \Pi_2, \quad \Gamma_1 = \Pi_1 - K, \quad \Gamma_2 = K - \Pi_2.$$

Notice that the value of K corresponds to the hypothesis that the investigator is assuming orthogonality between u_t and x_t. As with (11), the aggregate equation is got once denominators and common factors have been eliminated.

2.2 Some results on the dynamics of the macroequation

In equation (15) the way the dynamics of the aggregate equation is affected by the dynamics of the independent variables can be explicitly observed. In particular, if $\pi_i(L) = \Pi_i$, i.e. if microbehaviors are static, the aggregate equation dynamics is entirely due to the dynamics of the independent microvariables.

Moreover, a simple inspection of formulas (15) shows the dependence of the macroparameters on the parameters belonging to the microprocesses generating the x_{it} variables, and not only on their 'natural' micro counterpart (that is the coefficients of equations (2)).

Furthermore, unless the microparameters assume special values (see 2.3 below) we shall have $a(L) \neq c(L)$ while the ratio $b(L)/a(L)$ will not be a (finite) polynomial. Thus the aggregate equation is a rather general one. In fact we cannot write it in the rational distributed-lag form:

$$y_t = \frac{b(L)}{a(L)} x_t + u_t,$$

nor in the form of a finite distributed-lag model with a ARMA disturbance:

$$y_t = \pi(L) x_t + \frac{c(L)}{a(L)} u_t,$$

where $\pi(L)$ is a polynomial.

In the two-agent model we are examining, the possibility of a feedback from the variables y_{it} to the x_{it} is not ruled out. This is not immediately evident from the W.R. of $(X_{1t} X_{2t})$, whereas it would be in the W.R. of z_t or in system (7).[14] However, both when a microfeedback is present and, in the opposite case, the term in the lower left-hand corner of the $D(L)$ matrix is:

$$\frac{1}{\Pi_1 - \Pi_2} [(a_{11}(L) - a_{22}(L)) + (a_{21}(L) - a_{12}(L))];$$

thus, for the aggregate variables a feedback is always present unless, as noted for the other aggregation effects, the microparameters assumed special values.[15]

Finally the aggregate disturbance, being a linear combination of the disturbances belonging to the W.R. of $(X_{1t} X_{2t})$, has no behavioral meaning. Nor has it an expectational meaning since microequations (2) are already, by assumption, in a solved form, with respect to possible expected variables.

We conclude this subsection by applying formulas (15) to the example we considered in the Introduction. For $(x_{1t} x_{2t})$ we have:

$$\begin{pmatrix} 1 - \alpha_1 L & 0 \\ 0 & 1 - \alpha_2 L \end{pmatrix} \begin{pmatrix} x_{1t} \\ x_{2t} \end{pmatrix} = \begin{pmatrix} v_{1t} \\ v_{2t} \end{pmatrix}.$$

From (15) we get:

$$\left(1 - \frac{\Gamma_1 \alpha_1 + \Gamma_2 \alpha_2}{\Gamma} L\right) y_t = K \left(1 - \frac{\Gamma_1 \Pi_2 \alpha_1 + \Gamma_2 \Pi_1 \alpha_2}{K\Gamma} L\right) x_t + u_t,$$

where the coefficients Γ, Γ_1 and Γ_2 are defined as in (15). The coefficients of L in the polynomials are different weighted averages of α_1 and α_2 and are therefore in general different.

2.3 Differences between agents' behaviors and between independent variables

The two-agent exact microequation model lends itself to some considerations easy to extend to non-exact microbehaviors and to more than two different agents.

Needless to say, in order to have any aggregation effect $\pi_1(L)$ must be different from $\pi_2(L)$.[16] For instance, in the case of a consumption equation, if the consumers follow static rules, aggregation effects arise only if there are differences in the propensities to consume. But rather serious aggregation effects arise also in the case where the propensities to consume are equal, provided there are differences in the time shape of the response: for instance, assume consumers can be gathered in two groups, such that for the first we have $y_{it} = ax_{it}$, while for the second $y_{it} = ax_{it-1}$; or, the first microequation being unchanged, for the second group $y_{it} = (a/4)(1 + L + L^2 + L^3)x_{it}$.

Also in the case of a price–cost equation, if individual prices are set following the rule of a fixed mark-up over the unit cost, then the more different the mark-ups the more relevant the aggregation effect; or the more different the periods of production across firms within the aggregate (assuming firms are charging the mark-up over the historical or the average cost), the sharper the aggregation effect.[17]

Yet it must be underlined that behavioral differences among agents are necessary but not sufficient in order for the aggregation effects listed in 2.2 to occur. As a matter of fact, condition (d) (see 2.1) regards the independent microvariables, not the microbehaviors. Its meaning can be conveniently clarified by showing significant examples on both what it does and what it does not rule out.

First, the case $X_{1t} = rX_{2t}$, i.e. X_{1t} is equal to X_{2t} up to a scalar, is excluded. This, in turn, means that we are ruling out not only that for any i and j, $i \neq j$, we have $x_{it} = x_{jt}$ (up to a scalar), but also the following, much less trivial, case: given an agent i in group 1, there exists an agent j in group 2 such that $x_{it} = rx_{jt}$, and vice versa, given an agent h in group 2, there exists an agent k in group 1 such that $x_{kt} = rx_{ht}$ (r is the same for all agents). For instance, in the consumption–income case, assume all incomes stem from two sources (say two firms), so that either $x_{it} = z_{1t}$ or $x_{it} = x_{2t}$, where z_{1t} and z_{2t} are, by way of example, orthogonal stochastic processes.

Then if the consumers belonging to behavioral groups 1 and 2 are equally distributed within each of the two firms, we shall get:

$$X_{1t} = \frac{N}{2} z_{1t} + \frac{N}{2} z_{2t} = X_{2t},$$

where N is the number of agents.

More generally, in order to have $X_{1t} \neq X_{2t}$ (up to a scalar), it is necessary that the x_{it}, as stochastic processes, be not distributed among individuals quite independently of the $\pi_i(L)$.

With the prototypes contained in the next section we shall try to show how differences in the micro background can make plausible such a non-independence assumption, which is implicit in condition (d) above. Here we limit ourselves to the following two observations.

If the x_{it} processes are mutually independent then so are X_{1t} and X_{2t}. Moreover in representation (12) we have $\mathrm{cov}(v_{1t}, v_{2t}) = 0$. This is the opposite case with respect to the one analyzed in 1.1. In general there will be both common causes affecting all x_{it} variables, even though with differences in intensity and phase, and local or sectoral or individual causes of variation for the x_{it}. Secondly, we observe that the presence of common causes is not inconsistent with a representation (12) for which (d) is fully valid. Consider the following example:

$$X_{1t} = U_t$$
$$X_{2t} = LU_t + v_t'$$

where $U_t = (1 - \beta L) v_t$ is the common cause, v_t and v_t' are orthogonal white-noise processes. The asymmetry, that is the absence of a stochastic term affecting only X_{1t}, is for reasons of mathematical convenience. Actually, the W.R. is immediately obtained:

$$\begin{pmatrix} X_{1t} \\ X_{2t} \end{pmatrix} = \begin{pmatrix} 1 - \beta L & 0 \\ L(1 - \beta L) & 1 \end{pmatrix} \begin{pmatrix} v_{1t} \\ v_{2t} \end{pmatrix}.$$

Here we see the way a simple phase difference in the action of the common cause can produce a sizeable effect (in as much as a sizeable difference between $\pi_1(L)$ and $\pi_2(L)$ is also present).

More generally, if there are several common causes affecting with different lags and intensities all of the x_{it}, and causes affecting only x_{it} variables corresponding to individual or groups of agents belonging to particular geographical or economic areas, we may write:

$$X_{1t} = \gamma_1(L) U_{1t} + \gamma_2(L) U_{2t} + \cdots + \gamma_n(L) U_{nt} + V_t'$$
$$X_{2t} = \gamma_1'(L) U_{1t} + \gamma_2'(L) U_{2t} + \cdots + \gamma_n'(L) U_{nt} + V_t'',$$

where the U_{it} are the common causes while V_t' and V_t'' gather the local, sectoral and individual causes of variation. The existence of differences between the $\gamma_i(L)$ and the $\gamma_i'(L)$, and between V'_t and V''_t entails, in general, a representation (12) fulfilling condition (d).[18]

Lastly, the aggregation effects vanish if the microparameters assume special values. For instance, if $a_{11}(L) = a_{22}(L)$, $a_{12}(L) = a_{21}(L)$ then no feedback arises from aggregation (note that in this case aggregation destroys even an existing microfeedback). The prototypes in the next section will show that such equalities (as the one ruling out the other aggregation effects) are quite unlikely when differences in the micro background are adequately taken into consideration.

3. Prototypes

The following simple models have an illustrative purpose both of the assumptions we adopted and of the results obtained. In order to avoid analytical complications we limit ourselves to equations with only one independent variable. Also for this reason, the models below must be considered primarily as prototypes and have no claim to realism. The reader will notice that while in the first model the dynamics comes, so to speak, from outside, the second model is 'closed' and contains a microfeedback.

3.1 A price–cost equation

Consider an economy in which two consumer goods are produced by means of two imported commodities. Let s_{ij} be the quantity of imported commodity j necessary to produce one unit of consumer good i. Assume further that an index number of consumer prices is available in which the weights are both equal to 1; and that an index number for import prices is also available in which the weights are $s_{11} + s_{21}$, $s_{12} + s_{22}$. With no loss of generality we can assume that $s_{11} + s_{21} = s_{12} + s_{22} = 1$. Thus the index numbers are $p_t = p_{1t} + p_{2t}$, p_{it} being the price of consumer good i, and $c_t = p_{1t}^\mu + p_{2t}^\mu$, where p_{it}^μ is the price of imported commodity i. Note that c_t is the import price index and the aggregate cost index as well.

Assume now that for price p_{it} we have:

$$p_{it} = \Pi_i c_{it}, \quad c_{it} = s_{i1} p_{1t}^\mu + s_{i2} p_{2t}^\mu,$$

that is the price p_{it} is obtained by applying the constant mark-up $m_i = \Pi_i - 1$ over the unit cost. For the prices of the imported commodities we assume two orthogonal AR(1) processes:

$$(1 - \alpha_i L) p_{it}^\mu = \xi_{it},$$

where $0 \le \alpha_i < 1$, ξ_{1t} and ξ_{2t} are orthogonal white-noise processes.

Moreover, we assume that the two techniques (s_{1i}) and (s_{2i}), being independent, are non-proportional: $s_{11} s_{22} - s_{12} s_{21} \ne 0$; that $\Pi_1 \ne \Pi_2$ and, finally, that $\alpha_1 \ne \alpha_2$. It is easy to obtain the equation linking aggregate price to aggregate cost. First, for the individual costs:

$$\begin{pmatrix} c_{1t} \\ c_{2t} \end{pmatrix} = \begin{pmatrix} \dfrac{s_{11}}{1 - \alpha_1 L} & \dfrac{s_{12}}{1 - \alpha_2 L} \\[2mm] \dfrac{s_{21}}{1 - \alpha_1 L} & \dfrac{s_{22}}{1 - \alpha_2 L} \end{pmatrix} \begin{pmatrix} \xi_{1t} \\ \xi_{2t} \end{pmatrix}.$$

The W.R. is:

$$\begin{pmatrix} c_{1t} \\ c_{2t} \end{pmatrix} = \frac{1}{(1 - \alpha_1 L)(1 - \alpha_2 L)} \begin{pmatrix} 1 - ML & QL \\ RL & 1 - N \end{pmatrix} \begin{pmatrix} v_{1t} \\ v_{2t} \end{pmatrix},$$

$$\begin{pmatrix} v_{1t} \\ v_{2t} \end{pmatrix} = \begin{pmatrix} s_{11} & s_{12} \\ s_{21} & s_{22} \end{pmatrix} \begin{pmatrix} \xi_{1t} \\ \xi_{2t} \end{pmatrix},$$

where, taking $S = \det(s_{ij})$:

$$M = \frac{s_{11} s_{22} \alpha_2 - s_{12} s_{21} \alpha_1}{S}, \qquad N = \frac{s_{11} s_{22} \alpha_1 - s_{12} s_{21} \alpha_2}{S},$$

$$Q = \frac{- s_{11} s_{12}(\alpha_2 - \alpha_1)}{S}, \qquad R = \frac{s_{21} s_{22}(\alpha_2 - \alpha_1)}{S}.$$

Using (15) the aggregate equation is easily seen to be:

$$(1 - FL)p_t = K(1 - GL)c_t + u_t,$$

where:

$$F = \frac{\Gamma_1(N - Q) + \Gamma_2(M - R)}{\Gamma},$$

$$G = \frac{\Gamma_1(\Pi_2 N - \Pi_1 Q) + \Gamma_2(\Pi_1 M - \Pi_2 R)}{K\Gamma},$$

$$K = \frac{\operatorname{cov}(v_{1t}, v_{2t})}{\operatorname{var}(v_{2t})},$$

$$u_t = v_{1t} - K v_{2t}.$$

Thus a purely static behavior has been transformed by aggregation into a dynamic macroequation. To the signs of F and G and their relative magnitude, and hence to the smoothness of the distributed-lag function implicit in the aggregate equation we shall return in the next section. Here it must be pointed out that the knowledge of the way firms operate does not help dynamically to specify the macroequation, unless the aggregation problem is explicitly taken into consideration. On the other hand, an investigator sticking to the commonly accepted representative agent practice, who were able to correctly specify and estimate the aggregate equation linking p_t and c_t, would seek an explanation for a non-existing dynamic behavior.

Using (15) the reader will easily analyze the consequences of different lags in the response to cost variations due to different periods of production.[19]

The following further example may deserve some interest. Consider a single industry producing one homogeneous good. Suppose there exists a firm acting as a leader, to whom the pricing function is left. The price is fixed according to:

$$p_t = \Pi(s_1 p_{1t} + s_2 p_{2t}),$$

where the cost on the right hand side is, of course, relative to the leader firm, and for p_{1t} and p_{2t} we have:

$$(1 - \alpha_i L) p_{it} = \xi_{it},$$

$\alpha_1 \neq \alpha_2$, ξ_{1t} and ξ_{2t} being orthogonal white-noise processes. Now assume that, in addition to p_t, an index of the industry unit cost is available based on the industry averages:

$$c_t = s_1' p_{1t} + s_2' p_{2t}.$$

The W.R. of $(p_t \, c_t)$ is easily obtained from:

$$\begin{pmatrix} p_t \\ c_t \end{pmatrix} = \begin{pmatrix} \dfrac{s_1}{1 - \alpha_1 L} & \dfrac{s_2}{1 - \alpha_2 L} \\ \dfrac{s_1'}{1 - \alpha_1 L} & \dfrac{s_2'}{1 - \alpha_2 L} \end{pmatrix} \begin{pmatrix} \xi_{1t} \\ \xi_{2t} \end{pmatrix},$$

and the same happens for the empirical equation linking p_t and c_t. A dynamics generated by aggregation is present if $s_1 s_2' \neq s_2 s_1'$.

3.2 A multiplier-accelerator model

In the previous example the dynamics of the microvariables is, so to speak, exogenous to the system. We now insert an aggregation problem into a simple version of the multiplier-accelerator model: the dynamics here propagates from the investment decisions to the consumption–income equation. The model is:

$$C_t = C + h_W W_t + h_P P_t + \varepsilon_t \tag{a}$$

$$I_t = I + a(1 - L) C_t + v_{1t} \tag{b}$$

$$M_t = M \tag{c}$$

$$X_t = M + v_{2t} \tag{d}$$

$$W_t = K_C C_t + K_I I_t + K_X X_t \tag{e}$$

$$P_t = Y_t - W_t \tag{f}$$

$$Y_t = C_t + I_t + X_t - M_t, \tag{g}$$

where $a > 0$; ε_t, v_{1t} and v_{2t} are mutually orthogonal white-noise processes. Equation (g) defines the aggregate income as the sum of consumption, C_t, investment, I_t, net exports, $X_t - M_t$. Equation (f) defines profits P_t. Imports are a constant (equation (c)); exports are given by the same constant plus a white noise: the average of the net trade balance vanishes. Investment is determined by an accelerator on consumption (equation (b)); in equation (a) aggregate consumption is obtained as the sum of wage-earners and of profit-earners behaviors. In equation (e) aggregate wage-earnings equal the sum of sectoral wage-earnings: K_C is the labor–product ratio for the consumption goods sector, times the wage per worker; analogously for K_I and K_X. Since we are interested in deviations from the mean, we assume $M = I = C = 0$. It must be pointed out that we are assuming homogeneity for each group of consumers (wage-earners and profit-earners) and for each group of firms (consumption goods, investment goods, exports). Finally, we suppose that the propensity to consume on wages is very high, and very low for profit-earners: for simplicity, $h_W = 1$, $h_P = 0$.

Let us now assume that: (1) only the variables C_t, Y_t, X_t, M_t, I_t are available; (2) an investigator is reasoning on the basis of a theory leading to a dynamic relationship linking agents' consumption to their income; (3) such a relationship is transferred as usual to aggregate data. Thus the problem consists in the specification and estimation of an equation whose general form is:

$$a(L) C_t = b(L) Y_t + c(L) u_t.$$

We assume further that u_t is given a behavioral meaning, that is u_t is interpreted as the aggregate of all those fractions of individual consumptions that are not explained by current and past income nor by past consumption. Moreover we assume that the investigator is aware of equation (g), so that he will not consider the equation $\mathrm{cov}(u_t, Y_t) = 0$ as a correct way of closing the model. From his point of view, a solution can be found by considering the variable X_t. The latter, although correlated with C_t via Y_t, is not correlated with W_t (because of the interpretation given to u_t by the investigator). Therefore X_t can be considered by the investigator as a valid instrumental variable.

The model can now be solved. First we obtain by substitution the following representation for $(C_t \ Y_t)$:

$$\begin{pmatrix} (1 - K_C - aK_I) + aK_I L & 0 \\ -(1+a) + aL & 1 \end{pmatrix} \begin{pmatrix} C_t \\ Y_t \end{pmatrix} = \begin{pmatrix} 1 & K_I & K_X \\ 0 & 1 & 1 \end{pmatrix} \begin{pmatrix} \varepsilon_t \\ v_{1t} \\ v_{2t} \end{pmatrix}.$$

The stationarity condition is:

$$aK_I < |1 - K_C - aK_I|.$$

The generic aggregate equation is:

$$(1 - \beta L) C_t = H Y_t + u_t,$$

where

$$\beta = \frac{a(H(1 + K_I - K_C) - K_I)}{1 - K_C - a K_I},$$

$$u_t = g\{(\varepsilon_t + K_I v_{1t} + K_X v_{2t}) - H[(1 + a) u_t + (1 + K_I - K_C) v_{1t}$$
$$+ (1 + a(K_X - K_I) + K_X - K_C) v_{2t}]\},$$

$$g = (1 - K_C - a K_I)^{-1},$$

as is easily seen by starting from the above representation of (C, Y_t). Finally, to determine H we multiply the above generic aggregate equation by X_t and take expected values assuming $\text{cov}(u_t, X_t) = 0$. We get:

$$H = \frac{K_X}{1 + a(K_X - K_I) + K_X - K_C}.$$

Notice that $\beta \neq 0$ provided $K_X \neq K_I$. Therefore, also in this case, different techniques and microbehaviors yield a dynamic equation in spite of static microbehaviors. The only dynamic behavior in the model regards the investment decisions and is a simple finite distributed lag, whereas the macroequation has an infinite distributed-lag structure.[20]

4. Extension of some results to the general model

4.1 The macroparameters as analytic functions of the microparameters

We pointed out in 2.1 that in the general case, that is when we drop the assumptions of only two agents and of exact microequations, the dependence of the macroparameters on the microcoefficients is not easy to be analyzed. Yet elsewhere we have been able to prove that the former are analytic functions of the latter, i.e. the parameters of the aggregate equations are analytic functions of the coefficients of the system (7) (including the coefficients of the variance–covariance matrix of ξ_t).

This entails that if the vector of the microcoefficients of (7) is contained in an open connected set $S \subset R^M$, where M is the number of microparameters, then given an algebraic relationship E among macroparameters, the following alternative holds: (1) E is true for any $s \in S$, or else: (2) the subset of S where E is true is nowhere dense in S (that is non-dense in any open set contained in S), thus negligible.[21]

For instance if $A(s)$ and $B(s)$ are macroparameters and there exists a $\bar{s} \in S$ such that $A(\bar{s}) \neq B(\bar{s})$, then the subset of S where $A(s) = B(s)$ is negligible.

A simple model will clarify the possible use of the above statement. Consider a three-agent model whose microequations are:

$$y_{it} = \Pi_i x_{it} + u_{it},$$

while for the x_{it} we have:

$$(1 - \alpha_i L) x_{it} = v_{it},$$

where the u_{it} and the v_{it} are mutually orthogonal white-noise processes. The model depends on 12 microparameters. If no further restriction on them is imposed S is the subset of R^{12} defined by: $|\alpha_i| < 1$, $\sigma_{u_i}^2 \geq 0$, $\sigma_{v_i}^2 \geq 0$, $i = 1, 2, 3$. Now let $\bar{s}$ be any point defined by $\Pi_1 = \Pi_2$, $\alpha_1 = \alpha_2$, $\Pi_2 \neq \Pi_3$, $\alpha_2 \neq \alpha_3$, $\sigma_{u_i}^2 = 0$, $i = 1, 2, 3$. Since we have again a two-agent case with exact microequations, the results of Section 2 apply. Thus, in $\bar{s}$ we have $a(L) \neq c(L)$, $a(L)$ is not a factor of $b(L)$, there is a feedback from y_t to x_t. Now, thanks to the analyticity of the coefficients of $a(L)$, $b(L)$, $c(L)$, these results can be extended to the whole S with the possible exception of a negligible subset (obviously containing all points for which $\Pi_1 = \Pi_2 = \Pi_3$).

It must be pointed out first that such an outcome corresponds to what could be expected on the basis of intuition: that is, the aggregation effects should not vanish when the microbackground becomes more complicated. Second, if in the above example there are reasons to assume that $\alpha_1 = \alpha_2 = \alpha_3$, then S is no longer the adequate set for s, nor is $\bar{s}$ an acceptable point. Some of the results on the polynomials $a(L)$, $b(L)$, $c(L)$ do not hold in this restricted set: in particular, $a(L)$ will be a factor of $b(L)$ and there is no macrofeedback.

Lastly we note that some obvious statements about the two-agent model can be easily transferred to the general model. Thus, while in the former the aggregation effects will be, so to speak, proportional to the difference between $\pi_1(L)$ and $\pi_2(L)$ and between X_{1t} and X_{2t}, in the latter the size of the aggregation effects will depend on the dispersion of the $\pi_i(L)$ and on the dependence of the x_{it} microparameters on the $\pi_i(L)$.

4.2 The shape of the aggregate equation

One may wonder whether the macromodels generated by aggregation of different agents do possess some typical characteristics of the estimated macroequations. In particular, in a macromodel like (1) (see the Introduction) the coefficient α is usually between zero and one, and is therefore interpreted as deriving from the presence of some adjustment cost. In a model as simple as the two-agent one we set up in the Introduction and worked out in 2.2, if $0 < \alpha_i < 1$ then α is also positive. Yet it must be pointed out that the corresponding lag distribution is not necessarily smooth. As a matter of fact, we have:

$$p_t = \frac{1 - \beta L}{1 - \alpha L} c_t + \cdots,$$

where:

$$\frac{1-\beta L}{1-\alpha L} = 1 + (\alpha - \beta)L + \alpha(\alpha - \beta)L^2 + \alpha_2(\alpha - \beta)L^3 + \cdots,$$

so that the result depends on $\alpha - \beta$. If the latter is negative the adjustment of p_t consists in an overadjustment in the first period followed by a monotonic opposite correction. For the actual values of α and β and therefore the possibility of a negative $\alpha - \beta$ see 2.1.[22]

But as soon as we consider a slightly more complicated model, like the example in 3.1, we see that not even the result on the sign of α is guaranteed. The aggregate equation was:

$$(1 - FL)p_t = K(1 - GL)c_t + u_t.$$

While the coefficient K is definitely positive, since v_{1t} and v_{2t} are positively correlated, the coefficients F and G can have both signs. For instance, if $S > 0$, $\alpha_2 = 0$, then Q and N are positive while M and R are negative. Since:

$$N - Q = s_{11}(s_{22} - s_{12})\alpha_1, \quad M - R = s_{21}(s_{22} - s_{12})\alpha_1,$$

then F is negative if $s_{22} - s_{12}$ is negative. Thus we have the possibility of an aggregate equation with no usual interpretation, arising from simple microbehaviors.

The foregoing result cannot be ascribed to an odd behavior of the independent variable, which is smooth, nor to an odd behavior of the two microvariables (costs): in fact, each one of them is smooth and reacts positively and smoothly to variations of the other (the autocovariance matrix of the vector $(c_{1t}\ c_{2t})$ is strictly positive and almost geometrically declining). Notice, also, that the same is true for the vector $(p_t\ c_t)$.

The problem of an unusual shape for the aggregate model is still present for a model in which the independent variables are generated by the same vector process as above, but the microequations are:

$$(1 - \theta L)p_{it} = \Pi_i c_{it}^\mu$$

with $0 < \theta_1 < 1$. In the simple case in which $\theta_i = \theta$, $i = 1, 2$, on the left-hand side of the aggregate equation we have:

$$(1 - \theta L)(1 - FL)$$

and therefore possibly a root having the wrong sign.

Moreover, if the microequations are less simple we can have a nontrivial $c(L)$ (the polynomial operating on u_t). For instance, if

$$\pi_1(L) = \frac{0.7 + 0.1L}{1 - \theta L.}$$

$$\pi_2(L) = \frac{0.3 + 0.3L}{1 - \theta L}$$

the p_{it}^H being still generated as in 3.1, we shall have:

$$c(L)=1-0.5L, \quad a(L)=(1-\theta L)(1-FL).$$

Now, it must be pointed out that equations estimated on the basis of finite realizations of the y_t and x_t processes can be no more than approximations of the underlying relationships. Moreover, we should remember that the specification and estimation process usually starts with an equation of the form:

$$\gamma(L)p_t = \delta(L)c_t + \tilde{u}_t,$$

where $\gamma(L)$ and $\delta(L)$ are polynomials of a sufficiently high degree to ensure that the hypothesis of a (approximately) white-noise $\tilde{u}_t$ is not rejected. Thus, if the underlying model is;

$$a(L)p_t = b(L)c_t + c(L)u_t,$$

then the estimated $\gamma(L)$ and $\delta(L)$ represent approximations to the expansions, respectively, of $a(L)/c(L)$ and $b(L)/c(L)$. In our case, the polynomial $\gamma(L)$ will be a truncation of:

$$(1-FL)(1-\theta L)(1+0.5L+0.25L^2+\cdots),$$

If a first-order truncation is chosen, the coefficient of L, namely $-(F+\theta-0.5)$, is not unlikely to be negative.

In conclusion, aggregation yields dynamically complex models but their shape is not easily predictable on the basis of the microequations.

4.3 Aggregation of time series relationships in econometric literature

In the econometric literature of time series the possibility of dynamic complications due to aggregation is only seldom mentioned, and in the few cases known to the present author the model implicitly considered seems to be the simplest one, namely: $x_{it} = r_i x_t$. See, for instance, Nickell (1985, p. 128), Layard and Nickell (1985, p. 66), Sargent (1978b, p. 1016), Hendry *et al.* (1984, pp. 1938–9). By contrast, the possibility of a feedback arising from aggregation — so that implicitly a more complex model is assumed — is noted in Sims (1972, p. 34).

Also the model analyzed by Trivedi (1985) — in which the aggregation problem is explicitly considered — is based on $x_{it} = x_t$ too. Thus knowledge of the model generating x_{it} is superfluous and aggregation is immediate (the difficulties in Trivedi's work lie elsewhere).

Dynamic complications arising with aggregation of microrelationships are analyzed in Granger (1980), who starts with a micromodel already containing the lagged dependent microvariable:

$$y_{it} - \alpha_i y_{it-1} = x_{it} + \beta_i W_t + e_{it}.$$

Granger is not interested in the explicit form of the macroequation linking y_t, x_t and W_t, but in the spectral density of the variable y_t corresponding to distributions of the parameter α_i, where $|\alpha_i| < 1$ but there is no α, $0 < \alpha < 1$, such that $|\alpha_i| < \alpha$ for any i (the number of agents is infinite in Granger's model).

Recently in Stoker (1986), the possibility of a dynamic aggregate equation due to different but static microbehaviors jointly with differences in the independent microvariables is explicitly stated. Yet Stoker limits himself to the dynamic form:

$$y_t = ax_t + \frac{u_t}{1 - \alpha L},$$

while, as we have seen, aggregation yields general dynamic macromodels.

An analogy between aggregation and rational expectations models has been pointed out in the present work: in both cases the parameters belonging to the independent processes contribute to the determination of the parameters of the equation linking observables. In the case of rational expectations a noticeable effort has been made to implement tests on joint hypotheses (rational expectations plus maximization of intertemporal functions) by making the above dependence explicit. Yet such attempts are confined to the representative agent. The existence of an aggregation problem is recognized, for instance, in a paper by Sargent devoted to testing for rational expectations in a demand for labor equation (see Sargent, 1978b, p. 1016, footnote). Sargent appears to believe that the problem could easily be dealt with. Actually, in his case, if one accepts that all firms face the same variable for the wage-rate, which is the only independent variable in Sargent's model, a test taking explicitly into account aggregation could be constructed along the lines of 1.1.[23]

However, when the assumption of identical independent variables across different agents is no longer acceptable even as a working hypothesis, the problem is much more difficult to deal with. If we consider, by way of example, the case in which the variables are consumption on the left- and income on the right-hand side, the construction of a test for, say, permanent income under rational expectations is incomparably more complicated.[24] In fact, the parameters of the aggregate equation depend on the parameters of the disaggregate model of incomes and, thus, the knowledge of the aggregate income parameters is no longer sufficient: a test for rational expectations could not even be set out without some idea of a disaggregate model for individual incomes.

The whole issue of testing theories is beyond the scope of the present work. We only observe that aggregation will obviously make it difficult to implement any test also for theories grounded on simple routinized, rather than maximizing, behaviors.

Concluding remarks

We have shown that serious consideration of the aggregative nature of the macrovariables can cast grave doubts on current interpretations of the dynamic form of estimated macroequations and of their parameters. As we have seen, the dynamics of the independent microvariables propagates to the macroequations, the latter turning out with a general dynamic shape, even though the microbehaviors are perfectly static or quasi-static. Moreover, aggregation is likely to introduce feedback relationships, whereas no feedback is present at the micro level. Finally, the macroparameters are not invariant with respect to change in the parameters belonging to the stochastic microprocesses generating the independent variables the agents are facing.

Yet it must be pointed out that the macroequations obtained by aggregation do not necessarily possess some of the most typical characteristics of estimated macroequations: as we saw in 4.2, if the aggregate macroequation has the following form:

$$(1 - \alpha L) y_t = K(1 - \beta L) x_t + u_t,$$

it is not unlikely that α is negative, contrary to what normally happens. We also saw that such an odd shape for the macroequation is not the outcome of unlikely cases for the microprocesses generating the independent microvariables. Nor does the outcome necessarily change if the microequations have autoregressive polynomials such as $(1 - \alpha_i L)$ with $0 < \alpha_i < 1$.

Further research on this problem could be carried out along the lines followed above. However, we conjecture that not much progress could be made within the narrow limits of the Slutsky–Frisch approach we adopted to model the dynamics of individual behaviors, not any development within those limits would be very interesting in our opinion. On the contrary, as we argued in the Introduction, in order to come to grips both with micro–macro problems and microbehaviors, the issue of individual microvariables and individual behaviors should be re-examined by dropping the dynamic regularity assumption, as well as the constancy of individual microbehaviors, and trying to model non-regular dynamic environments on the ground of specific information corresponding to economic problems. Thus we get back to one of the main issues raised by this book, namely the need of microfoundations of macroeconomic regularities much more embedded in the analysis of the institutional context in which the agents operate and of the actual decision-rules that they follow. We hope that the present work can give a contribution to the statement of the problem, just by showing how an important difference in dynamic shape between micro and macro can arise even under a very slight departure from the common practice of macroeconomics, in which the problem of the micro–macro correspondence is ignored altogether.

Notes

1. Nelson and Winter (1982), p. 134. See also, with reference to the pricing problem, Coutts *et al.* (1978): 'A useful analogy to the behavioral problems of

a firm would be to say that firms have (metaphorically or literally) developed computer programs over the years in order to cope with the stresses and challenges of the environment in which they live. The typical computer routine for pricing is very simple and not responsive in an optimizing way to fairly frequent environmental shocks (p. 98).'

2. More precisely, we shall assume that the x_i's are stationary stochastic variables, either after the subtraction of a regular trend or up to the application of a suitable difference operator.

3. To get an idea of the extent to which the problem of aggregate dynamic is identified with the problem of the dynamic behavior of a single agent, see among others, Nerlove (1972), Sims (1974) and, for a recent review, Hendry *et al.* (1984), pp. 1937–40.

4. That is, v_{1t-k} is orthogonal to v_{2t-h} for any k and h. We recall that orthogonality for two stochastic variables means that their covariance vanishes.

5. The proofs of some mathematical results we shall refer to are contained in the unpublished paper by Lippi (1986), available on request from the author.

6. 'Empirical lag distribution' is used in Nerlove (1979), p. 167, for the lag distribution corresponding to the aggregation of unobserved components (see Section 6 below).

7. See Lippi (1986), Lemma 1.

8. The unknowns are α and σ_u^2, the variance of u_t. As for the equations we have only to write down the variance of $(1 - \alpha L)u_t$ and the covariance of it with $(1 - \alpha)u_{t-1}$, thus getting two non-linear equations. It is possible to show that there exists a solution with $|\alpha| \leq 1$, $\sigma_u^2 \geq 0$. This is a particular case of a general result, enabling to deal with any number of agents and any degree for the polynomials $a_i(L)$, $b_i(L)$. We shall return to this question in 1.3.

9. Since u_{it} is orthogonal to x_{jt-k}, any i, j, k, and as u_t is a linear combination of u_{it}, $k \geq 0$, then u_t is orthogonal to x_{t-k}, any k. The orthogonality to y_{t-h}, $h > 0$, is easily found by considering the expression of y_{t-h} resulting from (4).

10. The other solutions of (7) contain terms like $\alpha \beta^{-t}$, where β is a root of the determinant of $A(L)$. The above assumption on the modulus of the roots of $\det(A(L))$ can be relaxed to include roots of modulus equal to one. These latter have been excluded for simplicity of exposition.

11. Let us stress the distinction, already made in the Introduction, between easily treatable non-stationarity, as represented for instance by the presence of unit modulus roots in $\det(A(L))$, and more radical forms of non-stationarity.

12. The rationality of $M(L)$ is a consequence of z_t being generated by system (7), thus having a rational spectral density. See Rozanov (1967), Chapters 1 and 2, and Hannan (1970), pp. 61–6. This is the general result we refer to in Note 8.

13. Actually, from the rationality of the spectral density of z_t the rationality of the spectral density of $(y_t\ x_t)$ follows easily.

14. If there were a microfeedback from the y_{it} to the x_{it} then the parameters of the W.R. of $(X_{1t}\ X_{2t})$ would not be invariant for variations of the parameters of equations (2). When speaking of a microfeedback we include both the case in which for each agent i the variable y_{it-k} enters the determination of x_{it} for some $k > 0$, and the case in which y_{t-k}, or subaggregates of it, determines all the x_{it}.

15. We are still assuming $\Pi_1 \neq \Pi_2$ and therefore $\pi_1(L) \neq \pi_2(L)$. If $\pi_1(L) = \pi_2(L)$, the representation (14) degenerates. Notice also that the feedback disappears

if $a_{11}(L) = a_{22}(L)$, $a_{12}(L) = a_{21}(L)$. Such a possibility, to which we shall return in 2.3, should not be confused with the case in which $X_{1t} = X_{2t}$ (up to a scalar) as stochastic processes. In the latter case (13) would degenerate, that is the variance–covariance matrix of v_t would be singular.

16. If $\pi_1(L) = \pi_2(L)$ our model degenerates and equations (15) are no longer valid. Yet by letting $\pi_1(L)$ and $\pi_2(L)$ tend to the common limit $\pi(L)$, while assuming that the limit of

$$\frac{\pi_1(L) - \pi_2(L)}{\Pi_1 - \Pi_2}$$

is finite, $b(L)/a(L)$ tends to $\pi(L)$ while u_t tends to zero.

17. The period of production is here defined, according to Coutts *et al.* (1978), as 'the length of time between the first purchase of the input used for the production process and the sale of the finished product' (p. 37).

18. There is an intermediate case between (d) and the case analyzed in 1.1. It is possible that $X_{1t} = X_{2t}$ (up to a scalar) is false but the variance–covariance matrix of v_t in (12) is singular: it is sufficient to assume, for instance, that $X_{1t} = v_{1t}$, $X_{2t} = v_{1t} + a v_{2t}$. Such cases do not appear very important. However aggregation is nearly as easy as in 1.1.

19. See Note 17.

20. Alternatively, if the equation linking C_t to Y_t were interpreted as deriving from a relation between C_t and expected values of Y_t, u_t could be interpreted as resulting from the difference between expected and actual values. See, for instance, Hendry and Ungern-Sternberg (1981). Lastly, no difficulty arises, as the reader can verify, if the model is closed by $\mathrm{cov}(Y_t\, u_t) = 0$.

21. See Lippi (1986). Actually, it is not necessary that S is open. The assumption that S is contained in the closure of an open connected set is sufficient.

22. The possibility of non-smooth lag distributions as an outcome of rational expectations is noted in Sims (1974), p. 314. The lag distribution Sims refers to is the orthogonal projection of p_t over the present past and future of c_t; thus it differs from ours, which implies only the past (on this point see 4.3 below). However, our result could easily be obtained for the bilateral projection.

23. It must be pointed out, however, that some assumption on the distribution of the vector of microparameters among firms is necessary in order to deal with the finiteness of the sample size. Either a small number (as compared with the sample size) of different firms or a continuous distribution depending on a small number of parameters must be assumed.

24. However, for a test of permanent income under rational expectations based on the representative agent, see Sargent (1978a). In this case the aggregation problem is not even mentioned.

References

Coutts, K., Godley, W. and Nordhaus, W. (1978), *Industrial Pricing in the United Kingdom,* Cambridge, Cambridge University Press.

Granger, C. W. J. (1980), 'Long-memory relationships and the aggregation of dynamic models', *Journal of Econometrics,* vol. 14, pp. 227–38.

Hannan, E. J. (1970), *Multiple Time Series*, London, Wiley.

Heiner, R. A. (1983), 'The origin of predictable behavior', *American Economic Review*, vol. 73, pp. 560–95.

Hendry, D. F., Pagan, A. R. and Sargan, J. D. (1984), Dynamic specification, in *Handbook of Econometrics*, vol. 2, van Nostrand.

Hendry, D. F. and von Ungern-Sternberg, T. (1981), 'Liquidity and inflation effects on consumers' behavior', Chapter 9 in A. Deaton (ed.), *Essays in the Theory and Measurement of Consumers' Behaviour*, Cambridge, Cambridge University Press.

Layard, R. and Nickell, S. (1985), 'The causes of British unemployment', *National Institute Economic Review*, February, pp. 62–85.

Lippi, M. (1986), 'Aggregation and dynamics in one-equation econometric models', Dipartimento di Economia Politica, Università di Modena.

Nelson, R. R. and Winter, S. G. (1982), *An Evolutionary Theory of Economic Change*, Cambridge, Mass., The Belknap Press of Harvard University Press.

Nerlove, M. (1972), 'On lags in economic behavior', *Econometrica*, vol. 40, pp. 221–51.

Nerlove, M., Grether, P. M. and Carvalho, J. L. (1979), *Analysis of Economic Time-Series*, New York, Academic Press.

Nickell, S. (1985), 'Error correction, partial adjustment and all that: an expository note', *Oxford Bulletin of Economics and Statistics*, vol. 47, no. 2, pp. 119–29.

Rozanov, Y. (1967), *Stationary Random Processes*, Holden Day.

Sargent, T. J. (1978a), 'Rational expectations, econometric exogeneity and consumption', *Journal of Political Economy*, vol. 86, no. 4, pp. 673–700.

—— (1978b), 'Estimation of dynamic labor demand schedules under rational expectations', *Journal of Political Economy*, vol. 86, 1009–44.

Sims, C. A. (1970), 'Discrete approximations to continuous distributed lags in econometrics', *Econometrica*, vol. 38, pp. 545–64.

—— (1972), 'Are there exogenous variables in short-run production relations?', *Annals of Economic and Social Measurement*, vol. 1, pp. 17–36.

—— (1974), 'Distributed lags', Chapter 5 in M. Intriligator and D. Kendrick (eds), *Frontiers of Quantitative Economics*, Vol. 2, Amsterdam, North Holland.

Stoker, T. M. (1986), 'Simple tests of distributional effects on macroeconomic equations', *Journal of Political Economy*, vol. 94, pp. 763–93.

Trivedi, P. K. (1985), 'Distributed lags, aggregation and compounding: some econometric implications', *Review of Economic Studies*, vol. LII, pp. 19–35.

9 Evolutionary theories in economic thought

Norman Clark and Calestous Juma
SPRU, University of Sussex, Brighton and African Center for Technology Studies, Nairobi

Introduction

The stand one takes on epistemological issues—i.e. on what we expect theories to tell us and therefore on how we judge their respective merits—is never an easy one to explain. Nor is it something that academic researchers, especially professional economists, have ever been encouraged to explore in detail, possibly because such an exploration is almost certain to threaten all sorts of established positions—ideological, cognitive, economic, bureaucratic—which have not been reached without some considerable expenditure of effort (and other resources) and which have often become enshrined in established institutions (like university departments) that have seldom been noted for their propensities towards rapid cognitive change. There are, of course, enormous advantages inherent in such intellectual inertia since it is doubtful if disciplined scholarship could take place at all under more anarchic conditions.

And yet every so often such conditions do not only arise, they are clearly necessary as an essential feature of the advancement of knowledge. We do not understand precisely how this process functions. It is certainly not only through some explicit confrontation between 'fact' and 'theory' (or through the sheer weight of Kuhnian 'anomalies'), but rather also as a result of some more subtle set of mechanisms which impress upon intellectual communities that something is wrong, that existing theories just do not work and that attempts to make them work, to re-establish the viability of existing theory, increasingly leads to intellectual clumsiness and 'baroque' explanations.

However, we do know that an important factor influencing adherence to particular theoretical positions lies in the character of underlying metaphysical positions, positions which are often not fully appreciated by practising scientists themselves. In his Lowell Lectures, brought out as *Science and the Modern World* in 1926,[1] A. N. Whitehead made this point in terms of the following broad propositions:

1. Intellectual thought in any field is always conducted through a process of abstraction whereby 'reality' is expressed in terms of specific entities and their relationships to each other.
2. This process of abstraction both excludes what is felt to be unimportant for the analysis and gives the entities specific characteristics.

3. Provided these abstractions are used carefully—i.e. constantly confronted by experience—then they have great scientific usefulness. Where, however, they get taken for reality itself they will have a profoundly deadening effect on scientific development.
4. It is the job of philosophy (and philosophers) to make sure that this does not happen by constantly reviewing the nature of the abstractions made within any given context both conceptually and empirically.

However, it is all too easy to get caught in the grip of one's abstractions. According to Whitehead,

We all know those clear-cut trenchant intellects, immovably encased in a hard shell of abstractions. They hold you to their abstractions by the sheer grip of personality. [Nevertheless] . . . the disadvantage of exclusive attention to a group of abstractions, however well-founded, is that, by the nature of the case, you have abstracted from the remainder of things. Insofar as the excluded things are important in your experience, your modes of thought are not fitted to deal with them. You cannot think without abstractions; accordingly, it is of the utmost importance to be vigilant in critically revising your modes of abstraction. It is here that philosophy finds its niche as essential to the healthy progress of society. It is the critic of abstractions. A civilisation which cannot burst through its current abstractions is doomed to sterility after a very limited period of progress.[2]

What follows is an exploration of the history of economic ideas with a view to understanding better the underlying 'influential metaphysics' and how dominant ways of thinking emerge and evolve. These are major ideas and 'visions' which organize the development of scientific models, the nature of the theoretical 'abstractions' made, the choice of variables, the 'facts' that are held to require exploration, and the heuristics guiding 'scientific progress'. One can discern many examples of such 'visions' which have influenced the ways economists have tried to model the temporal growth of economic systems and whose characteristics may be seen in dialectical terms.

For example, a 'short-term' perspective stresses the properties of the economic system *given* an unchanged parametric structure (in the neoclassical formulation, the 'givens' are the so-called 'fundamentals'—technologies and tastes). To a considerable extent the short-term perspective coincides with 'static' analysis. Conversely, the 'long-term' perspective centres on dynamics and changing structures (including, of course, technologies, institutions, beliefs and behaviours). A second example, which is discussed at length in various chapters of this volume, lies in the dichotomy between an 'equilibrium' and an 'evolutionary' perspective. Such a dichotomy is partly related to the relative emphasis on the *result* of a process compared to the process itself. However, it is in fact more than that, and in the history of economics the former vision has often implied an almost exclusive attention to the existence and properties of equilibria and equilibrium paths neglecting completely the question of how precisely the system gets there. On the other hand, the 'evolutionary' perspective places attention on a careful definition of the relevant processes (selection, innovation, etc.).

A third dichotomy on which this chapter is mainly focused is the tension between 'mechanistic' and 'organic' visions of the behaviour of economic systems. Essentially, the 'mechanistic' view entails the belief that the 'whole' can be simply described in terms of properly quantifiable and stable 'equilibrium' relationships amongst its constituent 'parts' (the 'watch' metaphor, quoted also in Allen's chapter, is a useful example). On the contrary, the 'organic' vision argues that the 'whole' cannot be reduced in this way, but rather the properties of complex systems evolve from non-linear interactions among its components and 'disequlibrium micro-states'. It is also a vision consistent with Prigogine's theory of dissipative structures in chemical systems, whereby crucial systemic properties emerge as a result of micro fluctuations and coupled dynamics between (disequilibrium) processes at the level of individual parts.

It is our intention to explore aspects of the evolutionary tradition in economics with a view to understanding why it is that the discipline has not become an evolutionary and 'organic' one but has instead become increasingly mechanistic throughout the twentieth century. Beginning, briefly, with the early classical economists it is possible to trace a strong (albeit sometimes implicit) 'organic' tradition in the history of economic thought, particularly with Marx and institutional thinkers such as Veblen. However, from Marshall onwards the prevailing approach has become progressively dominated by the notion of equilibrium even where it engages with evolutionary ideas. It is only relatively recently that several economists, including some represented in this volume like Freeman and Perez, Nelson, Dosi and Orsenigo, and Silverberg, building upon the work of Schumpeter, have begun to develop a more systemic view of the nature of technological and economic change.

It is at least arguable (cf. also Allen, chapter 5) that the biases towards quantification, reductionism and equilibrium behaviour associated with early thinkers such as Bacon, Descartes, Galileo and Newton, have had a considerable (if unconscious) influence on the minds of professional economists right from the very beginning. But, of course, while the fountainhead itself, classical physics, began to change course during the nineteenth century towards a more 'organic', 'indeterminate' perspective on natural events, precisely the opposite is the case with professional economics.

Classical antecedents: from Smith to Marshall

Evolutionary views of socio-economic development in general, and technological change in particular, are not a recent academic enterprise. Their antecedents are to be seen in the work of the classical economists. For example. Darwin's work was partly inspired by reading Malthus' essay on human population and according to Schumpeter 'the terms static and dynamic were . . . introduced by John Stuart Mill. Mill probably heard them from Comte, who, in turn, tells us that he borrowed them from the zoologist de Brainville.'[3]

Darwin's *Origin of Species* consolidated a long tradition of evolutionary thought. But the application of Darwin's theory to economic development was impeded by three main factors. First, limited knowledge on evolution and human behaviour opened the way to arguments mainly by analogy; such arguments are often fallacious. Second, social change was not obviously gradualist and therefore the theory was not particularly consistent with the observations of social historians (especially of the Marxists). Third, the rules of the hard sciences (especially Newtonian physics), combined with the Cartesian philosophy of nature as automata and the Baconian appeal to empirical rigour, had become a legitimate view of reality. And economics mostly adopted a mechanistic world-view.

Classical economists did not know as much as we do today about evolutionary concepts.[4] However, they recognized the dichotomy of static and dynamic systems. But this recognition was influenced more by mechanical dynamics than by organic evolution. It is in this context that the dynamics of Mill and Smith can be understood. Much of Smith's use of the terms 'equilibrium', 'laws of motion' and 'scientific objectivity' are drawn from Newtonian physics. Smith, as well as other early economists, is fascinated by the 'order' of the economic system and an obvious analogy is the 'order' of the physical world, generated irrespective of the 'intentions' of the individual units (which, of course, in the physical world are not there at all). The economic sphere could be seen as a microcosm of the celestial arena: forces of supply and demand, guided by the invisible hand, would generate a balance despite, or better *because* of, individual selfishness as market forces 'gravitate' in the right direction. The metaphor of economic order as a 'gravitation process' also underlies Ricardo's theory value. Of course, the physical metaphor with 'forces', 'gravitation', 'natural' (i.e. equilibrium) prices, distributive shares, etc., is not the only possible one. Somewhat earlier than Smith, Mandeville, in his *Fable of the Bees*, describes the economic order with a seemingly biological metaphor, the beehive, whereby coordination is generated by division of labour and specialisation. However, the 'biology' of the metaphor does not go much beyond the nature of the example. What, in fact, Mandeville wants to stress is the mechanics of an ordered interlocking among different economic functions.

Smith was obviously not at home with biological metaphors. He stressed that, unlike animals, human beings had specific attributes which enabled the division of labour to emerge: the ability to truck, barter and exchange. These abilities could be brought into a common stock 'where every man may purchase whatever part of the produce of the other man's talent he has occasion for'.[5] But not for animals:

The strength of the mastiff is not . . . supported by either the swiftness of the greyhound, or by the sagacity of the spaniel, or by the docility of the shepherd's dog. The effects of those different geniuses and talents . . . cannot be brought into a common stock, and do not . . . contribute to the better accommodation and conveniency of the species.[6]

Starting from selfish goal-motivated individuals raises the question of the social assessment of collective outcomes. The 'forces' of supply and demand may well 'order' the general mechanics of the system (the Invisible Hand properties) but are these outcomes socially desirable? One must recognize that in Smith there is a tension between the institutionalist influence of the early Scottish social philosophers (Ferguson, Stuart, etc.), revealed particularly in his *Theory of Moral Sentiments*, which pushes him to 'investigate' the nature of the social and moral context in which the market system is embedded[7] on the one hand, and the natural optimality of the 'celestial harmony' from the Newtonian metaphor, on the other. Certainly, one does not find in Smith the acritical optimism of contemporary Pareto-optimality theorems, but it is also true that neo-classical economics can reasonably claim to have Smith among its ancestors. Relatedly, the 'individual'—in his abstract autonomy—was, and still is, at the centre of the economic universe.[8]

Darwin's influence on economic thought is particularly interesting in the context of the development of Marx's concept of technological change. When Marx first read Darwin's *Origin* in 1860, he wrote to Engels that 'although it is developed in the crude English style, this is the book which contains the basis in natural history for our view'.[9] But later, Darwin and his followers became victims of Marx's hostility. There are two main reasons for this. First, the Malthusian content of the theory (on populations and within-population selection) was inconsistent with Marx's own ideological position. He saw Malthusianism as an apologia for the establishment and Engels asserted that Darwinism was more scientific without its Malthusian content. Second, Marx and Engels contended that their conception of history as a series of class struggles was much richer in content than the 'weakly distinguished phrases of the struggle for existence'.[10] Marx rejected the application of Darwinian views to socio-economic evolution with their implicit gradualism, preferring a Hegelian approach which allowed also for sudden ruptures and 'quantitative change that becomes qualitative change'. However, he adapted Darwinian concepts to his analysis of technological change.[11]

His view of socio-economic evolution involved transition from one mode of production to another. These transitions resulted from internal antagonisms or conflicts which resolved themselves in a new synthesis where the ultimate transformation (for example, from feudalism to capitalism) was seen as a dialectical leap. This is clearly inconsistent with Darwin's evolutionary gradualism, though not with modern notions of punctuated evolution. Indeed, Marx was committed to the overthrow of the political system and therefore any appeal to gradualism was not welcome. And Darwin was equally uninterested in his revolutionary ideas.[12] But despite this hostility towards Darwinian concepts, Marx consistently used biological or organic metaphors in his analysis of socio-economic transition in general, and technological change in particular. Technology evolves from crude designs to more refined manufacturing systems that benefit from scientific disciplines:

The power loom was at first made . . . of wood; in its improved modern form it is made of iron . . . It is only after considerable development of the sciences of mechanics, and an accumulation of practical experience that the form of a machine becomes settled entirely in accordance with mechanical principles, and emancipated from the traditional form of the tool from which it emerged.[13]

This evolution occurs in a social and economic environment. Both the technology and the environment influence each other:

Social relations are closely bound up with productive forces. In acquiring new productive forces men change their mode of production; and in changing their mode of production, in changing the way of earning their living, they change all their social relations. The handmill gives society with the feudal lord; the steam mill, society with the industrial capitalist.[14]

In this process, the role of individuals adds little to the broader pattern of evolution: 'A critical study of technology would show how little any of the inventions of the eighteenth century are the work of a single individual.'[15] Marx equates the development of technology to that of organs in species:

Darwin has directed attention to the history of natural technology, i.e. the formation of the organs of plants and animals which serve as the instruments of production for sustaining their life. Does not the history of the productive organs of man in society, or organs that are the material basis of every particular organisation, deserve equal attention?[16]

His view of technological change is akin to the co-evolution of species in a given ecosystem and their mutual transformations. The tone is clearly evolutionary.

As simple tools evolve, they are adapted to the requirements of particular applications and used by specific workers.

In Birmingham alone 500 varieties of hammer are produced, and not only is each one adapted to a particular process, but several varieties often serve exclusively for the different operations in the same process. The manufacturing period simplifies, improves and multiplies the implements of labour by adapting them to the exclusive and specific functions of each kind of worker.[17]

This functional differentiation, according to Marx, creates a combination of simple instruments that forms one of the material conditions for the existence of machinery. Here we see evolutionary theory applied to technical change. But where does technical change come from? Marx himself reveals the source linking technological change with the division of labour. Darwin's law of variation:

As long as the same part has to perform diversified work, we can perhaps see why it should remain variable, that is, why natural selection should not have preserved or rejected each little deviation of form so carefully as when the part has to serve for some one special purpose. In the same way that a knife which has to cut all sorts of things may be of almost any shape; whilst a tool for some particular purpose must be of some particular shape.[18]

Marx recognized that technical evolution continued long after the machinery had been installed, a fact that underscores the evolutionary nature of technological progress. As noted elsewhere, he paid particular attention to the role of working experience, or the accumulation of disembodied technical change. But he also anticipated modern studies of technical change in the capital goods sector by pointing to plant-level technical improvements: 'When machinery is first introduced . . . new methods of reproducing it more cheaply follow blow by blow, and so do improvements which relate not only to individual parts and details of the machine, but also to its whole construction.'[19] He was able to blend Darwin's notions of random mutation with Hegelian dialectics to provide a methodological analysis of technical change that is unparalleled among classical thinkers. Studies which have ignored this fact have missed the vital interactions and feedbacks between technology and social change and have erroneously viewed Marx as a technological determinist. These studies have also alluded to some imagined ambiguity in Marx's analysis of technological change. The perceived ambiguity is a result of confusing the role and position of technology in the various transitional stages along the path of socio-economic evolution.[20] In fact, Marx tries to capture what other authors in this book would call the 'matching' or 'mis-matching' between technological systems and forms of social organization, labelling it as the 'contradiction between productive forces and the relations of production'.

The main problem with Marx is that he recognized the significance of evolutionary factors but returned to a sort of 'long-term equilibrium' world-view in his prognosis for future social systems. In Marx's world, the socio-economic system has been experiencing moments of extreme fluctuations, of class struggles, but will tend towards a stable end-state, governed by socialist principles—classless societies in which the sources of fluctuations and struggle are eliminated. Society settles into an equilibrium as the underlying social laws that Marx sought to lay bare prevail over individual action and inter-group conflict.

A different type of ambivalence is manifested by Marshall.[21] For Marshall the 'Mecca of economics lies in economic biology rather than economic dynamics'.[22] He argued that economics was like biology because they both dealt with 'a matter, of which the inner nature and constitution, as well as the outer form, are constantly changing'.[23] For Marshall the subject-matter was 'human beings who are impelled, for good or for evil, to change and progress'.[24] However, although he advocated the use of biological concepts, his own work paid only token allegiance to the approach. Much of his *Principles of Economics* is non-evolutionary except for the sections which deal with industrial organization and the division of labour where he draws on the concepts of survival of the fittest and the physiological view of human behaviour. He sees large-scale industries as trees of the forest which grow, compete for light and water, lose vitality, grow old and die; except for 'vast joint-stock companies, which often stagnate, and do not readily die'.[25] Interpreting his views in terms of contemporary biology, one could say that he conjectured (but did not demonstrate) that both short-term and long-term equilibria are the 'hill-climbing' results of selection processes.

Marshall's evolutionary views also differed from Marx's in terms of their 'gradualist' content. In Marx we find cumulative transition mediated through class antagonism which reaches a critical moment and makes a dialectical leap, a revolutionary overthrow of one class by another. In contrast Marshall adopts Darwinian gradualism: 'Economic evolution is gradual. Its progress is sometimes arrested or reversed by political catastrophes: but its forward movements are never sudden . . .'[26] Nevertheless, both Marx and Marshall (and implicitly unlike Smith) agree that the contributions of individuals add only little to the cumulative changes which have been in the making long before them. Thus

any inventor, or an organizer, or a financial genius may seem to have modified the economic structure of a people almost at a stroke; yet the part of his influence which has not been merely superficial and transitory, is found on inquiry to have done little more than bring to a head a broad constructive movement which has long been in preparation.[27]

Marshall's Darwinian metaphors led him to visualize some form of selection equilibrium in the growth of the firms. He states that

a business firm grows and attains greater strength, and afterwards perhaps stagnates and decays; and at the turning point there is a balancing or equilibrium of the forces of life and decay . . .[28]

But although such balances appear dynamic, Marshall did not abandon the Cartesian–Newtonian world-view. For a volume of the foundations of economics must 'give a relatively large place to mechanical analogies'.[29] Later, he offered an economic methodology under which mechanical analogies would be used in the early stages of economic development and biological explanations would take over in later stages.

There is a fairly close analogy between the early stages of economic reasoning and the devices of physical statics . . . I think that in the later stages of economics better analogies are to be got from biology rather than from physics; and, consequently, that economic reasoning should start on methods analogous with those of physical statics, and should gradually become more biological in tone.[30]

Marshall's insistence on mechanical analogies probably reflects the influence of the Cartesian–Newtonian appeal to mathematical rigour. Mathematics was only useful to economics if it could throw 'a bright light on some small part of the great economic movement rather than at representing its endless complexities',[31] and where the subject-matter was stable enough in its parameters, or their derivatives, to be reduced to entities that validate the use of mathematics. Marshall's tone was thus somewhat Newtonian. Like celestial bodies, parts change while the whole remains stationary: individuals grow old and die while the population remains the same; grain prices fluctuate with every harvest but the average value of the grain remains stable.

The growing command of mankind over nature changes the character and magnitude of economic and social forces. To Marshall this is analogous with Newtonian mechanics:

Our planetary system happens . . . to be a stable equilibrium; but a little change in circumstances might make it unstable, might for instance, after a time cause one of the planets to shoot away from the sun in a very long ellipse, and another to fall into it.[32]

For example, the law of supply and demand also takes on at an early stage a clear Newtonian perspective:

In the earlier stages of economics, we think of demand and supply as crude forces pressing against one another, and tending towards a mechanical equilibrium; but in the later stages, the balance or equilibrium is conceived not as between crude mechanical forces, but as between the organic forces of life and decay.[33]

Thus Marshall manifests a commitment to the mechanical thinking of the day despite his appeal to biological analogies. At the same time, however, since society is not an ordinary combination of inanimate material, we have to revert to an organic view of economic activity. This ambivalence is reflected in his analysis of competition, leading to some confusion over perfect and imperfect competition. His approach was later reinterpreted by the neo-classical school, especially with the now standard formulations of monopolistic competition and imperfect competition.[34]

By the late nineteenth century it is clear that economics was being progressively purged of its organic content, prompting Veblen to ask: 'Why is economics not an evolutionary science?'[35] There are several answers, some of which have been alluded to above. First, biology was still embryonic at the time economics was consolidating itself. Darwin came to the scene a century after Adam Smith and development in the biological sciences was partly retarded by the emphasis on classification rather than on measurement and analysis. But even more important were the efforts made in the eighteenth and nineteenth centuries to adopt the Cartesian–Newtonian world-view to economic analysis.

This became the tradition that economists sought to belong to—the tradition of hard sciences, of irreducible and stubborn facts. The post-Smithian economics relied increasingly on particular forms of abstraction or units of analysis, and the best mathematical minds endeavoured to make the discipline an exact science. This process reached a significant peak with the publication in 1874 of Leon Walras's *Elements of Pure Economics*, whose general equilibrium theory had strong mechanical underpinnings. He visualized 'the pure theory of economics or the theory of exchange and value in exchange' simply as a 'physico-mathematical science like mechanics or hydrodynamics'.[36] The need to make economics an exact science was a strong drive during the period. Walras says that 'the establishment . . . of economics as an exact science is no longer in our hands and need not concern us. It is . . . perfectly clear that economics, like astronomy and mechanics, is both an empirical and rational science'.[37]

It is interesting to note how closely the modern tradition in economics echoes precisely this mechanistic framework. Economic systems are conceived of in terms of *units of production* (firms) and *units of consumption* (households) exchanging commodities and factor services in *markets* and *prices* which reflect the forces of supply and demand. Markets always are predisposed to clear since competition amongst buyers and sellers ensures that prices will *equilibrate* at precisely the point at which there is no excess or deficiency of goods and services in the market place. The system is then 'idealized' to reveal the conditions under which it will function in a 'perfect' way—there are many buyers, many sellers, perfect knowledge of all alternatives, no production/consumption complementarities and so on. Under such an idealized system all economic actors will behave perfectly predictably. The forces involved are those of competition, themselves determined by specific behavioural postulates of a psychological character and by technical conditions. Prices provide all the necessary information to allow the entities (households and firms) to behave optimally and, provided the system is suitably isolated, its internal behaviour can be described mathematically in a deterministic way.

Finally, historic time is effectively abolished in the sense that markets are assumed to clear instantly, there are no transactions costs, and future states of nature are either perfectly known or can have probabilities of their occurrence assigned to them.

Where system conditions are not such as to allow the economic system to behave in this idealized way, economists tend to talk in terms of 'market imperfections'. And, of course, that is what reality is all about. The point is, however, that the idealized system becomes the ultimate reference point against which all real states of the system are judged. In Whitehead's language a set of logical abstractions becomes a normative standard. The idealized system is turned from an analytic device into what nature *really is or should be*. Where the evidence does not seem to support such a view, which is practically all the time, then 'institutions' are routinely wheeled in to explain deviations from the mechanistic ideal.

But the very discipline that set the 'metaphorical' pace for economics started changing its course in the last century. The limitations of Newtonian physics started being felt with the theories of electromagnetism and thermodynamics. The process was later complemented by the theories of relativity and quantum physics, and with the acceptance of these theories Newton started to lose his grip on the natural sciences. It can therefore be argued that conventional economics was well ahead of the other social sciences, but in a misleading direction; even the pace-setter and archetype of the natural sciences, physics, had changed course. Georgescu-Roegen puts it as follows:

By the time Jevons and Walras began laying the cornerstones of modern economics, a spectacular revolution in physics had already brought down the mechanistic dogma both in the natural sciences and in philosophy. And the curious fact is that none of the architects of 'the mechanics of utility and self-interest' and even none of the latter-day model builders seem to have been aware at any time of this downfall.[38]

Veblen's argument, that if 'economics is to follow the lead or the analogy of the other sciences . . . the way is plain so far as the general direction in which the move will be made'[39] (i.e. the evolutionary route), was not needed. Instead, evolutionary concepts in the post-Marshallian period sought refuge in other theoretical camps and co-existed with cartesian and Newtonian frameworks.

The post-Marshallian era

Although post-Marshallian economic thought was dominated by mechanistic notions, efforts were made to inject some dynamic elements into its content. One of these areas was market competition. Competition was viewed in conventional economics as analogous with Newtonian motions where resources 'gravitated' towards their most optimal pattern of utilization and prices were 'forced' to the lowest possible levels which could be sustained over the long run. Competition therefore guaranteed order and stability in the market just as gravitation did among Newtonian bodies.[40] However, this view did not adequately account for the competitive behaviour of firms. Economic theory was bedevilled by the paradoxical concepts of monopoly and perfect competition: 'Both are situations in which the possibility of any competitive behaviour has been ruled out by definition.'[41] In fact, in the pre-Second World War period, several attempts were made to introduce alternatives to the equilibrium/short-term analysis of economic systems. For example, Sraffa[42] criticized the logical foundations and empirical plausibility of the Marshallian compromise between U-shape cost curves and longer-term, non-decreasing returns. And, of course, since 'scarcities' and decreasing returns are fundamental elements of the neo-classical representation of the economy, Allyn Young's article on increasing returns[43] must be seen as a contribution (unjustly neglected) to the understanding of dynamic economies (implicitly or explicitly, economies with technological change).

Other elements of economic dynamics relate to product changes. In this respect, Chamberlin attempted to reorientate economic theory by introducing dynamic concepts. His analysis sought to synthesize monopoly and competition in a way that is akin to chemical processes[44] in so far as chemical synthesis requires continuous movement and change in which dynamic and static characteristics may be clearly distinguished. Although he remained in the orthodox economic mainstream, his work carried elements of evolutionary thinking: the dominant role of continuous product differentiation and the wide range of product possibilities suggests an implicit evolutionary content.

Although product variation plays a significant role in Chamberlin's model, it is not clear whether technology was to be held constant or not. But since he stressed product variation, it is reasonable to assume that innovation would be important. Indeed, he subsequently admitted that an entrepreneur would need to innovate to break away from the established order of things:

> The appearance on the market of any new products creates pressure in some degree on the markets for others, and when products are variable and determined by profit maximization some of this pressure is bound to be exerted on quality in order to maintain prices which people can afford to pay.[45]

Despite these dynamic aspects, Chamberlin did not seek to recast his theory of competition on an explicit evolutionary forge. This was left to other economists such as Alchian, who sought to replace the notion of explicit maximization with the biological concept of natural selection.

> The suggested approach embodies the principles of biological evolution and natural selection by interpreting the economic system as an adaptive mechanism which chooses among exploratory actions generated by the pursuit of 'success' or 'profit'.[46]

Competitive behaviour among firms, he argued, was not determined by the motive of profit maximization, but by 'adaptive, imitative, and trial-and-error behaviour in search for profits'.[47] Success was largely influenced and reinforced by previous success, not motivation. The fact that successful firms were still in the market was not a result of their 'conscious' profit-maximizing behaviour but rather an outcome of the fact that a whole lot of other firms had been selected out. The situation is clearly Darwinian: '[T]hose who realize *positive profits* are the survivors; those who suffer losses disappear.'[48] Alchian rejects the relative importance of Schumpeter's entrepreneur because even in a world of fools there would still be profits.

However, a limitation of Alchian's analysis is that, while giving a comprehensive assessment of the behaviour of firms in a competitive environment, he does not offer a convincing account of the role of technical change in the process of natural selection. Part of the problem results from excessive emphasis on imitative behaviour to which much of innovation is attributed.

> Adapting behavior via imitation and venturesome innovation enlarges the model. Imperfect imitators provide opportunity for innovation, and the survival criterion of the economy determines the successful, possibly because imperfect, imitators.[49]

He argues that

Innovation is provided also by conscious wilful action, whatever the ultimate motivation may be, since drastic action is motivated by the hope of greater success as well as the desire to avoid impending failure.[50]

But his view neglects the conditions under which technical change becomes a critical tool for competition in so far as it sets in motion the conditions which call for its constant improvement.

As in neo-classical approaches, Alchian often seems to treat technical change as exogenous to economic evolution. It is merely brought into play for purposes of adaptation to the changing market environment but does not necessarily shape those conditions. Hence it is reasonable to conclude that Alchian did not seek to reframe all economic theory into an evolutionary outlook. Rather he restricted his analysis to firm behaviour by showing the irrelevance of the notion of profit maximization. Indeed, it has been argued (albeit never demonstrated) that evolutionary processes of adaptation and selection lead precisely to those equilibria analysed by neo-classical economists.

Boulding, on the other hand, attempted to restructure economics and bring it in line with ecological dynamics. He conceived micro-economics as a 'study of particular economic quantities and their determination'.[51] Firms or households, in his view, are analogous with economic organisms. He builds a theory which attempts to show the functional relationship between the behaviour of these organisms and the external environment.

By developing a theory of the interaction of organisms through exchange, micro-economics also develops a theory of the determination of the main quantities of the system—prices, outputs, consumption, and so on.[52]

In a similar fashion macroeconomics is viewed as dealing with the national aggregates of individual quantities.

Boulding sought in ecology those elements which were analogous with existing economic abstractions such as population equilibrium and homeostatic mechanisms. This led him to a 'balance sheet' approach to economic analysis in which he expanded the Marshallian forest to include other organisms. It is a

complex pattern of organisms, trees, grasses, flowers, birds, mammals, insects, reptiles, bacteria; subsisting, growing, propagating, dying in a maze of complementary and competitive relationships, all founded on the physical environment of earth, air, sun, water.[53]

But this reformulation remained ineffective in explaining economic transitions because it sought simply to replace static 'mechanical' equilibria with 'ecological' equilibria. Concepts such as homeostasis became crucial to the theory because they provided arguments for some form of balancing mechanism among economic organisms.

Economic organisms drift towards some steady-state situation. In his view, there is some state 'of the organism which is organized to maintain, and any disturbance from this state sets in motion behaviour on the part of the organism which tends to re-establish the desired state'.[54] This argument suggests that there are some inherent forces in economic organisms which direct it towards 'a homeostasis of the balance sheet'. The latter, however, may tell us a little of what happens in the structure of industry, but does not explain the dynamics of economic evolution.

The institutionalist tradition

Institutional economics, or institutionalism, provided one of the earliest expositions of evolutionary thinking. Institutionalism was not itself a coherent package of analytical tools, but a diverse collection of critical ideas built on a theoretical and methodological rejection of conventional economics. It revolved around Veblen, Mitchell and Commons, although, as Blaug says, the three economists had little in common:

Veblen applied an inimitable brand of interpretative sociology to the working creed of businessmen; Mitchell devoted his life to the amassing of statistical data, almost as an end in itself; and Commons analyzed the working of the economic system from the standpoint of its legal foundations.[55]

They were dissatisfied with the narrowness of neo-classical thinking, demanded the integration of other social sciences into economic thought, and rejected the casual empiricism of conventional economics.

Institutionalism was rooted in dissent. In his post-mortem, Boulding sees some elements of suicidal criticism in the movement:

Veblen is the type of dissenter of the sourest kind, whose weapons are irony and sarcasm and sardonic innuendo, but who . . . almost deliberately brings his own house on his head in the process of general destructiveness.[56]

In his critiques, Boulding generalizes on the basis of other forms of dissent, a type of reasoning which many would find fallacious. What is more important, however, is the fact that Boulding's own image ignores Veblen's contribution to evolutionary thinking in general and to the significance of technological change in particular. As with many critical attacks on the establishment, Veblen did not develop his ideas into a solid and consistent analytical framework, but he left behind interesting insights into economic systems that deserve attention.

He argued that economic activity evolves in an unfolding sequence, but that conventional economics had remained at the stage where 'the natural sciences passed through some time back'.[57] What could then replace the law of supply and demand, the theory of price equilibrium, marginal utility and the rest of the tools in the neo-classical kit? The answer lay in a reformulation of the contextual setting of economics, whose subject matter had to be seen as an unfolding sequence embodying evolutionary realism: 'There is the economic life process still in great measure awaiting theoretical formulation.'[58]

Industry and technology are the motive power behind this economic life process:

The active material in which the economic process goes on is the human material of the industrial community. For the purpose of economic science the process of cumulative change that is to be accounted for is the sequence of change in the methods of doing things—the method of dealing with the material means of life.[59]

Veblen was writing at the turn of the century when the role of techno-logical change in economic evolution had become apparent, but was largely unexplained. And to him, everyone was unavoidably trapped in the evolutionary sweep of technological advancement.

Under the stress of modern technological exigencies, men's every-day habits of thought are falling into the lines that in the sciences constitute the evolutionary method; and knowledge which proceeds on a higher, more archaic plane is becoming alien and meaningless to them. The social and political sciences must follow the drift for they are already caught in it.[60]

Veblen emphasized the role of technological change, broadly defined to include both hardware and know-how. He stressed industrial arts to a point that bordered on determinism. The adage, necessity is the mother of invention, was reversed; invention had become the mother of necessity. Technological change was an inherent aspect of social evolution and still took place irrespective of economic factors. However, the issue at hand is the self-propelling dynamism that is accorded to technological change. Veblen often suggested new directions for analysis but left them un-developed. It is in this sense that the role of technological change in the process of economic evolution had therefore to await the analysis of Schumpeter.

The Schumpeterian heritage

Schumpeter is one of the few economists who both questioned the static underpinnings of neo-classical economics and at the same time suggested an alternative approach. By locating economic transition within the broad context of social change, Schumpeter adopted, like Marx, an evolutionary model in which technological change and the efficacy of the entrepreneur as an innovative agent played the most significant role. However, he acknowledged the importance of Walrasian equilibria as 'ordering mechanisms' of the economy and, especially in his early work, presented a continuous tension between these two aspects of his writings—a tension which he never really resolved (on this issue see also Chapter 2 by Dosi and Orsenigo).

The Schumpeterian economic system carried strong evolutionary notions: 'The essential point to grasp is that in dealing with capitalism we are dealing with an evolutionary process.'[61] He goes on:

The fundamental impulse that sets and keeps the capitalist engine in motion comes from the new consumer's goods, the new methods of production or transportation, the new market, the new forms of industrial organization that capitalist enterprise creates.[62]

These changes

illustrate the same process of industrial mutation—if I may use that biological term—that incessantly revolutionalizes the economic structure *from within*, incessantly destroying the old one, incessantly creating a new one. This process of Creative Destruction is the essential fact about capitalism.[63]

In his early work, Schumpeter set out to analyze not the process of evolution itself, but the dynamics which bring it about.

Not how the economic process developed historically to the state in which we actually find it, but the workings of its mechanism or organism at any given stage of development, is what we are to analyse.[64]

The influence of Walras and Marx can be noted at this metaphorical level in his reference to the 'mechanism or organism' of the economic process. He attempts to blend the two. Interestingly enough, Schumpeter follows Marx's cue by rejecting the hasty generalization arising from the Darwinian 'postulate that a nation, a civilisation, or even the whole of mankind, must show some kind of uniform unilinear development'.[65] He also rejects the Newtonian view of society by asserting that historical 'changes constitute neither a circular process nor pendulum movements about a centre'.[66] Moreover, both Marx and Schumpeter conjecture on the long-term outcomes of the evolution of capitalist economies. For Marx socialism would emerge from the collapse of capitalism, while for the later Schumpeter it would result from its success as investment opportunities shrink and the role of entrepreneurs becomes obsolete.

Schumpeter's theory of economic develoment emphasized the endogenous forces which bring about economic evolution and qualitative change. For economic development to occur, a society has to do more than just adapt to changing market conditions. If

the phenomenon that we call economic development is in practice simply founded upon the fact that the data changed and that the economy continuously adapts itself to them, then we shall say that there is no economic development.[67]

In the Schumpeterian system, development is understood as 'changes in economic life as are not forced upon it from without but arise by its own initiative, from within'.[68] The transition is both cumulative and sequential:

Every concrete process of development finally rests upon preceding development . . . Every process of development creates the prerequisites for the following.[69]

His evolutionary theory of development thus transcends the notions of circular economic flows and the tendency towards any general equilibrium. The changes in the circular flow and the destabilization of equilibrium originate in the sphere of industry and commerce (on the supply side), not in the area of 'wants of the consumers of final products' (on the demand side). The shift is not, by definition, minor; it is one

which so displaces its equilibrium point that the new one cannot be reached from the old one by infinitesimal steps. Add successively as many mail coaches as you please, you will never get a railway thereby.[70]

Schumpeter emphasizes further the evolutionary view of economic change in his Business Cycles:

As a matter of fact, it is to physiology and zoology—and not to mechanics—that our science is indebted for an analogous distinction which is at the threshold of all clear thinking about economic matters.[71]

He defines economic evolution as the 'changes in the economic process brought about by innovation, together with all their effects, and the responses to them by the economic system.'[72]

Hence we have a picture which is both *co-evolutionary* and *far from equilibrium*. The creation of 'economic space' or a market niche leads to the swarming towards new innovations by imitators as the copying or modification of newly introduced technologies become increasingly possible. In the Schumpeterian system such opportunities come in clusters and are unevenly distributed, so that the changes which result from these disequilibria are not relatively smooth, as a Darwinian process would tend to be, but proceed in jerks and rushes. Nevertheless, it is still possible to locate their epicentre.

In every span of historic time it is easy to locate the ignition of the process and to associate it with certain industries and, within these industries, with certain firms, from which the disturbances then spread over the system.[73]

However, as the capitalist system matures Schumpeter visualizes a situation where investment opportunities vanish and the entrepreneurial function becomes obsolete, forcing the economy into near-equilibrium 'socialist' practice.

Technological progress is increasingly becoming the business of teams of trained specialists who turn out what is required and make it work in a predictable way. The romance of earlier commercial adventure is rapidly wearing away, because so many more things can be strictly calculated that had of old to be visualised in a flash of genius.[74]

Finally Schumpeter delivers his ultimate prognosis:

Since capitalist enterprise, by its very achievements, tends to automatise progress, we conclude that it tends to make itself superfluous—to break to pieces under the pressure of its own success.[75]

This return of the economic system to a near-steady state associated with socialist organization suggests that the appeal to stable or near-stable systems that has characterized the post-seventeenth-century intellectual tradition influenced Schumpeter's thinking just as it affected Marx's.

Schumpeter's work, however, forms a significant starting point for the analysis of non-equilibrium economic structures and has been built upon by a number of modern economists, as discussed in more detail by Dosi and Orsenigo (Chapter 2) and by Silverberg (Chapter 24). While in our view there are still strong strains of 'mechanistic' thinking permeating this work (for example, his fascination with Walrasian theory as the description of ideal equilibrium conditions of the economy), nevertheless Schumpeter remains a major source of inspiration for those economists who begin to engage more directly with socio-economic complexity in theory building. For example, the work of Freeman and Perez, Silverberg and Arthur illustrates quite clearly (see Chapters 3, 24, 26) the systematic and non-equilibrium dynamics of modern industrial production.

Some concluding points

In this chapter we have provided a survey of some of the 'classic' historical literature in evolutionary economics. While not complete (for example, we have not mentioned the German Historical school which influenced the early American economists), our survey appears to indicate that this tradition, despite giving many useful insights, has never engaged systematically with technological change as a *process*. Instead, most of its practitioners have tended at best to erect an evolutionary canopy over a conceptual structure which remains fundamentally a mechanistic one.

It remains for us, finally, to speculate briefly upon the reasons for this trend. One possible set of reasons is *ideological* in that the appeal of 'private selfishness' mechanically yielding harmony was well suited to match the 'common-sense' justifications of the status quo and also to defend the benefits that derive from it. It is our view, however, that a more important set of reasons is *cognitive*. The elegance, and early success, of classical physics appeared to validate a view of nature in which discrete 'entities' are linked together by 'forces' according to simple laws. However, we now know that although classical physics has been very successful in describing the gross behaviour of inert macro-systems, it has, as Allen points out in Chapter 5, been singularly unsuccessful in explaining living systems at whatever level of size or complexity. Nor does it always explain very well changes of form and structure even in inert macro-systems. Conversely, although their views are still in a minority amongst natural scientists, modern theories which stress the non-linear and self-organizing dynamics of complex structures (associated with Bohm, Haken, Prigogine and others) seem more suited to the essentially systemic nature of technological change.[76]

What is certain, however, is that a fresh look should be taken at many of these matters. Our own view, which we have developed in detail elsewhere,[77] is very much in accordance with that of Allen (see Chapter 5), who argues the need for a dynamic systems approach integrating many disciplines. We believe that by portraying the evolution of new technologies as complex and unstable systems based upon flows of information and guided by socially agreed paradigms, not only is it possible to open up the 'black box' of technical change (normally reduced to an exogenous 'catch up' in standard models); it is possible also to give economic growth and development a content of detailed causation. Much, however, still remains to be done.

Notes and References

1. A. N. Whitehead, (1985), *Science and the Modern World*, London, Free Association Books.
2. ibid., p. 73.
3. J. Schumpeter (1934), *The Theory of Economic Development*, Cambridge, Mass., Harvard University Press, p. xi.
4. With the exception arguably of Malthus. See, for example, N. von Tunzelmann (1986), 'Malthus' "total population system": a dynamic re-interpretation', in D. Coleman and R. Schofield (eds), *The State of Population Theory*, Oxford, Blackwell, pp. 65–95.
5. A. Smith (1961), *The Wealth of Nations*, Vol. I (Cannon (ed.)), London, Methuen, p. 20.
6. ibid., p. 20. Students of entomology would take issue with Smith for not considering the division of labour among bees and ants. In fact, in his day, Linnaeus had already described aphids as ants' cows, recognising the division of labour among insect societies. Houthakker (1956) had provided economic arguments showing that the Smithian notion that the division of labour was limited by the extent of the market was analogous to speciation, or the formation of species among animals. See H. Houthakker (1956), 'Economics and biology: specialization and speciation', *Kyklos*, vol. 9, pp. 180–9.
7. On these points, see G. Dosi (1985), 'Institutions and markets in a dynamic world', Brighton, SPRU, University of Sussex, DRC Discussion Paper No. 22, forthcoming in *The Manchester School*.
8. See A. Hirschman (1982), *Shifting Involvements: Private Interest and Public Action*, Oxford, Martin Robertson.
9. D. Meek (ed.) (1953), *Marx and Engels on Malthus*, London, Lawrence & Wishart, p. 172.
10. ibid., p. 187.
11. We shall return to the Darwinian stand in our review of Marshall.
12. See R. Colp (1982), 'The myth of the Marx–Darwin letter', *History of Political Economy*, vol. 14, no. 4, pp. 416–82, for detailed assessment of the contacts between Marx and Darwin, especially on the myth that Darwin rejected Marx's requests to dedicate *Capital* to him.
13. K. Marx (1976), *Capital*, Vol. I, Harmondsworth, Penguin, p. 505. Marx captured the ultimate organic metaphor in the 'attempt made to construct a locomotive with two feet, which raised it from the ground alternatively, like a horse.'
14. K. Marx (1976), *The Poverty of Philosophy*, Moscow, Progress Publishers, p. 102.

15. Marx, *Capital*, Vol. I, op. cit., p. 493.
16. ibid., p. 493. Marx attempted to develop these ideas in unpublished note-books. See E. Colman (1971), 'Short communication on the unpublished writings of Karl Marx dealing with mathematics, the natural sciences and technology and the history of these subjects', in N. Bukharin (ed.), *Science at the Crossroads*, London, Frank Cass, pp. 234–5.
17. Marx, *Capital*, Vol. I, op. cit., pp. 450–61.
18. C. Darwin, *Origin of Species*, quoted in ibid., p. 461. It is interesting to note that while Darwin uses a mechanical metaphor, Marx uses organic ones.
19. ibid., p. 528.
20. See, for example, A. Hansen (1921), 'The technological interpretation of history', *Quarterly Journal of Economics*, vol. 36, pp. 72–83; R. Heilbroner (1967), 'Do machines make history?', *Technology and Culture*, vol. 8, no. 3, pp. 335–45; D. MacKenzie (1984), 'Marx and the machine', *Technology and Culture*, vol. 25, no. 3, pp. 473–502; W. Shaw (1979), 'The handmill gives you the feudal lord: Marx's technological determinism', *History and Theory*, vol. 18, pp. 155–76. For a contrary view, see N. Rosenberg (1982), 'Marx as a student of technology', in *Inside the Black Box*, Cambridge, Cambridge University press, pp. 34–51.
21. For a detailed review of Marshall's assertion that economics is a branch of biology, see J. Hirschleifer (1977), 'Economics from a biological viewpoint', *Journal of Law and Economics*, vol. 20, no. 1, pp. 1–52. See also J. Hirschleifer (1982) 'Evolutionary models in economics and law', *Research in Law and Economics*, vol. 4, pp. 1–60. For an assessment of the use of economic models in ecology, see D. Rapport *et al.* (1977), 'Economic models in ecology', *Science*, vol. 195, p. 4276, 28 January, pp. 367–73.
22. A. Marshall (1959), *Principles of Economics*, London, Macmillan, p. xii.
23. ibid., p. 637.
24. ibid., p. xiii.
25. ibid., p. 263. For an empirical test of these ideas of Marshall, see R. Lloyd-Jones *et al.* (1982), 'Marshall and the birth and death of firms: the growth and size distribution in the early nineteenth century cotton industry', *Business History*, vol. 24, no. 2, pp. 141–55.
26. Marshall, op. cit., p. xi.
27. ibid., p. xii.
28. ibid., p. 12.
29. ibid., p. 12.
30. A. Marshall (1925), 'Mechanical and biological analogies in economics', in A. C. Pigou (ed.), *Memories of Alfred Marshall*, London, Macmillan, p. 314.
31. ibid., p. 313.
32. ibid., p. 317.
33. ibid., p. 318.
34. Particularly by Chamberlin and Robinson. See E. Chamberlin (1962), *The Theory of Monopolistic Competition*, Cambridge, Mass., Harvard University Press, and J. Robinson (1933), *The Economics of Imperfect Competition*, London, Macmillan.
35. T. Veblen (1898), 'Why is economics not an evolutionary science?', *Quarterly Journal of Economics*, vol. 12, pp. 374–97.
36. L. Walras (1954), *Elements of Pure Economics*, London, Allen & Unwin, p. 71.

37. ibid., p. 47.
38. N. Georgescu-Roegen (1971), *The Entropy Law and the Economic Process*, Cambridge, Mass., Harvard University Press, pp. 2–3.
39. Veblen, op. cit., p. 388.
40. P. McNulty (1968), 'Economic theory and the meaning of competition', *Quarterly Journal of Economics*, vol. 82, pp. 639–56, has extended the physical analogy to equate the concept of perfect competition to that of a perfect vacuum: 'not an "ordering force" but rather an assumed "state of affairs" ', ibid., p. 643.
41. ibid., p. 641.
42. P. Sraffa (1926), 'The laws of returns under competitive conditions', *Economic Journal*, vol. XXXVI, no. 144, December.
43. A. Young (1928), 'Increasing returns and economic progress', *Economic Journal*, vol. XXXVIII, no. 152, December.
44. Chamberlin, op. cit., see p. 3.
45. E. Chamberlin (1957), 'The product as an economic variable', in E. Chamberlin, *Towards a More General Theory of Value*, Oxford, Oxford University Press, p. 131.
46. A. Alchian (1950), 'Uncertainty, evolution and economic theory', *Journal of Political Economy*, vol. 58, p. 211. For an enlargement on Alchian's approach, see S. Enke (1951), 'On maximizing profits: a distinction between Chamberlin and Robinson', *American Economic Review*, vol. 41, pp. 566–78. E. Penrose (1952), 'Biological analogies in the theory of the firm', *American Economic Review*, vol. 42, no. 5, pp. 804–19, provides a critique of Alchian's model emphasizing the pitfalls of relying on biological metaphors. The critique did not undermine Alchian's main arguments.
47. Alchian, op. cit., p. 212.
48. ibid., p. 213.
49. ibid., p. 219.
50. ibid., p. 220.
51. K. Boulding (1962), *Reconstruction of Economics*, New York, Science Editions, p. 3.
52. ibid., p. 4.
53. ibid., p. 6.
54. ibid., p. 26–7.
55. M. Blaug (1968), *Economic Theory in Retrospect*, London, Heinemann, p. 678. For a detailed review of the history of institutionalism since Adam Smith, see J. Spengler (1974), 'Institutions, institutionalism: 1776–1974', *Journal of Economic Issues*, vol. 8, no. 4, pp. 877–96.
56. K. Boulding (1957), 'A new look at institutionalism', *American Economic Review*, vol. 47, May, p. 2. More recently Boulding has changed his position on these issues and has developed a much more organic perspective. See Boulding, K. (1978), Ecodynamics, A New Theory of Societal Evolution, Beverly Hills, London, Sage, and (1981), *Evolutionary Economics*, Beverly Hills, London, Sage.
57. Veblen, op. cit., p. 384.
58. ibid., p. 387.
59. ibid., p. 387.
60. ibid., p. 397. Veblen placed his evolutionary conception in an institutional context thus: 'From what has been said it appears that an evolutionary economics must be the theory of a process of cultural growth as determined by the

economic interest, a theory of a cumulative sequence of economic institutions stated in terms of the process itself' (ibid., p. 393).

61. J. Schumpeter (1943), *Capitalism, Socialism and Democracy*, London, Allen & Unwin, p. 82.
62. ibid., p. 83.
63. ibid., p. 84.
64. J. Schumpeter, *The Theory of Economic Development*, op. cit., p. 10.
65. ibid., p. 57.
66. ibid., p. 58.
67. ibid., p. 63.
68. ibid., p. 63.
69. ibid., p. 64.
70. ibid., p. 64.
71. J. Schumpeter (1939), *Business Cycles*, Vol. I, New York, McGraw-Hill, p. 37.
72. ibid., p. 86.
73. ibid., p. 102.
74. J. Schumpeter (1943), *Capitalism, Socialism and Democracy*, op. cit., p. 133.
75. ibid., p. 133.
76. See, for example, D. Bohm (1980), *Wholeness and the Implicate Order*, London, Routledge; F. Capra (1983), *The TAO of Physics*, London, Fontana, 2nd ed.; I. Prigogine and I. Stengers (1984), *Order Out of Chaos*, London, Heinemann.
77. N. Clark and C. Juma (1987), *Long Run Economics: An Evolutionary Approach to Economic Growth*, London, Pinter Publishers.

Part IV Innovation and the evolution of firms

Preface to Part IV

Richard R. Nelson
Columbia University, New York

Over the past century the locus of inventive activity has shifted from the workshops of individuals to the organized laboratories of business firms. There are several factors behind the shift. First, in many if not all industries inventing has become an activity requiring special skills and training at an advanced level in science and engineering, the use of expensive instruments and other equipment, and often a group of people working collaboratively. Second, knowledge about prevailing technology and its strengths and weaknesses, and about user-needs, has tended to become proprietary, not readily accessible to someone not connected with a firm and lacking special access. Third, invention has become a prominent component of the competitive weaponry of firms.

In recognition of the central importance of industrial R & D, if not always with understanding of the factors behind it, for many years economists have concerned themselves with the character of firms and of industry structures that are conducive to industrial innovation. The questions explored have included prominently the following. Does modern industrial invention and innovation require the presence of large and well-established firms? What are the circumstances in which small firms, or new firms, are the principal sources of industrial innovation, rather than large established firms? Is an industry structure in which only a few firms control a large share of the market, and are relatively immune from short-run liquidity crises, conducive to innovation? How to explain the instances in which rapid technical change was created through an industry structure where entry is easy and external financial sources inclined to bet heavily on promising ideas? These kinds of questions have been on the research agenda of economists at least since the publication of Joseph Schumpeter's *Capitalism, Socialism and Democracy* in 1942.

As the kinds of questions indicate, until recently the focus of economic research has been on how market structure influences industrial invention. There also has been considerable attention to the role of demand, what users will buy and how much they will pay for it, in influencing the kinds of technical advances firms bring forth. However, in recent years certain new or strengthened understandings have significantly changed the research agenda, adding new questions, and changing the way older ones are posed. Scholars have come to recognize better that in many industries the process of technological advance has a strong internal logic, which influences what demands can and cannot be met. Also, it may be much easier for firms to appropriate the returns to certain kinds of inventions than to others. These understandings have enriched, but also made more complex, analysis of the forces influencing the rate and direction of industrial invention.

In many cases it is apparent that scientists and technologists clearly see certain directions, avenues, down which they believe technology can be advanced relatively reliably, while attempts to advance the technology in other directions may be much more problematic. Where these easily pursued directions correspond to user-needs, and where innovators have some mechanism for assuring that they receive a non-trivial fraction of the use-value of their innovations, technological change tends to proceed down those tracks.

This new understanding that technology tends to unfold in particular directions in turn led to awareness that firm behavior, and industry structure, may be molded by the way technology is unfolding, at least as much as the character of innovation depends on firm behavior and market structure. The causal links go both ways, not just in one. Thus in recent years the natural ways to advance recombinant DNA technology have, in general, not required massive resources and giant laboratories, but have been pursuable by small companies, or even by individuals with access to modern laboratory equipment. And judicial decisions regarding patentability have made it possible for small-scale innovators to hold off large-scale potential imitators, and to be in a strong position regarding bargaining about patent rights. In contrast, the advance of modern passenger-jet aircraft technology has required large-scale research and development efforts on the part of teams of experienced scientists and engineers. Further, jet engine and air-frame design, while not protectable by patents, is very difficult to reverse-engineer. This is a context in which large established firms have a major advantage over newcomers.

The chapters in this section develop various of these themes. Dosi's chapter elaborates the discussion above, and presents a broad picture of recent findings on the nature of the innovative process. The chapter by Willinger and Zuscovitch is concerned with the new information-intensive production systems. They discuss what is required if firms are to be effective in their R & D, and effective in their use of these new technologies. The chapter by Teece focuses on the firm more narrowly, and explores the question of how conditions of appropriability, and of technological opportunity, affect what it is profitable for firms to do, and the most profitable way for them to pursue various technological options. Kay focuses on the nature of research and development and identifies several key characteristics that influence how it is organized and managed. Coombs is concerned with the new understanding about the reciprocal relationship between technological advance and market structure.

10 The nature of the innovative process*

Giovanni Dosi
Faculty of Statistics, University of Rome, Rome and
SPRU, University of Sussex, Brighton

Introduction

The attempt in this book to place technical change at the centre of theory of economic change can draw from a widening empirical evidence on the sources, procedures and microeconomic effects of technical change. Here, I shall try to organise and interpret some of that evidence.

The growing attention to innovation-related phenomena is probably due to various factors, partly internal to the dynamics of the economics discipline and partly related to the increasing empirical perception of the importance of technological factors in competitiveness and growth. For example, an increasing number of industrial case studies has highlighted the importance of technological innovation for industrial competitiveness (for reviews, see Freeman, 1982; Dosi, 1984; Momigliano and Dosi, 1983; OECD, 1984). Moreover, the experience of Japanese competition in international trade and the very rapid productivity gains in Japanese firms have focused attention on a number of features of the Japanese 'national system of innovation' (Aoki, 1986; Altschuler *et al.*, 1985; Freeman, 1987; and Freeman's chapter in this book). Finally, the intuitive perception of the importance of the so-called 'microelectronics revolution', with varying degrees of pessimism on its employment outcomes, has induced a re-appraisal of the possible 'compensation mechanisms', on macroeconomic grounds, between the labour-saving and employment-creating effects of innovation (for critical surveys, see Momigliano, 1985; Freeman and Soete, 1985, 1987; Stoneman, Blattner and Pastré, 1982). Whatever the motivations for the analyses of innovation and technological change, this field of inquiry increasingly highlights the characteristics of a fundamental ingredient of the process of growth and transformation of the economy, which is discussed from different angles in several chapters of this book.

Here, I shall limit my discussion to what I consider some of the 'stylised facts' and fundamental properties associated with the innovative process

*A more detailed and extensive analysis of the origins, nature and effects of innovation—on which this chapter is partly based—can be found in G. Dosi, 'Sources, procedures and microeconomic effects of innovation', SPRU, University of Sussex, Brighton, DRC Discussion Paper. Comments from the participants at the Lewes and Maastricht meetings of the project which led to this book, and in particular those of C. Freeman and R. Nelson, are gratefully acknowledged.

(next section): in doing that, I shall draw from several empirical contributions, over the past decade, on the economics of innovation, including those of Abernathy and Utterback (1975, 1978), Freeman (1982), Klein (1977), Nelson and Winter (1977, 1982), Rosenberg (1976, 1982), Sahal (1979, 1981, 1985), Pavitt (1979, 1984a), von Hippel (1979, 1982), and also some contributions of the author (Dosi, 1982, 1984). Second, I will try to provide an interpretation of technological innovation and its relationship with scientific advances, on the one hand, and market processes, on the other. Finally, I shall argue that such an interpretation of the innovative process is useful to the understanding of inter-industry differences in the modes and degrees of innovativeness, which are further analysed in other chapters of this book.

Some stylised facts on innovation

In an essential sense, innovation concerns the search for, and the discovery, experimentation, development, imitation, and adoption of new products, new production processes and new organisational set-ups. Almost by definition, what is searched for cannot be known with any precision before the activity itself of search and experimentation, so that the technical (and, even more so, commercial) outcomes of innovative efforts can hardly be known *ex ante*. Certainly, whenever innovative activities are undertaken by profit-motivated agents, they must involve also some sort of perception of yet unexploited, technical *and* economic, opportunities. However, such perceptions and beliefs rarely entail any detailed knowledge of what the possible events, states-of-the-world, input combinations, product characteristics will be. Putting it another way, innovation involves a fundamental element of *uncertainty*, which is not simply lack of all the relevant information about the occurrence of known events but, more fundamentally, entails also (a) the existence of techno-economic problems whose solution procedures are unknown (more on it in Nelson and Winter, 1982, and Dosi and Egidi, 1987), and (b) the impossibility of precisely tracing consequences to actions ('. . . if I do this, that will occur . . .', etc.). These uncertainty features of innovative activities are the *first* 'stylised fact'.

Of course, the perception or belief that 'some unexploited opportunity is there' is not always disappointed: the record of technological advances of modern economies, at least since the Industrial Revolution, presents impressive testimony in this respect. In fact, technological innovation has been able to draw, and increasingly so in this century, from novel opportunities stemming from scientific advances (from thermodynamics to biology, electricity, quantum physics, mechanics, etc.). The increasing reliance of major new technological opportunities on advances in scientific knowledge is, in my view, the *second* property of contemporary innovation.

The nature of the *search activities* leading to new products and processes has also changed over the last century: the increasing complexity of research and innovative activities militates in favour of formal organisations (firms' R & D laboratories, government laboratories, universities, etc.) as opposed to individual innovators as the most conducive environment to the production of innovations. Moreover, the formal research activities in the business sector tends to be integrated within more or less integrated manufacturing firms (Mowery, 1983; Teece's and Nelson's chapters in this book). This is the *third* major feature of innovative activities.

However, in addition to the previous point, and in many ways complementary to it, a significant amount of innovations and improvements are originated through 'learning-by-doing' and 'learning-by-using' (Rosenberg, 1976, 1982). That is, people and organisations, primarily firms, can learn how to use/improve/produce things by the very process of doing them, through their 'informal' activities of solving production problems, meeting specific customers' requirements, overcoming various sorts of 'bottlenecks', etc. This is the *fourth* 'stylised fact'.

Fifth, it seems that the patterns of technological change cannot be described as simple and flexible reactions to changes in market conditions: (i) in spite of significant variations with regard to specific innovations, it seems that the directions of technical change are often defined by the state-of-the-art of the technologies already in use; (ii) quite often, it is the nature of technologies themselves that determines the range within which products and processes can adjust to changing economic conditions; and (iii) it is generally the case that the probability of making technological advances in firms, organisations and often countries, is among other things, a function of the technological levels already achieved by them. In other words, technical change is a *cumulative activity*.

How does one interpret these phenomena and link them with the intuitive fact that in market economies particular patterns of innovations find a necessary condition in some sort of (actual and/or expected) economic reward to the innovators? How does one account for the possibility for someone (individuals or firms) being systematically 'better', on technological grounds, than others? What explains the relatively ordered patterns which technical change appears to show and its 'momentum', seemingly propelled by a strong internal logic, despite quite diverse and varying market conditions? I shall now turn to these issues.

Knowledge, opportunities and search: technological paradigms and trajectories

Let me start by observing that the solution of most technological problems (e.g. designing a machine with certain performance characteristics, developing a new chemical compound with certain features, improving the efficiency of a production input, etc.) implies the use of pieces of knowledge of various sorts. Some elements represent widely applicable understanding: it might be direct scientific knowledge or knowledge related to well-known and pervasive applicative principles (e.g. on electricity, mechanics, more recently, informatics, etc.). Some other pieces of knowledge are specific to particular 'ways of doing things', to the experience of the producer, the user, or both.

Moreover, some aspects of this knowledge are well articulated, even written down in considerable detail in manuals and articles and taught in schools. Others are largely tacit, mainly learned through practice and practical examples (of course, 'training' and 'apprenticeship' relate also to this aspect of technology): there are elements of being a 'good engineer', a 'good designer', or even a 'good mathematician' that cannot be entirely transmitted in an explicit algorithmic form.

Finally, some of the knowledge involved in the use and improvement of technologies is open and public: the most obvious examples are scientific and technical publications. However, other aspects are private, either 'implicitly' because they are tacit anyway, or explicitly in the sense that they are protected by secrecy or legal devices such as patents.

All three aspects (universal versus specific, articulated versus tacit, public versus private) are essential in the conceptualisation of 'what is technology'. More precisely, technological advances normally draw on some *sub-set* of the publicly available knowledge, which is shared and improved upon by the community of engineers/applied scientists/ designers, etc. However, in the activities aimed at technological innovations, such a shared use of highly *selected* scientific and technological knowledge (related, for example, to selected physical or chemical principles, materials, properties, etc.) is coupled with the use and development of specific and often partly private heuristics and capabilities.

Elsewhere (Dosi, 1982, 1984) as recalled in Chapter 2, I suggest a broad similarity, in terms of definition and procedures although not in objectives or career structures, between 'science' and 'technology'. More precisely, as modern philosophy of science suggests the existence of scientific paradigms (or scientific research programmes), so there are *technological paradigms*. A 'technological paradigm' defines contextually the needs that are meant to be fulfilled, the scientific principles utilised for the task, the material technology to be used. In other words, a technological paradigm can be defined as a 'pattern' for solution of selected techno-economic problems based on highly selected principles derived from the natural sciences. A technological paradigm is both a set of *exemplars*—basic artefacts which are to be developed and improved (a car—of the type we know—an integrated circuit, a lathe, etc., with their particular techno-economic characteristics) and a *set of heuristics*—'Where do we go from here?', 'Where should we search?', 'On what sort of knowledge should we draw?', etc. (consider, for example, general search rules of the kind: 'strive for an increasing miniaturisation of the circuit', 'if an heterocyclic compound worked as a pesticide, fiddle around with the various atomic rings trying to improve its effectiveness', etc.). Putting it another way, technological paradigms define the technological opportunities for further innovations and some basic procedures on how to exploit them. Thus they also channel the efforts in certain directions rather than others: *a technological trajectory* (Nelson and Winter, 1977, and Dosi, 1982) is the activity of technological progress along the economic and technological trade-offs defined by a paradigm (Gordon and Munson, 1981; Saviotti and Metcalfe, 1984). One can take as fairly evident examples of such paradigms the internal combustion engine, oil-based synthetic chemistry, or microelectronics. A closer look at the patterns of technical change, however, suggests the existence of 'paradigms' and 'trajectories' with different levels of generality, in many industrial sectors.

Freeman and Perez (1986) use the expression 'techno-economic paradigm' to describe those pervasive technologies which influence the behaviour of firms and industries throughout the economic system (see Chapter 3). Note, however, that a 'techno-economic paradigm' (or 'regime') in Freeman–Perez's sense, is a *macro-technological* concept and refers to broad clusters of 'paradigms' in the sense I suggest here: for example, the electronics 'techno-economic paradigm' or 'regime' captures the common characteristics, complementarities and inter-linkages between several 'micro' paradigms—related to semiconductors, computers, industrial automation, etc.

Whatever name is chosen, the concept of 'paradigm' points to interpretations broadly consistent with Rosenberg's 'focusing devices' (Rosenberg, 1976) or Sahal's 'technological guide-posts' (Sahal, 1981, 1985). The crucial hypothesis is that innovative activities are strongly *selective, finalised* in rather precise directions, often *cumulative* activities. This is very different from the concept of technology as information that is generally applicable and easy to reproduce and reuse (Arrow, 1962), and where firms can produce and use innovations mainly by dipping freely into a general 'stock' or 'pool' of technological knowledge. Instead we have firms producing things in ways that are differentiated technically from things in other firms, and making innovations largely on the basis of in-house technology, but with some contribution from other firms, and from public knowledge. Under such circumstances, the search process of industrial firms to improve their technology is *not* likely to be one where they survey the whole stock of technological knowledge before making their technical choices. Given its highly differentiated nature, firms will instead seek to improve and to diversify their technology by searching in zones that enable them to use and to build upon their existing technological base. In other words, technological and organisational changes in each firm are cumulative processes, too. What the firm can hope to do technologically in the future is heavily constrained by what it has been capable of doing in the past. Once the cumulative and firm specific nature of technology is recognised, its development over time ceases to be random, but is constrained to zones closely related technologically to existing activities.

Thus, in general, technological progress proceeds through the development and exploitation of both public elements of knowledge, shared by all actors involved in a certain activity, and private, local, partly tacit, firm-specific, cumulative forms of knowledge.

First, there are certainly 'free-good' elements in technological progress essentially stemming from the free flow of information, readily available publications, etc.

The second aspect of the 'public' characteristics of technology relates to the *untraded interdependences* between sectors, technologies and firms and takes the form of technological complementarities, 'synergies', and flow of stimuli and constraints which do not entirely correspond to commodity flows. All of them represent a structured set of technological externalities which can be a *collective asset* of groups of firms/industries within countries/ regions (see, for example, Lundvall, 1984, and Chapter 17 of this book) and/or tend to be internalised within individual companies (see, for example, Teece, 1982, and Chapter 12 of this book; Pavitt, 1984c). In other words, technological bottlenecks and opportunities (Rosenberg, 1976), experiences and skills embodied in people and organisations, capabilities and 'memories' overflowing from one economic activity to another, tend to organise *context conditions* which (i) are country-specific, region-specific or even company-specific; (ii) are a fundamental ingredient in the innovative process; and (iii) as such, determine different incentives/stimuli/ constraints to innovation, for any given set of strictly economic signals.

These untraded interdependences and context conditions are, to different degrees, the *unintentional* outcome of decentralised (but irreversible) processes of environmental organisation (one obvious example is 'Silicon Valley') and/or the result of explicit strategies of public and private institutions. (In this sense one can interpret, for example, the strategies of vertical and horizontal integration of electrical oligopolies into microelectronics technologies or the efforts of various governments to create 'science parks', etc.).

To the extent that innovative learning is 'local' and specific in the sense that it is paradigm-bound and occurs along particular trajectories, but is shared—with different competences and degrees of success—by all the economic agents operating on that particular technology, one is likely to observe at the level of whole industries those phenomena of 'dynamic increasing returns' and 'lock-in' into particular technologies discussed in Arthur's chapter (see also Arthur, 1985; David, 1975, 1985).

Conversely, to the extent to which learning is also local and cumulative at the level of *individual firms*, one is likely to observe also firm-specific trajectories, involving the cumulative development and exploitation of internalised (and thus 'private') technological competences, through those strategies discussed in Teece's chapter.

It is important to remark that what has just been said does *not* imply irrelevance of the inducement mechanisms to changes of techniques stemming from the levels and changes in relative prices (in particular, the price of labour to the price of machines (for some recent evidence, cf. Sylos-Labini, 1984) and also to the price of energy and materials, or from changing demand conditions. On the contrary, these factors are likely to be fundamental ones, influencing both the rate and direction of technical progress, but *within the boundaries* defined by the nature of technological paradigms. Moreover, innovation yields new techniques which are likely to be superior to the old ones irrespective of relative prices, either immed-iately, as often is the case of many microelectronics-based processes (see Soete and Dosi, 1983), or after a learning period (as, for example, in the case of agricultural machinery discussed by David, 1975). If the new techniques had existed before they would also have been adopted at the 'old' relative prices. In other words, technical progress generally exhibits strong *irreversibility features*.

Take the example of microelectronics. As discussed at greater length in Freeman and Soete (1985, 1987), Momigliano (1985), Soete and Dosi (1983), Coriat (1983, 1984), electronics-based production technologies are (i) labour-saving; (ii) fixed-capital saving (i.e. they often induce a fall in the capital/output ratio (for sectoral evidence in the United Kingdom, see Soete and Dosi, 1983); (iii) circulating-capital saving (i.e. the optimisation of production flows allows a fall in the stocks of intermediate inputs per unit of output); (iv) quality-improving (i.e. they increase the accuracy of production processes, allow quality testing, etc.); (v) energy-saving (in so far as the energy use generally is also a function of mechanical movements of the various machineries, the substitution of information processing equipment for electromechanical parts reduces the use of energy). Taking all these characteristics together, it is clear that electronics-based pro-duction techniques are generally unequivocally superior to electro-mechanical ones irrespective of relative prices. That is, the new wage/profit frontiers associated with the new techniques do not intersect for any positive value of the 'old' one (see Dosi, Pavitt and Soete, 1988).

It is important to distinguish between the factors which *induce, stimulate or constrain* technical change from the *outcomes* of the changes them-selves. As we analyse in Dosi, Pavitt and Soete (1988), and following the suggestions of Rosenberg (1976), inducement mechanisms may involve a broad set of factors, including:

(a) technological bottlenecks in interrelated activities;
(b) scarcities of critical inputs; or, conversely;
(c) abundance of particular inputs (e.g. energy, raw materials, etc.);
(d) composition, changes and rates of growth of demands;
(e) levels and changes in relative prices (first of all, as mentioned, the relative price of machines to labour);
(f) patterns of industrial conflict.

Where the critical stimuli come from depends on the nature of the techno-logies and on the economic and institutional context of each country: one can find plenty of evidence on the role of each of these factors. However, irrespective of the immediate triggering factor(s), the patterns of innovation present some remarkable common properties. First, the 'normal' patterns of technological change, to repeat, tend to follow 'trajectories' defined by specific sets of knowledge and expertise. Second, major discontinuities in the patterns of change are associated with changes in technological paradigms (as defined above). Third, irreversibility in the technological advances means also that, using a neo-classical language, the changes *of* the production possibility sets *dominate* over changes *within* any given set. More precisely, at any given time, instead of a well-behaved set we are likely to observe only one (or very few) points corresponding to the best-practice techniques, while, over time, the dominant process of change will imply improvements in these (very few) best-practice techniques (along the 'trajectories'), rather than processes of 'static' inter-factoral substitution.

The conceptualisation of technology and technical change based on 'paradigms', 'guide-posts' or whatever name is chosen, helps also in resolving the long debate in the innovation literature about the relative importance of 'demand pull' (cf. Schmookler, 1966; and, for critical discussions, Mowery and Rosenberg, 1979; Freeman, Clark and Soete, 1982) versus technology push: environment-related factors (such as demand, relative prices, etc.) are instrumental in shaping (a) the rates of technical progress; (b) the precise trajectory of advance, within the (limited) set allowed by any given 'paradigm'; and (c) the selection criteria amongst new potential technological paradigms. However, each body of knowledge, expertise, selected physical and chemical principles, etc. (that is, each paradigm) determines both the opportunities of technical progress and the boundaries within which 'inducement effects' can be exerted by the environment. Moreover, the source of entirely new paradigms is increasingly coming from fundamental advances in science and in the (related) 'general' technologies (e.g. electricity, information-processing, etc.).

So far, I have discussed an interpretation of what I consider fundamental characteristics of the innovative process *in general*. However, at a finer level of analysis, one empirically observes a significant inter-sectoral variety in the rates of technical progress, modes of search, forms of knowledge on which innovation draws. In some areas paradigms are powerful in that they generate rapid sustained technical change. Others are weak, in that they provide relatively little guidance as to where fruitfully to search. Moreover, the fact that a certain kind of technical advance can be achieved cheaply and easily, does not in itself make it profitable for a firm to pursue that advance. I will now discuss these issues.

Opportunities, market conditions and the inter-sectoral differences in innovativeness

On the grounds of the foregoing analysis, the interpretation that I suggest (developing, in particular, on Nelson and Winter, 1982; Freeman, 1982;

Rosenberg, 1976) of the observed differences, over sectors and over time, in the rates and modes by which innovations are generated, diffused and used, traces them back to inter-sectoral and inter-temporal differences in (a) the *opportunities* of innovation that each paradigm entails; (b) the degrees to which firms can obtain economic returns to various kinds of innovation, that is the *degree of appropriability* of innovation; and (c) the *patterns of demand* that firms face.

I have mentioned earlier, among the 'stylised facts', the increasing reliance of major new technological advances upon scientific progress. However, as discussed in detail in Nelson's chapter, only in some techno-logies and sectors is the link direct and powerful: scientific inputs are, there, an essential part of the momentum of technological advances. In other sectors and technologies the links are much more indirect and may simply relate to the use of science-based equipment and intermediate inputs, or to the generic science-based knowledge acquired by researchers, engineers, etc., during their formal training.

In general, I suggest, the linkages between scientific advances and technological opportunities are likely to be much more direct at the early stage of emergence of new technological paradigms. In these cases, pro-gress in general scientific knowledge yields a widening pool of *potential* technological paradigms. In another work (Dosi, 1984), I analyse the specific mechanisms through which a much smaller set of paradigms are actually developed, economically applied and often become dominant. Here, suffice to say that this process of selection depends, in general, on (a) the nature and the interests of the 'bridging institutions' (Freeman, 1982) between pure research and economic applications; (b) quite often, especially in this century, strictly institutional factors, such as public agencies (the military, space agencies, the health system, etc.); (c) trial-and-error processes of exploration of the new technologies, often asso-ciated with 'Schumpeterian' enterpreneurship; (d) the selection criteria of the markets and especially the techno-economic requirements of the users (see Chapter 17 by Lundvall). Certainly, new paradigms become attractive as the cost and difficulty of further progress within existing paradigms increase. However, note that increasing obstacles to progress within a certain paradigm do *not* automatically induce the emergence of new ones; scientific advances are often a necessary condition of their development. Whatever the precise selection mechanisms which produced them, new paradigms reshape the patterns of opportunities of technical progress, in terms of both the *scope* of the innovations and the *ease* with which they are achieved. As examples, the reader may think of the clusters of new technological opportunities associated with electricity, those asso-ciated with synthetic oil-based chemistry, or, more recently, micro-electronics and bioengineering. Whilst, after a period of intensive development, there might be diminishing returns to innovative efforts within the limits of a *specific* paradigm (the so-called Wolf's Law), new technological paradigms, directly and indirectly—via their effects on 'old' ones—prevent the establishment in general of decreasing returns in the search process for innovations. New paradigms spread their effects well beyond their sector of origin and provide new sources of opportunity, via input/output flows and technological complementarities, to otherwise stagnant activities. The emergence of new paradigms and the diffusion of their effects throughout the economy is possibly the main reason why decreasing returns do not set in throughout the economy: on the contrary, static and dynamic economies of scale are the general rule. Contrary to the most pessimistic expectations of classical economists and contrary also to many contemporary formalisations of problems of allocation of resources in decentralised markets, decreasing returns historically did not emerge even in those activities involving a given and 'natural' factor such as agriculture or mining: mechanisation, chemical fertilisers and pesticides, improved techniques of mineral extraction and purification prevented 'scarcity' from becoming the dominant functional feature of these productive activities. *A fortiori*, this applies to manufacturing.

To summarise: sectors and technologies differ in the easiness and scope of technological advances; these varying technological opportunities depend on the nature of each technological paradigm, on the degrees to which it is able directly to benefit from scientific progress and/or from other new technological breakthroughs, and on its 'maturity'. In turn, paradigm-specific opportunities are a first determinant of the observed inter-sectoral differences in the rates of innovation.

However, for any level of notional opportunities, private, economically motivated agents will invest resources in their exploration only if there is an actual or expected market ultimately willing to pay for it, and if these agents (typically firms) will be able to capture a significant fraction of what the market is willing to pay. In other words, innovative efforts are also a function of *the structure of demand and of the appropriability conditions*: examples of very low innovative efforts by business firms due to lack of appropriability, despite the existence of significant technological opportunities, are discussed in Nelson's chapter.

In general, appropriability conditions differ between industries and between technologies: Levin *et al.* (1984) study the varying empirical relevance as appropriability devices of (i) patents; (ii) secrecy; (iii) lead times; (iv) costs and time required for duplication; (v) learning-curve effects; and (vi) superior sales and service efforts. To these one should add the more obvious forms of appropriation of differential technical efficiency related to scale economies. Of course, the easier it is for firm B to pick up and duplicate the innovative achievements—in terms of product performances or production efficiency—of firm A, the lower the appropriability of innovation. Clearly, with perfect, costless and immediate duplicability no business firm would have any incentive to innovate. Conversely, with very high appropriability only a very little share of the benefits from innovation would spread throughout the economic system in the form of efficiency improvements, learning through imitation and price changes. As it happens, in contemporary mixed economies one observes, at least within manufacturing, degrees of appropriability which are generally sufficient to provide an incentive to business firms to sustain relatively high rates of technical progress without, however, preventing, sooner or later, imitation, diffusion and distribution of economic benefits to other firms, users and consumers (of course, this is a quite loose proposition since one can hardly define what is the 'sufficient', let alone the 'optimal', degree of appropriability, or how much different innovation would have been under different appropriability regimes, etc.).

In fact, as discussed in Nelson's chapter, Levin *et al.* (1984) find that for most industries 'lead times and learning curve advantages, combined with complementary marketing efforts, appear to be the principal mechanisms of appropriating returns for product innovations' (p. 33). Moreover, there appears to be a quite significant inter-industrial variance in the importance of the various ways of protecting innovations and in the overall degrees of appropriability, with around three-quarters of the industries surveyed by the study claiming the existence of at least one effective means of protecting process innovation and more than 90 per cent of the industries claiming the same regarding product innovations.[1]

If, as suggested, inter-sectoral differences in technological opportunities, appropriability regimes and demand patterns jointly account for the observed inter-sectoral differences in the rates of innovations, these same variables, together with the sector-specific nature of the knowledge on which innovations are based, explain also the sectoral differences in the typical organisational forms of innovative search. For example, some sectors and technologies may mainly rely on 'informal' processes of learning-by-doing and design improvements; others rely heavily on formal search activities undertaken in R & D laboratories; in some sectors innovations are primarily generated by big firms, in others by relatively smaller firms.

Scherer has recently developed an inter-sectoral matrix of the origin and use of R & D in the US economy based on the inter-sectoral generation and use of a large sample of patents (Scherer, 1982). On the grounds of a data base on innovation in the United Kingdom from 1945 to 1979 collected at the Science Policy Research Unit of the University of Sussex, Pavitt (1984a) has developed a sectoral taxonomy of sectors of production and use of innovation. This evidence, and that from Levin *et al.* (1984), seems broadly consistent with the interpretation put forward here of 'why sectors differ in their rates and modes of innovation'.

Pavitt (1984a) identifies from major groups of sectors, namely:

(i) *'Supplier-dominated' sectors* (which include textile, clothing, leather, printing and publishing, wood products). Innovations are mainly process-innovation: innovative opportunities are generally embodied in new varieties of capital equipment and intermediate inputs, originated by firms whose principal activity is outside these sectors themselves. Thus the process of innovation is primarily a process of diffusion of best-practice capital-goods and of innovative intermediate inputs (such as synthetic fibres, etc.). The knowledge base of innovation in these sectors mainly relates to incremental improvements in the equipment produced elsewhere, to its efficient use and to organisational innovations. Appropriability of firm-specific technological capabilities is rather low and firms are typically not very big (with some exceptions in those activities which present economies of scale in production or marketing such as textiles and clothing).

(ii) *'Scale-intensive' sectors.* Innovation relates to both processes and products; production activities generally involve mastering complex systems (and, often, manufacturing complex products); economies of scale of various sorts (in production and/or design, R & D, etc.) are significant; various appropriability devices operate (e.g. lead times, product complexity, etc.); firms tend to be big, produce a relatively high proportion of their own process technology, devote a relatively high proportion of their own resources to innovation, and tend to integrate vertically into the manufacturing of some of their own equipment. This group includes transport equipment, some electric consumer durables, metal manufacturing, food products, parts of the chemical industry, glass and cement. Moreover, within this group one can make a finer taxonomic distinction, according to the nature of the production process, between (a) assembly-based industries (generally characterised by Taylorist/Fordist automation, such as cars, electrical consumer durables, etc.) and (b) continuous process industries (cement, several food products, etc.).

(iii) *'Specialised suppliers'.* Innovative activities relate primarily to product innovations which enter other sectors as capital inputs. Firms tend to be relatively small, operate in close contact with their users and embody a specialised knowledge in design and equipment-building. Typically, this group includes mechanical and instruments engineering. Opportunities are generally high and are often exploited through 'informal' activities of design improvements, introductions of new components, etc. Appropriability is based to a good extent on partly tacit and cumulative skills.

(iv) *'Science-based' sectors.* This group includes the electronics industries and most of the chemical industries. Innovation is often directly linked to new technological paradigms made possible by scientific advances; technological opportunity is very high; appropriability mechanisms range from patents (especially in chemicals and drugs) to lead times and learning curves (especially in electronics); innovative activities are formalised in R & D laboratories; a high proportion of their product innovation enters a wide number of sectors as capital or intermediate inputs; firms tend to be big (with the exception of new 'Schumpeterian' ventures and highly specialised producers.

Admittedly, the empirical evidence on the sectoral patterns and characteristics of the innovation is far from complete. However, my conjecture is that these empirical patterns can be interpreted by means of a few fundamental variables derivable from the relatively general conceptualisation of the process of innovation, outlined above.

Some conclusions

In this chapter, I have tried to analyse some general characteristics of the process leading to the search and economic exploitation of technological innovations in contemporary mixed economies and to apply such a framework to the interpretation of the evidence stemming from a growing number of empirical studies.

The innovative process—it has been argued—entails an intrinsically uncertain activity of search and problem-solving based upon varying combinations of public and private (people-specific or firm-specific) knowledge, general scientific principles and rather idiosynchratic experience, well-articulated procedures and rather tacit competences. I have called a technological paradigm each specific body of knowledge which guides these search and development activities, grows out of the trials and errors of individuals and firms, and is often shared by the entire community of technological and economic actors as the basis upon which one looks for improvements in process efficiency and product performances. Moreover, each paradigm implies different opportunities for innovation, defined in terms of (1) the 'ease' with which technological advances, however defined, can be achieved; (2) different possibilities for the innovator to appropriate economic benefits from it in terms of profits, market shares, etc.; and (3) diffeent degrees of cumulativeness of technological advances in terms of dynamic increasing returns to innovative effort and auto-correlated probabilities of innovative success, either at the level of single firms or industries.

On the basis of this analytical framework, I have suggested some broad conjectures on how inter-technological differences in innovative opportunities, appropriability regimes, knowledge bases, modes of search, etc., might explain the observed variety in the rates and forms of organisation of innovation in contemporary economies.

This interpretation of the innovative process—which draws heavily from the works cited in the introduction and throughout the text—has, in my view, also relevant implications at the levels of both theory and historical analysis.

The theoretical approach with which the present analysis of innovation is consistent (indeed, it is perhaps a necessary microeconomic ingredient) is sketched elsewhere in this book (see, in particular, the chapters in Part II and Part IV) and also, of course, in Nelson and Winter (1982). Here, let me just mention a few implications which might help the reader to grasp some of the analytical threads which hold together the contributions to this book.

First, the foregoing survey of the characteristics of technology and innovation implies a fundamental distinction between *information and knowledge*. Certainly, innovative activities imply imperfect and asymmetric information. However, for whatever available information, the problem-solving activity involved in search and discovery is based on competences, 'visions', and heuristics which are a logical precondition to information processing. Thus this view departs also from any theory of production based on a view of technology, based only or primarily on freely available blueprints (more on this in Winter, 1982; Nelson and Winter, 1982; Amendola, 1983; Dosi and Egidi, 1987).

Second, and relatedly, innovation is generally based on a variety of knowledge sources which inevitably include public institutions, firm-specific experiences and other forms of institution-specific accumulation of competences. Thus the institutional analyses of the chapters that follow in this part and elsewhere in the book are essential to the understanding of the 'anatomy' of the capitalist machine for technological change (cf. especially Nelson's chapter).

Third, as discussed in the chapters by Dosi and Orsenigo, Teece, and Kay, any satisfactory theory of the firm must involve also an institutional (and history-based) analysis of how organisational structures affect the accumulation of competences, and the appropriation of specific rent-earning assets (on this see also Williamson, 1985; Rumelt, 1987; Teece, 1982; Kay, 1984; Pavitt, 1984c).

Fourth, innovative opportunities and their economic exploitation co-evolve in ways that are at least partly endogenous to the process of discovery, development and production, so that the system very seldom hits any 'hard constraint' whereby all available opportunities are fully known and thoroughly optimised. On the contrary, one is likely to observe permanently a variety of search efforts, strategies and results. One can permanently expect to observe (a) inter-firm *asymmetries* in production efficiency and product technologies (cf. the chapters by Metcalfe and Dosi–Orsenigo) and (b) at least equally wide asymmetries among countries. As a consequence, inter-national differences in innovative capabilities, as well as inter-sectoral differences in the patterns of technical change, can be considered as parts of the foundation of a rather general theory of international trade, whereby the sources of competitiveness of each country are not in any meaningful sense a 'primary endowment', but the outcome of processes of innovation, learning, imitation and diffusion (see the chapters by Dosi-Soete, Fagerberg and Perez-Soete; Pasinetti, 1981; Freeman, 1987).

Fifth, and finally, the interpretation of innovative processes briefly outlined in this chapter entails, and is strictly complementary with, a representation of a changing economy as an *evolutionary environment* (cf. in particular the chapters by Silverberg, Metcalfe, Dosi–Orsenego, Coombs,

Nelson), wherein economic agents continuously try new things, pay for but also learn from their (and others') mistakes, earn quasi-rents and gain market shares from their success, and, ultimately, contribute to the endogenous evolution of their environment.

Note

1. For detailed discussions of appropriability mechanisms, see also Taylor and Silberston (1973), von Hippel (1979, 1980, 1982), and Buer (1982). The relative costs of innovation versus imitation—clearly a good proxy for appropriability—are studied by Levin *et al.* (1984) and Mansfield (1984). A detailed company-level study of patenting strategies is presented in Wyatt (1985) and Wyatt and Bertin (1985).

References

Abernathy, W. J. and Utterback, J. M. (1975), 'A dynamic model of product and process innovation', *Omega*, vol. 3, no. 6.

—— (1978), 'Patterns of industrial innovation', *Technology Review*, 80, June–July, pp. 2–29.

Altschuler, A., Anderson, M., Jones, D. T., Roos, D. and Womack, J. (1985), *The Future of the Automobile*, Cambridge, Mass., MIT Press.

Amendola, M. (1983), 'A change of perspective in the analysis of the production of innovation', *Metroeconomica*, vol. 35, no. 3, pp. 261–74.

Aoki, M. (1986), 'Horizontal vs vertical information structure of the firm', *American Economic Review*, vol. 76, no. 5, pp. 971–83.

Arrow, K. (1962), 'Economic welfare and allocation of resources for invention', in NBER (1962).

Arthur, W. B. (1985), *Competing Techniques and Lock-in by Historical Events: The Dynamics of Allocation Under Increasing Returns*, Stanford, Stanford University, CEPR.

Baker, M. J. (ed.) (1979), *Industrial Innovation*, London, Macmillan.

Buer, P. (1982), *Investigation of Consistent Make or Buy Patterns of Selected Process Machinery in Selected US Manufacturing Industries*, Cambridge, Mass., Sloan School of Management, MIT, Ph.D. dissertation.

Coriat, B. (1983), *La Robotique*, Paris, La Découverte/Maspero.

—— (1984), 'Crise et électronisation de la production: robotisation d'atelier et modèle Fordien d'accumulation du capital', *Critiques de l'Économie Politique*.

David, P. (1975), *Technical Choice, Innovation and Economic Growth*, Cambridge, Cambridge University Press.

—— (1985), 'Cliometrics and QWERTY', *American Economic Review, Papers and Proceedings*.

Dosi, G. (1982), 'Technological paradigms and technological trajectories: a suggested interpretation of the determinants and directions of technical change', *Research Policy*, vol. 2, no. 3, pp. 147–62.

—— (1984), *Technical Change and Industrial Transformation*, London, Macmillan.

Dosi, G. and Egidi, M. (1987), *Substantive and Procedural Uncertainty: An Exploration of Economic Behaviours in Complex and Changing Environments*, Brighton, SPRU, University of Sussex, DRC Discussion Paper, presented at the Conference on Flexible Automation and New Work Modes, Paris, 1–4 April 1987.

Dosi, G., Pavitt, K. and Soete, L. (1988), *The Economics of Technical Change and International Trade*, Brighton, Wheatsheaf, forthcoming.

Freeman, C. (1982), *The Economics of Innovation*, London, Frances Pinter, 2nd edn.

—— (1987), *Technology Policy and Economic Performance* , London, Frances Pinter.

Freeman, C., Clark, J. and Soete, L. (1982), *Unemployment and Technical Innovation: a Study of Long Waves and Economic Development*, London, Frances Pinter.

Freeman, C. and Perez, C. (1986), 'The diffusion of technical innovation and changes of technoeconomic paradigm', presented at the Conference on Innovation Diffusion, Venice, 17–21 March 1986.

Freeman, C. and Soete, L. (1985), *Information Technology and Employment: An Assessment*, Brussels, IBM-Europe.

—— (eds) (1987), *Technical Change and Full Employment*, Oxford, Basil Blackwell.

Gardiner, P. (1984), 'Design trajectories for airplanes and automobiles during the last 50 years'; 'Robust and lean designs', in C. Freeman (ed.), *Design, Innovation and Long Cycles in Economic Development*, London, Royal College of Arts (2nd edn. London, Frances Pinter, 1986).

Gordon, T. J. and Munson, T. R. (1981), *Research into Technology Output Measures*, Gladstonebury, Conn., The Future Group.

Griliches, Z. (1984) (ed.), *R & D, Patents and Productivity*, Chicago, NBER/ Chicago University Press.

Hippel, E. von (1979), 'A customer active paradigm for industrial product idea generation', in Baker (ed.) (1979).

—— (1980), 'The user's role in industrial innovation', in B. Dean and J. Goldhar (eds), *Management of Research and Innovation*, Amsterdam, North Holland.

—— (1982), 'Appropriability of innovation benefit as a predictor of the source of innovation', *Research Policy*, vol. 2, no. 2, pp. 95–116.

Kay, N. (1984), *The Innovating Firm*, London, Macmillan.

Klein, B. (1977), *Dynamic Competition*, Cambridge, Mass., Harvard University Press.

Levin, R., Cohen, W. M. and Mowery, D. C. (1985), 'R & D appropriability, opportunity and market structure: new evidence on some Schumpeterian hypotheses', *American Economic Review, Papers and Proceedings*, vol. 75, no. 2, pp. 20–4.

Levin, R., Kleverick, A. K., Nelson, R. and Winter, S. (1984), *Survey on R & D Appropriability and Technological Opportunity: Part 1—Appropriability*, New Haven, Yale University, mimeo.

Lundvall, B. A. (1984), 'User/producer, interaction and innovation', paper presented at the TIP Workshop, Stanford, Stanford University (also printed by Aalborg University Press, Denmark).

Malerba, F. (1985), *The Semiconductor Business: The Economics of Rapid Growth and Decline*, Madison, University of Wisconsin Press.

Mansfield, E. (1984), 'R & D and innovation: some empirical findings', in Griliches (ed.) (1984).

Mansfield, E. *et al.* (1971), *Research and Innovation in the Modern Corporation*, New York, Norton.

Metcalfe, J. S. (1985), 'On technological competition', Manchester, Department of Economics, University of Manchester, mimeo.

Momigliano, F. (1985), 'Le tecnologia dell'informazione: effetti economici e politiche pubbliche', in A. Ruberti (ed.), *Tecnologia Domani*, Bari, Laterza-Seat.

Momigliano, F. and Dosi, G. (1983), *Tecnologia e Organizzazione Industriale Internazionale*, Bologna, Il Mulino.

Mowery, D. (1983), 'The relationship between intrafirm and contractual forms of industrial research in American manufacturing, 1900–1940', *Explorations in Economic History*, vol. 20, no. 4, pp. 351–74.

Mowery, D. and Rosenberg, N. (1979), 'The influence of market demand upon innovation: a critical review of some recent empirical studies', *Research Policy*, vol. 8, pp. 102–53.

National Science Foundation (1983), *The Process of Technological Innovation: Reviewing the Literature*, Washington DC, National Science Foundation.

NBER (National Bureau of Economic Research) (1962), *The Rate and Direction of Inventive Activity*, Princeton, Princeton University Press.

Nelson, R. (1980), 'Production sets, technological knowledge and R & D: fragile and overworked constructs for analysis of productivity growth?', *American Economic Review, Papers and Proceedings*.

—— (1981), 'Research on productivity growth and productivity differences: dead ends and new departures', *Journal of Economic Literature*, vol. 19, no. 3, pp. 1029–64.

—— (1982), 'The role of knowledge in R & D efficiency', *Quarterly Journal of Economics*, vol. 96, no. 3, pp. 453–70.

Nelson, R. and Winter, S. (1977), 'In search of a useful theory of innovations', *Research Policy*, vol. 6, no. 1, pp. 36–77.

—— (1982), *An Evolutionary Theory of Economic Change*, Cambridge, Mass., The Belknap Press of Harvard University Press.

OECD (1984), *Committee for Scientific and Technological Policy, Science, Technology and Competitiveness: Analytical Report of the Ad Hoc Group*, Paris, OECD/STP (84) 26.

Pasinetti, L. L. (1981), *Structural Change and Economic Growth*, Cambridge, Cambridge University Press.

Pavitt, K. (1979), 'Technical Innovation and Industrial Development: The New Causality', *Futures*.

Pavitt, K. (1984a), 'Patterns of technical change: towards a taxonomy and a theory', *Research Policy*, vol. 13, no. 6, pp. 343–74.

—— (1984b), 'Chips and "trajectories": how will the semiconductor influence the sources and directions of technical change?', in R. Macleod (ed.) (1986), *Technology and the Human Prospect*, London, Frances Pinter.

—— (1984c), *Technological Innovation and Strategic Management*, Brighton, SPRU, University of Sussex, mimeo.

Perez, C. (1985), 'Microelectronics, long waves and the world structural change: new perspectives for developing countries', *World Development*, vol. 13, no. 3, pp. 441–63.

Rosenberg, N. (1976), *Perspectives on Technology*, Cambridge, Cambridge University Press.

—— (1982), *Inside the Black Box*, Cambridge, Cambridge University Press.

Rothwell, R. *et al.* (1974), 'SAPPHO Updated. Project SAPPHO, Phase 2', *Research Policy*, vol. 3, no. 3, pp. 258–91.

Rothwell, R. and Gardiner, P. (1984), 'The role of design in product and process change', *Design Studies*, vol. 4, no. 3, pp. 161–70.

Rumelt, R. (1987), 'Theory, strategy and enterpreneurship', in D. Teece (ed.) (1987).

Sahal, D. (1979), *Recent Advances in the Theory of Technological Change*, Berlin, International Institute of Management.

—— (1981), *Patterns of Technological Innovation*, New York, Addison Wesley.

—— (1985), 'Technology guide-posts and innovation avenues', *Research Policy*, vol. 14, no. 2, pp. 61–82.

Salter, W. (1960), *Productivity and Technical Change*, Cambridge, Cambridge University Press.

Saviotti, P. and Metcalfe, J. S. (1984), 'A theoretical approach to the construction of technology output indicators', *Research Policy*, vol. 13, no. 3, pp. 141–52.

Scherer, E. (1982), 'Inter-industry technology flows in the US', *Research Policy*, vol. 11, no. 4, pp. 227–46.

Schmookler, J. (1966), *Invention and Economic Growth*, Cambridge, Mass., Harvard University Press.

Soete, L. (1979), 'Firm size and innovative activity: the evidence reconsidered', *European Economic Review*, vol. 12, pp. 319–40.

Soete, L. and Dosi, G. (1983), *Technology and Employment in the Electronics Industry*, London, Frances Pinter.

Stoneman, P., Blattner, N. and Pastre, O. (1982), 'Major findings and policy responses to the impact of information technology on productivity and employment', *Microelectronics, Robotics and Jobs*, Paris, ICCP, OECD.

Sylos-Labini, P. (1984), *Le Forze dello Sviluppo e del Declino*, Baris, Laterza (English translation: *The Forces of Development and Decline*, Cambridge, Mass., MIT Press, 1985.

Taylor, C. and Silberston, A. (1973), *The Economic Impact of the Patent System*, Cambridge, Cambridge University Press.

Teece, D. (1982), 'Toward an economic theory of the multi-product firms', *Journal of Economic Behaviour and Organisation*, vol. 3, no. 1, pp. 39–64.

—— (ed.) (1987), *Strategy and Organisation for Industrial Innovation and Renewal*, New York, Ballinger.

Williamson, O. (1985), *The Economic Institutions of Capitalism*, New York, Free Press.

Winter, S. (1982), 'An essay on the theory of production', in S. H. Hymans (ed.), *Economics and the World Around It*, Ann Arbor, University of Michigan Press.

—— (1984), 'Schumpeterian competition in alternative technological regimes', *Journal of Economic Behaviour and Organisation*, vol. 5, no. 3–4, pp. 287–320.

Wyatt, S. with Bertin, G. and Pavitt, K. (1985), 'Patents and multinational corporations: results from questionnaires', *World Patent Information*, vol. 7, no. 3, pp. 196–212.

Wyatt, S. and Bertin, G. (1985), *The Role of Patents in Multinational Corporations Strategies for Growth*, Paris, AREPIT.

11 Towards the economics of information-intensive production systems: the case of advanced materials*

Marc Willinger and Ehud Zuscovitch

Bureau d'Economie Théorique et Appliquée, Université Louis Pasteur, Strasbourg

Introduction

The ongoing shift from one technological system to another is not just a matter of setting up a new configuration of advanced technologies. A qualitative change in the nature of economic activity is under way and the industrial system already looks radically different compared with the post-war system (see Freeman and Perez, and Boyer in this volume). One of the main features of the new technical system appears to be its 'information intensity' meaning, firstly, that the system is capable of creating and dealing with increasing amounts of information, and, secondly, that it becomes more and more able to adjust itself to a growing and changing variety of signals generated by the economic environment. In this chapter we shall study the implications of these features for the behaviour of firms. We shall show how the management of technology changes under Information-Intensive Production Systems (IIPS). Efforts to achieve scale economies partly shift from standardisation of R & D and production technologies to the coordination of specialities with a view to dominating increasing complexity.

In order to grasp this qualitative change, we shall analyse in the first section, 'likely technological trends', the management of technological options and the accumulation of technological knowledge during the development of a usual technological paradigm. The emphasis on information, learning and the kind of technical properties that one looks for during the diffusion process will prepare the ground for the question of dealing with growing information intensity.

We shall try to tackle this issue in the subsequent section, 'Permanent variety and changes in firms' strategies', after a proper characterisation of IIPS. With less standardisation, the selection process operates less

---

*The research whose results are reported here was performed under the FAST project (Forecasting and Assessment in Science and Technology) of the EEC DG XII, which we gratefully acknowledge for support. See 'New Advanced Materials', P. Cohendet, M.J. Ledoux & E. Zuscovitch Eds, Springer-Verlag 1988. We have benefited from discussions with participants in the IFIAS meeting at Maastricht in May 1987. The editorial work of R. Nelson and G. Dosi helped much towards the reshaping of this chapter into its present form; as did the remarks by C. Freeman and N. Kay.

vigorously so that technological options become less and less mutually exclusive. Two major problems arise. The first is that no firm is singly capable of mastering the growing informational requirements (with regard to both technological knowledge and markets information). Indeed, various types of cooperation have been developing rapidly for some time now. The second is that with fewer scale economies of the standard type one needs another; otherwise, the whole system is not viable. Informational scale economies, linked to flexible integration of decisions and routines, may offer an alternative.

The area in which we have done the research leading to this chapter is that of advanced materials. The choice was not random. On the one hand, substitution and diffusion mechanisms can be very nicely illustrated with materials because each of them has a large spectrum of product applications. On the other hand, new materials are an essential component of the new technological system. While information technologies generate flexibility, advanced materials support the induced product variety. One development, we suggest, reinforces the other.

Likely technological trends

Increasing variety of products and their management, or what we call IIPS should be carefully delimited because increasing variety is also a typical property of transition situations. Actually, whenever the economy goes through a structural change caused by the modification of the technological basis upon which it is established, numerous new technical options are tested before the selection process, partly through lock-in mechanisms and partly by scaling-up and cost reduction, establishes the new standard that will become the dominating technological paradigm. In transition periods, as uncertainty rises, agents reconsider the composition of their R & D activities so as to be, if possible, at the right place when important choices in development trends are to be made. This adjustment attitude in itself tends to increase variety because most firms combine passive behaviour of 'just keeping oneself informed' with active R & D behaviour generating new options. Using diversification to reduce uncertainty was one of the driving forces behind the rapid penetration of information technologies. Yet the latter, once introduced, increase variety by their own nature, and push the system towards growing information intensity. It is, then, necessary to distinguish between the set of arguments relative to *transitional variety*, which disappears once the paradigm is stabilised, and the one that develops out of the very nature of IIPS.

Therefore we shall study here the emergence and management of variety in transitory situations, that is, at the pre-paradigmatic stage (see next sub-section). We shall then analyse the nature of the substitution process which takes place through the change from one paradigm to another. This will highlight the technology management problem as a function of the knowledge requirements before and after the stabilisation of the new paradigm.

Technological learning and technological options

Let us consider the example of new materials. Their development generates a growing variety in the material industries, thereby increasing the number of technological options. How these options are gradually revealed and defined depends on the particular way new materials are introduced in an already existing technological framework. As we shall see, this is done in a piece-by-piece substitution process in which learning effects lead to a global reconception of complex products such as cars or aeroplanes. Firms try to manage the overall process by a broadening of their range of activities, thus generating technological variety in order to prepare (and to be prepared for) selection. They often aim at *horizontal integration* within a whole set of materials. Synergy effects of being familiar with the relevant markets, as well as a knowledge of neighbouring production processes, are more likely to be profitable than purely random diversification (see Teece's chapter). This, for example, partly explains why the chemical industry goes into ceramics activities, or why some steel producers take part in the plastics industry.

Maintaining variety is also part of the strategies through which firms try to manage substitution phenomena. Some firms specifically invest in new materials in order to slow down their diffusion. This behaviour may seem paradoxical, but it can be illustrated by an example from the aluminium industry. Composite materials in the aerospace applications are a major threat to aluminium producers, who are the traditional suppliers of the market. To match the challenge, aluminium producers invest in composite materials (especially carbon fibres), while simultaneously developing new and improved aluminium-lithium alloys (Al-Li).[1] As a result they control and reduce the range of substitution possibilities between composites and aluminium alloys. However, aluminium producers are aware of the fact that, in the long run, major substitutions may well occur just the same. Their investment in carbon fibres can also be viewed as a long-term strategy to enter the composite market. In the short run, however, their diversification behaviour is directed towards valorization of both past and current research on new alloys (Al-Li) and appears as a means to secure profitability of existing capital and thus to recover past investment.

Nevertheless, generally speaking, investment in new materials and new technologies is made in order to acquire knowledge about them. If firms expect that in the near future most of today's technical problems will be solved, there is an incentive to gather production knowledge today. There is an *economic advantage in being ready* at the moment when the market selection process reveals its outcome. To illustrate this principle let us take the case of newly developed ceramics. Among the wide field of potential applications for these materials, those of particular interest are the thermo-mechanical applications (engines, turbines, etc.) in which ceramics may progressively replace metallic alloys. In the short run, however, most expectations conclude that metallic alloys will keep their dominant position. This is mainly due to the fact that, facing a risk of substitution, the metal industry develops improved alloys with better properties (recall Rosenberg's example of sailing ships).[2] But the industrial control of ceramics production is an immediate challenge and, indeed, Japanese firms have already started industrial production of ceramics for thermo-mechanical applications, in spite of the fact that today the market is still very narrow. This production is not actually intended to be sold as such, but is primarily made in order to learn how to produce ceramics. It is merely a kind of *technological simulation*. Scientific and technical knowledge-acquisition is one thing, but in view of competition the crucial stake is production-knowledge.

It is important to note that such strategies act in favour of the emergence of new materials and play an important role in the rate and direction of the innovating process (it is a kind of self-fulfilling expectation in technical progress).

Diffusion patterns: complementarities, substitution and the redesign of systems

At any one time the field for material applications can be divided into two types of area. There are areas in which only one specific material can resolve the relevant technical problem. There are others in which a number of materials compete in order to fulfil the same function. In an area where only one material imposes itself there is obviously no economic problem of inter-technological rivalry, which, on the contrary, is important in the latter cases and operates also through the relative prices of resources employed in the manufacturing of various materials.

The simplistic description that we have just presented helps one to grasp the dynamics of the development of a new material. The technical needs which stimulate the emergence of a new material are clearly those for which the existing materials, produced in well-established technologies, give neither technically nor economically satisfying solutions. It is in the periphery of the field of existing technical paradigms that solutions are not very effective and are consequently expensive (these are the zones of diminishing returns for standard materials). Facing this stimulus, some firms begin to develop new materials which can respond to technical challenges which are either insoluble or not economically viable through the usual means. The cost of development of these new materials is important but, in spite of that, their advantage is that they could potentially compete with the traditional materials in some special applications.

The R & D carried out at this stage of emergence of a new material is of a particular nature. Given the high cost of the new elements, an incremental procedure is generally adopted. The designer will typically insert a new piece made of new materials in *existing technical devices* and the new item will have to match up to the old ones. For example, some parts such as piston heads will use new ceramics in an otherwise metallic engine. Another example is the use of elements made of composite materials in an aircraft within the existing aluminium design. This piece-by-piece substitution process implies that the R & D will have to handle compatibility properties, and *complementarity* links are created between old and new materials.

Through this incremental process learning occurs. As scientific and technical problems are progressively solved, new processing techniques are elaborated and thus knowledge and know-how are created, skill networks and industrial standards emerge, scale economies appear, and cost reduction along with it. At a certain stage, the diffusion process goes through a *threshold*. Technical devices are completely reconceived as a function of the properties of the new compounds: consequently, the R & D will look for *substitution* properties in order to be able to compete with other materials, even in the fields which were hitherto exclusively reserved for them. This 'materials war' involves phenomena of irreversibility (in this area, as well as more generally in several other technologies, see David, 1975; Rosenberg, 1982). If at a given moment, in order to satisfy a particular need, a specific material imposes itself with some scale it will tend to exclude others by the mere fact that R & D budgets are limited and options that are not actually in practice are not improved. Consequently, they cease their evolution and, very often, become impossible (or too expensive) to reactivate (Zuscovitch, 1986; and Arthur's chapter).

A technical system such as an aeroplane is a system of interdependence of technical constraints favouring the incrementalism of innovations. The variability in the innovative options on any one component depends on the constraints coming from the features of other components. The place which was formerly occupied with a metal piece, and in which one wishes to insert another made of composite material, was defined as a function of the whole (metallic) system. Now, there is no reason why a composite should behave like a metal and so using it within the system will make the users discover the new properties such material exhibits. To take full advantage of these properties one would have to *redesign*:

It is not just simply a case of substituting a composite for a metal, but rather of completely redesigning each element, profiting from the (directional or multi-directional) characteristics of the composites used, and very quickly we realize that the rational use of composites brings upon the reconsideration of the very way one conceives and manufactures structures.[3]

Examples of such reconceptions can, of course, be found not only in aeronautics (the rotor boss of the SA 365 c helicopter), but also in the car industry (Bertin's suspension), and in the railways (the bogie elaborated by MBB). In most cases these reconceptions are characterised by a new integration of pieces and a simplification of the system.

This simplification is no trivial operation and, in general, the reconception of technical systems such as an aircraft, in order to take into account the properties of a new material, is a complex operation. The computerisation of conception methods, thanks to CAD, has made a qualitative jump possible in the field. In spite of this, however, the reconception of systems remains above all a function of the constitution of new bodies of knowledge. The latter is only possible through a cumulative process which can only start precisely by a 'piece-by-piece' substitution. The emergence of a threshold effect working in favour of the complete reconception of a system is only realised after the exhaustion of gains from an incremental type of logic. It is often at the moment when expected marginal returns from the incremental innovation are negligible that the technical knowledge, accumulated at the time of the 'piece-by-piece' substitution process, reaches the critical mass necessary for the global reconception of the system.

This critical amount of knowledge is reached through the growth of the number of links, which one has to master in order to integrate pieces made of one material into systems originally created for different ones. The complexity of both system and knowledge increases to the point where a simplification of the system is called for (and allowed). During the 'step-by-step' substitution periods, firms search and, consciously or not, relax the technical constraints of the 'old' optimal solution. As the process goes on, knowledge concerning advantageous reconception opportunities is gained. When the field of such opportunities is sufficiently opened, a qualitative jump becomes possible on the technical level as well as on that of economic performance.

This reinterpretation of the diffusion process in terms of technological learning and the management of technological options suggests that an important problem may arise. Under IIPS, where increasing variety and the capacity *permanently* to maintain many options are decisive, the usual capital-increasing scale economics are likely to operate less effectively. This will consequently alter the nature of economic activities within and among firms. We shall study this problem in depth in the next section.

Permanent variety and changes in firms' strategies

The learning process described in the first section involved a selection mechanism which reduced the number of technological options. The latter were actually mutually exclusive, at least after some stage of development. It follows that the information was intensive (in knowledge and know-how variety) only before selection. Growing flexibility and induced product variety modifies this basic tendency. We shall first try to characterize the technological and market knowledge requirements in IIPS. With many coexisting alternatives, diffusion curves should become smaller and flatter and the problem of economic viability will immediately arise. The issue can be divided into two separate questions. The first is the question of the viability of the resource allocation process in IIPS. The second concerns the dynamic aspect and the possible existence of a sort of 'increasing returns to information', somewhat equivalent to the capital-scale economies in the mass production system.

Characteristics of IIPS

The keystone of the technical system which is still dominant today is *the standardisation of production*. It relies upon a process of technical and organizational changes in order to scale up operations and to satisfy a growing demand. However in the post-war period, the quick growth and the constant increase of welfare in industrial countries had its price. The logic of standardisation has often implied a very limited flow from science to technology and production: only a tiny part of science-based knowledge could be implemented. Moreover, the satisfaction of consumer needs occurred through standardised products so that consumers could benefit from the advantages of mass production.

The characteristics of the materials industries are very typical of that industrial context. The post-war technical system was built up on quite a large set of materials such as various metals, plastics, concrete, glass, wood, etc. The production of these materials was, nevertheless, highly standardised, each one being produced in large quantities and representing an essential component of the general mass-production nature of the economic system. In actual fact, the larger part of manufacturing as a whole was based upon, and often structured around, a limited number of materials (e.g. metal products). While suitable for a large spectrum of applications, that set-up nevertheless restricted the scope for product variations and the industry's capacity for adjustment. Specialised materials of course already existed in order to match specific needs and applications, but more often than not they were primarily produced as standard commodities and then subsequently adapted and 'functionalised'.

Since the late 1960s, production technologies have undergone a qualitative change. The change was partly induced by endogenous technological developments and partly by more general economic factors. First, during the period of fast growth per capita income rose constantly: a richer society demands more variety and Western countries exhibit the rich man's problems. Second, following the oil crisis, the deep uncertainty about both energy prices and the nature of the ongoing technical change has considerably increased the need for flexibility. Yet without the technological push of both information technology and advanced materials the working rules of the economic system would not change that much.

In effect, the origin of the changes in the production system goes back to the early programmable automation. From the start, numerically controlled machines showed that, along with the usual benefits of automation, smaller series also became competitive and allowed a larger product variety than before. In the late 1970s and even more so in the 1980s, a rapid diffusion of micro-computer technologies in production took place in the forms of computer-aided design, computer-aided manufacturing, robotics, artificial intelligence applications and flexible manufacturing systems. In almost all industrial sectors this embodiment of 'intelligence' in production tools considerably lowers the overall set-up costs and thus enables the producer to switch more often from one product to another. Increasingly it seems that efficiency and variety are no longer rival objectives. In a growing part of the industry, from clothing to leather, plastics processing, metal products, etc., it becomes increasingly profitable to produce small batches with a wide spectrum of combinations of properties.

In the materials industry a parallel evolution supplies the necessary condition for the new system. When the variety of products increases, materials have to adjust and offer 'tailor-made' solutions which exhibit the required properties for each particular application, optimising both users' and producers' constraints. While some adaptation in the materials used has always been necessary, it was usual practice to choose the material whose features best suited the most important technical requirement and then took the other features of that material as constraints upon design and processing. Now the materials choice itself has become increasingly an endogenous design variable, that is, a dimension subject to programming. In turn, this has become possible due to both a growing understanding of the microscopic properties of matter and the development of new processing technologies. In other words, new materials loosen one of the tightest constraints on the evolution of the global technical system.

As a consequence, in the new economic system which is gradually emerging, the firm plays the role of *coordination of inputs and outputs properties through network management*. The firm is increasingly trying to match the variety of properties demanded by the user with its own technological 'data base'. Such a task requires permanent research into the characteristics demanded by the user, on the one hand, and the development of the scientific and technical knowledge that is likely to be used in fulfilling this demand, on the other. The definition of the product can no longer be made without the active cooperation of the user, who must reveal his needs and preferences and participate in the definition of the necessary technical solution.[4]

The informational viability of the firm

In an Information-Intensive Production System (IIPS) firms have to face increasing information costs. A growing amount of resources and effort is required for informational activities, namely (a) gathering information on specialised and changing micro-markets, and (b) searching for new technical solutions adapted to the specific needs revealed by these micro-markets. As a result firms have to cope with higher transaction costs to implement refined market searching and with higher R & D expenditures. Hence, one arrives at a basic viability question: how do the required resources for developing such activities become available?

One part of the possible answer comes from the consumer's willingness to pay: tailor-made products are higher priced than standardised products.

Indeed, lower price-elasticity of demand and quasi-monopoly power in differentiated-product industries lead to higher selling returns than in competitive industries. However, whether these higher returns will fall short of or exceed the increased informational costs ultimately depends on *the size of each 'micro' market*. In general, for any given micro-market size, and level of the quasi-rent on the specific product-service package, the basic question is whether there exists a reallocation of resources within the firm which is economically viable, i.e. which can at least offset the increased informational costs.[5]

Of course, the question of viability of a *variety-based, information-intensive production system* is directly linked to the question of its permanence. When such viable reallocations do not exist, variety can only appear as a transitory phenomenon that will vanish after the market selection process has elicited some new standards. If, for example, small series are less efficient within a given market, despite potential variety in demand, such a selection process would push towards scale industries and standardisation of products.[6] The post-war technical system should be considered as a result of such a process which favoured large-scale production in most industries. We shall try to tackle the question of viability of IIPS by discussing, first, increasing transaction costs and, second, growing R & D expenditure.

(a) Transaction costs of micro-markets and economies of scope. Increasing transaction costs arise mainly because of specialised demands which, in a dynamic context, are frequently changing. In a variety system such costs are no longer entirely fixed but are mainly variable, and arise because of the time and costs required to locate, define and satisfy more specialised needs. In the post-war technical system, transaction costs were a relatively small proportion of the total cost of the firm. In addition, they could be shared among a large number of identical products. Economic viability was granted through scale economies obtained with specific capital goods. In a variety-based system, however, large series of identical products are replaced by small batches of a broad range of different products. With small series, scale economies are severely reduced if specific capital goods are employed. Unit costs will increase as well as transaction costs. However, new equipment such as CAD/CAM, robotics and flexible manufacturing systems (FMS) exhibit a kind of advantage that could be compared to scale economies. For example, robot production lines incorporate enough flexibility to handle a variety of different products. More generally, by sharing a given set of inputs *economies of scope*[7] may be obtained. Economies of scope arise mainly when the 'horizontal constraint', i.e. specialisation in the use of capital equipment, is removed. This is indeed the case with FMSs which are not designed for specific tasks. Their scope of operation is quite large and such equipment easily adapts to new production lines simply by modification of the software. As a consequence variety and efficiency no longer appear as rival objectives. Joint

production costs obtained by sharing the same capital inputs are lower than the sum of specific production costs. To put it another way, product-specific economies of scale are smaller than economies of scope. Such a property, called 'transray convexity'[8] of the firm's cost function, means that 'as a firm changes the composition of output while holding fixed the level of some aggregate measure of output, costs will be lower for diverse rather than specialized output mixes' (Bailey and Friedlaender, 1982).

Traditional economies of scale still appear when aggregate output increases, as the result of physical indivisibilities of capital goods. But if full capacity is not attained with given equipment and for some product mix, it will be efficient to fill the gap by adding a new product to the mix. Now if economies of scope are high enough, they compensate, at least to some extent, the increasing costs resulting from information-gathering activities. Thus one can argue that economic viability is likely, at least for certain degrees of variety. However, economic viability does not depend only on the general properties of a technological system (in our case, the IIPS), but also on the firm-specific, and path-dependent, abilities of individual firms (cf. in this volume the chapters by Teece and Arthur). The viability of IIPS for each firm crucially depends on its success in adjusting its behavioural routines—especially with regard to R & D activities—and in acquiring the right kind of knowledge. We shall now discuss these fundamental requirements.

(b) R & D management in IIPS and organisational flexibility. In a standardised production system, R & D expenditures are mainly fixed costs for a given product and research costs are distributed among a great number of identical products. In addition, informational economies of scope within R & D activities occur and indeed many improvements are readily applied to products and technologies belonging to the same family. Output of R & D activities are shared inputs for production activities. As an example, take the case of the French nuclear power industry. All power stations were built according to the same standards. As a result, any improvement made in one station, or knowledge acquired within a given process, was automatically applied or used in others.

We suggest that such advantages no longer hold (or are less important) within an IIPS. First, R & D costs are distributed only over quite a narrow set of identical products. Second, improvements made in a given process are not easily applied to other processes. Because of greater variability of R & D expenditures firms are faced with a new cost constraint, and the question is once again one of viability in dealing with these increasing R & D costs.

At a first glance, a high variety of R & D projects under these circumstances seem hardly viable. Indeed, this is likely to be the case if R & D is managed the same way as in the 'standardised' production system. However, one may conceive of different organisational developments capable of handling an increased output variety and input specificity. One such development involves a recombination of standardised intermediate consumption in order to obtain output variety. As a result, final products will be of variable design but will incorporate mainly standardised components. Only some characteristics of the products will be more variable at the expense of higher standardisation of other characteristics. Such a possible evolution was pointed out by Cohendet and Llerena (1987), and is well exemplified by some material industries, such as silicium production, for example. In this case new technologies and materials would only affect the distribution of variety and standardisation among industries without affecting the average degree of variety within the technical system.

However, increasing variety in some industries does not necessarily imply higher standardisation in others. Another development with full exploitation of IIPS is nevertheless possible, subject to two conditions. The first is the formation of technological partnerships; the second is the capacity to internalise efficiently external information. These two points will be developed.

First, under these circumstances, R & D viability rests upon a radical change in its organisation. If variety is an economic objective, concentrated research activities are less efficient because the results of each R & D project are distributed over a small set of products each with relatively short production runs. This is the main reason that induces firms to collaborate with others instead of integrating new activities or doing 'in-house' research, illustrating Teece's observations on the limits of integration (Chapter 12). Thus firms will have to develop more cooperative research, especially with other firms possessing complementary knowledge and skills. This is indeed the case with composite materials. Development of composite products involves quite different bodies of technical knowledge. Most R & D activities are undertaken by teams organised through partnership of different firms. As a result firms also try to develop their ability to organise such cooperative research activities, obviously involving, for these tasks, resources and organisational effort. In turn, this has some major implications concerning the organisation of the firm, and especially its communication system, i.e. its internal and external system of interactions.

A firm will try to set up an optimal communication network internally in order to save on communication costs within the firm and to take into account the economic environment. Once such a communication network is installed, set-up costs are not easily recovered because such networks are highly firm-specific, depending in particular on the firm's 'culture'. There is then a natural tendency towards specialisation of networks in order to achieve efficiency with respect to a given environment. On the other hand, an already existing network can generate economies of scope because it can be used for a great deal of different messages. But as Arrow noted, optimality of the firm's communication system is no longer granted if external conditions change:

Eventually the communication system may be very inefficient at handling signals, and the firm may vanish or undergo a major reorganization. To put it in another way, the firm's organization is designed to meet a more or less wide variety of possible signals. The wider the range planned for, the greater is the flexibility of the firm in meeting the unforeseen (that is what flexibility means) but the less efficient it is in meeting a narrower range of possibilities . . . [Arrow, 1973]

A similar point is made in relation to user-producer communications by Lundvall in Chapter 17. He relates the rigidity of the communication system to the efficiency of innovations. A given set of communication systems may eventually lead to 'unsatisfactory innovations' when consumer needs change. However, firms must not only be flexible in their handling of the information from the environment. They must also be able to draw from the appropriate technical knowledge and skills distributed in the environment. Let us call such threads of technological flows and inter-dependences (cf. the chapters by Lundvall and Dosi) the *skill network* of an environment.

In IIPS, in order to secure viability, firms have to create new relations with the outside skill network in order to produce new and adapted solutions for evolving needs. This means that firms have to develop organisational flexibility, i.e. the capacity to generate and organise new relations within their environment and especially with the skill network.[9] Such organisational flexibility seems to be a main issue for competition in IIPS.

The firm in IIPS and the 'internalisation of the environment'

Higher product variety and rising information intensity imply that firms have to manage growing complexity in information-processing and problem-solving (cf. Dosi–Orsenigo in this volume). This can only be dealt with by *simplifying internal procedures*, and by developing *coordination skills*. Such integration is capable of liberating the firm's human resources required to deal with external information.

(a) Informational scale economies through algorithmisation. The capacity permanently to process new information, which also amplifies the strategic reach of the firm, implies the capacity to transform an increasing number of choices and assessments into routinised procedures. There must be a continous transformation of problems that belong to the field of decision-making into that of standardised responses. It is only in so far as such a transformation operates with a certain ease and autonomy that the full IIPS is viable. We call such a process the 'algorithmisation' of information-processing, decision-making and organisational coordination. We conjecture that, on the grounds of the new technologies, such a process (a) leads to the economic viability of IIPS, and (b) embodies a momentum of its own, like a 'trajectory', in the terminology of Dosi's chapter, towards higher levels of efficiency with flexibility. This trajectory is, loosely speaking, the equivalent in IIPS of the trajectory toward mechanisation, automation and economies of scale in the earlier 'standardised' production system.

It is necessary, in a way, to prove whether the new functioning principle based on the processing of information is capable of *generating a surplus*. During industrialisation the principle of surplus creation, and hence of economic development, relied on a chain reaction that linked *standardised* organisation of work, dispossession of individual qualifications by automisation and opening of bigger and bigger markets. The static expression given in economics textbook to this process is increasing returns to scale. For the new information-intensive production regime to be viable, a new chain reaction must take place without being conditioned by standardisation in the usual sense.

One is already able to see some steps in the 'chain-reaction' which led the evolution of information technologies. With the diffusion of central computers in the 1960s, firms were able, by batch processing, to improve the efficiency of their routine functions (accounting, stock management, billing, etc.). At the end of the 1970s and at the beginning of the 1980s, this was followed by the development of more decentralised computer systems and the integration of computerisation of production, via CAD, robotics and, finally, the flexible workshop. The latter step brings about a change, we suggest, in the general logic of production organisation, capable of dealing more efficiently with frequent changes. However, this second stage has been largely conditioned by the previous ones. Indeed, the capacity to move from one production sequence to another requires the optimisation of each. This optimisation is itself a result of the accumulation of knowledge and control of the processes generated by the previous stages of informatisation. For example, when in the cost-accounting area the use of computers creates better knowledge of, say, factors that influence material consumption, new instructions to production management are given. In turn, codified instructions mean that, in areas where decisions had previously to be made, a routine procedure is implemented. The rate of 'algorithmisation' consequently increases in the workshop, bringing it closer to the level at which it can integrate its own computers. It is the control of the production organisation via computerisation that allows codified changes in products and processes and hence makes a wider variety of management possible.

The computerisation of standardised functions generates a 'surplus of information' on less well-organised functions. As a consequence this allows a more accurate determination of the behavioural norms related to these functions, whereas before their decision-making was more uncertain. These more 'discretionary' functions become in turn standardised, and thus more apt to absorb information technologies in their own right. Apparently what appears here is a chain-reaction process in which each computerised stage prepares the necessary conditions for the implementation of a new generation of computers. At each stage, this process implies setting up procedures which allow the analysis of the internal logic of the activities concerned. This progressively transforms the structures of firms and goes in the direction of an increased automatisation of decision procedures. Such an evolution tends to reduce the uncertainty of strategic decisions because it increases the control of the firm over the environment and in this sense 'internalises' it within the strategic scope of the firm (Simon, 1980). The introduction of more sophisticated means of storing, processing and communicating information tends to displace the limit which exists between the 'algorithmical' and the 'non-algorithmical' part of the firm. At each further step, as codification (algorithmisation) proceeds, discretionary decision capabilities can be applied to problems of higher complexity.[10]

Obviously this description of such a cumulative process is a simplification. In fact it may not be so continuous. Threshold effects appear each time that the algorithms underlying the functioning of a part (or the whole) of the firm can no longer react to the evolution of the environment. In a sense, organisational failures and bottlenecks in information accumulation are the equivalent to the physical limits in 'scaling up' in the standardised system of production.

(b) The control of the external environment: the emergence of the coordination function. Whether the potential future growth regime is regular or not, the cumulative character of the integration of information by successive 'algorithmisations' will not stop too soon. Flexible equipment is of no value without constantly renewed information. Each time the variety of products augments somewhere in the system, there will be a tendency to multiply the variety of the related components in order to respond to increasingly differentiated and specific needs. Consider again the case of advanced materials. In order to conceive and produce a growing variety of objects, the knowledge of *zones of compatibility* of different properties becomes of major importance. *Flexibility does not mean convexity of the properties space.* The ability to master potential combinations will be a future firm-specific asset among competitive firms in developed countries. Between equally flexible systems, the difference will be made by the possibility of stretching these zones of properties beyond the frontiers defined by standard data banks. It is in this respect that R & D activities will certainly become the most constraining (and rewarding) activity because it will be able to ensure an informational specificity, and thus be of comparative advantage to particular firms.

If this is so, it is necessary to ask what are the determinants of competitiveness in a complex system such as this one. Who will best control technical progress? How will the results be appropriated? Who will control the most strategic areas? The system constructor or the materials suppliers? The system constructor (car or aircraft industry, for instance) is well aware of the range in which constraints are compatible for a given technical object. The materials suppliers, traditionally associated with a number of user industries, dominate the complete spectrum of properties. Inter-industrial technological partnerships provide evidence that the question remains unanswered, and indeed that it probably does not have any single answer. We are at the beginning of this transformation and thus it is too early to foretell the precise articulation of the new industrial system. One characteristic is, nevertheless, clear. The growing complexity of the system will make the coordination function very important both within and among firms.

In fact, there is a field in which the complex network has already been very important for some time, namely the space programme. Space technology does not have a unique scientific body of knowledge, as is the case with chemistry or electronics. Space technology is essentially organisational with no 'production' of its own. It is merely a kind of agency (e.g. the European Space Agency) which organises an international network of different industries. It is through a process of coordination and imposing of technical and organisational constraints (command delays, charge books, defined standards, etc.) that the space network weaves itself. The spillover of knowledge from the space departments to other technological and commercial fields comes from the nature of the participation in the immense technical and organisational coordination network.[11] According to their role in the network the firms do not develop the same learning profile, and thus the induced benefit categories are of a different qualitative nature. This example, we suggest, can be generalised. Hence, looking beyond the traditional dimensions of sectoral stratification and market structure, the role of the firm in the 'skill network' will become increasingly decisive for competitiveness.

Conclusion

The growing integration of information technologies, aided by the potentially tailor-made new materials, shifts the economic emphasis from capital-intensive to information-intensive production. We have tried to show how technological learning and the management of technological options differ in this context. If scale economies diminish in importance, inputs and outputs variety increase and transaction costs rise. To overcome transaction costs induced by the continuous redefinition of micro-markets and rising R & D costs, such 'Information-Intensive Production Systems' should prove their economic viability by finding some means of increasing efficiency. We have argued that, indeed, new technologies provide such a potential. Statically, the economies of scope of flexible equipment may compensate for information costs. Dynamically, a process of 'algorithmisation', that is, codification and routinisation of decision-making via more and more information-processing, may increase organisational efficiency, widen the strategic scope of the firm, and 'internalise' more control over the environment.

Notes

1. The advantage of the Al-Li alloys is that they do not require, up to a certain percentage of lithium, a costly redesign of both the aircraft and of the processing machines as in the case of composite materials. Therefore their diffusion does not imply high fixed costs. As we shall see, reconception thresholds are a very important feature in the competition among technological alternatives. Avoiding them, or at least postponing them, may have a large impact on the effectiveness of competing technologies. (See, on the issue of competing alternative technologies, the chapter by Arthur in this volume.)

2. 'Factors affecting the diffusion of technology', in N. Rosenberg (1972).

3. See Zuscovitch and Arrous (1984).

4. Problems raised by the interaction between user and producer are extensively discussed by Lundvall in Chapter 17.

5. Remember, however, that here we treat micro-market size and quasi-rent as given while they are equally determined by the nature of the income distribution. Income distribution, however, is partly determined in a macroeconomic setting, as are the optimality and welfare properties. An IIPS will certainly not have the same macro overall adjustment properties as the standard mass-production regime. Severe segmentation of markets, of labour and of goods would probably be less mean-dependent and more variance-dependent in all respects. Unions rightfully dread a structural deterioration in their power but also, more importantly, in the very capacity of workers to defend their basic rights once this segmentation is pushed too far. The only guarantee against exploitation is that the human capital is an essential component of the whole. In the same way that the product will be partly defined by the consumer so that he can expect to share consumer surplus, white- or blue-collar workers will also enter product definition. Apparently partnership is the name of the new game and everybody should be happy—except for those who are excluded, of course. The unemployed within and outside the developed countries will still call for standard solutions, provided that there will be solutions. Variety is the rich man's problem. Redistribution of resources will be even more needed than before in order to ensure minimal social integration.

6. For recent progress on selection processes in economics of technological change, see Nelson and Winter (1982) and Gibbons and Metcalfe (1986). In this book, this issue is discussed in the chapters by Silverberg, Metcalfe, Dosi–Orsenigo and Allen.

7. For a complete definition and analysis, see J. Panzar and R. Willig (1981).

8. See E. Bailey and A. Friedlaender (1982) for a formal definition.

9. This has also some implications for the organisation of the firm and particularly for its hierarchical structure. As Kay points out in Chapter 13, highly flexible structures, or what he calls 'organic systems', are better suited to meet the quickly changing environment of IIPS. 'Mechanistic systems', characterised by functional specialisation and formal hierarchical relationships, appear less efficient in managing dynamically fluctuating environments.

10. See Zuscovitch and Brendle (1985) for a detailed analysis of this process.

11. See Cohendet and Zuscovitch (1985).

References

Arrow, K. J. (1973), 'Information and economic behavior', in *Collected Papers of K. J. Arrow*, Vol. 4, *The Economics of Information*, Oxford, Basil Blackwell (1984).

Bailey, E. E. and Friedlaender, A. F. (1982), 'Market structure and multiproduct industries', *Journal of Economic Literature*, vol. XX, September, pp. 1024–48.

Cohendet, P. and Llerena, P. (1987), 'Flexibilité, complexité et intégration dans les processus de production', Actes du Seminaire International 'AMES', Paris, April, pp. 101–22.

Cohendet, P. and Zuscovitch, E. (1985), 'L'apprentissage techno-économique du programme spatial européen', SITEF, Toulouse, October.

David, P. A. (1975), *Technical Choice, Innovation and Economic Growth*, Cambridge, Cambridge University Press.

Gibbons, M. and Metcalfe, J. S. (1986), 'Technological variety and the process of competition', Conference on Innovation Diffusion, Venice, March 1986.

Nelson, R. R. and Winter, S. G. (1982), *An Evolutionary Theory of Economic Change*, Cambridge, Mass., Harvard University Press.

Panzar, J. C. and Willig, R. D. (1981), 'Economies of scope', *American Economic Review*, vol. 71, no. 2, May, pp. 268–72.

Rosenberg, N. (1972), 'Factors affecting the diffusion of technology', *Explorations in Economic History*, Fall.

—— (1982), *Inside the Black Box*, Cambridge, Cambridge University Press.

Simon, H. A. (1980), *Le nouveau management*, Paris, Economica.

Williamson, O. (1985), *The Economic Institutions of Capitalism*, New York, Free Press.

Zuscovitch, E. (1986), 'The economic dynamics of technologies development', *Research Policy*, vol. 15, pp. 175–86.

Zuscovitch, E. and Arrous, J. (1984), 'La diffusion intersectorielle des matériaux synthétiques', in P. Cohendet (ed.), *La Chimie en Europe*, Paris, Economica.

Zuscovitch, E. and Brendle, P. (1985), 'Informatisation: l'impact sur l'organisation des enterprises', *La Revue Française de gestion*, No. 51, mars–avril–mai.

12 Technological change and the nature of the firm*

David J. Teece

School of Business Administration, University of California, Berkeley

Introduction

Modern capitalist economies have a variety of organizational forms within which research and development is conducted. They include universities and government and private laboratories. Research and development laboratories differ in size, in the scope of scientific disciplines represented within them, and in the mechanism by which they are funded. These institutions both cooperate and compete to varying degrees and transfer know-how in and out.

The predominant mode of industrial research in the private sector, at least in the United States, is the integrated research organization, part of a business enterprise which engages in at least one other activity vertically related to research and development such as manufacturing, marketing, distribution, sales and service. This chapter focuses on this particular component of the research infrastructure of modern American capitalism. It attempts to explain the reluctance on the part of innovating enterprises to rely on external research facilities to procure new products and processes via the market.

In view of the historical reluctance of firms to contract for technology, the sudden and recent rise in external acquisition activities by certain US corporations warrants an explanation. Relatedly, the 'hollowing' of the corporation—that is, the outsourcing of components and in some case whole systems—is explored with respect to possible ramifications for the appropriability of returns from innovation.

A second and subsidiary theme explored in this chapter is the relationship between technology and technological change, and the growth or diversification activities of the business enterprise. Given the current state of economic theory, one should be equally surprised by the diversification as by the coherence—that is, the tendency for firms *not* to be pure conglomerates with their activity randomly spread across a variety of product lines—of the modern corporation. It is hypothesized here that a good deal of the coherence of the corporation can be understood in terms of techno-

*I am especially grateful to Richard Nelson, Giovanni Dosi, Sidney Winter, Gary Pisano and Oliver Williamson for helpful discussions that have shaped my thinking on the issues addressed in this chapter.

logy, technological change and the differences between technologies in their managerial requirements.

Historical perspective on the organization of private-for-profit R & D activities

During the late nineteenth century and the first half of the twentieth century, American manufacturing firms bought an increasing share of R & D in-house. Previously, practically all of it had been conducted outside of the firm in stand-alone research organizations. Thomas Edison's industrial research laboratory in Menlo Park, New Jersey, was one such structure, and from it flowed the light bulb and many other inventions.[1] Even as late as 1945, there were hundreds of such organizations employing over 5,000 scientists and engineers.

Throughout the early decades of the twentieth century, however, the independent, stand-alone labs were in relative decline (see Figure 12.1); and during certain decades, they probably actually declined in absolute number. In 1911, for instance, Arthur D. Little organized for General Motors a laboratory for materials analysis and testing. But the main component of G.M.'s research organization came from an independent lab—the Dayton Engineering Laboratories Company—which was absorbed by G.M. after being organized by Charles Kettering and E. A. Deeds (Sloan, 1964).

Table 12.1:   Employment of scientific professionals in independent research organizations as a fraction of employment of scientific professionals in all in-house and independent research laboratories, 1921–46

1921	15.2%
1927	12.9%
1933	10.9%
1940	8.7%
1946	6.9%

Source: Mowery (1983, Chapter 2).

This is not to imply that contract research and in-house research are substitutes. Mowery (1983) has suggested that they were complements, in the sense that as in-house research facilities grew in size and number during 1900–40 they also developed as the primary clients for the stand-alone research organizations. This may indicate that they were subcontractors bearing a vertical relationship to the in-house labs. Firms without in-house laboratories, moreover, used contract research only for the simplest types of research projects (Mowery, 1983, p. 363), a characteristic still evident today (Teece and Armour, 1977, p. 56).

Mowery's case studies of Arthur D. Little (founded 1896), the Mellon Institute (1911), and Batelle (1929) are instructive. Mellon's contract research was primarily concerned with the improvement of existing processes or the utilization of by-products. Nearly 25 per cent of Batelle's projects undertaken during the period 1929–40 were analyses or tests of metals, minerals or coal (few mining firms had in-house labs). Chemical analyses were a mainstay of ADL's activities. The evidence seems to indicate that the independent research organizations did not engage significantly in new-product development and did not offer a wide menu of contract research services.

In-house research thus came to be the dominant mode for supporting corporate research in America, for small as well as for large organizations. By the 1970s, there were very few stand-alone research organizations, and these typically performed a very limited kind of research. In the petroleum industry, only one such firm—Universal Oil Products—remained by 1970, and it has subsequently lost its stand-alone status. Teece and Armour (1977, pp. 56–7) noted the rather narrow range of research activities that were conducted under contract—typically, those where the research objectives are simply and obvious, and where the risks are low.[2]

The integration of R & D with production

Contractual analysis

The internalization of research and development warrants theoretical explanation. Why is it that in the modern capitalist corporation R & D generally nestles in close to marketing and manufacturing? Put differently, why do non-market modes rather than market (contractual) modes appear to dominate as a mechanism for securing the output of research establishments? After all, Stigler (1956, p. 281) has remarked that, 'We may expect the rapid expansion of the specialized research laboratory which sells its services generally. The specialized laboratories need not be in the least inferior to captive laboratories.' In order to explore these matters, a stylized organizational framework is assumed for an industry experiencing technological change (Figure 12.2). The figure shows the kinds of transactions/interactions which must exist between the organization if new technology is to be developed and implemented.

If one begins with the premise that there are gains associated with organizational specialization and that markets provide workable mechanisms for linking organizations, then Stigler's presumption that the stand-alone lab supported by contracts would outperform in-house labs naturally follows. Indeed, in most advanced industrial economies one observes a considerable amount of defense-related research being procured via contractual mechanisms. At the same time, most firms in industries experiencing rapid technological change have in-house R & D capabilities. An exploration of the relative efficiency properties of the two modes thus appears to be warranted.

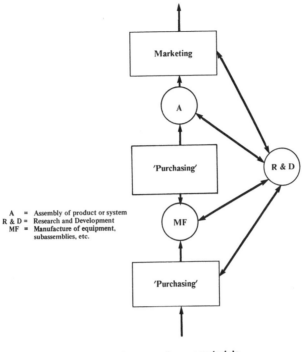

Figure 12.1

Two sets of factors are relevant. The first set of factors relates to economies of scale and specialization. The second set of factors relates to the workability of contractual mechanisms. Both issues will be examined from the perspective of the relative merits of A (assembly) or MF (manufacturing) being integrated into R & D. The contractual issues are essentially the same whether it is the assembler or the manufacturer purchasing R & D services.

If a purchaser (such as A or MF) of R & D services is comparing in-house and contract research alternatives, and if the R & D activity in question involves significant scale economies or capabilities which the purchaser does not possess, then standard microeconomic analysis would indicate that contracting for R & D services from an established low-cost provider will be the superior alternative, just as it would be for any other service or component. However, a more sensitive analysis reveals that contractual mechanisms for procuring R & D services are shot through with hazards, so that the costs and practicality of relying on the market for R & D services will be tightly circumscribed in many important circumstances. This is because contracts encounter difficulties as the degree of uncertainty increases. The greater the uncertainty, the more difficult it is to specify a workable contract. There are just too many unknown contingencies, which means that contracts are necessarily incomplete. According to one observer:

it is inherent in an industry experiencing rapid technological improvement that a new product, incorporating the most advanced technology, cannot be contracted for by detailed specification of the final product. It is precisely the impossibility of specifying final product characteristics in a well-defined way in advance which renders competitive bidding impossible in the industry. To attempt such a specification would, in itself, constitute a serious impediment to technical progress. [Miller and Sawyers, 1970]

Contractual difficulties are not, however, limited to specification problems. There are disclosure and 'lock-in' problems which are invariant to the mode of contracting chosen, whether it is of the fixed-prices or the cost-plus variety. Each of these two fundamental modes of contracting is now explored further.

Fixed-price contracts. The use of fixed-price contracts to procure new products which are state-of-the-art or beyond exemplifies the difficulties associated with the use of unassisted markets. A number of problems can be identified. First, there are problems associated with the production of precontract information. In competitive bidding for complex contracts, conveyance of information at the precontract stage is likely to be a substantial problem (Goldberg, 1977). Formulating specifications will require interaction with the potential providers at the precontract stage which will be both time-consuming and costly. The costs of transferring the information will influence both the relative efficacy of alternative bidding mechanisms and the nature of the output itself. They will also, of course, influence the relative merits of competitive bidding versus vertical integration.

A second problem the purchaser faces in relying on markets is obtaining the appropriate level of protection of proprietary information — his own and that of the potential suppliers. Conveying accurate information to potential bidders can decrease the likelihood that some valuable trade secrets will be protected. Likewise, a solicitation which requires suppliers to reveal confidential information might induce those suppliers to forgo the bidding or demand costly safeguards.

A third problem is 'lock-in'. That is, there are limited options for changing developers, as well as limited options for using a supplier (other than the original developer) to perform subsequent production. This is due largely to the fact that in order to secure competitive bidding at the production stage, detailed manufacturing drawings and specifications must be created. Yet drawings executed for development purposes are often necessarily incomplete. Short-cuts may be taken and engineers often rely upon verbal communication with production foremen to ensure that the proper manufacturing sequences and tolerances are satisfied. The tacit component (Teece, 1981; Nelson and Winter, 1982) is often high. Errors might, of course, be minimized through intimate contact and cooperation between manufacturer and developer, but if the developer has lost out on the production contract to a competitor, it may be difficult to achieve the kind of cooperation needed for the successful transfer of technology from the developer to the manufacturer/producer.

Of course, the transfer of production away from the developer to another enterprise does not remove the 'lock-in' problem—it merely transfers the dependence from one potential supplier to another. This can be relieved, at least in part, by second-sourcing strategies, but this is also expensive as manufacturing drawings and know-how must be conveyed by the original producer to the new second-source producer with attendant costs and delays. Furthermore, if economies of scale are present, considerable production cost savings may be sacrificed by a dual-sourcing strategy. Similarly, when learning is an important factor, experience curve advantages may be lost by second sourcing. Also, quality control and standardization are more difficult to achieve when multiple supply sources are involved.

The above problems are softened once the design of a new product has been stabilized. It may then be possible to rely on contractual mechanisms to achieve efficient supply. When specifications define in detail the product to be procured, the buyer has a better chance of assuming that the contractor delivers what was promised, and the contractor can in turn ensure that it will be asked to deliver no more than was promised.

Cost-plus contracts. Because of the above problems, and because R & D costs are subject to enormous uncertainty, it is hazardous if not impossible to determine the price for a product which has yet to be created. Unless both parties are risk-neutral, there may be a reluctance to enter fixed-price contracts. An alternative is the cost-plus contract.

However, the cost-plus contract is unlikely to be superior to integration, except where a one-shot transaction is contemplated—in which case it may not be cost effective to build the requisite internal capabilities. The reason is that the cost-plus contract has only weak incentives for least cost performance. In fact, in order to ensure that the gross abuses of this mechanism do not occur, it may be necessary to set up an administrative structure which replicates many of the features of vertical integration.[3]

For instance, in 1955 the Consolidated Edison Company of New York used a cost-plus contract with Babcock and Wilcox for the development and construction of a 235,000 kW atomic energy plant where the relationship involved major technological uncertainties. But the relationship was hardly arms-length. Consolidated Edison exerted detailed supervision over Babcock and Wilcox, auditing all their invoices, approving all engineering changes, and authorizing any variations that might affect the level of cost. This was a highly detailed control by the buyer of the contractor's activities.[4] In short, in order to monitor cost-plus contracts, an administrative mechanism must be set up which is tantamount to vertical integration.

Indeed, when the procurement of technologically advanced products and systems is contemplated, the key organizations responsible for delivering advanced products and systems will need to have an in-house research and development capability.

Contracting for R & D exposes the enterprise not only to an R & D 'lock-in' in that valuable knowledge may be required which will give the R & D organization an advantage with respect to subsequent R & D contracts, but to a manufacturing 'lock-in' as well if the R & D service procured involves the design of equipment or components which will then be embedded in a product (or service) which the procurer is manufacturing. The lock-in problems stem, at least in part, from the costs of technology transfer from the developer to the producer. The developer thereby obtains a first-mover advantage in production which can be used to advantage by the developer if the developer is also a potential supplier at the production stage. This is true for both fixed-price and cost-plus contracts. The reason is that during development activities a considerable amount of tacit knowledge is acquired in a learning-by-doing fashion. If the development work is extensive and costly to replicate, then the procurer is exposed to a 'lock-in' in the sense that subsequent production cannot be contracted in a fully competitive fashion. The developer will have acquired a first-mover advantage and may be able to price subsequent production above long-run costs because of the advantage it has acquired, relative to its rivals, at the development stage. The phenomenon has been commented upon in the context of weapons acquisition:

Consider two firms, A and B. Firm A is the sole developer of the weapon; both firms are capable of producing it. Now, since firm A has developed the weapon, it is reasonable to assume that A has garnered some knowledge from the development process which will be useful in the production process. Consequently, the original developer, in this case A, is capable of producing the first x units at a lower cost than any other producer. [Arditti, 1968, p. 320]

Arditti presents supportive data from the airframe industry. In a different context, data have also been assembled which suggests that the switching costs are especially high before the new preoduct has gone into production. The available evidence strongly supports the contention that it is knowledge and the high cost of its transfer which yields the advantage to the first mover. Furthermore, the less codified is the relevant know-how, and the closer it is to the state-of-the-art, the more costly it is to transfer (Teece, 1977). In short, when the amount of development activity involved is large, the procurer may well provide the supplier with a non-trivial first-mover advantage if the work is performed at the procurer's expense. In these circumstances, the procurer can avoid the 'lock-in' problem via the vertical integration of production.

Integration between research and the user. Contractual analysis makes it clear that integration between the manufacturer and R & D is usually necessary both because of the difficulties associated with specifying the R & D services which are to be procured as well as subsequent lock-in. In the above discussion, it was assumed that the organizational unit desiring R & D services had a clear perception of what was needed, even if that perception could not be translated into workable specifications.

The identification of market requirements is, however, a complex process itself. An essential feature of successful innovation is that it must be responsive to user needs. The available evidence indicates that successful attempts at innovation are distinguished frequently from failures by greater attention to the understanding of user needs. Innovation involves a complex series of events. A number of interfaces must be crossed in the process of technological innovation. Each interface becomes a potential barrier to innovation unless spanning mechanisms are put into place. At least three different kinds of spanning or gatekeeping functions are commonly acknowledged as critical to innovative success (Roberts, 1979): the technical 'gatekeeper', the market 'gatekeeper' and a manufacturing 'gatekeeper'. The technical gatekeeping function bridges the organization to the scientific community at large. The market gatekeeper function must understand what competitors are doing, what the regulators are up to, and what is happening with respect to changes in the customer marketplace. The person or persons communicating these sources of information to the R & D environment is a critical contributor who keeps the technical organization on target towards the kinds of activities that will eventually be successful in the marketplace (Roberts, 1979, p. 27). The manufacturing gatekeeper function develops understanding of the real and hard-nosed environment of the manufacturing plant so as to keep R & D up to date on the realities of materials, of assembly processes, and to keep marketing and R & D up to date on the cost of doing things different ways. This function helps ensure that what gets designed and developed in R & D is targeted towards producibility at a cost sufficiently low to generate meaningful volume and profitability.

These functions are best performed by specialists who understand each other's problems and needs, who share common objectives, and who can collaborate and exchange the information that each needs freely and without corporate or proprietary barriers. Integration clearly facilitates the activities of such specialists. Intra-organizational boundaries are typically more permeable than market boundaries—in part because secrecy is not jeopardized, and a common internal language can be employed. The existence of a common coding system and the attendant dialogue among organizations facilitates both technology transfer and the formulation of appropriate research objectives. As a result, the research activity is likely to be better directed and hence more productive.

Cumulative learning and spillovers in R & D

The analysis presented in the previous section sheds light on considerations which very often compel integration of the R & D activity or grounds of contractual efficiency. In most cases, however, there are additional factors which are not fully elucidated by focusing on contracting and technology transfer issues alone, although in a theoretical sense they can possibly be thought of in contracting terms.

As was indicated above, the phenomenon of 'lock-in' is likely to characterize the relationship between the R & D provider and the unit utilizing the results of the R & D process. 'Lock-in' has its roots in high switching costs, often due to the fact that much of the technology generated by R & D activities is of the tacit kind, and this is costly to transfer.

This tacit knowledge, moreover, tends to be cumulative, which is all the more reason why it is often desirable to deepen and stabilize the relationship among the buyer/user and the seller/provider. As Nelson and Winter (1982) have explained:

> In many technological histories the new is not just better than the old; in some sense the new evolves out of the old. One explanation for this is that the output of today's searches is not merely a new technology, but also enhances knowledge and forms the basis of new building blocks to be used tomorrow. [pp. 255–6]

Because the knowledge acquired in the course of one project often has implications for the next round of R & D projects, it is important that the entity which is sponsoring the R & D activity keep a close liaison with the R & D unit, not only to access valuable technology and possibly firm-specific knowledge that the R & D unit will have generated, but also for reasons of preventing this from 'spilling over' to competitors. Spillover would almost certainly occur if the R & D unit was free standing.

This 'neighborhood' characteristic of discovery not only explains why firms need to keep the R & D activity in-house; it also explains why there is a certain natural trajectory associated with a firm's *de novo* product migration and diversification activity. This is the topic of the next section.

Determining product boundaries with technological change

The firm's 'core business'

A firm's core business, it can be argued, stems from the underlying natural trajectory embedded in the firm's knowledge base. New product development thus usually proceeds 'close in' to previous successes. A wave of improvements, often dramatic in their significance, may follow the introduction of a major new technology. The desirability of hunting for improvement depends, of course, upon the commercial promise which first commercialization may have yielded or at least signalled. Previous commercialization histories may indicate the most promising technological neighborhoods to explore in terms of market acceptance. Sometimes, however, there may be a kind of inevitability to the direction of search, driven by what Rosenberg (1969) has referred to as 'technological imperatives'.

A change in technological regime—where regime is defined by the convergence of engineer beliefs about what is feasible or at least worth attempting—or the simultaneous coexistence of several related technological regimes (as with both CMOS and NMOS technologies in semiconductors) may soften technological imperatives, making them less path-dependent. Of course, technological discontinuities may blow path dependencies asunder.

There are important implications for economic theory, for the organization of research, and for the organization of economic activity more generally. First, because promising areas of research inquiry lie 'close in', and because a set of production/manufacturing activities are typically implied by a particular research focus, a firm's 'core business' (or possibly core businesses)—by which is meant the set of competences which define its distinctive advantage—can be expected to display a certain stability and coherence. Path dependencies inherent in technological progress can be expected, at least partially, to drive the definition of a firm's capabilities, and therefore the businesses in which it has a comparative advantage.

Buttressing path dependency as a limiting factor with respect to a firm competency are the set of organizational routines which develop once a particular research endeavor bears fruit. Whereas the creative part of research is at least partly *ad hoc*, routines characterize efficient post-development behavior in production, marketing, distribution and sales. A routine is defined by putting a skill, or set of skills, to use in a particular or distinctive environment in a repetitive way. As mentioned earlier, path dependencies define the neighborhoods/environments in which skills can be most productively applied. Hence, a firm's initial point of entry in a technological regime, and the trajectories/paths which are initially selected, will define in large measure the kinds of competences that the firm will generate, and the products it will develop and commercialize. After first commercialization, a set of routines will develop which will lead to a deepening of competencies in certain areas. The skilful performance of organizational routines provides the underpinnings for what is commonly thought of as the distinctive competence of an enterprise. 'These people at company X are good at Y' summarizes views which outsiders may develop with respect to these competences. These competences, coupled with a modicum of strategic vision, will in turn help define a firm's core business. A firm's core business is necessarily bounded by particularized competences in production, marketing and R & D. Employees will tend to form natural teams, where regrouping is difficult and the ability to absorb new members limited.

Routines, since they cannot be codified, must be constantly practised to exhibit high performance. This in turn implies that the firm must remain in certain activities in which short-run considerations would indicate that abandonment is desirable. Put differently, core business skills need to be constantly exercised to retain corporate fitness.

Because a firm's learning domain is defined in part by where it has been, and the technological imperatives and opportunities which that implies, it is readily apparent that a firm has a limited but by no means a non-existent ability to change its business. The products it can produce and the technologies it employs are highly path-dependent, at least at the level of an individual business unit. At the level of the corporation, more can be done, but this typically involves entering the corporate control market (i.e. buying and selling businesses) and not the market for factors of production.

Implications for the theory of the firm are apparent. Except by entering the market for corporate control, profit-seeking firms have limited abilities to change products and technologies. The notion of a smooth, twice differentiable production function would appear to be at odds with the conceptualization of the firm outlined above. In addition, economics of scope would appear to be constrained by the limited ability to apply routines across different product and technological environments/neighborhoods. 'Related' diversification would appear to be feasible so long as it is consistent with the underlying path dependencies and/or imperatives, a matter which is to be discussed in more detail later.

The analysis has so far assumed relative stability with respect to technological regimes. Suppose, however, that the firm experiences a technological discontinuity which obsoletes its skills, and possibly renders its downstream assets valueless. In these circumstances, established firms will be lacking in many of the relevant research competences. However, 'downstream' competences, particularly in sales and distribution, more often than not are still relevant to the new technological regime.

In these circumstances—that is where the technology necessary for survival lies distant from the neighborhood of the firm's traditional research inquiry—it may be extremely difficult to utilize existing in-house research competences within the new paradigm. This is because of the path dependencies noted earlier. Accordingly, the relevant competences may have to be purchased *en masse*, or technology transfer programs must be employed to educate existing personnel in the assumptions and logic of a new paradigm. In these circumstances, in-licensing and collaboration with the organizations (typically universities or new business firms) responsible for pioneering the new paradigm will be common.

Incumbent firms can thus be expected to display permeable boundaries when technological regimes shift, unless of course incumbents have been responsible for the shifts. However, if the know-how in question is not protected by intellectual property law, then the collaboration at issue is likely to be more in the form of imitation rather than in licensing. However, if the technology has a large tacit component, know-how licensing may still be necessary. Needless to say, transactions-cost issues also enter the equation, with collaboration more likely less difficult than contractual problems.

Multiproduct diversification

Technological change is often driven, so it seems, by certain imperatives in a trajectory which, considered in light of the firm's market-entry strategy, helps define the firm's 'core business'. However, the diversity of application areas for a given technology are often quite large, and the possibility of applying the firm's capabilities to different market opportunities is often available, especially after growth opportunities in existing markets are exhausted.

Suppose application areas outside of the core business do in fact open up. The question arises as to whether potential scope economies deriving from the application of generic know-how in new markets add more to the innovating firm's value if they are served through licensing and related contractual arrangements to unaffiliated firms who then serve the new product markets in question, or by direct investment, either *de novo* or by merger/acquisition. This is an important question, the answer to which ought to help shape a positive theory of the scope of the firm's activities.

Whether the firm integrates or not is likely to depend critically on four sets of factors:

1. whether the technology can be transferred to an unaffiliated entity at higher or lower cost than it can be transferred to an affiliated entity;
2. the degree of intellectual property protection afforded to the technology in question by the relevant statutes and laws;
3. whether a contract can be crafted which will regulate the sale of technology with greater or less efficiency and effectiveness than department-to-department or division-to-division sales can be regulated by internal administrative procedures;
4. whether the set of complementary competences possessed by the potential licensee can be assessed by the licensor at a cost lower than alternatives. If they are lower, the available returns from the market will be higher, and the opportunity for a satisfactory royalty or profit-sharing arrangement accordingly greater.

These matters are explored in more detail elsewhere (Teece, 1980, 1983, 1986). Suffice to say that contractual mechanisms are often less satisfactory than the alternative. Proprietary considerations are more often than not served by integration, and technology transfer is difficult both to unaffiliated and affiliated partners, with the consequences that integration (or multiproduct diversification) is the more attractive alternative, except where incumbents are already competitively established in downstream activities, and are in a position to render *de novo* entry by the technology-based firms unattractive. Hence, multiproduct firms can be expected to appear as efficient responses to contractual, proprietary and technology transfer problems in an important set of circumstances. Mixed modes, such as joint ventures and complex forms of profit-sharing collaboration, will also be common according to how the set of transactions in question stacks up against the criteria identified above.

Vertical integration

Technological change also has implications for the vertical structure of the business enterprise, and the level of vertical integration also has implications for the rate and direction of technological change expected to characterize the business enterprise. However, the literature linking the rate and direction of technological change and the boundaries of the firm is still in its infancy.

Economic historians have long suggested that there may be links. For instance, Frankel (1955) has argued that the slow rate of diffusion of innovations in the British textile and iron and steel industries around the turn of the century was due to the absence of vertically integrated firms. Kindleberger (1964) has gone so far as to suggest that the reason why West Germany and Japan have overtaken Britain may be due to 'the organization of [British] industry into Separate Firms dealing with each other at arm's length'. This 'may have impeded technological change because of the possibility that part of the benefits of that change would have been external to the separate firms' (pp. 146–7). General Motors' early dominance in the diesel electric locomotive industry has also been attributed to the fact that it was integrated into electrical supply while its competitors were not (Marx, 1973). Clearly a systematic exploration of the relationship between technological innovation and enterprise boundaries is needed. This can be done by comparing the properties of integrated structures with non-integrated structures which rely on arms-length contractual relations to achieve the requisite degree of coordination.

For present purposes, it is useful to distinguish between two types of innovation: autonomous (or 'stand-alone') and systemic. An autonomous innovation is one which can be introduced without modifying other components or items of equipment. The component or device in that sense 'stands alone'. A systemic innovation, on the other hand, requires significant readjustment to other parts of the system. The major distinction relates to the amount of design coordination which development and commercialization are likely to require. An example of a systemic innovation would be electronic funds transfer, instant photography (it required redesign of the camera and the film), front-wheel drive, and the jet airliner (it required new stress-resistant airframes). An autonomous innovation does not require modification to other parts of a system for first commercialization, although modification may be necessary to capture all of the advantages of the innovation in question. The transistor, for example, originally replaced vacuum tubes and the early transistor radios were not much different from the old ones, although they were more reliable and used much less power. But one did not have to change radio transmission in order to commercialize transistor radios. Another example would be power steering—the automobile did not have to be redesigned to facilitate the introduction of this innovation, although it did permit designs which placed more weight over the front wheels. A faster microprocessor or a larger memory would be further examples.

When technological interdependencies are important, it is likely that the commercialization of an innovation will require new investments in several different parts of the industry or the system. Thus, suppose that a cost-saving (equipment) innovation has been generated which can enhance efficiency if successfully introduced into an industry, and suppose that introduction into one part requires that complementary investments be made in other parts. If the subparts are independently owned, cooperation will have to be obtained in order for the innovation to be commercialized.

There are two powerful reasons why common ownership of the parts will speed both the adoption and the subsequent diffusion of the innovation. Where there are significant interdependencies, introduction of an innovation will often result in differing benefits and costs to various parties. This effect makes it difficult if not impossible to coordinate the introduction of such an innovation. While a system of frictionless markets could overcome this problem—the firms obtaining the benefits could compensate those incurring the costs so that the introduction of the innovation would not depend on the degree of integration in the industry—it is commonly recognized that it may be extremely difficult to engineer a workable compensation agreement, in part because all relevant contingencies are not known when the contract would need to be drawn up.

Therefore, in the absence of integration, commercialization can be slowed or completely stalled. Considerable cost disparities can open up between old and new methods, yet the new method may not be implemented because the individual parties cannot agree upon the terms under which it will be introduced. There can be a reluctance on the part of both parties to make the necessary investments in specialized assets, and to exchange information about each other's needs and opportunities—even if cooperation would yield mutual gains, and certainly if the gains will go to one party at the expense of the other. Hence, in the absence of integration, there can be a reluctance on the part of one or more of the parties in an industry to develop or commercialize a systemic innovation requiring the participation of two or more firms.

To summarize, it is hypothesized that integration facilitates systemic innovations by facilitating information flows, and the coordination of investment plans. It also removes institutional barriers to innovation where the innovation in question requires allocating costs and benefits, or placing specialized investments into several parts of an industry. In the absence of integration, there will be a reluctance on the part of both parties to make the necessary investments in specialized assets, even if this would yield mutual gains. One reason is that both parties know that the exercise of opportunism might yield even greater benefits to one of the parties. Hence, in the absence of common ownership of the parts, there will be reluctance on the part of one or more of the parties to adopt a systemic innovation.

Comprehensive evidence with respect to the above concepts has yet to be assembled. The only statistical test performed to date relates to the petroleum industry (Armour and Teece, 1978). These findings indicated that firm and R & D expenditures for basic and applied research in the US petroleum industry, 1951–75, were statistically related to the level of vertical integration which the enterprise possessed.[5] Anecdotal historical evidence is surveyed below.

According to Frankel (1955, pp. 312–13), the lack of vertical integration in the British iron and steel industry hindered the introduction of technical innovation in the latter part of the century because the innovations in question displayed interrelatedness. In the 1860s, 1870s and 1880s, a number of technical changes evolved which offered the prospect of substantial economies in various phases of production. New and commercially feasible methods of steel ingot production were possible through introduction of the Bessemer converter and the open hearth and electric furnaces; advent of the rolling mill made possible phenomenal savings in the shaping and finishing of steel products; the optimum size of the blast furnace was greatly increased; and significant fuel economies all along the line became possible. Most important, no single one of these changes would yield its potential savings in full except in conjunction with the others, thereby compelling coordinated design of investment and the assembling of the various parts of the industry at a single location. The economies attainable from coordinated design and centralization derived from several sources: from a reduction in transport and handling charges; from higher capacity utilization; from easier and more accurate control over product quality; and from fuel economies. But to attain this, these had to be in such proportions and on such a scale that the whole plant could work effectively and economically. There had to be a sufficient number of coking ovens, blast furnaces and steel furnaces both to keep one another employed and to meet the requirements of the rolling mills. The technical changes that made possible the economies in question materialized in an era when the ownership structure in Britain had crystallized in a pattern inconsistent with the new technological need for integrated operation. As a result, in part at least, those changes had hardly begun to be assimilated in the United Kingdom by the end of the century.

Frankel (1955, pp. 313–14) provides further supporting evidence for the general proposition from the textile industry. He argues that the failure of the British to put the automatic loom into place in the cotton industry was due to the lack of vertical integration. The loom was first introduced around the turn of the century, and by 1914 represented 31 per cent of the looms in operation in the United States. By 1919, the figure was 51 per cent and by 1939, 95 per cent. In Britain, by 1939, only 5 per cent of the looms were automatic. Introduction of automatic looms demanded more than replacement of one machine by another. For a great many firms it required redesign of the weaving shed—often its complete rebuilding, strengthening of flooring, elimination of pillars, and respacing of machinery. It called for equipment and method changes in the preliminary processing of yarn; idiosyncratic investments were required in both the spinning and weaving. Furthermore, the innovation created a need for product simplification and for a change in the traditional practices of converters in allocating orders to weavers, so that long runs of given fabric types could be attained. Certain of the interconnections were external to the firm. Frankel (ibid.) concludes that 'Their presence, together with those internal to the firm, constitute a part of the explanation for Lancashire's continued reliance on the old power loom', while the automatic loom diffused very rapidly in the vertically integrated US industry.

Other historians share this perspective. Kindleberger has studied the reasons for the failure of the British railroads to abandon the 10-ton coal wagon in favor of the more efficient 20-ton wagon. One hypothesis considered is that the retention of the 10-ton car was due to the impossibility of changing it without also modifying terminal and switching facilities, which might have made the cost prohibitive. Another hypothesis—and the one which Kindleberger comes to favor—is that the lack of integration blocked the adoption of the larger cars. (The British railroads were peculiar in that the coal wagons were owned by the coal mines and not the railroad companies.) In this regard, it is of interest to note that in this period two of the British railroads—the Great Western and the Great Eastern—adopted 20-ton wagons for their own use for locomotive coal as early as 1897; the Northeastern had used 20-ton, bottom-discharge mineral wagons for iron ore and 40-ton bogie wagons since the beginning of the century. But as Kindleberger (1964) notes:

These wagons were all owned by the railroads, not the coal or iron companies. The Great Western Railway failed, however, to persuade colliery owners to change to a larger wagon when it offered a rebate of 5 percent on freight cars for coal in fully loaded 20-ton wagons in 1923 and, in 1925, reduced charges on tipping and weighing these wagons. Only 100 came into use. [p. 143]

Kindlberger (1964) concludes that the reason for the slow rate of diffusion was institutional and not technical. In short, it stemmed from the absence of vertical integration.

Technical aspects of interrelatedness do not seem to have held up the movement to more efficient size, either through making such a change uneconomic because of the enormity of the investment required or by adding amounts too great for any one firm to borrow. The sums involved were not large, and railway finance was rarely a limiting factor in the period up to 1914. Private ownership of the coal cars by the collieries, on the other hand, posed a type of interrelatedness that was institutional rather than technical. [ibid.]

Kindleberger (1964) does not advance a satisfactory explanation of why market mechanisms could not achieve the requisite coordination, but he hints at the difficulties of devising a mechanism for sharing the gains from the innovation.

For the railroads to guarantee new low rates on larger wagons would have been to take all the risk of the new investment, and that of the collieries, on themselves. To indicate that they would consider new and lower rates only if these were justified by operating economies would assign the risk to the collieries. An attempt to apportion the risk between the two would have been equitable but not likely to arouse much enthusiasm. [ibid.]

An alternative reason might well be that the collieries had no guarantee that the lower rates would prevail. In the absence of competition from other railroads or modes offering competitive rates, the railroads could raise the rates again once the collieries had made the requisite investments. Furthermore, to the extent that the economies could not be captured until substantially all of the mines had adopted the larger cars, the rate reduction offered may have been insufficient to entice the mines to make the needed investments.

A more general impediment to innovation has been identified in the British distribution system. British industry in the nineteenth century displayed very little in the way of forward integration—there was a layer of merchants between the manufacturer and the final customer. While enabling specialization economies to be obtained in a static market, Kindleberger suggests that 'the separation of selling from production may have the drawback of slowing down technical change by imposing barriers of communication between the ultimate customer and the producer' (1964, p. 148). Furthermore, 'it may be significant that the woolen industry, which did much better than cotton in maintaining its rate of technical change, moved to direct trading' (ibid.). His final conclusion is that:

There is the distinct possibility, whose complete demonstration would require a separate book, that the merchant system bears a significant share of the responsibility for slowing down technical change because it renders a large proportion of the benefits of technical change external to the firms that must effect or sell it. [p. 149]

A more contemporary episode which is instructive is how General Motors' integration between locomotive manufacture and electrical equipment supply facilitated GM's commercialization and subsequent success with its diesel electric locomotive program. The diesel locomotive revolution began in 1934 when General Motors produced the first diesel electric passenger locomotive. The domestic diesel electric locomotive building industry currently consists of GM and General Electric. GE did not enter the industry as a fully integrated builder, producing both the diesel engine and the electrical components, until the early 1960s. Previously, GE had confined itself to the electrical equipment supplier end of the business. The electrical equipment in a diesel electric locomotive represents approximately one-third of the total locomotive cost. GM, on the other hand, originally purchased its electrical equipment from others but, in the late 1930s, it integrated upstream into electrical supply. From the 1930s until the 1960s when GE entered, GM was the only integrated producer. The producers of steam locomotives, including Alco, Baldwin, Lima-Hamilton and Fairbanks Morse, had all abandoned locomotive production by the 1960s.

One effect of GM's integration was the elimination of duplicate personnel.

The locomotive builders maintained in-house electrical engineering staffs even though they sourced their electrical equipment externally. These in-house staffs were apparently maintained because of the problems of information exchange associated with market contracts.

The maintenance of in-house electrical engineering staffs facilitated the reception of technical engineering and price data, and reduced the extent of undetected data distortion. These market transactions costs arise from the small number of producers and the uncertainty that marked the locomotive building industry . . . Uncertainty and market transactions costs are greater when technology is changing rapidly. In this case, advance specification of final product design and cost was impossible. [Marx, 1976, pp. 45–6]

Another advantage of integration was that it eliminated costly disputes with respect to warranty responsibility. Haggling and the opportunistic interpretation of contractual ambiguities marked the Alco–GE relationship, which was often described as 'antagonistic' by railroad executives. A particularly difficult problem was the identification of the source and responsibility for engine failure. Because of the systems nature of the technology, it was never very clear whether the problem was mechanical or electrical. Locomotives requiring service were frequently shuffled back and forth between the building and electrical equipment supplier. Because of the costliness of locomotive downtime, the availability of timely after-sales service is a critical factor in procurement decisions. The railroads frequently cited the superiority of General Motors' post-sales service as an important factor in its sales record.

Thus, by facilitating coordination and timely post-sales service, vertical integration appears to have contributed to the market success of the GM diesel electric locomotives. Furthermore, integration also facilitated rapid technological development. According to Marx (1976), one of the biggest problems with the electrical equiment suppliers was:

their commercially cautious and slow rate of development. The electrical suppliers were more risk averse than the builders because of different commitments and alternatives. This produced different rates of development for mechanical and electrical equipment and, because of the interdependence, technological bottlenecks. [p. 47]

Vertical integration also helped solve appropriability problems. The locomotive builders which were not vertically integrated typically funded a portion of the electrical equipment supplier development cost, depending on the exclusivity of the work. The identification, sharing and pricing of intellectual property generated by such development activities turned out to be difficult and costly.

Contract terms notwithstanding, the indirect benefits of contract execution (accumulation of knowledge, staff development, and the like) accrue to the supplier, and enforcement through secrecy is seriously impaired. General Motors also needed to exclude rivals from sharing in the results of its own in-house mechanical and electrical research. The exclusion problem was difficult because of the close technical contact required between builders and electrical equipment suppliers, who also manufactured for competing builders (Marx, 1976, pp. 49–50). Vertical integration, by harmonizing the divergent interests of the locomotive and electrical equipment producers, helped overcome many of the problems associated with the exclusivity and appropriability of the technology. Attention could then be focused on getting the job done at the lowest cost.

In conclusion, it appears that GM's integration into electrical equipment supply reduced costs by internalizing market exchange under circumstances (uncertainty, technological interdependence) which generated significant contractual difficulties. This integration also stimulated the pace of product development by promoting harmonious information exchange. The experience with vertical integration in the diesel electric locomotive building industry suggests that technological innovation displaying interdependencies among the parts is greatly facilitated by common ownership of the parts.

The above analysis has concerned itself with the organizational mechanics of getting an innovation commercialized. The post-commercialization market performance of the innovator is also a very significant matter, which has been dealt with elsewhere (Teece, 1986). Suffice to say that ownership by the innovator of the supporting assets and skills needed to ensure competitive supply of the new product, or of existing products based on the new process, is often required to ensure that the rent stream from the innovation is shielded from capture by 'fast seconds'. The exceptions are where the appropriability regime—that is, the protection afforded the new product or process by patents, copyrights, trade secrets and inherent 'hard-to-copy' aspects of the innovation—is extremely tight. When property rights are difficult to establish and where imitation, either through 'inventing around the patent' or reverse engineering or other activities is relatively easy (i.e. the appropriability regime is weak), then the innovator needs to own or otherwise control the relevant cospecialized assets to be able to impede the imitator's efforts to take the product/service to market or more advantageous terms than the innovator (Teece, 1986). Since cospecialized assets in marketing, distribution and manufacturing are often aligned vertically, vertical integration may be required in order to assist the innovator in capturing the rent stream generated by the innovation.

This analysis is consistent in part with an alternative argument which has been made. Several writers, including Utterback (1978), have speculated that older, vertically integrated firms will have a greater commitment to old technology because of the large technology-specific investments they have made upstream and downstream. The phenomenon to which Utterback refers is simply that innovators may resist cannibalizing the value of their own irreversible investments. Put differently, innovating firms, integrated and otherwise, that have laid down innovation-specific investments will generally not be the first to commercialize new innovations which will impair the value of existing assets. They will do so only under competitive threat, or if by doing so the present value of the profits from the new innovation will outweigh the losses from the old.

Since vertically integrated firms often have specialized investments in place and since a primary rationale for vertical integration is to protect specialized investments from recontracting hazards, it is to be expected that vertically integrated firms will have a higher proportion of their asset base which is dedicated to particular technologies than do non-vertically integrated firms. Thus a monopolist which is vertically integrated and has assets specialized to the old technology may indeed delay the commercialization of new technology if it is confident that it does not face competitive threats. Were such delay to occur, it is caused not by vertical integration as such, but by the fact that the innovator, by assumption, owns assets dedicated to the old technology—assets whose value will be impaired by the new technology. Hence, it is theoretically possible that vertically integrated firms, because they own assets dedicated to the old technology, may retard the commercialization of new technology when the following conditions hold: the vertically integrated firm is the innovator; the vertically integrated firm is a monopolist or possibly a colluding oligopolist; the vertically integrated firm has made investments in the old technology which will be impaired in value by introduction of the new; the innovation destroys a rent stream with a net present value to the innovator greater than the rent stream that it would serve io create.

Such instances are likely to be infrequent and, moreover, the impairment to the commercialization of innovation flows fundamentally from a combination of market power in the presence of sunk costs. Whether the dampening of commercialization is socially as well as privately desirable will swing on the magnitude of the externalities generated by the new technology relative to the old.

Transacting for know-how across enterprise boundaries: collaborative arrangements and technological change

The analysis so far has examined the properties and stressed the virtues of organizational arrangements in which research and development proceeds as an in-house activity. As indicated at the outset, however, contract research is in some cases viable. Moreover, once technology is produced, in many cases it can be traded (licensed) in the market for know-how which is increasingly international in its scope (Teece, 1981).

Indeed, the vertically integrated enterprise with in-house research and its own manufacturing, distribution and sales is in some industries being joined by almost pure research enterprises. Relatedly, incumbent firms are increasingly engaged in extensive collaborative dealings with other firms, especially research-oriented, new business enterprises. In this section, various reasons for these developments are explored and the implications for the organization of research assessed.

The organizational arguments (section on 'The integration of R & D with production') favoring in-house research in order to avoid contractual difficulties rests on a fundamental assumption, namely that the firm has the inventive capacity to develop competitive technology in-house. However, given that the institutional loci of new technology in the US are diverse and include the universities, other not-for-profit institutions, and government laboratories, there is a high probability that from time to time established firms will have to source technology externally. When knowledge accumulation is cumulative, then established enterprises can generally build upon existing competences in order to develop new technologies in a timely and cost-effective fashion. Occasionally, fundamental break-throughs in science and technology occur which do not build upon incumbent firms' competences. Such developments constitute what was referred to earlier as paradigm shifts. When these shifts cause the institutional locus of innovation to lie external to incumbent firms and the new knowledge in question is proprietary and difficult to copy, then the opportunity for licensing and other forms of collaboration become manifest. This appears to be the case with biotechnology where the key breakthroughs have been generated within the universities, and this in turn has spawned several hundred, small biotechnology firms usually founded by scientists.[6] Incumbent pharmaceutical firms, such as Eli Lilly, Merck, and Johnson & Johnson, have seen both the opportunity and the threat posed by the new biotechnology[7] and the new enterprises that have been spawned to develop it.

The opportunity stems from the ability to develop and commercialize new products which will open up new markets while employing at least part of the incumbent firms' fixed costs in plant, equipment, distribution and human capital. The threat stems from the possibility that the new techno-logy will render obsolete incumbent firms' products, facilities and capa-bilities. Research collaboration (such as in licensing, joint R & D) is attractive to the incumbents for those reasons and more; to the new business firms it is often a source of capital. It also can provide access to downstream assets, particularly marketing channels. In short, collabora-tive research can occur alongside in-house research in order to bolster the technological capabilities of incumbents and in order to enable new busi-ness firms—which may begin as stand-alone research ventures—to continue to fund research and to acquire the ability to integrate vertically into manufacturing, marketing and distribution. Needless to say, the market for know-how is likely to encounter many of the contractual diffi-culties described in the section on 'The integration of R & D with pro-duction' in this chapter; as the biotechnology industry evolves, it is to be expected that the new business firms will take on a more classical structure. Indeed, the two leading biotechnology firms, Genentech and Cetus, are actively pursuing a vertical-integration strategy with respect to their key businesses.

A shift in technological paradigm is not the only reason why in-house research gets displaced as the main driver of a firm's technological capability. Scale issues, as with the development of new jet engines or large central office telecommunication switches, may require collaboration. So may pure incentive considerations, as when a salaried scientific position is no match for the outcome-driven incentives of the new business firms.[8] But the pervasiveness and durability of in-house research is worthy of comment. The 1970s and 1980s have certainly exhibited important changes in the way that research is organized, but even the new enterprises seem rapidly to adopt structures which eschew contract research, except in the very early stages of industry development. The robust nature of the organization of research in the modern corporation would thus appear to be apparent, even though the corporation is taking on certain 'postmodern' features.

Implications and conclusions

The above analysis of the firm and its relationship to technological change helps us understand not only the nature of the firm, but also sheds light on some topical managerial and public policy issues raised in the introduction. Some of these implications are briefly summarized below.

Stand-alone laboratories and hollow corporations

The natural organizational home for research appears to be inside the corporation, alongside production/operations. This model seems to be dominant for large corporations, and to a lesser extent for smaller corporations, as it facilitates interaction between the users and providers of new technology. It also avoids the difficulties associated with writing, executing and enforcing R & D contracts. Relatedly, managerial decisions to 'hollow out' the corporation by out-sourcing components and other subsystems may have the indirect effect of impairing the innovation process by establishing barriers to the transfer of information between research and manufacturing, possibly causing future designs to be less sensitive to manufacturability concerns. It may also serve to enhance the capabilities of competitors and potential competitors. Out-sourcing runs the risk of creating circumstances whereby innovators are no longer able to profit from innovation, despite the fact that they are highly innovative.

Diversification economies

The evolution of technology is often driven by certain technological imperatives which induce firms to gravitate in certain technological directions. This technological drift is often highly constrained, causing firms to articulate focused competences ('core' businesses). Sometimes scope economies become available when a key internal competence affords multiple application. Diversification is often a desirable organizational response for a set of reasons similar to why research is better supported in-house rather than via contracts. This suggests that the core business of an enterprise typically has a technological underpinning, and that efficient diversification is likely to be driven by technological imperatives. Hence the focused or laterally diversified enterprise—where corporate diversification tracks underlying technological imperatives—is likely to be a characteristic of economies in which efficiency concerns drive diversification decisions. Unless tax and technology transfer issues are visible drivers of corporate diversification decisions, one may be entitled to suspect that corporate diversification is driven by factors not consistent with stockholder, wealth-seeking behavior.

Vertical integration and technological innovation

The analysis presented in this section indicates that when a stream of innovations has significant systems ramifications, then vertical integration is likely to facilitate the commercialization of an innovation, if not its initial development. Of course, not all technology possesses strong systems interdependencies, and many that do involve interdependent organizations which do not afford vertical integration opportunities.[9] However, when the relevant organizational domain is within the range of feasible integration, vertical integration is likely to facilitate innovation, and may well be required if a stream of systematic innovations is to be commercialized in a timely fashion. Vertically integrated firms may also thwart the introduction of new technologies when the innovation would have the effect of destroying the value of investments in place, and the vertically integrated developer of the innovation is not threatened by a competitive technology.

New business firms and research collaboration

The analysis earlier in this chapter suggested the importance of performing research in-house. Contract research is usually but not always a poor substitute. However, opportunities for many other forms of collaboration, such as R & D joint ventures, do exist. Indeed, they may represent an imperative in instances where the firm contemplating conducting research lacks the desired skills and is unable to acquire them in the labor market. This might actually characterize even research-intensive firms when a shift in the technological paradigm renders the existing skill base of the enterprise obsolete or irrelevant.

Collaboration between established firms and universities, and between established firms and new business firms that possess the relevant skills may therefore be necessary. The incumbent firms are likely to possess marketing and manufacturing assets of great value to a new business firm, while the new business firm may have research findings, capabilities, or possibly even products of great value to the established firms. Circumstances such as these provide opportunities for collaboration.

Collaboration by definition falls into neither the 'contract research'[10] nor the 'in-house research' categories identified earlier. Its ubiquity in no sense destroys the argument made earlier in favor of in-house research. The presumption in favor of in-house research can be readily overturned, for a transitory period, when the sources of know-how lie external to the firm and cannot easily be acquired through 'hiring in' technical and scientific personnel. In these instances, co-development activities and R & D joint ventures may make good sense. Often collaboration in research and development is part of a larger arrangement involving production and marketing. Clearly, a more complete understanding of the organization of research in a capitalist economy requires our assessment of a broader set of institutions, including universities, that condition the environment in which technological change proceeds.

Notes

1. Edison's Menlo Park laboratory, which exmployed sixty-four people by February 1880, has been called the world's first industrial research laboratory, but it was not a prototype of those to follow. It was organized to give vent to the creative genius of one man only—Thomas Edison (Friedel and Israel, 1986).

2. Specifically, Teece and Armour (1977, pp. 56–7) noted: 'Universal Oil Products—Houdry is a similar example; Scientific Design would be an analogous example in the chemical industry—is an engineering, design, and research company that is not integrated into production, refining, transportation, or marketing, and yet has made important contributions to technological innovation in the petroleum industry. The rather narrow research activities of Universal Oil Products should, however, be indicated here, lest it be assumed that this example could represent an appropriate model for the entire industry. First, it would seem that where the research objectives are simple and obvious, a nonintegrated research and development firm like Universal Oil Products may not be particularly disadvantaged. For instance, the development of higher octane gasolines, or the development of processes to meet new environmental standards, do not involve the formulation of complex research objectives. Universal Oil Products' research seems to have been confined to meeting simple objectives relating to the refining function: the company has not been responsible for innovations on lubricants, petrochemicals, or exploration and production. It mainly performs applied research and avoids high risk endeavors. The nonintegrated research and development firm, though performing useful services for the industry and consumers, does not seem a sufficiently robust organization to absorb the full gamut of current research and development activities in the industry. The specialization that has emerged seems to have advantages, and an assumption that a nonintegrated research and development structure could successfully perform the current industry portfolio of research and development projects would not seem to be grounded on an understanding of the many subtleties of the research and develoment process.'

3. Richard Tybout (1956) succinctly characterizes the cost-plus contract as follows: 'The cost-plus fixed fee contract is the administrative contract par excellence. For the market mechanism, it substitutes the administrative mechanism. For the profit share of private entrepreneurs, it substitutes the

fixed fee, a payment in lieu of profits forgone. And for the independent private business unit, it substitutes the integrated hierarchical structure of an organization composed of an agency . . . and its contractors' (1956, p. 175).

4. 'Consolidated Edison Company of New York: the development of an atomic power plant', Weapons Acquisition Project, Harvard Business School, December 1959.

5. Despite the fact that the ultimate objective of R & D programs is to produce innovations, not simply to dissipate resources on R & D activities, expenditure data can be viewed as a useful proxy for innovative performance in that it reveals the intensity of innovative activity. Furthermore, if the discount rate facing non-integrated firms is similar to that facing integrated firms and if similar risk preferences exist across the management of these firms, the higher productivity per dollar of research expenditure posited in vertically integrated firms implies that, *ceteris paribus*, such firms will devote more resources to R & D.

6. Over 400 by 1987 in the US alone.

7. The new biotechnology consists of three general techniques: recombinant DNA (rDNA), cell fusion (monoclonal antibody technology), and the novel bioprocessing technology.

8. Williamson (1985) traces these differences to the 'low powered' incentives of large organizations versus the 'high powered' incentives of smaller entrepreneurial firms.

9. See Horwitch and Prahalad (1981) for a discussion of the variety of institutions that are most often involved in the innovation process.

10. Note that contract research is different from licensing. Patent licensing, for instance, involves the sale of intellectual property rights, usually subject to certain restrictions. General licensing involves the sale of scientific and technological assets already developed. Contract research involves the development, for fee, of technological assets.

References

Arditti, F. D. (1968), 'On the separation of production from the developer', *Journal of Business*, vol. 41, no. 3, pp. 317–32.

Brown, G. S., Davidson, F. P. and Little, H. F. (1976), 'The systems perspective: concepts related to sustained efficiency of the United States telecommunications network', F.C.C. Docket 20003, Bell Exhibit 62.

Dosi, G. (1982), 'Technological paradigms and technological trajectories', *Research Policy*, vol. 11, pp. 147–62.

Frankel, M. (1955), 'Obsolence and technological change in a maturing economy', *American Economic Review*.

Friedel, R. and Israel, P. (1986), *Edison's Electric Light*, New Brunswick, NJ, Rutgers University Press.

Goldberg, V. (1977), 'Competitive bidding and the production of accountant information', *Bell Journal of Economics*.

Horwitch, M. and Prahalad, C. K. (1981), 'Managing multi-organization enterprises: the emerging strategic frontier', *Sloan Management Review*, Winter.

Kindleberger, C. P. (1964), *Economic Growth in France and Britain, 1851–1950*, Cambridge, Mass., Harvard University Press.

Malmgren, H. (1961), 'Information, expectations, and the theory of the firm', *Quarterly Journal of Economics*, vol. 75, August, pp. 399–421.

Marx, T. (1976), 'Vertical integration in the diesel-electric locomotive building industry: a study in market failures', *Nebraska Journal of Agricultural Economics*, vol. 15, no. 4, Autumn, pp. 37–51.

Miller, R. and Sawyes, D. (1970), *The Technical Development of Modern Aviation*, New York, Praeger.

Mowery, D. C. (1983), 'The relationship between intrafirm and contractual forms of industrial research in American manufacturing, 1900–1940', *Explorations in Economic History*, vol. 20, pp. 351–74.

Nelson, R. R. and Winter, S. G. (1982), *An Evolutionary Theory of Economic Change*, Cambridge, Mass., Harvard University Press.

Roberts, Edward (1979), 'Stimulating technological innovation: organizational approaches', *Research Management*, November, pp. 26–30.

Rosenberg, N. (1969), 'The direction of technological change: inducement mechanisms and focusing devices', *Economic Development and Cultural Change*, vol. 18, pp. 1–24.

Scherer, F. M. (1965), 'Size of firm, oligopoly and research: a comment', *Canadian Journal of Economics and Political Science*, May, pp. 256–66.

—— (1980), *Industrial Market Structure and Economic Performance*, Chicago, Rand McNally.

Schumpeter, J. A. (1942), *Capitalism, Socialism and Democracy*, New York, Harper.

Sloan, A. P. (1964), *My Years with General Motors*, New York, Doubleday.

Stigler, G. J. (1956), 'Industrial organization and economic progress', in L. D. White (ed.), *The State of the Social Sciences*, Chicago, University of Chicago Press.

Teece, D. J. (1976), *Vertical Integration and Vertical Divestiture in the U.S. Petroleum Industry*, Stanford, Institute for Energy Studies.

—— (1977), 'Technology transfer by multinational firms: the resource cost of international technology transfer', *Economic Journal*, June.

—— (1980), 'Economies of scope and the scope of the enterprise', *Journal of Economic Behavior and Organizations*, vol. 1, no. 3.

—— (1981), 'The market for know how and the efficient international transfer of technology', *The Annals of the Academy of Political Social Science*, November.

—— (1983), 'Towards an economic theory of the multiproduct firm', *Journal of Economic Behavior and Organizations*, vol. 3.

—— (1986), 'Profiting from technological innovation', *Research Policy*, December.

Teece, D. J. and Armour, H. O. (1977), 'Innovation and divestitute in the U.S. oil industry', in D. J. teece (ed.), *R & D in Energy Implications of Petroleum Industry Coorganization*, Stanford, Stanford University Institute for Energy Studies.

Thompson, J. D. (1967), *Organizations in Action*, New York, McGraw-Hill.

Tybout, R. (1956), *Government Contracting in Atomic Energy*, Ann Arbor, University of Michigan Press.

Utterback, J. M. (1978), 'Management of technology', in A. Hax (ed.), *Studies in Operations Management*, Amsterdam, North Holland, pp. 137–60.

White, L. (1971), *The Automobile Industry since 1945*, Cambridge, Mass., Harvard University Press.

Williamson, O. E. (1975), *Markets and Hierarchies*, New York, Free Press.

—— (1985), *The Economic Institutions of Capitalism*, New York, Free Press.

13 The R & D function: corporate strategy and structure

Neil Kay

Department of Economics, Herriot-Watt University, Edinburgh

R & D in the firm: function, strategy and structure

The purpose of this chapter is to examine the R & D function, strategic problems, internal organisation, and the interrelationship between them, from the perspective of economics. We shall analyse the economics of R & D activity in terms of four basic features or characteristics, and then consider the implications of these characteristics for function, strategy and structure. We hope to show that these characteristics are recurring features of analysis, often underlying a wide variety of issues and problems that have frequently been treated independently of each other in separate literatures and approaches. We start by examining the four characteristics, before examining in turn their implications for R & D activity, strategy and internal organisation.

The characteristics of R & D activity

The four characteristics or features that have central importance for the economies of R & D acxtivity are non-specificities, lags, uncertainty and costliness. *Non-specificity* in this context is relevant at the level of the product and the firm. Much R & D is not product-specific in so far as a particular piece of work may feed into a variety of end products, the R & D generating technological synergies, or economies of scope. Also, much R & D activity is not firm-specific, generating externality and property right problems. Both questions are likely to be very important for the firm; low product-specificity may allow the firm to spread R & D costs over a variety of product lines, while low firm specificity may signal a weak or low competitive advantage for the firm in its R & D activity. *Lags* and delays are a typical feature of R & D activity, a given piece of R & D often taking many years before it is embodied in commercial ventures, if at all. In themselves, lags are not necessarily an intractable problem, but they may directly contribute to other problems such as dangers of losing proprietary knowledge (low firm specificity), cost and uncertainty. *Uncertainty* is also a pervasive problem, uncertainty in this context meaning unmeasurable or non-insurable uncertainty (Knight, 1921), in contrast to predictable or measurable risks of an actuarial nature. Uncertainty here can be classified into general business uncertainty, which refers to all decisions concerning the future; technical uncertainty, which is concerned with achievement of specified performance and cost level; and market uncertainty, which refers to the possible achievement of a commercially viable product or process. R & D work can be faced with problems of uncertainty of all three types (Freeman, 1982, Chapter 7). *Cost* levels and associated resource commitment also tend to pose problems, though this can vary from sector to sector. The barriers to entry, or even to continuance, posed by high and/ or increasing R & D economies of scale and scope have become a major issue in some sectors like aerospace and automobiles. Just as lags may not pose insuperable problems in certain circumstances, so also cost level itself should not be a problem if there are no significant problems of knowledge and information in the market-place. Such issues do become important, however, if R & D cost levels exceed the internal financing capability of the firm, and there are information barriers to external capital market financing of corporate projects.

The impact of these factors generally varies as a project moves from basic research through applied research into development and then final introduction or innovation. Generally, non-specificities, lags and uncertainty tend to decrease, while cost levels and associated resource demands tend to increase, as a project moves downstream through the various stages towards final innovation. As far as non-specificities are concerned, both product- and firm-specificity of R & D tends to increase as a project moves towards final launch. For example, in laser R & D, basic research may be ultimately applicable to a wide range of applications in laser technology, applied research is likely to be concerned with a narrower range of potential applications, say in measuring devices, while resulting development work is liable to be specific to a specific measuring device or highly related group of devices. This tendency for product specificity to rise as a project moves through the various R & D stages may also create parallel tendencies for firm specificity to rise in the same direction; the extent of external applications due to leakage of technical information is likely to be directly related to product non-specificity. Thus, externalities may be more important for earlier, upstream research activity, especially basic research. Any tendency for firm-specificity to vary in this fashion may be reinforced to the extent that development work reflects tacit knowledge that may not easily diffuse externally, and also to the extent that basic research involves appropriability problems such as inapplicability of patent protection.

The other features tend to vary in a more obvious fashion as projects move along basic research, applied research, development, to introduction. Lags to final innovation will tend to be cumulative through the various stages and will tend to shorten towards and through development (Kay, 1979, pp. 23–4). Uncertainties tend to increase the further a stage is removed from final innovation (Freeman, 1982, p. 150), and so degree of uncertainty in its various manifestations is likely to diminish as a project moves through its various stages to completion. Finally, the cost of R & D activity tends to increase as projects move from earlier stages through to development and from laboratory experimentation to prototypes and pilot plants (Mansfield, 1968, p. 78; Schon, 1976, pp. 40–2).

In the next section we shall examine how these characteristics individually and collectively contribute to important issues and problems in R & D management and behaviour.

The four characteristics and R & D behaviour

It follows therefore that non-specificity, lags, uncertainty and costliness are each common features of R & D, though the relative importance of respective characteristics may vary with technology, firm or even time period. The extent and significance of the first three characteristics will tend to diminish as projects move from earlier upstream stages towards eventual innovation, while costliness of projects and associated resource commitments frequently increase in the same direction. Any reasonably innovative project is likely to encounter issues of non-specificity, lags, uncertainty and cost that could have important implications for their competitive position in the market-place. For example, are product specificities low enough to provide synergies and spread R & D costs? Are firm specificities strong enough to avoid appropriability problems? Are lags short enough to facilitate first-mover advantages? Are uncertainties sufficiently controllable to guide resource direction and reassure the capital market? Will cost considerations be low enough to permit internal financing?

Not only will questions like these vary in importance from project to project; they will vary in importance as projects and related or derived projects move downstream towards final completion. In this section we explore the implications of these general issues for a number of problems in R & D behaviour.

The financing of R & D and the importance of uncertainty

Uncertainty is a dominant characteristic influencing the financing of R & D both at project level and at the level of the R & D function overall. To start with, very little R & D work is financed by the external capital market, most being internally financed (Freeman, 1982, p. 149). However, this may conceal a greater level of capital market response to R & D activity than is apparent at first sight, since the external capital market may be strongly influenced in their overall level of support for the company by general R & D performance, as well as signals relating to proposed activity.

One element that may impede efficient linking of external capital and internal R & D is possible conflict of interest in information disclosure as far as capital market and product market is concerned. Improving the quality and detail of R & D plans available to the capital market may have a detrimental effect on a firm's competitive advantage in the product market. These conflicts may constitute limiting factors on the potential efficiency of external financing, and the problems may be exacerbated to the extent that corporate actors are liable to indulge in opportunistic behaviour and mis-representation. If, despite these problems, external financing is under-taken, say, by government agencies, uncertainty creates problems in contract design. A cost-plus system would leave the sponsoring agency vulnerable to moral hazard and opportunism, while fixed-price systems might make it difficult to find R & D-conducting firms willing to bear the uncertainties and associated costs (see Chapter 12).

The frequently observed optimistic bias in estimating R & D costs and lag times (Freeman, 1982, pp. 151–6) is also attributable to uncertainty, either because no allowance is made for uncertainties, 'bugs' and surprises, or because project estimators may opportunistically abuse an information-ally superior position to gain project approval by deliberately under-estimating costs and lags.

Uncertainty also creates time-cost trade-offs; if a target is required urgently, as in cancer research, many tasks may have to be carried out simultaneously, increasing the chances of duplicated learning, dead-ends and diminishing returns (Mansfield, 1968, p. 72; Freeman, 1982, p. 151). If the target can be approached more slowly, many R & D tasks can be carried out sequentially, permitting transference of learning and exper-ience, with consequent economising on resources. Finally, the same problems of uncertainty encountered in this problem area also impede construction of R & D budgets in a rational, aggregative, bottom-up fashion. As a consequence, most large firms allocate annual funds to the R & D function on a rule-of-thumb basis such as percentage of sales (Mansfield, 1968, p. 62; Kay, 1979, pp. 72–7). The actual budget rule often evolves through decision-makers learning what is the 'appropriate' budget for their firm (Freeman, 1982, p. 163).

Basic research: the extreme case

The further upstream a project is located in the basic research–applied research–development–introduction progression, the more lags, uncer-tainties and non-specificities assume importance in the resource allocation process. This is especially the case for basic research activity. The lags and uncertainties involved may discourage private investors (Freeman, 1982, p. 168) and these problems are likely to be compounded by the existence of non-specificities in the form of externalities. Consequently, government intervention or support for basic research is likely as a result of these market failure problems, though government support for basic research has traditionally been biased towards support for universities rather than corporations. For those firms that do conduct basic research, the diversi-fied firm is likely. to have an advantage, since a broad portfolio of businesses means that the various unpredictable and unexpected results are more likely to be internalised within corporate businesses (Nelson, 1959).[1] The 3M Corporation is an example of a highly diversified firm which has a successful track record of exploiting radical, innovative opportunities in this way, often within divisions unrelated to those that developed the original idea.

Demand-pull[2] theories of innovation are likely to be less relevant the further upstream a project is located. If demand-pull theories are relevant at all, it is likely to be in the development stage when work is close to completion, less uncertain, and more specific and precise in its output; Freeman (1982, p. 103) points out the pull of the market operated as a complementary force to technological momentum in many cases where the market demand was *urgent* and *specific*. The further back towards basic research a project is located, the more supply-side science and technology-push arguments are likely to be relevant.[3]

Winners and losers

Being first to introduce a new product or process does not guarantee success, and indeed the four characteristics of R & D may combine against the first-in. The first-in may incur severe problems of uncertainty, delay and cost, while non-specificities may contribute to rapid leakages of technical knowledge externalities to potential competitors. Mansfield (1985) produces evidence to show that information on technical developments typically leaks out very rapidly to competitors in a wide range of technologies. The second-in may exploit such non-specificities to cut down on the uncertainties, delays and costs incurred by the pioneer. The pioneer may have first-mover advantages, but these factors may erode them partially or totally. Sperry's loss of an early lead in commercial computer development to IBM was a major example of this type.

Consequently, the link between a firm's own R & D and its subsequent growth is highly tenuous at best, though for a given industry as a whole there is typically a stronger and observable relationship between industries R & D and industry growth (Freeman, 1982, p. 164). The instabilities associated with firm level tend to smooth out at industry level, while many of the externalities will work themselves out within industry boundaries, strengthening the link between industry R & D and growth.

Implications of possible recent changes in the characteristics

The cost factor has become an even more important influence in some sectors in recent years. Previously, merger and takeover represented strategic devices for spreading escalating R & D costs and exploiting internal economies. In some sectors, such as aircraft and automobiles, mergers and takeovers may have reached saturation point for nationalistic and anti-trust reasons. Joint ventures and licensing agreements have grown in importance in recent years and, in at least some cases, represent attempts to spread R & D costs in cases where merger is not feasible or desirable. R & D consortia or clubs have also evolved for similar reasons in some sectors such as electronics.

The chapter by Teece discusses joint ventures in more detail, but there are also issues of relevance to the analysis of this chapter. The creation of such R & D consortia or clubs may provide cooperative gains for the participating members in the form of technological advantages that would have been difficult or too costly for individual members to develop alone. We would expect such cooperative ventures to emphasise more upstream non-product-specific activity, since research of this nature is more likely to benefit the group as a whole, or a significant proportion of its members. More downstream product-specific development activity might lead to possible direct competitive conflict between group members and could have a zero-sum quality for participants in the venture. Consequently, Nelson (1984) suggests that such ventures are more likely to be appropriate for the exploitation of generic research programmes applicable to a variety of subsequent development programmes. Some evidence of this is provided by Peck (1986), who cites the example of MCC, a private microelectronics and computer technology joint R & D project involving twenty-one US companies. Its research programmes are generally consistent with Nelson's definition of generic research; Peck gives as an example the VLSI/CAD programme in MCC which does not design specific circuits but instead seeks to develop methods of computer designing circuits (p. 220).

Another possible change that may have significance for the conduct of research is that the perceived lag between conduct of basic research and eventual commercial application may have shortened in some cases, such as certain areas of biotechnology. Scientific norms of openness and active dissemination of research results may be compromised if commercial applications are expected in the relatively near future; the compartmentalisation of the historically distinct traditions and norms of science and commerce has traditionally been facilitated by the existence of buffers in the form of long lags weakening the profit implications of basic research for individual researchers.

Therefore, the four characteristics, and changes in these characteristics, have fundamental implications for the conduct of R & D activity. In the next section we shall see that these same characteristics have similarly profound implications for corporate strategy and internal organisation.

Strategy and structure implications

In this section we shall look at some implications of the four characteristics for the strategy and structure of individual corporations. We shall devote more attention to problems of structure or internal organisation, since many of the problems relating to strategy have already been introduced and discussed in the previous section. Freeman (1982) provides a synopsis of strategy types that incorporate or reflect a number of problems discussed in the last section. As far as analysis of strategy itself is concerned, Freeman (1982) produces a useful basis for analysing different types of R & D strategy. The *offensive* strategy will be appropriate if there are particular advantages to being first in with a particular innovation. Here protection of property rights (especially non-specificities) and lags required for competitive response are critical elements in deciding whether or not to adopt an offensive strategy. The *defensive* strategy is still likely to involve a high level of R & D, but the firm is prepared to react and follow offensive innovators, possibly with some degree of product differentiation. Obviously, if an offensive innovator finds that non-specificities benefit other firms in the form of externalities, this facilitates defensive strategies, and, as we saw in the previous section, such circumstances may be the norm rather than the exception. The ability to respond quickly and reduce lags is also important. As Freeman points out (1982, p. 178), a science-based firm's R & D strategy may contain mixtures of offensive and defensive strategies. IBM is an example of a company which has successfully and fairly consistently pursued a defensive strategy, mobilising considerable technical and marketing resources to respond to external technological threats. The *imitative* strategy does not attempt to match the offensive and defensive innovators in terms of skills and is prepared to follow some way behind if it enjoys particular advantages in terms of cost, tariffs or supplies. The *dependent* strategy is usually followed by smaller firms with sub-ordinate subcontracting roles in which they do not initiate new products but accept specifications and conditions imposed by dominant firms. Component manufacturers in the automobile industry have typically adopted such a role, though there are interesting signs that even in this sector the threat from Japanese manufacturers is likely to lead to merger and consolidation amongst parts-makers. Amalgamation would help create the critical mass necessary to take a more active and leading role in component and sub-system innovation (*The Economist*, 23 May 1987, p. 80). The *traditional* strategy is based on absence of technological innovation in a market which is benign and slow changing, while the *opportunist* strategy is based on entrepreneurial perception of niches that may not require substantial in-house R & D.

The four characteristics discussed earlier may all influence the possible strategies a firm will choose. For example, cost, uncertainty and lags may dissuade smaller, specialised firms from adopting offensive or defensive strategies, while non-specificities and second-in advantages discussed earlier may persuade firms to adopt a defensive rather than an offensive strategy. On the other hand, if it is possible to disengage the relatively cheaper upstream inventive stages from the more expensive downstream development work, small firms may have a comparative advantage on these cheaper, earlier stages. Large firms may be better placed to indulge in costly full-scale development (Freeman, 1982, p. 137; Williamson, 1975, p. 142). The role of structure or internal organisation in R & D activity is also influenced by the four characteristics. Williamson (1975), building on Chandler (1962), provides an analysis that will help introduce basic ideas which we can then develop further using our earlier analysis of the four basic characteristics.

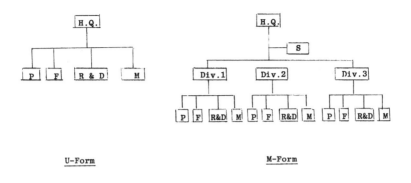

Figure 13.1   Basic hierarchies

Williamson contrasts the functional, or U-form, structure which is more appropriate for smaller, specialised firms with the multi-divisional, or M-form, structure which is likely to evolve in large diversified firms. In a specialised firm, the similarities and synergies between groups of products are so strong that functional specialists are liable to have to spend considerable time talking to each other and coordinating plans and schedules. Consequently, it is logical to group them together in a functional home as in the U-form example in Figure 13.1.

The M-form structure will tend to be more appropriate for a large, diversified firm. Divisionalisation creates natural decision units in the diversified corporation, putting together those functions responsible for a product or group of products. The divisions are assigned responsibility for operating and short-term strategic decisions, so as to reduce the number of levels in the hierarchy that have to be crossed before an inter-functional decision is arrived at, reducing delay, loss and distortion of information, and permitting top-level management to concentrate on long-run, strategic decision-making. Further, a competitive internal capital market may be created, comparability of divisions being facilitated by the existence of a uniform project yardstick for performance at middle (divisional) levels.

Therefore, the M-form creates a rational structure for the management of large, diversified firms. The problem that R & D poses for this solution is that of all the functions it is the least likely to be amenable to such treatment. We can see why by comparing the characteristics of reasonably innovative R & D work with the characteristics of economic activity appropriate to divisional operations. On the four characteristics of time, uncertainty, non-specificity and cost, reasonably innovative R & D work scores badly on the first three counts as far as divisional implications are concerned. Profit-centre operation tends to be short run; divisional managers are not only commonly assessed on the basis of annual performance, they are typically highly qualified and mobile general managers for whom divisional performance in a few year's time would often represent an externality, and consequently be disregarded. Highly uncertain and long-term returns may also be discounted heavily by a managerial set for whom the penalties for failure may be greater than the rewards for success.[4] The product non-specificity aspect would also reinforce the tendency for divisional management to under-invest in, or neglect, R & D due to externality considerations, if most of the benefits accrue to other profit centres.

The problems of long-time horizon, non-specificity (or synergy) and high uncertainty are more appropriate to levels in the firm responsible for strategic overviews rather than short-term, specific responsibilities as in divisions. The further we move upstream towards basic research activity, the more these problems become exacerbated for divisional management. Therefore, the tendencies towards centralisation of R & D are accentuated the further upstream the R & D is located. This is indicated at 'S' level for the M-form in Figure 13.1. The fourth characteristic, cost, may work against the inclusion of even development work in some divisions if the system under development is extremely costly and complex. Divisions often have extremely limited discretionary access to internal funds, and costly development plans may exceed their discretionary limits. Accordingly, financing decisions, or even the development work itself, may have to be shoved further up the corporate hierarchy.

In those circumstances, it is reasonable to ask why *any* R & D should be conducted at divisional level. Low product-specificity, long lags, extreme uncertainty and high cost all provide barriers to the effective divisionalisation of R & D. If even one of these characteristics is present in a particular R & D project, it impedes divisionalising the project and provides pressure for incorporation at 'S' level in Figure 13.1. Further, even if some projects do not possess any of these characteristics to a significant extent, there may still be incentives to allocate them to 'S' level to avoid diseconomies from splitting the R & D function.

There are, in fact, counteracting pressures to leave some or all R & D at divisional level. Firstly, removing a major function such as R & D from divisional responsibility impairs the internal capital market in so far as R & D cost is now shared between divisions, reducing the extent to which divisions can be treated as independent profit centres. Secondly, in a major study of factors influencing success or failure of innovation,[5] the factor which discriminated most clearly between success or failure was whether or not users' needs were understood (Freeman, 1982, p. 124). Separating R & D from divisional marketing could inhibit the integration of technological possibilities and designs with consumer requirements. Therefore, the location of R & D in the corporate hierarchy is likely to be a complex problem in practice, involving trade-offs between divisionalisation/ centralisation advantages and disadvantages. Different companies evolve different solutions to these conflicts. At a relatively early stage in its post-war development. General Electric discovered that its divisions were not innovating largely for the reasons discussed earlier, and responded by reallocating much of its R & D to 'S' level. Du Pont's solution to similar problems was to split its divisions' budgets into two components, one for operations and one for innovations, and monitor the respective components separately.

In fact, the formal hierarchical designs discussed above face potentially severe limitations imposed by the nature of R & D and product life-cycle considerations. Hierarchical bureaucracies of the type described above fall into the category of mechanistic systems as defined by Burns and Stalker (1968).[6] *Mechanistic* systems are characterised by functional specialisation, precise roles, vertical interaction between managers and formal hierarchical relationships. This form was identified by Burns and Stalker as being appropriate to technologically stable conditions. *Organic* systems are characterised by informal lateral relationships, networks rather than hierarchies, continual redefinition of tasks, and broadly specified responsibilities. These characterisations are ideal types and in practice organisations operate along a continuum on which these descriptions represent polar extremes.

Mechanistic systems encounter problems in incorporating innovative decisions on their agenda, and are likely to face extreme difficulties in rapidly changing environments. Since innovation constitutes a break in existing standard operating procedures and programmes, mechanistic structures typically have great difficulty in accommodating relevant decisions within existing routines.

Relevant information is liable to be ignored or mistreated because it does not fit into existing classifications or may face delays in being acted on as it is referred up the hierarchy. Even if the system is set up to signal significant data on innovation, in a highly innovative environment this would lead to the senior management fire brigade facing a number of alarm bells ringing simultaneously. Innovation, especially in turbulent environments, is characterised by non-programmable, surprising, routine-breaking information, and the mechanistic structure typically encounters severe difficulties in this area of decision-making. The characteristics of R & D uncertainty and non-specificity discussed earlier are particularly relevant here; Burns and Stalker point out that the mechanistic system is designed to deal with tasks that are *precise* and *specific*; uncertain, surprising tasks with a high degree of non-specificity will be ignored or mishandled by such a system.

The organic system, with its absence of pre-set rules, roles and responsibilities, is better equipped to facilitate innovativeness in rapidly changing environments. The form sacrifices the possibilities of static economies from functional specialisation and division of labour, but this can be a cheap sacrifice in conditions of rapid technological change, since these economies may not be obtainable in any case. What it provides instead is flexibility and responsiveness; the non-specificity and uncertainty inherent in innovation finds parallels in the non-specificity and uncertainty typically surrounding relationships and roles in the organic system.

The principles differentiating organic from mechanistic systems in Burns and Stalker's early analysis have been embodied in a variety of organisational designs that have evolved in recent years. For example, project teams or task forces with limited life spans may be set up to deal with innovative opportunities, cutting across formal organisational hierarchies and dealing with non-specificities by focusing on 'the innovation' as the unifying concept. Matrix management is a more elaborate and complex solution displaying both mechanistic and organic features and has been adopted by firms facing turbulent environments, including ITT, Monsanto, ICI and Lockheed. In a matrix structure an individual typically has simultaneous responsibilities to a functional home (e.g. R & D, production, marketing) and to a specific project. In principle, the functional line of responsibility provides mechanistic static economies from functional grouping and specialisation, while the project line of responsibility provides organic dynamic efficiency gains by focusing and integrating at the level of the particular project or innovation. In practice, dual responsibilities and confusion of responsibilities may inhibit the extent to which firms operating a matrix system can pursue dynamic and static efficiency goals simultaneously.[8]

To summarise, the characteristics that were important in shaping issues at *project* level in innovative activity (i.e. uncertainty, non-specificity, lags and cost) have also proved central in analysing problems of R & D strategy and organisation design. Non-specificity, uncertainty, lags and cost are major considerations affecting R & D strategy and the incorporation of R & D within formal hierarchies, while non-specificity and uncertainty are particular features that may encourage adoption of an organic rather than a mechanistic mode.[9]

Thus, probing beneath the surface differences of conventional analysis of R & D behaviour, business and corporate strategy, and organisational form reveals interesting similarities and parallels in terms of the general relevance of the four common concepts. This encourages optimism as to the possibility of pursuing a policy of integrating the historically separate literatures, to a greater or lesser extent.

This line of possible development finds further justification in recent arguments by some organisational theorists that work in their field would be enriched and strengthened by adoption of an evolutionary perspective on the development of organisational forms (McKelvie and Aldrich, 1983). They argue that existing studies tend to suffer from over-simplistic assumptions, presuming that organisations are either all alike or unique. They argue that systematising analysis of organisational forms, and introducing notions such as variation, selection and competition into analysis, would create a more coherent analytical basis in this area of study.

Again, at a surface level, McKelvie and Aldrich's argument is symptomatic of the Balkanisation of analysis in this area, since they make no reference to the extensive economic literature on evolutionary approaches to the study of organisation. However, at a deeper level, it suggests the possibility of commonalities and even convergence in terms of methods and frameworks between economics and organisational approaches, possibly complementing and building on the four common characteristics discussed throughout this chapter.

Concluding remarks

Non-specificity, uncertainty, delay and cost are important attributes affecting the economics of R & D activity. This chapter has attempted to show that it is possible to synthesise apparently disparate threads as far as issues in analysis of the R & D function, corporate strategy and structure are concerned. It is argued that analysis of function, strategy and structure should be rooted in the same core issues and problems.

We are also optimistic that it is possible to discern kinship relationships in approaches, such as evolutionary theory,[10] transaction cost economies[11] and organisational decision-making[12] in those subjects. If so, it offers interesting possibilities for cross-fertilisation between economic, business and organisational approaches.

Notes

1. This implicitly assumes that the specialised firm would not be able to appropriate a high level of gains through market transactions, e.g. joint venture and licensing. The reasonableness of this assumption may depend on the transaction costs associated with these alternatives in particular industrial environments.
2. The demand-pull approach is most commonly associated with Schmookler (1966). Mowery and Rosenberg (1979) have, however, questioned the legitimacy of many of the demand- or market-pull approaches to empirical interpretation.
3. However, the market still has an important role as an *ex post* selection device. See Nelson and Winter (1977) and Dosi (1982).
4. Freeman (1982, p. 167) points out that failure of divisional management to look far enough ahead was one consequence of the short-time perspective in profit-controlled divisions. Hayes and Abernathy (1980) identify the short-term orientation of divisional profit centres as a contributory factor towards what they perceive as the neglect of technological change in the US economy.
5. This was termed the Sappho project and is discussed in more detail in Freeman (1982, Chapter 5).
6. Since Burns and Stalker's seminal work, a great deal of theoretical and practical analysis has been undertaken regarding organic system design. Child (1984) provides an excellent coverage of both these aspects.
7. This does not mean that R & D lags and cost are not important in organic systems as they are in mechanistic. They will of course still be of relevance.

However, what the organic system does appear to offer is a particularly appropriate system for dealing with the other two characteristics of non-specificity and uncertainty.

8. See, in particular, Nelson and Winter (1982).
9. Williamson (1985) presents a recent statement of his development of trans-action cost economics. Kay (1982, 1984) utilises transaction cost economics to analyse problems in corporate strategy and structure. For an analysis of problems associated with Williamson's existing framework, see Kay (1987).
10. For a survey of recent work in this field, see March and Shapira (1982).

References

Burns, T. and Stalker, G. M. (1968), *The Management of Innovation*, London, Tamstock.

Chandler, A. (1962), *Strategy and Structure*, Cambridge, Mass., MIT Press.

Child, J. (1984), *Organisation: A Guide to Problems & Practice*, 2nd edn., London, Harper & Row.

Dosi, G. (1982), 'Technological paradigms and technological trajectories', *Research Policy*, vol. 11, pp. 147–62.

Freeman, C. (1982), *The Economics of Industrial Innovation*, 2nd edn., London, Frances Pinter.

Hayes, R. H. and Abernathy, W. J. (1980), 'Managing our way to economic decline', in Steiner, G. A. *et al.* (eds), *Management Policy and Strategy*, 2nd edn., New York, Macmillan.

Kay, N. M. (1979), *The Innovating Firm, A Behavioural Theory of Corporate R & D*, London, Macmillan.

—— (1982), *The Evolving Firm: Strategy and Structure in Industrial Organisation*, London, Macmillan.

—— (1984), *The Emergent Firm: Knowledge, Ignorance and Surprise in Economic Organisations*, London, Macmillan.

—— (1987), 'Markets and false hierarchies: some problems in transaction cost economics, European University Institute Working Paper.

Knight, F. M. (1921), *Risk, Uncertainty and Profit*, Boston, Houghton Mifflin.

McKelvey, B. and Aldrich, H. (1983), 'Populations, natural selection and applied organisational science', *Administrative Science Quarterly*, vol. 28, pp. 101–28.

Mansfield, E. (1968), *The Economics of Technological Change*, London, Long-man.

—— (1985), 'How rapidly does new technology leak out', *Journal of Industrial Economics*, vol. 34, pp. 217–23.

March, J. G. and Shapira, Z. (1982), 'Behavioural decision theory and organisa-tional decision theory', in G. R. Ungson and D. R. Braunstein (eds), *Decision-Making: An Interdisciplinary Perspective*, Boston, Kent Publishing.

Mowery, D. and Rosenberg, N. (1979), 'The influence of market demand upon innovation: a critical review of some recent empirical studies', *Research Policy*, vol. 8, pp. 102–53.

Nelson, R. R. (1959), 'The simple economics of basic scientific research', *Journal of Political Economy*, vol. 67, pp. 297–306.

—— (1984), *High Technology Policies: A Five Nation Comparison* American Enterprise Institute.

14 Technological opportunities and industrial organisation

Rod Coombs
Department of Management Sciences, University of Manchester Institute of Science and Technology, Manchester

On the significance of technological regimes

During the 1960s and 1970s research on the details of the technical-change process tended to focus on particular innovations. One of the central questions studied was the relative importance of demand-pull versus technology-push as determining why particular innovations or clusters of them came about when they did. However, the idea of demand-pull was then much better worked out than the idea of technology-push. Perhaps partly because of this, most of the empirical studies were able to document the importance of the former but not the latter. The perception by scholars of the importance of demand-pull, and the ambiguity of the influence of technology-push, had a noticeable influence on the policy discussions, which tended to stress the possible roles of government in influencing the character of demand, and to downplay direct government R & D support.

The last decade has seen a significant increase in understanding, or at least a change in perception, regarding the nature and significance of 'technological opportunities'. The change has been associated with a change in the unit of observation from particular innovations to the development of technologies more broadly. Put another way, innovations came to be seen as connected, and the attention focused on the connecting structure, rather than on particular innovations in that structure. Nelson and Winter (1977, 1982) have used the terms 'technological regimes' and 'technological trajectories' to refer to the intellectual structure guiding technical change in a field at any time, and to the associated internal dynamics through which technology unfolds. Dosi (1982) has employed 'technology paradigm' to refer to the intellectual structure associated with a given technological regime. Sahal (1981) and Saviotti and Metcalfe (1984) have developed similar ideas. The underlying notion regarding all of these intellectual developments is that innovations should not be considered in isolation, but rather must be understood in terms of an evolving technological structure.

There has been a parallel shifting in thinking about national policies, from the stimulus of (more) individual innovations, to the fostering of advance of broad technologies, like information technology, biotechnology, etc. With this shift of focus has come more careful analysis of the appropriate roles of government and the finance of R & D aimed at advancing particular technologies.

These theoretical, empirical and policy developments have had influence on a wide variety of topics. One important one, and a central concern of this chapter, is the analysis of connections between technical change and industrial organization. During the 1950s, 1960s and 1970s, there was considerable research on this topic. However, almost all of it presumed that the causal flow was from industrial organization to technical advance. The notion of the technological regime which is common to a number of firms in the same industry calls attention to the possibility that causality may flow at least as much from the nature of technology and the character of technical change to industrial organisation, as from industrial organization to technical change.

The associated concepts of technological regimes, paradigms and trajectories have been explored in an earlier chapter. Here the focus is on the relationship between these notions and the connections between market structure and technological change.

Market structure and innovation: the two-way causality

The Schumpeterian tradition

The literature on the relationships between market structure, firm size and innovation is voluminous but has not been able to come to a firm conclusion. Both on theoretical grounds and on the grounds of casual observation it is easy to propose both advantages and disadvantages in innovation for monopolised and competitive market structures, and for large and small firms. In each case it is the unequal distribution of the incentive to innovate and the capacity to innovate which causes the ambiguity of prediction. Nevertheless, the force of the Schumpeterian position on market power and size, coupled perhaps with the industrial economists preference for exploring relationships in which conduct is derived from structure, has led to considerable empirical work testing this view. The two relationships most commonly tested are that research intensity increases with market concentration, and that research intensity also increases with firm size. Kamien and Schwartz (1982) review a large number of studies on these relationships. In the case of market concentration they find that there is little consensus, but remark that there appear to be strong industry effects and that the degree of *technological opportunity* at industry level may be a major influence on research intensity (first shown by Scherer, 1967). In the case of firm size, they suggest some consensus around the view that research intensity increases with size up to a certain point and then falls again. But once more they add the caution that the picture is probably more fundamentally affected by industry-specific variables which have not been included in the analysis. More recent work on market structure by Angelmar (1985), and on firm size by Rothwell and Zegveld (1981) and

Kaplinsky (1983), has confirmed that the patterns vary considerably between industries. This no doubt explains why no clear pattern is visible above the industry level of aggregation.

This conclusion—that variations by industry in technological opportunity are the primary variables explaining variations in research intensity —undermines the view that industry structure variables are a primary determinant of patterns in innovative behaviour. Indeed, it suggests that a strong causality runs from technological opportunity, through innovative behaviour, to industrial structure itself, thus reversing the previous orthodoxy (Momigliano and Dosi, 1983). In fact this represents a more general statement of an observation first made by Phillips (1971) in a case study of the aircraft industry; namely that rapid technical change and difficult imitation conditions in an industry tend to generate powerful pressure towards concentration. Subsequently, a number of other studies of particular industries have added weight to this view: see, for example, Katz and Phillips (1982) on computers, Dosi (1984) and Malerba (1985) on semiconductors, and Altshuler *et al.* (1984) on automobiles.

Industry life cycles

Somewhat separate in its origins from the debate on market structure and innovation, there has been a significant tradition of theoretical and empirical studies which have argued that many of the features of an industrial sector, including concentration, are related dynamically to the evolution of the dominant technology of the industry, in some form of product or industry life cycle. Variations in productivity growth rates between industries were explained in part by reference to the 'age' of the industry and its technical base by Salter (1966). Varying rates and interactions between radical product and process innovation were placed at the centre of the life cycle by Abernathy and Utterback (1975).

The detailed work of Walsh (1984) on the chemical industry and its subsectors from the middle of the nineteenth century to the 1970s has shown the subtle shifts in the nature of technological change in an industry which accompany its evolution. The early stages of the dyestuffs, plastics and pharmaceuticals industries were all characterised by bursts of discontinuous scientific and technical discovery, which were partly serendipitous, and partly resulted from broadly targeted scientific research activity. These were the Schumpeterian 'impulses' which led to reallocation of resources and structural change. As the markets for these products began to develop the character of technical change shifted to improvements, branchings and extensions of initial technical paradigms, and towards process change. Furthermore, the fine structure of technical change begins to reveal a closer 'tracking' of shifts in patterns of demand as the industries mature. This pattern of a technical *opportunity* being exploited through a group of technological *trajectories* is a very robust feature of industrial dynamics. It is a reflection of the path-dependence, or directionality, of technical change, which exercises such a powerful influence on the evolution of the industry itself. In later sections we explore further the evidence on the mechanisms which link these patterns of technical change to changes in industrial organisation.

We therefore see a contrast between two approaches to the relationships between technical change and industrial organisation. These two approaches emphasise different directions of causality between market structure and patterns of innovation. In part this arises from their differing starting points. In the traditional view, which emphasises the effects of market structure on innovation, the analysis tends to be fairly static, analyses incentives to innovate in different market structures, and is ultimately concerned with the normative issues of efficiency and welfare. Where models have been made more complex, to include such variables as retaliatory innovation and R & D spending, such as in the work of Dasgupta and Stiglitz (1981), the primary focus nevertheless remains on the issue of whether the effect of market power on innovative patterns is or is not socially desirable. The question of how that market structure has arisen is not addressed; indeed, in their basic model the number of firms in the industry and the R & D to sales ratio are determined simultaneously, rather than any causal relationship being suggested.

As we noted above, the main reason for questioning the traditional approach is the lack of fit with the empirical evidence. Stoneman (1983, p. 46) reviews several empirical studies which indicate that product market and technological characteristics seem to be operating alongside structure as determinants of R & D allocations and innovative behaviour, and that the specific combination of influences varies from industry to industry.

Those approaches which, by contrast, emphasise the causality from technical change to market structure, tend to take a more dynamic view of the issue. The *evolution* of industrial structure rather than its effects becomes the object of study, and hence the process of technical change, viewed as a sequence of related innovations, becomes a natural candidate for incorporation into the analysis. We now examine these issues more closely.

Stochastic growth models and industry structure

An interesting phenomenon in the field of industrial economics which is an important instrument for clarifying the relationship between technical change and market structure is the observation of serial correlations in the growth rates of firms. This has been observed in general studies of firm growth (Singh and Whittington, 1968) and has been given a more specific technical component by Mansfield (1968), who argues that successful innovators enjoy higher than average growth rates.

Nelson and Winter (1982) explore the causes of serial correlation by setting up and analysing a number of dynamic models. In all of their models, R & D aimed at innovation is distinguished from R & D aimed at imitation. Some firms spend on both, some only on imitation. The former are called innovators, the latter imitators. Both kinds of firms have target

R & D to sales ratios. As they grow or decline, their R & D spending does too. This is important because in these models the probability that an innovator will achieve an innovation is proportional to its R & D spending. A successful innovation gives a firm a production cost advantage over its competitors. The expected time before an imitator is able to latch on to the innovation is proportional to its imitative R & D spending. Thus in these models large firms are more effective innovators and imitators than small ones. In turn, the size of a firm at any time is related to its past innovative and imitative successes, since profitable firms are tempted to expand, although they may be dissuaded by concerns about spoiling the market, and unprofitable ones are forced to contract. The production cost advantages conferred by innovators can be set in the model to reflect either a regime of incremental innovation on the basis of the industry's existing technology, or a regime of radical, science-based technical change resulting in high rates of 'latent productivity growth'. Firms who have achieved size advantages can be modelled as behaving aggressively or with restraint in their investment decisions. Equilibrium is not a feature of the model.

The model takes the form of a computer simulation in which the initial conditions, including the number of firms, is set; and then the simulation is run for a number of decision periods. Amongst the results the following are particularly noteworthy.

1. In the simulations based on sixteen firms the level of concentration always increases over time.
2. The rate of increase of concentration and the final level achieved are modified by the rate of technical change and its regime, by the ease or difficulty of imitation, and by the degree of investment restraint of large firms.
3. Where the rate of technical change is fast, and imitation difficult, the tendencies towards concentration are most powerful, thus confirming the observation of Phillips (1971) in a more general sense.
4. Where firms in concentrated industries pursue aggressive growth policies, imitators tend gradually to achieve ascendancy over innovators. Where restraint is shown, innovators and imitators survive with innovators predominant.

Space precludes a fuller discussion of the detailed features of this model, but the results which are most salient to the issue of causality in the relationship between market structure and innovation can now be summarised.

Firstly, the model does demonstrate some traditional (and some more surprising) features of the causality which runs from market structure to innovation. Large firms in industries where small firms are also present do have innovative advantages which result in greater than average growth. Concentrated industries achieve a given rate of technical change for less total R & D expenditure, but give rise to a higher price level. Concentrated industries can shelter innovators if investment restraint is shown, or they can drive innovators out of business to the benefit of imitators if less restraint is shown, thus halting technical advance.

Secondly, however, and more striking, the forces of concentration are very strongly dependent on the rate and character of technical change. This confirms the original empirical finding of Scherer (1967) that differences in technological opportunity between industries are a more important factor than structure in explaining differences in innovative activity. Particularly interesting is the finding of a stronger result for the simulation of radical as compared to incremental technical change regimes. This is strong support for the Schumpeterian insight that the dynamics of industrial growth create powerful incentives for innovators and for imitators. Furthermore, it suggests a picture of a multiple set of contingencies affecting the two-way nature of the relationship between innovation and market structure.

Complicating factors

There are a number of complicating factors which now need to be considered, in order to move beyond the simplifying assumptions made in the discussion so far. The first of these, which is not incorporated into the Nelson and Winter model, is the question of entry. They acknowledge its importance (1982, p. 328) and argue that their results would not be fundamentally affected by entry of small imitative firms, but note that entry by large and technically progressive firms would change the picture considerably. In an extension of the basic model, Winter (1984) introduces a treatment of entry. He finds that in the 'cumulative' or incremental regime of technical change established firms can defend against entry better than they can in a more radical, 'science-based' technical regime. A more explicit treatment of entry is that of Gort and Klepper (1982) who offer a five-stage model of the patterns of entry during the evolution of a market as follows.

1. rapid growth of entry following the first innovation; conditioned by ease of entry and number of potential entrants;
2. increase in the number of producers;
3. entrants and exits cancelling out with net entry zero;
4. negative entry, or shake-out;
5. zero entry as the industry becomes mature.

This model has features in common with a number of other discussions of the industry life cycle. The essential principle is to contrast the nature of technical possibilities at the beginning and end of the process. At the beginning the technology is seen as volatile. External technologies possessed by potential entrants may facilitate entry, and disable existing producers. At the end of the process; technology-led entry is more difficult because the existing technology is mature, and the accumulated experience of the existing producers adds to the other mechanisms for deterring entry. This latter point is consistent with the analysis of Winter (1984). Gort and Klepper's work supports the view that the dynamics of innovation will promote concentration over time, as in the Nelson and Winter model, though it starts from different assumptions. Furthermore it has significant empirical support. However, it perhaps oversimplifies the phases of evolution of the market by implicitly suggesting that the technology base of the industry will always be sufficiently well defined as to allow existing producers to maintain sovereignty over it into the mature phase of the industry. This may not be the case where there are multiple technologies embodied in the product.

If we acknowledge that complex products comprise a *range* of component technologies, and that radical change in one of them may alter the relative entry potential of outsiders, then the neat sequence of stages could be upset, or even periodically reversed. In other words, the contingent factors which affect the evolution of concentration, both in this model and in the Nelson and Winter model, are subject to variation not only *between industries*, but also *within* industries over time. Thus the evolution of market structure may not follow one clear path; but rather a zigzag of paths, reflecting variations in the conditioning factors of rate of technical change, ease of imitation, range of technologies employed in the industry, etc. We shall return to this point later.

A second complicating factor in developing the insights of the Nelson and Winter model and the Gort and Klepper model is the issue of economies of scale, economies of scope, and the multi-product firm. The latter point is particularly important since Nelson and Winter explicitly restrict their model (for good reasons) to single-product situations. Stoneman (1983) summarises the arguments on this point as follows. There is no reason to expect technical change to push the minimum efficient scale of plants in one direction or the other. However, the arguments of Williamson (1975) on the organisational benefits of the M-form company, and on its ability to utilise unexpected R & D gains, together with the advantages of such large firms in financing R & D, may have increased the minimum efficient scale of firms. If markets have not grown at the same rate then this process could increase concentration. However, since the flexibility of M-form firms is not infinite (and indeed the unrelatedness of diversification is correlated with diminishing performance) we can assume that such firms do not completely obliterate the significance of industrial boundaries, nor do they remove the upper bounds on concentration.

These issues have also been examined in a rather more general framework by Kay (1986). He argues that markets for capital, and for cooperative agreements concerning innovation, both between firms and within large diversified firms, play an important role in facilitating innovations in circumstances where product market structure would theoretically reduce incentives. Thus, for example, the availability of capital, and innovative opportunities, for deployment within diversified M-form organisations should reduce the effect of the apparent constraint on innovativeness implied by the structures of the product markets in which the organisation operates. Similarly, licensing agreements, joint ventures and other forms of agreement should in principle allow innovative opportunities to be realised in spite of market structure constraints. The caveat on both these mechanisms is that the markets in capital and in agreements have to function with sufficient efficiency to allow this flexibility of innovation to be realised. Clearly, this flexibility is not complete; but Kay argues convincingly that cooperation mechanisms and capital markets are able significantly to free the direction of innovative activity from the constraints which product market structure might otherwise impose.

Summarising this discussion of economies of scale and scope, we can say the following. The traditional analysis of the relationship between industrial organisation and technological change, in the context of the well-defined, single-product industry, hinges on the view that the capacity to innovate and the incentives to innovate are dissociated. The capacity lies with the larger firms and those with market power. The balance of incentive lies with the smaller firms. We have seen first that this dissociation is not black and white, and, secondly, that institutional innovations such as the multi-product firm can significantly *recombine* the capacity and the incentive to innovate. Thus the issue of industrial organisation becomes much more complex than in the traditional view.

The effect of this discussion of complicating factors such as entry, multi-product firms and collaboration, on our diagnosis of the innovation market structure relationship, is paradoxical. Whilst it strengthens the intrinsic importance of causalities flowing from technical opportunities to market structure, it highlights the fact that the sources of these technical opportunities, and the mechanisms through which they are applied, are complex and have multiple relationships to any industry being analysed. Clearly, then, the issue can only be resolved by recognising the need to define time periods, levels of aggregation, product characteristics, and bundles of technical characteristics, in such a way that the problem is constrained and made more manageable. For example, if we were to insist on conducting the analysis on an object defined as the transport industry, the problems would be immense, and any results might not be very meaningful. If we, however, restrict the problem to railways, or road haulage, or private cars, the issue becomes more tractable.

Technological opportunities and technological trajectories

The preceding discussion has identified the fact that the links between innovation and market structure can best be approached by seeing the problem dynamically, and by seeing innovations not as discrete, but as sequences of related innovations which intersect from time to time in complex ways. Technological opportunities come into existence, have a fruitful phase, and subsequently diminish in fruitfulness. These strongly directional processes are what have been variously referred to as technological trajectories, paradigms, etc.

If innovative opportunities do indeed arise in a structured form, in part as a result of the evolution of technological trajectories, then the foregoing observations suggest that product market structures will respond adaptively to them, through the behaviour of collaborating groups both within and between firms. Market structures will, however, exercise a significant influence on the rate at which trajectories are exploited, and new ones identified.

But, as was briefly mentioned above, a significant moderating influence should be taken account of at this point. Whilst technological opportunities and trajectories occur in the domain of *technology*, innovations occur in the domain of *products*. Products vary greatly in terms of their complexity; the range of technologies which they incorporate; and in terms of their sequential position with respect to other production and consumption activities. These variations condition the way in which related technological opportunities are realised in different types of product. Thus it is not possible to 'read off' a set of industry structure characteristics and dynamics directly from a diagnosis of technological opportunities. Proper attention must be paid to the range of interacting technologies relevant to the product or service, and to the position of the product in the input/output structure. This point can be illustrated through use of Pavitt's (1984) taxonomy of sectoral patterns of innovation. He identifies distinctive characteristics of the innovation process in 'supplier-dominated' sectors; 'production-intensive' sectors (sub-divided into 'scale-intensive' and 'specialised equipment suppliers'); and in 'science-based' sectors. The extent to which technical change is product- or process-centred, internally or externally generated, radical or incremental, varies between these types of industrial sector. It seems likely therefore that the patterns in the relationship between technological opportunities and market structures will vary between these types of industry. This represents a step in the direction of defining levels of aggregation and product characteristics which was earlier noted as a precondition for further clarifying the relationships between innovation and market structure.

It is also important, however, to consider the time period chosen for analysis of change in industrial structure. In the short to medium term, industries within Pavitt's categories may exhibit relatively stable patterns of causality. In the longer run, however, Pavitt's taxonomy from supplier-dominated through to science-based is one in which age of industry decreases and research intensity increases. Pavitt's categories of sector therefore have a dynamic relationship to technological opportunities as well as the cross-sectional relationship to which he draws attention.

In the next section we briefly consider technological trajectories a little further. One objective of the discussion is to identify those aspects of trajectories which are intimately connected to the experience and skills of particular firms, and contrast them with those aspects of trajectories which exist more independently, and which are available to groups of firms in industries. In making this analysis we are therefore assuming a frame of reference within theory of the firm which is essentially behavioural, drawing on the traditions of Penrose (1959) and Cyert and March (1963).

In so doing we are adopting a framework which is sympathetic to the microeconomic foundations of the evolutionary model of industrial dynamics discussed in this chapter so far. Earlier chapters in this book have discussed technological trajectories in more depth.

Firm-specific resources and technological opportunities in innovation

Institutionalised R & D departments have as their objective the creation of technology, but not of all possible technologies. Their possibilities are limited first and foremost by the objective characteristics of the knowledge bases within which they are working. A useful way of presenting this is in terms of the parameters which describe any particular system.

Most technical systems can be defined in terms of some performance characteristics which embody the function of the device and some physical specifications which determine the level of performance achieved. A simple example is the case of microelectronic circuits. One important performance parameter is the speed of operation of the circuits, which is of significance to users. This performance variable is a function of a specification, namely the degree of miniaturisation of the circuit. (The smaller the distance the electrons have to travel between parts of the device, the quicker the circuit can operate.) There is obviously a physical limit to this reduction in size. In this case it is determined by the laws of quantum mechanics which do not allow the device to function in a stable manner if certain elements are placed closer than a given distance. This limit is independent of any technical difficulties which may arise in achieving it. Other examples abound; the relationship between drag coefficient and fuel efficiency in motor vehicles is another one.

If the physical limit to any physical specification is still distant, and there remains considerable scope to operate on that specification to increase performance, then there exist substantial '*intensive*' technological opportunities in that system. By contrast, '*extensive*' technological opportunities will exist if the system in question has numerous possible functional applications in a variety of products or processes, where its performance characteristics will be of value. This latter is clearly the case with microelectronics. This approach to specifying technologies has been developed recently for the purpose of constructing indicators of technical change (Saviotti and Metcalfe, 1984). What is significant for the present discussion is that the technological frontier has some definite structure, and that technical reasons exist for expecting some strategies for altering that structure to be easier than others. This is a way of capturing the directionality of technical change.

However, the relative difficulty of different strategies for altering the technical frontier has to be expressed in terms of some unit; and the natural one is consumption of resources. It would seem appropriate to express some relationship between the cost of achieving some unit of technical change and the benefit which falls to the firm which makes the change.

Following Stoneman (1983), we can use the simple identity:

$$G = p \cdot x - c \cdot x - E$$

where G is profit

    p is the price of the commodity incorporating the technical change

    x is the level of output of the commodity

    $x = sM/p$

    s is the market share for the producer

    M is the size of the total market

    c is the cost of production of one unit

    E is the expected cost of achieving the technical change

If a mark-up pricing policy is assumed then the expression becomes:

$$G = s \cdot M \, (l - k) - E$$

where $k = c/p$

Thus profit is positively related to size of market, share of market and mark-up, and is negatively related to the cost of achieving the technical change. This expression now allows some useful insights into the significance of different regimes for technological innovation.

Consider first the case of a radical innovation which opens a new market or serves an existing market with a product based on new technological principles. The technological opportunity, now measured in terms of the profit expectation, will be high where s and M are high; which may be the case if the performance or the cost of the new item offer substantial advantages with respect to previous products, and/or if entry barriers are low. But for the profit to be high s and M have to be high in relation to E. E will be low to the extent that the knowledge required to achieve the technical change is easily available to the firm involved. This will be a function of the R & D specialisation of the firm, and its collaborative possibilities.

Consider now the contrasting case of subsequent improvement innovations within the parameters of the technical system defined by the first innovation. These may increase the performance or reduce the price with respect to the initial state. The values of M and s for each incremental step will depend on the growth rate of the performance parameter. This will perhaps increase in the short run as a result of learning but will decrease in the long run as a result of encountering the intrinsic performance limit of the technical system, as described earlier. For these incremental innovations E may also diminish initially as a result of learning, but may increase ultimately as more complex methods are needed to modify specifications and increase performance. Thus the technological opportunities evolve in a manner which is related to the diffusion process initiated by the first innovation; an issue also analysed by Metcalfe (1981).

There are a number of overlapping concepts here. The first case discussed above—that of the radical innovation—closely resembles the concept of 'extensive' technological opportunities mentioned earlier, though the relationship is not exact. The second case—that of the succeeding incremental innovations—appears to be identical to the notion of 'intensive' technological opportunities and closely resembles the idea of a natural trajectory of technical change. Furthermore, the radical innovation/extensive opportunities scenario is essentially the same as the 'science-based and the cumulative regimes in the Nelson and Winter model are cussed above, and the incremental innovation intensive opportunities scenario corresponds to the 'cumulative' regime in that model.

This is an important conclusion which links the Nelson and Winter model with the industry life-cycle tradition. It is likely that the science-based and the cumulative regimes in the Nelson and Winter model are frequently linked together sequentially, given the appropriate choice of boundary conditions of time and product characteristics. An initial science-based regime would give a powerful 'internal' impetus to the process of concentration. A gradual shift to a cumulative regime can allow a relative attenuation of the causal mechanisms running from innovation to market structure, and an emergence of some of the reverse mechanisms. The Penrosian firm-specific character of much of the technical change in the cumulative regime can act as a defence against entry, as Winter (1984) suggests. However, this will be balanced by the enhanced danger of entry by science-based firms, especially if markets for capital and cooperation lower entry barriers. Hence a particular product function could become the site of a conflict between a decaying cumulative technical regime and an emerging new science-based regime. In the light of the increasing role of multi-product firms, and the strategic use of R & D, it is now possible for this conflict between technologies to be conducted not only through competition between firms but also through strategic choices made within firms.

These topics of firm-specific resources, theory of the firm, and technological trajectories are dealt with in more detail elsewhere in this book, and will not be developed further here. The purpose of this brief discussion has been to illustrate the argument that it is through this route that further progress can be made in exploring the structure and directionality of technical change. Such an exercise might then develop the insights into the links between directional technical change and market structure which emerged prominently from the models discussed in the earlier part of this chapter.

Conclusion

If it seems that the diagnosis in this chapter reduces our power to make general statements and to deduce public policy, then this is only partly true. The power to make certain kinds of general economic statements— such as 'oligopoly might be the optimum industrial structure for technical change'–is indeed reduced, since the theoretical basis for such statements has been undermined by the preceding arguments. But the power to make general statements about technological trajectories is reinforced, since their significance has been underlined by the arguments. This returns us to the point made in the first section, namely that policy-making as well as analysis has tended to swing back towards technology type as the focus of discussion and intervention in recent years. Despite the difficulties with making policy in this way, it seems to be the least unsafe method available.

It is worth recording another implication of the foregoing analysis which links to the macroeconomic sphere, also mentioned in the first section. If sectoral rates of technical change are relatively independent, and if they condition industry dynamics to a significant extent, then this closely resembles the supply side conditions of Pasinetti's (1981) approach to macroeconomics, in which the levels of output and employment growth are primarily determined by the structural change process, and equilibrium is only possible as a fluke. However, this does not preclude some linking of sectoral rates of technical change, through a mechanism such as Freeman's 'New Technology Systems', thus permitting long-run fluctuations in structural change, and hence in economic growth. Such connections between the industrial and macroeconomic dynamics of technological trajectories are also discussed elsewhere in this book.

References

Abernathy, W.J. and Utterback, J.M. (1975), 'A dynamic model of process and product innovation', *Omega*, vol. 3, no. 6.

Altschuler, A. *et al*. (1984), *The Future of the Automobile*, Cambridge, Mass., MIT Press.

Angelmar, R. (1985), 'Market structure and research intensity in high-technological-opportunity industries', *Journal of Industrial Economics*, vol. 36.

Coombs, R.W., Saviotti, P.P. and Walsh, V. (1987), *Economics and Technological Change*, London, Macmillan.

Cyert, R.M. and March, J.G. (1963), *A Behavioural Theory of the Firm*, London, Prentice-Hall.

Dasgupta, P. and Stiglitz, J. (1981), 'Entry, innovation, exit: towards a theory of oligopolistic industrial structure', *European Economic Review*, vol. 15.

Dosi, G. (1982), 'Technological paradigms and technological trajectories', *Research Policy*, vol. 11.

—— (1984), *Technical Change and Industrial Transformation*, London, Macmillan.

Freeman, C. (1982), *The Economics of Industrial Innovation*, London, Frances Pinter.

Freeman, C., Clark, J. and Soete, L. (1982), *Unemployment and Technical Innovation*, London, Frances Pinter.

Gort, M. and Klepper, S. (1982), 'Time Paths in the Diffusion of Product Innovations', *Economic Journal*, 92.

Hay, D. and Morris, D. (1979), *Industrial Economics, Theory and Evidence*, Oxford, Oxford University Press.

Kamien, M.I. and Schwartz, N.L. (1982), *Market Structure and Innovation*, Cambridge, Cambridge University Press.

Kaplinsky, R. (1983), 'Firm size and technical change in a dynamic context', *Journal of Industrial Economics*, vol. 32.

Katz, B. and Phillips, A. (1982), 'Innovation, technological change and the emergence of the computer industry', in H. Giersch (ed.) *Emerging Technology*, Tübingen, J.C.B. Mohr.

Kay, N.M. (1986), 'Industrial structure, rivalry and innovation, theory and evidence', Herriot-Watt University Working paper.

Malerba, F. (1985), *The Semi-Conductor Business: The Economics of Rapid Growth and Decline*, Madison, University of Wisconsin Press.

Mansfield, E. (1968), *Industrial Research and Technological Innovation*, New York, Norton.

Metcalfe, J.S. (1981), 'Impulse and diffusion in the study of technical change', *Futures*, vol. 13.

Momigliano, F. and Dosi, G. (1983), *Tecnologia and Organizzazione Industriale Internazionale*, (1985), I Mulino, Bologna.

Nelson, R. (1985), 'Policies in support of high technology industries', Yale University, Institute for Social and Policy Studies, Working Paper 1011.

Nelson, R. and Winter, S. (1977), 'In search of a useful theory of innovation', *Research Policy*, vol. 6.

—— (1982), *An Evolutionary Theory of Economic Change*, Cambridge, Mass., Harvard University Press.

Pavitt, K. (1984), 'Patterns of technical change: towards a taxonomy and a theory', *Research Policy*, vol. 13.

Pasinetti, L. (1981), *Structural Change and Economic Growth*, Cambridge, Cambridge University Press.

Penrose, E. (1959), *The Theory of the Growth of the Firm*, New York, Wiley.

Phillips, A. (1971), Technology and Market Structure: A Study of the Aircraft Industry, Lexington D.C., Heath.

Rothwell, R. and Zegfeld, W. (1981), *Industrial Innovation and Public Policy*, London, Frances Pinter.

Sahal, D. (1981), 'Alternative conceptions of technology', *Research Policy*, vol. 10.

Salter, W. (1966), *Productivity and Technical Change*, Cambridge, Cambridge University Press.

Saviotti, P.P. and Metcalfe, J.S. (1984), 'A theoretical approach to the construction of technological output indicators', *Research Policy*, vol. 13.

Scherer, F.M. (1967), 'Market structure and the employment of scientists and engineers', *American Economic Review*, vol. 57.

Schmookler, J. (1966), *Invention and Economic Growth*, Cambridge, Mass., Harvard University Press.

Singh, A. and Whittington, G. (1968), 'Growth, profitability and valuation', DAE Occasional Paper No. 7, Cambridge, Cambridge University Press.

Stoneman, P. (1983), *The Economic Analysis of Technological Change*, Oxford, Oxford University Press.

Walsh, V. (1984), 'Invention and innovation in the chemical industry: demand-pull or discovery-push?', *Research Policy*, vol. 13.

Williamson, O.E. (1975), *Markets and Hierarchies: Analysis and Anti-Trust Implications*, New York, Free Press.

Winter, S. (1984), 'Schumpeterian competition and alternative technological regimes', *Journal of Economic Behaviour and Organisation*, vol. 5.

Part V National systems of innovation

Preface to Part V

Richard R. Nelson
Columbia University, New York

The chapters in this section follow on naturally from those in Part IV. In Part IV the focus was on the evolution of particular technologies, and on how technical change was both shaped by and shaped firm behavior and industry structure. Here the focus is wider, being concerned with national systems of technical change spanning the full spectrum of industries. And the institutional concerns are broader.

The thrust of both Nelson's chapter on the United States and Freeman's on Japan is that modern national innovation systems are complex institutionally. While they involve the institutional actors and activities considered in the chapters of Part IV, they include as well institutions like universities dedicated to public technological knowledge, and government funds and programs. While these two chapters deal only with the United States and Japan, a description and analysis of the innovation systems of any of the other major industrialized nations would show a similar complex structure. Private-for-profit firms are the heart of all of these systems. They compete with each other, but they also cooperate. In all nations universities play an important role in the innovation system. And in all modern nations, public funds account for a significant fraction of total R & D spending, in some cases being nearly as great as total private funds.

There are certain essential similarities among the innovation systems in advanced industrial nations. There also are certain interesting and important differences. The contrast between the United States and Japan brings this out strikingly. A comparison of the two national systems is particularly interesting because throughout much of the post-war period the United States has been the clear technological leader in most fields, but over the last decade Japan has caught up in many, and now is ahead in a few, technologies.

As noted, in both nations there is vigorous technological competition among firms in the same industry. However, in Japan, under the auspices of MITI, there also has developed a tradition of inter-firm cooperation in certain kinds of research. In the United States, university—industry interaction has been close for a long time in many industries, and in some technologies universities have been an important source of invention. This seems to be much less the case in Japan, where the distance between industry and universities seems to be greater. In both nations, the government has played an important role, but the nature of the roles has been strikingly different. In the United States, defense and space R & D programs accounted for a large share of total industrial R & D during the 1960s, and spillover to civilian technology was considerable during that era in the fields of aircraft, semiconductors and computers. In recent years the evidence suggests that spillover has been much less substantial. In Japan, government industrial R & D support has been very small compared with the level in the United States, and in particular there is very little defense R & D spending. On the other hand, principally through MITI, the Japanese government has played a significant role in trying to direct and orchestrate the Japanese industrial R & D effort in certain key industries. Much of the current public policy debate in the United States, in Europe and in Japan is concerned with the efficacy of, on the one hand, significant government R & D support for the advancement of particular technologies, in the style of the US Department of Defense, and, on the other, MITI-like coordination of industrial research.

The chapter by Lundvall takes a different cut at analyzing national systems of innovation. His focus is on user–producer interactions, which he argues is an important if often overlooked feature of the innovation process. He argues plausibly that geographical and cultural closeness facilitate effective interaction, and goes on to propose that national borders tend to enclose networks of technological interaction which define national innovation systems. He puts forth several reasons why there are such national systems—common government, as well as common heritage and education (at least in the relatively homogeneous Nordic countries), and obstructions to cross-national flow of labor being prominent on his list. The Nelson and Freeman chapters simply assume that there are national systems, and that borders matter. Lundvall presents a theory as to why this might be the case. Actually, rather little is known about just how borders affect the flow of technological information and capabilities, which is what many governments are concerned about, or the patterns of interaction between upstream and downstream firms, which is Lundvall's focus, or university industry connections, which is another interesting topic. It seems clear that borders matter, but not clear how much, or in what ways.

The chapter by Pelikan is concerned with a theoretical exploration of whether a capitalist innovation system can be out-performed by a socialist one, where by the latter he means one in which officials appointed by a central authority control the use and creation of technology. He argues that it cannot, because of the likelihood that incompetent people will control the process in socialist regimes, whereas under capitalism pluralism and competition tend to assure good management, or at least that there are ports of entry with good management. While Pelikan does not consider in any detail the inefficiencies of the pluralistic capitalist system that have been stressed in several places in this book, or the large potential gains from some centralization in some cases, his stress on the dangers of centralization echo some observations in Nelson's chapter. Of course, one could look at the real question as being not about the relative merits of a fully decentralized versus a fully managed system, but about how much centralization or decentralization is appropriate for what kind of work. This is implicitly the way the matter is being treated nowadays in so-called capitalist economies. And many socialist economies are experimenting with a certain amount of decentralization and even competition. The results of these experiments will be interesting to watch.

15 Institutions supporting technical change in the United States*

Richard R. Nelson

Columbia University, New York

Economists, from Marx to Schumpeter, have touted capitalism as an engine of technical progress. But what kind of an engine is it? What are its key components? How does it work?

This chapter is a preliminary report on my theoretical and empirical research on innovation systems in capitalist economies. That research has been powerfully shaped by the understandings about the nature of technical progress, and perceptions of the role and organization of corporate R & D, discussed earlier. The emphasis here is on mapping and trying to comprehend the wider institutional structures within which corporate R & D and technical change proceed in capitalist economies. If technical change is far more complicated and variegated than it is depicted in standard economic theory, so too are the institutional structures supporting it.

The focus here is on the contemporary US scene. The following chapter is concerned with modern Japan. There are many similarities between the two national innovation systems, but some important differences as well. They will be initially signalled here, and developed at greater length in the following chapter.

Also, one of the striking features of national innovation systems is that they change over time, usually gradually, but sometimes sharply. The occasional large changes in innovation systems are part and parcel of the occasional sea changes in technical–economic paradigms discussed earlier by Freeman and Perez. While I shall sketch where the current US system came from, and how it is different from what it used to be and why, space precludes giving that subject adequate treatment here. And while I will speculate a bit about where it is going, how the new technologies discussed in several places in this book will drive it, I cannot here consider that matter at any length.

The complex capitalist innovation system

Particularly in comparison with Soviet-style systems, there are three rather obvious characteristics of national innovation systems in capitalist

*The research on which this chapter is based has been funded partly by PRA-NSF, and partly by the American Enterprise Institute.

economies. One is the privatization of much of new technology, which harnesses profit incentives and market forces to its creation. A second striking feature is the existence of multiple, independent, generally rivalrous sources of new technology. A third, and related, characteristic is heavy reliance on *ex post* market forces to select on the innovations offered by different firms, and on the firms themselves.

Put tersely, in capitalist countries, technical change is set up as an evolutionary process. The research on technical change, discussed earlier in this book, increasingly is explicitly analyzing it as such.[1] The fact that the process is that way in good part reflects the particular institutional structure of capitalist countries. Technical change proceeds in quite different ways in Soviet-style economies.

Evolutionary processes in general, and technical change in particular, are inherently wasteful, at least with the vision of hindsight. Due to the unplanned, uncoordinated nature of industrial R & D in capitalist economies, R & D allocation is doomed to be inefficient, compared with any kind of an ideal. Looking backward one can see a litter of failed or duplicative endeavors that probably never would have been undertaken had there been effective overall planning and coordination. Economies of scale and scope that might be achieved through R & D coordination are missed. Certain kinds of R & D that would have high social value simply are not done. Also, because technology is to a considerable extent proprietary, one can see many enterprises operating inefficiently, even failing, sometimes at considerable social cost, for want of access to the best technology.

It is something of a puzzle, therefore, why the capitalist innovation system has performed so well. There certainly is nothing like the twin theorems around to support an argument that capitalism 'can't be beat'. But, of course, the key question is: what are the alternatives? Compared with what? Various socialist scholars have observed the wastefulness of capitalism and proposed that a centrally planned and coordinated system, which treated technology as a public good, ought to be able to do better at generating and using new technology. The troubles socialist economies have been having with their innovation systems suggests that this is easier said than done.

What is it about technical change that makes effective central planning so difficult, or perhaps impossible? The basic matter, I would argue, is the uncertainty that almost always surrounds the question, where should R & D resources be allocated, in a field where technology is fluid? There generally are a wide variety of ways in which existing technology could be improved, and several alternative paths toward achieving any of these — not simply uncertainty about where the bets ought to be laid, but also disagreement among exprts. Under such circumstances, attempts to get *ex ante* consensus are likely to be futile or counter-productive. What the capitalist innovation system provides is multiple sources of initiative, and a competition among those who place their bets on different ideas. And it does so in a context where, as I shall elaborate later, there is widespread access to the basic generic knowledge one needs to understand the techni-cal possibilities, and strong incentives to heed market signals. It is left to the market to decide, *ex post*, what were the good ideas. This is an inefficient and wasteful way to do things, and painful for the losers, but, given the nature of technological uncertainties and the way humans and organizations seem to think and behave, it may be hard to do much better than to set up technical change as an evolutionary process.

Also, there is another feature of capitalist innovation systems that par-tially mitigates the problems discussed above. In capitalist economies technology, or aspects of it, is partly a public good. These public and private faces of technology both complement each other and are at odds. The public aspect of technology helps to control the inefficiencies associated with the private rivalrous aspect, but at the same time builds other problems into the system.

Schumpeter's perceptive analysis about how new technology gets generated and spread in capitalist countries clearly recognizes both the private and public sides.[2] He saw the lure and reward for innovation in the quasi-rents on the private temporary monopoly associated with the intro-duction of a new product or process. However, in Schumpeter's analysis the monopoly normally is limited. Sooner or later competitors will be able to imitate, or invent around, the initial innovation. The fact that techno-logy ultimately goes public has three benefits.[3] First, this assures that a healthy share of the benefits of innovation go to users, and that 'triangle' costs are kept down. Second, knowledge of the new innovation provides a base and a spur for further innovation by others. Third, by facilitating subsequent competition, the dangers that a company can build a wide and durable industry monopoly out of a particular innovation are kept under control. However, all of these public benefits will come to naught if fear of rapid imitation damps incentive to innovate in the first place.

From one point of view, the job of institutional design is to get an appropriate balance of the private and public aspects of technology, enough private incentive to spur innovation, and enough publicness to facilitate wide use. Access to an innovation by competitors should not be so rapid or complete as to dull incentives to innovate. On the other hand, the stronger the restrictions on access and the longer their lasting, the higher the social costs in terms of less than optimal use.[4]

However, while this simple view of trade-offs is illuminating, it is too simple. It represses that different kinds, or aspects, of technology differ significantly in terms of latent publicness. Also, the institutional structure of real capitalist systems is much richer than that depicted in simple models.

It is important to distinguish between two different aspects of a techno-logy. On the one hand, a technology consists of a body of generic know-ledge, in the form of generalizations about how things work, key variables influencing performance, the nature of currently binding constraints and approaches to pushing these back, widely applicable problem-solving heuristics, etc. Dosi (1982) has called these packages of generic knowledge 'technological paradigms'. On the other hand, a technology also comprises a collection of specific ways of doing things, or artefacts, which are known to be effective in achieving their ends if performed or used with reasonable skill in the appropriate context. Much, if not all, of the generic knowledge tends to have properties of a latent public good. Such knowledge tends to be widely applicable, and germane to a variety of users. Access to generic knowledge may be essential if one hopes to advance further the technology with any force. Also, in a system where there is considerable inter-firm mobility of scientists and engineers, generic knowledge is very difficult to keep proprietary. On the other hand, while portions of the set of extant techniques possess latent public good properties, in the sense that certain techniques are widely applicable, a good part of it is not appropriately so characterized. As Keith Pavitt (1984) has stressed, a good portion of technique is of rather narrow application, being tailored to the attributes of the products and processes of particular firms. Thus restriction of access entails little cost.

Also, there is much more to the capitalist innovation system than for-profit firms in rivalrous competition. There are, as well, a variety of mechanisms through which firms share technological knowledge, and cooperate on certain kinds of R & D. There are universities in it, and professional societies. There are public monies, as well as private funds.

Once institutional richness is recognized, along with different aspects and kinds of technological knowledge, the simple 'trade-off' view of the matter needs to be supplemented by another one. One can see the task of institutional design as somehow to get the best of both worlds. Establish and preserve property rights, at least to some degree, where profit incentives are effective in stimulating action, and where the costs of keeping knowledge private are not high. Share knowledge where it is of high cost not to do so, and the cost in terms of diminished incentives is small. Do the work cooperatively, or fund it publicly, and make public those aspects of technology where the advantages of open access are greatest, or where proprietary claims are most difficult to police. Put another way, the design problem involves institution creation and task assignment at least as much as simple trade-offs taking institutional structure as given.[5]

This chapter is organised as follows. In the next section I describe the proprietary parts of the capitalist system, with particular emphasis on the means through which firms appropriate returns to their investments in innovation, and consider some consequences of the uneven effectiveness of these means across industries, and across different kinds of innovation. The subsequent section is concerned with technology sharing, and R & D cooperation among firms. Universtities, a very important part of the institutional structure, are considered in the following section. Next is a treatment of government programs in support of R & D. In the concluding section I pull these strands together.

Proprietary technology: mechanisms, domains and consequences

R & D carried out by business firms, in rivalry with other firms in the same industry and looking to innovation to get ahead or stay up, is the heart of the modern capitalist engine. Christopher Freeman (1982), Nathan Rosenberg (1985), David Mowery (1984) and others have told the story of the growth of employment of scientists by industry, and the rise of industrial research laboratories. Such laboratories proved profitable for the firms because they served to link the increasingly powerful generic knowledge and methods of modern science to the problems and opportunities of industrial technology, in an environment where both kinds of knowledge could be brought to bear on project selection and execution. However, for a modern industrial research laboratory to be profitable for a firm investing in one, it was not sufficient that organized, focused scientific research be able to push forward industrial technology in directions the market would pay well for. The firm had to be able to appropriate a non-trivial share of those benefits. In particular, a firm undertaking expensive R & D had to have assurance that its competitors would not reap on the cheap what they did not sow.

Historians and economists studying technical change in capitalist countries have recognized a wide variety of means through which firms appropriate returns to their investments in innovation. However, until my colleagues and I designed a questionnaire with the purpose of exploring exactly where different means of appropriation were effective, there was no systematic map of the terrain. Since the details of the questionnaire, and the broad results of our probes about appropriability, have been reported in several other places, here I will simply summarize some of our findings that are most relevant to the topic of this chapter.[6]

To oversimplify somewhat, we distinguished three broad classes of means through which firms can appropriate returns to their innovations — through the patent system, through secrecy, and through various advantages associated with exploiting a head start — and asked our respondents in different lines of business to score on a scale from one to seven the effectiveness of these means for product innovation and for process innovation.

There were significant cross-industry differences regarding the means rated most effective for appropriating returns to product innovation. Contrary to widespread lay beliefs, patents were rated the most effective instrument in only a small number of industries.[7] Those tended to be of two types: those producing chemical products, and those producing relatively simple mechanical or electrical devices. In industries like semiconductors and computers, a head start and related advantages were reported as the most effective means through which firms appropriated returns. But while there were significant inter-industry differences in the means reported most effective, most of our industries reported at least one of the means as being very effective in enabling a firm to appropriate returns from product innovation. However, our respondents from the food-processing and metal-working industries tended to report that there was no effective means for them to protect their product innovations. It is interesting to note that these industries are characterized by very low levels of product R & D relative to sales.

Most industries reported that, with the exception of secrecy, the standard means for capturing returns from innovation were less effective for process innovation than for product innovation. A significant fraction of industries reported that no means was particularly effective. It is interesting to learn that in most industries firms spend very little on process R & D.

My colleagues and I have studied the effect of the ability to appropriate returns on the R & D intensity of an industry through regression analysis. We measured ability to appropriate through the means discussed above by the score assigned to the most effective means. Since a firm that accounts for a large share of a market can appropriate returns, even if the means considered in our questionnaire are not effective, we also included a measure of industry concentration in the regression equations. The bulk of industrial R & D is aimed at new or improved products, and the ability to appropriate variable had a positive and significant effect in the cross-industry product R & D intensity regression. The ability to appropriate returns to process innovation variable had a positive sign in the process R & D intensity equation, but it was not significant. In contrast, industry concentration had a much larger positive coefficient in the process R & D regression than it did in the product R & D regression.[8]

These findings are consistent with an important structural feature of capitalist economies. Except in highly concentrated industries, process innovations come largely in the form of new machines and materials (products) made by upstream suppliers. If one reflects on it, one can see that this 'institutional assignments' solution has some efficiency advantages. Except for highly concentrated industries, if the process R & D is done upstream, innovators will be able to get their innovations applied to a larger fraction of industry production than if the process innovations are done in-house and use is restricted (say by secrecy).

In our questionnaire we asked our respondents to assess the contribution made to technical change in their line of business from various outside sources, particularly upstream suppliers. Our regression analysis suggests that upstream contributions are greater, the less concentrated the user industry. Also of interest is the fact that the contribution of upstream firms was strongly positively correlated with the reported contribution of professional and technical societies. These latter would appear to be important vehicles for sharing information about new process technology, and about technological needs. I turn now to consider this sharing, cooperative aspect of capitalist innovation systems.

Technology sharing and R & D cooperation

Private R & D yields proprietary knowledge, initially. But that knowledge does not stay private; it leaks away and becomes public. The fact that proprietary technology ultimately goes public enhances the ability of the economy to use new technology, both in production and as a base for further research and development. However, to the extent that a significant share of the benefits of a company's R & D goes to competitors, or consumers, its incentives to do such R & D are diminished.

At first thought, one might presume that firms that create new technology ought to exert strong efforts to hold back that technology from going public, and in the normal run of things they clearly do. However, in some cases firms take positive action to make their proprietary knowledge available to others.

Patent licensing, of course, is a widespread practice. Here, while there are exceptions, society gains by enlarging the range of firms that can use a new technique, and the licensor collects a portion of those gains. This is easy enough to explain.[9]

Not quite so easy is the practice of implicit patent pooling, which exists in a number of industries, under which rivalrous firms apparently have an agreement not to sue each other for infringements. Such arrangements reflect an apparent agreement among a group of firms that they are all better off if they make a common, big pool of at least some of their technological knowledge, than if they all try to keep their individual pools strictly private. It seems that, within limits at least, rivalrous companies can and do recognize the 'public good' properties of technology. There is a possible problem here, of course, of free riders. My conversations with people in industries where these arrangements exist indicate that patent pools tend to be limited to firms that are active in R & D and hence are contributing to the pool, and that patent suits are likely to arise when non-contributors to the pool are known to be drawing significantly from it.[10]

Technical and professional societies provide formal structures for the sharing of technological information. As noted earlier, these societies seem to serve as vehicles for communication between suppliers and users. They also facilitate the spread of certain kinds of information among rivals. Industrial scientists and engineers, like academics, take pride in their professional reputations, which to a considerable extent are enhanced, and recognized, through publication of articles in journals associated with professional societies, through giving talks at their meetings, etc. For the members of these societies, new technology is the news they gather to hear about. Their operation almost certainly speeds the 'going public' of new generic technological knowledge.[11] R & D cooperation among firms also long has been a part of the capitalist system. Cooperation between user and supplier has been discussed in an earlier chapter. Firms in the same line of business, but operating in separated markets, sometimes have combined cross-licensing with exchange of information about technological problems and opportunities thus engaging in a form of *de facto* R & D cooperation. This pattern has long been common among firms operating in different national markets. In recent years there has been a surge of explicit joint R & D ventures among companies in different countries, particularly in aircraft and electronics.[12]

Even rivalrous firms may forge agreements to have certain kinds of research carried out cooperatively where the results are difficult to keep proprietary, or where it would be disadvantageous to the group as a whole to do so. Typical examples are industry-wide problems, like learning how better to grade and test raw materials, or to establish appropriate standards for inputs. There is a tradition in some industries of trying to fund this type of work collectively, through some kind of an agreed-upon voluntary tax formula for contribution to a trade association, which can support research at universities, or at independent laboratories. There are obvious free-rider limits on this mechanism, however.

In industries closely linked with science, the results of generic research have strong, latent public-good properties and are difficult to keep private for long. As a result only a few, generally very large, firms engage in much of this work. Most of it is undertaken at universities, as I shall elaborate in the following section.

However, in the past ten years or so in several different industries, groups of firms have come together to finance and have generic research carried out through formal cooperative research arrangements. These have been particularly prominent in the United States in the semiconductor and computer industries. Some, like the Microelectronics and Computer Technology Corporation, involve a group of member firms who jointly fund an agreed-upon body of research in special laboratories. Others, like the North Carolina Microelectronics Center, have been organized by state government, and involve public, as well as private, funds. NCMC and the Center for Integrated Systems at Stanford University are associated with universities.[13]

These new cooperative R & D organizations clearly were motivated by the belief that cooperative generic research was an important reason for Japan's technological and economic success in high-technology industries. This part of the Japanese innovation system is discussed at some length in the following chapter. As will be stressed, in Japan universities play little role in such endeavors; indeed, with certain exceptions, the connections between university and industry research are relatively weak. In contrast, in the United States university research and industrial research often have been intertwined closely. I turn now to that part of the United States' innovation system.

The role of universities

Since the last part of the nineteenth century, universities have become an increasingly important part of the capitalist engine. They are a recognized repository of public scientific and technological knowledge. They draw on it in their teaching; they add to it through their research.

Within the United States, university science and engineering and our science-based industries grew up together.[14] Chemistry took hold as an academic field at about the same time that chemists began to play an imporant role in industry. The rise of university research and teaching in the field of electricity occurred as the electrical equipment industry began to grow up in the United States. In both cases the universities provided the industry with its technical people, and academic research provided many of the ideas about product and process innovation.

It is important to recognize that these are two quite distinct kinds of contribution. Academics may be able to teach what new industrial scientists need to know, without having their research be particularly relevant to industry. It may be necessary for young scientists to learn the basic principles and research techniques of a field before being able to work effectively in an industrial laboratory, even if the research being done by academics stands at some distance from what is going on in industry. In some technologies, academic research may be illuminating the opportunities and providing the key insights for industrial R & D, but in others the cutting edge of industrial R & D may be far away from academic research.

The situation is dynamic, not static. There is evidence that academic research in chemistry and electrical engineering has over the years diminished as a source of important new knowledge for industry. Academic researchers were very important to technological developments in the early days of the semiconductor industry, but as time went by research and development in industry increasingly separated itself from what the academics were doing. As I shall document in a moment, at the current time certain areas of academic biology and computer science are very important sources of new ideas and techniques for industry. The latter is a new field; the former is experiencing a renaissance.

To probe at some of these issues, in our survey my colleagues and I asked our respondents to score, on a scale from one to seven, the relevance of various fields of basic and applied science to technical advance in their line of business. We also asked them to score, on the same scale, the relevance of university research in that field.

The fact that an industry rated a field of science highly relevant by no means implies that it rated university research in that field so. Thus while seventy-five industries out of 130 rated the relevance of chemistry as a field at five or greater, only nineteen industries rated university research in chemistry that highly. Forty-five industries rated the relevance of physics at five or greater, but only four gave that high a score to university research in physics. This does not mean that academic research in physics is unimportant over the long run to technical advance in industry. However, the impact will likely be stretched out and indirect, operating through influences on the applied sciences and the engineer disciplines, with the ultimate impact on industrial R & D occurring through these.

What fields of university research have widespread reported relevance to industry, in the sense that a number of industries accredited university research in that field with a relevance score of five or more? Computer science and materials science head the list, followed by metallurgy and chemistry. The industries for which these sciences are important tend to look to universities for new knowledge and techniques, as well as training.

Biology, and the applied biological sciences (medical and agricultural science) appear somewhat special today. While these scientific fields were deemed relevant by only a narrow range of industries, those industries that scored these fields at five or higher almost always rated university research in these fields at five or higher too.

Industries where technological advance is being fed significantly by academic science naturally look for close links with university scientists and the laboratories where that work is going on. In recent years there have been a large number of new arrangements established whereby a single firm or a group of firms funds research at a university laboratory, and receives some sort of advantaged access to that research or its findings. Not surprisingly, the industries most engaged in these activities are ones where firms are large and academic research is rated as highly important to technological change. The major such industries are pharmaceuticals, computers and semiconductors. And the fields of university science being tapped tend to be those where academic research was judged highly relevant to technological advance in those industries—the biological sciences and computer sciences.

My conjecture is that in the United States these kinds of new arrangements for support of industry-oriented generic research will prove more durable than the self-standing industry cooperatives. The same free-rider problems are there, and this limits the magnitude of industry funding. However, the universities themselves are interested in sustaining these programs, and federal and state governments are likely to provide funding for them.

In contrast, because of the presence of MITI, in Japan there is a mechanism for pulling together and subsidizing groups of firms to do generic cooperative research, without involving a university connection. And, as noted, Japan's efforts in this area have preceeded largely without university involvement. Which route will turn out to be more effective in the long run is hard to say.

Government programs in support of technical change in industry

Particularly since the Second World War, government R & D support has been an important part of the capitalist innovation system. However, there are major differences across countries in the roles played by government. In Japan, in certain key industries MITI has orchestrated the R & D attack, getting companies to think through together which directions ought to be followed and what goals pursued if commercial primacy were to be achieved. The United States has no organization like MITI, and the government role generally has not been to try to plan and coordinate the development of broad technologies, except in fields highly relevant to the military, and where it has tried to do so the experience usually has been bad. Rather, the governmental involvement, while large and important in some areas, has tended to be quite selective. In good part this is because where firms are rivalrous, government R & D is viewed with latent hostility as potentially helping one's competitors. To be accepted, government funding must be viewed as benefiting the industry as a whole, or as being justified by overriding natural interests.

I have found it analytically useful to distinguish three different kinds of government R & D support programs. One kind is concerned with basic research. The second is tied to government procurement needs. A third class, of relatively modest importance in the United States, is expressly aimed to advance the commerical competitiveness of a particular industry, or group of firms.[15]

While acceptance of a governmental responsibility for broad funding of basic research at the universities was reached in the United States only after the Second World War, the tradition of governmental support of selected kinds of research at universities developed much earlier. Thus the Hatch Act of 1887 provided for federal funding of agricultural research. During the 1930s there began to be a trickle of federal funds into health-related research. Prior to the Second World War, the armed services funded a considerable amount of research at universities to foster the development of computers.

However, government funding of research at universtities was piecemeal until after the Second World War. During the 1920s and 1930s various influential scientists in industry were trumpeting the importance of university research, as well as teaching, to the health of their industries, but the policy message they and their academic colleagues gave was that industry should band together to support universities. For reasons that are obvious to economists, this call for industrial voluntary contributions to finance a public good failed to achieve its purpose. By the end of the Second World War, industry scientists and university scientists were ready to appeal for public funding for university basic research, and they got it.

Despite a popular impression that the National Science Foundation is the principal governmental source of funds for academic research in the United States, in fact a significantly larger amount of government research support to universities comes from government agencies with particular applied missions, which are seeking to build the scientific understanding to advance those missions. Thus the National Institutes of Health are the dominant source of university funding in the biological sciences. The Department of Defense and the Department of Energy are the major sources of university research support in the fields of concern to them. It is interesting that the fields of academic research deemed most relevant to technical advance in industry by our questionnaire respondents have tended to be those in which a mission-oriented government agency, as well as the National Science Foundation, has been providing significant support.

Of course, governmental funding of academic research presently is puny compared with governmental support of R & D on products and systems which it wants to procure for its own purposes. The massive defense-procurement-related R & D programs of the last quarter century are so familiar to contemporary observers that it seldom is recognized that this phenomenon, like government support of university research, dates from the Second World War. Prior to then, much less R & D went into the design of military equipment, and a large share of what did was financed by companies themselves as an investment in possible future government sales.

There are various issues about the efficacy of the post-Second World War military R & D programs that can be raised. The central one is the effectiveness of these programs in assuring US and world security. This issue involves both the appropriateness of the goals of the programs, and the effectiveness with which these were pursued. This is a massive complex topic and I cannot address it here in any detail. However, a strong case can be, and has been, made that many of these programs have been frighteningly misguided and disgracefully mismanaged. One major alleged problem is lack of a sophisticated mechanism for appraisal of objectives, of the sort provided by customer markets. Another is lack of serious competition among producers, once an R & D contract has been let.

Another issue is the effect of these programs on the character of US civilian technology. While prior to the Second World War there were many instances where defense demands served to pull into existence technologies of subsequent value to the civilian economy, only a few of these were of major importance. Usually advances in military technology exploited advances originally achieved for other purposes. In the two decades following the Second World War, however, military R & D pulled into place a number of technologies of enormous civilian significance, including modern semiconductors, the electronic computer, and jet aircraft. Various observers have remarked on this and have gone on to argue that DOD R & D has been the key to US technological supremacy during the 1960s and 1970s.

However, during the post-war period military R & D has absorbed a large share of total industrial R & D in the United States, and likely has squeezed out a certain amount of civilian R & D by bidding away scarce scientific and technical resources. Also, with few exceptions, the civilian pay-off per dollar of military R & D certainly has been very small. The technologies pulled into place in the two decades after the war may be exceptional; since 1972 it is arguably the case that military R & D has cost the US considerably in terms of foregone civilian alternatives.

While NASA funding of new technologies has been far smaller than

DOD funding, project Apollo complemented DOD R & D funding and procurement in pulling into existence important advances in semiconductor and computer technologies, and a variety of new materials of subsequent widespread use. The NASA programs have differed from the DOD programs in one very important respect. From its beginnings NASA has advertised itself as a vehicle for advancing American technology across a broad front through technology-stretching procurement.

Perhaps because political support for NASA has not proved durable, in recent years a number of observers have come to see DOD R & D support programs as a vehicle to be used explicitly to enhance civilian technology. However, national security needs to have a strong imperative of its own, and the DOD is unlikely to be willing to see its programs diverted much to generate more 'spillover'. And, as noted, in recent years at least the civilian harvest from military R & D has been thin. Nonetheless, it is likely that a new governmental role, that of advancing civilian technology across a broad front by financing ambitious technology-stretching projects, is gaining political currency. In Japan, MITI has played that role. The United States has no MITI. Just how the United States will organize the provision of government funding for stretching civilian technology, in particular whether it will find a different instrument than the DOD, is hard to say.

Compared with the magnitude of DOD R & D, public finance of R & D to develop civilian technologies has been small change. However, two such programs warrant attention.

One is the long-standing support of nuclear power reactor R & D. This program has been closely controlled from Washington, has tended to concentrate resources on a small number of designs liked by government officials, and arguably has led the nuclear power industry of the United States into a dead end. This, and similar programs in Europe, provide strong support for my earlier warnings about problems of trying to plan and control technical advance centrally.

The other is the more-than-century-old program of support of R & D to lift agricultural productivity. This program has been highly decentralized and quite responsive to farmers' demands. Various studies show that the rate of return has been very high.

While many observers have looked to the agricultural R & D support program as a model that might be widely extended, in fact most industries have resisted government R & D support, not welcomed it, for the reasons suggested earlier.

What is it about farming that has led the 'firms' in this industry actively to demand, not resist, government R & D support of applied as well as generic, work? A principal factor is that individual farmers, unlike individual firms in industries such as pharmaceuticals, are not in rivalrous competition with each other. It does not hurt one farmer if his neighbor becomes more productive. Put another way, there is very little proprietary knowledge among farmers. At the same time, regional groups of farmers perceive that their sales can be enhanced and their profits increased if their productivity and the quality of their crops are improved. Thus a regional group of farmers has a strong interest in getting effective applied research and development undertaken aimed to enable them, as a group, to become more competitive. The circumstances here clearly are rather special. It is unlikely that the agricultural model can be used in many industries.

Reprise

This essay has been concerned with laying out the institutional structures supporting technical advance in modern capitalist countries, with particular focus on the current US scene. I hope I have been persuasive that capitalist innovation systems are far more complex than commonly recognized, and far more complex than their depiction in extant economic models.

I began this essay by observing that, while the capitalist engine obviously has been a powerful one, inefficiency is built into its basic design. While privatization of new technology harnesses the profit motive to its creation and leads innovators to be sensitive to market opportunities, privatization causes waste both in the use and generation of technology. While I do not believe that the power that has been generated could have been with an engine of radically different design, that is far from saying that the engine is optimal in any way.

However, the engine undoubtedly is less inefficient than simple models of it, which miss the complexity, would suggest. The system has managed to avoid a good share of the costs of privatization, while preserving the profit motive for industrial innovation, by treating as public large parts and aspects of technology, through involving institutions like universities and providing liberal amounts of public money. In my view the capitalist innovation system has solved the institutional assignment problem not optimally, but tolerably well.

Of course, the institutional assignment problem never is solved once and for all. As science and technology change, and as the nature of research and development in different areas of science and technology change, so too do the institutional structures appropriate to the endeavor. In the United States there is no single agency responsible for looking at the national innovation system as a whole and recommending or mandating needed changes. Rather, new institutions and institutional assignments are created pluralistically, and the structure itself changes through an evolutionary process.

The modern corporate R & D laboratory itself, the heart of the system, grew up during the early twentieth century as a result of bets made by a few scientists and businessmen. Events proved them right, and the lesson was learned by other firms. The nature and the source of funding of university research in the United States have also followed an evolutionary pattern, with different kinds of universities doing different things and being open to different kinds of initiatives on the part of business and government. As noted earlier, the system of government funding of university research arose only after various other proposals for funding had been tried and failed.

At the present time there are a lot of organizational experiments going on. Industry cooperation in the finance of generic research is now the rage. In the United States there has been a surge of new arrangements linking industry to university research, in some cases initiated by industry, and in some cases initiated through government programs. It is too early to judge which new departures will be fruitful and survive and which will not. But they are going on. Such institutional experimentation may be the most durable strength of the system.

As noted, at the present time there are many voices in the United States suggesting that the country experiment with a structure like MITI. Others have suggested that MITI, while appropriate to catching up techno-logically, is not a useful institutional vehicle for a country at the frontier. Still others argue that it is, but that is hard luck for the United States because our historical traditions and political structure make it impossible for us to put in place such a structure, or not to abuse it were it in place. Whether the DOD should be used in a MITI-like way in technological fields of national security concern is, as observed, a matter of current dispute.

I shall make a strong bet that over the coming decade, through one route or another, that the US innovation system will adopt a number of features that are noteworthy on the Japanese scene. The following chapter des-cribes some of these features.

Notes

1. Earlier chapters have noted that this view of technical change is flatly at odds with the treatment of technical change contained in virtually all neo-classical models that address the topic. This conflict is discussed at length in Nelson and Winter (1982), where we also attempt to lay out a general structure for formal evolutionary models of technological change.
2. The basic Schumpeterian model was mapped out in his *Theory of Economic Development*, first published in 1911. The characterization in *Capitalism, Socialism, and Democracy* (1942), published nearly thirty years later, differs mainly in that large corporations have replaced individual entrepreneurs as the locus of innovation.
3. This and subsequent characterizations of the benefits and costs of making technology public are based on Nelson and Winter (1982), particularly Chapter 14.
4. Perhaps the best analysis that views this problem in terms of balance of trade-off is by Nordhaus (1969).
5. Thus this is a study in the spirit of 'the new institutional economics'. Oliver Williamson's work in this area (1975, 1985) has been particularly influential,

but many other economists now are concerned with the details of institutional structures and how the present ones came into being. For a survey of much of this work, see Langlois (1986).

6. A description of the questionnaire and a preliminary report of some of the findings is contained in Levin *et al.* (1984).

7. Taylor and Silberston (1973), Scherer *et al.* (1959), and Mansfield, Schwartz, and Wagner (1981) also have provided evidence of the limited number of industries where patents are important.

8. These results are consistent with those of Pavitt (1984) in his more systematic study bearing on upstream–downstream relationships.

9. Unfortunately, economists have only begun to map out the domain of patent licensing. For a sketch, see Caves *et al.* (1983).

10. For case studies of technology sharing, see von Hippel (1986) and Allen (1983).

11. Unfortunately, there is very little published research on just what technical societies do, and the nature of the information passed around. My observations above are based on limited evidence.

12. For the story of aircraft, see Mowery (1986); for electronics, see Haklisch (1986).

13. These and other partnerships between universities and industry are described in *New Alliances and Partnerships in American Science and Engineering*, put out by the Government-University-Industry Research Roundtable, National Academy Press, 1986. See also the survey by Peters and Fusfeld (1982).

14. See Thackray (1982), Noble (1977), and Rosenberg (1985).

15. This section draws heavily on Nelson (1982, 1984).

References

Allen, R.C. (1983), 'Collective invention', *Journal of Economic Behavior and Organization*.

Caves, R., Crookell, H. and Killing, J.P. (1983), 'The uncertain market for technology licenses', *Oxford Bulletin of Economics and Statistics*, August.

Cohen, W. and Leventhal, D. (1985), 'The endogeneity of appropriability and R and D investment', Carnegie Mellon University, mimeo.

Dosi, G. (1982), 'Technological paradigms and technological trajectories', *Research Policy*, vol. 11.

Freeman, C. (1982), *The Economics of Industrial Innovation*, London, Frances Pinter.

Haklisch, C.S. (1986), *International Alliances in the Semiconductor Industry*, Center for Science and Technology Policy, New York.

Haklisch, C.S., Fusfeld, H.D. and Levenson, A.D. (1984), *Trends in Collective Industrial Research*, Center for Science and Technology Policy, New York.

Hippel, E. von (1982), 'Appropriability of innovation benefit as a predictor of the source of innovation', *Research Policy*.

—— (1986), 'Competition between competing firms: informal know-how trading', Sloan School MIT Working Paper No. 1759–86.

Langlois, R.W. (ed.) (1986), *Economics as a Process: Essays in the New Institutional Economics*, New York, Cambridge University Press.

Levin, R.C. Klevorick, A.K., Nelson, R.R. and Winter, S.G. (1984), 'Survey research on R and D appropriability and technological opportunity: Part I—Appropriability, Yale University, mimeo.

Mansfield, E., Schwartz, M. and Wagner, S. (1981), 'Imitation costs and patents: an empirical study', *Economic Journal*, December.

Mowery, D.C. (1983), 'The relationship between the contractual and intra-firm forms of industrial research in American manufacturing, 1900–1940', *Explorations in Economic History*.

—— (1984), 'Firm structure, government policy, and the organization of industrial research: Great Britain and the United States, 1900–1950', *Business History review*.

—— (1986), 'Multinational joint ventures in product development and manufacture: the case of commerical aircraft', Carnegie Mellon University, mimeo.

Nelson, R.R. (ed.) (1982), *Government and Technical Progress: A Cross-Industry Analysis*, New York, Pergamon Press.

—— (1984), *High Technology Policies: A Five Nation Comparison*, American Enterprise Institute, Washington D.C.

Nelson, R.R. and Winter, S.G. (1982), *An Evolutionary Theory of Economic Change*, Cambridge, Mass., Harvard University Press.

Noble, D. (1977), *American by Design*, New York, Knopf.

Nordhaus, W.D. (1969), *Invention, Growth and Welfare: A Theoretical Treatment of Technological Change*, Cambridge, Mass., MIT Press.

Pavitt, K. (1984), 'Sectoral patterns of technical change: towards a taxonomy and a theory', *Research Policy*, vol. 13.

Peck, M.J. (1986), 'Joint R and D: the case of the MCC', *Research Policy*.

Pelikan, Pavel (1986), *Institutions, Self Organization, and Adaptive Efficiency: A Dynamic Assessment of Private Enterprise*, The Industrial Institute for Economic and Social Research, Stockholm, May.

Peters, L. and Fusfeld, H. (1982), *Current U.S. University and Industry Research Connections in University and Industry Research Relationships*, National Science Board, Washington, DC.

Polanyi, M. (1962), *Personal Knowledge: Towards a Post-Critical Philosophy*, New York, Harper Torchbook.

Polsby, N.W. (1984), *Political Innovation in America: The Politics of Policy Initiation*, New Haven, Yale University Press.

Reich, L. (1985), *The Making of American Industrial Research: Science and Business at G.E. and Bell*, New York, Cambridge University Press.

Rosenberg, N. (1985), 'The commercial exploitation of science by American industry', in K.B. Clark, R.H. Hayes and C. Lorenz (eds.), *The Uneasy Alliance: Managing the Productivity and Technology Dilemma*, Boston, Harvard Business School Press.

Scherer, F.M. *et al.* (1959), *Patents and the Corporation*, Boston, privately printed.

Schumpeter, J.A. (1934), *The Theory of Economic Development*, Cambridge, Mass., Harvard University Press (first published in Germany, 1911).

—— (1942), *Capitalism, Socialism, and Democracy*, New York, Harper.

Taylor, C.T. and Silberston, Z.A. (1973), *The Economic Impact of the Patent System: A Study of the British Experience*, Cambridge, Cambridge University Press.

Teece, D.J. (1986), 'Capturing value from technological innovation: integration, strategic partnering and licensing decisions', Berkeley, mimeo.

Thackray, A. (1982), 'University—industry connections and chemical research: an historical perspective', in *University—Industry Research Relationships*, National Science Board, Washington, DC.

Williamson, O.E. (1975), *Markets and Hierarchies*, New York, Free Press.

—— (1985), *The Economic Institutions of Capitalism*, New York, Free Press.

16 Japan: a new national system of innovation?

Christopher Freeman

Science Policy Research Unit, University of Sussex, Brighton and MERIT, State University of Limburg, Maastricht

Technology gaps and institutional innovation

When Britain opened up a major 'technological gap' in the first industrial revolution, this was related not simply to an increase in invention and scientific activities, and to a cluster of innovations in the textile, iron and engineering industries, but to novel ways of organising production, investment and marketing and novel ways of combining invention with entrepreneurship (see Chapters 2 and 3). Similarly, when Germany and the United States overtook Britain in the latter part of the nineteenth century and in the twentieth century, their success was also related to major institutional changes in the national system of innovation, as well as to big increases in the scale of professional research and inventive activities and new clusters of radical innovations. In particular both countries developed new ways of organising the professional education of engineers and scientists and of organising research and development activities as specialised departments within firms, and employing the new graduate engineers and scientists in design, production, marketing and management as well as in research.

Again today, when Japan is drawing ahead in some important new technologies, this is related not simply or even mainly to the scale of R & D, but to other social and institutional changes. Japan drew ahead of the United States in the relative intensity of *civil* industrial R & D already in the 1970s and is now well ahead (Patel and Pavitt, 1987). But more significant are the measures of 'output' of the science and technology system which suggest a Japanese lead in exploiting the *results* of R & D (Freeman, 1987). Japanese trade performance in the 1970s and 1980s is further indirect evidence of this success, based as it is on new product and process design, and high quality.

This chapter therefore considers the nature of this new 'technology gap' and those qualitative aspects of the Japanese 'national system of innovation' which might help to explain it.

It seeks to identify some of the distinguishing features of the Japanese 'national system of innovation', not because they are unique, but on the contrary because they are likely to be emulated increasingly as international technological competition intensifies. This chapter first of all discusses the role of central government, especially MITI; it then considers the role of firms, especially the 'Keiretsu'; and finally other social and educational innovations.

The role of MITI

Recently, a voluminous literature has grown up on the role of MITI in explaining the technological performance of the post-war Japanese economy. Some of this literature tends to attribute Japanese success mainly to government policies inspired by MITI, while another part concentrates on debunking this notion. It is clear that a large part of the Japanese success must be attributed to the management of technical change by numerous Japanese enterprises, but this success was related to social and institutional changes promoted and sometimes initiated by MITI, and to the persistent pursuit of certain long-term strategic goals.

The not-so-invisible guiding hand of MITI shaped the long-term pattern of structural change in the Japanese economy and this influence was largely exerted on the basis of judgements about the future direction of technical change and the relative importance of various technologies. The central point of interest from the standpoint of this analysis is that in the immediate post-war period, after an intense debate, Japan specifically rejected a long-term development strategy based on traditional theory of comparative advantage (Shinohara, 1982). This was apparently at that time being advocated by economists in the Bank of Japan and elsewhere who subscribed to the free-trade doctrines of the classical school. They had advocated a 'natural' path of industrial development, based on Japan's relatively low labour costs and comparative advantage in labour-intensive industries such as textiles. One of the central points at issue was whether Japan could hope to compete in the automobile industry and whether special steps should be taken to encourage its growth, but the debate affected industrial and trade policy in its entirety.

In the early days, according to G.C. Allen (one of the few European economists who consistently attempted to study and learn from Japanese experience), the views of the Bank of Japan had some influence. But on the whole the bureaucrats and their advisers at the Ministry of International Trade and Industry (MITI) prevailed. According to Allen:

Some of these advisors were engineers who had been drawn by the war into the management of public affairs. They were the last people to allow themselves to be guided by the half-light of economic theory. Their instinct was to find a solution for Japan's post-war difficulties on the supply side, in enhanced technical efficiency and innovations in production. They thought in dynamic terms. Their policies were designed to furnish the drive and to raise the finance for an economy that might be created rather than simply to make the best use of the resources it then possessed. [Allen, 1981]

Thus, MITI saw as one of its key functions the promotion of the most advanced technologies with the widest world market potential in the long term. In this respect MITI differed from almost all other analogous Ministries and Departments in Western Europe or North America, which mostly did not see themselves as responsible for long-term technology policies until much later (i.e. in the 1970s or 1980s) and were guided by very different conceptions of comparative advantage. Even today most do not accept the same responsibility for technology as MITI does.

As early as 1952 the 'Enterprises Rationalisation Promotion Law' provided direct government subsidies for

> the experimental installation and trial operation of new machines and equipment, plus rapid amortisation and exemption from local taxes of all investments in research and development; second, it authorised certain industries (to be designated by the cabinet) to depreciate the costs of installing modern equipment by 50 per cent during the first year; and third, it committed the central and local governments to building ports, highways, railroads, electric power grids, gas mains and industrial parks at public expense and make them available to approved industries. [Johnson, 1982]

From this and many other examples it is clear that MITI (and some other ministries) saw it as one of their main responsibilities to encourage the introduction of new technologies through new investment. Furthermore this law is particularly significant in its clear recognition of the crucial role of externalities and infrastructure for innovative firms (see Chapter 21 by Perez and Soete), and of the role of government in ensuring the availability of the necessary infrastructural investments. This tradition has continued right through to the 1980s in the development of regional policies which lay great stress on the development of science, education, communications and transport infrastructure (Kuwahara, 1985). Regional policies have consistently sought to strengthen technological capability throughout the country, particularly in small and medium-sized firms. There are nearly 200 'prefecture laboratories' (i.e. an average of four in each prefecture) which offer research and technical advisory services, varying with the structure and needs of local industry (Ergas, 1984).

However, although the young generation of aspiring technocrats in MITI espoused enthusiastically their role in charting and promoting the adoption of advanced technology in post-war Japan, they never attempted to do this alone. On the contrary, they established a mode of working which depended upon a continuing dialogue on questions of technological development, both with industrial R & D people and with university scientists and technologists. This meant that they were well informed about the broad trend of new developments and were well placed to form an overall view or 'vision' of what was required. Later, this mode of continuous consultation with the Japanese scientific and technological community was systematised and this has been described by Irvine and Martin (1984) in their book, *Foresight in Science Policy: Picking the Winners*.

The informal mode of continuous consultation remains, however, even more important and has been vividly portrayed by Vogel (1980). In his book, *Japan as No.1*, he lays great stress on these informal contacts as fundamental to MITI's success in restructuring the Japanese economy and orienting the leading firms to a desired course of action.

The agreements they promote among companies in a given industrial sector require a higher level of trust than can be achieved through formal contacts. When a specific issue arises, interested parties schedule even more informal gatherings than usual. When necessary, bureaucrats from other ministries join these meetings and other knowledgeable experts and men of influence are called in . . . American government officials and business men negotiating economic matters feel at a great disadvantage because Japanese officials are much better informed, not only about Japanese companies but often about American companies . . . [p. 76]

Although the *responsibility* for promoting advanced technology was accepted throughout the post-war period, the *mode* of fulfilling this responsibility changed over time. The policies of MITI have been nothing if not pragmatic and eclectic in their choice of *means*, although quite consistent in the long-term goals. Consequently there have been big changes in the methods and instruments of industrial technology policy, as both external and internal circumstances changed. As Koshiro (1985) has shown, the post-war period can be divided into distinct phases: in the 1950s direct physical controls, allocations and priorities were still important, but in the 1960s indirect fiscal and other incentives were used to stimulate and channel the huge investment boom. In the 1970s and 1980s there has been a clear recognition of the strategic importance of information technology.

Clearly the success of such a system must depend on a reasonably accurate identification of the key areas in which to concentrate techno-logical effort and new investment, both at national level, at 'Keiretsu' level and at company level. Serious mis-specification for new areas of invest-ment could lead to enormous waste of resources and clearly 'accuracy' in this context refers both to future trends in technology and future trends in world markets and society generally. A lot of effort in Japan goes into the preparation of such long-term 'visions' of the future, both at national level and company level, as well as in universities and in numerous think-tanks (e.g. STA, 1972). There is no other society where financial institutions, banks and even the Ministry of Finance devote such attention to the future direction of technical and social change.

The Japanese system of informal and formal technological forecasting permits the formulation of technological and industrial policies not so much on the basis of particular products or of existing industrial statistics or the weight of established firms and industries, but rather on the basis of those new technologies which are likely to transform the established exist-ing pattern.

The recognition of the importance of information technology occurred very early in Japan. Of course there were individual experts and companies in Europe and America who recognised it at least as early. But the impor-tance of the national Japanese system of forecasting lay in the diffusion and generalisation of these expectations through a large number of companies in a great variety of industries. This helped to create a climate where firms would make investments in new products and processes associated with the new technology on a much larger scale than elsewhere in the OECD area,

where this confidence was sometimes lacking. This was especially important in the diffusion of information and communication technology (see
Chapter 3 on uncertainty and investment at times of change in techno-
economic paradigm).

The promotion of 'generic' technologies, especially information technology, has now become a regular feature of technology policy and industrial
policy in almost every member country of the OECD in the course of the
1970s and 1980s. The extent to which such efforts are successful will
depend not simply on the scale of resources, which are committed in the
public and private sectors of the economy, but also on social conditions and
attitudes and appropriate institutions, particularly the 'national system of
innovation'. The Japanese system seems particularly well adapted to take
advantage of the enormous potential of information technology for several
reasons:

(1) the systems approach to process and product design;
(2) the flexibility of the industrial structure;
(3) the capacity to identify crucial areas of future technological advance at
    national and enterprise level;
(4) the capacity to mobilise very large resources in technology and capital
    in pursuit of strategic priorities;
(5) the horizontal flow of information within and between firms.

We now turn to consider the role of firms, especially the 'Keiretsu' in
relation to these five points.

The role of firms in the Japanese national system of innovation

Ever since 1868 Japanese central government had worked closely with
industry in modernising the Japanese economy and importing foreign
technology. But Japanese national policies for technology in the 1930s
were driven mainly by military imperatives. Dependence on imported oil,
rubber and other industrial materials and the early development of a war
economy led to a one-sided concentration on the promotion of technologies primarily designed to strengthen autonomous Japanese military
capability.

As Yamauchi (1986) pointed out,

the government and industrialists did not pay as much attention to reducing
production costs or increasing productivity as to how they could modify imported
technology to produce first class defence equipment and adjust it to Japanese raw
material sources. . .

It would of course be a mistake to underestimate the technological
advances already achieved in Japan before and during the Second World
War. Japanese industry was not only capable of independent design,
development and production of complex military equipment, such as air-

craft and tanks, but also of a wide range of machinery. However, Japan lagged behind in the techniques of mass production of cars and consumer durables and in some branches of the chemical industry such as flow processes in petrochemicals and synthetic materials.

In the post-war period it was recognised from the outset that the import of mass and flow production techniques was crucial for economic success. It is not so widely recognised that from the earliest days this was accompanied by a systematic policy designed to improve these technologies.

The method of assimilating and improving upon imported technology was mainly some form of 'reverse engineering' (Tamura, 1986; Pavitt, 1985). This involved trying to manufacture a product similar to one already available on the world market but without direct foreign investment or transfer of blue-prints for product and process design. The widespread use of reverse engineering in the 1950s and 1960s had several major consequences for the Japanese system of innovation.

(a) Japanese management, engineers and workers grew accustomed to thinking of the entire production process as a system and of thinking in an integrated way about product design and process design. This capability to redesign an entire production system has been identified as one of the major sources of Japanese competitive success in industries as diverse as shipbuilding, automobiles and colour television (Jones, 1985; Sciberras, 1981; Peck and Wilson, 1982). Whereas Japanese firms made few original radical product innovations in these industries they did make many incremental innovations, as shown for example, by the Japanese lead in vehicle patenting in the United States. They also redesigned and reorganised many processes so as to improve productivity *and* raise quality. The automobile industry is probably the most spectacular example (Altschuler *et al.*, 1985; Jones, 1985).

(b) Japanese engineers and managers grew accustomed to the idea of 'using the factory as a laboratory' (Baba, 1985). The work of the R & D department was very closely related to the work of production engineers and process control and was often almost indistinguishable. The whole enterprise was involved in a learning and development process and many ideas for improving the system came from the shop-floor.

Since almost all studies of the management of innovation in Western Europe and the United States point to the lack of integration between R & D, production management and marketing as a major source of failure, the integrative effect of learning by creative reverse engineering conferred a major competitive advantage on many Japanese firms. It also gave production engineering a much higher status than is usually the case in Europe or the United States. These horizontal links are probably the single most important feature of the Japanese national system of innovation at enterprise level.

(c) Reverse engineering in such industries as automobiles and machine tools also involved an intimate dialogue between the firm responsible for assembling and marketing the final product and numerous suppliers of components, sub-assemblies, castings, materials and so forth. The habits, attitudes and relationships engendered during this prolonged, joint learning process did much to facilitate the high degree of cooperation with subcontractors which finds expression, for example, in the 'just-in-time' system. Another factor fostering such intimate relationships was the conglomerate 'Keiretsu' structure of much Japanese industry (see below).

(d) The emphasis on high quality of products which is characteristic of Japanese technology policy also owed much to the experience of reverse engineering. In the 1950s, the first production models, whether in automobiles, TV sets or machine tools, were often of relatively poor quality (Jones, 1985; Baba 1985). A determined effort to overcome these defects led to a widespread acceptance of such social innovations as 'quality circles' (originally an American innovation) and to the development of greatly improved techniques of quality control not simply at the end of the production run but at every stage, including all components from subcontractors. Some of the most important (and most closely guarded) Japanese innovations have been on-line inspection, test and quality control equipment and instrumentation arising in this process. Where the quality of components from subcontractors was particularly bad, as in the case of castings, this led to intense pressure from MITI for the restructuring of the entire industry and a drastic change in its techniques. In other cases these problems were dealt with by joint technical effort between assemblers and subcontractors.

This Japanese approach to the import of technology may be compared and contrasted with the methods used on the one hand in the Soviet Union and on the other hand in many Third World countries. The Soviet Union was also engaged in the large-scale development and import of technology in the twentieth century (Sutton, 1971) and also used reverse engineering, but in the Soviet system much of the responsibility for diffusion and development rested with central research institutes or Project Design Bureaux. This meant that much of the 'technological learning process' took place there, rather than at enterprise level, and acute problems were experienced in the transfer of technology from the specialised R & D institutes to factory level management. This weakness has been increasingly recognised and the institutional arrangements have been changed considerably in the 1970s and 1980s to strengthen R & D at enterprise level and to regroup research activities in close relationship with enterprises. This process has probably gone furthest among the socialist countries in the DDR, where in the 1980s responsibility for R & D, design, production and world marketing is now under one management system in the large groups called 'Kombinats'.

In many Third World countries, on the other hand, the method of technology transfer was very often either through subsidiaries of multi-nationals or by the import of 'turn-key' plants designed and constructed by foreign contractors. Neither of these methods is likely to result in an intense process of technology accumulation in the (relatively passive) recipient enterprise. Dissatisfaction with both these methods has led, on the one hand, to pressures on multinationals to set up local R & D activities in addition to training, as in Brazil. On the other hand, it has led to efforts to 'unpackage' imported technology and to devolve part of the design and development to local enterprises. The Japanese policy of reject-ing foreign investment and putting the full responsibility for assimilating and improving upon imported technology on the enterprise is more likely to lead to 'systems' thinking and to total systems improvement.

At an earlier stage in economic development, by establishing specialised in-house R & D departments in the chemical and electrical industries, German and American firms were able to achieve a world lead in the newest technologies in the latter part of the nineteenth century. At that time the R & D department provided a point of entry for the findings of fundamental scientific research to be assimilated and used in contemporary industrial technology and for some of the brightest scientists and engineers to be recruited into the new industries. However, as the R & D department became a part of the regular organisation of most large industrial firms, some of the disadvantages of specialisation began to be apparent, espe-cially the cultural barriers between 'academic' R & D, and the production and marketing divisions of companies (see, for example, Burns and Stalker, 1957). One of the reasons for the relatively successful performance of small entrepreneurial firms in areas where development costs were low was that they were able to overcome the internal communication and cultural barriers much more easily through the integration of research, production and marketing by the innovative entrepreneur working with a few colleagues.

The Japanese success, however, seems to have been based far more on an integrative approach within *large* firms. Their approach to product and process design, often originally developed through reverse engineering, created a new style of innovation management which reintegrated R & D with engineering design, procurement, production and marketing even in the largest organisations. As development, production and marketing went ahead, the whole organisation was committed to the new products and processes in a way that was relatively uncommon in other countries. Moreover, once development work began, lead times were often very short, especially in the electronics industry.

Horizontal information flows increasingly characterised Japanese management organisation rather than the vertical flows so characteristic of the hierarchical US corporation (Aoki, 1986). It is interesting that this feature of Japanese management was singled out not only by an academic economist (Aoki) but also by the head of research of one of the most

successful world-wide competitors of the Japanese electronics companies—
Northern Telecom—in his centenary address to the Canadian engineering
institutes.

These horizontal information flows are also an important feature of the
inter-company cooperation within the 'Keiretsu', as was emphasised by the
MIT study of the world automobile industry (Altschuler *et al.*, 1985):

> The Japanese practice of group coordination, simultaneously attains the scale and
> coordination advantages of Western-style vertical integration and the flexibility of
> decentralisation. Its aim is cooperation and mutual information flow between the
> parts rather than rigid top-down hierarchy . . . Because the members of an indus-
> trial group are coordinated through their equity links and management working
> groups, they are able to share research facilities, support staff (such as accountants
> and marketing responsibilities) and production capacity . . . Finally, the Japanese
> have developed relationships among the automotive industrial groups, their financ-
> ing sources, and industrial groups in other sectors that seem to carry competitive
> advantages over the typical arrangement in the United States . . . [p. 148]

Clearly, the Japanese model of competition has some distinctive features. It permits and encourages a long-term view with respect to research,
training and investment. For this reason it is a vital element in the national
system of innovation. Firms which are in more perfect competitive market
situations would not be able so easily to amass or to allocate resources for
these long-term objectives. Indeed there would be strong pressures from
the capital markets for them to improve short-term profitability by sacrificing long-term investments. This model does not appear to correspond very
closely to the model of a competitive capital market and evolutionary
competitive survival of competence postulated in Chapter 18.

The formation of large conglomerates and of vertically integrated groups
of companies is of course not confined to Japan. But most commentators
on the Japanese economy agree with the MIT study that they have a
specially important role there particularly in relation to technology, finance
for long-term investment and world marketing strategies and networks (the
'Shosha').

Goto (1982), in an original analysis of the 'Keiretsu' explains the
peculiar success of the Japanese groups in terms of Williamson's (1975)
theory of transaction costs:

> resource allocation in a market economy is implemented within the firm under the
> direction of the manager, or through the market by the market mechanism. The
> division of labour between these two modes is determined by their comparative
> efficiency as an instrument to implement all transactions. Here we can see there is a
> third possibility. From the standpoint of the firm, by forming or joining a group, it
> can economise on the transaction costs that it would have incurred if the transaction
> had been done through the market, and at the same time, it can avoid the scale
> diseconomies or control loss which would have occurred if it had expanded intern-
> ally and performed that transaction within the firm.

He notes that Williamson refers to the Zaibatsu as an alternative mode in a
footnote but does not develop the point because he regards them as a

'culturally specific' phenomenon. Goto argues that they are not a uniquely Japanese type of institution and that they have a wider economic significance. Chapter 12 by Teece strongly confirms this.

Imai and Itami (1984) have given a review of other ways in which Japanese firms use the 'organisational' mode of resource allocation rather than the market mode. The lower cost of capital for strategically important areas of long-term investment is recognised by many other commentators as one of the most important.

Education, training and related social innovations

None of the developments at enterprise level which have been described above would have been possible without changes in the education and training of the work-force and a set of related social changes which broke down the barriers between 'blue-collar' and 'white-collar' types of employment.

The Japanese education and training system is remarkable for two features: first of all, in the absolute numbers of young people acquiring secondary and higher levels of education, especially in science and engineering; secondly, in the scale and quality of industrial training, which is carried out mainly or entirely at enterprise level. Japan is now, together with the United States and the Soviet Union, among the leading countries in the world in the extent of educational opportunity, both at secondary and tertiary level. However, this provision for secondary and higher education has been complemented increasingly by an intensive system of education and training in the large firms. The high level of training intensity goes back a long way in the leading firms and was directly related to their efforts to assimilate foreign technology. Thus, for example, Fukasaku's (1987) study of training and research in Mitsubishi shipbuilding before the First World War shows that already then the company had its own training establishments providing a high level of technical education. Sakurai's (1986) study of Mitsubishi's diversification from mining and shipbuilding to chemicals and electrical engineering between the two world wars shows again that the training and retraining of their own employees from the mining companies was a crucial element in their success, as well as the setting up of a central R & D laboratory to develop new products and processes, which also acted as a training establishment.

The combination of a high level of general education and scientific culture with thorough practical training and frequent up-dating in industry is the basis for flexibility and adaptability in the work-force and high-quality standards. The Japanese system of industrial training is distinguished further by its close integration with product and process innovation. The aim is to acquaint those affected by technical change with the problems that are likely to arise, and give them some understanding of the relationship between various operations in the firm. This again greatly facilitates the horizontal flow of information. Thus the 'systems' approach is inculcated at all levels of the work-force and not only at top management level. Obviously, the availability of a large number of good-quality professional engineers, not just in R & D but in production engineering and management too, generally has played a vital part in the Japanese success in the import of technology, the redesign of processes and products, and increasingly now in autonomous innovations.

This success was also based on a high level of *general* education. Prais (1987), in his comparison of Japanese and British education, concludes that the standard of attainment is higher in Japan especially for the average and below-average pupils. One of its consequences is to encourage all-round capability at lower levels in the work-force so that problems of breakdown and maintenance are more rapidly dealt with. Another advantage of this approach is a smoother assimilation and readier acceptance of new process technology. Finally, it has facilitated the participation of the work-force in the improvement of quality, which is widely acknowledged as one of the outstanding successes of Japanese innovation management in the post-war period.

The huge increase in the scale of education and training in Japan since the Second World War was accompanied by a number of other major social innovations which reinforced the capacity of Japanese society to implement technical change at a high rate. Some of these were only indirectly related to the national system of innovation but Aoki (1985) and Dore (1985) are probably right in seeing them as complementary to those changes which directly affected the management of technical innovation.

The abolition of the distinctions between blue- and white-collar workers started earlier and has probably gone further in Japan than most other industrial countries. Before the Second World War the distinctions in both status and income were probably at least as rigid as in other industrial countries. But immediately after the Second World War, a rather curious combination of circumstances led to a social levelling process which went further and faster in Japan than in most other countries. During the period of direct American military occupation and government, a number of radical 'New Dealers' were able to put into practice tax reforms, which they were unable to implement during Roosevelt's 'New Deal' in the United States. At the same time the strength of the Communist-led unions in some industries was sufficiently great in the immediate post-war period to induce the newly restructured large Japanese firms to make major concessions to blue-collar workers with respect to their status and forms of remuneration. The change of management in many of the larger firms also facilitated a new approach both to social and technical issues. This unique combination of circumstances led to rather low income differentials between management, white-collar and blue-collar workers—probably lower than almost any other capitalist industrial country—and to the abolition of most of the status differentials, which continued to characterise British and some other European firms (such as different hours of work, different eating arrangements, etc.). It should be remembered, however, that income statistics do not tell the whole story since the upper groups receive many 'perks' and benefits in kind.

These social changes, together with the system of annual bonuses related to company performance and the 'lifetime employment' system in the large company sector, provided a powerful combination of incentives. Like the education and training system and the systems approach to technical innovation, they provided a basis for continuous improvement in productivity through work-force involvement in technical change, although 'lifetime employment' never covered the entire work-force even in the large firms (McCormick, 1985). This certainly did not mean any form of 'workers' control'. The social system remained hierarchical and deferential but with considerable opportunities for climbing ladders.

The new techno-economic paradigm

It has been argued that, with respect to the role of central and local government, the organisation of firms for the management of innovation and the role of education and training, the Japanese national system of innovation has some important competitive advantages. These advantages are likely to be particularly important in relation to the change of techno-economic paradigm which is such an important feature of contemporary structural change in the world economy (see Chapter 3). Indeed the developments in the Japanese national system of innovation have received an important stimulus from information technology as well as reciprocally promoting its diffusion.

Although Japanese firms were not the major contributors to the original radical innovations in computers and telecommunications, the Japanese technological forecasting system did indeed identify the main elements of the emerging 'ICT' paradigm earlier than elsewhere, and this enabled Japanese firms to exploit the potential of the new paradigm in such areas as robotics, CNC machine tools, flexible manufacturing systems, construction and financial services more rapidly than most other countries. Japanese policy-makers recognised the crucial importance of information technology at a very early stage and the goal of a 'knowledge-intensive' economy was proclaimed already at the beginning of the 1970s. The OPEC crisis accelerated a trend in the policy-making of Japanese government and industry, which was already well articulated.

Various measures to support the computer industry, the semiconductor industry and the electronics industry go back to the 1950s, but at that time they were not regarded as part of a new technological paradigm which would pervade the entire economic system, but simply as important new sectors with very high growth rates and very big world market potential. The need to economise in space and materials were also important considerations. Originally, it was the consumer-goods electronics industry which was the main focus of attention, as one part of the overall expansion of the then dominant assembly-line, mass-production technology. The semiconductor industry was seen as important mainly in this context. The capacity of the Japanese semiconductor industry to overtake the US industry provided the basis for an increasingly original contribution to innovations in consumer electronics.

The first computer development programmes were initiated in Tokyo University, the laboratories of the Japan Telegraph and Telephone Corporation (NTT), and MITI institutes in the 1950s, and a succession of laws were passed from 1957 onwards giving MITI broad powers to promote electronics industry developments including computers.

The combined effect of these various measures, persistently pursued by MITI and other agencies for more than two decades, was to establish a semiconductor industry which was drawing ahead of the US industry by the 1980s and a viable Japanese computer industry able to compete with IBM when trade was liberalised (Gregory, 1986). No European companies had comparable success.

But the explicit and successful fostering of these two strategic industries was only one strand of Japanese information and communication technology policy in the 1970s and 1980s, albeit a very important one. Two other strands were equally, if not more important from the standpoint of the economy as a whole: the diffusion of IT *outside* the electronics industry itself and the policy for the telecommunications network.

The distinctive feature of a new techno-economic paradigm (see Chapter 3) is that it has effects in every sector of the economy, providing scope everywhere for renewal of productivity increases through a combination of organisational, social and technical innovations and for a broad range of new and improved products and services. The main problem in periods of change of paradigm is not so much in the leading-edge industries (in this case, computers and VLSI) as in the adaptation of the rest of the economy. It is here that the type of structural and institutional inertia problems identified by Perez (1983, 1985) are acute, and that national policies and new regulatory regimes are especially important.

The Japanese economy has been particularly successful in adapting the new paradigm to the needs of some other industrial sectors, especially mechanical engineering, vehicles and now construction. Kodama (1985, 1986) points out that the expression 'Mechatronics' was first coined in Japan in 1975 and that even before that in 1971 an explicit policy designed to induce 'fusion' was initiated with the 'Law on Temporary Measures for the Development of Specific Machinery and Electronics Industries', which spoke of 'consolidation of machinery and electronics into one', and 'systematisation' of them.

The successful Japanese development of robotics, CNC machine tools and flexible manufacturing systems has also owed a great deal to the group structure of Japanese industry. The collaboration of the leading Japanese vehicle firms with 'their own' robotics suppliers and similar collaboration with electronic firms in the same groups is one obvious instance.

In the long run perhaps even more significant is the Japanese infrastructural policy with respect to telecommunications. Both before and since its privatisation the telephone utility (NTT) has pursued its programme for an 'Integrated Network System' (INS). This is envisaged as ultimately providing a connecting web for information services to private and industrial users throughout the country. It will 'put a digital broadbased infrastructure in place in anticipation of its uses, while simultaneously developing those uses through model programmes and pilot projects' (Borres et al., quoted in Arnold and Guy, 1986, p.97).

This appears to be a bolder strategy than that of most other OECD countries, which is largely based on responding to current new business opportunities and is therefore more conservative in the scale and scope of new infrastructural telecommunications investment. The INS concept 'represents a discontinuous shift in the character of telecommunications networks' since it will enable broad-bandwidth services using video signals or other forms of very rapid data transmission to use the same network as telephone services. It will ultimately permit a wider range of new information service provision, linking computer and telecommunication networks as a digital technology. The Japanese strategy therefore tackles the key strategic problems of diffusing information technology both to the service and manufacturing industries and to household consumers. This is not simply 'deregulating' and 'privatising'. It is an important step in establishing a new 'regulation regime' as well as a new infrastructure.

As Melody (1986) has forcefully pointed out, in all OECD countries during the 'era of "deregulation"' more regulatory activity has been generated than ever existed in the so-called "regulation" era'. National and international policies will have an enormous influence on the provision of new services, on technical standards, on terminal and systems interconnection, on value-added network services (VANS), on the radio frequency allocation and on prices. Japanese policy has clearly recognised the fundamental strategic importance of this regulation underpinning the whole change of techno-economic paradigm in the same way as an electric power distribution system, a highway network or a railway network in previous periods.

In the case of the Fordist mass-production paradigm, as Yamauchi (1986) insists, Japan was two decades behind in the 1950s but had the great advantage of following a production system already well established in the United States and elsewhere, and improving upon it. In the case of information and communication technology, Japan is among the leaders. This was already evident in consumer electronics in the 1970s and is now increasingly apparent in capital goods, manufacturing systems, information systems and infrastructure.

Conclusions

In this context the organising and energising role of the Japanese forecasting system is important. The 'Visions' of the future produced by STA, MITI, NIRA and other government and private sources do not pretend to be accurate predictions, nor do they commit companies to inflexible plans. They chart the broad direction of advance for the economy and for technology and give companies sufficient confidence in this vision to make their own long-term investments in research, development, software, equipment and training. In this respect technological forecasting plays a role similar to that of project evaluation in sophisticated research-intensive companies. Nobody believes that it is possible to eliminate uncertainty, but a thorough discussion within the firm of the range of probabilities and alternative strategies serves to mobilise resources, to expose difficulties and bottle-necks, and above all to energise the participants, secure consensus and heighten awareness.

It may be that this consensus tends to diminish the pluralism and range of evolutionary alternatives which Nelson distinguishes as so important in the US system. Nevertheless, the contemporary success of the Japanese national system of innovation in catching up and moving ahead in information technology confronts other countries with a formidable challenge and has had severe disequilibrating effects in the world economy (Chapter 3). But catching up with Japan is certainly not an impossible task. Nor does this mean simply imitating Japan. Potentially there are a variety of different social and institutional alternatives: Japanese solutions are certainly not perfect. In some respects Sweden has found equally good or better solutions.

The Swedish example is of special interest because this is a case of a small European country with fairly limited resources which is nevertheless among the leading countries in the production and the diffusion of robotics, in the design and manufacture of telecommunication equipment and generally in computer applications. Sweden's successful diffusion of ICT has been achieved whilst maintaining excellent social services, a rather high degree of consultation with trade unions and safeguards for civil liberty. Swedish industry has made particular efforts to keep in touch with Japanese developments and in general to take the best from world technology. Sweden was also committed fairly early on towards giving ICT a high priority and probably has the most advanced training and retraining system in Europe. This clearly demonstrates the feasibility of catching up with Japan and perhaps of doing better.

In the case of the US national system of innovation analysed by Nelson in Chapter 15, there are clearly some important similarities and some major differences. The strength of the Japanese challenge in world markets has already led to determined effort in the United States to recover the US technological lead in many industries and services. The US automobile industry, for example, is striving in a variety of ways to assimilate Japanese organisational and technical innovations and emulate its success. At a more general level there is increasing evidence of the emergence of a national technology policy with respect to the semiconductor and computer industries. As Nelson observes, a whole number of initiatives for joint government-sponsored R & D programmes linking industry and universities have been taken in the 1980s. However, a distinguishing feature of the newly emerging technology and industrial policies in the United States is that they are mainly conducted under the auspices of defence agencies such as DARPA (Arnold and Guy, 1986). This limits their effectiveness and their strategic objectives in terms of the performance of the civil economy. As we have seen, the priority given to strategic defence objectives in Japan in the 1930s delayed the assimilation of the most advanced civil mass-production technology (Yamauchi, 1986).

Another significant difference between the Japanese and US national systems of innovation lies in the area of fundamental research. The United States has clearly been the world leader in basic scientific research since the Second World War and, as Nelson's chapter has shown, the interaction between this (largely university-based) research and the private industry-financed applied research and development has been an extremely fruitful source of radical innovation in the post-war period, although the intensity of this interaction varies very much by industry and field of sciences.

It is sometimes suggested that the relative weakness of Japanese fundamental research by comparison with the United States may now prevent the Japanese economy from further strengthening its technological competition. This is indeed an important topic of debate and policy-making in Japan and some of the most powerful leading companies have taken major decisions in the 1980s to build up their basic research. However, there is widespread agreement with Nelson's thesis that successful fundamental research probably flourishes most in an environment which stimulates controversy and pluralism, and when is conducted mainly in universities and publishes in open scientific literature. Lundvall (Chapter 17) has also shown how important are the interactions between 'users' and 'producers' in the national system of innovation. These links are particularly strong in the Japanese system.

But while there would be much agreement in Japan with Nelson's thesis on the advantages of the United States (and Europe) in fundamental university research, there are two qualifications which should be taken into account in considering the performance of the two systems.

The first is that the contribution of Japanese universities both to world scientific research and to Japanese industrial innovation is often under-estimated. Whilst it is certainly true that Japan's contribution to world science is relatively much less significant than her contribution to world technology, it is by no means negligible and, more importantly, it is increasing rapidly. Even in the 1940s, 1950s and 1960s, Japanese universities were making major contributions which were an essential basis for the development of new technologies in Japanese industry. For example, Tokyo University played a leading part in the work which ultimately led to the success of the Japanese robotics and computer development programmes. There is much more interaction between Japanese universities and industry than is commonly realised in the West even though the networks operate under different financial arrangements than those customary in the United States. It would have been impossible for Japanese industry to succeed in mastering new technologies without a fairly strong interaction with university basic research in some ways very similar to that described by Nelson.

The second qualification is that it is not actually essential to be the world leader in basic science in order to be a world leader in technology. It is necessary to have a strong capability in basic research in order to assimilate and advance most important new technologies today, but since world scientific literature is an open literature and since world-wide exchange of ideas is still a characteristic of the world's scientific community, it is not essential to *lead* in science in order to develop and exploit new technologies in advance of competitors, as the United States itself demonstrated in the latter part of the nineteenth century.

References

Allen, G.C. (1981), 'Industrial policy and innovation in Japan', in C. Carter (ed.), *Industrial Policy and Innovation*, London, Heinemann, pp. 68–87.

Altschuler, A., Anderson, M., Jones, D. and Womack, J. (1985), *The Future of the Automobile: The Report of MIT's International Automobile Program*, Cambridge, Mass., MIT Press.

Aoki, M. (1985), 'The Japanese firm in transition', Japan Political Economy Research Committee Conference, Department of Economics, Stanford Center for Economic Policy Research, Stanford University, Publication No. 39, mimeo.

—— (1986), 'Horizontal vs vertical information structure of the firm', *American Economic Review*, vol. 76, no. 5, pp. 971–83.

Arnold, E. and Guy, K. (1986), *Parallel Convergence: National Strategies in Information Technology*, London, Frances Pinter.

Baba, Y. (1985), 'Japanese colour TV firms: decision-making from the 1950s to the 1980s: oligopolistic corporate strategy in the age of micro-electronics', D.Phil. dissertation, University of Sussex.

Burns, T. and Stalker, G.M. (1961), *The Management of Innovation*, London, Tavistock.

Dore, R. (1985), 'The social sources of the will to innovate', Papers in Science, Technology and Public Policy, no. 4, Imperial College Lecture, London.

Ergas, H. (1984), 'Why do some countries innovate more than others?', Centre for European Policy Studies, Brussels.

Freeman, C. (ed.), (1986), *Design, Innovation and Long Cycles in Economic Development*, London, Frances Pinter.

—— (1987), *Technology Policy and Economic Performance: Lessons from Japan*, London, Frances Pinter.

Freeman, C. and Perez, C. (1986), 'The diffusion of technical innovation and changes of techno-economic paradigms', paper prepared for the Conference on Innovation Diffusion, Venice, DAEST, March 1986.

Fukasaku, Y. (1987), 'Technology imports and R & D at Mitsubishi Nagasaki Shipyard in the pre-war period', *Bonner Zeitschrift für Japanologie*, vol. 8, pp. 77–90.

Goto, A. (1982), 'Business groups in a market economy', *European Economic Review*, pp. 53–70.

Gregory, G. (1985), *Japanese Electronics Technology: Enterprise and Innovation*, New York, John Wiley.

Imai, K. and Itami, H. (1984), 'Inter-penetration of organisation and market: Japan's firm and market in comparison with US', *International Journal of Industrial Organisation*, pp. 285–310.

Irvine, J.H. and Martin, B.R. (1984), *Foresight in Science Policy: Picking the Winners*, London, Frances Pinter.

Johnson, C. (1982), *MITI and the Japanese Miracle: The Growth of Industrial Policy, 1925–1975*, Stanford, Stanford University Press.

Jones, D.T. (1985), 'Vehicles', Chapter 2 in C. Freeman (ed.), *Technological Trends and Employment: 4: Engineering and Vehicles*, Aldershot, Gower.

Kodama, F. (1985), 'Mechatronics technology as Japanese innovation: a study of technological fusions', Graduate School for Policy Science, Saitama University, Tokyo.

—— (1986), 'Japanese innovation in mechatronics technology', *Science and Public Policy*, vol. 13, no. 1, pp. 44–51.

Koshiro, K. (1985), 'Japan's industrial policy for new technologies', Centre for International Trade Studies, Yokohama National University, Yokohama.

Kuwahara, Y. (1985), 'Creating new jobs in high technology industries', in OECD (1985), *Employment Growth and Structural Change*, Paris.

McCormick, K. (1985), 'The flexible firm and employment adjustment: fact and fable in the Japanese case', Unit for Comparative Research in Industrial relations, University of Sussex, mimeo.

Melody, W.H. (1986), 'Telecommunication policy: directions for the technology and information services', *Oxford Surveys in Information Technology*, vol. 3, pp. 77–106.

Patel, P. and Pavitt, K. (1987), 'Is Western Europe losing the technological race?', *Research Policy*, vol. 16, nos. 2–3–4, pp. 59–86.

Pavitt, K. (1985), 'Technology transfer among the industrially advanced countries: an overview', in N. Rosenberg and C. Frischtak (eds.), *International Technology Transfer: Concepts, Measures and Comparison*, New York, Praeger, pp. 3–23.

Peck, M.J. (1986), 'Joint R & D: the case of microelectronics and computer technology cooperation', *Research Policy*, vol. 15, no. 5, October, pp. 219–31.

Peck, M.J. and Goto, A. (1981), 'Technology and economic growth: the case of Japan', *Research Policy*, vol. 10, pp. 222–43.

Peck, M.J. and Wilson, R. (1982), 'Innovation, imitation and comparative advantage: the case of the consumer electronics industry', in H. Giersch (ed.), *Emerging Technology: Consequences for Economic Growth, Structural Change and Employment in Advanced Open Economies*, J., Mohr, Tübingen, J. Mohr, pp. 195–212.

Perez, C. (1983), 'Structural change and the assimilation of new technologies in the economic and social system', *Futures*, vol. 15, no. 4, October, pp. 357–75.

—— (1985), 'Micro-electronics, long waves and world structural change: new perspectives of developing countries', *World Development*, vol. 13, no. 3, pp. 441–63.

Prais, S.J. (1987), 'Educating for productivity: comparisons of Japanese and English schooling and vocational preparation', *National Institute Economic Review*, no. 119, February, pp. 40–56.

Sakurai, H. (1986), 'Metamorphosis of the mining company: a case study of Mitsubishi Metal Corporation', International Symposium on Japanese Technology, Saitama University, Tokyo, mimeo.

Schumpeter, J.A. (1928), 'The instability of capitalism', *Economic Journal*, pp. 361–86.

Sciberras, E. (1981), *Technical Innovations and International Competitiveness in the Television Industry*, Omega, pp. 585–596.

Shinohara, M. (1982), *Industrial Growth, Trade and Dynamic Patterns in the Japanese Economy*, Tokyo, University of Tokyo Press.

STA (1972), *Science and Technology Developments up to AD 2000*, Science and Technology Agency, Tokyo, Japan Techno-Economics Society.

Sutton, A.C. (1971), *Western Technology and Soviet Economic Development*, 3 volumes, Hoover Institute, Stanford.

Tamura, S. (1986), 'Reverse engineering as characteristic of Japanese industrial R and D activities', International Symposium on Japanese Technology, Saitama University, Tokyo.

Tanaka, M. (1978), 'Industrialisation on the basis of imported technology: a case study of the Japanese heavy chemical industry, 1870–1930', M.Phil. thesis, Science Policy Research Unit, University of Sussex.

Vogel, E.F. (1980), *Japan as No.1*, Tokyo, Tuttle.

Williamson, O.E. (1975), *Markets and Hierarchies: Analysis and Anti-Trust Implications*, New York, Free Press.

Yakushiji, T. (1986), 'Technological Emulation and Industrial Development', paper presented at the Conference on Innovation Diffusion, Venice, DAEST, March 1986.

Yamauchi, I. (Nomura Research Insitute) (1986), 'Long range R and D', in C. Freeman (ed.), *Design, Innovation and Long Cycles in Economic Development*, London, Frances Pinter, pp. 169–85.

17 Innovation as an interactive process: from user–producer interaction to the national system of innovation

Bengt-Åke Lundvall
Institute for Production, Aalborg University, Aalborg

Introduction

In this chapter the focus is upon the interactive aspects of the process of innovation.[1] The analysis takes as its starting points two important characteristics of an industrial economy: the highly developed vertical division of labour and the ubiquitous and all-pervasive character of innovative activities. It follows that a substantial part of innovative activities takes place in units separated from the potential users of the innovations.[2]

Here we shall argue that the separation of users from producers in the process of innovation, being 'a stylized fact' of a modern industrial society (capitalist or socialist), has important implications for economic theory. When we focus upon innovation as an interactive process, theoretical and practical problems tend to present themselves differently than in mainstream economic theory.

The interactive aspects of the process of innovation can be studied at different levels of aggregation. In the first part of the chapter we discuss 'the microeconomics of interaction'. In the second part we present some preliminary ideas on how a model of a national system of innovation can be developed.

The micro-foundation: interaction between users and producers

In standard microeconomics the agents—firms and consumers—are assumed to behave as maximizers of profits and utility. Perfect competition with numerous buyers and sellers, the flow of information connecting them, encompassing nothing but price signals, is the normative and analytical point of reference of the theory. Monopolistic structures and complex client relationships are regarded as deviations from this normal and ideal state.

The kind of 'microeconomics' to be presented here is quite different. While traditional microeconomics tends to focus upon decisions, made on the basis of a given amount of information, we shall focus upon a *process of learning*, permanently changing the amount and kind of information at the disposal of the actors. While standard economics tends to regard optimality in the allocation of a given set of use values as the economic problem, *par préférence*, we shall focus upon the capability of an economy to produce and diffuse *use values with new characteristics*. And while standard economics takes an atomistic view of the economy, we shall focus upon the *systemic interdependence* between formally independent economic subjects.

Product innovations in a pure market?

In an economy characterized by vertical division of labour and by ubiquitous innovative activities, a substantial part of all innovative activities will be adressed towards users, outside the innovating units. In such an economy successful innovations must be based upon knowledge about the needs of potential users, and this knowledge is as important as knowledge about new technical opportunities (Freeman, 1982, p. 124, *passim*). When an innovation has been developed and introduced, it will diffuse only if information about its use value characteristics are transmitted to the potential users of the innovation. Within organizations and firms, this constitutes an intra-organizational problem, to be solved through inter-action and information exchange, involving different individuals and departments belonging to the same organization.

Here, however, the focus will be upon those innovative activities which are oriented towards new products to be presented to a market. For simplicity, we shall label such innovations 'product innovations', keeping in mind that they might constitute new materials and new process equip-ment, as well as new consumer products. Further, we shall not primarily treat innovations as single events. By using terms such as 'the process of innovation' and 'innovative activities', we indicate that the traditional separation between discovery, invention, innovation and diffusion might be of limited relevance in this specific context.[3]

How can the mutual information problem be solved when the producer and the user are separated by a market? If the market is 'pure', in the neo-classical sense, the problem must remain without a solution. In such a market the only information exchanged relates to products already existing in the market and it contains only quantitative information about price and volume. Anonymous relationships between buyer and seller are assumed. In such a market the innovating units as well as the potential users will operate under extreme uncertainty. Producers have no information about potential user needs and users have no knowledge about the use-value characteristics of new products. If the real economy was constituted by pure markets, product innovations would be haphazard and exceptional.

It is interesting to note that the pure market—hailed by some neo-classical economists for its ability to establish an efficient allocation of resources on the basis of very limited amounts of information—forms an environment hostile to innovative activities, and that product innovations would be all but absent in a capitalist economy characterized by perfect competition. At an abstract level, a socialist economy would be expected to overcome this crucial information problem more easily through a planning mechanism, taking into account the need for the exchange of qualitative information. According to a recent study of innovations in the Soviet Union, however, the lack of efficient user–producer interaction seems to be a major problem in the 'real existing socialist countries' (Amann and Cooper, 1982).

Anne P. Carter (1986) has recently pointed to the neglect of product innovations in production models as a general and serious weakness. But this neglect might be said to be fully consistent with the microeconomic assumption of pure markets as the norm. In a world where all products were characterized by constant use-value characteristics, pure markets could survive, and those pure markets would tend to reproduce the existing set of use values. Introducing product innovations into economic models cannot but erode the traditional concept of the pure market.

Product innovations and transaction costs

One well-established alternative conception of the process of exchange is the transaction cost approach presented by Oliver E. Williamson (1975). What are the implications of product innovations if we take this approach as our point of departure? According to Williamson, markets characterized by small numbers, uncertainty, limited rationality and opportunistic behaviour will tend to become hierarchies. High transaction costs will induce vertical integration. A market where product innovations were frequent would involve true uncertainty at both sides of the market, the uncertainty emanating not from the external conditions for transaction but from qualitative change in the commodity itself. It would also imply what Williamson calls 'informational impactedness'—an uneven distribution of information. The innovating unit would, typically, have much more, and more certain, information about the use value characteristics of the new product than the potential user.

In the Williamson framework, as in the neo-classical world, we would expect product innovations to be exceptional. They should become internalized and transformed into process innovations through vertical integration.

It is, of course, quite difficult to measure the proportion of innovative activities directed towards product innovations in the sense of the concept used here. One of the few systematic innovation data banks is the one developed at the Science Policy Research Unit, Sussex University. Among the more than 2,000 important post-war innovations reported in Pavitt (1984), more than a half were developed for outside firms (ibid., p. 348). OECD data on the allocation of R & D activities confirm that product innovation is as important a phenomenon as process innovation in the OECD area.

Thus neither standard microeconomics nor the original transaction cost approach are easily reconciled with the stylized facts of a modern industrial economy. In order to explain the actual importance of product innovations we must take a closer look at the (assumed) market–hierarchy dichotomy.

The organized market as a solution?

If all transactions in the real world took place either in 'pure markets' or in 'pure organizations', innovative activities would be less frequent than they are, and they would mainly take the form of process innovations. The fact that product innovations are frequent in the real world demonstrates that most real markets are 'organized markets' rather than pure markets. The actually observed relative efficiency of the capitalist system, in terms of innovative behaviour, can only be explained by the fact that the invisible hand of the pure market economy has been replaced by bastard forms, combining organization elements with market elements.

The organized market is characterized by transactions between formally independent units and by a flow of information on volume and price. But it also involves relationships of an organizational type. Those relationships might involve flows of qualitative information and direct cooperation. They might take a hierarchical form, reflecting that one party dominates the other, by means of financial power or of a superior scientific and technical competence. As we shall see, a purely hierarchical relationship will, however, often prove insufficient. Mutual trust and mutually respected codes of behaviour will normally be necessary in order to overcome the uncertainty involved.[4]

User–producer interaction in the process of innovation

We shall now take a closer look at the specific forms of user–producer interaction in relation to the process of innovation. The producer will have a strong incentive to monitor what is going on in user units. First, process innovations within user units might be appropriated by producers or represent a potential competitive threat. Second, product innovations at the user level may imply new demands for process equipment. Third, the knowledge produced by learning-by-using can only be transformed into new products if the producers have a direct contact to users. Fourth, bottlenecks and technological interdependencies, observed within user units, will represent potential markets for the innovating producer. Finally, the producer might be interested in monitoring the competence and learning potential of users in order to estimate their respective capability to adopt new products.

The user, on the other hand, needs information about new products, and this information involves not only awareness but also quite specific information about how new, use-value characteristics relate to her/his specific needs. When new user needs develop—for example, when bottleneck problems occur—the user might be compelled to involve a producer in the analysis and solution of the problem. This can only be done successfully if the user has a detailed knowledge about the competence and reliability of different producers.

When complex and specialized equipment is developed and sold to users, there will be a need for *direct cooperation* during the process of innovation. The cooperation is not a single act but takes place at different stages of the process (Rothwell and Gardiner, 1985). First, the user may present the producer with specific needs to be fulfilled by the new product. Second, the producer might install it and start it up in cooperation with the user. At this stage, the producer might offer specific training to the user. After the product has been adopted there might follow a period where the producer would have obligations regarding repair and updating of the equipment.

The uncertainty involved in this kind of transaction will be considerable. Not only is the user buying a product with unknown characteristics. He is also buying the cooperation of an external party for a future period. It should be obvious that the room for an opportunistic producer to cheat is considerable. Conversely, this implies that 'trustworthiness' becomes a decisive parameter of competition. If a user has a choice between a producer known for low-price and technically advanced products, but also for having a weak record in terms of moral performance, and one well known for trustworthiness, the first will be passed by. This implies limits to opportunistic behaviour. Those limits are reinforced when users pool their information about the reliability of different producers.

The exchange of information between user and producer also involves uncertainty and room for cheating and disloyal behaviour. The user must disclose her/his needs to the producer in order to get workable solutions. The producer has an interest in disclosing the full capacity of his product and in giving the user insight into his technical competence as a potential cooperator. But in both cases a full disclosure might be abused by the other party. Information might be spilled to competitors and each party may invade the market of the other party. Again, the abuse can only be restrained if codes of behaviour and mutual trust form an element of the relationships. Without any such restraints, transaction costs would become prohibitive and vertical integration would become a necessary outcome.

How strong is the element of organization?

The element of organization might be quite weak in certain markets. If the product is simple, its use-value characteristics changing but slowly, and the expenditure for its procurement forms a negligible part of the user's budget, the market might become quite 'pure'. When its use-value characteristics are changing rapidly, are complex and the product is expensive, the element of organization will be strong. The former type of goods will, typically, be developed by the producer alone and bought 'off the shelves', while the latter will be developed in an interaction between the user and producer, and the act of exchange will involve direct coopera-tion and exchange of qualitative information.

The flow of information

In markets where the element of organization is strong, the flow of information might be analysed in terms parallel to those applied in the theoretical analysis of pure organizations. Here we shall use some elements from a conceptual framework developed by Kenneth Arrow (1974). The flow of information can only take place if there exist *channels of information* through which the message can pass. Further, a *code of information* is necessary in order to make the transmission of messages effective. The establishment of channels of information may, according to Arrow, be regarded as parallel to a process of investment in physical capital. It is a time-consuming process involving costs. The development of a common code is also time-consuming and involves learning. The more the code is used in transmitting information, the more effective it becomes. 'Learning-by-interacting' increases the effectiveness of a given set of channels and codes of information.

The selectivity of user–producer interaction

The organizational element will not link every single producer to every single user—here we disregard pure monopolistic and pure monopsonistic situations. Normally, each producer will have a close interaction with a subset of all potential users and each user will be attached to only one, or a small subset of all potential producers. This selectivity reflects the need to develop non-economic relationships of hierarchy and mutual trust. It also reflects the need to develop effective channels and codes of information.

User–producer relationships in time

It takes time to develop selective relationships involving elements of hierarchy and mutual trust. It also takes time to develop effective channels and codes of information. Once those relationships have become established, it will not be cost-less to sever the connections. Inertia—a general resistance to change and risk aversion—combines with rational motives in reinforcing existing user–producer relationships. *Ceteris paribus*, the user will prefer to trust producers, known from her/his own experience, rather than getting involved with a new producer. The investment in information channels and codes will be lost if the old relationships are severed and new investment in the creation of new relationships will be required. Therefore user–producer relationships will tend to become enduring and resistant to change. Only if the costs of keeping the existing relationships going are apparent, or the economic incentives offered by new relationships are substantial, will a reorganization of the markets take place.

User–producer relationships in space

The user–producer relationship is defined in 'economic space' coupling units, close to each other, in an input–output system. The selective user–producer relationships will involve units more or less distant from each other in geographical and cultural space. The importance of distance will vary with the type of innovative activity involved. When the technology is standardized and reasonably stable, the information exchanged may be translated into standard codes, and long-distance transmission of information can take place and involve low costs. Here, user–producer relationships involving units located far away from each other might be effective.

When the technology is complex and ever changing, a short distance might be important for the competitiveness of both users and producers. Here, the information codes must be flexible and complex, and a common cultural background might be important in order to establish tacit codes of conduct and to facilitate the decoding of the complex messages exchanged. The need for a short distance will be reinforced when user needs are complex and ever changing.

When the technology changes rapidly and radically—when a new technological paradigm (for a discussion and a definition, see Dosi, 1982) develops—the need for proximity in terms of geography and culture becomes even more important. A new technological paradigm will imply that established norms and standards become obsolete and that old codes of information cannot transmit the characteristics of innovative activities. In the absence of generally accepted standards and codes able to transmit information, face-to-face contact and a common cultural background might become of decisive importance for the information exchange.

Vertical integration as a means of overcoming geographical and cultural distance

The development of transnational capital and of vertically integrated firms operating all over the world reflects that 'organizational proximity' may overcome geographical and cultural distance. But vertical integration may have its price. It tends to exclude integrated units from the interaction with producer units and user units outside the integrated firm. Such independent firms will tend to guard themselves against an open information exchange with a vertically integrated unit. As users, they risk to get less efficient technology than their integrated counterpart and competitor. As producers, they fear that the know-how built into their product innovations will become expropriated by the integrated user and transferred to an integrated competing producer.

Also, the vertically integrated units may prove to be more rigid and less susceptible to new technical opportunities and new user needs than the parties operating in an organized market. The tendency towards vertical integration is strong, but there are also certain counter-tendencies at work. The trade-off between saved transaction costs and the loss in terms of a more narrow interaction with external parties will differ between different parts of the economy. It will, among other things, reflect the state of the technology and the character of the process of innovation.

User and producer characteristics and the innovative potential of interaction

Not all user–producer relationships promote innovative activities. Being closely linked to conservative users having weak technical competence might be a disadvantage for a producer, and vice versa. The innovativeness and the competence of users and producers are important qualities which might stimulate the other party. The degree of standardization among users might also be important. Being dependent upon a set of users with very diversified needs might make it difficult for the producer to accumulate experience and to exploit scale economies.

The effectiveness of the user–producer relationships grows with time. As a subset of users and producers gets more experience from interaction, the elements of hierarchy and mutual trust are strengthened and the exchange of information becomes more open. The code of information becomes more effective in transmitting complex messages related to the process of innovation. As we shall see below, this 'effectiveness' does not, however, guarantee *efficiency* if the criterion is user satisfaction at a low cost. The negative side is inertia and resistance to change.

'Unsatisfactory innovations'

Traditional welfare economics tends to disregard innovative activities. It analyses the allocation of a given set of use values with given characteristics. Nor are the concepts used easily adapted to a normative analysis of the process of innovation. There is no point in asking how actual innovations deviate from 'an optimum'. Innovations not yet conceived are not known to us, and therefore we do not have any well-defined points of reference for such an analysis.

In certain instances it might, however, be possible to demonstrate how innovative activities and technological trajectories deviate systematically from user needs. When deviations cannot be ascribed either to a lack of technical opportunities or to an unwillingness among users to pay the costs for an adaption to the user needs, we might label the innovations 'unsatisfactory'.

When the user–producer relationships are characterized by a strong dominance of producers in terms of financial strength and technical competence, such deviations become more likely. In the field of consumer goods the producer dominance is very accentuated. The producer organizes both the process of innovation and the information exchange with users. In this field we should expect 'unsatisfactory innovations' to be frequent (Freeman, 1982, p. 202ff). A pattern of dominance and hierarchy might be found also when the user is a professional organization. If a few big firms produce scientifically based, complex and systemic products for a great number of small, independent user units—each with a low technical and scientific competence—producers will dominate the process of innovation and the likelihood of unsatisfactory innovations becomes great. In a study of the Danish dairy industry, such a pattern, resulting in 'hyperautomation', was found to characterize the relationships between producers and users of dairy equipment (Lundvall *et al.*, 1983).

In such situations coordination among users might develop and resources might be pooled in order to develop a counter-competence. Such a co-ordination will often be more difficult to make efficient when the users are consumers than when they are professional units. Government regulation or government support to user organizations might be necessary in order to rectify an unsatisfactory trajectory in consumer technology.

Another background for unsatisfactory innovations might be inertia in user–producer relationships and the 'effectiveness' of already established channels and codes of information. In a historical period characterized by the development and introduction of basic radical innovations, the rigidity of the existing set of user–producer relationships tends to become manifest. A basic radical innovation will often be produced by a new sector with weak forward linkages. The potential users of the innovation will be found in most parts of the economy, and those users will have backward linkages to producers, having little experience and competence in relation to the new technology. Existing user–producer networks will prove to be tenacious and it will take considerable time for a new network to become established. During such a period of transition, productivity might be stagnating, while new technological opportunities seem to flourish.

Here, the problem is not only specific unsatisfactory technical innovations, but rather a general 'mismatch' in the whole economy. Christopher Freeman and Carlota Perez (1986) have discussed how a 'technological revolution', based upon information technology, might provoke mismatch problems related not only to capital and labour but also to the existing socio-economic institutional set-up. The rigidity of user–producer relationships might be regarded as one important aspect of this last type of mismatch. It is important because it has its roots in the very core of the market system, in markets producing innovations. Policy strategies, putting all the emphasis upon flexibility through the market mechanism and minimizing the role of government in the process of adjustment, seem to be somewhat off the point when rigidities are produced and reproduced within the markets themselves.

Is innovation induced by supply or by demand?

One of the classical disputes in innovation theory refers to the role of demand and supply in determining the rate and direction of the process of innovations (Mowery and Rosenberg, 1979; Freeman, 1982, p. 211). The user–producer approach puts this question in a new perspective. On the one hand, it demonstrates that demand does play an important role in the process of innovation. On the other hand, it puts the emphasis more upon the *quality of demand* than upon demand as a quantitative variable. The very substantial user expenditure channelled into the demand for private transportation has not resulted in radical product innovations in the automobile industry. Conversely, very competent and demanding users have provoked radical innovations in areas where the volume of expenditure has been miniscule. The role of users in relation to the development of new scientific instruments is illustrating in this respect.

Individual innovations might appear as unrelated to user needs, such as innovations emanating from science. In the second part of this chapter it will be argued that even science has its users and that many innovations, appearing as purely supply-determined, have their roots in a user–producer interaction placed early in the chain of innovation. In this perspective *general* statements about the role of 'demand' and 'supply' do not seem very relevant.

Some implications for industrial and technology policy

The fact that technology is influenced by the demand side has been used to argue for a *laissez-faire* technology policy. If demand is provoking the innovations called for, there is no need for state intervention. Those arguing that the supply side plays the dominating role will often recommend government support to R & D activities and education, combined with an active manpower policy. The implications of a user–producer approach are somewhat more complex.

First, technology policy should take into account not only the competence and innovativeness of units placed early in the chain of innovation. The lack of competence of users and the tendency of producers to dominate the process of innovation might be as serious a problem as a lack of competence on the producer side. Even when the state itself acts as a user, one will often find that the competence will be too weak and this might result in 'unsatisfactory innovations'. Two Danish case studies, looking into the role of local government as user of waste-water technology and office technology, demonstrated how a lack of local user competence had a negative effect upon the systems developed and used (Gregersen, 1984; Brængaard *et al.*, 1984).

Second, government may intervene, directly or indirectly, in relation to the establishment and restructuring of patterns of user–producer relationships. In a period characterized by gradual technical change and incremental innovations, a national government might sustain national and international user–producer linkages which already exist. It might also support the establishment of specific organisations, intermediating between groups of users and groups of producers, pooling information, and thereby stimulating the production and diffusion of innovations.

In a period characterized by radical innovations and a shift in technological paradigm, the task of government becomes vastly more complex and important. In such a period, there is a need for a transformation of the existing network of user–producer relationships. The inertia originating in the organized markets will at the national level be supported by the political power of strong interest groups, closely associated with the prevailing structure. The difficult task for government will be to stimulate the renewal, or severance, of well-established user–producer relationships and the establishment of new relationships.

Standard microeconomics and the user–producer approach

Some of our results can now be confronted with the kind of microeconomic theory presented in standard textbooks. We make the following observations:

— The element of organization will be different, in terms of content and strength, between different markets and it will change over time. Some markets will be more susceptible to an analysis based upon the concepts of optimizing agents acting at arms-length distance than others. This raises some doubt about the intentions to construct one single model of micro-behaviour, assumed to be generally valid for all markets—a problem discussed by Kornai (1971, p. 207ff).

— The standard approach will be most relevant when technological opportunities and user needs remain constant. When product innovations are continuously provoked by changing technological opportunities and users needs, it is no longer meaningful to assume optimizing behaviour. 'Short-run' decisions, by producers to become involved in certain lines of innovating activities, and by users to choose among new products, will be characterized by true uncertainty, as will, *a fortiori*, 'long-run' decisions, referring to the establishment of (and investment in) new relationships and information channels.

— Standard microeconomics regards technical change as an exogenous process and its outcome as technical 'progress', indicating growing efficiency. In organized markets the existing set of user–producer relationships may produce technological trajectories, deviating systematically from what is 'satisfactory', even when users and producers act according to profit motives.

— In standard microeconomics, changes in relative prices will influence the decisions taken by users and producers automatically and instantaneously. A world characterized by organized markets will be sluggish in this respect. The existing set of user–producer relationships and the continuous qualitative change in products will reduce the responsiveness to changes in relative prices.

National systems of innovation

In the first part of this chapter, we found that the microeconomic framework, as presented in standard textbooks, is not easily reconciled with certain stylized facts of the modern economy. A highly developed vertical division of labour, when combined with ubiquitous innovative activities, implies that most markets will be 'organized markets' rather than pure markets. In this second, and final, part we shall sketch some of the implications of our micro-approach for the national and international level. Elements of a model of a national system of innovation will be introduced.

The subdisciplines in economics most relevant in this context are theories of economic growth and international trade. Standard growth models are developed under the assumption of a closed economy. This is a natural assumption in so far as the models regard new technology as falling 'as manna from heaven' and as equally accessible for all actors, sector, regions and nations. Standard foreign-trade theory assumes labour and capital to be perfectly immobile and commodities to be perfectly mobile across national borders. It has the assumption of perfectly free and mobile technology in common with standard growth theory.

This last assumption is at odds with what can be observed in the real world, where some countries establish themselves as technological leaders, generally or in specific technologies, while others tend to lag behind. According to the user–producer approach, geographical and cultural distance is a factor which may impede the interaction between user and producers. This might contribute to an explanation of why different national systems display different patterns of development.

The nation as a framework for user–producer interaction

The tendency towards internationalization of trade, capital and production has been strong during the post-war period. Some would even argue that nations tend to become obsolete as economic subjects. But this process of internationalization has not wiped out idiosyncratic national patterns of specialization in production and international trade. The fact that Denmark is strongly specialized in dairy machinery, Sweden in metal-working and wood-cutting technology, and Norway in fishery technology cannot be explained by the general factor endowments in those countries. Rather, we should look for the explanation in the close interaction between producers of such machinery and a competent and demanding domestic user sector (Andersen *et al.*, 1981).

Interaction between users and producers belonging to the same national system may work more efficiently for several reasons. Short geographical distance is part of the explanation; more important may be a common language and the cultural proximity. It is thus interesting to note that firms in the Nordic countries tend to regard all the Nordic countries as their 'home market'. This might reflect that those nations have very much in common in terms of culture and social organization (Dalum and Fagerberg, 1986).

Another factor of importance is, of course, national government. The role of government in relation to the process of innovation has been seriously underestimated according to recent historical studies (Yakushiji, 1986). Besides more direct interventions in relation to specific innovations, government imposes standards and regulations, making domestic inter-action more efficient. In important instances the state intervenes directly in the network and supports existing user–producer relationships.

The fact that national economies have idiosyncratic technological capa-bilities reflects that international transfers of technology is neither cost-less nor instantaneous. Some parts of knowledge can be embodied in traded commodities, while other parts are embodied in the labour force. The limited mobility of labour across national borders can partly explain why technology is not easily transferred internationally. The structure of the national systems of production and innovation is a product of a historical process and it cannot be transferred as easily as 'factors of production'. It might be here that we find the most fundamental restriction to international learning and international transfer of technology.

The importance of nations as frameworks for user–producer interaction does not rule out transnational interaction, however. In some industries and technologies the required scale of the R & D effort is so enormous that not even the biggest of the transnational firms can afford to go alone when developing a new product. This is the case for civil aircraft, space technology and nuclear power. Here the pattern of user–producer interaction transcends national borders. But even in these areas, national interests related to international competitiveness and military goals put certain limits to the actual cooperation taking place, according to recent case studies (OECD, 1986).

Applying a user–producer perspective to international relations brings forward the structural interdependency, characterizing the process of innovation within and between nations. On this background we shall sketch the outlines of 'a national system of innovation'. Earlier research involving international comparisons of innovative capabilities has demonstrated important international differences at the micro level, in terms of management strategies and firm behaviour, sometimes taking into account differences in the environment of firms, financial institutions and labour relations, for example. Such studies, useful as they are, might underplay the importance of the structure of the full system of innovation, however. When the process of innovation is regarded as the outcome of a complex interaction, it is obvious that the whole system might be more than a sum of its parts.

The concept of the national system of innovation will be developed step by step, using earlier contributions on systems of production and on the division of labour within systems of innovation as some of its elements.

National systems of production

While Anglo-Saxon Industrial Economics tends to regard national economies as 'a bunch of industrial sectors', the French tradition has been more oriented towards the systemic interdependence between different parts of the economy. Verticals of production or 'filières', encompassing all stages of production from raw materials to final products, are important units of analysis in this tradition (de Bandt and Humbert, 1985). A broader concept, also bringing in public agencies and financial institutions, industrial subsystems or 'mésosystèmes industriels', has recently been developed and proposed as the units, most adequate, for industrial policy (de Bandt, 1985).

An even more ambitious approach, presented by some French marxists, and inspired by the work of François Perroux, defines 'the national system of production' as a unit of analysis. The national industrial system is divided into a small number of sections, defined by the economic function of the output and by its sector of use (investment goods, semi-manufactured goods and consumer goods) (GRESI, 1975). Some of the contributions in this tradition assume the section producing investment goods for the production of investment goods to be the strategic one for economic growth and development. National systems, having a strong position in this area, will tend to have a strong international competitiveness and vice versa. The national system of production is thus not assumed to be a closed system. On the contrary, it is the specific degree and form of openness which determines the specific dynamics of each national system of production.

Production and innovation

In order to judge the relevance of this model it is necessary to look into the relationship between the process of production and the process of innovation. These processes differ in important respects but they are also mutually interdependent.

Production is a repetitive process where routines tend to develop. The flows of goods and services between different subsystems can—if use-value characteristics remain constant—easily be quantified in terms of value and volume. The process of innovation might be continuous and cumulative, but it will always have a unique element, stressing the importance of creativity, as opposed to routine decision-making. The flows between the subsystems will be complex and systemic information, difficult to translate into quantitative terms.

The interdependency between production and innovation goes both ways. On the one hand, learning taking place in production—as 'learning-by-doing' or as 'learning-by-using'—forms an important input into the process of innovation. 'Learning-by-interacting' will, typically, take place between parties, linked together by flows of goods and services originating from production (this is a prerequisite for user–producer relationships to become enduring and selective). On the other hand, the process of innovation might be the single most important factor restructuring the system of production, introducing new sectors, breaking down old, and establishing new, linkages in the system of production.

This interdependency between production and innovation makes it legitimate to take the national system of production as a starting point when defining a system of innovation. But the division of labour in the system of innovation is not just a reflection of the division of labour in the system of production. Some parts of the production system will be more productive in terms of innovations while others primarily will be users of innovations developed by others. This is documented in some recent contributions to innovation theory.

The vertical division of labour in the national system of innovation

Most innovation studies, focusing upon vertical interaction, have put the emphasis upon the division of labour in the process of innovation. The pioneering studies of the sector producing scientific instruments, made by von Hippel (1976), demonstrated that process innovations were often developed by the sector itself. Even when independent producers were involved the users played an important active part in the process of innovation.

In Pavitt (1984), a taxonomy, referring to different types of industries according to their respective role in the process of innovation, is presented. Using a data base for important UK innovations, containing information of origin and address of each innovation, three different types of sectors were identified—supplier-dominated, production-intensive and science-based. This taxonomy and the further subdivisions made are extremely useful in defining the division of labour within the national system of innovation.

Flows and stocks in the national system of innovation

Earlier we pointed out that the flows within the system of innovation take the form of complex and systemic information—messages difficult to translate into quantities. This is also true for the stocks of the system. Knowledge, scientific as well as know-how and tacit knowledge, is difficult to measure. Other important 'stocks' may be the inventiveness and creativity of individuals and organizations and those are even more difficult to assess in quantitative terms.

In standard economics there is a strong tendency to define scientific analysis as synonymous with the establishment of quantitative and mathematical models. If we accepted this dictum, important aspects of the national system of innovation would be regarded as being outside the realm of economic science. As pointed out by Georgescu-Roegen (1971, p. 316ff), this ideal of science is not uncontroversial, however. It reflects an epistomology imported from Newtonian physics. Georgescu-Roegen demonstrates that 'dialectical concepts'—along with arithmomorphic concepts—must be a part of any science analysing change.

Further, there have been different attempts to develop a quantitative analysis of the flows within national systems of innovation. As a matter of fact, the already mentioned study by Pavitt (1984) may be regarded as a quantitative approach using the number of 'important UK innovations' as the unit of account. Another interesting contribution in this field is Scherer (1982). Here a detailed input–output matrix for the US industrial system is developed on the basis of information gathered on patenting and R & D activities.

In both of these papers it is the industrial system which is at the centre of the analysis. This is natural in so far as most innovations emanate within this system. But when we look at the system of innovation from a user–producer perspective it becomes interesting to take a closer look at the interfaces between industry and the academic community and at the interfaces between industry and some of the 'final users' of industrial innovations— workers, consumers and the public sector.

In a recent paper by Nelson (1986) the division of labour in, and performance of, the US system of innovation is discussed. It is demonstrated that universities and other public institutions involved in the production of science are important parts of this system, acting in a way which makes them complementary to the innovative activities going on in the private sector. It is obvious that any model of a national system of innovation must take into account the interaction between universities and industry.

Science and technology in a user–producer perspective

In the first part of this chapter we focused mainly upon the interaction between firms producing goods and services. The user–producer perspective might, however, be applied to early stages in the chain of innovation—basic research, applied research and developmental activities. It is almost built into the definition of 'basic research' (as non-applied) that it should take place without any specific purpose or address. This picture is too simple, however. Even pure science, as mathematics and logics, has its users, and the agenda of science will often be determined by users in applied science. Also in this area the innovativeness and competence of users may influence the rate and direction of scientific discovery. In a case study referring to Bell Telephone Laboratories. Nelson (1962) has demonstrated the close interaction between basic and applied research.

What separates pure science from technology is primarily the institutional framework. Science will, typically, be produced in universities according to an academic 'mode of behaviour', while technology primarily will be produced in private firms according to a profit-oriented 'mode of behaviour'. The academic mode will typically be characterized by non-pecuniary incentives—the 'search for excellency' will be a strong motive power (sometimes even combined with an urge to understand what is going on). The output of science will be widely dispersed because the world-wide diffusion of research results is a precondition for recognition of excellency (David, 1984). This mode of behaviour implies a different culture from the one predominating in profit-oriented firms. Norms, values and incentives are different, as well as the language and the codes of information used in the two spheres.

It is not surprising that the link between universities and industry has become a political issue. The growing recognition of the role of science in relation to technology and production has made it a national priority to strengthen this link. The flourishing of 'Silicon Valleys', characterized by a close interaction between 'excellent' universities and high-technology firms in different parts of the world, has given the debate further impetus. In most OECD countries the establishment of 'sicence parks' and 'technopolises' has become a part of industrial policy.

The efforts made to integrate and subordinate academic activities in relation to industry may not be cost-less, however. If the academic mode of production is undermined and replaced by a profit-oriented mode of behaviour, where pecuniary incentives become more important and where secrecy regarding the output becomes more frequent, the academic mode of behaviour may lose one of its principal merits—its tradition for world-wide diffusion of knowledge. In the field of biotechnology this process seems already to have reached a critical level (Chesnais, 1986). National systems of innovation may temporarily become strengthened when universities become subordinated to industry. In the long run, the production and world-wide distribution of knowledge may become weakened.

Introducing the final users of technology into the system

The classical actors in innovation studies are individual entrepreneurs and the R & D laboratories of big firms. Secondary parts may be played by scientists and policy-makers. The user–producer approach points to the fact that 'final users' in terms of workers, consumers and the public sector may have a role to play in relation to innovation.

The fact that workers and consumers tend to be absent from the scene in most innovation studies reflects, to a certain degree, the reality of a modern industrial system. Both in planned and market economies the process of innovation tends to become a professionalized activity and workers and consumers tend to become passive beneficiaries or victims in relation to new technology, rather than subjects taking an active part in the process of innovation. It is, however, not self-evident that such a division of labour is 'natural' and appropriate. Active and competent final users might enhance the innovative capability of a national system of innovation.

Further, the actual participation of 'final users' may be underrated in the literature on innovation. Workers play an important part in the daily learning process taking place in production and many incremental innovations may be the product of skilled workers improving on the process equipment. Where workers are directly involved in the process of innovation, the outcome in terms of productivity and efficiency might be more satisfactory than when they are excluded from this process. Some studies of the Japanese experience seem to point in this direction.

Among consumers we find some interesting examples in the user clubs established in relation to specific brands of personal computers. Here private consumers act as professional users, developing new software in an interaction with producers of hardware and software. But for most consumer goods the interaction is organized exclusively by producers gathering information about, and manipulating, consumer needs. An interesting theoretical contribution giving consumer learning an important role in the overall development of the national economy is made by Pasinetti (1981), who maintains that the learning of new needs are of crucial importance for the maintenance of full employment. When productivity is growing and demand for existing consumer goods becomes satisfied, the learning of new needs by consumers is a necessary condition for avoiding 'technological unemployment'.

We have already pointed out the importance of the public sector as a final user in relation to technology policy. The most comprehensive and important historical example might be the military industrial complexes in the United States and the Soviet Union. In both these cases, the state has acted as a competent and very demanding user on a very big scale. Through long-term contracts radically new and advanced products have been developed. In the Scandinavian countries there is a growing debate on the possibilities of building 'welfare–industrial complexes' oriented towards the fulfillment of social needs in relation to energy, housing, environment, transport and the health service. Such complexes might, if the public sector acts as a competent user with a long-term perspective, be as effective as 'warfare–industrial complexes' in provoking new technology. There is no reason to believe that the positive impact upon the well-being of citizens should be less.

Social innovation as the basis for technical innovation

In a period characterized by radical change in the technological basis of the economy, established organizational and institutional patterns might prove to be important obstacles to the exploitation of the full potential of new technology. In such a period, social innovations might become more important for the wealth of nations than technical innovations. The Gorbachev drive for social change and democratization in Soviet Union might be seen in this light. In the capitalist countries the focus is still narrowly oriented, either towards the manipulation of financial variables or towards an 'acceleration of technological progress'. Institutional change, strengthening the competence and the power of final users, might be one of the social innovations which can give national systems of innovation a stronger position in the world economy. It would also imply that unsatisfactory innovations became less frequent.

The need for social innovations and institutional change is even more urgent at the world level. The enormous and growing gaps between rich and poor countries reflect that the international transmission of knowledge and technology is not working as assumed by standard economy theory. In so far as specific technological capabilities are rooted in national networks of user–producer relationships, 'technology transfer' can only solve part of the problem, however. There is a need for strengthening the whole national system of innovation, including science, industry and final users.

Notes

1. The basic ideas presented in this chapter have many different and heterogeneous sources. They reflect a collective effort among the IKE group, at Aalborg University, where a research team, studying Industrial Development and International Competitiveness, has pursued theoretical and empirical work, based upon a dual inspiration from French industrial economics and British innovation theory. An earlier, but more extensive, presentation of those ideas and their different sources can be found in Lundvall (1985). This booklet was worked out in 1984, during my stay as a visiting fellow at the Science

Policy Research Unit, Sussex University, and at the Department of Economics, Stanford University, and financed by a grant from the Social Research Council in Denmark. Christopher Freeman, Carlota Perez, Luc Soete, Keith Pavitt, Kenneth Arrow, Nathan Rosenberg, Paul David and many others at SPRU and in Stanford commented generously upon my work. This version has benefited not only from discussions with the participants at the Lewes and Maastricht meetings but also from comments from my colleagues and friends in Aalborg, Esben Sloth Andersen, Bjørn Johnson, Asger Brændgaard, Bent Dalum, Birgitte Gregersen and Lars Gelsing.

2. Adam Smith recognized the significance of this separation, presenting it as an important source of wealth and productivity growth: 'All the improvements in machinery, however, have by no means been the inventions of those who had occasion to use the machines. Many improvements have been made by the ingenuity of the makers of the machines, when to make them became the business of a peculiar trade' (Smith, 1776, p. 8).

3. We believe, however, that the user–producer perspective might be useful in clarifying how the different stages in the chain of innovation relate to each other in different parts of the economy.

4. It is interesting to note that Williamson, in his most recent work, recognizes that most transactions take place in organized markets. The dichotomy between pure markets and pure hierarchies is substituted by a scale where those two forms represent the extreme points. It is now argued that most transactions take place 'in the middle range' of such a scale (Williamson, 1985, p. 83). But still his analysis tends largely, to neglect the process of innovation *per se* as a factor reinforcing vertical integration and organized markets. Recent contributions by Japanese economists (Imai and Itami, 1984) do take into account technical innovation as a factor affecting the pattern of organized markets, but their focus is primarily management strategies rather than the implications for economic theory.

References

Amann, R. and Cooper, J. (eds) (1982), *Industrial Innovation in the Soviet Union*, New Haven, Conn., Yale University Press.

Andersen, E.S., Dalum, B. and Villumsen, G. (1981), 'The importance of the home market for the technological development and the export specialization of manufacturing industry', in *Technical Innovation and National Economic Performance*, IKE seminar, Aalborg, Aalborg University Press.

Arrow, K.J. (1974), *The limits of organization*, New York, W.W. Norton & Company.

Bandt, J. de (1985), 'French industrial policies: successes and failures', in *A Competitive Future for Europe?*, congress report, Rotterdam.

Bandt, J. de and Humbert, M. (1985), 'La mésodynamique industrielle', in *Cahiers du CERNEA*, Nanterre.

Brændgaard, A., Gregersen, B., Lundvall, B.-Å., Maarbjerg-Olesen, N. and Aaen, I (1984), *Besparelser eller beskæftigelse: en undersvegelse af danske kommuners anvendelse af EDB og ETB*, Aalborg, Aalborg University Press, 1984.

Carter, A.P. (1986), 'Diffusion from an input–output perspective', paper presented at the Conference on Innovation Diffusion, Venice, March 1986.

Chesnais, F. (1986), 'Some notes on technological cumulativeness: the appropriation of technology and technological progressiveness in concentrated market structures', paper presented at the Conference on Innovation Diffusion, Venice, March 1986.

Dalum, B. and Fagerberg, J. (1986), 'Diffusion of technology, economic growth and intra-industry trade: the case of the Nordic Countries', paper presented at the Second Knoellinger Seminar, Aabo, April 1986, mimeo.

David, P. (1984), 'On the perilous economics of modern science', paper presented at the TIP Workshop, Stanford University, August 1984, mimeo.

Dosi, G. (1982), 'Technological paradigms and technological trajectories: a suggested interpretation of the determinants and directions of technical change', *Research Policy*, vol. 11, no. 3, 1982.

Freeman, C. (1982), *The Economics of Industrial Innovation*, London, Frances Pinter.

Freeman, C. and Perez, C. (1986), 'The diffusion of technological innovations and changes of techno-economic paradigm', paper presented at the Conference on Innovation Diffusion, Venice, March 1986.

Georgescu-Roegen, N. (1971), *The Entropy Law and the Economic Process*, Cambridge, Mass., Harvard University Press, 1971.

Gregersen, B. (1984), *Det miljøindustrielle kompleks: teknologispredning og Beskæftigelse*, Aalborg, Aalborg University Press.

GRESI (Groupe de réflexions pour les stratégies industrielles) (1975), *La Division Internationale de travail*, Paris.

Hippel, E. von (1976), 'The dominant role of users in the scientific instruments innovation process', *Research Policy*, no. 5.

Kornai, J. (1971), *Anti-equilibrium*, Amsterdam, North-Holland.

Lundvall, B.-Å. (1985), *Product Innovation and User–Producer Interaction*, Aalborg, Aalborg University Press.

Lundvall, B.-Å., Maarbjerg-Olesen, N. and Aaen, I. (1983), *Det lanbrugsindustrielle kompleks: teknologiudvikling, konkurrenceevne og beskæftigelse*, Aalborg, Aalborg University Press.

Mowery, D. and Rosenberg, N. (1979), 'The influence of market demand upon innovation: a critical review of some recent empirical studies', *Research Policy*, no. 8, pp. 102–153.

Nelson, R.R. (1962), 'The link between science and invention: the case of the transistor', in National Bureau of Economic Research, *The Rate and Direction of Inventive Activity*, Princeton University Press.

Nelson, R.R. (1986), 'The generation and utilization of technology: a cross-industry analysis', paper presented at the Conference on Innovation Diffusion, Venice, March 1986.

OECD, (1983), 'Report on the results of the workshop on research, technology and regional policy', DSTI/SPR/83.117.

——, (1986), 'Technical cooperation agreements between firms: some initial data and analysis', DSTI/SPR/86.20, May.

Pasinetti, L. (1981), *Structural Change and Economic Growth*, Cambridge, Cambridge University Press, 1981.

Pavitt, K. (1984), 'Sectoral patterns of technical change: towards a taxonomy and a theory', *Research Policy*, vol. 13.

Rosenberg, N. (1976), *Perspectives on Technology*, Cambridge, Cambridge University Press.

—— (1982), *Inside the Black Box: Technology and Economics*, Cambridge, Cambridge University Press.

Rosenberg, N. and Mowery, D. (1978), 'The influence of market demand upon innovation: a critical review of some recent empirical studies', *Research Policy*, no. 8.

Rothwell, R. and Gardiner, P. (1985), 'Invention, innovation, re-innovation and the role of the user: a case study of British Hovercraft development', *Technovation*, no. 3.

Scherer, F.M. (1982), 'Inter-industry technology flows in the United States', *Research Policy*, no. 4, 1982.

Smith, A. (1776), *An Inquiry into the Nature and Causes of the Wealth of Nations*, Dent edn. (1910).

Williamson, O.E. (1975), *Markets and Hierarchies: Analysis and Antitrust Implications*, New York, Free Press.

—— (1985), *The Economic Institutions of Capitalism: Firms, Markets, Relational Contracting*, New York, Praeger.

Yakushiji, T. (1986), 'Technological emulation and industrial development', paper presented to the Conference on Innovation Diffusion, Venice, March.

18 Can the imperfect innovation systems of capitalism be outperformed?*

Pavel Pelikan
The Industrial Institute for Economic and Social Research, Stockholm

Introduction

In this chapter, capitalism will be considered in a somewhat broader perspective than in the rest of this volume. Rather than examining how technical innovations are handled within any given capitalist system, I propose to use a comparative approach. I will consider the entire class of capitalist systems, compare its potential with the potential of some non-capitalist systems, and then search to identify in more detail those systems where technical innovations would be handled relatively best.

To justify the usefulness of such a comparative approach and to formulate my main questions, Chapter 15 by Nelson is a convenient point of departure. Focusing on the US capitalist system, Nelson examines its ways of handling the great variety of kinds and stages of the innovation process. He points to the advantages as well as to the imperfections of this system, and suggests that it could be improved by changes in its institutional design. He leaves open the question, however, of how far and in which direction such changes should go.

Clearly, this question cannot be given a solid answer without comparative analysis. As most likely no economic system is perfect, one cannot judge what should be done with a given imperfect system without comparing its imperfections with the imperfections of alternatives. Two errors are to be avoided: the one of defending a given system if at least one alternative were better, and the opposite error of rejecting it if all alternatives were even worse.[1]

Given an imperfect capitalist system where technical innovations are handled in a suboptimal way, there are two specific questions which I wish to examine here:

— Is a superior system more likely to be found within the class of capitalist systems or outside it?

* The financial support of the Marianne and Marcus Wallenburg Foundation is gratefully acknowledged. I thank Piet-Hein Admiraal, Leszek Balcerowicz, Bo Carlsson, Pierre-André Chiappori, Gunnar Eliasson, Ken Hansen, Ronald Heiner, Albert Hirschman, Richard Nelson, Keith Pavitt, Tomas Pousette, Nils-Henrik Schager, Nick von Tunzelmann, Stephen Turner, Oliver Williamson, Sidney Winter and Bengt-Christer Ysander for valuable comments on earlier drafts. None of them is responsible for my conclusions and remaining errors.

— What properties should such a superior system have; in particular, what role in promoting technical progress should it assign to government?

Comparing economic systems for their technical innovativeness is, however, not easy. The problem is that a suitable approach must be not only comparative, but moreover dynamic. As Nelson and Winter (1982) emphasize, technical progress is an evolutionary process for which static analysis is insufficient. But with a few exceptions, the existing dynamic approaches have not been comparative, while the comparative ones have been largely static. Surprisingly enough, this is even true of Schumpeter (1942), who did discuss both capitalism and socialism, but when he came to his famous dynamic problem of 'creative destruction', it was only capitalism he examined with care.

Among the exceptions, the most valuable ones probably are the comparative study of organizational adaptability and technical innovativeness by Balcerowicz (1986), and the more empirically oriented survey of technical progress in East and West by Hanson and Pavitt (1986). In a somewhat parallel way, I have made my own attempts to develop a dynamic comparative approach to economic systems in Pelikan (1985, 1986, 1987).

But none of them provides a ready-to-use method for the present purposes. This means that this inquiry must pursue two objectives: besides comparing different economic systems for their technical innovativeness, it must also search for a theoretical method which would make such a comparison fruitful.

The context and the scope of the inquiry

There are many different questions which the two objectives involve. Given the limited space of one chapter, I can examine only a few of them here. To avoid misunderstandings, it is useful to present a brief survey of all the questions involved, situating the ones which will be examined in a broader context. This will also allow me to point to the limitations of the inquiry and to warn in advance about some of its unusual steps.

The questions involved in any comparative study can be divided into three main areas: *terminology*, *values* and *analysis*. As the central question usually is of the kind, 'is one economic system better than another system?', the three areas can be exemplified by the following questions: What is an 'economic system'? What is to be 'better'? How to find out which 'system' is 'better'?

The questions of terminology cannot be neglected, for the clarity and the productivity of the entire inquiry depends on the care with which its terms are selected and defined. As the present topic is broader than what the well-defined terms of neo-classical economics can handle, the use of some non-standard terms—in particular 'system', 'arrangement', 'structure', 'organization' and 'institution'—will be inevitable. The greatest difficulty with these terms is that they sound treacherously familar, but lack an operationally clear and generally accepted meaning.

As the following section will explain in more detail, one of the unusual steps I propose to take—and which I claim is essential for all dynamic comparative approaches—is to depict an economic system in a dual way, by what I term 'the regime–structure framework'.

In the short run, an economic system is depicted in the usual way, by the economy's 'structure'—e.g. by the specific mixture of markets and/or private and/or public hierarchies into which the economy's agents are arranged.

In the long run, when such a structure itself changes—e.g. as markets and hierarchies form, expand, contract, take over each other, or dissolve—the system is depicted by the set of the prevailing institutional rules, referred to as the economy's 'regime'. By itself, this is not so unusual either, for institutional rules are often discussed in modern economic literature.

What is less usual is to consider a regime together with the corresponding structure as a couple, putting them into a well-defined, dynamically interesting relationship. Intuitively, the regime can be thought of as the rules of a game, and the structure as the configuration of the players actually playing the game. The basis of the relationship is that each regime is largely responsible for the formation and the development of the corresponding structure, which in turn is directly responsible for the economy's performance, including technical innovativeness. (For the reader familiar with biology, a useful formal analogy is the modern dual view of a living organism—as a genotype and as a phenotype.)

When the meaning of the term 'economic system' is clarified, the next terminological question is, of course, to classify and provide with names the great variety of forms which economic systems can assume. But here is the first limitation of the present inquiry. Without giving this question any detailed satisfactory answer—such an answer would probably require a new Linné—most of the time I will limit myself to two rough classification principles. Following Williamson (1975), I will classify structures into markets, hierarchies and mixtures of the two. As to regimes, the basic classification will be into two large classes—capitalist and socialist. Following the marxist tradition, it is private ownership of capital, transferable through capital markets, which will be regarded as the main distinguishing feature of the capitalist regimes. Towards the end of the inquiry, however, some finer distinctions will also be made.

Two points should be emphasized. One is the difference between the two classifications. Under the influence of neo-classical economics, which is limited to studies of given, constant and simplified structures, this difference has been effaced and economic systems have been reduced to such structures. Typically, a capitalist system has been reduced to a set of markets and a socialist system to a hierarchy of central planning. Here, in contrast, capitalism is not identified with markets, nor socialism with hierarchies. The present view is that, in general, *the structures of both capitalist and socialist systems are variable mixtures of both markets and hierarchies*. Clearly—given the extensive use of markets in modern socialist economies and the presence of large hierarchies in modern capitalist economies—this view must be recognized as far more realistic. Only one kind of market is not allowed, by definition, to develop under a socialist regime—the market for capital.

Consequently, the technical innovativeness of capitalism is definitely not to be judged from the technical innovativeness provided for by pure markets. It will be fully recognized that hierarchies can often outperform markets—as witnessed by the example of large and successful capitalist firms, and theoretically exposed by Williamson (1975). What I will argue is that different regimes should be judged according to how conducive they are to the formation and the development of suitable structures, which in any modern economy will most likely contain both markets and hierarchies. The unusual problem to which I will then call attention is that *markets as well as hierarchies can be of very different qualities*, and that *some regimes may be conducive to the formation of markets and hierarchies of better qualities than other regimes*.

The second point of emphasis concerns the meaning of the terms 'capitalism' and 'capitalist regimes'. As already indicated, they do not refer to any specific regime, either real or idealized, but to an entire *class of regimes*. This class should be understood as containing a very large number of specific regimes, both real and idealized, with possible wide differences in performance capacities in general, and in technical innovativeness in particular. Their only common feature is that they all allow for private ownership of capital, transferable through capital markets. As regimes are only sets of rules, capital markets need not even actually exist; the only condition a regime must fulfil in order to be classified as capitalist is that its rules (in particular property rights) allow such markets to form and to develop, if entrepreneurship is supplied. This means that this class is far from limited to *laissez-faire* regimes. It also contains regimes which allow government to play a more or less significant role—to be discussed in the last section—provided that the above feature is maintained.

Regarding the questions of values—to decide what is 'better' and what is 'worse'—they are often considered to be the stumbling-block of all comparative studies. It is often claimed that such a study must depend more on the subjective values held by the student than on any objective analysis. For instance, any verdict in favor of a capitalist system is claimed to require liberal, individualistic or even egoistic values, whereas to value above all equity, solidarity and altruism is expected to yield a verdict in favor of a socialist system

Fortunately and somewhat surprisingly, however, this is not quite true, and especially not when different systems are to be compared for technical innovativeness. The general idea of how to avoid values is due to Nelson

(1981) and — in what may be regarded as another unusual step — I will apply it here. To begin with, each economic system is divided into two inter-related but separable parts:

— the system of final consumption, generating final demands;
— the system of production, determining the ways to meet these demands.

The focus is then reduced to comparing different *systems of production*, regarded as instruments for meeting some given final demands. These may be mostly demands for private goods, as generated by an individualistic consumption system with high income inequality, or contain high demands for subsidized merit goods — such as day care, education, public transport, medical care, health insurance and pension plans — as generated by a social welfare system with low income inequality. *If some systems of production can be shown to outperform other systems of production, regardless of what the final demands are, they can be said to be 'better' in a value-free fashion.*

As to innovation systems, they are simply regarded as parts of the production systems. Clearly, much of the abilities of any production system to adjust to and meet any final demands will depend on the abilities of its innovation system to supply it with suitable product and production process innovations.

The limitation here is that only those values which can be expressed in terms of final demands are respected — and avoided — in this way. Although 'final demands' can be given a very broad interpretation, even embracing items not usually regarded as goods to be produced — such as high employment, social security, and protection of nature and culture — some values may nevertheless not qualify. In particular, these are the values which one may have about systems of production *per se* — e.g. appreciating the freedom and the challenge of private enterprise or, on the contrary, the less free but possibly more stable and reassuring atmosphere of central planning.

Let me emphasize, however, that even if such values remain unsettled, they need not disturb the inquiry. The reason is that one can take them into consideration *ex post*, while fully recognizing any results which the inquiry might reach without them. For instance, if different systems of production were ranked according to 'pure' technical innovativeness, this ranking could easily be adjusted to any such values *ex post* by a suitable trade-off: the ranking of a highly innovative but little valued system would simply be somewhat lowered, and vice versa.

Finally, let me turn to the analysis employed. It has two features which should be noted and justified in advance. One is its roundaboutness. Although the main topic is technical innovativeness, not much will in fact be said about new products and production technologies. Instead, most attention will be paid to organizational and institutional problems.

To justify such a shift of focus, recall that, since Schumpeter, technical and organizational changes have been recognized as closely tied to each other. The regime–structure framework enriches this picture by showing that organizational changes moreover strongly depend on the prevailing institutional rules. The inquiry must thus consider a long loop of causes and consequences, leading from the rules ('regime') through changing organizations ('structure') to the evolution of products and production technologies, and back to the organizations—and, in the long run, to the rules themselves.

The evolution of products and production technologies is thus only one link in a long chain, and not even the most important one for the present purposes. As Nelson and Winter (1982) point out, this evolution is not entirely natural ('darwinian'), but more or less directed. What is most important here are the different ways in which the structures themselves evolve under different regimes. And in these areas, organizational and institutional problems clearly dominate.

The other notable feature of the present analysis is the lack of mathematical models. Although all the terms used have been defined with sufficient precision, I have not yet found suitable mathematical methods to embrace the complex relationship between regimes and technical innovativeness in its entirety, without assuming away some of its essential parts. Consequently, the analysis is purely qualitative, and its results only approximative. But hopefully it does throw some new light on the question of how an innovation system could, and how it could not, be improved upon.

The regime–structure framework and organizational dynamics

To begin with a well-known picture, recall that neo-classical microeconomics depicts a capitalist economy as a collection of maximizing private producers and consumers, linked together by a set of markets. In the same spirit, comparative economics often depicts a socialist economy as a collection of maximizing socialist producers and consumers, linked together by a hierarchy of central planning.

Generalizing slightly, I define *structure*—meaning 'organizational structure'—by three groups of parameters:

— a *collection* of economic agents (e.g. firms, agencies or individuals);
— their *behavior* (e.g. maximizing or satisficing);
— the (organizational) *arrangement* which links them together (e.g. a certain mixture of markets and hierarchies).

A structure can be visualized as an active device ('mechanism') or ('organism'), which *functions* in a certain specific way. The agents inform and motivate each other through exchanges (transactions) of signals and resources, either among themselves or between themselves and environments (e.g. nature, other economies). What the agents do is determined in part by the agents' own behavior and in part by the arrangement which links them together. As will be explained below, each such arrangement contains rules which constrain, but usually do not uniquely determine, the behavior of its participants.

Globally, the functioning of a structure can be measured and evaluated by various *performance indicators*, such as aggregate output, productivity, efficiency, transaction costs, or—what is of particular interest here—technical innovativeness.

Note the difference between a structure and its arrangement. An arrangement only describes the agents' interrelations, e.g. the markets and/or the hierarchies which link them together. A structure moreover specifies the agents' actual behavior—e.g. their response functions or routines—by which they have adapted to the constraints of the arrangement. Whereas *each structure implies a certain way of functioning, and certain performance abilities*, this need not be true of arrangements. An arrangement only has a certain potential to perform, but its actual performance also depends on the behavior of the participating agents. Only in the special case of identical agents (e.g. if all were equally perfect optimizers) would an arrangement determine performance. On the other hand, if the agents are not identical and their true behavioral characteristics are difficult to observe—and this case will be of much importance later in my argument—*identical arrangements may be observed to have different performance abilities*.

Nelson's chapter provides important examples of the potential of different arrangements in the area of innovation. Extending Williamson's (1975) comparative analysis of markets and hierarchies, he shows that different arrangements are differently advantageous in providing for different innovation activities. For instance, activities with high costs of technology transfer and easy-to-appropriate returns are shown to be best conducted by profit-seeking firms on markets, whereas various non-market arrangements are shown more suitable in opposite cases.

For the present argument, the most important lesson one can learn from these examples is that *there is no single-type arrangement—neither markets, nor hierarchies—which would be universally optimal for all innovation activities*. This extends into the area of innovation the well-known result of Williamson's that neither market nor non-market arrangements are universally superior, but have different comparative advantages and disadvantages for different kinds of transactions. The general conclusion here is that *technical innovativeness requires a variegated structure of different kinds of arrangements*—e.g. a mixture of several kinds of markets and several kinds of hierarchies—which could successfully handle the entire spectrum of innovation activities.

The greatest advantage of studying structures is that they are directly responsible for the economy's function and performance. In the long term, however, they are unsuitable to represent an economic system. Whereas 'system' should refer to some relatively stable parameters, structures rarely remain stable for a long time. For instance, every time a market forms or dissolves, or a firm enters, exits or merges with another firm, the structure changes.

The search for a relatively more stable set of parameters naturally leads to the set of institutional rules which, like the rules of a game, constrain the behavior of the economic agents involved. While the agents can enter, exit or change their arrangements in various by the rules permitted ways, the rules can stay put. Examples of such rules are property rights in the sense of Demsetz (1967), or the economic constitution in the sense of Buchanan (1975). The presently used term 'regime' is due to Hurwicz (1971) who formally defines it as the set of institutional constraints on the decision spaces of the agents within an economy.[2]

Note first that *each arrangement implies a regime*. For instance, each market implies certain transferable property rights and certain rules of signalling and contracting. Similarly, each hierarchy implies certain rules determining the rights and the obligations for each of its members. On the other hand, *each regime typically allows several alternative arrangements to form*. For instance, under the same property rights, differently competitive markets may form—including no market at all, if the agents do not supply enough entrepreneurship.

For a national economy, the regime is usually quite complex, including all the institutional rules which pertain to all parts of the economy's arrangement—such as labor law, corporate law, patent law, antitrust law, and also various customary and ethical norms, stemming from the underlying culture.

An important part of each such regime are the rules which specify the economic role of government. At one extreme, a *laissez-faire* regime may prohibit government from playing any significant economic role, while, at the other extreme, a socialist command regime may require government to organize and run the entire production, according to the rules of a certain planning procedure. Postponing the discussion of some more interesting intermediate cases to the last section, let me now only emphasize that the *economic* role of government under the given rules of a given regime is to be strictly distinguished from the *institutional* role of government in making and changing the rules and thus the regimes (e.g. through legislation). This corresponds to Hayek's (1967) classification of government activities into 'particular measures' and 'general rules'. Since the present inquiry is limited to comparing given regimes, without examining how they are, or could be, made or changed, only the former—the economic, or 'particular measures', role—will be discussed here.

The advantages and disadvantages of studying regimes are complementary to those of studying structures. Whereas a regime is relatively more stable, it is, on the other hand, less directly related to the economy's performance. The problem is that a regime does not actively perform, but only influences the performance of an interposed structure. What a regime needs, in order to show analysable effects, are some active, interacting agents whose behavior it would channel, through the specific constraints of its rules, towards certain actions rather than others. All known economic analysis of institutional rules refers indeed to an assumed structure—such as a set of perfectly competitive markets populated by perfectly rational agents, who always take maximum advantage of whatever institutional rules happen to exist, which is explicitly or implicitly referred to in most of the property rights literature.

The question then is what can be gained by considering regimes if structures are needed anyway. My guess is that not much, as long as one limits attention, as neo-classical analysis does, to initially postulated constant structures. But the situation becomes quite different when structures are regarded as variable, and their formation and development submitted to analysis. In such an organizationally dynamic view, regimes and structures play distinct and complementary roles, forming a promising theoretical framework. It is this view which Schumpeter (1942) advocated by saying: 'The problem that is usually being visualized is how capitalism administers existing structures, whereas the relevant problem is how it creates and destroys them.' This view will also be adopted here, with the notable difference from Schumpeter that other regimes than capitalism will be considered, too.

To see what organizational dynamics is about, consider first that in real economies both regimes and structures change and develop. The rules of a regime may change through legislation and/or a spontaneous evolution of custom. Structures may change, as already noted, through organization and reorganization of markets and/or hierarchies. The important point is that the two kinds of changes need not go together. In particular, a *regime need not change every time the corresponding structure changes*. For instance, a market, a firm or an entire industry may appear or disappear, while the prevailing institutional rules may stay put.

Consequently, the dynamics of economic systems can be divided into two relatively independent branches: *institutional* dynamics, studying changes of regimes, and *organizational* dynamics, studying changes of structures under a given regime. The former, which is about the political, legislative and cultural processes through which institutional rules form and reform, will not be considered here. It is the latter on which the present inquiry focuses.[3]

The basic principle of organizational dynamics is that each given regime, through the constraints of its rules, channels in certain specific ways not only the functioning of an existing structure (as standard analysis has studied), but also the formation and development of such a structure (as Schumpeter urges us to study).

This principle indicates the strategy for the present inquiry. If different regimes are to be compared for their technical innovativeness, and if this is part of the performance of the corresponding structures, the crucial problem is *which structures, of which performance, can form and develop under different regimes*.

One subtle point about the regime–structure framework should be noted. Although the principle is simple enough, a closer look discovers a complication. When using this framework, one cannot ignore the fact that *the structure of a real economy may involve several significant levels of organization.* This may seem upsetting for the theoretical economist who is used to dealing only with one such level at a time, e.g. only with firms but not with their internal organization, as the older microeconomics used to do, or with individuals but not with firms, as the more recent transactional analysis proposes to do. But the complication is not as serious as it may seem. The framework, if slightly adjusted, may depict any multi-level organization by its recurrent application.

To see the main idea, consider the following two levels of organization, which will be sufficient for the present inquiry:

— the internal organization of multi-personal agents, such as the internal hierarchies of firms and government agencies;
— the overall organization of all agents into a national economy, such as a set of markets or a hierarchy of central planning.

Clearly, both levels can be depicted by the regime–structure framework. For instance, a firm can be said to have a certain internal structure (including a certain internal arrangement) and a certain internal regime (the written and unwritten rules of conduct for its members); and the entire economy can be said to have a certain overall structure (including a certain overall arrangement) and a certain overall regime. Whenever necessary, to avoid confusion, the adjectives 'internal' and 'national' or 'overall' will denote the two levels of the same concepts.

Structures and arrangements of different levels are easy to relate to each other. One can simply say that lower levels add details to higher levels. For instance, the internal structures of firms and agencies add details to the overall structure of an economy, displaying some of its agents as arranged collections of smaller agents (e.g. plants, departments, and ultimately individuals). The overall structure (arrangement) can then be seen as a structure of structures (an arrangement of arrangements).

The relationships between regime of different levels is more subtle. In general, a higher-level regime contains rules which constrain the design of lower-level regimes. For instance, corporation law and labor law are rules of the national regime which constrain the design of the internal regimes of firms. Different national regimes may be differently restrictive, allowing for more or less variety of internal regimes. For instance, in many socialist economies, the national regime is so restrictive that it also determines most features of the internal regimes of all firms.

For the present purposes, the essential difference between a national regime and the internal regimes of multi-personal agents is in their origins. Only national regimes originate in the above-mentioned political, legislative and cultural processes. In contrast, internal regimes are designed and redesigned, under the constraints of the prevailing national regime, within the agents themselves—e.g. by the owners or top managers within a firm, possibly after voluntary or compulsory negotiations with the firm's employees. It is therefore natural to regard the formation and development of internal regimes as part of the organizational dynamics which is to be examined here. Institutional dynamics, from which inquiry abstracts, is thus limited to national regimes. This means that only national regimes, and not the internal regimes of firms and agencies, will be assumed given.

Economic self-organization

In the context of capitalist economies, the processes by which structures form and develop—the subject of organizational dynamics—have been studied under several names. For instance, besides 'creative destruction' used by Schumpeter (1942), Alchian (1950) and Nelson and Winter (1982) speak of 'selection', Eliasson (1984) of 'structural adaptation', and Marris and Mueller (1980), in a survey of earlier studies of these processes, of 'self-organization'.

For a comparative approach, I believe the latter term most suitable. It is more comprehensive than 'selection' or 'adaptation', and it also has the advantage of pointing to an interesting literature outside economics where helpful cues for understanding these processes can be found. This is the recent mathematically or biologically oriented literature about strange loops and self-organization. In the present volume, more on self-organization, including further references, can be found in the chapters by Allen and Silverberg, who address this problem in a broad methodological perspective.

In contrast to such broad approaches, the present discussion of self-organization is quite narrow and pedestrian. The processes by which the structure of an economy organizes and reorganizes under a given regime constitute only one limited stage of the processes by which the entire society organizes and reorganizes. In order to mark the limits, I will speak of *economic* self-organization.

This means that I leave aside several other stages, assuming that they have already done their work, somehow. These include the formation of regimes—possibly called 'institutional self-organization'—and the closely related formation of languages, values and customs—possibly called 'cultural self-organization'. And one should not forget, as social scientists tend to do, the historically preceding 'biological self-organization', which has formed the genetic potential of human brains to create and learn languages, cultures and institutions, on which the entire self-organization of societies ultimately reposes.

To narrow the focus on economic self-organization clearly involves the risk of missing some possibly significant feedbacks through which it relates to other stages of self-organization of societies. An important example is the feedback which, in somewhat different terms, the marxists like to emphasize: maladapted structures of economies produce crises which provoke institutional and cultural changes, resulting in a more or less different regime for the next round of economic self-organization. Admitting that such feedbacks may be significant, I nevertheless contend that a good understanding of how economic self-organization works under different given regimes is essential. Although it may not be sufficient, it is certainly a necessary basis for any more ambitious study where also the evolution of regimes is to be examined.[4]

To visualize economic self-organization in more concrete terms, recall the example of markets and hierarchies which organize, reorganize, expand, take over each other, contract or dissolve. In general, economic self-organization is made of processes which change at least one of the three components of a structure:

— the collection of economic agents (e.g. through entries, exits, take-overs or divestitures);
— their behavior (e.g. through internal self-organization of firms, or learning of individuals, conceivable as internal self-organization of brains);
— their arrangement (e.g. through formation, modification or dissolution of various communication and motivation channels of which different types of markets and hierarchies are made).

It is possible to provide for a relatively simple microeconomic model by abstracting from demographic changes—that is, by assuming a constant set of individuals of given learning potential (the competence to acquire competence). In this case, economic self-organization can be depicted as a game played by these individuals, under the rules of the prevailing regime. Such a game includes the following kinds of moves:

— designing and redesigning various (multi-level) arrangements;
— assigning and reassigning positions within these arrangements to specific individuals;
— learning of new individual behavior (new competence) within the given learning potentials.

These kinds of moves may be taken separately or simultaneously. For instance, an entrepreneur may design a firm, assign himself a certain position within it, and learn a new competence while doing so. As a result of these three kinds of moves, the given individuals keep organizing and reorganizing themselves into a series of structures.

For the present purposes I need not elaborate this model in detail, but only outline how it relates to, and differs from, standard analysis. Obviously, the main difference is that the formation (self-organization) of structures is considered at all. It is only when a structure is formed that standard analysis can start its work—to determine how such a structure functions and performs. This difference then entails several other differences.

First, the usual view of economic behavior must be enlarged by a new dimension. Traditionally, economic agents have been examined for their allocative behavior, that is, for their ways of transacting signals and resources within some already organized structures. To some degree, their learning behavior has also been studied, e.g. in the theory of learning by doing. The new dimension—which I propose to call *associative*—is the behavior by which the agents form, modify or dissolve the various inter-agent links of which structures are made, such as lasting contacts with business partners, long-term employment contracts, and the control of firms or agencies.[5]

Associative behavior involves its specific *associative constraints*—such as limited span of control, limited precision of languages, and limited trust—and *associative preferences*—such as favoritism, nepotism, and likings for rituals, status and control ('power'). Such constraints and preferences influence the behavior of economic agents side by side with the usually considered resource constraints and consumer preferences. To the surprise of conventional analysis, they may push economic self-organization towards structures which are far from allocatively efficient.

All economic agents are thus recognized as associatively active and selective. They all contribute to economic self-organization by influencing at least some links of the structures in which they become involved. But their contributions are likely to be asymmetric, in particular in complex structures. Such structures, in order to begin to form, usually need an entrepreneur–organizer—private or public—to provide an initial design and to trigger the formation. The model thus throws a new light on the role of entrepreneurs, making it comparable to the role of catalysts in the formation of chemical compounds.[6]

There is another additional problem that the model must solve. In the excitement over the new problem of self-organization, one must not forget (as some students of self-organization tend to do) that the old problem of resource-allocation does not disappear. The additional problem, then, is how these two problems relate to each other. Although formal modelling is difficult, the general principle is simple. To recall, economic self-organization forms organizational structures which determine how resources will be allocated. But since economic self-organization, in turn, needs resources—e.g. the capital which a firm needs for entering, expanding, taking over another firm, or simply surviving—the resulting allocation of resources becomes an important constraint on further self-organization.

An organizationally dynamic comparative analysis thus slowly begins to take shape. Although it agrees with traditional analysis that structures determine performance, it does not compare them directly. Instead, the focus of comparison is shifted to regimes. These are compared for their capacities to channel, by the constraints of their rules, economic self-organization towards structures of some desirable performance, which, in the present case, is a high technical innovativeness.

The strange loop of economic competence

The difficulty with this strategy is that it substantially prolongs analysis. It preserves the old question of how structures perform, and raises the new question of how structures self-organize. The strategy could hardly be fruitful, unless we can find a substantial short cut from properties of self-organization to the performance of structures. What we need is a characteristic feature of structures which is crucial for their performance, and at the same time easy to identify as a product of their self-organization. I now wish to argue that such a feature exists, giving it the name 'economic competence'.

My starting point is the concept of competence as introduced by Heiner (1983).[7] In essence, competence measures the capacities of an agent to solve difficult problems. Each level of competence implies a maximum difficulty of problems which can be solved optimally. If more difficult problems must be solved, their solutions are likely to contain costly errors, and thus be suboptimal. To refer to such a situation, Heiner coins the term 'competence-difficulty gap'.

As Heiner points out, limited competence is caused by imperfect ability to use information, which is to be distinguished from the usually considered case of imperfect information. One consequence of this distinction is that one can finally recognize in theory what has been commonplace in practice: the possibility of different results when the same information is used by agents of different competence. In order to refer to such a situation in terms close to the usual economic jargon, I shall say that competence is *scarce* and *asymmetric*.[8]

For the present purposes, it is essential to distinguish *economic competence* from competence in other fields, such as technology and politics. Such a distinction can be found already in Knight (1921), who insisted on the difference between economic problems, the subject proper of economic analysis, and technical problems, which call for the competence of natural scientists and engineers.

Economic competence can be regarded as a mixture of three basic components, corresponding to the above-mentioned three dimensions of economic behavior: *allocative* competence—e.g. the competence for deciding on the quantities and/or prices of inputs and outputs, or for choosing production techniques; *associative* competence—e.g. the competence for designing, joining, modifying or leaving organizations; and *learning* competence, with the meaning of 'economic or business talents', as the competence to learn these two kinds of competence. In contrast, technical competence is the competence for designing products and production processes in terms of physical variables, and includes also the competence to learn such competence, or 'technical talents'.

To be sure, technical competence can also be of much concern for an economist, in particular in studies of technical innovations. Moreover, it is often intimately interwoven with economic competence. Typically, the solutions of technical problems require economic evaluation, while the solutions of economic problems are constrained by available technologies. It may even be the same person—such as the Schumpeterian entrepreneur — who uses both. But a difference nevertheless exists and, as will become clear shortly, is of great importance for economic theorising. It is one thing to design a product or a production process in terms of physical parameters, and another thing to evaluate the private and/or social costs and benefits of such a design, in order to decide for or against its use in production. Whether the technical design and the economic evaluation are made by different persons or by the same person is clearly immaterial for the validity of the distinction.

The reason why this distinction is so important is that the two kinds of competence raise substantially different problems for economic theory. Paradoxically enough, it is technological competence which is easier to handle. As the well-known literature on human capital, learning by doing, and job assignment amply illustrates—and it is perhaps useful to emphasize that this literature is about technological and not economic competence— neo-classical theory has no difficulties in recognising that technological competence may be scarce and asymmetric. This kind of competence can simply be regarded as a property of human factors of production, and its production and allocation treated in a formally similar way as the production and allocation of any other capital good.

But the apparently innocent step from scarce and asymmetric technical competence to scarce and asymmetric economic competence demands a real somersault from economic theory. When acting as workers, engineers or scientists, people can be regarded as factors of production. But when acting as traders, investors, managers, policy-makers or planners, they must be recognized as economic agents. To admit that their competence may be scarce and asymmetric even for these roles undermines the entire neo-classical theorizing. It contradicts the fundamental neo-classical axiom that all economic agents are perfectly rational optimizers—that is, of equally abundant competence for solving economic problems.

To show how much the beautiful axiomatic building of neo-classical economics is damaged, let me elaborate. If economic competence is scarce and unequally distributed, it becomes a scarce resource and the problem of its allocation must be raised. But this problem is fundamentally different from all allocation problems for which neo-classical theory has been built. Whereas all other scarce resources are merely *objects* being allocated, economic competence determines at the same time the very *method of economic calculus* by which resource-allocation is governed.

The crucial role of the rationality axiom in neo-classical theorizing is thus exposed from a somewhat unusual angle. This axiom is needed to separate the objects from the method; what it implies is that all agents have abundant economic competence for which no allocation problem ever arises. But if economic competence is scarce and itself in need of allocation, this separation is destroyed and a strange loop, from the family of paradoxes which have scourged axiomatic building of modern mathematics, appears in full beauty. Economic competence spreads on both sides of the fence: *the already allocated economic competence determines the method by which further allocation of economic competence is governed.*[9]

This step, besides being theoretically disturbing, points to two important problems. The first is the possibility of path-dependency in economic self-organization, in particular in the formation of hierarchies. Initial accidents in the allocation of competence among the founders of a hierarchy may gradually amplify, possibly causing the entire hierarchy to become pervaded by exceptional competence, or exceptional incompetence.[10]

The second problem is the possibility of important failures of economic systems which have been well known in practice, but thus far neglected in theory. According to neo-classical analysis, all welfare losses in all systems must ultimately be ascribed to improper motivation of *perfectly competent egoists*. Even the losses due to imperfect or assymetric information must ultimately be ascribed to improper motivation of the agents who have the right information but do not communicate it, or who could obtain it but do not search for it—for instance, because of differences between private and social costs and benefits. But when this step is taken, we can moreover see the losses caused by possibly well-motivated but *not so competent egoists or altruists*. This means that economic systems can now be assessed not only according to how well they can cope with egoism, but also according to how well they can cope with incompetence. Since lack of competence can harm technical innovativeness at least as much as lack of motivation, this problem is of high relevance here.

The dependence of technical innovativeness on economic competence can now be summarized as follows. Although the competence at the fighting line of technical progress is technical, it is on economic competence that its production, recognition and deployment depends. Therefore, *the technical innovativeness of an economic system ultimately depends on its abilities to allocate efficiently economic competence.* In particular, this is the competence of entrepreneurs, managers, investors, policy-makers or planners to read and interpret economic signals, to estimate future supply and demand, to evaluate the probability of success of different research and production projects, to design contracts and organizations, and, last but by no means least, to estimate the competence limits of others and oneself.

Economic competence as an outcome of economic self-organization

To complete the short cut, I now need to establish that the use of economic competence in an economy is determined by economic self-organization. An essential element of my argument is the concept of 'tacit knowledge', as introduced by Polanyi (1967) and discussed in the context of evolutionary economics by Nelson and Winter (1982). In essence, this is knowledge which can be freely used by its owners, but cannot be expressed and communicated to anyone else. The point I now wish to make is that economic competence is tacit in this sense.

The best theoretical justification that some knowledge (information) must always be tacit can probably be found in computer theory. It clearly shows that in order to observe, interpret, act upon or communicate any information, some information must always pre-exist, such as working knowledge of concepts, codes (languages) and logic. Although some of such information might have been communicated on an earlier occasion, that communication inevitably required some pre-existing information, too. The upshot is that at least some of the information on which all communication and decision-making ultimately repose must be tacit, that is, inherent to the systems involved. As an example, think of a computer, where the entire hierarchy of treatment of software, communicable through its inputs and outputs, ultimately reposes on its hardware, inherent to its construction.

The claim that economic competence is tacit obviously depends on how this is defined. To choose the right definition, let me examine a little closer Heiner's distinction between information and ways of using information. Strictly speaking, a way of using information is also information (e.g. a program or a routine), and there may be ways of using this information (e.g. programming programs), and so on *ad infinitum*.[11] This discloses that the distinction is not uniquely determined, but offers a number of options. To fit my claim, I make the definition coincide with the distinction between communicable and tacit information. This means that not only data (e.g. prices and quantities), but also all communicable ways of using data as well as all communicable ways of using such ways (e.g. instruction books, computer programs), are regarded as (communicable) economic information. This means that I will use 'economic competence' to refer to *the (residual) ways of using information in economic decision-making which cannot be communicated, but are inherent to each economic agent* — such as the competence to understand and suitably apply instruction books and computer programs, but which cannot itself be put in an instruction book or a computer program.

The upshot of this definition is that the only way by which individuals can acquire economic competence is their own learning, based on their own experience, formal education, and the innate (and/or by early education determined) competence to learn economic competence 'economic talents'.

The next step I need to take is to define economic competence as a property of not only individuals, but structures in general. This will make it possible to speak, for instance, of firms, agencies and entire economies as being more or less competent.

Let me now define *the competence of a structure as the allocation of the individual competence involved in the structure*. This means that a structure's competence is made up of all the individual competence involved, but without being a simple sum of individual contributions. What also counts is the structure's arrangement, and the allocation of specific individuals over this arrangement. Clearly, the competence employed for top economic decisions—such as those of entrepreneurs, managers, investors, policy-makers and planners—must weigh more than the competence of the rank and file.

Two implications are of particular importance. First—and this is only another way of expressing conventional wisdom—the same individuals can form structures of different competence, if organized into different arrangements. Second—and this is a less usual point for economic theory—*the same arrangement can result in different competence if it involves different, or differently permuted, individuals.*

Economic competence has already been related to individual rationality. It is now moreover possible to relate it to *x-efficiency* of firms and allocative efficiency of economies. The three traditionally separate concepts—rationality, *x-efficiency* and allocative efficiency—are thus provided with a deep common meaning. At different levels of organization, they all refer to the economic competence of structures, determining the structures' performance abilities.

The conclusion that economic competence is allocated by economic self-organization is now easy to draw. That economic competence cannot be allocated through the usually studied inter-agent transactions obviously follows from its tacitness. And that it is precisely economic self-organization which must assume this task is nearly as obvious. As an inherent property of structures, economic competence must be allocated by the same processes by which structures are formed. And, by definition, these are the processes which constitute economic self-organization.

Economic self-organization under different regimes

What has thus been established is that technical progress depends on economic competence, which is allocated by economic self-organization. The next step is to examine how this is channelled by different regimes.

Let me begin with the behavior in a similar way as the rules of a game constrain the behavior of the players. Following the distinction between allocative and associative behavior, the rules of a regime can be divided into two corresponding categories:

— *allocative rules*, constraining the agents in their allocating of resources (e.g. in investment, R & D, production and trade);
— *associative rules*, constraining the agents in their associating and dissociating (e.g. in entries, exits, cooperation agreements, take-overs and divestitures).

As associating and allocating are interrelated, both categories influence economic self-organization. To the extent that resources are required, the allocative rules—such as property rights—play an important role. But the distinguishing feature of self-organization is that it not only uses resources, but moreover changes structures for the next round of resource-allocation.

It is for this additional area that the associative rules are specialized. They can be exemplified by antitrust law, corporate law, the rules regulating entry and exit, and the rules regulating the labor and capital markets—where most of the associating and dissociating of individual employees, managers and owners is conducted under a capitalist regime.

A regime thus influences economic self-organization in a double way. Its allocative rules do so indirectly, via their responsibility for economic results, determining which structural changes become economically feasible. Its associative rules do so directly, by determining which of the economically feasible changes are moreover institutionally permissible.

Although when new, a regime must begin with the structure inherited from its predecessor, its double influence on economic self-organization makes it increasingly responsible for the subsequent states and performance abilities of the structure—much as the genetic message of an organism is responsible for the development of the organism's anatomy and behavior. This discloses as illegitimate the neo-classical habit to assign an arbitrarily postulated structure to a given regime—such as a set of perfectly competitive markets to capitalism, or a hierarchy of optimal planning to socialism —without verifying whether the regimes in question are actually capable of engendering or at least preserving such structures.

To determine how economic self-organization would actually unfold under a single given regime is not easy: a complex simulation model would probably be required. But fortunately, and somewhat surprisingly, the question of how different regimes compare with each other in channelling economic self-organization can be given an approximative but meaningful answer by relatively simple means.

The key idea is to focus on failures of economic self-organization, and to assess different regimes for their abilities to resist them. Since economic self-organization is modelled here as (several levels of) selective associating and dissociating of economic agents, let me denote such failures as *associative failures*.

In general, to speak of failures of economic systems requires the choice of certain values, or performance criteria (e.g. Pareto optimality, or a more specific social welfare function), in order to determine what is a failure and what is a success (or an optimum). But here it is possible to avoid the question of values in the way described above in the second section. Economic self-organization can be assessed for successes and failures in adapting production structures to some given final demands, regardless of what these actually are.

Associative failures can be divided into two basic categories:

— *surviving errors*, consisting of mistakenly formed and afterwards neither corrected nor dissolved maladapted structures—such as an inefficient market, a poorly organized firm, or an incompetent policy-making or planning agency which survive for long periods of time;
— *absent successes*, consisting of potentially successful structures which,

although feasible given available competence, failed to form—such as new firms promoting new technologies, or otherwise superior to incumbent firms, whose entry has been hindered or not sufficiently encouraged.

Referring to these two categories, a simple method for comparing regimes can be devised. The main idea is to compare their resistance to associative failures, that is, their intolerance to surviving errors and their openness to associative trials. If regime A proves to be *relatively* more resistant to associative failures than regime B, the conclusion will be that the structures formed under A are likely to become better adapted, and therefore perform *relatively* better than the structures formed under B—and this regardless of final demands, and also regardless of how poorly adapted the structures under A might appear according to some absolute ('nirvana') criteria. Consequently, if it is technical progress which is demanded, it will also be better promoted under A than under B—in the sense that a suitable variegated structure, containing the right mixture of markets and hierarchies of the right qualities, is also more likely to form under A than under B.

Capitalism is necessary for superior technical innovativeness

After the somewhat long, but I believe inevitable, theoretical detour, it is now possible to outline the answer to the initially stated question. Let me expose the main points by way of justifying the following proposition: *the superior regimes, promoting technical progress better than all other regimes, belong to the class of capitalist regimes—that is, regimes allowing for private ownership of capital, transferable through capital markets.*

To avoid misunderstanding, let me emphasize what this proposition does not imply. First, it does not imply that technical progress would be successfully promoted by all capitalist regimes; the possibility that some of them may perform poorly is not at all excluded. Second, the proposition does not imply that a superior regime should be of the *laissez-faire* kind, excluding all active role of government. Private ownership of capital, transferable through capital markets, is claimed to be a *necessary, but possibly not sufficient*, condition for superiority.

This proposition clearly contradicts neo-classical analysis which formally proves—by constructing various methods of optimal socialist planning[13]— that *some* socialist systems can perform at least as well as *the best* capitalist systems. To justify the proposition I need to show why this proof no longer holds when economic self-organization enters the picture.

Recall that the two crucial assumptions for this proof are: the stocks of all resources can be measured, at least by their users; and all production units as well as the planning agency are perfectly competent optimizers. But neither holds for economic self-organization, specialized in allocating tacit, scarce and asymmetric economic competence.

Because of its tacitness, economic competence is a resource whose stocks cannot be directly measured, not even by their users, as the frequent cases of overestimation or underestimation of one's own competence amply demonstrate. Only indirect measuring, via actual performance, is possible. Such measuring requires competition, in the sense of contests or tournaments, conducted in the same field as the competence to be measured. Hence for measuring economic competence, the competition must also be economic, and not political or rhetorical.

Because of its scarcity and asymmetry, economic competence cannot be *a priori* assumed to be allocated in any favorable way. In particular, one cannot simply assume that socialist firms and planning agencies are competent at will. Their competence must be put in question and examined as a result of economic self-organization under a socialist regime.

But if the two assumptions do not hold, the following proposition does: *economic self-organization cannot be optimally planned in advance, but must involve experimentation through associative trials and errors.* The reason is easy to see. If economic competence, which economic self-organization is to allocate, cannot be directly measured, there is no reliable information base, neither centralized nor decentralized, for an optimal planning of its allocation. Moreover—and this is how the strange loop of economic competence manifests itself here—unless economic competence is optimally allocated already at the outset, the planning agency itself may be far from assembling the best available competence for this task. Consequently, any regime which is not sufficiently open to associative trials and ready to cope with associative errors *even at the highest organizational level* can easily cause the structure of the entire economy to become one huge surviving error.

This proposition thus exposes the crucial importance, *under any regime*, of the generation of associative trials and the elimination of subsequent errors or, alternatively, the selection of successes. A too lax selection will cause surviving errors, whereas a too constrained trial-generation will cause absent successes. Moreover, absent successes may also be caused by a severe but misdirected selection which prematurely eliminates future successes in temporary difficulties.

It is now easy to see why private ownership of capital and capital markets are so important. Consider the two basic alternatives for ruling them out, to which I refer as 'government socialism' and 'cooperative socialism'. Each alternative refers to a large class of regimes, both real and idealized, which may differ in many other rules, but have similar property rights for capital. Since much of economic self-organization is shaped by these rights, significant global conclusions can be drawn for each class, regardless of what the other rules are.

In all regimes of the government socialist class, capital is formally owned by central political authorities. Even if the decisions on its current use can largely be delegated to lower levels, economic self-organization must remain largely centralized. Balcerowicz (1985) speaks of 'centralized organizational rights', and Hanson and Pavitt (1986) describe this as a situation where any organizational reshaping requires prior approval from the central authorities. Note that such regimes may, but need not, require central planning of resource-allocation. This class is thus much larger than the usually studied socialist planning, for it also includes quite decentralized socialist regimes which allow for extensive use of product and labor markets, such as in Hungary.

There are several joint reasons why this way of channelling economic self-organization is inferior. First, it assigns to the central authorities a dominant role, for which they are unlikely to assemble the best available competence, given their origins in political and not economic competition. And even if the most competent entrepreneurs, managers and investors of the old regime were initially selected, such a selection would soon become obsolete in a dynamic world where new types of competence, including competence for judging competence, may continuously be required.

Second—and much of this is in fact a consequence of the first—economic competence will likely be misallocated also at all lower levels. The entire structure of socialist firms and their hierarchical and/or market arrangements is likely to contain more of both absent successes and surviving errors, because of a too constrained trial-generation and a too lax error-elimination. The most competent trials are likely to be prevented for lack of the necessary approval from the probably less competent central authorities. And too many errors ('lame ducks') are likely to keep surviving because of their monopolistic privileges and/or generous subsidies—or 'soft budgetary constraints', to use Kornai's (1980) term. The empirical findings of Hanson and Pavitt (1986) are in very good agreement with this theoretical argument.

Note that it is the low expected competence of the central authorities which is seen here as the main reason why soft budgetary constraints are unlikely to be used in a more clever way. To be sure, highly competent investors might be able to perceive the fine differences between 'permanent lame ducks' amd the recuperable ones, which can be transformed into future successes. They can then outperform the short-sighted product markets by helping the latter with selective investment as well as restructuring, often requiring important changes in the top management. But—and this is the essential point—*investors with such competence are unlikely to be found and kept without continuous economic competition on capital markets.*

Let me now turn to the regimes of the class of cooperative socialism, where the social ownership of capital is decentralized, each firm being owned by the collective of its employees. No central planning is required, and product and labor markets can extensively be used. But capital markets must be limited to credit markets, with no real stock exchange.

Following Ward (1958), neo-classical analysis sees the main problem with cooperative socialism in the perverse responses of employee-owned firms to changes in demand and profit. But in broader discussions, such as in Vanek (1970), this problem has not been recognized as decisive. Several ways to alleviate it have been proposed, and the principles of employee participation and profit-sharing have been claimed to more than compensate for it by other social and economic advantages.[14]

Let me therefore emphasize that the present argument is of quite a different kind. It does not put in question any of the claimed advantages. It admits that successful cooperatives may exist, and that many private firms might benefit from applying some of these principles within their internal structures. What the argument claims is that cooperative socialism *as a regime* is conducive to structures of lower technical innovativeness than what at least some capitalist regimes can achieve.

A scrutiny of associative failures can again justify this claim. At first sight, it seems that surviving errors need not worry cooperative socialism more than capitalism. Since product and labor markets can be used fully, competition and hard budgetary constraints seem able to keep eliminating lame ducks as rigorously as under the best capitalist regime. But this is not quite true. In order to see why, let me begin with absent successes which constitute a more obvious drawback of cooperative socialism.

Collective decision-making, as implied by the cooperative ownership of capital, acts as a constraint which discourages or prevents some new firms from entering and some small successful firms from expanding. On top of the problem of perverse incentives for growth of firms, as exposed by Ward, the present argument adds the problem of scarce, tacit and asymmetric competence. Successful entry and expansion of firms are often based on exceptional competence of innovators, entrepreneurs and investors, which, just because of their exceptionality, will often be misunderstood in any larger collective. That this problem will tax new industries and new technologies with particular severity is obvious.

A related problem arises with the supply of capital, in particular risk capital, on which associative trials often strongly depend. As is well explained by Neuberger and Duffy (1976), cooperative socialism not only precludes stock markets, but strongly constrains the entire banking sector. Only government, and under certain restrictions existing production cooperatives, can be allowed to enter. As a consequence, this sector is likely to suffer not only from absent successes, but also from surviving errors, to the detriment of its resulting competence. It is not only that no potentially competent investors from outside government and existing production cooperatives can ever try, but also that government banks may grow bureaucracy, lose competence and yet keep allocating much of the scarce capital.

With the low expected competence of the banking sector in mind, it is easy to see the high probability of surviving errors also in production. The survival of a firm does not depend only on its customers, but also, and sometimes above all, on its investors. Unless these are extremely competent, they will more often than not fail to recognize lame ducks from future successes in need of capital. Consequently, the production structure will likely contain more of the former and less of the latter, in comparison with regimes which allow more competent investment structures to self-organize. And it is precisely here that private ownership of capital and room for fully fledged capital markets prove essential.

Nelson's qualified praise of capitalism is thus strengthened in a comparative context. It is not markets, but the potential for efficacious experimentation with both market and non-market structures at *all* levels of economic organization which is shown to be the crucial comparative advantage of capitalism *as a class of regimes.*

Note that this argument differs from the usual pro-capitalist arguments of the public choice or the neo-austrian varieties. As to markets, they are not claimed to be always superior to non-market arrangements; the risk of market failures in resource-allocation as well as in self-organization is recognized as real. As to government, it is not *a priori* regarded as the villain of the piece. In contrast to Public Choice, government is here accorded the benefit of the doubt as to its intentions, and only its economic competence is, in a probabilistic way, put in question. Moreover, the discussion is limited to the role of government in production, in particular in R & D, and in the corresponding investment. The areas of macroeconomic policies and policies concerning income transfers and consumption, both public and private, are left aside. A wide variety of policies in these areas—ranging from what may be called 'conservative capitalism' to 'advanced welfare society'—may thus be fully compatible with the present argument.

How to improve upon capitalist regimes?

Since the claimed advantage of capitalism is only comparative and concerns the potential of only a subclass of capitalist regimes, it is fully legitimate to suspect any given capitalist regime—as Nelson does with the US capitalism—of leaving room for improvements. To conclude, let me briefly address the question which Nelson notes but leaves open—of where to search, and where not to search, for such improvements.[15]

Two kinds of institutional rules are central to such a search: those about economic competition, and those about the economic role of government. According to the present argument, the main task of competition is to select and promote persons and multi-personal structures of the best available competence, or at least to demote the persons and to dissolve the structures of insufficient competence. As has been shown, the selection of highly competent investors and, with their help, of highly competent hierarchies is crucial. Whereas highly competent hierarchies can much improve upon the short-sighted selection of producers and innovators by product markets, mediocre hierarchies can, on the contrary, do much worse than these markets.

The implication is, in essence, that economic competition should be modelled after tournaments in organized sports, in order to discover and promote specific competence (rather than general ruthlessness).

The old intuition of the US legislators is thus given a somewhat unusual theoretical support. The main point—which is simple in principle but involves a host of subtle problems in practice—is to keep the entry to and the exit from all markets, including capital markets, reasonably open, and the competition itself reasonably fair-play. The search for improvements is thus directed in part to removing institutional barriers to entry and exit, and in part to prohibiting predatory (strategic) behavior of incumbent competitors, e.g. by suitable legislation on antitrust and fair business practices. Another task is to neutralize perverse incentives to associating, such as the likings of managers for corporate control *per se*, or the incentives of stockbrokers to push for any mergers, whether efficient or not.

As to government, the present argument exposes its low expected economic competence, regardless of its intentions.[16] The general implication is that government should be institutionally prevented from intervening by selective measures in production, R & D and the corresponding investment, *whenever it is possible* to organize economic competition in such a way that more competent private agents for taking such measures (e.g. sponsoring and coordinating research or redressing failing firms) are likely to emerge.

The emphasized clause is of much significance. It may justify a non-negligible agenda of selective measures (which would not be welcome by either the public choice or the neo-austrian approaches). It calls attention to the possibly important category of such measure for which private agents are unlikely to emerge, *and which are better taken with relatively low expected competence than not taken at all*.

One example is the application of antitrust to particular cases. Even if the government agencies in charge are of imperfect competence for this task, their intervention can be justified on similar grounds on which imperfect umpires are preferred to no umpires at all in organized sports.

Another example is government entrepreneurship in some socially important areas where private entrepreneurs are slow in appearing. As the supply of private entrepreneurship is, at least in part, culturally conditioned, such areas may be of more importance in some cultures than in others. The crucial, but often violated, requirement is that the entry to such areas remain open and the government initiated units be exposed to competition, on comparable terms, from potential private entrants. The society will then gain in one of two ways: such a unit may succeed—which the present argument does not exclude but only shows as somewhat unlikely—or provoke, by its poor performance, more competent private entrepreneurs to enter and take over such a previously neglected area.

The coordination and sponsoring of research, in particular generic (or basic) research, is probably one such area in any culture. To be sure, not even here should private entrepreneurship be underestimated; in Chapter 15, Nelson gives several examples of private foundations supporting basic research, as well as of privately organized cooperative agreements among firms and universities for various R & D ventures. But private entrepreneurship here is likely to be insufficient—in some cultures more than in others—which means that some government policies may help, *even when conducted by poorly motivated government agencies of relatively low expected competence.*

Such policies include—and many theoretical economists should acknowledge this case personally—government subsidies to basic research. One may very well admit that the subsidies are likely to be misallocated—e.g. because of favoritism and/or a lack of highly competent foresight, more subsidies may go to conventional lines of research, yielding 'lower marginal contribution', than to emerging scientific innovators, capable of producing 'higher marginal contribution'. Nevertheless, even the disappointed innovators will probably agree that this is a better solution than if no basic research were subsidized at all.[17]

Another promising candidate for government policy is the choice of technical norms, especially when it matters less *which* norm is chosen than that a norm *is* chosen.[18]

In general, the list of candidates worth examining is quite long. France and Japan provide perhaps the best-known examples of capitalist systems where government engages, with variable success, in a particularly long list of policies intended to promote technical innovativeness. As I cannot examine such a list in detail here, let me briefly summarize the main principle implied by the present approach:[19]

— Policies with high coordination effects and low competence requirements—such as the choice of a technical norm among equally good alternative norms—imply high social gains at a low risk, and can be safely recommended.
— The more the effects of a policy—in terms of social gains or losses—depend on the competence employed, the riskier it is to allow a government agency to conduct it.[20]

Paradoxically enough—and this is perhaps the only definite conclusion I can draw here—many such risks can be reduced only in capitalism. It is only there that successful innovations can also be supported by independent private investors, in spite of possible policy errors.

Notes

1. The second error is the one Demsetz (1969) warns against in his discussion of what he calls 'the nirvana approach' and 'the grass is always greener fallacy'. In part, this chapter can be seen as corroborating, extending and qualifying Demsetz's argument.
2. Institutional rules, as any rules of a game, raise the problem of their observance. Here I abstract from this problem by assuming for each of the regimes considered that the agents involved effectively observe, and expect each other to observe, all its rules. Since such rules originate partly in written law and partly in unwritten custom (ethics), one can imagine that their observance is

achieved by a mixture of formal law enforcement, informal social sanctions, and internalized ethical norms.

3. Referring to the above-mentioned analogy with the genotype–phenotype framework of modern biology, organizational dynamics can be considered analogues to ontogeny, and institutional dynamics to phylogeny. The differences in time-scales are, of course, not the same. Phylogeny is so much slower than ontogeny that the phenotype of an organism can usually form and fully develop under a constant phenotype. Although the present simplifying assumption of given regimes corresponds to this case, in real economies the two dynamics are often interwoven (cf. also the discussion on economic v. institutional self-organization below).

4. Although the evolution of regimes may also depend on many non-economic factors (e.g. religious, ideological or cultural), the evolutionary potential of each regime is strongly constrained—and the marxists should be first to agree—by its economic performance. But as this performance depends on the structures formed, it is the economic self-organization under each regime that will eventually determine much of the regime's fate in the broader process of institutional self-organization.

5. The failure to see associative behavior as a separate dimension of economic behavior seems to be the main reason why theory has made so little progress in studies of economic self-organization. In economic literature, the closest topics probably are coalition formation, long-term employment contracts, and the issue exit v. voice as examined by Hirschman (1970). Balcerowicz (1985) has a similar concept in mind when he speaks of 'organizational actions'.

6. It is instructive to note that such an enlarged view of economic behavior can no longer refer to the paradigm of mechanics, on which neo-classical economics has been built, but is closer to that of chemistry or biochemistry. Economic agents can no longer be regarded as passively accepting their roles in a given 'mechanism', but must be recognized as actively and selectively 'reacting' with each other (cf. the affinities of atoms and molecules, and the role of catalysts). They must be recognized as themselves forming and reforming the 'mechanism'—and one should now rather say 'organism'—of which they are parts.

7. See also Heiner's chapter in the present volume.

8. To term unequally distributed competence 'asymmetric' has been suggested to me by Heiner in a personal communication. 'Asymmetric competence' thus nicely complements the familiar 'asymmetric information'.

9. The most inspiring reference about strange loops is probably Hofstadter (1979).

10. The chapter on 'Injelitis' in Parkinson (1957) provides an excellent example of a path-dependent process through which an entire hierarchy can become pervaded by incompetence.

11. Winter (1971) was probably the first economist who exposed such an infinite regression in economic decision-making. This problem has been recently elaborated by Mongin and Walliser (1987).

12. Whereas many students of self-organization use this new field to combat reductionism and methodological individualism, I believe, and hopefully demonstrate by the present discussion, that the two principles can fruitfully be used even in this field.

13. See Heal (1973) for a pedagogically excellent survey of these methods. The paradox that it is neo-classical analysis which provides such a strong defense of socialism is pointed out in Nelson (1981) and elaborated in Pelikan (1985).

14. During the discussions on the economic reform in Czechoslovakia, I helped to elaborate one of such ways in Kocanda and Pelikan (1967).
15. This question has in fact two components: the theoretical knowledge of such improvements, and the political means for implementing them. I will briefly address only the former, fully aware of the fact that there is no direct way from theoretical knowledge to practical implementation.
16. The conjecture that government lacks this type of competence has often been made (see, e.g. Eliasson, 1984), but the present argument seems to be first to provide it with theoretical justification.
17. As Cazes (1986) points out in his revealing comparison of Tocqueville, Cournot, and Schumpeter, it was already Tocqueville who advocated government support to basic research as a necessary condition for avoiding decadence of a democratic society.
18. See Arthur's chapter in this volume for a more detailed discussion.
19. From a somewhat different point of view, the case of Japan is examined in detail by Freeman in Chapter 16.
20. This proposition corroborates and extends in an organizationally dynamic context the conclusion about the limits of government policy-making reached by Heiner (1983).

References

Alchian, A.A. (1950), 'Uncertainty, evolution and economic theory', *Journal of Political Economy*, vol. 58, pp. 211–22.
Berlcerowicz, L. (1986), 'Enterprises and economic systems: organizational adaptability and technical innovativeness', in Leipold H. and A. Schiller (eds.), *Zur Interdependenz von Unternehmens-und Wirtschaftsordnung*, Schriften zum Vergleich von Wirtschaftsordnungen, Band 38, Stuttgart, G. Fisher Verlag.
Buchanan, J.M. (1975), *The Limits of Liberty*, Chicago, University of Chicago Press.
Cazes, B. (1986), *Histoire des futurs*, Paris, Seghers.
Day, R.H. and Eliasson, G. (eds.) (1986), *The Dynamics of Market Economies*, Amsterdam, New York, Oxford, North Holland.
Demsetz, H. (1967), 'Toward a theory of property rights'. *American Economic Review*, vol. 57, Proceedings 347–59.
—— (1969), 'Information and efficiency: another viewpoint', *Journal of Law and Economics*, vol. 12, pp. 1–22.
Eliasson, G. (1984), 'The micro-foundation of industrial policy', in A. Jacquemin (ed.). *European Industry: Public Policy and Corporate Strategy*, Oxford, Oxford University Press.
Hanson, P. and Pavitt, K. (1986), The comparative economics of research development and innovation in East and West: a survey, Science Policy Research Unit, University of Sussex, mimeo.
Hayek, F.A. (1967), *Studies in Philosophy, Politics, and Economics*, Chicago, University of Chicago Press, and London, Routledge & Kegan Paul.
Heal, G. (1973), *The Theory of Economic Planning*, Amsterdam, New York, Oxford, North Holland.
Heiner, R.A. (1983), 'The origin of predictable behavior', *American Economic Review*, vol. 83, pp. 560–95.

Hirschman, A.O. (1970), *Exit, Voice and Loyalty: Responses to Decline in Firms, Organizations and States*, Cambridge, Mass., Harvard University Press.

Hofstadter, D.R. (1979), *Gödel, Escher, Bach*, New York, Basic Books.

Hurwicz, L. (1971), 'Centralization and decentralization in economic processes', in A. Eckstein (ed.), *Comparison of Economic Systems*, Berkely, University of California Press.

Knight, F. (1921), *Risk, Uncertainty and Profit*, Boston, Houghton Mifflin.

Kocanda, R. and Pelikan, P. (1967), 'The socialist enterprise as a participant in the market', *Czechoslovak Economic Papers*, vol. 9.

Kornai, J. (1980), *Economics of Shortage*, Amsterdam, North Holland.

Marris, R. and Mueller, D.C. (1980), 'The corporation, competition and the invisible hand', *Journal of Economic Literature*, vol. 18, pp. 32–63.

Mongin, P. and Walliser, B. (1987), 'Infinite regressions in the optimizing theory of decision', in B. Munier (ed.), *Risk, Rationality and Decision*, Dordrecht, D. Reidel.

Nelson, R.R. (1981), 'Assessing private enterprise: an exegesis of tangled doctrine', *The Bell Journal of Economics*, vol. 12, pp. 93–111.

Nelson, R.R. and Winter, S.G. (1982), *An Evolutionary Theory of Economic Change*, Cambridge, Mass., Harvard University Press.

Neuberger, E. and Duffy, W. (1976), *Comparative Economic Systems: A Decision-Making Approach*, Boston, Allyn & Bacon.

Parkinson, C.N. (1957), *Parkinson's Law and Other Studies in Administration*, New York, Ballantine Books.

Pelikan, P. (1985), 'Private enterprise v. government control: an organizationally dynamic comparison', Working Paper 137, Industriens Utredningsinstitut, Stockholm.

—— (1986), 'Institutions, self-organization, and adaptive efficiency: a dynamic assessment of private enterprise', Working paper 158, Industriens Utrednings-institut, Stockholm.

—— (1987), 'The formation of incentive mechanisms in different economic systems', in S. Hedlund (ed.), *Incentives and Economic Systems*, London, Sidney, Croom Helm.

Polanyi, M. (1967), *The Tacit Dimension*, Garden City, NY, Doubleday-Anchor.

Schumpeter, J.A. (1934), *The Theory of Economic Development*, Cambridge, Mass., Harvard University Press.

—— (1942), *Capitalism, Socialism, and Democracy*, New York, Harper & Row.

Simon, H.A. (1955), 'A behavioral model of rational choice', *Quarterly Journal of Economics*, vol. 69, pp. 99–118.

Vanek, J. (1970), *The General Theory of Labor-Managed Market Economies*, Ithaca, NY, Cornell University Press.

Ward, B. (1958), 'The firm in Illyria: market syndicalism', *American Economic Review*, vol. 48, pp. 566–89.

Williamson, O.E. (1975), *Markets and Hierarchies: Analysis and Antitrust Implications*, New York, Free Press.

Winter, S.G. (1971), 'Satisficing, selection and the innovative remnant', *Quarterly Journal of Economics*; vol. 85, pp. 237–61.

Part VI International diffusion of technology and international trade competition

Preface to Part VI

Luc Soete
MERIT, Faculty of Economics, State University of Limburg, Maastricht,

In this section we bring in more explicitly some of the international implications of our analysis. The question as to the relationship between
technical change and the international competitiveness of a country or
industry is now a crucial item on any policy agenda: in the context of the
international economic debate between industrialized countries as well as
in the context of the industrialization (or lack thereof) of the newly
industrialising and less developed countries. The five chapters in this
section provide only a broad, impressionistic picture of the variety and
diversity of questions which arise from the theoretical approach sketched
out in the previous sections. The issues addressed here start all from the
(by now) strong evidence, both of an empirical and historical nature, that
the international patterns of competitiveness of the industrialized as well as
less developed countries have been strongly influenced by their relative
technological capabilities.

These international differences in technological levels and innovative
capabilities are not only a fundamental factor in explaining differences in
inter-country trade competitiveness; they are also an essential factor in
explaining inter-country differences in macroeconomic growth as emphasized in the chapter by Dosi and Soete. Giving a broad overview of the
voluminous literature in this area, Dosi and Soete's chapter illustrates how
consideration of the dynamic implications of trade, and in particular of the
allocative patterns induced by trade, will lead one to focus far more on the
virtuous or vicious macroeconomic feedbacks which international specialisation will imply in the long run.

The point is made much more explicitly in the following chapter by
Fagerberg, more empirical in focus, which looks at the 'classic' question of
'why growth rates differ' between countries. As Fagerberg illustrates, from
a dynamic perspective the relative international competitiveness of a
country has itself a strong influence on the relative rate of growth of its
economy. The chapter provides further evidence that in the last three
decades following the Second World War, this interactive growth process
led within the group of OECD countries to a pattern of convergence:
convergence in terms of technological levels, industrial structures,
commodity composition of domestic production, per capita incomes,
wages, and even forms of corporate organisation. With regard to technical
change, the dominant pattern was one of a process of catching up with the
American levels, or, put in other words, one where the rates of techno-

logical diffusion to other OECD (and non-OECD) countries was significantly higher than the American rates of innovation.

Whether this process of international technology diffusion can also lead to industrialization 'short cuts' within the development context is the general issue addressed in the next two chapters. The first one, by Perez and Soete, brings to the forefront the distinction between the technology 'transfer' or technology using costs and the actual technology assimilation 'entry' costs. The latter will be substantial and for most developing countries prohibitive and will exclude them from effectively 'catching up'. However, the Perez and Soete chapter, in line with the Freeman and Perez chapter in Part II, points to the existence of some temporary 'windows' of opportunity during periods of paradigm transition.

The next chapter by Unger is more pessimistic in tone. The developing world in Unger's view finds itself 'locked in' in a vicious circle of lack of entrepreneurship, increased protectionism in the developed world, a poorly developed capital goods sector, considered to be the main carrier—if not with regard to the origin, then certainly with regard to the effective assimilation—of technical change, and finally the dominant role of multinational enterprises in 'transferring' increasingly 'packaged' technology abroad.

This last issue is the focus of the chapter by Chesnais which discusses in more detail the patterns in foreign investment and international inter-firm technology agreements over the last decades. For Chesnais the reasons for the significant increase in inter-firm licensing agreements has to do with the increase in the scientific base, complexity and diversity of present technological advances. The international 'sourcing' of scientific and technological knowledge has also to be viewed from this perspective. No firm, not even the largest multinational corporation can rely on its own technological and scientific efforts. Chesnais's chapter calls for further integration of the issues of foreign investment and cross-country technology flows in economic growth and trade theory.

As we have already indicated, the chapters in this section certainly do not cover the full spectrum of subjects which could be addressed under an 'international' heading. Particularly with regard to the problems confronting developing countries, the list of subjects could be vastly enlarged. Also the international finance side, in line with the rest of this book, has not been covered. The aim of this section, however, was to provide no more than a selective overview of topics and questions where technical change and economic theory in their international dimension are in need of 'revision'.

19 Technical change and international trade

Giovanni Dosi

Faculty of Statistics, University of Rome, Rome and SPRU, University of Sussex, Brighton

Luc Soete

MERIT, Faculty of Economics, State University of Limburg, Maastricht

Introduction

In contrast to many other fields of economic theory, international trade theory has traditionally kept the importance of technical change in explaining international trade flows or the international 'competitiveness' of a country or an industry at the centre of much economic debate. This can be explained to a large extent by the almost unique influence of 'classical' thinking in the area of international trade, with many contemporary trade theorists even expressing today, and particularly with regard to the technology assumption, strong doubts as to the actual contribution of 'neo-classical' thinking.

The fact that 'pure' neo-classical trade theory is still so prominent in international trade textbooks and is still held in such esteem by policy-makers (at least until recently) has indeed little to do with the way that 'factor endowments' (pure Heckscher–Ohlin–Samuelson) trade theory explains international trade flows. Its value as a *descriptive* theory—i.e. national differences in endowments of productive factors form the basis for trade—is regarded as very limited.

Like so many other fields of economic analysis, the 'strength' of the pure orthodox theoretical framework lies primarily in the relatively straight-forward normative implications—in terms of the gains from trade for both trading partners, as well as international factor price equalization—which can be built around the model. The fact that in order to do so it has to rely on a set of extreme 'heroic' assumptions is then generally justified in terms of cost–benefit analysis: the insights gained by such a simple but complete trade/welfare picture outstrip by far the disadvantages of more realistic but more complex and less clear analyses.

Such a view requires, however, first that a 'reasonably accurate' explanation is offered for the main interdependencies identified by the theory, and, second, that the distortions and imperfections of the real world lead only to minor or 'short-lived' aberrations with relatively little consequence for the normative or policy conclusions of the theory. In the case of 'orthodox' trade theory and rather uniquely amongst nearly all fields of economic inquiry there has been growing recognition from all sides that both conditions do not hold.

Nowhere is this more clearly illustrated than in the seminal review which Hufbauer (1970) presented nearly twenty years ago on the emerging and growing evidence and support in favour of the so-called 'neo-technology' accounts of international trade flows. In interpreting his neo-technology results, Hufbauer, himself author of one of the most detailed technology 'gap' trade studies on synthetic materials (1966), remained, if anything, rather schizophrenic. His 'neo-technology' results, while powerful in explaining the actual trade flows and admittedly closer to the real world, represented an approach which, in Hufbauer's words, was not 'geared to answering the traditional questions of economic inquiry'. And Hufbauer added with some irony: 'It can as yet offer little to compare with Samuelson's magnificent (if misleading) factor-price equalisation theorem' (Hufbauer, 1970, p. 192).

While Hufbauer's contribution was exceptional in its frankness, it was in no way exceptional in bringing out the dilemma between relevance and consistency with a general and established theoretical framework which has characterized the analysis of technical change in economic theory.

Some authors privilege the first criterion (relevance) and find in the evidence on technological change a powerful challenge pushing toward the search for a radically different theory. As Rosenberg puts it,

in a world where rapid technological change is taking place we may need an analytical apparatus which focuses in a central way upon the process of technological change itself, rather than treating it simply as an exogenous force which leads to disturbances from equilibrium situations and thereby sets in motion an adjustment process leading to a new equilibrium [Rosenberg, 1970, pp. 69–70]

Conversely, other economists stress as a necessary condition for the theoretical consideration of the phenomena related to technological change precisely their tractability within the traditional model or simply consider the absence of any alternative as a sufficient condition for their neglect. In Bhagwati's words,

the 'realistic' phenomena . . . such as the development of new technologies in consumption and production involve essentially phenomena of imperfect competition for which, despite Chamberlin and Joan Robinson, we still do not have today any serious theories of general equilibrium . . . Unless therefore we have a new powerful theoretic system . . . we cannot really hope to make a dent in the traditional frame of analysis [Bhagwati, 1970, p. 23]

These two positions illustrate in many ways also two archetypes of scientific strategies, the first focusing on the search for alternative models conforming more to reality and the second pursuing a gradual and progressive incorporation of an increasing number of phenomena into modified forms of neo-classical general equilibrium analysis. It may be useful to use such theoretical benchmarks to review a highly selected literature which presents a high variance in its 'degree of orthodoxy', scope and realism of the assumptions.[1] We shall in this short review start from what could be called an 'incrementalist' analysis of technology-related phenomena broadly along the lines of the neo-classical approach.

The 'pure' theory: neo-classical extensions and the revisionists

Consider first the neo-classical 'pure' theory of trade in its simplest text-book form. There are generally four fundamental assumptions:

(i) *On technology*. Differences in technologies can be adequately repre-sented by production functions. The latter are assumed to represent the real world, are well behaved, continuous, differentiable, exhibit non-increasing returns to scale, etc. Moreover, they are assumed identical across countries.

(ii) *On behaviours*. Perfect competition prevails throughout. Agents are maximisers under budget constraints.

(iii) *On demand*. Identical tastes across countries and well-behaved utility functions.

(iv) *On adjustment mechanism*. Adjustments are such as to guarantee *ex hypothesi* the clearing of all commodity and factor markets.

These assumptions lead to the following subsidiary assumption: hypotheses (i)–(iv) offer a reasonably accurate description of the prevailing 'state of the world' and the main interdepencies in the international arena, so that any possible distortions or imperfections of the real world lead only to minor or 'short-lived' aberrations with relatively little consequence for the interpretative and normative conclusions of the theory.

In its simplest form, the 'pure' theory of international trade then goes on to prove some of the most 'classic' theorems of economic theory: on relative specialisation determined by relative factor endowments (Heckscher–Ohlin–Samuelson theorem),[2] on factor–price equalisation, and the theorem of comparative statics on the effects of changing prices on factors' returns (Stolpher–Samuelson theorem) and of changing endowments upon commodity outputs (Rybczynski theorem).

We will not consider here the developments and refinements of all four above hypotheses,[3] but will limit our review to some of those contributions which do not entirely subscribe to the derived hypothesis that distortions are short-lived, and have tried therefore to modify some of the assump-tions (i)–(iv). Typically, the scientific strategy is to hold the rest as true and work out the implications of the additional (more 'realistic') hypo-thesis. Assumption (iv) remains, however, *the* core proposition which is generally kept untouched, since the entire model, irrespective of how it is precisely defined, needs a link of some kind between relative scarcities and relative prices.

One way of relaxing the simplest technological assumptions has been by allowing production functions to be different between countries. Jones

(1970) analyses some of the implications: factor price equalisation does not occur any longer, 'differential rates of technical differences between countries come to dominate the determination of comparative advantages' (p. 84), but the Heckscher–Ohlin theorem on specialisation still applies in a modified form. Berglas and Jones (1977) embody in their model a mechanism of learning-by-doing characterised by 'local learning' (Atkinson and Stiglitz, 1969) on the techniques effectively in use. Findlay (1978) develops a steady-state dynamic model including technology transfers between an 'advanced' country and a 'backward' one. Chipman (1970) considers the case of moving production functions whereby technical progress is itself endogenous along Kennedy–von Weizsäcker–Samuelson lines (cf. Kennedy, 1964; von Weizsäcker, 1965; Samuelson, 1965). Purvis (1972) present a model with international technological differences and capital mobility, illustrating that in this case, contrary to the standard model, factor mobility and trade may be complementary. The issue of capital mobility is also considered by Ferguson (1978) and Jones (1980): interestingly, the patterns of trade turn out to be essentially determined by technology gaps and relative labour costs.

Another way of relaxing the standard assumption with regard to the production function is by introducing economies of scale. Since the analysis of the latter must be generally associated with behavioural assumptions different from the pure competitive model,[4] one may consider these two variations on the standard model together.[5] First, as Drèze (1960, 1961) and Ohlin (1933) himself, already fifty years ago, pointed out, economies of scale taken on their own can be an explanatory variable of trade patterns. Second, from a more normative point of view, they may well influence the welfare effects of trade so that a country may even lose from trade, as suggested originally by Graham (1923).

More recently several interesting theoretical developments have been produced in this area (see Dixit and Norman, 1980; Chapter 9). Krugman (1979, 1984a, 1982a) has explored the conditions under which Graham's arguments hold: they depend on the nature of the increasing returns (which are either 'national' or 'international') and the pattern of change in relative prices due to the transition from autarky to trade. Imperfect competition due to increasing returns *may* imply gains from trade for both trading partners (cf. Melvin, 1969, and Krugman, 1979a) but may also imply losses (cf. Kemp, 1969). In the case of 'imperfect competition' a large number of conclusions emerge which may be diametrically in conflict with the standard Heckscher–Ohlin–Samuelson model:[6] for example, factor prices will not be equalised, but, on the contrary, the price of the factor used intensively in the production of the export good may actually be high in each country (cf. Markusen and Melvin, 1980, p. 3). Similarly, factor mobility instead of substituting for trade (trade in factors as opposed to trade in commodities), as in the standard model, will be complementary to trade, with each country achieving an equilibrium where it is well endowed with the factor used intensively in the production of its export good. As Markusen and Melvin (1980) note: 'In the Heckscher–Ohlin model this is, of course, the basis for trade whereas in the present model it is the result of trade' (p. 3).

In general, as shown by Markusen and Melvin (1984), sufficient conditions for the gains-from-trade theorems to hold are (i) on the behavioural side, marginal pricing, and (ii) on the technological side, the convexity of the production possibility sets.

The analysis of differentiated products, on the other hand, has led to attempts at synthesis between theories of monopolistic competition, intra- and inter-industry trade. Differentiation is supposed to come from a demand for a variety of product characteristics (cf. Barker, 1977; Dixit and Stiglitz, 1977; Krugman, 1979, 1980, 1981) or from different combinations of some fundamental attributes (cf. Lancaster, 1979) embodied in each product. Thus whereas intra-industry trade (see Grubel and Lloyd, 1975) is explained on the grounds of monopolistic competition, the explanation for the inter-industry trade flows will be left to the traditional Heckscher–Ohlin model. These models predict that intra-industry trade will be highest between similar countries in terms of per capita income and patterns of demand (Linder, 1961), whereas inter-industry flows will be more important the greater the difference between countries in terms of their 'endowments'.[7] An alternative (Ricardian) model of intra-industry trade is provided by Petri (1980), where intra-industrial specialisation for any given pattern of demand is determined by relative labour productivities and cost conditions within sector-specific and country-specific structures of production.

Another line of analysis of those market structures different from pure competition has been pioneered by Caves (1971, 1974) in an attempt to link instruments and concepts of industrial organisation (multinational corporations, oligopolistic competition, strategic behaviours) with a general equilibrium trade model. A growing literature on industrial organisation and international trade has emerged since.[8] While some of the results can be formally represented in terms of the traditional model with specific factors,[9] this line of enquiry has more clearly drawn attention to the significance of the link between industrial structures and trade flows (given whatever 'endowments') and to a different adjustment mechanism (international capital mobility in the form of multinational investment rather than intra-national, inter-sectoral mobility). This line of analysis allows therefore, at least in principle, the consideration of *country-specific* variables, both institutional and economic in nature which as such represent absolute advantages/disadvantages and hence also incentives/obstacles to the location of international capital (see Jones, 1980).

Under the broad heading of 'industrial organisation and international trade', one must also mention parts of the vast literature on the origins and effects of multinational corporations. Some of the studies are quite far in spirit and construction from the neo-classical assumptions listed above (e.g. Hymer, 1976): technological differences between companies and countries, country-specific absolute advantages and high degrees of 'imperfection' of markets in general and the market for technology in particular are implicit from the start. These features of the world are indeed the necessary structural conditions for the existence of multinationals. Other interpretative models try to incorporate also some neo-classical elements. This appears to be the case of Dunning's 'eclectic theory' (see Dunning, 1977, 1981a, 1981b; Buckley and Casson, 1976) wereby Heckscher–Ohlin mechanisms of adjustment in prices, quantities, and relative specialisation are considered as *one of* the processes at work, whose relative importance depends on the sectors, the degree of development of the countries, and the nature of the technology. Finally, other interpretations—such as Rugman (1980)—try to reconcile the existence of multinationals, intra-firm trade, etc., with traditional analysis. Rugman recognises the widespread existence of 'imperfections' (and thus the limited validity of assumptions (i) and (ii) above). However, he assumes that companies face and overcome these imperfections by internalising the relevant transactions. Therefore multinationals become some kind of 'second-best approximation' to the working of the standard model.

None of these theories has been thoroughly formalised. It is safe to say though that all of them, to different degrees, lead to conclusions at variance with the canonic model: factor prices are not generally equalised, there are oligopolistic rents, trade patterns do not depend only on countries' endowments, the degrees and forms of market 'imperfections' become a determinant on their own of productive locations and trade.

Some models adopt 'Ricardian' hypotheses on technology—with coefficients of production fixed and different between countries—while generally retaining general equilibrium assumptions on prices, determined through a market clearing process. Dornbusch, Fisher and Samuelson (1977) present a two-country Ricardian model with a 'continuum' of commodities and the patterns of specialisation determined by relative wages and relative productivities. Wilson (1980) extends the model to many countries and non-homotetic demand schedules. Jones (1979) considers the conditions under which technical progress may produce 'immiserizing growth' for either of the trade partners.

A simple but illuminating picture of the technology–trade relationship emerges from Krugman's North–South trade model (1979a, 1982). Starting from an innovative North and a non-innovative South, where the North's innovations take the form only of new products produced immediately in the North, but only after a lag in the South, Krugman (1979a) shows how new industries have to emerge constantly in the North in order to maintain its living standards since the new industries decline and disappear sooner or later in the face of low-wage competition from the South. In Krugman's model, this is because the North's wages reflect the rent on the North's monopoly of new technology: 'This monopoly is continually eroded by technological borrowing and must be maintained by constant innovation of new products. Like Alice and the Red Queen, the developed region must keep running to stay in the same place' (Krugman, 1979a, p. 262). In other words, while the North will be able to achieve some 'moving equilibrium' through a large enough rate of innovation, acceleration of technology transfer will narrow the wage differentials between North and South and might even lead to an absolute decline in living standards in the North. The most interesting aspect of Krugman's model is, maybe paradoxically, the set of simplistic and, from a traditional trade point of view, totally 'unrealistic' assumptions behind the model: there are no differences in factor endowments, because there is only one factor of production (labour); and all goods, old and new, are produced with the same cost function, leaving no room for differences in labour productivity. Neither neo-classical nor Ricardian trade explanations are relevant, there is no fixed pattern of trade, but trade is determined by a continuing process of innovation in the North and technology transfer to the South. Yet despite these simplifications, some of the conclusions, which emerge from the model are very appealing, not least because, as Krugman observes: 'The picture of trade seems in some ways more like that of businessmen or economic historians than that of trade theorists' (Krugman, 1979a, p. 265).

It is obviously very difficult to provide a synthetic assessment of these quite heterogeneous streams of literature, characterised as they are by very different directions and degrees of 'revisionism'. Three general conclusions, however, may be drawn.

First, there is probably little disagreement, even among neo-classical trade theorists, about the inadequacy of the 'canonic' factor proportions theory to explain *by itself* international trade flows. As Krugman (1979c) puts it: '. . . casual observation seems to militate against a simple factor proportions theory. The emphasis on factor proportions in international trade is . . . not the result of an empirical judgement' (p. 14).

Second, most of the studies we reviewed implicitly highlight the lack of robustness of the major Heckscher–Ohlin–Samuelson results in terms of both predictions and welfare implications. Relaxation of the least realistic assumptions (i.e. perfect competition, constant returns to scale, factor immobility, immediate and free diffusion of technology, existence of well-behaved production functions) leads, generally speaking, to indeterminate predictions in relation to the direction and volume of trade. Moreover, the factor-price equalisation theorem does not generally follow. In terms of welfare implications, depending on which assumption is relaxed, conclusions on the 'gains from trade' are sometimes in accordance and sometimes at variance with the orthodox model.

Third, and from our perspective of more direct interest, quite interesting results sometimes emerge, *despite* the continuing presence of highly restrictive assumptions. This set of conclusions could prove to be even more important when placed in an alternative theoretical framework: for example, the role of technology gaps, country-specific absolute advantages and different forms of industrial organisation; the importance of economies of scale and various types of learning; the absence of any general tendency towards factor-price equalisation.

It was already mentioned at the beginning of this survey that a core assumption shared by most of the models reviewed so far is a *scarcity* link between factors, commodities and prices, irrespective of the particular hypotheses on technology, forms of competition, etc. In this sense, the contributions reviewed above share all the points of strength and weakness of general equilibrium analysis. The strength, in our view, relates to the capability of handling with a simple and general theoretical device the question of *interdependence* among national and international markets. Not surprisingly, the main question addressed by the standard Heckscher–Ohlin–Samuelson theory and by most of its 'revisionist' developments concerns the *patterns of specialisation* of each country in relation to some country-specific characteristics.

The other side of this coin is that such analyses, undertaken in terms of equilibrium positions, take as given that (i) there are adjustment mechanisms which generally lead to such equilibria, and (ii) that these mechanisms based on price/quantity adjustments—as in the standard Walrasian model—lead to the clearing of all markets. Both points are difficult to accept on either theoretical or empirical grounds. The difficulties in accounting for the adjustment processes in the standard general equilibrium framework when neither the fantastic 'auctioneer' nor a complete set of contingency markets exist (see Hahn, 1984; Leijohnuyfud, 1981) are well known and discussed at greater length in some of the other contributions to this volume. There is, however, no reason to believe that such adjustment processes are any easier in the open economy case.

On more empirical grounds, it is difficult to believe that relative prices are explained by relative scarcities in a world generally characterized by various forms of static and dynamic economies of scale, continuous technical progress, national economies often characterised by some degrees of unutilised labour or labour *and* capital.

The very formulation of the standard model in its 'timeless' form becomes even harder to accept whenever one of the factors of endowment—capital—is as such a set of reproducible (and heterogeneous) commodities. The question has been discussed in a 'capital controversy',[10] with many points in common with the famous 'Cambridge Debate' on capital theory, focusing on the problems ranging from the heterogeneity of capital goods[11] to the measurement of that 'aggregate capital' which must appear among the 'endowments'.[12]

Another feature common to practically all the models reviewed so far is the behavioural assumption concerning maximising agents.[13] Particularly with regard to technical change, this assumption becomes rather questionable. As argued at greater length elsewhere (Dosi, 1984) and following Nelson and Winter (1982), it is difficult to maintain that maximisation procedures are an adequate representation of the global behaviours of the agents whenever one properly accounts for the fundamental features of technical change (including uncertainty about choices and outcomes, patterns of search generally embodying tacit heuristics, various kinds of irreversibilities, etc.). It is not only or even primarily a matter of realism of assumptions. The fundamental point is that behaviours are directly relevant also in terms of the equilibrium positions towards which the system might tend to converge. In other words, even the 'static attractor' of the system may well be *path-dependent* and *behaviour-dependent* (cf. Nelson and Winter, 1982; Dosi and Orsenigo, 1985).

The less pure theory: the 'heretics'

The discussion so far has focused upon that stream of economic analysis concerned primarily with one theoretical question, namely *the determinants of specialisation*, and one functional mechanism, namely the adjustment processes induced in the latter by the *interdependences between markets*, both within each country and between countries. It is a line of enquiry which—despite the great differences in the assumptions on technology, demand, nature of the markets—links Ricardo, the neo-classical school and all those 'revisionist' contributions based on a general equilibrium framework. One of the fundamental premises of such a stream of thought is that trade (or the notional transition from autarky to trade) affects the inter-sectoral (and, sometimes, inter-national) allocation of inputs, quantities and prices, but *does not* affect the rate of utilisation of the stocks of inputs themselves (and thus the rates of macroeconomic activity).[14] This is straightforward in modern general equilibrium analysis where, as already discussed, full employment of all factors is assumed by hypothesis. It is equally true for that part of Ricardo's *Principles* concerned with international trade, based as it was on the assumption that

no extension of foreign trade will immediately increase the amount of value in a country, although it will very powerfully contribute to increase the mass of commodities, and therefore the sum of enjoyments. As the value of all foreign goods is measured by the quantity of the produce of our land and labour, which is given in exchange for them, we should have no greater value if, by the discovery of new markets, we obtained double the quantity of foreign goods in exchange of a given quantity of ours, [Ricardo, 1951, p. 128].

Since in Ricardo's model production techniques are given, the assumption concerning an unchanged 'amount of value in a country' is precisely equivalent to an assumption of constancy of the rates of macroeconomic activity throughout the notional transition from autarky to trade. In the history of economic thought, however, one can identify also another group of contributions, highly heterogeneous in scope and nature, seldom thoroughly formalised, heretic in spirit and often produced by outsiders to the dominant economic tradition. In this composite group one may include early economists from the eighteenth and nineteenth centuries, such as the

Reverend Tucker, Count Serra of Naples, Ferrier, List, Hamilton, as well as parts of the analysis of Adam Smith. In more recent times one finds an equally heterogeneous set of writers ranging from some technology-gaps and product-cycle authors (Posner, Freeman, Vernon, Hirsch) to Kaldor, Cornwall and Thirlwall, broadly in the post-Keynesian tradition; 'structuralist' writers in development economics, especially within the Latin American tradition; economic historians, such as Gerschenkron and Kuznets; some modern French writers such as Bye, de Bernis, Lafay and Mistral. Obviously, these contributions are highly different in nature and scope. However, one may state that they have in common, explicitly or implicitly, one or several of the following assumptions:

(i)   International differences in technological levels and innovative capabilities are a fundamental factor in explaining the differences in both levels and trends in export, imports and income of each country.

(ii) General equilibrium mechanisms of inter-national and inter-sectoral adjustment are relatively weak, so that trade has important effects upon the rates of macroeconomic activity of each economy. Putting it another way, the growth of each economy is often balance-of-payments-constrained and this constraint becomes tighter or looser according to the levels and composition of the participation of each country in world trade flows. The weakness of price/quantity adjustments between sectors and between countries has to do partly with the nature of technology (fixed coefficients, irreversibilities, etc.) and partly with the nature of demand (sticky baskets of consumption, etc.) As a result, what adjusts in the international arena is world market shares within each sector and, through that, the levels of macroeconomic activity generated by foreign demand.

(iii) That same weakness of general equilibrium adjustments is such that the intra-sectoral distribution of trade shares between countries and their evolution through time can be explained by a set of country-specific absolute advantages and without explicit reference, at least in a first approximation, to price/quantity adjustments between sectors and between factors' returns.

(iv) Technology is not a free good.

(v)   The allocative patterns induced by international trade have dynamic implications which may either yield 'virtuous' or 'perverse' feedbacks in the long term.

These assumptions have generally been stated in a rather confused way by the early writers, who did not share the rigour and depth of any Ricardo or Samuelson, and were often motivated simply by policy issues such as protection versus free trade. Nonetheless, they had precious if confused insights into complex problems of economic dynamics which were later neglected in the cleaner but more restrictive formalisations of modern trade theory. For example, Tucker (1774) (quoted also by Hufbauer, 1970) assumes that there is a macroeconomic link between technological advantages, international competitiveness and incomes, and discusses whether the product-cycle effects induced by the lower wages of the 'poor country' will eventually reverse the competitive position of the 'rich' *vis-à-vis* the 'poor'. His answer is reassuring for England: continuous technical progress, higher capabilities of accumulation and institutional factors will keep an absolute advantage there, despite the lower wages of the more backward countries. Ferrier (1805) deals with the relationships between trade and rates of macroeconomic activity in the light of the historical experience of the Continental Blockade, arguing that there is a direct negative link between import penetration and employment levels in the relatively backward country due to a generalised technological disadvantage and to the long term effects that de-specialisation in the most advanced products (in that case, manufactures) exerts upon the capability of progress and accumulation: '. . . I compare a nation which with its money buys abroad commodities it can make itself, although of a poorer quality, with a gardner who, dissatisfied with the fruits he gathers, would buy juicier fruits from his neighbours, giving them his gardening tools in exchange'. (Ferrier, 1805, p. 288).

Interestingly, Adam Smith was equally aware of the dynamic implications of trade and his position appears almost symmetrical to Ferrier's, from the 'advanced country' point of view. First, he argues, trade has a beneficial effect upon the rates of macroeconomic activities and employment because, in contemporary words, exports increase aggregate demand. This is close to what Myint (1958) later defined as a 'vent-for-surplus' model of trade. Second, the enlargement of the market due to international trade feeds back upon the domestic division of labour and thus on the trends in productive efficiency.

The argument of List (1904), German and nationalist, is directly against Ricardo and Say. The practical matter at stake, as known, was the political advocacy of protectionism and industrialisation. In List's view, there is nothing in the adjustment mechanisms on the international market (in List's terminology, the adjustments 'based on the theory of exchange values') which guarantees dynamic convergence between nations in terms of productive capabilities and incomes (the 'growth of productive forces of a Nation'). In several respects, this view involves much more than an 'infant industry argument', the idea being that the long-term position of each country depends jointly on its degrees of capital accumulation, its global technical and learning capabilities,[15] and a set of institutional factors (social consensus, factory discipline, political conditions). According to List, the adjustment processes set in motion by international trade might well be detrimental to the development of these aspects of the 'national productive forces'. Putting it in modern words, static and dynamic economies of scale and differing income elasticities of the various commodities will lead under free-trade conditions to divergence rather than factor-price equalisation, and to growth polarisation with the concentration of production in one country rather than welfare gains for both partners. In a similar perspective, these points have been emphasised in much of the early development/trade/dependency literature (cf. Prebisch, 1950), and in the historical analysis of the early industrialisation/opening of trade process in the United Kingdom.

More recently and along the lines suggested by Kaldor (1970, 1975, 1980), Thirlwall and Vines (1983) have formalised such views in a multi-sector North–South model and have studied the 'consistency conditions' between the two countries and the various sectors. The Kaldor–Thirl-wall–Vines approach, while incorporating some ideas similar to earlier 'two-gap' models of development—whereby the growth of the industrialis-ing countries is shown to be constrained by either saving/investment capacity or by the foreign exchange requirements[16]—embodies a general hypothesis that world growth is determined by 'asymmetrical' patterns of change in technical coefficients and demand composition. In this view, processes of inter-factoral and inter-commodity substitution in response to relative prices and excess factor supplies are of minor importance. What adjusts is the level of sectoral and macroeconomic activity.

An ambitious multi-sector model along similar lines is that of Pasinetti (1981), whose open-economy version determines the relative rates of growth between economies in terms of evolution of relative productivities and income elasticities of the commodities each country produces.

In all these models the difference in the income elasticity of the various commodities plays a fundamental role and is assumed to dominate upon the price/quantity adjustments in consumption baskets. Thus, as Thirlwall (1980) shows, the income elasticities enter into the determination of the foreign-trade multiplier of each economy (via import propensities and export elasticities to world income). The other factor is obviously techno-logy. 'Polarisation' in innovativeness is shown to imply 'polarisation' in growth.

Interestingly, while both the Ricardian and neo-classical perspectives focus upon the determinants of the *patterns of specialisation*, the set of contributions reviewed above focuses on the relationship between trade, levels of activity and growth. In terms of adjustment mechanisms, both Ricardo and the neo-classical school hold the rates of activity constant and study trade-induced changes in relative prices and relative quantities; conversely, the 'heretic' stream often assumes away price/quantity adjust-ments and studies the link between trade and rates of activity in both the short and long term.

In order to highlight these differences, one may represent the early heretic model as follows. Imagine two countries, Portugal and England, producing two commodities, (wine and cloth) with only one production factor: labour. Suppose that, at the beginning, the two countries are absolutely identical: the same technical coefficients, same relative prices, same patterns of consumption, same absolute prices as expressed in their respective currencies whose exchange rate is equal to one. Suppose also the existence of a non-reproducible asset, say, gold, or alternatively

tradable shares representing titles of ownership over the productive activities. Finally, suppose that each economy has some surplus labour which
can be mobilised without any extra cost whenever required. Clearly, the
two countries, even if opened to the international markets, will not trade.
Assume now an across-the-board improvement in the Portuguese technical
coefficients which leaves *unchanged relative* productivities and *relative*
prices. In the perspective of both Ricardo and the neo-classicals still no
trade will occur. As Findlay puts it, '. . . greater technological efficiency
cannot be the cause of trade if the relative difference is the same in both
goods' (Findlay, 1973, p. 57).

On the contrary, in what could be called a Smith–Ferrier–List model of
trade a *one-way* trade will occur with Portugal progressively gaining
market shares on the English market in *both* wine and cloth. Correspondingly, gold or ownership titles will move from England to Portugal. The
rates of macroeconomic activity will grow in Portugal and fall in England.
The adjustment process to the Portuguese technological advance will not
stop until the exchange rate will have entirely adjusted to the new purchasing power parity determined by the new levels of productivities in
Portugal as compared to English ones. It is easy to define the dynamic
counterpart of the model. Imagine a *continuous* flow of technical improvements in Portugal. One will observe a continuously increasing market
penetration of Portugal on the English markets. The adjustment process
takes essentially three forms.

First, the English currency continues to devaluate. Second, gold or
ownership titles continue to flow out of England. Third, the rates of
activity in Portugal continue to grow and the English ones to fall. Notably,
the increasing technological gap is reflected in the changing world market
share in *each* commodity, even if no international specialisation occurs.
One could broaden the model, for example, by introducing a third commodity, whisky, which only England can produce due to some natural
advantage. Then, under the above assumptions, England will slowly
converge toward an absolute specialisation in whisky while her short-term
rate of activity and her long-term growth will depend upon the levels and
changes in the Portuguese propensity to drink whisky as compared with the
English propensity to drink wine and wear clothes.

Needless to say, such a model embodies gross over-simplifications.
However, it illustrates probably better the evidence on the free-trade
adjustment processes following major technological polarisations than the
Ricardian alternative. This is precisely what continental writers from the
early nineteenth century had in mind: given the European backwardness
vis-à-vis England, *laisser-faire* regimes would not have yielded mutual
gains from trade, but rather would have reduced Europe to a condition
more similar to India.

A major factor counteracting this link between polarisation in technology and in income levels is, of course, the international diffusion of
technology. Indeed, most modern technology-gap models focus on the

crucial time element between innovation and imitation abroad as the trade and income-polarising 'reversal' factor.

The basic assumption of modern technology-gap trade accounts is that technology is not a freely, instantaneously and universally available good, but that there are substantial advantages in being first. Thus in Posner's seminal model it is suggested that while technical changes and developments may influence some industries and not others, it is the technical change originating in one country and not in others which will induce trade 'during the lapse of time taken for the rest of the world to imitate one country's innovation' (Posner, 1961, p. 323).

A similar point is made in Freeman's case study of the plastic industry: 'Technical progress results in leadership in production in this industry, because patents and commerical secrecy together can give the innovator a head start of as much as 10–15 years' (Freeman, 1963, p. 22). Once imitation has taken place, more traditional factors of adjustment and specialisation would again take over and determine trade flows. In Hufbauer's words: 'Technology gap trade is . . . the impermanent commerce which initially arises from the exporting nation's industrial breakthrough and which is prolonged by static and dynamic scale economies flowing from the breakthrough' (Hufbauer, 1966, p. 23). There is, of course, nothing necessarily 'impermanent' about these static and dynamic scale economies. Coupled with new or improved product innovations they might well lead to a more or less continuous trade flow.

Product life-cycle theories (Hirsch, 1965; Vernon, 1966) provide an articulated trade picture along similar lines. They also integrate foreign direct investment and view technology as part of a wider set of market structure factors, including entry, product differentiation/standardisation, nature of demand. Vernon's original model is primarily demand-determined: high levels of income and sophisticated demand patterns induce innovative responses of domestic firms. More recently, the introduction of supply factors has dealt with some of the weaknesses of the original model (for a critical assessment see, Walker, 1979). The contributions here relate primarily to theories of innovation and can be seen as an extension of post-Schumpeterian 'evolutionary' models (see Nelson and Winter, 1982; Dosi, 1984) to the international field, where the emphasis is on the dynamic/biological nature of international competition.[17]

Another recent direction of investigation relates to the importance given to the import and export of technology in shaping a country's future trade pattern. It opens the way to a further integration of foreign investment theories (cf. Buckley and Casson, 1976, 1981, Dunning, 1981), technology transfer and catching-up models (cf. Cornwall, 1977; Gomulka, 1971, 1978; Kotzumi and Kopecky, 1980), and dynamic diffusion models (see Nelson, 1968; Nelson, Winter and Schuette, 1976; Nelson and Winter, 1982; Metcalfe and Soete, 1984) within a theoretical trade framework.

The empirical evidence

The picture which emerges out of the innumerable number of empirical trade studies is, as one might expect, far from uniform. Moreover, the correspondence between theoretical models and empirical tests is generally poor. As Deardorff notes in his thorough review of trade studies,

Empirical tests of the theories are often faulted on the grounds that they test propositions that do not derive rigorously from the theories. The reason is not usually that empirical models are sloppy. Rather, the problem seems to lie in the theories themselves, which are seldom stated in forms that are compatible with the real world complexities that empirical research cannot escape. [Deardorff, 1984, p. 468]

We will organise our review of an even more selected literature with reference to the same themes and approaches discussed above.

A major stream of research, not surprisingly, has been concerned with the explanation of the so-called 'Leontief paradox' within a by and large, orthodox factor-proportions framework. As is well known, Leontief (1953) found that the composition of trade of the United States, clearly a capital-abundant country, was biased in favour of labour-intensive exports and capital-intensive imports. While the typical research strategy in the theoretical field was simply to neglect the potentially disruptive implication of such a falsification of the theory, the empirical strategy focused upon additional variables which could explain away the 'paradox'. This has been one of the analytical procedures which has drawn attention toward technology-related variables, typically labour skills and what has become known as 'human capital'. Many empirical studies, primarily concerned with the US case, found these latter variables to be significantly correlated with the American composition of trade (see, amongst others, Keesing, 1965, 1967; Baldwin, 1971; Harkness and Kyle 1975; Branson and Monoyios, 1977; Stern and Maskus, 1981). Moreover, Leamer (1980) has argued that a proper test of the Heckscher–Ohlin model must not be based on the factor content of trade but on the relative factor intensity of production as compared to consumption. Using this criterion, Stern and Maskus (1981) found that the Leontief 'paradox' did hold for 1958 but not for 1947 or 1971. These empirical findings and refinements seem, at first sight, comforting to the prevailing theory in its generalised version, including a 'technology-production' factor and extending the concept of capital not only to human capital but also to 'intellectual capital', defined as the 'capitalised value of productive knowledge created by research and development' (Johnson, 1970, p. 14). However, one must have severe reservations about these 'revisionist' attempts to accommodate the evidence with a traditional factor-proportion view of trade flows.

First, with regard to the conclusions based on Leamer's methodological suggestions, the results are far from 'non-paradoxical' and depend crucially on the chosen years. They therefore appear not particularly robust.

Second, as argued by Deardorff, the 'acknowledgement of additional factors of production cannot in theory explain Leontief's paradoxical results regarding capital and labour' (Deardorff, 1984, p. 481)

Third, the higher the distance of the underlying model from the original labour/land framework, the lower appears the plausibility of the basic assumptions. As already discussed in the previous section, one can hardly consider 'capital' as an endowment whenever it is actually produced under conditions of non-decreasing returns. It is even harder to define R & D as an endowment, for its 'size' depends on highly discretionary decisions of firms and public institutions.

Fourth, proper 'tests' of the Heckscher–Ohlin model must be based on direct *plus* indirect factor contents. As discussed at length by Momigliano and Siniscalco (1984), this correct procedure has been followed only by a few studies.[19] The majority of them simply consider direct product characteristics. This methodological difference matters. Thus Italy's trade performance is *negatively* correlated with the direct R & D content of each commodity but is *positively* correlated with the total content (direct plus indirect, via input/output flows) (see Momigliano and Siniscalco, 1984).

Finally, there is the question whether empirical analyses of trade flows can be usefully carried out at the level of intra-country, inter-sectoral studies only. This methodological issue has been raised at a general level by Leamer (1974) and Leamer and Bowen (1981). The problem stems from different technology-specific characteristics which are likely to influence trade flows and can be accounted for only in inter-country, intra -sectoral analysis.

Given all these methodological problems and caveats, it is fair to conclude that most of the empirical studies based on cross-sectoral analyses relating trade flows (either measures of comparative advantages or net exports) to a menu of product characteristics, while useful in presenting the possible *regularities* in the structural features of domestic supply and their statistical correlation with the patterns of competitiveness, are far from useful in highlighting any causal mechanism *explaining* international competitiveness and specialisation.[20]

The empirical validity of the endowment-based theory of trade remains therefore very much subject to debate.[21] As Hufbauer puts it,

Leontief's findings dealt an apparently telling blow to the simplistic two-factor version. Various authorities have sought to repair the damage; their work in some respects resembles the tortured efforts of pre-Copernican astronomers. [Hufbauer, 1970, pp. 267–8]

A different line of empirical enquiry has been concerned with the patterns of relative inter-sectoral specialisations based on a simple Ricardian framework. MacDougall (1951–52) showed that the sectoral ratio of US to UK exports was well correlated with relative American and British labour productivities. These results, confirmed by Stern (1962) and Balassa (1963), do not, however, explain the *sources* of inter-sectoral differences in productivity and—as has been argued—could be consistent also with a Heckscher–Ohlin model of trade.[22] On the other hand, they could also highlight the mechanisms leading to comparative advantages on the ground of sector-specific gaps or leads in technolgy.

Empirical studies using the technology-gap trade framework or product life-cycle theory, on the other hand, emphasise in the first instance the inter-country differences in innovativeness as the basis of international trade flows. Rather than inter-industry variations in the technological 'endowment' of a specific country, it is the variation across countries in innovativeness within each sector which seems crucial (see, among others, Freeman, 1963, 1965; Hirsch, 1965; Hufbauer, 1966; Tilton, 1971; Dosi, 1984). Most sectoral studies (e.g. on chemicals, plastics, process plants, electronics products, semiconductors; see the authors just mentioned) high-light the dynamic relationship between early innovative leads, economies of scale, learning by doing, oligopolistic exploitation of these advantages, and international competitiveness. As referred to in the introduction, one of the most ambitious attempts of inter-country and inter-sectoral compari-son of technology-based and product-cycle-based models as compared to the other explanations of trade flows was carried out by Hufbauer (1970).

Hufbauer found that the commodity characteristics by country were related to a set of country characteristics including variables related to technology, economies of scale, product differentiation and patterns of domestic demand. Whereas some of the proxies used implied high levels of 'heroism', they pointed to the widespread existence of country-specific advantages/disadvantages related to technological innovation, national 'context' conditions and forms of corporate behaviour different from 'pure competition'.

Similarly, the findings by Gruber and Vernon (1970), while broadly in line with the Leontief 'paradox', highlighted the homogeneity in the structure of exports (and production) among the major industrial countries and their general correlation with per capita GDP. Walker (1979) critically analysed the sectoral evidence on product-cycle patterns of production and exports, finding that there are groups of products which do conform with the prediction of a shift from advanced to intermediate and backward low-wage countries, while other groups appear more in line with straight-forward technology-gap theories, whereby the advantage remains over long periods in the most innovative country(ies).

Irrespective of whether the analysis deals with intra-country, inter-sectoral comparisons or inter-national, inter-sectoral ones, an important methodological issue concerns the proxies used for the technology vari-able.[23] With the exception of Davidson (1979), Pavitt and Soete (1980), and Soete (1980, 1981), most empirical studies use technology *input* proxies, such as R & D expenditure or R & D employment. Yet the exact relationship between technology input and technology output remains unclear. Most technology-gap models, however, by emphasising the crucial role of new products and process innovations, make explicit the need for using a technology output proxy instead of an input proxy in explaining international trade flows.

Some interpretative suggestions

As we have discussed at greater length elsewhere (Dosi, Pavitt and Soete, 1988), the empirical evidence on the composition and dynamics of trade flows can be interpreted within what we consider to be a more satisfactory interpretative framework based on wide–spread technological gaps among countries, generally non-clearing markets, 'Keynesian–Kaldorian' links between international competitiveness and macro-economic rates of domestic activity. We also tried there to account for a few 'stylized facts' on which this interpretation is based.

First, the international distribution of innovative efforts and innovative results is far from homogeneous, even with the OECD countries, The 'club of the innovators' comprises not much more than a dozen countries, has been relatively stable in its membership for almost a century—with only one major entry (Japan), and shows interesting patterns of evolution in the internal ranking of countries (e.g. Germany and the USA overtaking England at the turn of the century as the major source of innovations, a very quick catching–up process by Japan and to a lesser extent some European countries, such as Italy after the second world war).

Second, these differences in innovative capabilities correspond to equally wide differences in labour productivities. Remarkably, as much as one can infer from imperfect statistical evidence, these differences do not correlate with analogous differences in capital/output ratios. That is, differences in the 'production functions' rather than differences in 'endowments' appear to be the fundamental feature of the international system of production.

Third, cross-sectoral analysis shows a high sectoral specificity in the opportunities and propensities to innovate and patterns of inter-sectoral distribution of one country's innovative strength and weakness which defy traditional explanations (e.g. why is Switzerland strong in pharmaceuticals and Sweden in mechanical engineering?).

Fourth, as regards trade flows, one obviously observes long term changes in the patterns of national 'revealed comparative advantages' but these changes are often inter–linked with country-wide changes in world market shares which often occur in all (or most) sectors, although at different rates (e.g. the British generalised decline or the Japanese rise).

It is against this background of stylised facts that we have started constructing an alternative model of technology and trade.

Technology, we argue in line with several other chapters in this book, cannot be reduced to freely available information or to a set of 'blueprints': on the contrary, each 'technological paradigm' with its forms of specific knowledge yields relatively ordered cumulative and irreversible patterns of technical change, which are also *country–specific*.

A fundamental implication of such an analysis of technical change is also a theory of production whereby different ('better' and 'worse') techniques, products and firms co–exist at any point in time.

Thus, the main mechanisms of change over time are evolutionary processes of innovation and diffusion of unequivocally better techniques and products. This interpretation, partly modelled elsewhere (Dosi, Pavitt, and Soete, 1988) can account for the continuous existence of technology gaps between firms and between countries and for the conditions of *convergence* or *divergence* in inter-firm and inter–national technological capabilities, according to the degrees of opportunity, cumulativeness and appropriability that each technology presents.

In this view, the degrees of innovativeness of each country in any one particular technology are explained—as regards their origin—through the inter–play between (i) science-related opportunities, (ii) country–specific and technology-specific institutions which foster/hinder the emergence of new technological paradigms, and, (iii) the nature and intensity of economic stimuli, which stem from abundance of particular inputs, or, alternatively, critical scarcities of inputs, specific patterns of demand and levels and changes in relative prices. In this sense, the interpretation suggested here accounts for the taxonomic evidence presented by the particular theories of 'market–induced' innovations (e.g. product-cycles, demand-pull, relative-price inducements) and incorporates them in what we believe to be a more general view of the innovative process: certainly there is a wide variety of economic inducements to innovation, but these belong to the necessary although not sufficient conditions. Sufficiency is provided by the degrees of matching/mismatching between these generic market opportunities and the institutional conditions related to the scientific/technological capabilities available in each country, the 'bridging institutions' between pure science and economic applications, the expertise embodied in the firms, the patterns of organisation of the major markets, the nature and impact of public policies.

Over time, capital accumulation and technological accumulation are inter-linked so that irreversible improvements in input efficiencies and search/learning processes feed back on each other. In some respects, our analysis overlaps with the question concerning 'why growth rates differ' (cf. the next chapter by Fagerberg). However, our interpretation is the polar opposite to the traditional one (but consistent with Fagerberg's): instead of explaining differences between countries in terms of differential endowments, we argue that the fundamental inter-national differences relate to the country-specific conditions of technological learning and accumulation.

The model of trade, only briefly hinted at here, takes these regularities as its starting point, and is based on the general existence of technological differences—that is: differences in input efficiencies, in product qualities and in performance—between countries. These gaps, we argue, are the equivalent of the Smithian/Ricardian 'absolute advantages' and determine two fundamental processes of adjustment between and within countries.

First, inter–sectoral intra–national differences in technology gaps/leads yield a tendency toward relative specialisations in the sectors of 'comparative advantages'. This is the familiar mechanism of adjustment described in the Ricardaian and, under different assumptions, neo-classical literature.

Second, and at least as important, intra–sectoral gaps/leads between countries yield adjustments in world market shares, as suggested by some of the 'heretic' contributions reviewed above. This adjustment process relates to the notion of 'absolute' or 'structural' competitiveness of each country. It is an 'absolute' notion in the sense that it does not relate to any inter-sectoral comparison ('I am relatively better in this or that'), although it is obviously relative to other countries ('I am better or worse than country B or C').

The link between absolute advantages/disadvantages and world market shares (or per capita exports), within each sector and for each country as a whole is empirically quite robust: in previous tests (Soete, 1981, Dosi and Soete, 1983), different degrees of innovativeness and differential productive efficiency perform as a good predictor of the inter–national distribution of export flows in more than three quarters of the forty industrial sectors that we considered, despite the admittedly imperfect nature of our statistical proxies.

Moreover, country-wide changes in innovativeness and input efficiencies are a significant part of the explanation of the long term changes in national export shares in the world markets.

In our interpretation and in line with the arguments advanced by Pasinetti (1981), comparative advantages are obtained only as a by-product of both intra-national inter-sectoral changes in inputs allocations and changes in the absolute amount of inputs each economy employs to produce for changing shares in the world market. That is, from a dynamic perspective, revealed comparative advantages appear to be the *ex post* result of sector-specific and country-specific learning dynamics, and of the related inter-national intra-sectoral changes in competitiveness of firms and countries.

This analysis can easily be linked with a 'Keynesian' view of the determination of the rates of macroeconomic activity of each economy. Unlike neo-classical trade analyses—which impose market-clearing in the model—and unlike also Ricardian trade models—which, in order to identify equilibrium specialisations, generally assume steady-state growth, our interpretation requires changes in the levels of macroeconomic activity of each economy in response to changes in international competitiveness (i.e. relative changes in innovativeness, input efficiency, organisational competence of domestic firms, etc). Thus, the link between absolute advantages/disadvantages and world market share (or per capita exports) is theoretically consistent with a determination of domestic aggregate demand via the foreign trade multiplier.

Elsewhere (Dosi, Pavitt and Soete, 1988), with the help of a simple formal model, we show that international gaps in technology define the boundaries of both 'Ricardian' processes of adjustments in specialisations and 'Keynesian' adjustments in the rates of macroeconomic activity. From a dynamic point of view, it is the evolution in the innovative/imitative capabilities of each country which shapes the trends in the relative and absolute rates of growth of the *tradeable* sector of each economy.

These theoretical propositions are broadly consistent with the empirical evidence reported and presented in Pavitt and Soete (1981) and in the next chapter Fagerberg: the links between innovativeness and macroeconomic growth, in cross-country analyses over the past eighty years, appear to be rather strong, although the precise forms of that relationship depend on each particular phase of development (i.e. each particular 'regime of international growth', as hinted in Boyer's chapter).

Conclusions

There are as will be obvious from the review section still major gaps in our understanding of the role of innovation in international trade. One is only beginning to analyze (i) the determinants of different national capabilities to innovate, imitate, and, generally exploit competitively the innovative efforts: (ii) the nature and relative importance of the various adjustment mechanisms within and between countries following such innovative processes; (iii) the relationship between sector-specific patterns of competitiveness and 'general equilibrium' factors, in the broader sense, linked to relative prices, inter-sectoral capital and labour mobility, etc; (iv) the implications of economies of scale, dynamic increasing returns (see in particular Arthur's chapter in this book), oligopolistic forms of market organisation, international investment and all the factors which generally go under the heading of 'imperfect competition'; (v) the long-term relationship between innovation, trade and growth. All these issues are as much in need of empirical research.

Our own approach as sketched out above, can be summarized by the following propositions: *First*, the 'microfoundations' of international trade analysis, consistent with the available evidence, should be found in the extension of an 'evolutionary' interpretation to the international arena. *Second*, in such evolutionary dynamics, what appears to be, *ex post*, a 'comparative advantage' is in no proper sense the result of any 'endowment' but the outcome of processes of learning—innovation, imitation, organisational change—which have both sector and country specificities. *Third*, the innovative process, by allowing various sorts of (static and dynamic) increasing returns generally entails also forms of market interactions different from perfect competition. *Fourth*, these same properties of technical change imply the possibility of those *irreversible processes* discussed in Arthur's chapter, and, thus, also, from a normative point of view, the possibility of 'virtuous' or 'vicious' circles in innovativeness, competitiveness and growth. *Fifth*, the *micro*-economic and sectoral levels and changes in international competitiveness, determined under conditions of continuous technological learning and limited short-term substitution in both production and consumption, appear also to represent the micro-foundations of many *macro*-economic analyses, in particular those with some 'Keynesian' ascendancy whereby economic systems seldom hit any powerful scarcity constraint, but are limited in their growth by aggregate demand and foreign balance requirements.

The largest part of the theoretical analysis of these processes is still to be done. However, we would argue that these contain some of the most promising links between the evidence on trade flows and patterns and the interpretations of innovation, industrial evolution and patterns of growth discussed in the other chapters of this book.

Notes

1. Extensive reviews of the trade literature can be found in Bhagwati (1964), Chipman (1965/66), Stern (1975), and Jones and Kenen (1984), and more specifically on the issues related to technology and international trade, in Hufbauer (1966, 1970), Chesnais and Michon-Savarit (1980), Aho and Rosen (1980), Dosi and Soete (1983), Soete (1985) and Lyons (1986).
2. That is the Heckscher–Ohlin theorem, stating that the relative specialisation of each country is in those commodities which use intensively those factors which are relatively abundant in that same country.
3. Such as, for example, the analytical treatment of those cases with more commodities than factors, etc.
4. Of course this is necessarily so if the economies of scale are internal to each firm.
5. For a thorough review, see Helpman (1984). An interesting collection of some of the 'state-of-the-art' contributors in the field is in Kierzkowski (1984).
6. For 'imperfect competition' models see, among others, Markusen (1980), Lancaster (1980), Helpman (1981). Helpman and Razin (1980), Melvin and Warne (1973). The implications of economies of scale in a neo-classical, open-economy growth model are analysed in Krugman (1984). For an overview see Helpman and Krugman (1985).
7. This line of enquiry is in many ways an attempt at a synthesis between the Heckscher–Ohlin–Samuelson model and Linder's model (cf. Linder, 1961). For a model accounting also for multinational investment, see Helpman (1984).
8. cf. the special issue of *The Journal of Industrial Economies* edited by Caves (1980), Brander (1981), Jacquemin (1982), Brander and Krugman (1983), Dosi (1984), Momigliano and Dosi (1983), Caves, Porter and Spence (1980).
9. That is, a general equilibrium model with sector-specific and inter-sectoral immobile factors (see Jones and Neary, 1984).
10. On this issue, see, for a 'Cambridge view', Steedman (1979, 1980), Metcalfe and Steedman (1981), and the replies by Ethier (1981) and Dixit (1981).
11. Interestingly, the standard neo-classical way out of the difficulties with regard to capital measurement has been, in the closed economy case, through general equilibrium models of Walrasian ascendancy. This possibility is generally

precluded in the field of international trade, since the specification of a long vector of 'endowments' implies nearly tautological conclusions. It is of little interest, as Corden puts it crudely, to have a 'theory' which says 'that Switzerland has a comparative advantage in watches because she is watchmaker-intensive or that the United States export 747s because she is intensive in firms or engineers capable of making 747s' (Corden, 1979, p. 9.). In trade-related capital theory the standard procedure is simply to assume that the measurement problem does not exist *ex hypothesi*: 'Suppose that . . . the common technology has no factor-intensity reversal . . .' (Ethier, 1981, p. 274).

12. This is not the place to discuss these issues. Suffice to make one remark. With time and reproducibility of capital (in the form of machines, etc.), the 'dynamic' equivalent of the timeless Heckscher–Ohlin–Samuelson model becomes one where the 'scarcity constraints' are the rate of growth of the labour supply and the saving rate. This strictly pre-Keynesian view of the growth process raises many questions: how does one account for all periods and countries in modern history characterised by structural unemployment of one kind or another? Do 'scarcity constraints' functionally define the system even in the presence of continuous technical progress and widespread economies of scale? Where is there proof that it is the rate of saving which determines the rate of investment and not vice versa such as in the Keynesian–Kaleckian view? Where is the evidence that countries characterised by higher saving propensities also present higher capital 'endowments' and relatively capital-intensive exports?

13. This is equally true for the models of 'pure' competition as well as those based on imperfect competition or oligopolistic strategic interaction.

14. Obviously, this assumption is necessary to base the analysis on unit functions, indifference curves, isoquants, etc.

15. For a reappraisal of List's view on the importance of the national techno-scientific system, cf. Freeman (1987).

16. See Chenery and Bruno (1962), Chenery and Strout (1966), Findlay (1973). For a thorough critical analysis of the debate on North–South differences, terms of trade, development, see Bacha (1978). A review of the trade/development literature, cf. Findlay (1984).

17. See Klein (1977, 1978). Klein's work focuses on individual firm behaviours in relation to industrial innovation. For an overview of this line of enquiry, see Graham (1979).

18. Some scattered and less convincing evidence exists also for Sweden (Bergstrom-Balkestahl, 1979) and Canada (Hanel, 1976). Thorough reviews can be found in Deardorff (1984) and Onida (1984).

19. To our knowledge, since Leontief (1953, 1956), the total factor contents has been used only by Carlsson and Ohlsson (1976).

20. One can interpret in this way also the results of those studies which include among the 'independent' variables a lot of factors of which only few can be derived by a standard factor-proportion model; cf. for example, Wells (1969), Moral (1972), Finger (1975b).

21. Romney Robinson: '. . . in models which demand that all phenomena be subsumed either under production functions or under factor availability, it means that there is nothing left on the supply side but factor proportions to account for price differences. Yet if different production functions were admitted, then the theory, confronted with evidence of trade contrary to that

indicated by factor supplies, could always take refuge in the plea: 'different production functions'. But that would reduce it to a banality. *Any* pattern of trade could be explained in such terms' (Robinson, 1968, p. 6–7).

22. See Falvey (1981) and Deardorff (1984). Bhagwati (1964) challenged the theoretical foundations of these 'Ricardian' tests. The critique is somewhat surprising in the light of the relatively little amount of *ad hoc* assumptions required to derive the tests from the theory, especially as compared to those necessary to the factor-proportion models.

References

Aho, C.M. and Rosen, H.F. (1980), 'Trends in technology-intensive trade: with special reference to US competitiveness', Office of Foreign Economic Research, Bureau of International Labor Affairs, US Department of Labour, mimeo.

Atkinson, A. and Stiglitz, J. (1969), 'A new view of technological change', *Economic Journal*, vol. 79, pp. 573–78.

Bacha, E. (1978), 'An interpretation of unequal exchange from Prebish-Singer to Emmanuel', *Journal of Development Economics*, vol. 5, pp. 319–38.

Balassa, B. (1963), 'An empirical demonstration of classical comparative cost theory', *Review of Economics and Statistics*, vol. 45, pp. 231–8.

Baldwin, R.E. (1971), 'Determinants of the commodity structure of US trade', *American Economic Review*, vol. 61, pp. 126–46.

Barker, T. (1977), 'International trade and economic growth: an alternative to the neo-classical approach', *Cambridge Journal of Economics*, vol. 1, pp. 153–72.

Berglas, E. and Jones, R.W. (1977), 'The export of technology', in K. Brunner and A. Meltzer (eds.), *Optimal Policies, Control Theory and Technology Exports*, Carnegie-Rochester Conference on Public Policy.

Berstrom-Balkestahl, B. (1979), 'Efforts on R & D indicators in Sweden, second workshop on the measurement of R & D output', OECD, Paris, 5th and 6th December 1979, mimeo.

Bhagwati, J.N. (1964), 'The pure theory of international trade: a survey', *Economic Journal*, vol. 74, pp. 1–84.

Bhagwati, J. N. (1970), 'Comment' in R. Vernon (ed.), *The Technology Factor in International Trade*, New York, Columbia University Press.

Bodenhofer, H.J. (1976), 'Technischer Fortschrift, Forschung und Entwicklung und Internationaler Handel, der Fall der Bundesrepublik Deutschland', *Jahrbucher für Nationalekonomie und Statistik*, vol. 190, pp. 151–79.

Brander, J.A. (1981), 'Intra-industry trade in identical commodities', *The Journal of International Economics*, vol. 11, pp. 1–14.

Brander, J.A. and Krugman, P.R. (1983), 'Reciprocal dumping model of international trade', *The Journal of International Economics*, vol. 13, pp. 313–21.

Branson, W. and Monoyois, N. (1977), 'Factor inputs in US trade', *The Journal of International Economics*, vol. 7, pp. 111–31.

Buckley, P. and Casson, M. (1976), *The Future of the Multinational Enterprise*, London, Macmillan.

Buckley, P. and Casson, M. (1981), 'The optimal timing of a foreign direct investment', *The Economic Journal*, vol. 91, pp. 75–87.

Carlsson, B. and Ohlsson, L. (1976), 'Structural determinants of Swedish foreign trade', *European Economic Review*, vol. 7, pp. 165–74.

Caves, R.E. (1971), 'International corporations: the industrial economics of foreign investment', *Economica*, vol. 38, February 1971, pp. 1–27.

Caves, R.E. (1974), 'International trade, international investment and imperfect markets', Special papers in International Economic No 10, International Finance Section, Princeton University.

Caves, R.E. (1980), 'International trade and industrial organisation: introduction', *The Journal of Industrial Economics*, vol. 29, pp. 113–19.

Chenery, H.B. and Bruno, M. (1962), 'Development alternatives in an open economy: the case of Israel', *The Economic Journal*, vol. 72, pp. 79–103.

Chenery, H.B. and Strout, A. (1966), 'Foreign assistance and economic development', *American Economic Review*, vol. 56, pp. 679–733.

Chesnais, F. and Michon-Savarit, C. (1980), 'Some observations on alternative approaches to the analyses of international competitiveness and the role of the technology factor', Science and Technology Indicators Conference, OECD, Paris, 15–19 September 1980, mimeo.

Chipman, J.S. (1965–66), 'A survey of the theory of international trade', *Econometrica*, vol. 33, pp. 447–519, vol. 33, pp. 685–760, vol. 34, pp. 18–76.

Chipman, J.S. (1970), 'Induced technical change and patterns of international trade', in Vernon (ed.) *The Technology Factor in International Trade*, New York, Columbia University Press.

Corden, W. (1979), 'Intra-industry trade and factor proportions theory' in H. Giersch (ed.), *On the Economics of Intra-industry Trade*, Tubingen, J C B Mohr.

Cornwall, J. (1977), *Modern Capitalism: Its Growth and Transformation*, London, Martin Robertson.

Davidson, W. (1979), 'Factor endowment, innovation and international trade theory', *Kyklos*, vol. 32, pp. 764–774.

Deardorff, A.V. (1984), 'Testing trade theories and predicting trade flows', in R.W. Jones and P.B. Kenen (eds.), *Handbook of International Economics*, Amsterdam, Elsevier-North-Holland.

Dixit, A. (1981), 'The export of capital theory', *The Journal of International Economics*, vol. 11, pp. 279–94.

Dixit, A. and Norman, V. (1980), *The Theory of International Trade*, Cambridge, Cambridge University Press.

Dixit, A. and Stiglitz, J.E. (1977), 'Monopolistic competition and optimum product diversity', *American Economic Review*, vol. 67, pp. 297–308.

Dornbusch, R., Fisher, S. and Samuelson, P.A. (1977), 'Comparative advantage, trade and payments in a Ricardian model with a continuum of goods', *American Economic Review*.

Dosi, G. (1984), *Technical Change and Industrial Transformation*, London, Macmillan.

Dosi, G. and Soete, L. (1983), 'Technology gaps and cost-based adjustments: some explorations on the determinants of international competitiveness', *Metroeconomica*, vol. 35, pp. 197–222.

Dosi, G. and Orsenigo, L. (1985), 'Market processes, rules and institutions in technical change and economic dynamics', Brighton, SPRU, University of Sussex, DRC Occasional Paper, mimeo.

Dosi, G., Pavitt, K. and Soete, L. (1988), *The Economics of Technical Change and International Trade*, Wheatsheaf, Brighton.

Drèze, J. (1960), 'Quelques reflexions sereines sur l'adaptation de l'industrie belge au marche commun', *Comptes Rendus des Travaux de la Societe Royale d'Economie Politique de Belgique*, no. 275, December.

Drèze, J. (1961), 'Les exportations intra-CEE en 1985 et la position belge', *Recherches Economiques de Louvain*, vol. 27, pp. 717–38.

Dunning, J.H. (1977), 'Trade, location of economic activity and multinational enterprises: a search for an eclectic theory', in B. Ohlin *at al.* (eds.), *The International Allocation of Economic Activity*, London, Macmillan.

Dunning, J.H. (1981a), 'Explaining the international direct investment position by countries: toward a dynamic or development approach', *Weltwirtschaftliches Archiv*, Band 117, pp. 30–64.

Dunning, J.H. (1981b), *International Production and the Multinational Enterprise*, London, Allen and Unwin.

Ethier, W. (1979), 'Internationally decreasing costs and world trade', *Journal of International Economics*, vol. 9, pp. 1–24.

Ethier, W. (1981), 'A reply to Professors Metcalfe and Steedman', *Journal of International Economics*, vol. 11, pp. 273–77.

Ethier, W. (1982a), 'Decreasing costs in international trade and Frank Graham's argument for protection', *Econometrica*, vol. 72, pp.389–405.

Ethier, W. (1982b), 'National and international returns to scale in the modern theory of international trade', *American Economic review*, vol. 72, pp. 389–405.

Falvey, R. (1981), 'Comparative advantage in a multi-factor world', *International Economic Review*, vol. 11, pp. 495–511.

Ferguson, D. (1978), 'International capital mobility and comparative advantage', *Journal of International Economics*, vol. 8, pp. 373–96.

Ferrier, F. (1805), *Du Governement Considéré dans ses Rapports avec le Commerce*, Paris.

Findlay, R. (1973), *International Trade and Development Theory*, New York, Columbia University Press.

Findlay, R. (1978), 'Relative backwardness, direct foreign investment and the transfer of technology: a simple dynamic model', *The Quarterly Journal of Economics*, vol. 92, pp. 1–16.

Findlay, R. (1984), 'Growth and development in trade models', in R.W. Jones and P.B. Kenen (1984) (eds.), *Handbook of International Economics*, Amsterdam, Elsevier-North-Holland.

Finger, J. (1975a), 'Trade overlap and intra-industry trade', *Economic Inquiry*, vol. 13, pp. 581–9.

Finger, J. (1975b), 'A new view of the product cycle theory', *Weltwirtschaftliches Archiv*, vol. 111, pp. 79–98.

Freeman, C. (1963), 'The plastics industry: a comparative study of research and innovation', *National Institute Economic Review*, no. 26, pp. 22–62.

Freeman, C. (1965), 'Research and Development in Electronic Capital Goods,' *National Institute Economic Review*, no. 34, pp. 40–97.

Freeman, C. (1987), *Technology Policy and Economic Performance*, London, Frances Pinter.

Gomulka, S. (1971), *Inventive Activity, Diffusion and the Stages of Economic Growth*, Aarhus, Skrifter fra Aarhus Universtets Okonomiske Institut nr. 24, Institute of Economics.

Gomulka, S. (1978), 'Growth and the import of technology: Poland 1971–1980', *Cambridge Journal of Economics*, vol. 2, pp. 1–16.

Graham, F.D. (1923), 'Some aspects of protection further considered', *Quarterly*

Journal of Economics, vol. 37, pp. 199–227.

Graham, E. (1979), 'Technological innovation and the dynamics of the US comparative advantage', in C. Hill and J. Utterback (eds.), *Technological Innovation for a Dynamic Economy*, New York, Pergamon Press.

Grubel, H.G. and Lloyd, P.J. (1975), *Intra-industry Trade: The Theory and Measurement of International Trade in Different Products*, London, Macmillan.

Gruber, W., Mehta, D. and Vernon, R. (1967), 'The R & D factor in international trade and international investment of United States industries', *The Journal of Political Economy*, vol. 57, pp. 20–37.

Gruber, W. and Vernon, R. (1970), 'The technology factor in a world trade matrix', in R. Vernon (ed.), *The Technology Factor in International Trade*, New York, Columbia University Press.

Hahn, F. (1984), *Equilibrium and Macroeconomics*, Oxford, Basil Blackwell.

Hanel, P. (1976), 'The relationship existing between the R & D activity of Canadian manufacturing industries and their performance in the international market', Ottawa, Technological Innovation Studies Programme, Office of Science and Technology, Department of Industry, Trade and Commerce, mimeo.

Harkness, J. and Kyle, J. (1975), 'Factors influencing United States comparative advantage', *The Journal of International Economics*, vol. 5, pp. 153–65.

Helpman, E. (1981), 'International trade in the presence of product differentiation, economies of scale and monopolistic competition: a Chamberlain–Heckscher–Ohlin approach', *The Journal of International Economics*, vol. 11, pp. 305–40.

Helpman, E. and Razin, A. (1980), 'Monopolistic competition and factor movements', Stockholm, Institute for International Economic Studies, University of Stockholm, Seminar Paper no 155.

Helpman, E. (1984), 'Increasing returns, imperfect markets, and trade theory', in R.W. Jones and P.B. Kenen (1984) (eds.), *Handbook of International Economics*, Amsterdam, Elsevier-North-Holland.

Helpman, E. and Krugman, P. (1985), *Market Structure and Foreign Trade: Increasing Returns, Imperfect Competition and the International Economy*, Wheatsheaf, Brighton.

Hirsch, S. (1965), 'The US electronics industry in international trade', *National Institute Economic Review*, no. 34, pp. 92–7.

Horn, J-E. (1976), *Technologische Neuerungen und Internationale Arbeitsteilung*, Kieler Studien nr 139, Tubingen, J C B Mohr.

Hufbauer, G. (1986), *Synthetic Materials and the Theory of International Trade*, Cambridge, Mass., Harvard University Press.

Hufbauer, G. (1970), 'The impact of national characteristics and technology on the commodity composition of trade in manufactured goods', in R. Vernon (ed.), *The Technology Factor in International Trade*, New York, Columbia University Press.

Hulsman-Vejsova, H. and Koekkoek, K. (1980), 'Factor proportions, technology and Dutch industry's international trade patterns', *Weltwirtschaftliches Archiv*, vol. 116, pp. 162–77.

Hymer, S.H. (1976), *The International Operations of National Firms: A Study of Direct Foreign Investment*, Cambridge, Mass., MIT Press.

Jacquemin, A. (1982), 'Imperfect market structure and international trade—some recent research', *Kyklos*, vol. 35, pp. 75–93.

Johnson, H. (1970), 'The state of theory in relation to the empirical analysis', in R. Vernon (ed.), *The Technology Factor in International Trade*, New York,

Columbia University Press.

Jones, R.W. (1970), 'The role of technology in the theory of international trade', in R. Vernon (ed.), *The Technology Factor in International Trade*, New York, Columbia University Press.

Jones, R.W. (1979), *International Trade: Essays in Theory*, Amsterdam, North-Holland.

Jones, R.W. (1980), 'Comparative and absolute advantage', *Schweizerische Zeitzchrift für Volkswirtschaft und Statistik*.

Jones, R.W. and Kenen, P.B. (1984), (eds.), *Handbook of International Economics*, Amsterdam, Elsevier-North-Holland.

Jones, R.W. and Neary, J.P. (1984), 'The positive theory of international trade', in R.W. Jones and P.B. Kenen (1984) (eds.), *Handbook of International Economics*, Amsterdam, Elsevier-North-Holland.

Kaldor, N. (1970), 'The case for regional policies', *Scottish Journal of Political Economy*, vol. 17, pp. 337–348.

Kaldor, N. (1975), 'What is wrong with economic theory', *Quarterly Journal of Economics*, vol. 89, pp. 347–57.

Kaldor, N. (1980), 'The role of increasing returns, technical progress and cumulative causation in the theory of international trade', Paris, ISMEA, mimeo.

Katrak, H. (1973), 'Human skills, R and D and scale economies in the export of the United Kingdom and the United States', *Oxford Economic Papers*, vol. 25, pp. 337–60.

Keesing, D. (1965), 'Labour skills and international trade: evaluating many trade flows with a single measuring device', *Review of Economics and Statistics*, vol. 47, pp. 287–294.

Keesing, D. (1967), 'The impact of research and development on United States trade', *The Journal of Political Economy*, vol. 57, pp. 38–48.

Kemp, M. (1969), *The Pure Theory of International Trade and Investment*, Englewood Cliffs, Prentice-Hall.

Kennedy, C. (1964), 'Induced bias in innovation and the theory of distribution', *The Economic Journal*, vol. 74, pp. 541–47.

Kierzkowski, H. (1984) (ed.), *Monopolistic Competition and International Trade*, Oxford, Clarendon Press.

Kindleberger, C. (1970), 'Comments', in R. Vernon (ed.), *The Technology Factor in International Trade*, New York, Columbia University Press.

Klein, B. (1977), *Dynamic Competition*, Cambridge, Mass., Harvard University Press.

Klein, B. (1979), 'The slowdown in productivity advances: a dynamic explanation', in C. Hill and J. Utterback (eds.), *Technological Innovation for a Dynamic Economy*, New York, Pergamon Press.

Koizumi, I. and Kopecky, K. (1980), 'Foreign direct investment, technology transfer and domestic employment effects', *The Journal of International Economics*, vol. 10, pp. 1–20.

Krugman, P. (1979a), 'A model of innovation, technology transfer and the world distribution of income', *The Journal of Political Economy*, vol. 87, pp. 253–66.

Krugman, P. (1979b), 'Increasing returns, monopolistic competition and international trade', *The Journal of International Economics*, vol. 9., pp. 469–79.

Krugman, P. (1979c), 'Comment on Corden', in H. Giersch (ed.), *On the Economics of Intra-Industry Trade*, Tubingen, J C B Mohr.

Krugman, P. (1980), 'Scale economies, product differentiation and the pattern of trade', *American Economic Review*, vol. 70, pp.950–9.

Krugman, P. (1981), 'Intra-industry specialisation and the gains from trade', *Journal of Political Economy*, vol. 89, pp. 959–73.

Krugman, P. (1982), 'A technology gap model of international trade', International Economic Association Conference on Structural Adjustment in Trade-dependent Advanced Economies, Stockholm, Sweden.

Krugman, P. (1984), 'Import protection as export promotion: international competition in the presence of oligopoly and economies of scale', in H. Kierzkowski (ed.), *Monopolistic Competition and International Trade*, Oxford, Clarendon Press.

Lancaster, K. (1979), *Variety, Equity and Efficiency*, New York, Columbia University Press.

Lancaster, K. (1980), 'Inter-industry trade under perfect monopolistic competition', *The Journal of International Economies*, vol. 10, pp. 151–75.

Leamer, E. (1974), 'The commodity composition of international trade in manufactures: an empirical analysis', *Oxford Economic Papers*, vol. 26, pp. 350–74.

Leamer, E. (1980), 'The Leontief paradox reconsidered', *The Journal of Political Economy*, vol. 98, pp. 195–213.

Leamer, E. and Bowen, H. (1981), 'Cross-section tests of the Heckscher–Ohlin theorem: comment', *American Economic Review*, vol. 71, pp. 1040–3.

Leijonhufrud, A. (1981), *Information and Coordination*, Oxford, Oxford University Press.

Leontief, W. (1953), 'Domestic production and foreign trade: the American capital position re-examined', *Proceedings of the American Philosophical Society*.

Leontief, W. (1956), 'Factor proportions and the structure of American trade: further theoretical and empirical analysis', *Review of Economics and Statistics*, vol. 38, pp. 386–407.

Linder, S.B. (1961), *An Essay on Trade and Transformation*, New York, Wiley.

List, F. (1904), *The National System of Political Economy*, London, Longman, English Translation from German Original 1844.

MacDougall, G. (1951–52), 'British and American exports: a study suggested by the theory of comparative costs', Part I and II, *Economic Journal*, vol. 61, pp. 697–724.

Markusen, J. (1980), 'Trade and the gains from trade with imperfect competition', Stockholm, Institute for International Economic Studies, Seminar Paper no 153, University of Stockholm, mimeo.

Markusen, J. and Melvin, J. (1980), 'Trade, factor-prices and the gains from trade with increasing returns to scale', Stockholm, Institute for International Economic Studies, Seminar Paper no 154, University of Stockholm, mimeo.

Markusen, J. and Melvin, J. (1984), 'The gains-from-trade theorum with increasing return to scale', in H. Kierzkowski (1984) (ed.), *Monopolistic Competition and International Trade*, Oxford, Clarendon Press.

Melvin, R. (1969), 'Increasing returns to scale as a determinant of trade', *The Canadian Journal of Economics*, vol. 3, pp. 389–402.

Melvin, J.R. and Warne, R.D. (1973), 'Monopoly and the theory of international trade', *The Journal of International Economics*, vol. 3, pp. 45–72.

Metcalfe, J.S. and Steedman, I. (1981), 'On the transformation of theorems', *The Journal of International Economics*, vol. 11, pp. 267–71.

Metcalfe, J.S. and Soete, L. (1984), 'Notes on the evolution of technology and international competition', in M. Gibbons *et al.* (eds.), *Science and Technology*

Policy in the 1980's and Beyond, London, Longman.

Morral, J.F. (1972), *Human Capital, Technology and the Role of the United States in International Trade*, Gainesville, University of Florida Press.

Myint, H. (1958), 'The 'Classical Theory' of international trade and the underdeveloped countries', *Economic Journal*, vol. 68, pp. 317–37.

Nelson, R.R. (1968), 'A 'diffusion' model of international productivity differences in manufacturing industry', *American Economic Review*, vol. 58, pp. 1219–1248.

Nelson, R., Winter, S. and Schuette, H. (1976), 'Technical change in an evolutionary model', *Quarterly Journal of Economics*, vol. 90, pp. 90–118.

Nelson, R.R. and Winter, S. (1982), *An Evolutionary Theory of Economic Change*, Cambridge, Mass., The Belknap Press of Harvard University.

Ohlin, B. (1933), *Interregional and International Trade*, Cambridge, Cambridge University Press Revised Edition (1967).

Onida, F. (1984), *Economia degli Scambi Internazionali*, Bologna Il Mulino.

Owen, N., White, G. and Smith, S. (1978), 'Britain's pattern of specialisation', London, Department of Industry, Economics and Statistics, mimeo.

Pasinetti, L.L. (1981), *Structural Change and Economic Growth*, Cambridge, Cambridge University Press.

Pavitt, K. and Soete, L. (1980), 'Innovative activities and export shares: some comparisons between industries and countries', in K. Pavitt (ed.), *Technical Innovation and British Economic Performance*, London, Macmillan.

Pavitt, K. and Soete, L. (1982), 'International differences in economic growth and the international location of innovation', in H. Giersch (ed.), *Emerging Technologies–Consequences for Economic Growth, Structural Change and Employment*, Tubingen, J C B Mohr.

Petri, P.A. (1980), 'A Ricardian model of market sharing', *The Journal of International Economics*, vol. 10, pp. 201–11.

Posner, M. (1961), 'International trade and technical change', *Oxford Economic Papers*, vol. 13, pp. 323–41.

Prebish, R. (1950), *The Economic Development of Latin America and its Principal Problems*, New York, ECLA, United Nations.

Purvis, D.D. (1972), 'Technology, trade and factor mobility', *Economic Journal*, vol. 82, pp. 991–9.

Ricardo, D. (1951), *On the principles of Political Economy and Taxation*, P. Sraffa (ed.), Cambridge, Cambridge University Press.

Robinson, P. (1968), 'Factor proportions and comparative advantage', in R.E. Caves and H.G. Johnson (1968), reprinted from *Quarterly Journal of Economics*, 1956.

Rosenberg, N. (1970), 'Comments', in R.Vernon (ed.), *The Technology Factor in International Trade*, New York, Columbia University Press.

Rugman, A.M. (1980), 'Internalisation as a general theory of foreign direct investment: a reappraisal of the literature', *Weltwirtschaftliches Archiv*, Band 112, pp. 210–34.

Samuelson, P.A. (1965), 'A theory of induced innovation along Kennedy-Weizsacker lines', *The Review of Economics and Statistics*, vol. 47, pp. 343–56.

Soete, L. (1980), 'The impact of technological innovation on international trade patterns: the evidence reconsidered', Paper presented to the OECD Science and Technology indicators Conference, Paris, September 15–19, mimeo.

Soete, L. (1981), 'A general test of technological gap trade theory', *Weltwirtschaft-

liches Archiv, Band 117, pp. 638–66.

Soete, L. (1985), 'Innovation and international trade', in B. Williams and J. Bryan-Brown (eds.), *Knows and Unknowns in Technical Change*, Technical Change Centre, London.

Steedman, I. (1979) (ed.), *Fundamental Issues in Trade Theory*, Cambridge, Cambridge University Press.

Steedman, I. (1980), *Trade Amongst Growing Economies*, Cambridge, Cambridge University Press.

Stern, R.M. (1962), 'British and American productivity and comparative costs in international trade', *Oxford Economic Papers*, vol. 14, no. 3, pp. 275–96.

Stern, R. (1975), 'Testing trade theories' in P.B. Kenen (ed.), *International Trade and Finance, Frontiers for Research*, Cambridge, Cambridge University Press.

Stern, R. (1976), 'Some evidence on the factor content of West Germany's foreign trade', *The Journal of Political Economy*, vol. 84, pp. 131–41.

Stern, R. and Maskus, K. (1981), 'Determinants of the structure of US foreign trade, 1958–1976', *The Journal of International Economics*, vol. 11, pp. 207–24.

Thirlwall, A.P. (1980), *Balance-of-Payment Theory and the United Kingdom Experience*, London, Macmillan.

Thirlwall, A.P. and Vines, D. (1983), 'A general model of growth and development on Kaldorian lines', paper presented at the conference on 'The Dynamics of Employment and Technology: Theories and Policies', Udine, Italy, 1–3 September 1983, mimeo.

Tucker, J. (1774), *Four Tracts, Together with Two Sermons on Political and Commercial Subjects*, Gloucester.

Vernon, R. (1966), 'International investment and international trade in the product cycle', *Quarterly Journal of Economics*, vol. 80, pp. 190–207.

Vernon, R. (1970) (ed.), *The Technology Factor in International Trade*, New York, NBER/Columbia University Press.

Von Weizsäcker, C.C. (1965), 'Tentative notes on a two-sector model with induced technical progress', *The Review of Economic Studies*, vo. 32, pp. 85–104.

Walker, W. (1979), *Industrial Innovation and International Trading Performance*, Greenwich, Connecticut, JAI Press.

Wells, L.T. Jnr. (1969), 'Test of a product cycle model of international trade: US export of consumer durables', *Quarterly Journal of Economics*, vol. 83, pp. 152–62.

Wilson, C. (1980), 'On the general structure of Ricardian models with a continuum of goods: applications to growth, tariff theory and technical change', *Econometrica*, vol. 48, pp. 1675–702.

Winter, S. (1982), 'An essay on the theory of production', in S.H. Hymans (ed.), *Economics and the World Around it*, Ann Arbor, University of Michigan Press.

Wolter, F. (1977), 'Factor proportions, technology and West German industry's international trade patterns', *Weltwirtschaftliches Archiv*, vol. 113, pp. 250–67.

20 Why growth rates differ

Jan Fagerberg

Economics Department, Norwegian Institute of International Affairs, Oslo

Introduction

This chapter focuses on the importance of creation and diffusion of technology for differences in economic growth across countries.

The question of how technology and growth relate is not a new one. The classical economists have discussed this question extensively, but attempts to study this relation empirically on a cross-country basis are much more recent. In fact, with one exception (Tinbergen, 1942), the first attempts were made in the mid- to late 1960s (Domar *et al.*, 1964; Denison, 1967). The next section discusses how this question is treated in some influential post-war studies on 'why growth rates differ' between countries. Generally, these studies either ignore technological differences between countries or treat them as accidental and transitory. Diffusion is assumed to take place relatively automatically, either as free knowledge or through the addition of new vintages of capital to the capital stock. The role of innovation is normally ignored, except in the case of the technological leader country, and then treated in a very superficial way. Thus the models underlying most of these studies can generally be characterized as 'convergence-to-equilibrium models'. No surprise, then, that these studies have difficulties in explaining phenomena such as 'changes in technological leadership' or the existence of 'laggards'.

The remaining part of the chapter develops and tests a simple model of 'why growth rates differ' which is more in line with the approach of this book. In the model, economic growth is assumed to depend on three factors: creation of new technology, diffusion of technology, and efforts related to the economic exploitation of innovation and diffusion. Contrary to many other approaches to the subject, this model allows for both convergence and divergence between countries. In the final part of the chapter, the model is tested on a sample containing data for twenty-seven developed and semi-industrialized countries between 1973 and 1983.

Lessons from previous research

Studies of why growth rates differ between countries may roughly be divided in three groups: (a) 'catch-up' analysis; (b) 'growth accounting';

and (c) 'production-function' studies. Let us consider these approaches one at a time.[1]

(a) 'Catch-up' analysis

The idea that differences in economic growth between countries are related to differences in the scope for imitation is normally attributed to Veblen (1915). Since then, several economic historians have analysed problems related to industrialization and growth from this perspective.[2]

More recently, Abramovitz (1979, 1986) and Maddison (1979, 1982, 1984) have applied this perspective to the differing growth performance of a large sample of industrialized countries. According to these writers, large differences in productivity levels between countries (technological gaps) tend to occur from time to time, mainly for accidental reasons (wars, etc.). When a technological gap is established, this opens up the possibility for countries at a lower level of economic and technological development to 'catch up' by imitating the more productive technologies of the leader country. Since these writers hold technological progress to be partly capital-embodied, they point to investment as a critical factor for successful 'catch up'. They also stress the role of demand factors, since demand is assumed to interact in various ways with investment and the pace of structural change in the economy. For instance, the deceleration of productivity growth in the last decade is partly explained in this way. They mention the importance of institutions, but do not discuss this in detail because of the methodological difficulties that are involved.

The works by Abramovitz and Maddison are to a large degree descriptive, and as such they are very useful. They convincingly support their arguments by comparing data for productivity levels and economic growth/ productivity growth across countries, and these comparisons are sometimes supplemented by descriptive statistics/simple statistical tests. Other scholars working in this tradition have extended these tests in various ways and reached similar results (Singer and Reynolds, 1975; Cornwall, 1976, 1977). However, they all concentrate on diffusion processes and ignore innovation aspects. As pointed out already by Ames and Rosenberg (1963), writers in this tradition have great difficulties in analysing phenomena such as developments in leader countries[3], changes of leadership,[4] and the existence of 'laggards'.

(b) 'Growth accounting'

For many years, Kuznets and his colleagues devoted much effort to the construction of historical time series for GDP and its major components (national accounts). The post-war 'growth accounting' exercises grew more or less naturally out of this work. While national accounts presented decompositions of GDP, growth accounts attempted to decompose the growth of GDP. The first analysis of this type was carried out by Abramovitz (1956) in a historical study of the United States. What he did was to sum up the growth of inputs (capital and labor), using 'prices' or factor shares as weights, and compare the result with the growth of output as conventionally measured. The result, that about one-half of actual growth[5] could not be explained in this way and had to be classified as unexplained total factor productivity growth, surprised many, including Abramovitz himself:

> This result is surprising . . . Since we know little about the causes of productivity increase, the indicated importance of this element may be taken to be some sort of measure of our ignorance about the causes of economic growth. [Abramovitz, 1956, p. 11]

Abramovitz discussed briefly possible explanatory factors behind this large residual, emphasizing research, education, learning by doing, and economies of scale. From this, researchers have followed different paths in 'squeezing down the residual', as Nelson (1981) puts it. One has been to embody as much as possible of technological progress into the factors themselves, as suggested by Jorgensen and Griliches (1967).[6] Another, following Ambramovitz's suggestions, has been to add other explanatory variables, thereby reducing the unexplained part of the residual, which, following Solow (1957), is normally attributed to technical change.

Denison was the first to apply this latter methodology to the study of why growth rates differ between countries (Denison, 1967; Denison and

Table 20.1 'Why growth rates differ' (Denison)

	1950–62			1953–61
	US	Western Europe[1]	Italy	Japan
Growth[2] of which:	3.4	4.7	6.0	8.1
Labor	1.1	0.8	1.0	1.9
Capital	0.8	0.9	0.7	1.6
Residual (TFP) of which:	1.4	3.0	4.3	4.6
Technology	0.8	1.3	1.7	1.4
Resource allocation	0.3	0.7	1.4	1.1
Scale factors	0.4	0.9	1.1	2.0
For comparison: National income per person employed[3]	100	59	40	55

Sources: Denison (1967), Chapter 21; Denison and Chung (1976), Chapters 4 and 11.

[1] Belgium, Denmark, France, Germany, Netherlands, Norway and United Kingdom.
[2] The columns do not always add up because of rounding errors and other minor adjustments not reported here.
[3] In 1960 US prices (except Japan: 1970).

Chung, 1976). Regarding technology, Denison's work rests on a view very similar to the one which characterizes many 'catch-up' analyses,[7] but his conclusion differs from theirs. Some of his main results are summarized in Table 20.1. As is apparent from Table 20.1, the results indicate a close connection between the size of the residual and the level of development. This could, of course, be interpreted in support of the catch-up approach. But Denison attributes about two-thirds of the differences in residuals between the United States and the rest of the countries covered by his investigation to other factors (improvements in resource allocation and the exploitation of economies of scale). In fact, when these factors are adjusted for, only France and Germany among the Western European countries seem to catch up in terms of technology. In his 1967 study, he therefore concludes:[8]

On the surface, to reduce the gap greatly would not seem very difficult if the businessmen, workers and governments of a country really wished and were determined to do so . . . In contrast to this *a priori* impression of possibilities, the historical record up to the early 1960s, at least, suggests that either the desire is lacking or imitation is a very difficult thing; most countries seem to have made little progress. [Denison, 1967, p. 340]

However, when Denison discusses the contribution from increased exploitation of economies of scale, what he mainly refers to is increased aggregate productivity caused by increased productivity in the production of durable consumer goods. But where does the technology used to produce consumer durables come from, if not from the United States? In fact, the 1950s and 1960s are exactly the periods when the production of consumer durables spreads from the United States to Europe and Japan. A similar argument can be made for structural changes. Without the growth of new industries based on imported technology, such as, for instance, consumer durables, would these changes have taken place to the same extent? Thus we will argue that Denison's conclusions rest on rather shaky assumptions, and that it is quite probable that he seriously understates the importance of diffusion of technology from the United States to Europe and Japan in this period.[9]

On a more general level, this illustrates a major weakness in growth-accounting analysis. As pointed out by Nelson (1973, 1981), most of the variables which the growth accountants take into account are interdependent, and without a theory of how these variables interact, decompositions cannot claim to be more than mere illustrations of the growth process.[10] To explain differences in growth between countries, it would be necessary to distinguish between 'active factors' ('engines of growth'), and more 'passive factors' which, though permissive to growth, cannot themselves be regarded as causal, explanatory factors, and the relations between the various factors would have to be determined and explained. Furthermore, the contribution of innovation to economic growth, not only in the United States but everywhere, would have to be worked out and integrated into the analysis.[11]

'Production-function' studies

As noted, the growth accounting exercises relate the growth of output to various input factors. Solow (1957) was the first to provide a formal theoretical framework for this type of analysis.[12] Following standard neo-classical equilibrium assumptions (perfect competition, full capacity utilization, full employment, no economies of scale, etc.), he assumed that production (Q) could be related to technology (A) and the factors of production (capital (K) and labor (L)) in the following way:

(1) $Q(t) = A(t) F(K(t), L(t))$

Let small-case letters denote rates of growth. By differentiating, dividing through with Q, and substituting the partial elasticities of output with respect to capital and labor, El_{QK} and El_{QL}, into the equation, we arrive at:

(2) $q = a + (El_{QK})k + (El_{QL})l,$

Since under neo-classical assumptions the partial elasticity of output with respect to labor, El_{QL}, equals the workers' share (s_L), and the partial elasticity of output with respect to capital, El_{QK}, the capitalists' share (S_K) of net output, the rate of growth can now be written as the sum of the rate of growth in the capital stock, weighted by the capitalists' share in net output, the rate of growth in the labor force, weighted by labor's share in net output, and the rate of growth of 'technology' ('total factor productivity growth' (a)):

(3) $q = a + s_K k + s_L l$

Equation (3) obviously provides a theoretical justification for growth accounting, even if the underlying assumptions are much stronger than those which underlie most applied work in this area. But Solow's work did also represent the starting point for econometric studies of 'why growth rates differ' between countries. Chenery (1986) provides a summary of some of the main results from econometric applications of production functions on cross-country samples consisting of less developed, semi-industrialized or developed countries. Generally, these studies show that Solow-type production–function models explain very little of the observed differences in growth between semi-industrialized or less-developed countries. According to Chenery, the main reason for this is that the equilibrium conditions which underlie the neo-classical approach do not hold for these countries. He concludes that

In particular, disequilibrium phenomena are shown to be more significant for the former (semi-industrialized) than for the latter (developed). Thus, although neo-classical theory is a useful starting point for the study of growth, it must be modified substantially if it is to explain the essential features of economies in the process of transformation. [Chenery, 1986, pp. 13–14]

Following this line of argument, several attempts have been made to extend the production-function approach by adding other explanatory

Table 20.2   Sources of growth in semi-industrialized countries 1964–73

	Regression coefficient	Contribution to growth
Growth		6.4
of which:		
Labor	0.766	1.8
	(3.73)	
Investment	0.135	2.7
	(2.96)	
'Residual'		1.9
of which:		
Exports	0.246	0.5
	(2.96)	
Manufacturing	0.809	1.5
	(3.68)	
'Constant'	−0.002	−0.2
	(0.132)	
R^2 (adjusted) = 0.75; N = 29		

Source: Feder (1986), Tables 9.9–9.10, Model V'.
The contributions do not add up because of rounding errors. The numbers in brackets are *t*-values.

variables, reflecting various types of disequilibria which exist within countries.[13] The main arguments in favor of this may be summarized as follows. Many countries, especially developing countries, are often assumed to have a 'dual' economy, consisting of a high-productive modern sector and a low-productive traditional sector. In this case, it is argued, a mere transfer of resources from the traditional sector to the modern sector should raise growth. A similar perspective is often applied to the relation between the export sector and the rest of the economy, because the export sector is often assumed to be more productive than other sectors. A recent application of this methodology to a sample of semi-industrialized countries may be found in Feder (1986). He estimates a neo-classical production function, with variables reflecting the development of exports and manufacturing production added, on a cross-country data set for the period 1964–73 (see Table 20.2). When compared with Denison's estimates for countries on a comparable level of development (Italy and Japan), some important differences emerge. First, the combined contribution of capital and labor explains about two-thirds of actual growth, compared to between one-third and one-half in Denison's calculations. Second, the contribution of capital is relatively more important in Feder than in Denison. Third, Feder does not distinguish between economies of scale and other factors related to re-allocation of resources. Fourth, Feder totally ignores the contribution of innovation and diffusion. The latter is, of course, the most striking. Following this approach, the question of 'why growth rates differ' between countries can be answered without any references to technology.

However, there are important methodological problems here. To what extent can the introduction of disequilibrium conditions be defended within a framework which assumes equilibrium from the start? The pure neo-classical growth model, as set out by Solow and others, pretends to explain economic growth from factor growth and technological progress. But the explanatory power of the model rests solely on the underlying equilibrium assumptions. If these assumptions do not hold, it is not at all clear how an estimated neo-classical growth model should be interpreted. For instance, in a situation where unemployment prevails, it is not obvious that growth in the labor force should be assumed to add anything to economic growth.[14] Furthermore, to what extent can structural changes, though facilitated by the existence of large, low-productive sectors populated by 'surplus labor', be counted as independent, explanatory factors of growth in the same sense as capital accumulation or innovative efforts? Why is it not the other way around, that structural changes are caused by capital accumulation, innovative efforts and growth? Thus neo-classical students of why growth rates differ seem to be faced with the following dilemma: either stick to the traditional neo-classical assumptions—this produces a logically coherent explanation that predicts poorly; or add additional variables that destroy the original equilibrium framework—then predictions become much better, but the model ceases to explain anything.

Chenery and others should be credited for having shown that the equilibrium conditions on which the production-function approach is built cannot be defended in studies of why growth rates differ between countries. However, they miss their point when they mix together a model built on equilibrium assumptions and factors reflecting disequilibrium conditions, without showing explicitly how the various factors interact and what the fundamental causal factors are. It is disappointing, also, that they normally[15] ignore the differences in technological levels and innovative performances across countries, which we believe to be one of the most fundamental disequilibrium mechanisms of the world economy. In our view, what needs to be done is to study 'why growth rates differ' from a theoretical framework which assumes disequilibrium conditions right from the start.

A technology-gap theory of economic growth

Essentially, the technology-gap theory of economic growth is an application of Schumpeter's dynamic theory of capitalist development, which was developed for a closed economy, to a world economy characterized by competing capitalist nation-states. Following Schumpeter (1934, 1939, 1942), the technology-gap theorists[16] analyse economic development as a disequilibrium process characterized by the interplay of two conflicting forces: innovation, which tends to increase economic and technological differences between countries, and imitation or diffusion, which tends to reduce them. Thus, whether a country behind the world innovation frontier succeeds in reducing the productivity gap *vis-à-vis* the frontier countries does not only depend on its imitative efforts, but also on its innovative performance, and on the innovative performance of the frontier countries. Furthermore, even if a country behind the world innovation frontier may succeed in reducing the productivity gap through mainly imitating activities, it cannot surpass the frontier countries in productivity without passing them in innovative activity as well. In general, the outcome of the international process of innovation and diffusion—with regard to the economic development of different countries—is uncertain. The process may generate a pattern where countries follow diverging trends, as well as a pattern where countries converge towards a common mean.

To do full justice to the Schumpeterian theory outlined above, the world economy should be modelled both from the technology side, characterized by creation, diffusion and contraction of competing technological systems, and from the side of competing nation-states, characterized by different technological levels and trends, institutional settings, and internal structural disequilibria.[17] However, for the purpose of highlighting some of the reasons behind 'why growth rates differ', we will assume that a simpler approach may do.

Assume that the level of production in a country (Q) is a multiplicative function of the level of knowledge[18] diffused to the country from abroad (D), the level of knowledge created in the country or 'national technological activity' (N), the country's capacity for exploiting the benefits of knowledge (C), whether internationally or nationally created, and a constant (Z)

(1) $Q = Z D^{\alpha} N^{\beta} C^{\tau}$, where Z is a constant.

By differentiating and dividing through with Q, letting small-case letters denote growth rates:

(2) $q = \alpha d + \beta n + \tau c$

Assume further, as customary in the diffusion literature, that the diffusion of internationally available knowledge follows a logistic curve. This implies that the contribution of diffusion of internationally available knowledge to economic growth is an increasing function of the distance between the level of knowledge appropriated in the country and that of the country on the technological frontier (for the frontier country, this contribution will be zero). Let the total amount of knowledge, adjusted for differences in size of countries, in the frontier country and the country under consideration be T_f and T, respectively:

(3) $\quad d = \mu - \mu(T/T_f)$

By substituting (3) into (2) we finally arrive at:

(4) $\quad q = \alpha\mu - \alpha\mu(T/T_f) + \beta n + \tau c$

Thus, following this approach, economic growth depends on three factors:

— the diffusion of technology from abroad (imitation): the contribution of this factor increases with the distance from the world innovation frontier;
— the creation of new technology within the country (innovation);
— the development of the country's own capacity for exploiting the benefits offered by available technology, whether created within the country or elsewhere ('efforts').

The model developed above does, of course, present a very simplified picture of reality, especially with respect to diffusion. For a more thoroughgoing discussion of diffusion aspects, the reader is referred to chapters by Perez–Soete and Unger in this book. But the model differs from the one which until now has dominated most empirical work on technological gaps and economic growth in at least one respect: *it incorporates the effects of national innovative performance.* As pointed out by Pavitt (1979/80) and Pavitt and Soete (1982), the omission of the innovation variable in most applied work makes it difficult to explain diverging trends, whether represented by laggards or related to the questioned changes in technological leadership. However, the reasons for this neglect are probably not only rooted in the deep influence of equilibrium or convergence assumptions on current economic thinking, but also in problems related to the measurement of innovation and diffusion of technology across countries. The latter will now be considered more closely.

Productivity, patents and R & D

In the preceding section, we defined two concepts related to a country's level of economic and technological development, the total level of knowledge appropriated in the country (T), and the level of knowledge created within the country (N).

The first concept (T) refers to the total set of techniques in use in the country, whether invented within the country, or diffused to the country from the international economic environment. T cannot be measured directly. What can be measured, however, is the output of the process in which these techniques are used, or the level of productivity (Q/L). We have, therefore, as a number of earlier studies chosen to use Real GDP per capita as a proxy for T. However, since current prices and exchange rates are known to produce downward-biased estimates of Real GDP per capita for countries with productivity levels below the world productivity frontier; we adjusted the data on GDP per capita accordingly on the basis of results obtained by the 'United Nations International Comparison Project'.[19]

The second concept (N) refers to the country's own creation of technology, or its level of national technological activity. To find a proxy for this, we have to look outside the range of variables traditionally included in growth studies. It is customary to divide measures of technological activity into 'technology-input' measures and 'technology-output' measures (Soete 1981). Of the former type, expenditures on education, research and development, and employment of scientists and engineers may be mentioned; of the latter, patenting activity. Regarding the former type, these measures reflect to some degree both imitation and innovation, since a certain scientific base is a precondition for successful imitation in most areas (Freeman, 1982; Mansfield, 1982). Another problem with 'technology-input' measures is that data generally are of a poor quality, especially for non-OECD countries. Patenting activity, on the other hand, reflects the innovation process much more directly than 'technology-input' measures, even if the propensity to patent varies considerably across industries (Pavitt, 1983). Furthermore, data on patents exist for a large group of countries and long time-spans. Until recently, differences in national patenting regulations were considered to make it difficult to compare patenting activities across countries,[20] but this problem may be significantly reduced by limiting the analysis to patenting activities of different countries in one common (foreign) market (Soete, 1981). Contrary to Soete who used patenting in the United States as an indicator, this study uses patenting on the world market.[21] This has the advantage that it gives data for the United States.

Let us now take a closer look at the relation between the two concepts as well as the proxies chosen. What we should expect, following the technology-gap argument, is that the technologically most advanced countries, in terms of high levels of national technological activity (N), also are the economically most advanced, in terms of GDP per capita (T). Since the relation between own and foreign-produced technology should be expected to increase rapidly as the country moves towards the world innovation frontier, the relation between GDP per capita (T) and national technological activity (N) should be expected to be log-linear rather than linear, and steeper for patent-based than for R & D-based indices since the latter to a large degree reflects both imitation and innovation processes.

These hypotheses are tested on cross-sectional data (yearly averages) from the 1973–83 period. The sample consists of twenty-seven developed and semi-industrialized countries for which data are available (twenty-four for R & D). The following variables are used:

Table 20.3   The relation between productivity and technological activity

(1)	$T =$	5.72 + 0.02EPA	$R^2 = 0.45$ (0.42),
		(9.80)* (4.49)*	SER = 2.14, DW = 0.72
(2)	$T =$	−1.44 + 2.14 lnEPA,	$R^2 = 0.72$ (0.71),
		(−1.25) (8.06)*	SER = 1.52, DW = 1.58
(3)	$T =$	− 4.28 + 8.45 ln ln EPA,	$R^2 = 0.75$ (0.74),
		(−3.07)* (8.69)*	SER = 1.44, DW = 1.79
(4)	$T =$	4.16 + 0.32RD,	$R^3 = 0.53$ (0.51),
		(4.84)* (4.98)*	SER = 1.89, DW = 1.27
(5)	$T =$	0.49 + 3.21 ln RD	$R^2 = 0.55$ (0.53),
		(0.33) (5.18)*	SER = 1.85, DW = 1.21
(6)	$T =$	3.65 + 5.41 ln ln RD,	$R^2 = 0.45$ (0.43),
		(3.33)* (4.27)*	SER = 2.04, DW = 1.03
			N (1–3) = 27, N (4–6) = 24

* = Significant at the 1 per cent level at a two-tailed test.
SER = Standard error of regression.
DW = Durban–Watson statistics.
The numbers in brackets under the estimates are t-statistics. The numbers in brackets after R^2 are R^2 adjusted for degrees of freedom.

T   = GDP per capita in constant 1980 US dollar (adjusted for differences in purchasing power of currencies)

RD = Civil R & D as % of GDP

EPA = External patent applications per billion of exports[22] (constant 1980 dollars)

The results are given in Table 20.3. First, whatever the form of the independent variable, a positive relation between productivity and national technological activity exists, significantly different from zero at a 1 per cent level. Second, as expected, the best results are obtained for log-linear models (log for R & D and double-log for patents, which implies a steeper curve in the latter case). Third, the correlation between productivity and patenting is much closer than between productivity and R & D. Fourth, in the case of productivity and R & D, the residuals show signs of serial correlation.[23] This indicates that countries on almost the same level of productivity tend to have correlated residuals, i.e. that the estimated level of R & D deviates from the observed level in a systematic way depending on the level of productivity (see graph 2 below).

Figure 20.1 plots the actual and estimated number of patents per billion of exports against GDP per capita (model 3 above). As can be seen from the figure, with some exceptions, the countries of our sample fit the regression line quite well. The main source of variance is Japan and a group of small, developed countries headed by Norway. Figure 20.2, which plots actual and estimated R & D against GDP per capita (model 5 above), shows that the variance in this case is larger. In addition to Japan and the group of small, developed countries referred to above, the variance comes

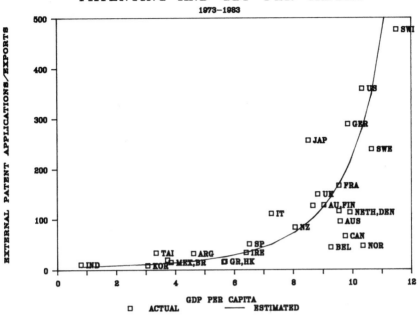

Figure 20.1 Patenting and GDP per capita (1973–83)

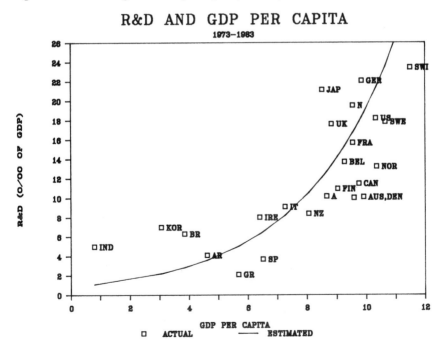

Figure 20.2 R & D and GDP per capita (1973–83)

from the semi-industrialized countries, which in most cases show much higher levels of R & D than should be expected, given their levels of GDP per capita. This latter phenomenon is in accordance with the assumption that a certain level of R & D is a necessary condition for imitation.

Patterns of development and growth

The general picture which emerges from Figures 20.1 and 20.2 suggests that the countries of our sample may be divided into three or four 'clusters' depending on the relation between productivity and technological activity.

Cluster A consists of four countries with high levels of productivity and high levels of technological activity: Switzerland, the United States, Germany and Sweden. These countries are the typical 'technological frontier' countries of our sample. Japan joins this group in terms of technological activity, but not in terms of productivity.

Cluster B consists of seven countries with medium levels of productivity and medium levels of technological activity: France, the United Kingdom, The Netherlands, Austria, Finland, Italy and New Zealand. This group of countries is less homogeneous than the other groups. In terms of R & D activity, some of them (France, the United Kingdom, and The Netherlands) are close to the leader countries, but they patent less, while others have more in common with the semi-industrialized countries or the countries in cluster C below.

Cluster C consists of five countries that have high levels of productivity, but relatively low levels of measured technological activity: Norway, Belgium, Canada, Australia and Denmark (Belgium is close to cluster B in terms of R & D, but not in terms of patenting activity). What most of these countries have in common, in addition to high productivity and low technological activity, is small size and an industrial structure based on natural resources.

Cluster D consists of the semi-industrialized countries of the sample (except India): Spain, Ireland, Greece, Hong Kong, Argentina, Brazil, Mexico, Taiwan and Korea. They have low levels of productivity and patenting, but their R & D efforts vary considerably.

Finally, Japan and India are in a sense 'freak cases'. Regarding Japan, the level of technological activity, measured through patents or R & D, is much higher than should be expected from the measured level of productivity. One way of interpreting this result is that it shows that the Japanese by the late 1970s had still not fully reaped the economic benefits of the country's high level of technological activity. In the case of India, this country fits the characteristics of cluster D in terms of technological activity, but the level of productivity is much lower.

Table 20.4 gives some further evidence on the patterns of growth of these countries in the last decade. This evidence confirms the type of interpretation of history that normally comes out of applied work on technological gaps and 'catch-up' processes. The frontier countries in cluster A show on average the weakest performance in nearly every respect: cluster A countries have lower economic growth, lower level of investments, lower growth in the labour force and less structural change than other countries. The medium-technology countries in cluster B, and the small, natural-resource-based economies of cluster C, come second and third worst, respectively, in most respects: economic growth, investments and growth of labour force. (But cluster B countries compete favorably with cluster C in two respects—growth of patenting activity and structural change). However, all developed countries become 'laggards' compared to the semi-industrialized countries of cluster D. On average, cluster D countries have rates of growth of GDP, patenting activity and labour force between two and three times that of the developed countries, and they also have much higher levels of investments and faster structural change.

It is important to note, however, that there are large differences in growth patterns within cluster D: the Asian NICs show a much better performance in all respects than Latin American and European NICs, even if the latter countries still have better performance than the developed countries in most areas (though not patent growth). But the distance is not all that large, especially to cluster C countries.

The growth pattern of Japan is an interesting mix of the patterns discussed so far. In terms of level of technological activity (and growth of labour supply), Japan belongs to cluster A, and in terms of productivity and structural change to cluster B. However, when it comes to GDP growth, patent growth and investment behavior, Japan shares many of the characteristics of cluster D countries. In fact, the share of investments in GDP is even higher than that of the Asian NICs.

'Explaining growth'

There are at least three important problems that have to be considered in an econometric test of the technology gap model.

(1) Are all relevant variables included?
(2) If so, what is the relation between these variables?
(3) How to quantify the variables.

The first problem refers to the section on technology-gap theory. Briefly, what we did was to develop a model where economic development is shaped by two conflicting forces—innovation, which tends to increase productivity differences between countries, and diffusion, which tends to reduce them. The fundamental (causal) factors of our model of economic growth are growth in national technological activity, diffusion of technology from abroad, and growth in the capacity for economic exploitation of these factors. However, there are other variables that could be considered as relevant. The most obvious candidates, to be considered below, are

Table 20.4 Patterns of growth 1973–83

	GDP growth	Patent growth[1]	Structural change[2]				Development level		
			Investment share in GDP	Export share in GDP	Agriculture as share of GDP	Population growth	GDP per capita[3]	External patenting/exports[3]	R & D per capita
All countries	2.8	5.0	23.6	6.0	-3.6	1.4	1.0	1.0	1.0
Cluster A	1.3	1.3	20.5	4.8	-1.0	0.8	1.4	3.0	2.0
Cluster B	1.8	4.6	22.1	7.3	-2.2	0.9	1.2	1.1	1.3
Cluster C	2.3	3.0	23.2	3.4	-2.0	1.1	1.3	0.6	1.2
Cluster D	4.4	8.1	25.6	7.5	-5.2	2.1	0.6	0.2	
of which:									
European NICs	2.7	1.1	23.2	8.8	-4.7	1.3	0.8	0.3	0.5
Latin-Am. NICs	3.2	0.8	24.3	3.2	-1.8	2.2	0.5	0.2	
Asian NICs	7.3	22.4	29.1	10.4	-9.2	2.9	0.5	0.2	
Japan	3.7	9.0	31.4	7.9	-2.6	0.8	1.1	2.2	2.1

[1] Growth in external patent applications relative to the frontier country (Switzerland).

[2] Annual change on 0%.

[3] Average = 1.

growth in labor supply (the neo-classical candidate) and changes in the sectoral composition of output and employment (the structural candidate). The neo-classical candidate, growth in labour supply, has already been discussed at some length. Our argument was that the existence of excess labour, or growth of labour supply, though permissive to growth, cannot be regarded as a causal factor of growth in the same sense as the technology-gap variables, especially not as long as unemployment prevails.[24] It is also questionable what role should be attributed to factors reflecting structural changes within the economy, even if one accepts the 'dual-economy argument' of large and persistent differences in productivity between sectors. To some degree, such changes should be regarded as effects, rather than causes, of economic growth. However, if institutional obstacles for transfer of resources from one sector to another exist, this may restrain growth. Thus, what we will do is to test the basic technology-gap model with and without variables reflecting structural changes, in order to decide to what degree these variables add something to the explanatory power of the model.

The next step in testing the theory is to find reliable proxies. This has already been discussed at some length in the previous sections. Following this discussion, we use growth in external patent applications (PAT) and growth in civil R & D (RDG) as proxies for growth in national techno-logical activity, and GDP per capita, adjusted for differences in purchasing power of currencies, as a proxy for the total level of knowledge appro-priated in a country, or 'productivity' (T). Since we have more observa-tions for patents than R & D, we will use the latter only to test the sensitivity for shift of proxy. As in most other studies, the investment share (INV) was chosen as an indicator of the growth in the capacity for econ-omic exploitation of innovation and diffusion. This is, of course, a simplifi-cation since institutional factors obviously take part in this process. But the share of investment may also be seen as the outcome of a process in which institutional factors take part, i.e. differences in the size of the investment share may reflect differences in institutional systems as well. For structural changes, we used changes in exports and agriculture as shares of GDP as proxies.

The problem of interdependence between variables relates to the dis-cussion in the preceding section on patterns of growth. Obviously, one of the impressions from this discussion is that the different factors that shape growth to some extent are interrelated. For instance, the fastest-growing countries of the sample, the Asian NICs, have a larger 'technological gap' vis-à-vis the technological leaders, higher growth in patenting activity, invest more and show faster structural change than most other countries. The opposite is true for the 'technological leaders' of cluster A. But the preceding section also shows that countries follow different patterns of development and growth. The Latin American NICs, for instance, have a 'technological gap' comparable to the Asian NICs, but they invest much less, their level of patenting activity grows much slower, and they show less structural change. In fact, their growth of patenting activity is inferior to all other groups of countries. Similar examples of different development patterns, though less spectacular (except Japan, of course), may be found among developed countries. Thus, even if it is difficult to deny that the variables to some degree may be interdependent, as most economic variables in fact are, we hold it as unlikely that this will cause multi-collinearity.

However, the problem is not only one of multi-collinearity, but also of interpretation. Therefore it is necessary to consider the possible feedbacks from the dependent to the independent variables, as well as the forms of interaction between the latter. We will limit this discussion to the basic model as outlined earlier. For theoretical reasons, we hold it as unlikely that differences in development levels and growth in national technological activity across countries can be analysed as mere reflections of, or be shown to depend strongly on, differences in economic growth or investments between countries. This is also supported by empirical evidence (Clark, Freeman and Soete, 1982).[25] An interaction between the two technology variables cannot be ruled out *a priori*, but seems less likely in light of the discussion above of differences in growth patterns between countries on comparable levels of development. The same holds for investments when related to the two technology variables. The most probable form of interdependence, therefore, runs from economic growth, interpreted as a demand variable, to investments. However, even if this may be true to some extent, available evidence suggests that differences in growth of domestic demand alone cannot explain the huge and persistent differences in investment ratios between countries (Fagerberg, 1986).

The following variables were used:

GDP   =   Average annual growth of GDP at constant prices
T =   GDP per capita at constant 1980 prices (dollars) adjusted for differences in the purchasing power of currencies
PAT   =   Average annual growth in external patent applications (abroad)
RDG   =   Average annual growth in Civil R & D (inflation adjusted)
INV   =   Investments as a share of GDP at constant prices
AGR/EXP =   Annual average change in agriculture (exports) as a share of GDP(‰))

The results of the test follow in Table 20.5 below. Generally, the results give strong support to the basic technology-gap model as a model of 'why growth rates differ' between countries. The degree of explanation is very high, above 80 per cent, and all variables turn up with the expected signs, significantly different from zero at the 1 per cent level. The results were not very sensitive to the choice of innovation proxy. Since Japan is often regarded as a special case, we also estimated the model with a dummy for Japan, but this did not influence the results.

Table 20.5   The model tested (27 countries, 1973–83)

1. Basic model

$$GDP = 0.38 - 0.24T + 0.12PAT + 0.20INV$$
$$(0.25) \quad (-3.74)^* \, (4.02)^* \qquad (3.47)^*$$

$R^2 = 0.83 \, (0.81)$
SER = 0.85
DW = 2.12

2. Basic model with dummy for Japan

$$GDP = -0.60 - 0.22T + 0.11PAT + 0.23INV - 1.22JAP$$
$$(-0.35) \quad (-3.40)^* \, (3.84)^* \qquad (3.67)^* \qquad (-1.24)$$

$R^2 = 0.84 \, (0.81)$
SER = 0.84
DW = 2.24

3. Test for effects of changes in agriculture as a share of GDP

$$GDP = 0.47 - 0.25T + 0.12PAT + 0.20INV + 0.005AGR$$
$$(0.26) \quad (-2.88)^* \, (3.68)^* \qquad (3.35)^* \qquad (0.10)$$

$R^2 = 0.83 \, (0.80)$
SER = 0.87
DW = 2.10

4. Test for effects of changes in exports as a share of GDP

$$GDP = 0.81 - 0.24T + 0.14PAT + 0.20INV - 0.07EXP$$
$$(0.53) \quad (-3.85)^* \, (4.54)^* \, (3.65)^* \qquad (-1.74)^{**}$$

$R^2 = 0.85 \, (0.82)$
SER = 0.82
DW = 1.85

$N = 27$

5. Test for shift of innovation proxy

$$GDP = 0.43 - 0.16T + 0.11PAT + 0.16INV$$
$$(0.28) \quad (-2.48)^{**} \, (3.21)^* \qquad (2.90)^*$$

$R^2 = 0.75 \, (0.71)$
SER = 0.80
DW = 1.41

$$GDP = -1.01 - 0.17T + 0.18RDG + 0.16INV$$
$$(-0.72) \quad (-2.54)^{**} \, (3.27)^* \qquad (2.97)^*$$

$R^2 = 0.75 \, (0.71)$
SER = 0.80
DW = 1.78

$N = 22$

---

*   = Significant at a 1 per cent level (two-tailed test).

** = Significant at a 10 per cent level (two-tailed test).
R^2 in brackets = R^2 adjusted for degrees of freedom.
SER = Standard error of regression.
DW = Durbin–Watson statistics.
N = Number of observations included in the test.

The results do not support the hypothesis of structural changes as independent, causal factors of economic growth. Both variables turn up with signs opposite of what should be expected, in the case of exports significantly different from zero at the 10 per cent level. The latter may be interpreted in support of the view that the influence of change in outward orientation on growth depends on international macroeconomic conditions, i.e. that the slow growth in world demand in the 1970s restrained the growth of outward-oriented countries.

Table 20.6   Actual and estimated differences in growth *vis-à-vis* the frontier countries, 1973–83

			Explanatory factors			
	Actual difference in growth	Estimated difference in growth	Diffusion	Innovative activity (growth)	Investment (level)	Export orientation (change)
Cluster A	–	–	–	–	–	–
Cluster B	0.5	1.0	0.4	0.4	0.3	−0.2
Cluster C	1.0	1.0	0.2	0.2	0.5	0.1
Cluster D	3.0	3.1	1.4	0.9	1.0	−0.2
of which:						
European NICs	1.3	1.2	1.0	−0.0	0.5	−0.3
Latin Am. NICs	1.9	2.3	1.5	−0.1	0.8	0.1
Asian NICs	6.0	5.7	1.6	2.9	1.7	−0.4
Japan	2.4	3.5	0.5	1.0	2.1	−0.2
All countries	1.5	1.7	0.7	0.5	0.6	−0.1

Table 20.6 decomposes the differences in growth between the frontier countries (cluster A) and the others (model 4). The following picture emerges:

(1) Differences in growth between the frontier countries and the other groups of developed countries (Japan excluded) were rather small in the period under consideration, about 1 per cent as a maximum (cluster C – cluster A). The model attributes this difference to a combination of factors, although technological factors seem to have greater significance for cluster B than for cluster C countries, while investments seem to matter more for the latter.

(2) The model attributes the higher growth of Japan, when compared to the frontier countries (around 3 per cent), mainly to Japan's high growth in national technological activity and the high level of investments in the country.

(3) Within the group of semi-industrialized countries, two distinctly different growth patterns may be observed. The European and Latin American NICs grow on average 1.5–2 per cent faster than the frontier countries, primarily because of diffusion of technology, but partly also because of a higher share of resources devoted to investments. The Asian NICs, however, grow on average about 6 per cent faster than the frontier countries, and 3–4 per cent faster than the other NICs. The model attributes this latter difference to the rapid growth of the Asian NICs' own technological activities, in combination with high levels of investments.

Concluding remarks

Most studies of 'why growth rates differ' between countries have in common the fact that they ignore innovation and lack a systematic theory of what causes growth to differ. Thus, while useful as descriptions, they do not really explain differences in growth performances across countries.

This chapter has developed a simple, testable model of economic growth based on Schumpeterian logic. Both this logic and the subsequent test point strongly in the direction of a close relation between economic growth and growth of national technological activities, a fact that is normally forgotten. Thus, to catch up with the developed countries, the results obtained here suggest that semi-industrialized countries cannot rely only on a combination of technology import and investments, but have to increase their national technological activities as well.

However, the limitations should also be stressed. For instance, the technology-gap model developed here has little or nothing to say on how to achieve higher growth in innovative activity or other efforts related to the exploitation of innovation and diffusion. Furthermore, sectoral as well as inter-temporal differences in the international process of innovation and diffusion, and the relation between these changes and similar changes in the institutional system, are ignored.[26] To do full justice to the theoretical perspective which underlines the model developed in this chapter, nothing less than a multi-sector, multi-country evolutionary model of technological and institutional change would be required.[27]

Appendix

Methods

Growth rates are calculated as geometric averages for the period 1973–83, or the nearest period for which data exist. Levels and shares are calculated as arithmetic averages for the period 1973–83, or the nearest period for which data exist. Changes in shares are calculated as total change in the share between 1983 and 1973, divided by the number of years (normally ten, sometimes less) $((s(t_1) - s(t_0))/n)$.

Sources

Real GDP per capita, 1980 market prices in US dollars, growth of gross domestic product at constant prices, agriculture, exports and gross fixed capital formation as a share of GDP:

OECD countries: *OECD Historical Statistics 1960–1983.*
Taiwan: *Statistical Yearbook of the Republic of China 1984.*
Other countries: *IMF Supplement on Output Statistics and UN Monthly Bulletin of Statistics.*

For Switzerland and New Zealand, data for Agriculture as a share of GDP were not available, so the data for these countries are estimates (based on employment).

External patent applications:
OECD countries: *OECD/STIU DATA BANK.*
Other countries: World International Property Organization (WIPO); *Industrial Property Statistics* (various editions) and unpublished data.
The OECD data are adjusted WIPO data. Data for the non-OECD countries are compiled from published WIPO statistics except for Hong Kong, Korea and Taiwan 1975–83 where data are compiled by WIPO from unpublished sources.

The R & D data are estimates based on the following sources:
OECD countries: *OECD Science and Technology Indicators, Basic Statistical Series (vol. B, 1982) and Recent Results (1984)).*
Other countries: *UNESCO Statistical Yearbook* (various editions) and various UNESCO surveys on resources devoted to R & D.
Military R & D expenditures were, following the OECD, assumed to be negligible in all countries except the United States, France, Germany, Sweden and the United Kingdom. The R & D data for these countries were adjusted downwards according to OECD estimates. The estimates were taken from OECD, Directorate for Science, Technology and Industry; 'The problems of estimating defence and civil GERD in selected OECD member countries' (unpublished). For other countries, civil and total R & D as a percentage of GDP were assumed to be identical.

Growth of labor force (population between 15 and 64):
OECD Historical Statistics 1960–1983, OECD National Accounts (various editions), *UN Monthly Bulletin of Statistics* (various editions), and *Statistical Yearbook of the Republic of China 1984.*

Notes

1. The purpose of the following is to discuss some main characteristics of postwar research in this field, not to give a complete survey. For survey articles covering the whole or parts of this field, the reader is referred to Choi (1983, Chapter 3), Nelson (1981), Chenery (1986) and Maddison (1987).
2. See, for instance, the works by Gerschenkron (1962) and Landes (1969).
3. '. . . the forces animating growth in the lead countries are more mysterious and autonomous than in the follower countries . . .' (Maddison, 1982, p. 29).

4. See, however, Abramovitz's instructive, but inconclusive discussion of possible factors influencing change of leadership (Abramovitz, 1986, pp. 396–405).

5. According to the numbers presented by Abramovitz, US GNP growth over the period 1869/78 – 1944/53 equalled 3.5 per cent, of which 1.8 per cent could be attributed to growth of inputs, and 1.7 per cent was left as unexplained. Similar, if not identical, results were reported by Solow (1957), Kendrick (1961) and Denison (1962).

6. Jorgensen and Griliches originally claimed that the residual could be eliminated altogether, but later retreated from this position. See the debate between them and Denison (Denison, 1969; Jorgensen and Griliches, 1972) on this subject.

7. cf., for instance, the following programmatic remark by Denison: 'Because knowledge is an international commodity, I should expect the contribution of knowledge—as distinct from the change in the lag—to be of about the same size in all the countries examined in this study' (Denison, 1967, p. 282).

8. However, in his 1976 study of Japan, he acknowledges that in this case, 'There was, in other words, a major element of 'catching up', . . . (Denison and Chung, 1976, p. 49).

9. More recently, Kendrick (1981b) has published a study of the growth of nine OECD countries between 1960 and 1979 based on Denison's methodology. But contrary to Denison's analysis, this study attributes a large part of the final residual to 'catching up', especially in the period 1960–73.

10. '. . .some of the recent studies seem to imply that somehow the growth accounts really explain growth. I do not see how they can. A growth accounting is not a tested theory of growth' (Nelson, 1973, p. 466).

11. It should be noted that Kendrick (1981b), in his study of nine OECD countries between 1960 and 1979, includes the contribution to growth from cumulative national R & D outlays. However, according to Kendrick's calculations, this contribution was almost negligible.

12. The purpose of what follows is only to discuss some problems related to applications of neo-classical production-functions to cross-country samples. We do not in any way attempt to survey the development of neo-classical growth theory or the theoretical controversies that followed. For a good (but old) survey of growth theory, see Hahn and Matthews (1964). Pasinetti (1974) provides an exciting introduction to the development of the neo-classical growth theory and the subsequent controversy from a post-Keynesian point of view.

13. For reviews of this literature, as well as empirical evidence, see Choi (1983), Chapters 5–6 and Chenery (1986).

14. Of course, the labor-force variable may still turn up with the expected sign significantly different from zero at the chosen level of significance. But this may simply reflect that the growth of labor force is positively correlated with other variables that affect growth positively, as, for instance, the level of development.

The correlation between growth in labor supply (*POP*) and GDP per capita measured in *PPPs(T)*, a much-used proxy for the potential for technology transfer, for the twenty-seven countries included in our sample (see the next sections) was (the numbers in brackets are *t*-statistics; one star denotes significance of test at the 1 per cent level):

$POP = 3.16 - 0.23T, \quad R^2 = 0.56(0.55)$
$(9.54) \, (-5.70)$

15. It should be noted that there are a few examples of researchers who have estimated neo-classical growth models with some kind of 'development-level' variable included (Chenery, Elkington and Sims, 1970; Parvin, 1975).

16. The major contributors to this development were Gomulka (1971) and Cornwall (1976, 1977), but the main arguments were outlined much earlier by Posner (1961), even if Posner's main concern was specialization, not growth. Krugman (1979) has recently constructed a formal model of north–south trade based on similar arguments. For a more thoroughgoing treatment of these aspects, see the preceding chapter by Dosi and Soete in this book.

17. For a general discussion of some of these issues, see Clark, Freeman and Soete (1982), Perez (1983), and the chapters by Freeman–Perez and Boyer in this book.

18. In the present context, knowledge means 'technological knowhow' (knowledge and skills on how to produce goods and services).

19. The UN study (Kravis et al., 1982) provides estimates for Real GDP (Nominal GDP adjusted for differences in the purchasing power of currencies) and Nominal GDP for thirty-four developing, semi-industrialized and developed countries for the year 1975. Since many of the countries included in our sample are not covered by the UN study, we used one of the short-cut methods developed there to estimate a relation between Real and nominal GDP per capita (r and n) for a sample of countries comparable to ours, and then used this estimated relation to predict Real GDP per capita for the countries of our sample. The estimated relation was (with a dummy for Jamaica (an extreme deviant) included):

$\ln r = 1.14 + 1.229 \ln n - 0.042 \, (\ln n)^2 - 0.372 \, \text{JAMAICA}$
$(1.52) \, (5.70)^* \qquad\qquad (-2.82)^* \qquad\qquad (-3.49)^*$

$N=27$
$R^2 = 0.99(0.98)$

(The numbers in brackets under the estimates are t-statistics; one star denotes significance at the 1 per cent level)

20. Nevertheless, Soete (1981) found quite a close correlation between levels of domestic patenting and R & D expenses in a cross-country study covering the business enterprise sector in nineteen OECD countries.

21. That is: total patent applications of residents in country x in all countries which report patent applications to WIPO (World Intellectual Property Organization) less patent applications by residents of x in country x.

22. For the sake of comparison with other variables, we will in this section deflate the total numbers of patent applications filed in other countries (external patent applications) by exports. The argument in favor of using exports as a deflator instead of GDP or population is that this adjusts for differences in export orientation, which could have biased the index (as a measure of innovating performance) upwards for countries where the share of exports in GDP is high, and downwards for countries where the share of exports in GDP is low, as, for instance, the United States and India.

23. The data are organized in descending order of GDP per capita (as it was in the early 1960s, though). This implies that the Durbin–Watson statistics can be

given a special interpretation: it shows whether countries on approximately the same level of GDP per capita tend to have correlated residuals.

24. This is not to deny that limitations in labour supply may restrict the growth of certain countries in certain periods, but this is not considered relevant in the period under consideration here (1973–83). Cornwall (1977), however, holds that it was not relevant in the pre-1973 period either.

25. On this point, see also Fagerberg (1987).

26. For a discussion of some of these issues (determinants of innovation, sectoral differences in innovation patterns, national systems of innovation and policy issues), the reader is referred to Parts IV–V of this book.

27. To the best of our knowledge, no attempts to construct international models along these lines have yet been made, but it certainly represents a path worth following. For a general discussion of evolutionary modelling, see the chapter by Silverberg in this book.

References

Abramovitz, M. (1956), 'Resources and output trends in the United States since 1870', *American Economic Review*, vol. 46, pp. 5–23.

—— (1979), 'Rapid growth potential and its realization: the experience of capitalist economies in the postwar period', in E. Malinvaud (ed.)(1977), *Economic Growth and Resources*, London, Macmillan.

—— (1986), 'Catching up, forging ahead, and falling behind', *Journal of Economic History*, vol. 66, pp. 385–406.

Ames, E. and Rosenberg, N. (1963), 'Changing technological leadership and industrial growth', *Economic Journal*, vol. 73, pp. 13–31.

Chenery, H. (1986), 'Growth and transformation', in H. Chenery *et al.* (eds.) (1986).

Chenery, H., Elkington, H and Sims, C. (1970), *A Uniform Analysis of Development Patterns*, Harvard University Center for International Affairs, Economic Development Report 148, Cambridge, Mass.

Chenery, H., Robinson, R. and Syrquin, M. (1986), *Industrialization and Growth*, Oxford, Oxford University Press.

Choi, K. (1983), *Theories of Comparative Economic Growth*, Ames, Iowa State University Press.

Clark, J., Freeman, C. and Soete, L. (1982), *Unemployment and Technical Innovation*, London, Frances Pinter.

Cornwall, J. (1976), 'Diffusion, convergence and Kaldor's law', *Economic Journal*, vol. 86, pp. 307–14.

—— (1977), *Modern Capitalism: Its Growth and Transformation*, London, Martin Robertson.

Domar, E. *et al.* (1964), 'Economic growth and productivity in the United States, Canada, United Kingdom, Germany and Japan in the post-war period', *Review of Economics and Statistics*, vol. 46, pp. 33–40.

Denison, E.F. (1962), *The Sources of Economic Growth in the United States and the Alternatives before Us*, New York, Committee for Economic Development.

—— (1967), *Why Growth Rates Differ: Post-War Experience in Nine Western Countries*, Washington, DC, Brookings Institution.

—— (1969), 'Some major issues in productivity analysis: an examination of estimates by Jorgenson and Griliches', *Survey of Current Business*, vol. 49: 1–28.

Denison, E.F. and Chung, W.K. (1976), *How Japan's Economy Grew so Fast: The Sources of Postwar Expansion*, Washington, DC, Brookings Institution.

Fagerberg, J. (1986), *Technology, Growth and International Competitiveness*, NUPI Rapport nr. 95, Oslo, Norwegian Institute of International Affairs.

—— (1987), 'A technology-gap approach to why growth rates differ', *Research Policy*, vol. 16, pp. 87–99.

Feder, G. (1986), 'Growth in semi-industrial countries: a statistical analysis', in H. Chenery *et al.* (1986).

Fellner, W. (ed.) (1981), *Essays in Contemporary Economic Problems*, Washington, DC, American Enterprise Institute.

Freeman, C. (1982), *The Economics of Industrial Innovation*, 2nd Edn., London, Frances Pinter.

Gerschenkron, A. (1962), *Economic Backwardness in Historical Perspective*, Cambridge (USA), The Bellknap Press.

Giersch, H. (ed.)(1981), *Towards an Explanation of Economic Growth*, Tübingen, J.C.B. Mohr (Paul Siebeck).

—— (1982), *Emerging Technologies: Consequences for Economic Growth, Structural Change, and Employment*, Tübingen, JCB Mohr (Paul Siebeck).

Gomulka, S. (1971), *Inventive Activity, Diffusion and Stages of Economic Growth*, Skrifter fra Aarhus universitets ekonomiske institutt nr. 24, Aarhus.

Hahn, F.H. and Matthews, R.C.O. (1964), 'The theory of economic growth: a survey', *Economic Journal*, vol. 74, pp. 779–902.

Jorgensen, D. and Griliches, Z. (1967), 'The explanation of productivity change', *Review of Economic Studies*, vol. 34, pp. 249–84.

Jorgensen, D. and Griliches, Z. (1972), 'Some major issues in growth accounting: a reply to Denison', *Survey of Current Business*, vol. 52, pp. 65–94.

Kendrick, J.W. (1961), *Productivity Trends in the United States*, New York, Princeton University Press.

—— (1981a), 'Why productivity growth rates change and differ', in H. Giersch (ed.) (1981).

—— (1981b), 'International comparisons of recent productivity trends', in W. Fellner (ed.) (1981).

—— (1984), *International Comparisons of Productivity and Causes of the Slowdown*, Cambridge, Mass., Ballinger Publishing Company.

Kravis, I., Heston, A. and Summers, R. (1982), *World Product and Income*, published by the World Bank, Baltimore, The John Hopkins University Press.

Krugman, P. (1979), 'A model of innovation, technology transfer and the world distribution of income', *Journal of Political Economy*, vol. 87, pp. 253–66.

Landes, D. (1969), *The Unbound Prometheus*, Cambridge, Cambridge University Press.

Maddison, A. (1979), 'Long-run dynamics of productivity growth', *Banca Nazionale del Lavoro Quarterly Review*, vol. 128, pp. 1–73.

—— (1982), *Phases of Capitalist Development*, New York, Oxford Unversity Press.

—— (1984), 'Comparative analysis of productivity situation in the advanced capitalist countries', in J.W. Kendrick (ed.) (1984).

—— (1987), *Growth and Slowdown in Advanced Capitalist Economies: Techniques of Quantitative Assessment*, Journal of Economic Literature, vol. 25, pp. 649–98.

Malinvaud, E. (ed.) (1979), *Economic Growth and Resources*, London, Macmillan.

Mansfield, E. *et al.* (1982), *Technology Transfer, Productivity and Economic Policy*, New York, Norton.

Nelson, R. (1973), 'Recent exercises in growth accounting: new understanding or dead end?', *American Economic Review*, vol. 63, pp. 462–68.

—— (1981), 'Research on productivity growth and productivity differentials: dead ends and new departures', *Journal of Economic Literature*, vol. 19, pp. 1029–64.

Pasinetti, L. (1974), *Growth and Income Distribution*, Cambridge, Cambridge University Press.

Parvin, M. (1975), 'Technological adaptation, optimum level of backwardness and the rate of per capita income growth: an econometric approach', *American Economist*, vol. 19, pp. 23–31.

Pavitt, K. (1979/80), 'Technical innovation and industrial development', *Futures*, vol. 11, pp. 458–70, vol. 12, pp. 35–44.

—— (1983), 'R & D, patenting and innovative activities', *Research Policy*, vol. 12, pp. 78–98.

Pavitt, K. and Soete, L.G. (1982), 'International differences in economic growth and the international location of innovation', in H. Giersch, (ed.) (1982).

Perez, C. (1983), 'Structural change and the assimilation of new technologies in the economic and social systems', *Futures*, vol. 15, pp. 357–75.

Posner, M.V. (1961), 'International trade and technical change', *Oxford Economic papers*, vol. 13, pp. 323–41.

Schumpeter, J. (1934), *The Theory of Economic Development*, Cambridge, Mass., Harvard University Press.

—— (1939), *Business Cycles I–II*, New York, McGraw-Hill.

—— (1942), *Capitalism, Socialism and Democracy*, New York, Harper.

Singer, H. and Reynolds, L. (1975), 'Technological backwardness and productivity growth', *Economic Journal*, vol. 85, pp. 873–76.

Soete, L. (1981), 'A general test of technological-gap trade theory', *Weltwirtschaftliches Archiv*, vol. 117, pp. 639–59.

Solow, R. (1957), 'Technical change and the aggregate production function', *Review of Economics and Statistics*, vol. 39, pp. 312–20.

Tinbergen, J. (1942), 'Zür Theorie der langfristigen Wirtschaftsentwicklung', *Weltwirtschaftliches Archiv*, vol. 55, pp. 512–49.

Veblen, T. (1915), *Imperial Germany and the Industrial Revolution*, New York, Macmillan.

21 Catching up in technology: entry barriers and windows of opportunity

Carlota Perez

UNIDO–Ministry of Industry, Caracas and SPRU, University of Sussex, Brighton

Luc Soete

MERIT, Faculty of Economics, State University of Limburg, Maastricht

Introduction

The importance of 'foreign' technology and its international diffusion is undoubtedly a historically well-recognised factor in the industrialisation of both Europe and the United States in the nineteenth century, and even more strikingly of Japan in the twentieth century. That importance emerges again and significantly stronger from the evidence of the rapid industrialisation of some so-called newly industrialising countries, such as South Korea, over the last two decades.

In fact, the great majority of developing countries continue to face enormous difficulties in their efforts to industrialise. This has lent credence to the theories of 'dependency' which hold that there is a structural gap between developing and developed countries that remains and widens. Thus the few recent examples of relative success which seem to counter that theory have, not surprisingly, aroused intense interest and demand a satisfactory explanation. In our view, what is required is a deeper understanding of the technological issues which underlie the process of development. More adequate attention must be given to the questions of how technologies evolve and diffuse and under what conditions a process of *effective* technological catching up can take place.

There is, of course, a voluminous literature on this subject which has been a focal point of research for economic historians (see, e.g. Landes, 1969; Rosenberg, 1976). We do not intend to review this literature here. Suffice to point out a fruitful convergence appearing between two streams of work: on the one hand, that based on in-depth case studies of countries catching up in the production and use of particular technologies (see especially Ames and Rosenberg, 1963; Habakkuk, 1962, von Tunzelmann, 1978; and many others); and, on the other, some of the recent international trade and growth models – reviewed in the chapter by Dosi and Soete—based on imitation and 'catching up' (see in particular Posner, 1961; Freeman, 1963, 1965, Gomulka, 1971, Cornwall, 1977, etc.). That convergence puts the emphasis clearly back on the historical context and the institutional framework (see also Section V) within which the process of imitation/technological catching up takes place. It includes the importance of 'developmental' constraints, be they primarily economic (such as the lack of natural resources) or more political in nature, the role of immigration (see Scoville, 1951) and other 'germ carriers', the crucial role of governments (for a broad overview, see Yakushiji, 1986), and, of course, the role of historical accidents.

From such a perspective, the international diversity in growth performance of countries—as illustrated in the previous chapter by Fagerberg—could well provide a case *par excellence* of the importance of path-dependent development, with possibilities of 'locked-in' development (see B. Arthur's chapter). It could mean that some industrialisation locations got 'selected' early on and, by appropriating the available agglomeration economies, exercised some 'competitive exclusion'—to use Arthur's (1986) term—on other locations. Indeed, and as also illustrated in Arthur's chapter, it is the increasing returns associated with industrialisation and development which make the conditions of development so paradoxical. Previous capital is needed to produce new capital, previous knowledge is needed to absorb new knowledge, skills must be available to acquire new skills, and a certain level of development is required to create the infrastructure and the agglomeration economies that make development possible. In summary, it is within the logic of the dynamics of the system that the rich get richer and the gap remains and widens for those left behind.

All development policies have in one way or another been geared to breaking away from this vicious circle. Most have concentrated on tackling the investment and infrastructure locational questions with some, but relatively less, direct attention to the knowledge and skills constraints.

The question we wish to tackle here is whether these constraints are always equally formidable or whether their intensity varies in time with some increasing and some decreasing, thereby opening windows of opportunity to escape the vicious circle. According to some of the neo-technology accounts of international trade, comparative advantage would shift to 'less developed' countries with the further international diffusion of technologies as they reach maturity. Thus through the 'use' of imported technologies these countries would acquire some comparative industrialisation advantage but only in mature products and industries.

Indeed at first sight, the choice of *mature* products as a point of entry is probably the only one available to initiate a development process. However (and leaving aside for the moment all aspects of technological 'blending' and other user-initiated technological change), in so far as mature products are precisely those that have exhausted their technological dynamism, this choice implies a clear risk of getting 'fixed' in a low wage, low growth, development pattern. A real catching-up process can only be achieved through acquiring the capacity for participating in the generation and improvement of technologies as opposed to the simple 'use' of them. This means being able to *enter* either as early imitators or as innovators of new products or processes. Under what conditions would this be possible?

To answer this question, the long term nature of technological change as a disruptive process with changes in direction and deep structural transformations needs to be far better understood. The notion of technological change as a global, more or less continuous process underlies the traditional way development is viewed. As long as technology is understood as a cumulative unidirectional process, development will be seen as a race along a fixed track, where catching up will be merely a question of relative speed. Speed is no doubt a relevant aspect, but history is full of examples of how successful overtaking has been primarily based on running in a new direction.

In this chapter we begin to look at some of the specific conditions under which technological catching up and imitation could take place. In a short introductory section, we set out, in line with the chapter by Metcalfe on diffusion, some of the most salient points with regard to diffusion theory which appear of relevance to theories of industrial development and economic growth. In the second section, we go in more detail into the conditions for imitators to enter and effectively catch up.

We begin with a static view of technologies in order to look at how the actual costs of developing, imitating or buying a production technology are influenced by the characteristics of the acquiring firm and by those of its location. We then introduce technological dynamism and examine how the various elements of those costs (and the barriers they erect for new entrants) increase or decrease as technologies evolve from introduction to maturity. This leads us to identify the importance of the timing of entry in terms of individual technologies. Finally, we introduce the interrelatedness of technologies in complex technology systems and the notion of changes in techno-economic paradigms, i.e. the emergence of radical discontinuities in overall technological evolution. This brings us to the concluding argument that catching up involves being in a position to take advantage of the window of opportunity temporarily created by such technological transitions.

Technology diffusion models and industrial growth and development

Some introductory comments

Diffusion models, at least in their simplest 'epidemic' representation, have, as already noted in Metcalfe's chapter, a striking level of methodological similarity with some of the models of industrial growth and economic development developed in the 1930s by Kuznets (1930) and Schumpeter (1912/34) among others. This is in many ways not surprising. The concepts of 'imitation' and 'bandwagons', so crucial to the diffusion literature, have been and still are central in many of the more structural accounts of economic growth, where the S-shaped diffusion pattern is similar to the emergence and long-term rise and fall of industries. An attempt at linking the two theories is made in Freeman *et al.* (1982). Here it is precisely the notion of 'clusters' of innovations including the follow-up innovations made during the diffusion period which are linked to the rapid growth of new industries, and will in the extreme case even provide the ingredients of an upswing in overall economic growth. In the more restrictive diffusion terminology, this could be viewed as an 'envelope' encompassing the diffusion curves of a set of closely interrelated clusters of innovations which, occurring within a limited time span, might tilt the economy in the early diffusion phase to a higher rate of economic performance.

Another similarity with diffusion models can be found in Rostow's theory of the stages of economic growth (1960) with again a distinct S-shaped pattern of take-off, rapid growth with the 'drive to maturity', and slower growth with the 'age of high mass-consumption' and standard-isation. Rostow phases contain many of the S-shaped development patterns assumed to exist for new products, as typified in the marketing and subsequent international trade literature on the 'product life cycle'. Similar notions underlie the argument put forward in the mid-1960s by Hirsch (1965), who showed how the relative importance of certain produc-tion factors would change over the different phases of the product cycle. Hirsch and after him Vernon (1966) and many other proponents of the product life-cycle trade theory illustrated how such changes could shift comparative advantage in favour of less developed countries as products reached the maturity phase.

Within the development literature, particularly the 'dependencia school', such views and particularly Rostow's theory were heavily criti-cised; the mechanistic, quasi-autonomous nature of the process of economic growth assumed by Rostow was seen as 'ahistorical'. Interest-ingly, though, the critique of Rostow's growth model finds its reflection in much of the recent diffusion literature, criticising the 'mechanistic, atheoretical' nature of the S-shaped, 'epidemic' technology diffusion models.

These recent diffusion contributions provide also a number of interesting insights into some of the broader industrial growth theories mentioned earlier. The first area of critique of the 'standard' diffusion model has led to the application of 'probit analysis' to develop a new model of inter-firm diffusion. Probit analysis was already a well-established technique in the study of the diffusion of new products between individuals. The central assumption underlying the probit model is that an individual consumer (or firm) will be found to own the new product (or adopt the new innovation) at a particular time when his income (size) exceeds some critical level. This critical, or tolerance, income (or size) level represents the actual tastes of the consumer (the receptiveness of the firm) which itself can be related to any number of personal or economic characteristics. Over time, though, with the increase in income and assuming an unchanged income distribu-tion, the critical income will fall with an across-the-board change in taste in favour of the new product, due both to imitation, more and better information, band-wagon effects. etc.

The probit model can be a useful tool for industrial growth theory. A 'critical' income *per capita* level is a concept which can be introduced in Rostow's theory of the stages of economic growth. Replacing the concept of individuals or firms by 'countries', different growth performances can be explained and expected. The problem is, of course, more complex. The example of the OPEC countries shows that even with a tremendous increase in income the absorptive capacity of a country might still be below the critical level needed for take-off. Thus, considering both the extreme variation in each country's ability to use and manage resources, to take risks and 'assess new innovations' (the variation in consumer tastes in the probit model), as well as the extreme income inequalities at the world level, it should come as no surprise that world-wide industrialisation (diffusion) has been so slow and uneven.

The second major set of criticisms against the standard diffusion model relates primarily to its *static* nature and the way the diffusion process is reduced to a pure demand-induced phenomenon. Metcalfe (1981, 1982) in particular has emphasised the limits of the standard model in this area. As many detailed studies of the 'innovation process' have indicated, there are plenty of reasons for expecting both the innovation and its surrounding economic environment to change as diffusion proceeds. At the techno-logical end, one may expect significant improvements to the innovation to occur as diffusion evolves. At the economic end the price of the innovation will change throughout the process of diffusion. In addition, the supply of the innovation will depend on the profitability of producing it.

Once the importance of the strong feedback between supply and demand factors in innovation diffusion is fully recognised, it is easier to see how past investment in the 'old' established technology can slow down the diffusion of the new innovation. This applies to past investment not just in physical capital but also in human capital, even 'intellectual' capital. As Rosenberg (1976) and von Tunzelmann (1978) have observed, the diffu-sion of steam power in the last century was significantly retarded by a series of improvements to the existing water power technology which further prolonged the economic life of the old technology. The process of decline and disappearance of an old technology is indeed slow, with the old technology firms often living off past, fully recovered investment and being sometimes able to underprice the innovation-adopting firms.

The implications for the international diffusion of technology and the potential for technological catching up are far-reaching. There is every reason to expect that the vast majority of new technologies will originate primarily within the technologically most advanced countries. There are also, however, good reasons to expect that the diffusion of such major new technologies will be hampered in some of those countries by the heavy investment outlays in the more established technologies, the commitment of management and the skilled labour force to them and even by the research geared towards improving them. This could mean that the new technology might diffuse more quickly elsewhere, in a country less committed to the old technology in terms of actual production, investment and skills. At the same time, as diffusion proceeds, some of the crucial, incremental innovations, resulting from user–feedback information and other dynamic factors, could tend to shift further the technological advantage to the country in which the new technology is diffusing more rapidly.

The industrialisation in the nineteenth century of Germany, France and the United States and a number of smaller European countries provides ample support for this view. The dramatic change in fortune in the United Kingdom's position from an absolute technological leadership, producing in the mid-nineteenth century more steam engines than the whole of the rest of the world put together, is a powerful illustration of this phenomenon. In recent times, this has been most obvious in the case of Japan in the 1960s and 1970s where world 'best-practice' productivity levels were achieved over a very short time in steel, cars, electronics, numerically controlled machine tools, and, in the most recent years, computers, largely on the basis of initially imported technology. More recently, and more strikingly, South Korea has achieved similar successes in some of these sectors.

These successful examples illustrate the existence of windows of opportunity for 'late industrialisers'. However, their scarcity highlights how 'non-automatic' and exceptional such processes of effective technological catching up are. The use of foreign, imported technology as an 'industrialisation' short cut depends on having the required conditions to undertake the difficult and complex process involved in its effective assimilation.

A first approach to the real cost of production technologies

There is a fundamental difference between the diffusion of a final consumer product in a population and the diffusion of capital goods or production technologies in general. In the first case, the product is developed with the clear intention of selling it. Thus the innovator will be pushing diffusion and trying to overcome obstacles to adoption. The price of the product is one of the tools to push diffusion. In the case of production technologies there is a whole range of situations. At one end of the spectrum, we find the innovator who develops the technology for his own use and wants to monopolise it, going to all lengths to avoid diffusion. At the other end, we find the supplier who develops a new machine or process with the intention of selling it to users, pushing, as in the case of consumer products, for widespread adoption. Metcalfe's diffusion models refer mainly to the latter part of the spectrum.

Yet, there is another, perhaps even more fundamental difference between the conditions for diffusion of innovations among consumers and among productive users. For someone to buy a personal computer and never learn to use it is certainly of little consequence. But for a firm buying a steel plant it is absolutely crucial that it be able to use the plant effectively to make steel, achieve a viable share of the market and make a profit. This means that besides having enough income to invest in the equipment, there are other more intangible assets that the would-be producer *must* possess or acquire. So the characteristics of the buyer (or imitator) will have enormous influence on the actual cost of the technology to that particular firm.

What this means is that production technologies have no single price tag. This is quite different from the assumption of most diffusion models that all adopters at a particular moment in time face the same cost. It will be argued here that the notion of a threshold for entry is not limited to the 'price' of the equipment but involves a set of interrelated conditions and leads in fact to vastly different costs of entry depending on the characteristics of the acquiring firm and of the environment in which it operates.

Beyond the fixed investment cost, there are at least three groups of elements which contribute to determine the actual cost of *entry* for each individual firm. One is the cost of the scientific and technical knowledge required to assimilate the innovation; another is the cost of acquiring the experience required to handle it and successfully bring it to the market; and third, but not least, is the cost of overcoming any 'locational' disadvantages related to the general infrastructure and other economic and institutional conditions surrounding the firm.

Consequently, also, the notion of an entry threshold for production technologies becomes much more complex than the straightforward income level of the probit model. Barriers to entry are then a fourfold combination where each of the elements mentioned above would impose a threshold below which costs for the would-be entrant become formidable. To take the most absurd limiting conditions, no one would consider setting up an automobile plant in the middle of the Sahara, and an illiterate peasant who hit the jackpot would be hard put to set up a firm to produce monoclonal antibodies.

All these cost elements are fully recognised in practice in many technology-transfer contracts to developing country firms. These generally include not only the cost of the 'turn-key' plant but also payment for the technology licence and for technical assistance or transfer of experience and 'know-how'. Additionally, government aid is usually expected to counteract locational disadvantages or provide tariffs to shield the higher local costs.

Threshold levels and entry costs: a simple world

To examine the way in which these various factors might influence the cost of entry, we start out with a simple world where technologies do not evolve and are of a 'free nature'. In other words, technologies are introduced in their final and only form and the innovator does not try to appropriate any part of the technology but is willing to sell the required information and equipment to imitators at their *net* cost.

By entry costs we now understand the total costs of everything the innovator or imitator requires for setting up production facilities, successfully launching the product, and reaching a viable market volume. For any innovation, the costs of entry for the innovator (C_a) could be represented as the sum of the following components: the fixed investment costs (I) in plant and equipment; the cost (S_a) incurred by the innovator in acquiring the scientific and technical knowledge relevant to the innovation which was not possessed by the firm at the beginning of the innovation process; the cost (E_a) incurred by the innovator in acquiring the relevant experience (know-how in organisation, management, marketing or other areas) required to carry the innovation through; the cost (X_a) borne by the innovator to compensate for whatever relevant externalities are not provided by the environment in which the firm operates. Finally, as regards the innovator, there would generally be certain costs (W), due to following 'wrong' leads in the trial and error process involved in innovating. Those extra costs could express themselves in terms of extra costs in each of the previous four components.

In the first instance, the difference with the imitating firm's costs (C_i) relates to W: i.e. the 'wrong' costs that will not be incurred. The imitating firm will know exactly where it stands and exactly where it is going. Given our assumptions, the imitator can purchase in the open market or from the innovator all the required equipment, plant, knowledge and know-how. Nevertheless, the savings in W are not enough to predict that the imitator will have lower costs of entry than the innovator. It all depends on the relative starting positions of the innovator and imitator in terms of relevant knowledge, experience and location. Let us briefly examine each of the components of the cost of entry.

(a) Fixed investment: the basic cost

With regard to the *fixed investment costs* (I), these are defined by the character of the innovation itself and can be very large or very small depending on the product. In our simple model they are fixed once and for all at the level determined by the net costs of the innovator. Since the innovation cannot be made without this investment, I represents the absolute minimum threshold of entry for any producer. If the innovator purchased or developed any unnecesary equipment, its costs would be included in W as W_k. An imitator then would enjoy a fixed cost advantage of W_k.

(b) The cost of closing the knowledge gap

The *scientific and technical knowledge* (S) required for an innovation generally includes a fair amount of what is called 'freely' available knowledge and information which serves as a platform for generating the new or innovation-bound knowledge (which in the real world would usually be patentable or kept secret). However, the fact that knowledge is freely available cannot be understood as having no cost of acquisition. Even if the information is in a library, a firm requiring it will incur various costs, in time, transportation and personnel to 'purchase' it. More likely the firm will have to hire consultants or qualified personnel as well as buy the relevant reference materials. The generation of new knowledge obviously has costs in time and personnel for design and experimentation as well as equipment and prototype expenses. The actual costs for the innovator will consequently include not only that of generating the new innovation-bound knowledge but also the cost of acquiring that part of 'freely' available relevant knowledge which the innovating firm did not possess to begin with.

To bring back the discussion to the concept of threshold levels, it should be clear that it would be absurd to assume that a firm can start with zero previous knowledge. There is a threshold level below which costs to the firm would be infinitely high. This threshold cannot be defined *a priori*, but would vary depending on how science-based or how truly 'new' the innovation is.

On the other hand, it is well established that the capacity to absorb new knowledge is greater the larger the amount of relevant knowledge already possessed. This in terms of cost would imply that the closer the firm is to the required frontier in terms of knowledge, the less costly it will be to acquire an additional 'unit' of information. Graphically, the relationship between the knowledge-related technology acquisition costs (on the vertical axis) and the various possible starting levels at which acquiring firms may find themselves in terms of the relevant scientific and technical knowledge required (on the horizontal axis) is represented in Figure 21.1

The minimum knowledge threshold s indicates the level at or below which the firm, whether innovator or imitator, would face infinite knowledge-related entry costs for lack of absorptive capacity. The level s_n is the total amount of relevant knowledge required for using the innovation, whereas the level s_p is the publicly available knowledge upon which the innovation-bound knowledge $(s_n - s_p)$ was built. Since there is no reason to assume that the innovator possessed all the relevant 'free' knowledge before generating the new, the firm's starting point s_a would be somewhere between s and s_p.

The knowledge-related entry costs for the innovator are then composed of the cost S_g of closing the gap between s_a and s_p, the cost S_n of generating the new knowledge $(s_n - s_p)$ and the costs incurred in following 'wrong' leads S_w. Obviously, the higher the level of relevant scientific and technical knowledge possessed by the innovating firm, the smaller the gap it has to close and the lower its entry costs. But this, of course, also holds for the imitator. Following our assumptions, an imitator with a starting knowledge level equivalent to that of the innovator would face equivalent costs S_g of closing the 'free' knowledge gap plus the net R & D costs S_n charged by the innovator who is assumed generously to spare him the 'wrong' development costs. So the imitator's cost curve would be lower (dotted line in Figure 21.1) for any starting level of knowledge than for the innovator. It is

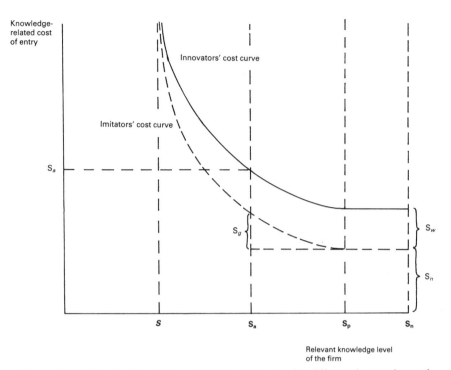

Figure 21.1   Varying knowledge-related cost of entry for different innovating and imitating firms.

clear, however, that even in our simple model the imitator's knowledge-related entry costs will depend crucially on his own initial scientific and technical knowledge base in the relevant areas. Consequently his entry costs may be much higher or much lower than the innovator's, depending on their relative starting positions on the horizontal axis.

(c) The cost of closing the experience and skills gap

With regard to the third set of entry costs, the *experience-related* costs, a similar argument could be put forward. For a product or process design to go beyond the prototype stage into a fully fledged innovation in the market, many skills must come together. From management, through production to distribution and marketing, experience is required and acquired. And the same holds for the success of an imitator.

Although the actual levels as well as the slope of the curves would be different within each particular technology, the entry costs curve for closing the varying gaps in experience levels could be of the same general shape as that discussed above where again a minimum threshold level of experience would exist below which the firm would face infinite costs. Again, a higher initial experience level would mean lower costs of closing the gap. We are, as in the case of knowledge, referring here to *relevant* experience. This creates an important difference between the two types of information discussed. Having a certain amount of 'irrelevant' knowledge does not harm the innovating firm. A wider knowledge base, even if in apparently unrelated fields, can be a source of originality and strengthen the absorptive capacity of the firm. By contrast, irrelevant experience, or rather experience in 'the old way of doing things', can be a dead weight when it comes to innovating and imitating. As already hinted at in the previous section, there could be a cost attached to getting rid of such 'wrong' experience.

So even in this simple view of the world there would be significant differences in the experience-related costs of entry, not only between innovators and imitators but also between new and old firms, i.e. between firms that have inertial 'wrong' experience and firms that do not.

(d) The cost of compensating for lack of externalities

Whatever the endowment of a firm, in financial resources, knowledge and experience, its capacity to innovate will be much influenced by the characteristics of the environment in which it operates or plans to operate. Moreover, every single entry-cost component will be affected by the surrounding advantages or disadvantages.

Even in the simple model discussed here where the cost I of the necessary plant and equipment is the same for all entrants, the locational (dis)advantages will produce big variations. Making realistic assumptions about economic geography, the distance from equipment suppliers, the adequacy of the transport infrastructure, and the local availability of competent design, construction and engineering contractors would result in vast actual cost differences for firms in different locations. So extra investment costs X_k accruing to each firm from disadvantages in location would increase I to $(I + X_k)$. Furthermore, the disadvantages can be so large, as in the extreme case mentioned of the automobile plant in the middle of the desert, that X_k erects a formidable entry barrier.

The same can be said for both scientific and technical knowledge and experience. There were obvious advantages for an electronics firm located in Silicon Valley in terms of access to relevant university research and researchers which made its knowledge-related costs of entry lower than those of an equivalent firm planning to set up in, say, Arkansas or Ecuador. It is also well known that these firms profited from a certain amount of synergy in terms of both knowledge and experience through the frequent communication between personnel of different nearby firms. Equally, the buying-in of personnel from other firms became a common practice to take experience short-cuts in both highly qualified staff and skilled workers in the field.

Thus, in more general terms it can be said that the quality and the quantity of scientific and technological capacity offered by the surrounding environment will result in variations in the cost of acquisition of the required relevant knowledge for otherwise equally endowed firms. The distance (both geographic and cultural) from these possible sources of knowledge (including in our simple case the distance from the innovating firm) will increase the entry cost component S to $(S + X_s)$. And, again, X_s could become large enough to erect an effective barrier to entry.

Similar considerations apply to the availability of experience and skills in the surrounding environment. It is clear that if the required skilled personnel is abundantly available locally the cost of acquisition is the going market rate for this type of labour (which, being different in each locality, would already determine differences in costs for firms in different locations). Otherwise, the skills must be imported from distant markets in the form of people or training or they must be acquired with time and practice and mistakes. The same can be said for consumer education. If surrounding consumers possess both the income level and the habit of using similar products, the cost of penetrating the market will be much lower than if the firm has to carry the cost of educating the consumers. So the experience-related costs of entry for an innovating firm will increase and will therefore depend not only on its own level of experience endowment but also on the endowment of the surrounding environment.

Yet the locational (dis)advantages which affect the cost of entry for a firm are not limited to the three categories related to our previous entry-cost elements $(X_k, X_s$ and $X_e)$. There are required services both for the investment process and for regular operation, ranging from financial services to transport facilities and basic utilities (water, electricity, telecommunications, etc.), which determine the general conditions for business and can have crucial or lesser importance depending on the specific nature of the innovation. The relative costs, efficiency and ease of access to those that are relevant among these services will influence both the cost and the possibility of entry. Another set of locational (dis)advantages includes those elements upon which more traditional economic analysis has concentrated, i.e. the relative prices of the required inputs, the relative wage rates and the size and characteristics of the domestic market.

Last, but not least, the firm operates within a legal, social and institutional framework. Numerous aspects of this framework such as government regulations, standards, taxes, subsidies, tariffs, and other relevant policies or laws; trade-union organisation and practices; the structure and policies of the financial system; even the values of the local population in terms of willingness to accept or reject the innovation or its consequences will have a strong bearing on the actual costs of entry for an innovator in that particular country or locality. Even issues relating to language can be significant depending on the nature of the innovation.

In general, it could be said that what determines the level of relevant (dis)advantages for a firm in a particular location is the previous history of development in that location. Each additional producer in a country, region or locality would benefit from the agglomeration economies created by its predecessors and from concomitant factors such as the educational level of the population, government experience in dealing with and supporting industry and services, development of distribution networks, etc. So there would be a minimum environmental threshold x which, depending on the specific nature of the innovation, can be either very low or very high. Below this threshold the extra costs confronting the firm could become prohibitive and above it they would decrease until they disappear (or even turn into savings).

There is, however, as in the case of the wrong' experience which created additional costs for the firm, the possibility of confronting inertial or negative conditions in the environment. In this case, extra costs W_x would accrue to the firm, whether innovator or imitator, to surmount such 'obsolete' conditions. A high level of consumer saturation in TV sets is an infrastructural advantage for introducing video-recorders but would become an inertial disadvantage for introducing a digital system of transmission requiring a change in reception equipment. So, in some cases, an environment with high commitment to the old products or a high development of the old type of infrastructure can hold back the diffusion of radical innovations.

Similar arguments could be put forward with regard to certain types of conditions which are also related to the environment and can result in significant savings to the firm, reducing its costs of entry and operation. This cost of entry 'rebate' is composed primarily of direct government 'help'. It comprises government subsidies of all sorts, preferential interest rates, R & D grants, tax reductions, protective barriers, and any other form of direct or indirect absorption of what would otherwise have been a cost to the firm. These are advantages that can be politically created, increased, reduced or eliminated by governments. They are not rooted in the environment as ports, roads, services or skills are, but they can certainly reduce the costs of entry for any producer in that particular country or locality.

To conclude the analysis of threshold levels and entry costs in this first, highly simplified case of a 'static' and freely available technology, it is clear that there is no single price tag for production technologies nor is it solely determined by the supplier. Furthermore, the absolute threshold level is not limited to the price of the technology. It includes minimum levels of scientific and technical knowledge, practical experience and locational advantages. Thus, given the great variety of possible initial conditions of would-be entrants, there is actually no way of determining beforehand whether the innovator or any particular imitator in any particular location will have the lower entry cost.

Yet this model seems to reinforce the difficulty of catching up. It is clear that the starting points of developing country firms in all four components, but particularly the last, would tend to be lower than those typical of firms in the more advanced countries.

To examine the question of development we must come closer to the real conditions in the 'technology market'.

The timing of entry

Technological evolution and the cost of entry as a moving target

Relaxing the freely available technology condition of the model will bring us closer to the real world. New entrants do affect both market share and profits of pre-existing producers. Consequently innovators will choose to sell or not to sell the relevant innovation-bound knowledge and experience as well as whatever equipment was directly designed for the innovation and is therefore not available in the market. Imitators will compare the cost of buying the technology with the cost of developing it themselves, if they can. Both these costs vary with the age of the techno-logy, the level of diffusion and the three additional factors discussed above. We shall, however, not dwell on this here.

Let us turn instead to the most unrealistic of the assumptions in our simple model, i.e. the one relating to the once-and-for-all static nature of the technologies. When a product or process is first introduced it is almost inevitably in a relatively primitive form and is submitted to successive incremental improvements which either reduce its cost of production and/ or increase its quality, performance, reliability, or whatever other aspect is important to the users or can contribute to enlarge the market. As discussed in the previous section, such improvements could follow what Nelson and Winter have termed a 'natural' trajectory and Dosi a 'techno-logical' trajectory. As in the product life-cycle model, the path of such successive incremental innovations from introduction to maturity of any particular technology, could be represented in the familiar S-shape fashion. Improvements are achieved slowly at first, then accelerate and finally slow down again, according to Wolff's law of diminishing returns to investment in incremental innovations. (See Figure 21.2).

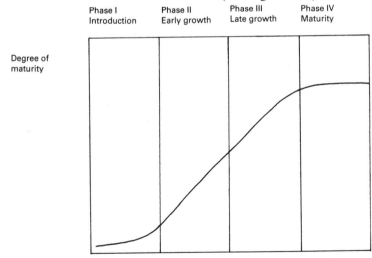

Figure 21.2   The life cycle of a technology

This means that the imitator does not always enter the 'same' technology as the innovator. Nor do later imitators enter at the same point in the technology's evolution or trajectory as earlier ones. All these improvements have a cost and they all imply the generation of additional, innovation-bound knowledge and experience. This implies that cost of entry curves vary in time. A reasonable assumption would be that they constantly shift upwards as they now cover the cost of the original investment plus all subsequent investment in incremental improvements. However, this is not necessarily so. As noted in the introduction, Hirsch (1965 and 1967) observed that requirements for entry vary in importance through the various phases of the product cycle. In our terminology, this would imply both that the various components of the cost of entry vary in relative importance, and that the minimum threshold levels move up or down as technologies evolve over the phases of the product life cycle.

Let us briefly examine what happens to each component in each of the four phases. Figure 21.3 illustrates graphically what we have in mind. Since different types of innovation can result in different evolutionary patterns, we shall take the simple case of a technology for producing a new final consumption product which eventually reaches massive diffusion.

Phase I is the period of first introduction where the focus is on the product itself. It has to perform its function adequately and break successfully into the market. It is a learning process for designers, plant engineers, management, workers, distributors and consumers. It is the world of the Schumpeterian entrepreneur. Since original design and engineering are involved, the s threshold is likely to be high, whereas e could be low. The level x of locational advantages required can be crucial and relatively high for successful introduction. Finally, investment costs I are likely to be low, if not always in absolute terms at least relative to what they will become as the technology evolves.

Phase II is the period of rapid market growth. Once the product is basically defined and its market tested and clearly capable of growing, the focus shifts to the process of production. Plant design becomes important and successive improvements are made to both the product and the process of production to achieve the optimal match between the two, in order to increase output and productivity. Materials and shape might be changed to lower costs and increase efficiency or respond to market demand. Plant organisation is gradually optimised and the most appropriate equipment chosen or specified. It is the world of the production engineer and the marketing manager. As the scientific and technical problems are gradually solved and their solution is embodied in both product and production equipment, the s threshold for imitators decreases. But the e threshold in terms of required skills increases rapidly as experience accumulates within the producing firm in relation to the product, the process of production and successful marketing. Locational and infrastructural economies of the sort generated by the innovation itself grow at the expense of the producers, so later entrants could find the relevant infrastructure more available than earlier ones. The cost of I is now higher than before as optimal plant size

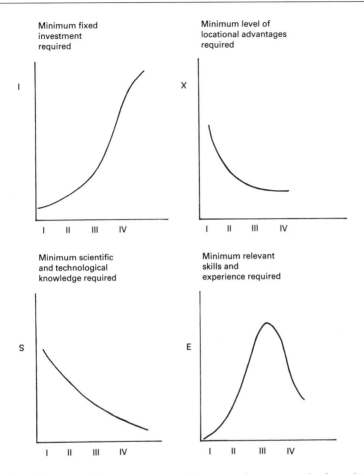

Figure 21.3   Variation in the components of the cost of entry over the four phases of the technology life cycle.

has grown and more sophisticated and better adapted equipment has been incorporated to handle the larger volumes.

By *Phase III* all the main conditions have been clearly established. Market size and rate of growth are well known, the relationship between product and process has been optimised, and the direction of further incremental innovations to increase productivity is clearly seen. The focus is now on managing firm growth and capturing market share. Scale-up of both plant and firm are the characteristics of this phase. As it proceeds many firms that were successful in the previous two phases might be eliminated. The actual capital costs and the management skills required to stay in the race in Phase III can be formidable. This is therefore no time for new entrants. The *S* component of entry costs is by now relatively low but the *E* and *I* components are at their highest and growing. Locational advantages become less important by comparison with the internalised economies that successful firms have accumulated in market and financial power by this time. Furthermore, regarding the price a firm would charge for selling the technology, one could say that in Phase I the price can tend to infinite due to an interest in monopolising the technical information of the S sort, but in Phase III it can again become relatively high in order to monopolize markets, through keeping the now much greater experience (E) within the firm.

Finally, in the maturity stage *Phase IV*, both the product and its process of production are standardised. Further investment in technological improvements results in diminishing returns. Since factor inputs are established and fixed, the advantage in costs of production goes to the firm or locality that can make the greatest comparative saving in any of them. This might lead the established firms to relocate some of their own plants even from the end of Phase III. But it can also lead them to concentrate on other innovations and to turn the technology acquired in the previous phases into a commodity, i.e. being willing to sell it at a discretionary price in the form of licences and 'know-how' contracts. This practice could eventually result in a buyer's market if there are competing suppliers. Thus, in the final or maturity phase of a technology the threshold of entry comes further down even though the actual costs of entry may still be high. The previous knowledge requirements are now very low because they are almost totally embodied in the product and the equipment. The required skills are well codified and can be purchased at a price, though their real acquisition for efficient production may not be guaranteed without enormous efforts on the part of the buyer (Bell, 1984). The relevant locational advantages continue to be important; those relating to the education of input suppliers and consumers are at their highest almost everywhere. Finally, the fixed investment costs are much higher than in Phase I but suppliers are available who have the experience and know the specifications for all the necessary equipment.

What this means is that, given the appropriate conditions, Phases I and IV provide the easiest-to-attain threshold conditions for new entrants, but with radically different costs and requirements. In Phase I with little capital and experience, but with the relevant scientific and technical knowledge plus an adequate provision of locational advantage or compensatory 'help', an innovator or imitator can enter the market at the early stages of the technology. By contrast, entry at Phase IV depends on traditional comparative and locational advantages. But it requires considerable amounts of investment and technology purchase funds. An important difference between the two entry points is that entry at Phase I does not guarantee survival in the race. Much further investment and technology generation efforts are required as competitors advance along the improvement path. A maturity entrance appears relatively safer as long as the product in question is not substituted by a newer one in the market. Profits will depend on how many other new producers struggle for a share at this stage.

This, then, appears to support both the view put forward by product life-cycle trade theory, illustrated in the success of export-led industrialisation strategies achieved on the basis of manufacturing mature traditional products, and the apparently contradictory early-entry 'events' of a number of industrialising countries in such technologies as digital tele-communications, electronic memory chips or PABX. The early-entry phenomenon is, as already mentioned in the introduction, further supported by much historical evidence with regard to the late but rapid industrialisation of many of the presently industrialised countries.

Windows of opportunity for catching up:

From product life cycles to techno-economic paradigms

One of the main shortcomings of the discussion above and indeed of the product life-cycle theory framework is that it assumes that products are independent of one another. Every new product is seen as a radical innovation, and the successive improvements to it and to its production process are the incremental changes which bring it to maturity, after which the next product is seen as a radical departure destined to follow a similar evolution.

In fact, as discussed at greater length in the chapter by Freeman and Perez and in Perez (1988), products build upon one another and are interconnected in technology systems. Each product cycle develops within a broader family which in turn evolves within an even broader system. In this sense, successive products within a system are equivalent to successive improvements to a product. This means that each 'new' product benefits from the knowledge and experience developed for its predecessors and its producer profits from the already generated externalities. It is clear that the electric can-opener is one of the last minor innovations in a long series of consumer durables made of metal or plastic with an electric motor, which began fifty years back with refrigerators, vacuum cleaners and washing machines. The entrants at the can-opener stage of the system find consumers with 'all-electric' houses, a fully developed range of optional equipment and parts suppliers, managers and workers with all the required skills and ready-made distribution systems. This is certainly not the case for biotechnology today which, as a system, is in its very early stages of development. And the same holds for some of the technology systems presently growing around microelectronics and its applications.

There are, then, two reasons why the notion of life cycles of technology systems is more relevant for development strategies than that of single product cycles. One is that, as mentioned above the knowledge, the skills, the experience and the externalities required for the various products within a system are interrelated and support each other. The other is that the analysis of technologies in terms of systems allows the identification of those families of products and processes which will provide the time for learning and catching up as well as a wide scope for development and growth.

If we go back to the various entry phases of the previous section, we find that the requirements for entry in Phase I, i.e. into new products (but now we add 'within new systems'), are relatively low with regard to experience or managerial ability and capital, which would make them ideal for some developing countries if it were not for the other two factors: the need for high levels of externalities and of scientific and technical knowledge. Assuming that government action could eventually compensate for the lack of locational and infrastructural advantages, let us concentrate on the type of barrier created by scientific and technical knowledge in the context of new technology systems.

In the industrialised countries, truly new technology systems do not necessarily originate in the most powerful, large and experienced firms. They often involve small firms started up by entrepreneurs with advanced university training in specialised areas, such as has been seen in micro-electronics and biotechnology, or revolutionary new ideas as those applied by Henry Ford. Much of the knowledge and skills which will later be required for the growth phase of the system and for subsequent products are developed within these firms as they evolve and either grow or are absorbed by large firms or simply disappear.

We are suggesting, then, that much of the knowledge required to enter a technology system in its early phase is in fact public knowledge available at universities. Many of the skills required must be invented in practice. It is only as the system evolves that it generates the new knowledge and skills which become increasingly of a private nature and are not willingly sold to competitors anywhere. With time, as discussed in the previous section, the system approaches maturity, and again both the knowledge and the skills tend to become public or are willingly sold at a price.

This implies that, given the availability of well-qualified university personnel, a window of opportunity opens for relatively autonomous entry into new products in a new technology system in its early phases. This partly explains the cases of electronic innovations occurring outside the main industrialised nations mentioned earlier on. The problem now becomes whether the endogenous generation of knowledge and skills will be sufficient to remain in business as the system evolves. And this implies not only constant technological effort but also a growing flow of invest-ment. Development is not about individual product successes but about the capacity to establish interrelated technology systems in evolution, which generate synergies for self-sustained growth processes.

If we follow the taxonomy put forward in the chapter by Freeman and Perez, it will be clear that the technology systems discussed here are in turn the elements of a larger whole—a techno-economic paradigm which also evolves in time from an early phase through growth to maturity. The 'life-cycle' of such a techno-economic paradigm is composed of a series of interrelated technology systems. There is no need to discuss this issue here, but it is clear that each new techno-economic paradigm requires, generates and diffuses new types of knowledge, skills and experience and provides a favourable environment for easy entry into more and more products within these systems. In this view, the present transition period identified with a change in techno-economic paradigm will affect the whole range of techno-logy systems which evolved and matured under the previous paradigm. Most of them will be profoundly transformed as the new information-intensive, flexible, systemic, microelectronics-based paradigm propagates across the productive system. Mature industries reconvert, mature pro-ducts are redesigned, new products and industries appear and grow, giving rise to new technology systems based on other sorts of relevant knowledge and requiring and generating new skills and new locational and infra-structural advantages.

This implies, however, that firms and countries that had accumulated great advantages in the now superseded technology systems face increasing costs in getting rid of the experience and the externalities of the 'wrong' sort and in acquiring the new ones. Newcomers that, for whatever reason, possess the new relevant knowledge and skills are lighter and faster. That is why these periods of paradigm change have historically allowed some countries to catch up and even surpass the previous leaders.

What this means for lagging countries is that during periods of paradigm transitions there are two sorts of favourable conditions for catching up. First of all, there is time for learning while everybody else is doing so. Secondly, given a reasonable level of productive capacity and locational advantages and a sufficient endowment of qualified human resources in the new technologies, a temporary window of opportunity is open, with low thresholds of entry where it matters most.

Of course, any developing country that can truly take advantage of this sort of opportunity has probably reached that position through decades of efforts at entering mature technologies and probably with some successes. But breaking the vicious circle requires growing systems and synergies. Mature technologies are by definition the less dynamic ones. Fast growth is based on interrelated technological dynamism, on the capacity to make successive improvements across a wide range of technologies and to generate externalities for an even wider range of related activities. It is such processes that result in lowering the cost of entry (and of operation) for other firms. So early entry into *new* technology *systems* is the crucial ingredient for the process of catching up.

The potential for technological catching up remains, however, subject to many of the various threshold levels and the entry cost components mentioned earlier on. Locational and infrastructural advantages do not fall from heaven, nor does a particular country's endowment in scientific and technical personnel and skills. They result from the previous history of development, plus natural resources, and social, cultural and political factors. And, depending on the nature of the new paradigm, these can be excellent, very good, bad or hopelessly inadequate in any particular country. Furthermore, taking advantage of new opportunities and favour-able conditions requires the capacity to recognise them, the competence and imagination to design an adequate strategy, and the social conditions and political will to carry it through.

The real chances of advance for any particular country may be very large or very small depending on all the factors mentioned, but they will also be affected by the ultimate shape taken by the socio-institutional framework at the international level. Our main point is that the present period has been and continues to be particularly favourable for attempting a leap in development of whatever size is possible. And this demands a complete reassessment of each country's conditions in the light of the new opportunities.

References

Ames, E. and N. Rosenberg (1963), 'Changing technological leadership and industrial growth', *Economic Journal*vol. 73, pp. 214–36.

Arthur, B. (1986), 'Industry location patterns and the importance of history', *Center for Economic Policy Research Paper No. 84*, June, mimeo.

Bell, M. (1984), ' "Learning" and the accumulation of industrial technological capacity in developing countries', in K. King and M. Fransman (eds), *Technological Capacity in the Third World*, London, Macmillan.

Cornwall, J. (1977), *Modern Capitalism: Its Growth and Transformation*, London, Martin Robertson.

Dosi, G. (1982), 'Technological paradigms and technological trajectories: a suggested interpretation of the determinants and directions of technical change', *Research Policy*, vol. II, no. 3, June.

—— (1984), *Technical Change and Industrial Transformation: The Theory and an Application to the Semi-Conductor Industry*, London, Macmillan.

Freeman, C. (1963), 'The plastics industry: a comparative study of research and innovation', *National Institute Economic Review*, no. 26, pp. 22–62.

Freeman, C. (1965), 'Research and Development in Electronic Capital Goods', *National Institute Economic Review*, no. 34, pp. 40–97.

Freeman, C., Clark, J. and Soete, L. (1982), *Unemployment and Technical Innovation: A Study of Long Waves and Economic Development*, London, Frances Pinter.

Gomulka, S. (1971), *Inventive Activity, Diffusion and the Stages of Economic Growth*, Aarhus, Skrifter fra Aarhus Universtets Okonomiske Institut nr. 24, Institute of Economics.

Habakkuk, H. (1962), *American and British Technology in the Nineteenth Century*, Cambridge, Cambridge University Press.

Hirsch, S. (1965), 'The US electronics industry and international trade', *National Institute Economic Review*, no. 34, pp. 92–4.

Hirsch, S. (1967), *Location of Industry for International Competitiveness*, Oxford, Clarendon Press.

Kuznets, S. (1930), *Secular Movements in Production and Prices*, Boston, Houghton Mifflin.

Landes, D. (1969), *The Unbound Prometheus*, Cambridge, Cambridge University Press.

Metcalfe, S. (1981), 'Impulse and diffusion in the study of technical change',

Futures, vol. 13, no. 5, pp. 347–59.

—— (1982), 'On the diffusion of innovation and the evolution of technology', paper prepared for the TCC Conference, London, January, mimeo.

Metcalfe, S. and Soete, L. (1984), 'Notes on the evolution of technology and international competition', in M. Gibbons and P. Gummett (eds), *Science and Technology Policy in the 1980s and Beyond*, London, Longman.

Nabseth, L. and Ray, G. (1974), *The Diffusion of New Industrial Processes*, Cambridge, Cambridge University Press.

Nelson, R. and Winter, S. (1982), *An Evolutionary Theory of Economic Change*, Cambridge, Mass., Harvard University Press.

Perez, C. (1983), 'Structural change and the assimilation of new technologies in the economic and social system', *Futures*, vol. 15, no. 5, pp. 357–75.

—— (1985), 'Micro-electronics, long waves and world structural change: new perspectives for developing countries', *World Development*, vol. 13, no. 3, March, pp. 441–63.

—— (1988), 'New Technologies and development' in C. Freeman and B-Å. Lundvall (eds), *Small Countries Facing the Technological Revolution*, London, Frances Pinter.

Posner, M. (1961), 'International trade and technical change', *Oxford Economic Papers*, vol. 13, pp. 323–41.

Ray, G. (1980), 'Innovation in the long cycle', *Lloyds Bank Review*, January, no. 135, pp. 14–28.

Rosenberg, N. (1976), *Perspectives on Technology*, Cambridge, Cambridge University Press.

—— (1982), *Inside the Black Box: Technology and Economics*, Cambridge, Cambridge University Press.

—— (1984), 'The commercial exploitation of science by American industry', paper prepared for the colloquium on Productivity and Technology, Harvard Business School, March, mimeo.

Rostow, W.W. (1960), *The Stages of Economic Growth*, Cambridge, Cambridge University Press.

Schumpeter, J.A. (1912), *Theorie der Wirtschaftlichen Entwicklung*, Leipzig, Dunker & Humbolt (English translation: Harvard University Press, 1934).

—— (1939), *Business Cycles: A Theoretical, Historical and Statistical Analysis of the Capitalist Process*, 2 vols, New York, McGraw Hill.

Scoville, W. (1951), 'Minority migration and the diffusion of technology', *Journal of Economic History*, vol. II, pp. 347–360.

Soete, L. (1981), 'Technological dependency: a critical view', in D. Seers (ed.), *Dependency Theory: A Critical Reassessment*, London, Frances Pinter.

—— (1985), 'International diffusion of technology, industrial development and technological leapfrogging', *World Development*, vol. 13, no. 3, March, pp. 409–22.

Teubal, M. (1982), 'Some notes on the accumulation of intangibles by high-technology firms', July mimeo.

von Tunzelmann, N. (1978), *Steam Power and British Industrialization to 1860*, Oxford, Clarendon Press.

Vernon, R. (1966), 'International investment and international trade in the product cycle', *Quarterly Journal of Economics*, vol. 80, no. 2, May, pp. 190–207.

Yakushiji, T. (1986), 'Technological emulation and industrial development', paper presented at the Conference on Innovation Diffusion Venice, 17–21 March.

22 Industrial structure, technical change and microeconomic behaviour in LDCs

Kurt Unger
El Colegio de Mexico, Mexico City

Introduction

The conventional analysis of import substitution industrialisation has by now produced a considerable number of studies accounting for the failure and successes achieved by many countries through that route. In spite of the broad coverage of these analyses there are still several major areas of dynamic analysis waiting to receive better attention. Two of these are the dynamics of competition (and what it implies with respect to the process of innovation) and the process of technological learning. It is my belief that the dynamics of competition and learning in less developed countries (LDCs) need to be better understood before we attempt to model the entrepreneurial reactions and attitudes towards innovation that would be necessary to accommodate together the micro and macro objectives of the new industrialisation strategies in those countries.

By examining the underpinnings of traditional import substitution industrialisation analysis in these two dynamic areas, we may be able to show that the very basic requirements of some of the new, more aggressive industrialisation policies, such as export promotion and/or technological leapfrogging with regard to microelectronics and biotechnology, are—and in line with the arguments set out in the previous chapter—very difficult to attain.[1] The most obvious factor missing to guarantee the success of these policies is that of the Schumpeterian entrepreneur, for whom the jump in quantum and quality of the 'domestic supply' required is so enormous that it seems unrealistic. Furthermore, the evolutionary sequence of entrepreneurial build-up of technological capabilities stressed by authors such as Nelson and Winter (1982) and Katz (1984) within the context of less developed countries suggests a gradual process not easily amenable to leapfrogging or to the sudden change to the export-oriented industrialisation argument. Here we intend to show that past experience with regard to entrepreneurial behaviour during import substitution industrialisation supports neither the demands nor the expectations now raised by the new strategies. In addition, we will argue that the user–producer interactive scheme of industrial innovation, as emphasized in various other contributions to this book but in particular in the chapter by Lundvall, is also rather weak in most LDCs due to the lack of a sufficiently strong capital-goods sector as well as the poor development of the institutional framework essential to the creation of the national system of innovation.

The chapter is divided into two sections. The first one summarises the characteristics of the industrial structure that developed during import substitution industrialisation: the preference for expanding the consumer-goods industries in oligopolistic markets, facilitated by the use of imported technology, and generating few incentives or rewards for entrepreneurial risk-taking. In the second section, the issue of technology transfer and related topics of technological change such as diffusion, packaging and learning are explored to explain the relatively slow development of technological capabilities taking place during this process. Some conclusions that bear on the prospects of the new strategies are briefly summarised at the end.

Industrialisation, entrepreneurship and the market system in LDCs

The choice of domestic production to substitute for imports implemented through import substitution industrialisation in most LDCs has meant the creation of two major negative results. One is a far less than competitive environment biased towards the development of consumer-goods industries (of relatively high profitability in spite of their inefficiency); the other is the continuing dependency of the economy on imports of production goods. Given the inefficiency of consumer-goods industries to compete in external markets through exports, a limit to the imports capacity of production goods has appeared as a result of foreign exchange constraints. Consequently, most LDCs have ended up with a stagnant, inefficient and non-integrated industrial sector.

The way in which such results were achieved, we will argue, must be analysed in a more rigorous manner than that conventionally adopted by simply attributing them to market inefficiencies induced externally to the proper (ideal) mechanisms that *ought* to conform to the neo-classical market paradigm. The fact that those results are more the rule than the exception demands from us an attempt to construct new forms of analysis. Here we adopt an approach similar to that suggested by some of the evolutionary writers reviewed in the rest of the book. The thread of the argument evolves around the way in which technical change is incorporated into and determines the industrial structures of LDCs during the process of import substitution industrialisation.

Such an outcome is far from being conducive to an equilibrating situation. For many countries, and especially the advanced countries, the proposition sustained in the introduction and in other chapters of this book may well be accepted: that the world is much more stable and ordered than what can be deduced on the grounds of the prevailing theory.[2] However, it is hard to conceive of such an automatic adjustment taking place in the LDCs in present times, and even less so if the market system is still assumed to guide the adjustment process into the near future.

Ever since the beginning, the price system has been denied its basic allocative function as the guiding post reflecting scarcity, quality and choice of priorities for the development of new industrial activities in LDCs. For one, the import substitution industrialisation strategy relied on a protection system to fix domestic prices, and that system gave rise to and *perpetuated* a set of pricing practices that discriminated against production goods and exports, favouring the continuing extension of the mix of consumer goods domestically produced. The profitability of the latter was not necessarily related to their efficient production, and was enhanced through a double mechanism that offered both high domestic prices to the protected consumer goods, while at the same time allowing those producers to import production goods at international or subsidised costs. These are in the end the main causes accounting for the failure of the import substitution industrialisation strategy to solve the balance-of-payments structural constraints which it was originally supposed to correct.

Although most people would agree on the poor implementation of protection in most countries,[3] there is still controversy about its future uses and about the extent to which the pure market system can be expected to substitute for it efficiently.

The major assumption behind the liberalisation proposals is usually related to the fact that in the absence of protection efficiency will appear everywhere (i.e. the old virtues of the market system will take over only if imperfections of this sort are removed), a result which is very unlikely to occur; more probably, some domestic industries will disappear in the face of open competition from imports. Whether the trade balance will as a result turn positive is unclear. More importantly, however, the validity of the infant industry argument will need to be retained if the logic of future industrial development of LDCs were to suggest priority to the production-goods (and particularly capital-goods) industries. This priority would seem to be reinforced when considering the diffusion of the new micro-electronics technologies, since these may have a considerable impact on the design, the production and the functioning of many capital goods.

The importance of developing a domestic capital-goods industry seems generally accepted as a necessary condition to enhance a country's capacity to develop successful innovations. This is well argued in the analysis of the innovation process as the result of effective user–producer interactions, as illustrated in Lundvall's chapter. It is also implicit in the taxonomy of technological trajectories developed by Pavitt (1984), and most clearly so in respect of the supplier-dominated group of industries. In both these accounts one discovers a key role for the machinery-producing sector in the development of the patterns of specialisation that are observed for most of the Scandinavian and Western European industrialised countries.

However, the user–producer approach also argues that inertia tends to consolidate the existing user–producer networks, an inertia that leads to decision-making on the basis of past experiences. This inertia develops not only within national systems of innovation, but also with regard to relationships involving domestic user firms and foreign producers well established in the international machinery or technology markets. This is a picture extremely familiar to many LDCs. Thus the permanent links reinforced through imported capital goods and technology create a degree of technological dependence that may not be overcome unless very specific policy measures are targeted to that end.

Several agents perform crucial roles that lead one to neglect the strategic importance of an endogenous user–producer interaction. Most of all, the entrepreneurial function is poorly performed from the view of a longer-term perspective of the host economies. This applies to transnational corporations (TNCs), locally owned firms and state enterprises. The subsidiaries of TNCs assume the technological leadership in the economy and become the major source of advanced technology, constituting the main vehicle to transfer technological changes originating from and conforming to the conditions in advanced countries. The TNCs replicate internally to each LDC the oligopolistic market structure of their countries of origin,[4] supplying their previous importers of finished goods with locally assembled goods using imported inputs and imported technology.

With regard to technology, private firms under local ownership have reacted less actively than TNC subsidiaries. They have chosen, even more significantly than the TNC subsidiaries, to concentrate on the most traditional niches of industrial production; food products, clothing, textiles, furniture, wood products and metal products, most of which are usually dominated by local firms. Their technology acquisitions are not differently guided from those of the TNCs, i.e. they search for the well-known and most reliable technology source, which means for the most part imported technology.[5] Price and the use of imported inputs and equipment are not particularly scrutinised, inasmuch as they can pass the costs involved on to the consumers. If these firms had previously been involved in foreign trade, it is yet more likely that their industrial activity and their technology acquisitions would have been limited to assemble or replicate the imported good.[6]

As industrialist the state has also acted rather poorly. First and foremost, the state has usually entered industries where private enterprises have not been interested due to the large amount of investment needed (e.g. steel) or where low-priced intermediate inputs (e.g. petrochemicals, fertilisers) or low-priced basic goods (e.g. maize and other staple goods for the basic diet) have not offered attractive returns to private investors. For the most part, state industries have developed rather inefficiently due to the absence of any competition, and have also been forced to offer those products at subsidised prices to the consumer-goods producers. In other words, not only can the origin of inefficiency be rooted in the inputs at the beginning of the production system—inefficiency which is then transmitted to the rest of the system—but in order to finance these inefficiencies, the state has developed structural deficiencies which it will be difficult to correct in the future.

On the technology side, much like the private sector, state enterprises have in general been passive importers of technology and capital goods. The state-owned enterprises choose their technology under criteria that do not conform to any conventional paradigm. According to James (1986, p. 21), the technological choices of state-owned enterprises are substantially at odds with the traditional theory of the firm. Management decision rules are highly simplified, poorly informed and subject to a variety of subtle motivations of unclear direction.[7] From a different perspective, though, the relatively high capital intensity of most of the industries where the state dominates should provide an interesting opportunity to develop a capital-goods industry.

The short-sighted guidance of the state has been verified again in recent periods, such as in the mid-1970s, when shortages of foreign exchange in many LDCs had already been clearly associated with their heavy dependency on imported production goods. Not long after, explicit policy proposals had appeared making state purchases a key instrument for the development of local capital-goods industries (see, for instance, the Mexican NAFINSA-UNIDO, 1977, programme), and the oil revenues of the late 1970s and early 1980s were wasted in imports of production goods along the same pattern that had characterised most of the previous import substitution industrialisation pattern. Similar behaviour was observed in some of the other oil-rich countries where the state controls the industry (e.g. Venezuela, Ecuador and some of the Arab countries).

Technology transfer and learning in LDCs

In spite of the substantial literature dealing with the transfer of technology and the involvement of TNCs in LDCs,[8] there are still several major issues that have attracted relatively little attention: the determinants and variety of technology transfer, the degree and extent of local learning *vis-à-vis* the continuing dependency on imported technology, the integration of local industry to domestic capital-goods producers, and the role of technology in the international division of TNCs activities. These issues are explored in the remainder of this chapter.

Technology transfer is an old but still inadequately tackled subject in most of the development literature. In so far as there has been in general poor treatment of the innovation and diffusion process in advanced countries, giving rise to the recent suggestions along post-Schumpeterian lines mentioned earlier (the evolutionary approach of Nelson and Winter, and the taxonomy of trajectories of technical change of Pavitt), there is a need to adjust the conventional view of technology transfer as a spontaneous, linear, static, neutral and homogeneous process that does not distinguish between sectors of activity, firms and countries involved. Some of the empirical studies in the early 1970s were already pointing to the necessity of recognising these different characteristics, sectoral conditions and consequences.[9] However, in so far as these were primarily sectoral and country-specific-type of analyses, these studies could not test for explanations on a more generally applicable basis. This remains one of today's major challenges.

In the first instance, one may be able to explain in a more comprehensive manner the determinants of technology transfer: why do firms engage in licensing? According to the dominant foreign investment theories (see in more detail the chapter by Chesnais), firms will choose the direct foreign investment mechanism as their first option, preferring foreign investment for its greater rent-extracting potential, and turning to licensing only if that potential cannot be realised (Caves, 1983, p. 204). Accordingly, it is mostly the circumstances that are relatively unconducive to foreign investment that need to be looked at when determining when licensing will occur (James, 1986, p. 13).

A number of factors may influence the preference for licensing rather than direct investment. According to Caves (1983, p. 224),

arm's-length licensing is encouraged by risks to foreign investors and barriers to entry of subsidiaries, by short economic life of the knowledge asset, by simplicity of the technology, by high capital costs for the potential foreign investor, and by certain types of product market competition that favour reciprocal licensing.

Thinking of technology transfer as transactions taking place in an organised market (in the sense used in Lundvall's chapter), and taking into consideration some of the factors encouraging the licensing, it would be plausible to expect market imperfections with regard to price-fixing; the extent of knowledge transferred; the degree and timing of diffusion likely to follow the knowledge transferred; and the conditions of packaging involving other elements of technology. The predominant role of TNCs in the technology transfer process adds further questions about the proper working of a market system as such, especially when the transfer is between parent and subsidiary firms.

The way in which prices are fixed for technology transfer contracts hardly resembles the demand–supply static scheme relating prices and quantities. The technological knowledge involved usually represents a whole set of 'indivisible' information which cannot be broken up into marginal quantities. Furthermore, prices, usually in the form of royalties, will be fixed rather arbitrarily, representing merely a compensation of past efforts invested in accumulating the know-how or experience related to the technology transferred. In other words, most of the time there will not be additional or marginal costs associated with the transfer operation.[10] If anything, there is an opportunity cost in the sense that the proprietor might have wanted to exploit the business himself directly, as argued by the direct foreign investment model reviewed above.

Nor is there a well-organised information system to compare the various possible suppliers. Thus even the arm's-length type of licensing may lead to a negotiated price fixed by mutual agreement from both parties, and even though the purchaser may not have complete information to consider less costly alternatives, these may not be of much relevance when he counts on transmitting that price to his domestic, captive (due to protection) customers. The degree of irregularity in price-fixing[11] was probably best illustrated during the first half of the 1970s, when most governments in LDCs were able to introduce legislation limiting royalty payments to less than half the previous percentages, without seriously inhibiting the licensing processes.[12]

One difficult aspect that will influence the technology price is the extent of diffusion of the knowledge transferred versus the exclusive appropriation by the licensee. Virtually all technologies will be subject, sooner or later, to a considerable degree of diffusion. The transfer of technology itself represents the initial step of a diffusion process that may further expand through copying, subcontracting and the like. In fact, access to technology has not been high in the ranking of barriers of entry in the last decade, and less so for older industrial activities where technology has matured.[13] Yet it is difficult to assess *a priori* the number of years during which a firm may be able to profit from the use of technology obtained on an exclusive basis; this period should be, in principle, the only one for which the licensor might have the right to a royalty in exchange.

The assessment of the extent of knowledge involved in the transfer of technology has remained a difficult issue both from a neo-classical perspective and the more explicit assumption of perfect information and from the technological development perspective. Perhaps the most significant contribution to the first is the well-known Arrow paradox on the lack of complete information when acquiring information (Arrow, 1962). If complete information existed, the need to acquire it would naturally disappear.

As far as the relationship between technology transfer and the accumulation of technological capability is concerned, there have been a large number of empirical studies showing a highly diversified pattern in this relationship, depending on the nature of the contract, the firms involved, the sectors of activity, and so on.[14] One needs also—as emphasised in the preceding chapter by Perez and Soete—to distinguish between transfer of knowledge merely related to the proper operation of the specific technology involved and the more ambitious transmission of the 'paradigm foundations' that may enable the licensee to produce for himself the new technologies implicit or likely to develop along the technological trajectory that may be anticipated for that industry or type of products.

Technology transfer studies have generally failed to account for the phenomenon of technological packages. Some studies, especially empirical sectoral studies,[15] have identified a variety of conditions linked to the technology packages. For some sectors, it is the packaging of technology elements as such (trademarks, patents, know-how, etc.) that is crucial. For other sectors, where technology diffusion has been general, technology acquisitions, if any, take place on the basis of single technology elements.

For other sectors, where the principle of producing and/or operating the equipment has not experienced such widespread diffusion, the package often includes the supply of capital goods. As we have already mentioned, and following Pavitt (1984), there will be a good number of sectors where technological trajectories will be crucially dependent upon (among other things) the complementary relations between producers and users of capital goods.

One major shortcoming of technology transfer studies in this area has been the inadequate (sometimes totally absent) treatment of capital goods as a crucial input into the transfer package, something increasingly recognised as important in the discussion on innovation and technological trajectories in advanced countries,[16] but probably even more important for LDCs in so far as it may inhibit their chances to initiate the development of their capital-goods industries. In this respect, earlier suggestions to treat the capital-goods industry both as a source of technology and as the locus for the accumulation of technological capacity (Rosenberg, 1976; Stewart, 1978) have been for the most part ignored. And recently, the sudden upsurge of literature advocating both export-oriented strategies and microelectronics as a vehicle into exports or leapfrogging in the context of the international process of industrial restructuring (see, e.g., Soete, 1985) has further obscured the crucial link between technological capacity and the development of the capital goods industries.

The social costs associated with the poor development of capital-goods industries are not properly captured by the price system used by the firm when comparing between domestic and imported capital goods. Two major social costs absent from that system are the chronic trade deficits of countries that do not produce capital goods and the lack of their own technological capability to innovate, adapt or copy technologies that are closely associated with the capital-goods industry. The rising trade deficits of the Latin American countries, for instance, are structural in the sense that they are derived from the interplay between two forces: the dependence on imports of production (and especially capital) goods in order to grow, and the lack of an export capability also associated to a large extent with a limited technological capability that could permit a more suitable exploitation of local resources. The successful experience of South East Asian exporters, on the other hand, seems to rest largely on the development of a capability to improve, adapt and innovate in order to take advantage of local conditions. What is probably most important to note here is that the development of such a capability may have been more related to the development of their capital-goods industries than generally recognised.[17]

Capital-goods production has been considered in the past as one of the main vehicles for the acquisition of a technological capability, as argued above. But the link becomes even stronger when one considers the present surge of innovations in microelectronics, since many of them take place as a result of the matching of microelectronics applications to capital goods.

Such applications cannot take place without the latter. In other words, if the diffusion of earlier electromechanical vintages of capital-goods production towards LDCs was taking place at a relatively slow pace, the development of capital goods based on the new technologies (or the upgrading of the previously developed machine producers)[18] will face much stronger bottlenecks if national policy does not play an active role. The discussion of an appropriate protection policy, to apply in a highly selective fashion that gives pre-eminence to learning objectives, becomes of relevance again.[19]

The need to have a strong technological national policy does not necessarily mean the introduction of wider state intervention across all industry. It certainly is necessary to make a careful and selective assessment of which sectors are likely to suffer most from the application of the new technology. The same can be said about the export prospects linked to the new technologies. Here the assessment of export-oriented strategies will need to include an estimate of the extent to which the new technology facilitates or opposes international sourcing. It has been argued that a declining trend in sourcing is to be expected given the benefits that may be derived from relocating production near the final markets.[20]

The analysis takes us beyond the microeconomic framework into issues of international trade, international location and the strategic responses of firms according to the structure of their markets—topics dealt within more detail in other chapters of this book. At the same time, though, the analysis calls for a more integrated analysis of the North and the South than what has been attempted so far. Here we introduce only a short list of arguments that point to some additional difficulties to be faced by LDCs in their attempt to follow open routes of industrialisation on an integrated basis with countries in the North.

If one is to give serious consideration to some of the recent trends of industrial restructuring in industrialised countries and their implications for LDCs, the outcome is more likely to be pessimistic in tone. Three major trends are commonly stressed in some of the recent literature: the locational effect of new technologies; the organisational changes accompanying the applications of microelectronics; and the protectionism of major importing countries as they face trade imbalances along their restructuring process.

The reconcentration of industrial activities close to the final markets has been a matter of recent observation both at the macro and micro levels. As discussed in more detail in Chesnais's chapter, the US economy has turned into a net recipient of foreign investment[21] in the 1980s in the search for one of the few remaining dynamic markets. At the micro level, both the application of microelectronics to production and the Japanese transformation of organisation systems have shifted the source of comparative advantage away from traditional concerns with relative labour cost, which represented the major attraction to base production in LDCs, to systems gains through savings of time, total quality control and lower inventory costs. These systems gains are better achieved if production of all parts and components takes place within a reasonable proximity.[22]

In order to expect a leapfrogging achievement from LDCs in this type of organisational innovation, it is necessary to assume that the institutional mismatch affecting all (or most) countries as a result of the new technologies (as repeatedly projected by Perez, 1985) will not confront LDCs as acutely.

Rather, we would need to assume that these countries may be able to jump a step further into the integration of the new organisation systems without having transited through the previous one and, in some cases, are able to start totally from scratch. Past experience with state enterprises and local entrepreneurial behaviour in times of relatively easier conditions seems, however, to deny such expectations. There only remains some hope that newly attracted TNCs may respond to internationally shaped demands, a result not likely to occur on a large scale for the reasons set out above and, in any case, possibly not a desirable trend either.

Finally, even if a few LDCs may find the necessary conditions to appropriate for themselves the new technological and organisational paradigms while retaining some of their traditional sources of comparative advantage (labour cost, natural resources, energy sources, etc.), the protectionist sentiment clearly prevalent in the major DC markets is going to limit a widespread effect of this type. In recent years, for instance, the United States has been increasingly introducing protection in sectors where its trade deficit has become more important or where the impact of imports is closely related to certain regions within the United States. Examples of such sectors are the automotive (though in the form of Japan's 'voluntary' export restrictions), clothing and textiles, shoes, steel and other industries.[23]

The EEC has also introduced protection for some of these sectors. In the absence of protectionism, these sectors would be among the most obvious sectors for LDCs to fit their future competitive advantage, if they could only couple with success some of the traditional factors of comparative advantage with the application of new technologies. But more likely the protectionist trends are here to stay, if not to be implemented even more widely.

Possibly one of the few open alternatives left to LDCs may be to resort again to greater integration among themselves. If the possibilities for enlarging North–South trade relations may not be so bright as argued above, there is always some room to enlarge the scale of operations by bringing together the markets of neighbouring countries. This is further stimulated if the countries involved are not too distant developmentally from each other, and if they consequently perceive the mutual gains for each in developing certain healthy complementarities. The bad experiences of Latin American integration efforts attempted on a large scale in the past, such as the Andean Pact and the Central American Common Market, have not prevented a more modest (though probably more promising) initiative for common projects recently launched by Argentina, Brazil and

Uruguay.[24] Notwithstanding the optimism with which these initiatives may be contemplated, the very selective number and type of neighbours that can be brought together in such conditions determines the limited scale on which these arrangements could take place in reality.

Conclusions

The LDCs find themselves on the verge of a new vicious circle, whereby the international conditions of competition are dramatically altered by the effect of new technological and organisational innovations which demand a new and even more active role from entrepreneurs than what was experienced in the recent past. Both neo-classical economics theory and conventional development economics theory have traditionally lacked a serious treatment of the imperfections that characterise entrepreneurial behaviour, while they both seem to rest on the unrealistic assumptions that if market signals (in the neo-classical view) or the infrastructural and incentives systems (in the conventional development view) are rightly devised, a sufficiently large supply of nationalistic and longer-term-oriented entrepreneurs will develop. The standard diffusion model, on the other hand, mistakenly assumes a mechanistic process whereby profit incentives move accordingly to the stage of diffusion and, in common with the other theories, entrepreneurial skills may never be in short supply. The latter assumption is particularly inadequate to the common LDC environment. The painful adjustment process taking place in many LDCs during the recent period has shown that entrepreneurs of this sort are as scarce as any other of the economic factors.

The conditions derived from the new innovations have not prevented the appearance of new strategies or the reshaping of old strategies for LDCs without a careful consideration of the new environment. Export-oriented strategies continue to be advocated, rather naïvely ignoring that they may be in direct conflict with two of the most direct results of those innovations: the relocation into industrialised countries of products where LDCs were developing a comparative advantage in terms of the older technological methods, and the rising trend of protectionism in the industrialised countries. The export-oriented or outward-outlook strategies in vogue have also failed to consider—for either exporters of new products or exporters who may incorporate the new technologies in their production in LDCs—the underlying marriage required between capital goods and microelectronics, which involves contradiction in the need to develop the capital goods industries *before* the marriage may take place. Needless to say, the development of capital goods and its qualification as the focus of technological capability accumulation have implicitly disappeared as a priority in the mainstream interpretations of outward-looking strategies.

Finally, our review of the sources of market imperfections detected for technology transfer operations suggests that those imperfections may become even more pronounced for transfers involving the new techno-logical innovations. Imperfections associated with price, quantity of knowledge, diffusion patterns and related aspects will continue, or may be worse, in the future. But probably most importantly, the conditions given rise to technological packages are going to deteriorate for LDCs, including the package of imports of capital goods, which in our view remains an important priority for the technological development of LDCs.

Notes

1. A somewhat similar approach is taken in other recent works, such as Schmitz (1984).
2. This is argued in spite of the limitations of conventional theory to account for the dynamic adjustment taking place over the long run with technical change acting at the same time as a disequilibrating factor—in a static sense—and a source of order for the directions of change.
3. Some important exceptions must be noted with respect to countries such as Japan (see, for instance, Weiss, 1986), South Korea (see Westphal et al, 1981) and Brazil. With regard to the latter, a recent study discovered the develop-ment of certain technological capabilities as a sequential process having to do with, among others, protection policies systematically maintained for at least two decades (Katz, 1984, p. 32). Other factors are size of market and plants, dynamism of the technological frontier, and the type of production processes.
4. The 'follow the leader' reaction observed in oligopolistic markets, as pointed out by Vernon (1973), and stressed in James's recent survey (1986, p. 9).
5. For some of the writers heavily devoted to empirical studies, large, locally owned firms are in fact on much the same footing as domestic subsidiaries of TNC as far as technological behaviour is concerned (see, for instance, Katz, 1984, p. 25). They may only retain a different type of technological behaviour when comparing domestic, family-owned firms and state enterprises. We also found supporting evidence of this sort in our Mexican food-industry study (Unger and Márquez, 1981).
6. For the late latecomers to import substitution industrialisation, as opposed to Gerschenkron's depiction of Germany, Russia and Italy, Hirschman general-ises: 'their industrialization started with relatively small plants administering "last touches" to a host of imported inputs, *concentrated on consumer rather than producer goods*, and often was specifically designed to improve the levels of consumption of populations who were suddenly cut off, as a result of a war or balance-of-payments crisis, from imported goods to which they had become accustomed' (1986, p. 9; author's emphasis).
7. References given by James (1986) cover studies on India, Brazil and Tanzania. For the Mexican context, Villarreal and Villarreal (1978) have also given evidence of the same nature.
8. Most of these studies have concentrated on Latin American countries and a few Asian countries. See, for instance, Vaitsos (1974), Chudnovsky (1974), Katz (1976), Fajnzylber and Martínez Tarragó (1976), and Lall (1983).

9. See the works of Nadal (1977), Cooper and Maxwell (1975), Wionsczek, Bueno and Navarrete (1974), IDRC (1980), Unger and Márquez (1981), Rattner (1977), etc.

10. The knowledge transferred could thus be characterised as a public good, as suggested by Fransman (1985).

11. For Fransman, the price of knowledge is indeterminate, ranging between a minimum level determined by the cost of producing that knowledge to a maximum amount determined by the buyer's estimate of the cost of the next best alternative (1985, p. 577). Alternatively, one could think that the maximum is determined by the buyer's perception (usually being a producer himself) of the limits of his market to bear higher costs.

12. In the Mexican case, for instance, a 3 per cent limit on royalties on sales was then imposed, while there were pre-legislation contracts on a 10 per cent basis (see Nadal, 1977). Not surprisingly, the AC are again pressing against royalty limits and in favour of the extension of patent rights periods, given the ongoing and further expected technological transformations of industry, and the competitive fears they raise. And at the other end, in LDCs facing recently depressed growth and investment, concessions are accordingly being granted under elusive arguments. For instance, since 1982 the Mexican authorities have relaxed the 3 per cent limit 'in order to permit the transfer of better [sic] technology' (Gustavo Gómez Bustos introducing G. Funes paper to the Austin meeting, April 1986). The limit is now relaxed up to 10 per cent again, though the assessment of the 'quality' of the technology involved is not specified.

13. The few typical exceptions may be electronics, biotechnology and new materials technologies, which are supposed to be in the earlier phase of their technological trajectories. Most other sectors are seen in the phase of wider diffusion of their technological principles and applications, which serves to explain the upsurge of some low-wage efficient LDC competitors.

14. Similarly to Pavitt's affirmation that 'most technological knowledge turns out not to be 'information' that is generally applicable and easily reproducible, but specific to firms and applications, cumulative in development and varied amongst sectors in source and direction[1] (1984, p. 343), the transfer of technological knowledge has to be examined in the context of a wide variety of specific conditions before we can assume that it will increase the technological capabilities of a firm or an industry. Among the interesting empirical studies, one should mention Katz (1984), Westphal et al. (1981), Lall (1983) and Unger (1985).

15. See Cooper and Maxwell (1974), Mercado (1980), Nadal (1977), Unger and Márquez (1981), Unger and Saldana (1984), Cortés (1977), Katz (1976, 1984), Vitelli (1985).

16. See, for instance, Pavitt's qualification to the evolutionary models on the basis of distinguishing the variety of conditions around the complementary relations between producers and users of capital goods.

17. Among the few exceptions, there is a recent reference explaining Singapore's advantage as the location for MNC production of computer disk drives as a direct consequence of the country's well-developed machining industry (James, 1986, p. 6).

18. Numerically controlled machine tools are a case in point where conventional machine-tools producers may be displaced if they do not respond actively (see the case of Romy of Brazil in Katz, 1984, p. 31–3). See also Jacobsson (1985).

19. A similar suggestion is found in Katz (1984, p. 30). In this respect, the strategic reserve of certain microelectronics activities to domestic firms, imposed for instance on the microcomputer industry of Brazil, seems coherent from a national, long-term perspective, in spite of the concern raised by user firms or individuals who may base their criticisms on short-term cost comparisons.

20. Thus, a reconcentration trend in the North is forecasted for sectors as dissimilar as automobiles (Jones and Womack, 1985) and clothing (Hoffman and Rush, 1984), even though in both cases the influence of microelectronics is at the forefront. See also Chesnais's chapter.

21. For an updated account of this process, see Scholl (1986).

22. The automobile industry, one of the traditional leaders in the search for post-costs reductions through world-scale distribution of components plants (what was known as the trend towards the world car), has recently shown a reversal trend to reconcentrate both in Japan and the United States. For a striking comparison of costs in favour of Japan's integrated plants over others in lower wage areas, see Jones and Womack (1985, p. 400).

23. I have given an account of recent protectionist moves for certain selected sectors in Unger (1986). Other references can be found there.

24. Though this is a recent initiative and no firm results can be reported yet, it shows in principle the will to define jointly policies and projects for specific sectors. For a list of projects agreed, see *Journal de Brazil*, 8 December 1986, p. 14.

References

Arrow, K. (1962), 'Economic welfare and the allocation of resources for invention', in N. Rosenberg (ed.) (1971), *The Economics of Technological Change*, Harmondsworth, Penguin.

Caves, R. (1983), *Multinational Enterprise and Economic Analysis*, Cambridge, Cambridge University Press.

Chudnovsky, D. (1974), *Empresas multinacionales y ganancias monopólicas*, Buenos Aires, Siglo XXI Editors.

Cooper, C. and Maxwell, P. (1975), 'Machinery suppliers and the transfer of technology to Latin America', Regional Scientific and Technological Development Program, OEA, Washington, DC, mimeo.

Cortés, M. (1977), 'Transfer to technology in petrochemicals in Latin America', unpublished Ph.D. thesis, University of Sussex.

Dosi, G. (1982), 'Technological paradigms and technological trajectories: a suggested interpretation of the determinants and directions of technical change', *Research Policy*, vol. 11, no. 3, June.

Fajnzylber, F. and Martínez Tarragó, T. (1976), *Las Empresas Transnacionales: expansión a nivel mundial y su proyección en la industria mexicana*, Mexico, FCE.

Fransman, M. (1985), 'Conceptualising technical change in the Third World in the 1980s: an interpretive survey', *Journal of Development Studies*, pp. 572–652.

Funes, G. (1986), 'Lineamientos de políticas de transferencia de tecnología', paper presented to the meeting on Mexican Policies of Technology Transfer and Foreign Investment, University of Texas, Austin, April.

Hirschman, A. (1968), 'The political economy of import-substituting industrialization in Latin America', *Quarterly Journal of Economics*, vol. 82, no. 1, pp. 1–32.

Hoffman, K. and Rush, H. (1984), *Microelectronics and Clothing: The Impact of Technical Change on a Global Industry*, Geneva, ILO.

International Development Research Centre (1980), *Science and Technology for Development, Policy Instruments for the Regulation of Technology Imports*, Ottawa, Ontario, IDRC-TS33e (STPI Module 6).

Jacobsson, S. (1985), 'Technical change and industrial policy: the case of computer numerically controlled lathes in Argentina, Korea and Taiwan', *World Development*, vol. 13, no. 3, March, pp. 353–70.

James, J. (1986), 'Microelectronics and the Third World: an integrative survey of literature', paper prepared for the United Nations University New Technologies Centre Feasibility Study, Maastricht, November.

Jones, D. and Womack, J. (1985), 'Developing countries and the future of the automobile industry', *World Development*, vol. 13, no. 3, March, pp. 393–408; *Journal do Brasil* (1986), dezembro 8 de 1986, Rio de Janeiro.

—— (1984), 'Domestic technological innovations and dynamic comparative advantage', *Journal of Development Economics*, vol. 16.

Katz, J. (1976), *Importación de tecnología, aprendizaje e industrialización*, Mexico, Fondo de Cultura Económica.

Lall, S. (1983), *The Multinational Corporation*, London, Macmillan.

Mercado, A. (1980), 'Estructura y dinamísmo del mercado de tecnología industrial en México: los casos del poliéster, los productos textiles y el vestido', México, El Colegio de México.

Nadal, A. (1977), *Instrumentos de política científica y tecnológica en México*, México, El Colegio de México.

NAFINSA-UNIDO (1977), *Mexico: Una Estrategia para Desarrollar la Industria de bienes de Capital*, México, Nacional Financiera, S.A.

Nelson, R. and Winter, S. (1982), *An Evolutionary Theory of Economic Change*, Cambridge, Mass., The Belknap Press of Harvard University Press.

Pavitt, K. (1984), 'Sectoral patterns of technical change: towards a taxonomy and a theory', *Research Policy*, vol. 13, no. 6, pp. 343–73.

Perez, C. (1985), 'Microelectronics, long waves and world structural change: new perspectives for developing countries', *World Development*, vol. 13, no. 3, March, pp. 441–63.

Rattner, H. (1977), 'Gestao tecnológica' (comp.), *Revista de Administracao de Empresas*, vol. 17, Nov–Dec., Fundacao Getulio Vargas.

Rosenberg, N. (1976), *Perspectives on Technology*, Cambridge, Cambridge University Press.

Schmitz, H. (1984), 'Industrialisation strategies in LDCs: some lessons of historical experience', *Journal of Development Studies*, vol. 21, no. 1, October, pp. 1–2.

Scholl, R.B. (1986), 'The International investment position of the United States', *Survey of Current Business*, vol. 66, no. 6, Washington, DC, June, pp. 26–35.

Soete, L. (1985), 'International diffusion of technology, industrial development and technological leapfrogging', *World Development*, vol. 13, no. 3, pp. 409–22.

Stewart, F. (1972), 'Choice of techniques in developing countries', *Journal of Development Studies*, vol. IX, October, pp. 99–121.

—— (1978), *Technology and Underdevelopment*, London, Macmillan.

Unger, K. (1985), *Competencia monopólica y tecnología en la industria mexicana*,

México, El Colegio de México.

—— (1986), 'La política industrial de los Estados Unidos y posibles implicaciones para México', in G. Szekely (comp.), *México–Estados Unidos 1985*, El Colegio de México.

Unger, K. and Márquez, V. (1981), 'La tecnología en la industria alimentaria mexicana', *Diagnóstico y procesos de incorporación*, México, El Colegio de México.

Unger, K. and Saldana, L.C. (1984), *La transferencia de tecnología y la estructura industrial en México*, México, Libros del Centro de Investigación y Docencia Económicas-CIDE.

Vaitsos, C. (1974), *Intercountry Income Distribution and Transnational Enterprises*, London, Clarendon Press.

Vernon, R. (1973), 'The location of economic activity', Cambridge, Mass., Harvard Business School, mimeo.

Villarreal, R. and Villarreal, R. (1978), 'Las empresas públicas como instrumento de política económica en México', *El Trimestre Económico*, vol. 45, no. 178, pp. 213–45.

Vitelli, G. (1985), 'Empresas industriales y empleo durante la industrialización sustitutiva: notas exploratorias', *Comercio Exterior*, vol. 36, no. 3, March, pp. 2250–67.

Weiss, J. (1986), 'Japan's post-war protection policy: some implications for less developed countries', *Journal of Development Studies*, vol. 22, no. 2, January, pp. 386–406.

Westphal, L., Rhee, Y.W. and Pursell, G. (1981), 'Korean industrial competence: where it came from', *World Bank Staff Working Paper*, no. 469, Washington, DC, IBRD.

Wionczek, M., Bueno, G. and Navarrete, J. (1974), *La Transferencia internacional de tecnología: El caso de México*, México, Fondo de Cultura Económica.

23 Multinational enterprises and the international diffusion of technology

François Chesnais

*Directorate for Science, Technology and Industry, OECD, Paris,
and Département des Sciences Economiques, Université Paris X, 92001 Nanterre*

Introduction

The last chapter in this section discusses some contemporary aspects of the relationships between science and technology and international investment (generally designated as foreign direct investment (FDI)), with special emphasis on the world-wide operations of multinational enterprises (MNEs). It is concerned with recent or ongoing changes in the overall pattern of FDI; in the international sourcing, creation and transfer of technology by MNEs; and finally in inter-firm technical cooperation agreements also involving such firms.

Considerable research and policy-oriented discussion have been directed towards the international dissemination or *transfer* of technology by MNEs (for a review and the appropriate references, see, *inter alia*, Caves, 1982). Rather *less* research and discussion have been devoted to the international *sourcing* of technology, and more broadly of scientific and technological knowledge, by MNEs, although this deficiency has now begun to be recognised by some (cf. Dunning and Cantwell, 1986; Bertin, 1986). This chapter will show that the international sourcing of technology includes, of course, the organisation of corporate R & D on an international level with laboratories in several countries, but covers also a wide variety of processes and mechanisms through which MNEs can organise the centralisation and appropriation of technology and technical knowledge. Today such mechanisms include a variety of inter-firm technical cooperation agreements which large corporations belonging to the MNE category are setting up with other enterprises, notably small, knowledge-intensive firms in 'high technology' industries, as well as with universities.

The chapter relates the new developments in the technological strategies of MNEs, both the ones they develop individually and those they organise through collective action, to the changes which have occurred internationally since the mid-1970s, notably: (i) the emergence and rapid generalisation of 'international' or 'world' oligopoly as the dominant form of supply structures in all R & D-intensive and scale-intensive industries; (ii) the world economic situation which has dominated since 1975; and (iii) last but not least, the important changes in science and technology with which the whole of this book is concerned.

Two theoretical traditions and a step towards a synthesis

The focus of the analysis is essentially on international investment and the MNEs. The setting of the analysis, however, is the wider process of internationalisation. This notion designates the wide set of economic mechanisms and relationships whereby previously fairly separate national economies become increasingly interrelated and interdependent with one another in all areas of economic activity. These mechanisms and relationships include the export and import of goods and services; outward and inward flows of direct investment and financial capital; outward and inward flows of embodied and disembodied technology; international movement of skilled personnel and transborder information flows; and, of course, the internationalised monetary and financial system.

The reference to the notion of internationalisation warrants a few indications concerning the theoretical underpinnings of this chapter. The conceptual approach which underlies the analysis is at the junction point between the most significant Anglo-Saxon work on foreign direct investment and the MNE, and the dominant French approaches towards the analysis of 'internationalization' (de Bernis, 1977), 'accumulation at world level' (Amin, 1970; Palloix, 1975), or 'world capitalism' (Michalet, 1976).

The approaches used by American and British scholars are essentially based on an extension of the decision to invest abroad either of the theory of the *firm* (Coase, 1937, as extended by Hymer, 1970; Horst, 1974; Buckley and Casson, 1976, with 'internalisation' and the interplay between 'markets' and 'hierarchies' (Williamson, 1975) as the key concepts, or else of the theory of *industrial organisation* and market structure theory (*inter alia*, Bain, 1956; Scherer, 1970; Caves, 1971; Knickerbocker, 1973; Vernon, 1974; and, more recently, Newfarmer, 1983, 1985). Here the extension of domestic oligopoly beyond national boundaries, prior to the emergence of global or international oligopoly, represents the main unifying trend in the analysis. Within the Anglo-Saxon tradition, Dunning's 'eclectic theory' 1981) represents an attempt to combine the two trends and impose a recognition of the *specificity* of the MNE as opposed to the traditional view of FDI, while seeking at the same time to bridge the gap between the theory of international investment and that of international location and trade.

French approaches are all different blends of what may be broadly defined as a 'neo-marxist' tradition. In contrast to the Anglo-Saxon approaches, all the French approaches essentially involve an extension at an international level of the theory of capitalist development (cf. Dobb, 1963; Sweezy, 1946), with the accumulation of capital and the related processes of (industrial) concentration and (financial) centralisation of capital as the key concepts. In all neo-marxist approaches government, e.g. the state, is also given a prominent central role as an institution shaping all aspects of modern capitalist society (cf. Mandel, 1975).

The blending of the French and the Anglo-Saxon approaches consists basically in the recognition that while MNEs are obviously active agents in the process of internationalisation and even architects of some aspects of the process, and *must consequently be analysed in their own right*, they are, nonetheless, *responding to an overall set of factors* over which they have in fact *little or no control*, and which *all stem from the basic mechanisms* driving the historical process of capitalist development. One of these mechanisms is the development (in a contradictory, antagonistic and unequal manner) of the forces of production, among which science and technology play an increasingly quite central role (see, *inter alia*, Rosenberg's essay on 'Marx as a student of technology', 1982, and Harvey, 1982, Chapter 4).

Once they are set against the background of the process of concentration and centralisation of capital and a situation where forces of production (notably those directly shaped by science and technology) have overrun national boundaries, a number of observations and concepts derived from the economics of technical change, the theory of the firm and the economics of industrial organisation and market structure acquire their full intelligibility and become necessary components of a global analysis. Set against such a background, empirical observations relating, for instance, to the close relationships between R & D intensity, industrial concentration and the scale of FDI in R & D- and scale-intensive industries take on a new dimension and can be interpreted as expressing a real *objective* constraint on firms in such industries to adopt the *world market* as the *only possible market* on which they can deploy and fully reap 'ownership advantages'.

The merging of the Anglo-Saxon approaches with the understanding derived from the extension at the world level of the process of capitalist development must *not* be interpreted, however, as implying a one-way process. For instance, while it is hard to establish a sound foundation for the analysis of global or international oligopoly without an understanding of the way in which the concentration and centralisation of capital will begin to take place at the international level with its tendency to englobe the advanced capitalist countries as a whole, through a process of 'mutual raiding' (Erdilek, 1985), international cross investment (Mucchielli and Thuillier, 1982), acquisitions and mergers, *conversely* the analysis of *firm behaviour in conditions of international oligopoly* (each firm backed by its home country government in one way or another), represents the *only way* of making *progress towards a better understanding* of the working of 'monopoly capital' and 'inter-imperialist rivalry'.

Similarly, once the concept of *internalisation* is set against the background of the twofold process of industrial concentration and financial centralisation of capital (as defined and distinguished in the marxist approach), and MNEs are defined in relation to their *group* structures and their *combined* industrial and financial attributes, it becomes possible to appreciate fully what Dunning has to say about the *organisation* of 'market failure' by large firms:

Where, for example, enterprises choose to replace, or not to use, the mechanism of the market, but instead allocate resources by their own control procedures, *not only do they gain* but, depending on the reason for internalisation, *others* (notably their customers and suppliers prior to vertical integration, and their competitors prior to horizontal integration) *may lose*. Internalisation is, thus, a powerful motive for takeovers or mergers, and a valuable tool in the strategy of oligopolists. [Dunning, 1981, p. 28]

In the same order of ideas, Dosi (1984) points out the importance of not considering internalisation as a passive response to 'market failure':

It would be misleading to consider internalization simply as an effect of and a reaction to some kind of 'market imperfection'. It is probably more accurate to consider it as one of the inner trends (and one of the 'rules of the game') in oligopolistic rivalry towards the transformation of the untraded features of technical change into proprietor assets which, as such, also represent entry barriers and differential advantages *vis-à-vis* other competitors.

The 'distinctive nature' of the multinational enterprise

A reference has been made to the financial dimensions of MNEs. This is a somewhat underlooked dimension of their scope and power, which has however been the object of a fair amount of attention and research in France and more recently in the United Kingdom (different French approaches include Morin, 1974, Pastré, 1980, Chesnais, 1979, and Grou, 1983; in the United Kingdom see Scott, 1979, 1986). These features are complementary to and indeed often an outcome of conglomerate organisation and are expressed *inter alia* in the 'portofolio' approach to assets, including industrial assets and the scale and significance of operations made by industrial MNEs as lenders in short-term international money markets (eurocurrencies) (Cohen, 1980). In this approach MNE must be viewed as a specific form of 'finance capital' (Hilferding, 1910; Lenin, 1915), e.g. a form which is predominantly engaged in industrial activity but in ways which are increasingly shaped by purely financial strategies as developed by financial analysts, financial market operators and bankers (see Minsky, 1982). This characteristic will be enhanced by the transformation of parent companies into 'holding' corporations, but is present today in all large multidivisional and multinational firms. It is a central factor in the emergence of the 'hollow corporation' as coined by *Business Week* which is now at the centre of debate in the United States (see Cohen and Zysman, 1987).

If due recognition is given to this dimension, and if the particular capacity of the MNEs to use world-based information technologies and systems to their own best advantage is also recognised (Antonelli, 1984), then Dunning's account of the 'distinctive nature' of the MNE (Dunning, 1981, p. 27) is a very acceptable one, namely that MNEs enjoy three combined and cumulative sets of advantages:

(i)   those which large firms may have over others 'producing in the same
       location' and which 'stem from size, monopoly power and better
       resource capability and usage';
(ii)   those pertaining to the advantage a branch plant or subsidiary can
       derive from belonging to a group, thus benefiting from many of the
       endowments of the parent company, 'for example, access to cheaper
       inputs, knowledge of markets, centralised accounting procedures,
       administrative experience, R & D, etc., at zero low marginal cost; or
       the *de novo* form will normally have to bear the full cost. The greater
       the non-production overheads of the enterprise, the more pronoun-
       ced this advantage is likely to be'; and
(iii) the particular type of advantage 'which arises specifically from the
       multinationality of a company, and is an extension of the other two.
       The larger the number and the greater the differences between
       economic environments in which an enterprise operates, the better
       placed it is to take advantage of different factor endowments and
       market situations'.

If these three aspects are used in combination, the MNE will be viewed as
a firm possessing a very wide range of opportunities simply not offered to
smaller domestic or regional firms, for *entry* into as well as *exit* from given
activities and markets; or again for 'internalising externalities', in our case,
for instance, the results of government or university-financed and executed R
& D. These firms also have special opportunities for reaping 'appropriable
rents' or quasi-rents (Klein *et al.*, 1978), and for exerting forms of monopolistic or monopsonistic 'market power' (falling short of outright
monopoly or monopsony) which can allow them to impose quasi-integra-
tion-type contractual arrangements of an essentially *predatory* nature on
smaller supplier firms, including specialised 'knowledge-intensive' small
firms.

But such firms are also oligopolists, in their home markets of course, and
also today in international markets, where oligopoly prevails in all 'science-
based' and in many 'scale-intensive' industries. The market power of each
firm is bounded by that of the other rivals which make up the oligopoly.
'Mutual recognition' and oligopolistic reaction and interaction, which are
the hallmarks of oligopoly, will take place in all spheres of activity, including technology, and may lead to situations where in the area of R & D and
the development manufacturing and marketing of high-technology products a considerable amount of cooperation between oligopolists occurs.
Once international oligopoly sets in, as is the case today, the 'endogenous
generation of market structure and technological performance' (Nelson
and Winter, 1982) will likewise start to become an international process.
Before turning to these hypotheses in the later part of the chapter, we first
discuss other important, albeit more traditional, aspects of the relationships between science and technology, FDI and MNEs.

Patterns of international investment in the 1980s

Major changes in the overall international pattern of foreign direct investment began to occur in the early 1970s. The fact that they started by *coinciding* with the deep changes in the world economic situation, before being later *accelerated* by the developments of the 1980s—in particular the collapse of profitable direct investment activity in most developing countries from 1981–2 onwards (the only exception being the Asian NICs) and the progressive extension of the new paradigms in science and technology and also manufacturing processes (notably Japanese—see Sciberras, 1980, for colour TV, and Jones, 1987, for automobiles)—helps to *explain the delay there has been in recognising the new international patterns* of FDI and in isolating them prior to adequate analysis.

The new patterns are the following: (i) a decline, later followed by a severe reduction, in the flow of FDI towards 'market economy' developing countries, in contrast with the People's Republic of China which has received the largest fraction of DC-orientated investment during the 1980s (UNCTNC, 1987); and (ii) more important still, the *recentring or reconcentration of the flow of FDI within the OECD area*, along with two major related changes, namely (a) the progressive shift in the role of the US economy from a 'home' to a 'host' country for FDI as European and later Japanese MNEs have developed their investment in the US market, and (b) the emergence since the late 1970s of Japan as a major 'home' country for MNEs and a large source of FDI directed towards the United States but also towards Europe.

The second, if not the first, of these two major developments was fairly foreseeable. It was announced in a Hymer and Rowthorn (1970) article, in which the authors predicted the emergence of global oligopoly as a result of the growth of European and Japanese FDI. The central finding of the Hymer–Caves strand of analysis (see also Knickerbocker, 1973) is that once a major firm in a concentrated industry has started to invest and manufacture abroad, its oligopolistic rivals are obliged to follow suit. While this may *start* as a rather unilateral process of oligopolistic rivalry between large firms based in the same economy (as it did in the 1950s and 1960s in the case of US-based foreign direct investment), *as soon as accumulation and the concentration and centralisation of capital have developed (or developed again) in other countries*, regions or poles of the internationalised capitalist world economy, the situation will *necessarily* increasingly be one of mutual cross-investment by MNEs, into one another's home markets and domestic technology bases.

This is the process that occurred increasingly in the 1970s and 1980s as a result of large-scale FDI by OECD-based MNEs into the US economy. Since the earlier 1980s, the United States has for the first time this century become a net importer of capital again. Part of this capital has had purely financial destinations, but a significant fraction has taken the form of investment into US manufacturing industry either through mergers or 'green-field' investment. At the same time as inward foreign direct investment has grown, outward US investment has somewhat declined. Consequently, if intra-Europe FDI is deducted from the European total, Europe and the United States now host approximately the same level of foreign investment (Fouguin, 1986). As in the case of trade flows, where Japan's imports are much lower than its exports, notably in high-technology industries, Japan's place in multipolar international investment is significantly different from that of Europe and the United States. Compared with Europe and the United States the level of foreign direct investment into Japan still remains extremely low. By contrast, Japanese *outward* foreign investment has been growing rapidly and will quite certainly be further accelerated by the changes in foreign exchange rates. Up to now a large part of Japanese investment in Europe and in the United States has been through joint ventures and inter-firm cooperation agreements of various sorts, one dimension of which is, as in the case of several US-based joint ventures, technical cooperation and the joint development of new technologies, and another the desire to overcome political and social sensitivities towards the entry of Japanese firms within the markets and domestic supply structures of US and European industry. When these sensitivities disappear, however, the preference of Japanese firms for majority-owned affiliates tends to reassert itself, as in the case of the United Kingdom (Dunning, 1985).

Trade, foreign investment and international flows of technology: the paucity of sound knowledge

In many instances, foreign direct investment has clearly recognisable trade-substituting effects: delocated production within a country replaces the exports previously made to that country from the MNE's home base. In other instances, foreign direct investment will create trade, along with new forms of dependencies and interdependencies. This is the case in particular when firms investing in a foreign economy continue to source capital goods and intermediary products from their home economy (as is often the case for Japanese firms at the moment) or when MNEs use affiliates to ship products (generally intermediary goods) to the parent company or to other affiliates.

An indication of the magnitude of the trade-substituting impacts which a unified theory would have to give an account of is given by UK data which show that in the case of the fifty largest corporations in 1981–2 the relation between overseas production of sales and export both as a percentage of sales was 3 to 1. Recent US Department of Commerce data show likewise that in 1983 the overall ratio of sales by the foreign affiliates of US MNEs to exports from the United States was a little over 2 to 1. This represents a drop in comparison to earlier periods and is due to the fall-back in US foreign direct investment since the end of the 1970s. However, in R & D-intensive industries where internationalisation has developed for many decades through direct investment rather than through exports, such as pharmaceuticals and chemicals, the ratio remains much higher: nearly 5 to 1 in pharmaceuticals and 3 to 1 in chemicals.

Even if the trade-substituting effects of foreign direct investment are quite substantial in some industries, in retrospect it is quite clear that the spectacular growth of exports and of internationalisation through trade would never have taken place on the scale it did in the absence of foreign direct investment. The trade-barrier-jumping capacity of foreign direct investment probably represents the strongest available deterrent to trade barriers, both tariff and non-tariff barriers. Foreign direct investment when coupled with trade also has a capacity to lower industrial entry barriers which trade alone does not possess. In the transitory period preceding the emergence of situations of world or international oligopoly in 'global market' industries and sectors, FDI in *combination with trade* succeeded in *lowering entry barriers*, reducing domestic concentration levels and weakening positions of domestic or regional oligopoly. In Europe notably, FDI increased United States competition significantly and had a positive effect on the competitiveness of European firms (Dunning, 1982). The need to *combine* the discipline stemming from low trade barriers with that resulting from *foreign direct investment* must be stressed. When foreign direct investment takes place behind high trade barriers, foreign affiliates, as shown by many industrial and country case studies and highlighted in Unger's chapter, tend to adapt themselves to reigning conditions of production and competitiveness and become a part of domestic oligopolistic supply structures. This, for instance, occurred in Spain in the 1960s and 1970s and of course in large Latin American countries like Brazil and Mexico (Connor, 1977, and Unger's chapter).

Another important theoretical issue in this area is the *relationship between intra-industry investment and intra-industry trade*. Discussing the case of industries in which 'there are a number of countries each home to a group of highly innovative firms' (e.g. in our terminology industries of the R & D-intensive, international oligopoly category), Dunning and Cantwell observe that:

Over the last 25 years, this is the kind of industry that has been characterised by the rise of the cross-hauling of investments between those countries harbouring the strongest firms. Such countries become hosts to the greatest levels of international production as well as being homes to MNEs of their own. This phenomenon is known as intra-industry trade and production; and, we might add, intra-industry technology trade and diffusion as well. [Dunning and Cantwell, 1986]

This, of course, remains an extremely general statement and amounts to a *plea for research* into those now extremely frequent situations where *intra-industry trade and intra-industry FDI occur simultaneously*, along with related two-way international flows of technology. In 1978, Dunning had already indicated that 'any theory of intra-industry trade must now take account of intra-industry investment. *We are only at the borders of research in this area*' (Dunning, in Giersch, 1979, p. 70, author's emphasis). Nearly ten years later we are still about at the same point: trade analysis *continues* to be carried out *separately* from that of investment. This was again the case for recent research at OECD during the structural adjustment study (OECD, 1987b), with resulting limitations on the usefulness of the findings. The latter confirm the continuation and strengthening of trends noted in earlier studies, but they would require an integration of the international investment variable to become really *meaningful*. The findings are the following (OECD, 1987b)

(i)   'OECD trade had increasingly involved products characterised by significant economies of scale in production, extensive product differentiation or close links to the science-base. Thus, from 1962 to 1985, the share of scale or production-intensive and science-based goods in total OECD manufacturing trade (exports plus imports) increased from 53 to 65 per cent, with growth rates of the latter category being particularly high in the most recent period.'

(ii)   The growth of trade has mainly entailed specialisation within industries. Using an index of intra-industry trade, based on the ratio of gross trade to net trade, the study finds that 'with the important exception of Japan, this index increased significantly for all the countries listed, the average for the group as a whole *rising by more than two-thirds* over the period 1959–1985'.

(iii)   This pattern of specialisation was accompanied by major shifts in the geographical structure of trade. 'Thus, throughout the 1950s and 1960s, trade occurred primarily between industrialised countries, sharing broadly similar factor endowments and patterns of demand. Trade grew particularly rapidly between closely located countries, mainly the United States and Canada on the one hand and the European OECD countries on the other'.

(iv)   Perhaps the most interesting finding, however, is the one concerning recent trends in the NICs which by 1985 accounted for fully 8 per cent of OECD manufactured imports. Regarding these countries, the study finds that 'the extension of interdependence to new trading partners did not weaken the major tendencies affecting the structure of manufactured trade. Thus, by the end of the period, nearly 40 per cent of OECD imports from the NICs were not in labour or resource intensive products, but in products characterised by significant scale economies or extensive product differentiation. And intra-industry trade—which had been a marginal factor in OECD trade with developing countries in the late 1960s—accounted for fully 31 per cent of the NIC's manufacturing trade with the OECD area in 1985: confirming that they too were increasingly drawn into the dynamic functions of trade'.

Such situations simply *cannot* be explained independently of FDI and the effects it has on the structure of trade. These effects are not limited to trade substitution (*inter alia* Vernon, 1979), but extend to other less well recognised phenomena, in particular:

(i)   the role FDI plays in gradually homogenising the organisation of production (pattern of industrial output and levels of productivity) in those countries in which the overall effect of such investment, through the combined influence of MNE strategies and host government policy, is (as in the Asian NICs) to integrate previous DCs into the 'North';

(ii) the role of international sub-contracting (Germidis, 1981) and other long-term commercial arrangements bearing on the supply of manufactured inputs to industrial production; and, of course,

(iii) 'intra-firm' trade, e.g. trade between affiliated firms within multinational corporate structures (Helleiner, in Giersch, 1979).

It is this type of structural impact, along the particular forms of integration of domestic economies into the world market it entails, which some authors have viewed as leading potentially to what Michalet (1976) has called 'le capitalisme mondial', i.e. a world wide set of economic relationships possessing systemic features, which might supersede the present pattern of national economies and international market relationships. In other recent work (Chesnais, 1988), we have argued that the end of Bretton Woods and the subsequent international monetary system, the onset of deep economic and trade instability (whether one decides or not to use the term economic crisis), along with the full restoration of the 'cumulative oppressive power' of *rentier* money capital (Keynes, 1936, pp. 375–76), have offset the emergence of any such system. Very strong liquidity preferences by money capital have been accompanied by increasingly 'footloose' strategies by MNEs and a premium on the part of FDI to industries and countries where *exit* barriers (Porter, 1985) are low. Contemporary microelectronics technology has given additional scope for such strategies by MNEs and wrecked previous industrialisation policies in almost all developing countries and most Latin American NICs (see Kaplinsky, 1987 for automobiles; Mytelka, 1988 for garments, as well as the chapter below by Unger). But this does not modify the essential fact that the structure of international trade *cannot be analysed independently of FDI and the worldwide strategies of MNEs.*

The internationalised sourcing of technology: an under-researched dimension of MNE operations

The organisation by MNEs of the *creation* and/or the *acquisition and appropriation* of technology on an *international* level, across national boundaries, is by no means a new phenomenom. It dates back to the period when attention was almost exclusively concentrated on the international *transfer* (i.e. dissemination) of technology by and in particular *within* the MNE. If little is known about world-wide sourcing operations by MNEs for technology, this is mainly because it has been the object of little research (see also Bertin, 1986): MNEs were thought of as simply (or mainly) transferring technology *outwards* and not also transferring it *inwards*. Discussing overseas R & D spending by MNEs, Caves (1982), for instance, simply mentions in passing that the 'basic research of MNEs is much more footloose than is applied research, and that some of it goes abroad to seek out particular scientific specialists'.

In a number of industries (cf. the studies produced at OECD in the late 1970s, Michalet and Delapierre, 1978; Chesnais, in OECD, 1979; Burstall, Dunning and Lake, 1981) there is evidence that MNEs, for instance, the European MNEs in pharmaceuticals and food processing and the US MNEs in the electrical, electronics and computer industries, were early to understand that foreign direct investment and internationalised group structures could form the basis not only for internalised transfer of technology conducive to the most advantageous exploitation of 'firm-specific advantages' across national frontiers, but also for the *sourcing and centralisation of scientific and technical knowledge and resources on an international scale*. The findings of a recent US survey (Fusfeld, 1986, pp. 132–3) regarding the motivations of US MNEs for setting up foreign laboratories have provided further information regarding the strategies of MNEs in this area. The most frequently quoted objective has been the desire to 'have a window on foreign science', first and foremost in Europe. Other objectives include access to special skills not easily available in the home country, developing new sources of technical concepts or simply establishing on an international stage of operations of corporations concerned with science and technology.

The telecommunications and computer and data processing industries have probably been those where the world-wide organisation of corporate R & D and sourcing of scientific and technical resources has experienced the greatest development. As early as the mid-1970s several large firms had a kind of international technical system with a foot in several national systems, but with identifiable autonomous features of their own, ensuring the international flow of technology within international group structures. IBM has, of course, often been studied in this respect (see Michalet and Delapierre, 1978). By the mid-1970s IBM had set up a world-based set of R & D activities organised independently of its manufacturing and marketing affiliates, in which the tasks assigned to laboratories did not necessarily match those of the subsidiary's production units to which given laboratories belonged formally. Few laboratories within the IBM group were engaged competitively or simultaneously in research, and then only in the exploratory stage before any heavy development expenses were involved. Their work was organised so as to maximise complementarities. At the end of the 1970s, IBM had three laboratories performing fundamental research, two in the United States and one in Switzerland. Development tasks were distributed on a world basis among all the other laboratories, i.e. fourteen major laboratories in the United States and eight in other countries: by order of establishment, The Netherlands, Germany, United Kingdom, Japan, Sweden, Austria, Canada and France.

To ensure that the R & D undertaken in affiliate laboratories geographically far removed from each other was consistent, IBM had set up a vast telecommunications network for regularly pooling all the group's technological resources, where laboratory computers were interconnected on a world-wide basis and a single data bank set up at the corporate R & D headquarters. In this respect again IBM has been exemplary. In particular since the emergence of world-wide telecommunication networks, its experience has been studied and partially followed by an ever more important number of firms. This is confirmed by the findings of the survey undertaken by Antonelli (1984) covering forty US and European MNEs, where replies show that among the seven main reasons given by firms for adopting the new international telecommunication equipment in their operations and undertaking the organisational changes required in corporate structures were the new possibilities offered for the 'international implementation of R & D capacities generated by increased interaction among affiliates and headquarters and greater division of labour, according to the technical requirements and scientific endowments of countries and affiliates'.

The centralisation of external scientific and technological knowledge is not limited to 'science-based' or R & D-intensive industries, but has been equally important in industries such as food processing, where innovation relies heavily on inter-industry transfers of technology. In our study of the technological activity of MNEs in this industry, we laid particular stress on the *horizontal coordination and management of inter-industrial technology transfers* by firms such as Unilever, Nestlé or CPC International and the role of engineering departments (Chesnais in OECD, 1979, Chapter XI).

The need to organise the sourcing of technological resources on an international basis and, in particular, to establish 'a window' on the world's most advanced science base, namely that of the United States, explains, of course, why large European firms, rapidly followed later by Japanese ones, have followed the road taken by the US MNEs in the preceding period. In the 1970s and 1980s non-US MNEs have increasingly sought to create laboratories in the United States as part of their investment in the US economy, in some instances as an important, if not a major component of the overall objective of this investment. This is particularly true in the chemical and chemicals-related industries, in particular in *pharmaceuticals*, where the need to gain direct access to the US science and technology base in the field of biotechnology has been a motive for much of the US investment made by non-US MNEs, which has generally taken the form of take-overs of existing firms, along with the acquisition of their R & D facilities which the new parent firms have often expanded. The process of 'international cross-investment in R&D', in the form of laboratories and other forms of scientific investments, including research contracts with universities, has been documented up to 1982 by Burstall in the case of the pharmaceutical industry (Burstall and Dunning, 1985). Since 1982, further European and Japanese investment has occurred in the United States, Japanese investment has grown in Europe, as has US and European investment in R & D facilities in Japan. Most firms still normally conduct the most sensitive and demanding types of work in centres located in their country of origin. Only still relatively few of the world's top thirty pharmaceutical MNEs have laboratories of the highest capacity situated elsewhere, but almost all now have some kind of 'window' open on the scientific capacity in their main competitors' home economies. This is all the more true since the emergence of biotechnology in the United States at the end of the 1970s and the expansion of inter-firm technological co-operation agreements, *inter alia* with the small genetic engineering firms, as a new mechanism for the acquisition of technology external to the large established MNEs (Chesnais, 1986; US Congress Office of Technological Assessment, 1984).

Increased pressures for an external technology sourcing by firms and the growth of inter-firm technical cooperation

Discussing the international flow of technology and technological balances of payments, the authors of the OECD Science and Technology Indicators No. 2 note that

problems of interpretation are raised not only by the mixed contents of the TBPs, but also by the elusive character of certain international flows of technological knowledge, i.e. those for which there is no visible form of payment (among others: cross-licensing, transfer of knowledge to a subsidiary, international co-operation of a non-commercial type). [OECD, 1986a, p. 54]

Today, on account of the rapid growth of inter-firm agreements, probably a very large part of outwards and inwards transfers of technology by firms now take this non-visible form.

In discussing the contemporary growth of inter-firm agreements it is important, of course, to keep a sense of *historical perspective*. International cross-licensing between large firms, which remains a fairly basic form of technical cooperation agreement in concentrated R & D intensive industries, was already a significant feature of the chemical and heavy electrical equipment industries in the 1930s (Newfarmer, 1978, 1985). Little-publicised technical cooperation has been a long-standing feature of the relationships between firms like Siemens and Philips, ICI and DuPont, or the three Swiss pharmaceutical majors in Basle.

Today, in addition to the deeply troubled world economic situation, there appears nonetheless to be *two series of major driving forces* explaining why present trends probably represent a qualitative development which will not be easily reversed. The first series of factors relate to the *point reached in the overall process of internationalisation*, along with the implications this has for firms, in the form of a continually growing requirement to wage what the business management literature calls 'global competition'. In all R & D-intensive industries, as well as in industries where scale economies are decisive, competition (e.g. oligopolistic rivalry) now takes place: (i) between a relatively small number of large firms (ranging from three in large commercial aircraft, and two or at best three in large civil aircraft engines, to ten or so in automobiles or in the main segments of the electronics sector); (ii) in a world arena which includes the respective home and host markets of rival MNEs as well as third markets, within and outside OECD; and (iii) through a wide array of means by which firms can gain access to technology and markets (notably 'reserved' government procurement markets). Such rivalry implies 'mutual recognition' and a variety of combinations between *competition* and *cooperation*.

The second set of factors concern contemporary developments in science and technology which help to explain why the access to a wide science and technology base that was an *advantage* in earlier phases is now a *necessity*. The overall trend is one where: (i) basic scientific knowledge is playing an increasingly crucial role in opening up new possibilities of major technological advance, or, to put it in another way, where the knowledge base of technology of firms is increasingly founded in basic science; (ii) many recent breakthroughs have occurred as a result of cross-fertilisation between scientific disciplines; (iii) technology has acquired stronger systemic features. These features are the hallmark not only of spectacular developments in space technology, telecommunications or military systems, but also of more mundane, albeit revolutionary, technologies in CAD/CAM, new materials, etc.

Ongoing paradigmatic changes in science and technology are accentuating all three aspects. Major innovations are based even more strongly on scientific knowledge; synergies and cross-fertilisation, both between scientific disciplines and between scientific and technological advances, play an ever more important role, notably through the advances continually occurring in computing technologies. The massive entry of computing into instrumentation has further strengthened the role played by the latter. The extension of the systemic features of technologies to a larger number of areas is a necessary and inevitable outcome and expression of these developments. Alongside these processes and as an expression of their pressure on firms, there has been a general tendency towards increases in R & D costs and outlays. This has been particularly noticeable in computers, electronics and components and pharmaceuticals, but would also be identifiable in areas such as new materials if detailed company data on costs were available.

In combination these developments in science and technology have created what Fusfeld (1986, p. 143) calls a 'capability squeeze' on firms, marked by: 'the increase in the number of technical fields relevant to corporate growth' and 'totally new requirements for significant technical advances'. These pressures can be met *partly* by increasing *in-house R & D* within corporate structures, both nationally and internationally, or by the establishment in cooperation with other firms of joint-venture corporations solely dedicated to R & D. In other cases, they will require the *external acquisition of knowledge*, know-how and skills located in *other* organisations, whether universities (when the knowledge is still close to basic research) or firms. These are the processes lying behind the observations made by Dunning and Cantwell (1986) that:

'there has been a historical shift away from technology being viewed by the firm as a specific and single purpose input towards the development of integrated technological systems which require coordinated governance for their economic deployment. The rise of such technological interdependence means that it is no longer appropriate to think simply in terms of a sequence which runs from technology creation to transfer and diffusion. The successful creation and application of new technology has become much more dependent upon the earlier dissemination of related technologies within the firm, and of the parallel technologies developed elsewhere by other firms.'

A wide range of interfirm agreements

The external acquisition of technology can be organised either through 'arm's-length' operations, notably straightforward licence agreements, through mergers and hierarchies (Williamson, 1975) (e.g. the outright acquisition of the firms possessing the desired technology or accumulated scientific and technical knowledge), or on the basis of a *wide range of inter-firm agreements* falling 'between markets and hierarchies', (Mariti and Smiley, 1983). The range of the main types of agreements established by firms with a view to producing, acquiring and/or commercially exploiting technology in common are set out in Table 23.1.

A. University-based cooperative research projects are collective R & D undertakings established and financed by firms in universities with or without public support. The distinctive characteristics of this type of agreement are location of the R & D in academic structures and extensive support and direction by firms (as opposed to governments) even if some public support is offered.

B. Government–industry cooperative national or international research projects are collective R & D undertakings with strong government backing, located in firms but also in universities and public research institutes. Here government initiative and financial support (national as in the case of Alvey or by the EC as in that of Esprit), and a much greater variety in the location and execution of R & D, are distinctive features.

C. Research corporations are *private joint-venture companies* financed on

Figure 23.1 Inter-firm R & D, technology and manufacturing co-operation agreements and the R & D, to marketing spectrum

Pre-competitive stage Research and development cooperation				Competitive stage				
				Technological cooperation		Manufacturing and/or marketing cooperation		
A	B	C	D	E	F	G	H	I
University based cooperative research financed by associated firms (with or without public support)	Government industry cooperative R & D projects with universities and public research institute involvement	Research and development corporations on a private joint-venture basis	Corporate venture capital in small high-tech. firm (by one or by several firms, otherwise competitors)	Non-equity cooperative research and development agreements between two firms in selected areas	Technical agreements between firms concerning completed technology *inter alia:* * technology-sharing agreements; * second-sourcing agreements; * complex two-way licensing; * cross-licensing in separate product markets	Industrial joint venture firms and comprehensive R & D, manufacturing and marketing consortia	Customer–supplier agreements, notably partnerships	One-way licensing and/or marketing agreements (including OEM sales agreements)
Many partners	Several partners		Few or very few partners	Few or very few partners		Few or very few partners		

Source: Chesnais in DSTI, 1986, *Technical Co-operation Agreements Between Firms: Some Initial Data and Analyses*, on the basis of typologies by Hacklisch (1986) and Ricotta and Mariotti (1986).

a shareholder basis by a number of firms, generally MNEs. Programmes focus on generic technology relating directly to the competitive interests of the joint-venture partners. The research results are proprietary and form a kind of pool of patents and know-how for partners.

D. Agreements involving the use of corporate venture capital (CVC) are used by large corporations, notably MNEs, to make small but strategic investments in new innovative processes, still belonging to small firms. Used in combination with R & D contracts, such investments prepared acquisition without interfering immediately with the activities of the small, innovative firms; these remain autonomous in their R & D and management decisions (Ricotta and Mariotti, 1986).

E. Non-equity cooperative research agreements are flexible forms of cooperation of limited duration, without shareholder participation, established between a very small number of firms (usually only two) to deal with specific technical problems. If the R & D is successful it can either be exploited commercially by the participating firms each in their own business, or lead to the establishment of a separate joint venture.

F. Technological agreements bearing on existing 'proven technologies' can take a variety of forms, depending on the specific characteristics of industries and technologies. They include: (i) technology-sharing agreements bearing on complementarity technologies; (ii) second-sourcing agreements between large MNE producers, otherwise competitors (as in semiconductors), involving access to proprietary technology; (iii) two-way exchanges of licences in directly complementary areas with clauses providing for the continuous exchange of improvements and developments; and (iv) two-way exchanges of licences or of scientific and technical knowledge produced by firms as a 'by-product' of their main lines of scientific and commercial specialisation.

G. Comprehensive R & D, manufacturing and marketing consortia are joint ventures with a number of partners, formed with the aim of creating, testing, producing and commercialising a product all the way from the R & D to the final market.

H. Customer–supplier partnerships, notably between MNEs, which represent 'the formalisation of a link that reflects a significant reliance of the partners on one another. It may or may not involve an equity interest or an exclusive relationship . . . It responds to the intensifying *systemic* dimension of components and provides a mechanism for leveraging critical technical and financial resources for the partners (Hacklisch, 1986).

I. Licence agreements and technology transfers forming part of a long term relationship between two firms, as in OEM agreements.

In search of useful interpretative analytical frameworks

The information base concerning inter-firm technical cooperation agreements includes a variety of industry case studies, some very detailed (Mowery, .1986; Hacklisch, 1986; Payne, 1986), others more limited in scope; a motley collection of statistical data bases; one or two Ph.D. theses containing some empirical testing (Hladik, 1984); articles written from the standpoint of the theory of the firm (Mariti and Smiley, 1983), and a rapidly growing but fairly heterogeneous literature by business management economists (Harrigan, 1985; Ricotta and Mariotti, 1986; Doz *et al.*, 1986). At present, there is really only one conclusion to be drawn from this material—that inter-firm agreements occur within a very wide variety of concrete situations, on the basis of a wide range of corporate strategies and with very differing consequences for the future of firms and the maintenance and/or strengthening of domestic technology bases.

Progress towards the development of appropriate conceptual frameworks for the interpretation of the existing data and the elaboration of new and hopefully more significant and/or easily usable studies than many of those made at present can take place along several alternative paths, on the basis of the different approaches discussed in earlier sections. The main theoretical question (which to our knowledge has not yet been really tackled) bears on the explanation of why MNEs, after giving priority to internalised modes of creation and dissemination of technology, have moved towards a much greater recourse to cooperation with other firms, e.g. why, *after* moving from the *market* to *hierarchies* (Williamson, 1975), they are now moving from *hierarchies* to the interfirm *organisation mode* (Imai and Itami, 1984).

Whatever the approach chosen, one essential condition must be satisfied, which is an adequate *understanding and account of technology and innovation*, along with the *particular constraints*, they place on firms to enter into agreement and the *particular advantages* which can be created by the *successful centralisation and appropriation of technology through such agreements*. While a purely scientific and technological interpretation developed independently of any theoretical basis *can only yield descriptive results at the best*, conversely no proper analysis of agreements can sidestep the economics of innovation and technical change.

Not many studies have yet succeeded in combining the reference to a well-defined economic approach with a sufficient detailed analysis of the technological constraints and opportunities pressing towards the establishment of agreements. Teece (1986) offers one example written from the standpoint of the theory of corporate strategy. Teece's central hypothesis is that:

in almost all cases, the successful commercialisation of an innovation requires that the know-how in question be utilised in conjunction with the services of other assets. Services such as marketing, competitive manufacturing, and after-sales support are almost always needed.

In some cases, firms (notably MNEs) will have internalised the specialised complementary assets through previous investments and mergers. In others, firms (notably small and medium enterprises or purely domestic or regional firms) will lack one or several of the necessary complementary assets and will be forced to find adequate partnerships and/or establish cooperation agreements. Other factors shaping corporate strategy are technological and rest on contemporary innovation theory as developed *inter alia* by Abernathy and Utterback (1978), Nelson and Winter (1982) and Dosi (1986). They concern in particular: (i) the appropriability regime, e.g. the degree to which an innovation can be protected (ranging from 'tight' regimes where technology is extremely difficult to imitate, to very 'weak' regimes where it is almost impossible to protect); and (ii) the degree to which a dominant design has been developed and imposed by one or several firms in an industry or, on the contrary, where there is a state of technological flux (a pre-paradigmatic stage with respect to dominant design).

In the Teece approach, as in all similar approaches influenced by the work of Porter (1984), the key strategic issue is the struggle 'to avoid handing over the lion's share of the profits from its innovation to imitators and/or owners of specialised and co-specialised complementary assets'. Which are the precise key assets required will obviously *vary* from industry to industry or even from product to product, while the degree of external dependence of firms and the risk that they fare badly in the distribution of value added and the flow of rent from innovation will obviously depend on their size, diversification and degree of multinational expansion.

Another analytical framework is the one developed by Bertin (1986) for the interpretation of data from the AREPTIT-SPRU questionnaire to MNEs concerning the *inward* as well as the outward transfer of technology through agreements involving patents (see Bertin and Wyatt, 1986, for a full account of this study). According to Bertin, MNEs must attempt to avoid two pitfalls: 'one is the transfer of advanced or sensitive technology to partners who might turn into dangerous competitors in the future; the second is the acquisition of such technology from a partner who may gain some type of control of a significant share of the firm's activity through its use'. In the face of rising R & D costs and the need to acquire technologies outside the firm, MNEs may be expected to develop strategies along two contrasting models:

In the *first model*, the firm holds a competitive position which is strongly centered in a main field of activity. It allocates the major share of its R & D expenses to this main field. It restricts itself to few transfers of technique, mostly with internal partners—subsidiaries or associates, whether foreign or domestic.

In the *second type*, closer to what we know as the industrial conglomerate model, the firm holds no such definite and strong competitive position or it has several distinct ones. Accordingly its R & D is not as specialised and it turns to external as well as internal partners for frequent technical transfers to complement its own research activity or to valorise its own technical output.

MNE strategies will also be shaped by certain features of the technology concerned, its availability (along with possible limitations set by sellers), the cost of acquisition and the expected returns. Bertin tests his model and comes up with results which show *extremely strong industry-specific features*, partially outriding the initial assumptions:

(i)   External transfer partners play a significant role in industries of the world-oligopoly type, such as automobiles and electronics. What is rather new is that such partners are also significant in the chemical industry. The increasing cost of research may exercise a strong influence on the firm's strategy, as suggested in various interviews, compelling the firm to increase technology exchange with competitors.

(ii) This is especially true of the electronics industry where more than two-thirds of firms have the same partners on sales and purchases of technology; the importance of cross-licensing is one possible explanation for this result, assuming a small number of suppliers of new technology.

(iii) Except for world oligopoly sectors, internal partners are given a strong preference in what could be called the core activities of MNEs . . . External partners are preferred in activities where they offer new potentialities for growth in the near future (markets) or in the distant one (new research fields). Uncertainty and heavy costs of entry are grave concerns in new fields of activity such as new materials, communications and advanced computing. These concerns induce firms, even the largest ones, to look for extensive external technical contacts and joint-ventures in research.

A taxonomy with the role of government, supply structures and key features of technology as parameters

As can be anticipated from the earlier sections of this chapter, our own attempt at establishing an interpretative analytical framework of taxonomy does not take the individual firm at its starting point of a theory of corporate strategy, but seeks to interpret inter-firm technical cooperation agreements in the context of the main 'exogenous' factors shaping the individual firm's environment: the progress of internationalisation, the tendency towards concentration and centralisation, the overall fall in the rate of return to capital (OECD, *Economic Outlook*, 1986c), the role of government, and the pace and direction of technological change.[1]

Ever since beginning to work on inter-firm technical cooperation agreements, we have been struck by *the extremely strong industry and/or technology-specific differences* in the type and range of agreements met within different industrial sectors (see OECD, 1986b). These must be related, of course, to the particular features of technology in different

Table 23.2 Main parameters shaping the types of agreements most frequently used by firms in different categories of industry

Main parameters / Types of agreement	Role of government in structuring the industry and its markets	International supply structure	Degree of novelty and sophistication of technology	Location of R & D and of 'technological capital' accumulation	Size of investment and rate of capital depreciation	Degree and nature of the systemic attributes of final product	Representative industries
Industrial consortia and international joint ventures aimed at world markets	Important or very important; industries considered as strategic	Highly concentrated (tending towards monopoly or duopoly)	New or very new and/or very sophisticated technologies	Large firms with privileged relations with government large public R & D labs	Very large investments with very long depreciation periods	Strong systemic with high technological content	Space launchers and satellites; long distance civil aircraft; jet engines; weapons and military systems; telecom. equipment
Complex international agreements pertaining to engineering, technology, financing and manufacture for domestic or regional market projects	Important in DCs, limited in advanced countries (except for export credits and foreign policy support during commercial negotiations)	World oligopoly with or without a dominant firm with trends towards cartel-type situations or fairly organised oligopolistic rivalry	Fairly well-known technologies requiring large accumulated know-how	Large firms belonging to the world oligopoly; engineering firms and heavy equipment manufacturers	Large investments and long or very long depreciation	Systemic with medium or low technological content	Large-scale bulk non-ferrous metal electrical power stations (including nuclear); large-scale public infrastructures
R & D joint-venture firms leading to patent pools open to corporate partners	Large buyer and/or purveyor of R & D funds	World oligopoly without a dominant firm and with very acute rivalry	Constantly and rapidly evolving technology	Large firms belonging to the world oligopoly	Large investments in particular in R & D requiring cooperation in generic technology	Not very systemic but sometimes significant technological complementarities	Electronic components
	As above	As above	As above	As above	As above	As above	Electronic components
Technology sharing agreements; complex two-way licensing, cross-licensing in separate product markets; second sourcing agreements	Weaker role	Medium to strong oligopolistic rivalry	Technology changing rapidly after a period of slow development	Ditto	Large investments still within the scope of large firms	Tech. complementarities and/or specialisation in sub-markets	Pharmaceuticals; specialised chemicals (high-grade plastics, composites)
R & D contracts between large and small firms, with or without the use of corporate venture capital	As above	As above	Rapidly evolving technology on the basis of radical paradigm change	Small knowledge-intensive high-tech firms with specialised skills; univ. or public laboratories	Investments in innovation not very costly but with very high risk	As above	Biotechnology; specialised electronics and software; certain new materials

sectors, and also to the nature of supply structures, the role of government in support, the very existence of certain industries, the subsidisation of R & D, and the establishment of non-tariff protection around 'reserved' public procurement markets (Chesnais 1987).

We have also observed that inter-firm technological cooperation across national frontiers invariably *combines* several dimensions or, again, *meets several objectives*, notably access to technology in combination with guaranteed access to certain semi-protected or threatened markets. In many industries, the exchange of technology is also an effective way of consolidating 'mutual recognition' and 'mutual forbearance' between oligopolists and of laying the basis for a strengthening of entry barriers, possibly paving the way for quasi-cartel-like behaviour. In instances where the main objective is access to technology, the type of agreement chosen will depend on the nature of the firm or institution where the technology is located and the steps to be taken to appropriate it. As a result, Table 23.2 has been built using six parameters:

(i)   The first concerns the role played by governments in shaping the structures of the industry (through R & D subsidies, large-scale procurement, open involvement in the organisation of the industry, and the division of tasks between firms).

(ii) The second parameter relates to the international supply structure (e.g. situations of near monopoly on duopoly: concentrated world oligopoly with a dominant firm (e.g. computers); concentrated world oligopoly with several firms of near equal strength; loose world oligopoly in combination or not with concentrated oligopoly in domestic or regional markets, etc.).

(iii) The *speed* of technical change, and the degree to which it has a *novel* or *radical* character and is therefore likely to have appeared outside established firms requiring them to resort to external acquisition.

(iv) The country location of the largest R & D outlays and the institutions (firms, government agencies and their laboratories, universities) within which the accumulation of technology has been proceding. In combination, (iii) and (iv) *influence* the easiness or, on the contrary, the obstacles to *external appropriation*.

(v)   The level of R & D and capital investment thresholds and the pressure they put on firms to cooperate.

(vi) The extent to which R & D- and scale-intensive products have *systemic* features, authorising a division of tasks and hence cooperation between firms in their conception and manufacture: this is an important dimension of some type of cooperation well illustrated by Mowery's study (1986) of the aircraft and engine industries.

Using the taxonomy: two examples

Industrial consortia and international joint ventures aimed at world markets (for instance, the General-Electric–SNECMA (France) joint ventures for the development production of the CFM 56 jet engine, see Baranson, 1976, and Mowery, 1986) are the form in which inter-firm cooperation (with which governments are also generally involved directly or indirectly) invariably takes place in industries such as *space products* (launchers and satellites), commercial *aircraft* of the large inter-continental categories, *jet engines*, and increasingly the *defence* industries, where international inter-firm agreements backed or initiated by governments have become more and more frequent.

This form of cooperation involves a carefully negotiated division of industrial responsibilities and workloads, financial risk, assets and profits. Agreements are almost invariably publicised in detail since they often involve the use of public funds. Membership is defined in terms of *percentages* of assets and liabilities and a precise definition of industrial roles.

The use of industrial cooperation as the preferred, if not exclusive form of cooperation can be directly related to

(i)   the 'strategic' and 'political' character of the industries concerned;
(ii) the way in which the pace and nature of world demand (including the size of the market and the particularities of market access), coupled with the extremely high costs and complexity of scientific and technical requirements for production, have created a situation where only a very limited number of producers are active, and where the threat of *outright* or *near-monopoly situations* is a real one and where alliance is the only choice open to almost all countries and to practically all firms; but also
(iii) where the strong *systemic*, but at the same time *high-technology features* of the end product allow a division of tasks, either among equals or near-equals (as in the case of the main participants in Airbus industries or Ariane), with all the complex problems of rivalry and coordination which this raises, or between firms in an unequal situation with one firm acting as prime contractor with sole final responsibility (as in the Boeing, TWR or Hughes Aircraft-led US consortia).

The semiconductor industry is one of those where the *greatest number and widest range of forms of agreements are used* by the large firms. The situation reflects, in part, the pace of technological progress in the industry (cf. Dosi, 1984, for a complete interpretation of the early 1980s). The close network of agreements which the major firms have established among themselves must, however, be related to the specific *supply structure of the industry*. The internationalisation and diversification strategies followed by all large electronics firms now place major manufacturers in a situation of oligopolistic rivalry generally involving competition on a combination of identical and/or complementary product markets. Electronics and in particular semiconductors are industries *par excellence* 'characterised by strong oligopolistic and technological competition' where 'MNEs . . . need a direct presence in all those countries which hold leading positions in the development of the industry and of associated technology' (Dunning and Cantley, 1986). As a result one finds:

— at the *stage of precompetitive R & D* a number of *national* alliances between oligopolists belonging to the same country: e.g. the Japanese example of the large industry—MITI projects, e.g. VLSI, the '5th generation computer project' (Sigurdson, 1986) which the United States and Europe have recently tried to imitate (e.g. the three US cooperative arrangements in microelectronics, the Semiconductor Research Corporation (SRC), the Microelectronics Center of North Carolina (MCNC), and the Stanford University Center for Integrated Systems (CIS), which belong to category A of Table 23.1; the UK Alvey, the Esprit project (examples of category B), or again the new private R & D joint-venture corporations (type C), such as the European Computer Research Center (ICL, Bull and Siemens) and, of course, the US Microelectronics and Computer Technology Corporation (MCC);

— at the *competitive stage* a considerable focus *on F-type agreements*, between oligopolists *of different nationality* bearing on already developed technologies. In semiconductors alliances very rarely take the form of consortia of joint ventures, but rather of *bilateral* agreements between oligopolistic rivals. Faced with continually increasing R & D costs, MNEs see at present considerable advantages in sealing mutual recognition through agreements involving a two-way exchange of technology, thus reducing some R & D outlays and at the same time raising the stakes for non-participants in the agreements. In combination and on account of their number, their bilateral agreements create a web-like network of agreements, at various points of which one finds (in a sort of nodal position) the firms which have established the largest number of linkages.

The most carefully documented research on this industry (Hacklisch, 1986) shows that technology-sharing agreements, second-sourcing with technological exchange and joint and/or complementary development accords are the forms of agreement most frequently encountered in semiconductors. Technology-sharing agreements generally involve a two-way exchange of comparable, but *complementary* technical expertise. Major examples are the US–Japan agreements in which US design capabilities have been shared in exchange for Japanese competence in CMOS fabrication technology. A major finding by Hacklisch is that 'The respective strengths of US companies in design and software microprocessor technology and of Japanese firms in CMOS are a prime characteristic in a number of US–Japan agreements in the area of MUCs/MPUs'. Examples given include the Intel–Oki, Intel–Fujitsu, Motorola–Hitachi, Zilog–NEC and Zilog–Toshiba agreements.

The pooling of patents (which will occur if corporations like MCC are successful) and reciprocal licensing confront potential competitors, notably smaller firms or firms contemplating entry into the industry, with formidable competitive stakes and entry barriers. The situation in semiconductors today presents both *similarities* and important *differences* with earlier examples of the 1930s (in heavy electrical equipment and chemicals). Technology-sharing and exchange between the largest firms in the industry are quite certainly increasing the advance of these firms over those which cannot hope to be parties to the most important types of partnerships. They represent one of the factors lying behind the continual increase in concentration at world level. At the same time, however, and this, of course, is the novel aspect, rivalry continues to be extremely acute within the small group of leading world firms, notably between the main US and Japanese manufacturers. This particular combination of cooperation and competition is one of the foundations for the fear sometimes expressed by some observers in the United States (cf. Reich and Mankin, 1986) that the technology agreements set up with US firms are, in fact, providing Japanese firms with an accelerated access to the technology of their US competitors.

Concluding remarks

These must necessarily be extremely brief. The first concerns our belief that there is need for a multi-form theoretical and analytical attack in all the areas discussed from the third section onwards, where important lacunae in our knowledge, due to gaps in theory which urgently require bridging, have been identified.

The second observation concerns the overall message stemming from our analysis, which is not extremely optimistic for developing countries (see also the chapter by Unger), nor indeed for the smaller or less developed OECD countries (Walsh, 1987). Much more research would be required to understand the medium and long-term effects of a situation where the *largest* and *most advanced firms*, technologically speaking, are exchanging *between themselves*, vital, *complementary* technologies. On the basis, however, of available data in the light of the understanding built up by earlier work on *barriers to entry* (Bain, 1956) and *technology gaps* (OECD, 1970), it can safely be stated that such cooperation creates *formidable new entry barriers* at the heart of the industry and with respect to its 'core technology' base (US National Research Council, 1983); thus creating new conditions of interfirm and intercountry dependencies, in the form of a whole new web of dependent technological links *vis-à-vis* the industry leaders. This is felt even by advanced small and medium-size OECD countries. It is certain to affect developing countries very strongly in the future. As Dunning and Cantwell (1986) have put it:

The change in the international environment has further compelled a move towards *integrated technological systems*. The advantages which stem from *such centralised co-ordination* has helped to strengthen the position of many MNEs *vis-à-vis* uninational firms, who are constrained to follow seriously only those activities in which their own countries have an existing or potential locational advantage. [author's emphasis]

The identification of such systems and the development of appropriate corporate strategies, (see the work of LAREA, GEST (1985) on 'Technology cluster Strategies') has already begun to create yawning new technological and industrial gaps between firms and countries, even within the most advanced OECD countries. The capacity on part of firms and countries to recognise (i) that core technologies may lie at the heart of technology *systems* (see Gille, 1978 and also with application to the Japanese situation Imai; 1984); (ii) that centralised coordination must start from a sound and firm domination of technological advance in these core core technologies; and (iii) that successful competition requires appropriate diversified large company industrial group structure, (of which the Japanese 'keiretsu' represents today the most successful example, see Freeman, 1987), *may represent* in coming years one of the most powerful instruments of *inequal development* at work in the world economy.

Note

1. *All* these factors of course are *endogenous* to the overall movement of the capitalist economy. The term 'exogenous' is used simply to designate the incapacity of any given firm, however large it may be and however much it contributes to their acceleration, to control the factors shaping the overall international economic, technological and political context in which it operates. The environment becomes increasingly 'exogenous' (e.g. constraining) as the size of firms become smaller, but *even the largest* MNE can never do more than *adapt*, with major advantages over small firms, *to the changes and challenges of the environment.*

References

Abernathy, H.L. (1978), *The Productivity Dilemna: Roadblock to Innovation in the Automobile Industry*, Baltimore, Johns Hopkins University Press.

Abernathy, H.L. and Utterback, J.M. (1978), 'Patterns of industrial innovation', *Technology Review*, no. 80, June–July.

Adam, G. (1973), 'Multinational Corporations and Worldwide Sourcing', in H. Radice (ed.) (1975), *International Firms and Modern Imperialism*, London, Penguin.

Amin, S. (1970), *L'accumulation à l'échelle mondiale*, Paris, Maspero.

Antonelli, C. (1984), *Cambiamento tecnologico e impresa multinazionali: il ruolo deli reti telematiche nelle strategie globale*, Milano, Franco Angeli.

——— (1987), 'L'impresa rete', *CESPE Papers*, CESPE Fondazione, Rome, mimeo.

Bain, J. (1956), *Barriers to New Competition*, Cambridge, Mass., Harvard University Press.

Baranson, J. (1976), *International Transfers of Industrial Technology by US Firms*, Lexington, Mass., Lexington Books.

Beaud, M. (1987), *Le système national mondial hiérarchisé*, Paris, La Découverte.

Bertin, G.Y. (1986), 'Multinational enterprises: transfer partners and transfer policies', in A.E. Safarian and G.Y. Bertin (eds), *Multinationals, Governments and International Technology Transfer*, London, Croom Helm.

Bertin, G.Y. and Wyatt, S. (1986), *Multinationales et propriété industrielle*, Institut de Recherche sur les Multinationales (IRM), Paris, PUF.

Buckley, P.J. and Casson, M. (1976), *The future of the Multinational Enterprise*, London, Macmillan.

Burstall, M., Dunning, J.H. and Lake A. (1981), *Multinational Enterprises Governments and Technology: The Pharmaceutical Industry*, OECD, Paris.

Burstall, M.L. and Dunning, J.H. (1985), 'International investment in innovation', in N. Wells, (ed.), *Pharmaceuticals Among the Sunrise Industries*, Croom Helm, London.

Caves, R.E. (1971), 'International corporations: the industrial economics of foreign investment', *Economica*, vol. 38, p. 149.

——— (1974), 'International trade, international investment, and imperfect markets', special paper in International Economics No. 10 (November) Dept. of Economics, Princeton University.

——— (1982), *Multinational Enterprise and Economic Analysis*, Cambridge, Cambridge University Press.

Centre de Prospective et d'Evaluation (CPE) (1985), *Rapport sur l'état de la technique*, numéro spécial de *Sciences et Techniques*.

Chesnais, F. (1979), 'Capital financier et groupes financiers: recherche sur l'origine des concepts et leur utilisation actuelle en France' dans *Internationalisation des Banques et des Groupes Financiers*, Séminaire CEREM, Nanterre, novembre 1979, Paris, Éditions du CNRS (1981).

Chesnais, F. et Michon-Savarit, C. (1980), 'Some observations on alternative approaches to the analysis of international competitiveness and the role of technology factor', Conférence sur les indicateurs de la science et de la technologie, OCDE, Paris, miméo.

——— (1984), 'Quelques remarques sur le contexte mondial de la dette des PED et la nature du capital prêté', *Tiers-Monde*, Tome XXV, no 99, juillet–septembre 1984 (numéro spécial sur La Dette du Tiers-Monde).

——— (1986a), 'Technological cumulativeness, the appropriation of technology and technological progressiveness in concentrated market structures', paper presented to the Conference on Technology Diffusion, Venice, March 1986.

——— (1986b), 'Science, technology and competitiveness', *DSTI Review*, no. 1, Autumn.

——— (1987), 'Les accords de coopération technologique et les choix des entreprises européennés', communication au colloque Europrospective, CPE, FAST, Commissariat général au Plan, La Villette, Paris, avril 1987.

——— (1988), 'Internationalisation, changement technique radical et compétitivité des systèmes productifs nationaux', dans J. Noisi (ed.), *Technologie et compétitivité internationale*, Actes du colloque international, Oligopoles, innovations technologiques et concurrence internationale, CREDIT, Montréal, octobre 1987, mimeo.

Coase, R.H. (1937), 'The nature of the firm', *Economica*, no. 4, November, CEPII (1987).

Cohen, S. and Zysman, J. (1987), *Manufacturing Matters: the Myth of the Post Industrial Economy*, New York, Basic Books.

Connor, J.M. and Mueller, W.F. (1977), *Market Power and Profitability of Multinational Corporations*, Report to the Senate Subcommittee on Multinational Corporations, Washington, DC, Government Printing Office.

Cotta, A. (1978), *La France et l'impératif mondial*, Paris, Press Universitaires de France.

Destanne de Bernis, G. (1977), *Relations économiques internationales*, 4e édn., Paris, Dalloz.

Dobb, M. (1963), *The Economic Development of Capitalism*, London, Routledge.

Dosi, G. (1982a), 'Technology industrial structures and international economic performance', paper prepared for the OECD Study on Technology and competitiveness, Paris, mimeo.

—— (1982b), 'Technical paradigms and technological trajectories: suggested interpretation of the determinants and directions of technical change', *Research Policy*, vol. 11, pp. 147–62.

—— (1984), *Technical Change and Industrial Transformation*, London, Macmillan.

Doz, Y., Hamel, G. and Prahalad, C.K. (1986), 'Strategic partnership: success or surrender: the challenge of competitive collaboration', mimeo, INSEAD (Fontainebleau), London Business School, University of Michigan, mimeo.

Dunning, J.H. (1981), *International Production and the Multinational Enterprise*, London, George Allen & Unwin.

—— (1985), *Japanese Participation in British Industry*, London, Croom Helm.

Dunning, J.H. and Cantwell, J.A., (1986), 'The changing role of multinational enterprises in the international creation, transfer and diffusion of technology', paper presented to the Conference on Innovation Diffusion, Venice, March 1980.

Erdilek, A. (ed.) (1985), *Multinationals as Mutual Invaders: Intra-Industry Direct Foreign Investment*, London, Croom Helm.

Fouquin, M. (ed.), (1986), *Industrie mondiale: La compétitivité à tout prix*, Centre d'Etude et Prospectives Internationales, Paris, Economica.

Freeman, C. (1982), *The Economics of Industrial Innovation*, 2nd edn., London, Frances Pinter.

—— (1987), *Technology Policy and Economic Performance: Lessons from Japan*, London, Pinter Publishers.

Fusfeld, H.T. (1986), *The Technical Enterprise, Present and Future Patterns*, Cambridge, Mass., Ballinger.

Germidis, D. (1981), *International Subcontracting: A New form of Investment*, Paris, OECD Development Centre.

Giersch, H. (ed.) (1979), *Proceedings of the 1978 Kiel Symposium on the Economics of Intra-Industry Trade*, Tübingen, J.C.B. Mohr.

—— (1982), *Proceedings of the 1981 Kiel Symposium on emerging Technology: Consequences for Economic Growth, Structural Change and Employment in Advanced Open Economies*, Tübingen, J.C.B. Mohr.

Gille, B. (1978), *Histoire des techniques*, Paris, La Pléïade.

Grou, P. (1983), *La Structure financière du capitalisme multinational*, Paris, Fondation des Sciences Politiques.

Haklisch, C.S. (1986), 'Technical alliances in the semiconductor industry', Center for Science and Technology Policy, New York University, mimeo.

Harrigan, K.R. (1985), *Strategies for Joint Ventures*, Lexington, Mass. Lexington Books.

Harvey, D. (1982), *The Limits to Capital*, Oxford, Blackwell.

Hilferding R. (1970 ed.), *Le capital financier*, Paris Éditions de Minuit.

Hladik, K.J. (1984), *International Joint Ventures*, Lexington, Mass., Lexington Books.

Horst, T. (1974), 'The theory of the firm', in J.H. Dunning (ed.), *Economic Analysis and the Multinational Enterprise*, London, George Allen & Unwin.

Hymer, S.H. (1960), *The International Operations of National Firms: A Study of Direct Foreign Investment*, Cambridge, Mass., MIT (published by MIT Press, 1976).

Hymer, S.H. and Rowthorn, R. (1970), 'Multinational corporations and international oligopoly: the non-American challenge', in C.P. Kindleberger (ed.), *The International Corporation*, Cambridge, Mass., MIT.

Imai, K. and Itami, B. (1984), 'Mutual infiltration of organization and market— Japan's firm and market in comparison with the US', *International Journal of Industrial Organization*, vol. 2, no. 4.

Imai, K. (1984), *Japan's Industrial Policy for High Technology Industries*, Conference on Japanese Industrial Policy in comparative Perspective, New York.

Jones, D. (1987), 'Structural adjustment in the automobile industry', *STI Review*, no. 3, Winter.

Kaplinsky, R. (1987), *'Technological Revolution' and the International Division of Labour in Manufacturing: A Place for the Third World?*, EADI Conference on New Technologies and the Third World, Institute of Development Studies, University of Sussex, Brighton.

Kemp, J. (1967), *Theories of Imperialism*, London, Routledge.

Keynes, J.M. (1936), *The General Theory of Employment, Interest and Money*, London, Macmillan.

Klein, B. (1979), 'The slowdown in productivity advances: a dynamic explanation', in C.T. Hill and J.M. Utterback (eds), *Technological Innovation for a Dynamic Economy*, New York, Pergamon Press.

Klein, B., Crawford, R.G. and Alchian, A.A. (1978), 'Vertical integration, appropriable rents and the competitive contracting process', *Journal of Law and Economics*, October.

Knickerbocker, F.T. (1973), 'Oligopolistic reaction and multinational enterprise', Graduate School of Business Administration, Harvard University.

LAREA/GEST (1985), *Grappes technologiques et stratégies industrielles*, Étude CPE no. 57, Centre de Prospective et d'Évaluation, Paris.

Lenin. V.I. (1970 ed.), 'Imperialism: the highest stage of capitalism', in *Selected Works*, Moscow, State Editions (First edition, Zurich, 1915).

Lundvall, B.A. (1986), *Product Innovation and User-producer Inter Action*, Industrial Development Research Series, no. 31, Aalborg University Press.

Mandel, E. (1975), *Late Capitalism*, London, New Left Books.

Mariti, P. and Smiley, R.H. (1983), 'Co-operative agreements and the organisation of industry', *Journal of Industrial Economics*, vol. XXXI, no. 4, June.

Michalet, C.A. (1976), *Le capitalisme mondial*, Paris, nouvelle édn. entièrement refondue, 1985, Paris, PUF.

Michalet C.A. and Delapierre, M. (1978), 'The impact of multinational enterprises on national scientific and technological capacities in the computer industry', mimeo.

Minskey, H.P. (1982), *Inflation, Recession and Economic Policy*, Brighton, Wheatsheaf Books.

Momigliano, F. (1981), 'Technological innovation, international trade and direct foreign investment: old and new problems for economic theory and empirical research', paper prepared for the OECD Study on Technology and Competitiveness, Paris, mimeo.

Momigliano, F. and Dosi, G. (1983), *Tecnologia e organizzazione industriale internazionale*, Bologna, Il Mulino.

Morin, F. (1974), *La structure financière du capitalisme français*, Paris, Presses Universitaires de France.

Mowery, D.C. (1986), 'Multinational joint ventures in product development and manufacture: the case of commercial aircraft, department of Social Sciences, Carngie Mellon University, Pittsburg, mimeo.

Muccielli, J.L. and Thuillier, J.P. (1982), *Multinationales européenes et investissements croisés*, Paris, Presses Universitaires de France.

Murray, R. (1971), 'The internationalisation of capital and the nation state', in H. Radice (ed.) (1925), *International Firms and Modern Imperialism*, London, Penquin.

Mytelka, L.K. (1988), 'New modes of competition in the textile and clothing industries: some consequences for the Third World', dans J. Niosi (ed.), *Technologie et compétitivité internationale*, Actes du colloque international, Oligopoles, innovations technologiques et concurrence internationale, CREDIT, Montréal, octobre 1987, mimeo.

Nelson, R. (1980), 'Competition, innovation, productivity growth and public policy', in H. Giersch (ed.), *Towards an Explanation of Economic Growth*, Symposium 1980, Tübingen, J.C. Mohr, 1981.

Nelson, R. and Winter, S.G. (1982), *An Evolutionary Theory of Economic Change*, Cambridge, Mass., The Belknap Press of Harvard University Press.

Newfarmer, R.S. (1983), 'Multinationals and the marketplace magic', in C.P. Kindleberger (ed.), *The Multinational Corporation in the 1980s*, Cambridge, Mass., The MIT Press.

—— (1985), *Profits, Progress and Poverty: Case Studies of International Industries in Latin America*, Indiana, University of Notre Dame Press.

OECD (1968), *Gaps in Technology, Analytical Report*, Paris, OECD.

—— (1979), 'Multinational enterprises and national scientific and technological capacities in the food processing industries', mimeo.

—— (1986a), *Science and Technology Indicators No. 2: R & D, Invention and Competitiveness, Paris, OECD.*

—— (1986b), 'Technical co-operation agreements between firms: some initial data and analysis', mimeo.

—— (1986c), *Economic Outlook*, no. 39, May, Paris, OECD.

—— (1987a), 'The contribution of science and technology to economic growth', mimeo.

—— (1987b), *Structural Adjustment and Economic Peformance*, Paris, OECD.

Ohmae, K. (1985), *Triad Power: The Coming Shape of Global Competition*, New York, The Free Press.

Oman, C. (1984), *New Forms of International Investment in Developing Countries*, Paris, OECD Development Centre.

Palloix, C. (1975), *L'internationalisation du capital*, Paris, Maspéro.

Papon, P. (1983), *Pour une prospective de la science: recherche et technologie, les enjeux de l'avenir*, Paris, Seghers.

Pastré, O. (1980), *La strategie internationale des groupes financiers américains*, Paris, Le Seuil.

Payne, B. (1986), *Co-operation and Technological in the International Machine Tool Industry: An Exploratory Analysis of Commercial and Technical Agreements*, London, Technical Change Center, mimeo.

Pavitt, K. (1984), 'Sectoral patterns of technical change: towards a taxonomy and a theory', *Research Policy*.

Porter, M.E. (1985), *Competitive Advantage*, New York, The Free Press.

Reich, R.B. and Mankin, E.D. (1986), 'Joint ventures with Japan give away our future', *Harvard Business Review*, March/April.

Ricotta, E. and Mariotti, S. (1986), *Diversification Agreements Among Firms and Innovative Behaviour*, Paper presented at the Conference on Innovation Diffusion, Venice, March 1986.

Rosenberg, N. (1976), *Perspectives on Technology*, Cambridge, Cambridge University Press.

—— (1982), *Inside the Black Box: Technology and Economics*, Cambridge, Cambridge University Press.

Sciberras, E. (1980), 'Technical innovation and international competitiveness in the television industry', Brighton, Science Policy Research Unit, mimeo.

Scherer, F.M. (1970), *Industrial Market Structure and Economic Performance*, (2nd ed., 1980). Chicago, Rand. McNally College Publishing Company.

Schumpeter, J.A. (1943), *Capitalism, Socialism and Democracy*, New York, Harper, (2nd ed. 1947).

Scott, J. (1979), *Corporations, Classes and Capitalism*, London, Hutchinson.

—— (1986), *Capitalist Property and Financial Power*, Brighton, Wheatsheaf Books.

Sigurdson, J. (1986), *Industry and State Partnership in Japan: The Very Large Scale Integrated Circuits (VLSI) Project*, Discussion Paper no. 168, Lund, Research Policy Institute.

Sylos-Labini, P. (1962), *Oligopoly and Technical Progress*, Cambridge, Mass., Harvard University Press (rev. ed., 1969).

Teece, D.J. (1986), 'Capturing value from technological innovation: integration, strategic partnering and licensing decisions', paper presented at the Conference on Innovation Diffusion, Venice, March 1986.

Telesio, P. (1979), *Technology Licencing and Multinational Enterprises*, New York, Praeger.

UNCTNC (United Nations Centre on Transnational Corporations) (1987), *Recent Developments Related to Transnational Corporations and International Economic Relations*, United Nations Economic and Social Council, New York, January, mimeo.

US National Research Council (1983), *International Competition in Advanced Technologies, Decision for America*, National Academy, Washington, DC.

US Congress, Office of Technology Assessment (1984), *Commercial Biotechnology: An International Analysis*.

US National Research Board (1985), *Science Indicators for 1985*, Washington, DC.

Vernon, R. (1966), 'International investment and international trade in the product cycle', *Quarterly Journal of Economics*, May.

—— (1974), 'The location of economic activity' in J.H. Dunning (ed.), *Economic Analysis and the Multinational Enterprise*, London, George Allen & Unwin.

—— (1979), 'The product cycle in a new international environment', *Oxford Bulletin of Economics and Statistics*, November.

Walsh, V. (1987), 'Technology, competitiveness and the special problems of small countries', *STI Review*, no. 2, September.

Williamson, O.E. (1975), *Markets and Hierarchies: Analysis and Antitrust Implications*, New York, Free Press.

Part VII Formal Modelling

Preface to Part VII

Gerald Silverberg
MERIT, Faculty of Economics, State University of Limburg, Maastricht

This volume is an attempt to articulate some of the dissatisfaction felt by at least some economists about the ability of current economic theory to deal with true economic change and development—in which technical change clearly plays a crucial role. And it certainly follows in a well-established, if somewhat heretical tradition in which the figure of Schumpeter stands out prominently. However, the heretical status of that tradition will remain its fate unless its positive insights can be translated into useful empirical hypotheses and a consistent and powerful theoretical framework truly appropriate to its task. In this respect the authors of this volume agree that it is time to go beyond the stage of lamentation and begin to lay the foundations of a new approach.

Taking its lead from the contributions in Part II on the need for a wider framework, the chapters that follow attempt to outline the formal, mathematical approaches which have already appeared scattered throughout the literature or are just now in the process of emerging, and demonstrate that they do indeed fall into a coherent pattern and represent a consistent alternative framework for doing economic analysis. Although the point of departure may originally have been dynamics, non-linearity, disequilibrium, stability analysis, selection, or the dialectic of chance and necessity, it is becoming clearer that these are all special aspects involved in the description of self-organisational and evolutionary systems. Our task is to identify the specific avenues of attack that will lead to a better understanding of the evolution of technologies, national economies and social relations situated at a deeper level than mere analogy. I hope the reader will be able to come away from this section with the feeling not only that these avenues exist, but that they lead to stimulating new insights into the economic process, many of which, though adumbrated in the past, begin to take on clearer contours when viewed in this perspective.

My own chapter attempts on the one hand to enumerate the different components of the overarching self-organisation framework while arguing for their essential interrelatedness, and on the other to make a prima-facie case for the relevance of this framework to economics. I then go on to examine in some detail a number of specific models which I classify under three headings: multi-equilibria and catastrophe-theoretic models, selection models and Schumpeterian dynamics, and models of the self-organisation of economic behaviour. There is a common thread underlying this sequence of models and it is extraordinary how a few basic mathematical structures can be adapted to such seemingly disparate applications when properly handled.

Metcalfe then focuses on the diffusion of innovations as an exemplary process at the core of technical change. After examining the equilibrium tradition in this field, he opts for an evolutionary approach, which leads him to a discussion of a number of selection models in some detail. These models progressively incorporate more detailed features of market competition and complement my discussion of the strengths and weaknesses of current selection models. Finally, he analyses what he calls the process of Marshallian diffusion, which allows the explicit derivation of substitution curves as a function of the characteristics of a new technology.

Arthur's chapter on competing technologies goes beyond this discussion of diffusion/selection by introducing a significant additional feature: a non-linear dependence of the relative rates of growth (or the probabilities of adoption) of the technologies on their present or even expected shares, whether due to learning, standards, increasing returns, etc. This apparently small change in the dynamics of the competitive process is significant for two reasons. First, it is a prime example of a collective phenomenon, in which the decision of the individuals is constrained by the collective in such a way that several possibly exclusive alternatives contend for dominance. Second, it underscores the crucial role of small historical events which can trigger the eventual choice between these alternatives. What is particularly impressive about Arthur's chapter is the invocation of a very general and rigorous analytical result on the asymptotic behaviour of non-linear stochastic processes. This result enables us to analyse a wide class of increasing returns phenomena on the basis of only a qualitative understanding of the relationships involved, and is a powerful complement to simulation results.

One implication of the evolutionary modelling presented in this section is the doubt it casts on the unambiguous nature of 'optimal' behaviour and strategic rationality. Lock-in to an inferior technology is also seen to be a real possibility, which may require action going beyond the capacity of individual agents acting without coordination to overcome.

Whereas Arthur and Metcalfe focus on the industry-level dynamics of technological evolution, Boyer's chapter is an attempt to integrate several different forms of technical change with distributional mechanisms to obtain a dynamic model of an entire economy. Taking his cue from the French 'régulation' school to which he has been a principal contributor, the analysis focuses on a number of fundamental 'regimes of accumulation' representing feedback networks between productivity, wages, consumption, investment and employment. He establishes links between these basic components by drawing on Schumpeterian and Kaldor–Verdoornian insights concerning productivity growth, and a generalised Phillips curve with respect to real wages. Qualitative changes in the resulting growth patterns are related to different constellations of the underlying parameters, which Boyer associates with long-term structural changes in the economy.

Obviously, this can only represent a simplified attempt to reflect important features of technical change and investment feedbacks in an overarching model of economic development. It remains a task for the future to work out a framework for analysing the economy-wide repercussions of concrete innovations in historical time, whether they be 'purely' technological or social as well.

24 Modelling economic dynmaics and technical change: mathematical approaches to self-organisation and evolution

Gerald Silverberg
MERIT, Faculty of Economics, State University of Limburg, Maastricht

Introduction: self-organisation and economic change

In this chapter we shall discuss some relatively new approaches to mathematical modelling which may loosely be subsumed under the heading 'theory of self-organisation'. Although this modelling philosophy and most of its early applications were originally inspired by problems in the natural sciences, as we shall argue, its relevance to the social sciences and in particular to questions of economic development and structure is more than accidental.

The theory of self-organisation deals with complex dynamic systems open to their environments in terms of the exchange of matter, energy and information and composed of a numbeɩ of interacting subsystems. Thus the 'behavioural environment' and the individual subsystems are conceived as undergoing a process of mutual coevolution which may admit a determinate joint outcome. Within certain domains, in particular, in the neighbourhood of a structural instability, these interactions can often be represented at an aggregate level by a small number of *order parameters* which summarise the net result of the complex of feedbacks constraining the behaviour of the subsystems. Many such systems have been shown both experimentally and theoretically to lead to the spontaneous emergence of coherent macroscopic structures (e.g. spatial, temporal, or in terms of other system attributes) from the seemingly uncoordinated behaviour of the component parts at the microscopic level. Moreover, self-organising systems can undergo a succession of such structural transformations in response to generalised changes in outside conditions coupled with internal fluctuations at the microscopic level. In some cases this can take on the character of an evolutionary progression. Good overviews of the field can be found in Ebeling and Feistel (1982), Haken (1983a), and Nicolis and Prigogine (1977). The relevance of the self-organisation concept to the social sciences has been discussed in Prigogine (1976) and Prigogine, Allen and Hermann (1977).

Before turning from this rather abstract description to details of specific methods and applications, one may rightly ask what makes the concept of self-organisation of interest to economic theory, and in particular to the incorporation of processes of technical change and economic development at the very centre of its reformulation. To begin with, the economic system in a biophysical sense is certainly open, dependent on inputs of energy and information to maintain the processes of circular flow traditionally analysed by economic theory. This point has been emphasised in particular by Georgescu-Roegen (1971, 1976) as well as by Boulding (1978, 1981), and even earlier by Lotka (1924) and Marshall (1890). This means that in some fundamental sense the laws applicable to the general process of biological evolution and ecological interaction will have their counterparts in the economic realm. This is not a question of superficial analogy, however, asserting a one-to-one correspondence between biological/ physical phenomena and economic ones. Rather, it implicates similar causal patterns of, for example, competition, cooperation, and the generation of variety operating in the 'deep structure' of both systems.

Second, it has become more clearly realised only in the last few years that both the mathematical richness and the empirical realism of the study of dynamical systems increases immeasurably when the focus shifts to intrinsic *non-linearities*. In economics this insight goes back to Richard Goodwin (1951), who showed that self-sustaining business cycles were only possible in the context of non-linear models. In addition to self-sustaining cycles, non-linearity introduces the possibility of systems with multiple equilibria, bifurcation of solutions of various types, and deterministic chaos, i.e. systems which, although deterministic, demonstrate no long-term regularities of behaviour and are highly sensitive to the choice of initial conditions. As we shall see, these features play an essential role in the mathematical theory of self-organisation and evolution. Conversely, it can be shown that non-equilibrium open systems can only display evolution if they are in the non-linear region. Once such non-linearities are admitted into economic modelling many traditional equilibrium approaches are called into question, while some qualitative thinking which has eluded formalisation until now can be given mathematical expression. Thus the theory of self-organisation also addresses the fundamental question raised by Adam Smith in economics: how do coherent market solutions emerge from the uncoordinated pursuit of self-interest of individual agents? But it makes clear that there may be a variety of answers to this question, many of them possibly suboptimal, and dynamically non-trivial.

A further departure from orthodox modelling philosophy, but one which also marks a reopening of scientific thought to historicity and the unique role of events, acts and individuals, is the place of stochasticity and ir-reversibility in processes of self-organisation. In contrast to mainstream econometrics, for example, which attempts to uncover unique structural laws from under the veil of stochastic noise, which simply serves to obscure them, stochasticity—the deviation of components and subsystems from mean values—is dialectically intertwined with deterministic regularities possibly to drive the system along new branches structurally distinct from past regimes. In biology this is what Jacques Monod (1970) called the interaction of chance and necessity. In economics it is not unrelated to the observation that a limitation of the large econometric models is their breakdown in the face of structural change, which they are not able to anticipate. The dialectic of chance and necessity impinges on the fundamental problem of the emergence of novelty. As against equilibrium models which see the economic process as one of adjustment to given conditions, which then may change for exogenous reasons and be continuously and almost timelessly tracked by the system, the theory of self-organisation examines the conditions under which departures from prevailing behaviour can become self-amplifying and modify the very environment hitherto dictating that behaviour. Since these departures are strictly speaking unpredictable at the macroscopic level, the cost is in terms of the precise ability to predict when, if and exactly which novelties may exert a significant effect on the system. The gain is, first, the open admission that the social sciences are indeed historical, but, second, the possibility of making educated statements about the kinds of change that may take place, patterns of regularity when it does, the existence of competing scenarios, and the magnitude of efforts needed to trigger a choice. This, of course, is the very stuff of political economy and economic history, which may now be open to an appropriate form of analytical treatment and more resistant to the kind of ideological scientism (in the sense of Hayek) model-guided theorising has been accused of in the past.

Finally, research on self-organisation has focused attention on the critical role of *collective phenomena* and *cooperative effects* in many systems. These features are of special relevance to applications in the social sciences and to the question of the relationship between individual behaviour and 'rational' choice, on the one hand, and the socio-economic environment (climates of opinion, social norms and institutions, herd effects, etc.), on the other. Systems displaying these properties converge to one or the other aggregate state depending on the distribution of initial states of the subsystems and possible thresholds and triggering events constraining deviant components to align themselves with the rest of the system. In a sense the system is able to 'vote' itself into a more structured or differentiated pattern because of the strong non-linearities mediating distributions of behaviour. Modelling approaches that proceed from the concept of a representative agent and unique self-consistent behavioural equilibria completely miss this point and thus are only able to account for institutional patterns of behaviour, implicit forms of cooperation apparently at odds with myopic self-interest, and pathologies like speculative bubbles, in highly artificial and *ad hoc* ways, if they recognise them at all.

In the following sections of this chapter we will illustrate these principles using a number of models which have been analysed in the economic, social science and biological literature. We will not present a detailed background to the mathematical methods themselves but instead refer the reader to the appropriate sources in the literature. Roughly speaking, these models fall into two categories. The first demonstrate how a social system moves between a small number of qualitatively distinct dynamic states, either cyclically or in response to input variables. The second show how such systems may encounter critical switch points which progressively and irreversibly drive them down a branching tree of specific development paths. This second class of models exemplifies the transition from self-organisation to evolution.

Multiequilibria and catastrophe-theoretic models

Consider a (multidimensional) dynamic system with state space vector $\mathbf{x}$ parameterised by a vector $\mathbf{a}$:

$$\dot{\mathbf{x}} = \mathbf{f}(\mathbf{x},\mathbf{a}).$$

If $\mathbf{f}$ is a linear function of $\mathbf{x}$ then in general only a unique stationary state X_0 is possible. Its stability properties depend on the eigenvalues of the matrix $\mathbf{f}$: if their real parts are all negative (or at least one is positive) then $\mathbf{x}_0$ is asymptotically stable (unstable) (see Hirsch and Smale, 1974, for a thorough introduction to dynamic systems and the associated linear algebra). If, however, $\mathbf{f}$ is a *non-linear function of* $\mathbf{x}$ then more than one stationary state can exist (for the moment we will leave aside the question of the existence of other 'attractors', i.e. other subsets of the state space such as closed curves, tori, and so-called strange attractors of fractal dimension invariant to the dynamic and exerting an 'influence' on other trajectories of the system). Their stability properties can be determined by linearizing the non-linear function $\mathbf{f}$ in the neighbourhood of the stationary points and examining the corresponding eigenvalues as in the linear case. In general, both the number and the stability of the stationary points may change as a function of the parameter vector $\mathbf{a}$. The values of $\mathbf{a}$ at which such qualitative changes take place are referred to as bifurcation or catas-trophe points. (In the mathematical literature one proceeds with greater generality by analysing the topological structure of the flow, i.e. the ensemble of all trajectories generated by $\mathbf{f}$, and determining for what values of $\mathbf{a}$ it changes. The concept of *structural stability* goes further and parameterises the system with respect to all possible small perturbations of the equations. The system is structurally stable if the topological structure of its flow is invariant with respect to all sufficiently small perturbations of a certain class. Otherwise it is structurally unstable.) For a certain kind of dynamical system, namely *gradient* systems, it is possible to classify com-pletely the kinds of bifurcations that can take place locally for parameter spaces of dimension less than or equal to four (cf. Poston and Stewart, 1978; Saunders, 1980; Thom, 1975). Gradient systems are characterised by the fact that they are derivable from a scalar function $V(\mathbf{x},\mathbf{a})$ (analogous to potential energy in mechanics):

$$\dot{\mathbf{x}} = \mathbf{f}(\mathbf{x},\mathbf{a}) = -\operatorname{grad} V(\mathbf{x},\mathbf{a}) = -(\partial V/\partial x_1, \partial V/\partial x_2 \ldots \partial V/\partial x_n).$$

The stationary points correspond to the extrema of V, with maxima being unstable and minima stable. One-dimensional systems are always gradient systems, but in higher dimensions gradient systems are a very restrictive special case. If we are only interested in the behaviour of the stationary states in response to changes in the parameters (thus regarding them as input or control variables) as an exercise in comparative statics, or if we can assume that the relaxation of the system to equilibrium occurs considerably more rapidly than the variations in the control parameters (the fast/slow or adiabatic approximation, of which more later), then catastrophe theory becomes applicable. Given the dimensions of the state and of the parameter space, the classification theorem says that if a qualitative change takes place, locally it must be topologically equivalent to one of a small number of 'canonical' polynomials relating the equilibrium values of the state space variables to the parameters. Topological equivalence means that the original parameters of the systems may have to be transformed via a possibly complicated but invertible and continuous mapping to the canonical variables. (This is a point that is often overlooked in naïve applications of catastrophe theory.)

Zeeman (1974) furnishes a non-trivial example of the kind of argument which can legitimately invoke the classification theorem and how it can be embedded in a more complete dynamic model. He considers the dynamics of a stock market under the influence of two kinds of agents (or one kind of agent with two differently weighted and possibly conflicting motives): fundamentalists, who orient themselves around some notion of a natural price (e.g. using price/earning ratios), and speculators, who react to the direction of change of market price levels. Depending on the proportion of money in the market of the two types of investor, Zeeman argues that the market will be characterised by either one or two possible equilibrium states. This is due to the fact that when speculative money dominates, speculators as a group will reinforce swings in price movements. This leads to a cusp structure for catastrophes in the parameter plane marking the transition from the region with a single stable equilibrium to one with two stable and one unstable equilibrium. As with many of the early catastrophe-theoretic models, Zeeman assumes that his economic parameters can be identified directly with the canonical cusp parameters. He then goes a step further by imposing a 'slow' cycling motion in the parameter space representing a market successively dominated by fundamentalists and speculators. The sudden catastrophic jumps correspond to the crisis typical of the switchover from a bull to a bear market. Characteristic features of catastrophe-theoretic models are, for example, hysteresis and sensitive dependence on intial conditions. Hysteresis means that when a trajectory in parameter space which crosses the catastrophe set and induces a jump in the system is reversed, a return jump is not induced at the same point but only later when another part of the catastrophe set is traversed. The system thus acquires a primitive path-dependent memory of its own past. Trajectories in parameter space may also split, i.e. two trajectories starting out very close together but running along either side of, say, the cusp point of the catastrophe set can lead to widely divergent system states over time. Thus certain initial configurations can be very crucial for the evolution of the system and can magnify the effect of random events occurring near such parameter values, enabling them to decide which divergent path the system will be committed to. Random events can also be decisive near 'overhanging cliffs' of the catastrophe surface, tripping the system over the edge so to speak and thus effecting a rapid switchover from one solution surface to another.

Another multi-equilibrium model of direct relevance to the macro-dynamics of technical change was first presented by Mensch *et al.* (1980) and subsequently reformulated and extended in Haag, Weidlich and Mensch (1985). This model was inspired by the observation that the relationship between investment, employment and national product seems to have broken down in the early 1970s. A number of authors suggested that this had something to do with the composition of investment and not only its absolute magnitude. Thus investment in modernising, rationalising, or accelerated replacement of equipment (possibly due, for example, to investment in more energy-efficient machinery in the wake of the oil crisis) would have a different effect on employment than pure expansionary investment. This fact had not been explicitly taken into account by macroeconomic models. (In fact, most models assumed that replacement investment was a fixed percentage of the capital stock, something which can only be justified in the long run in a golden age, steady-state growth universe.) Mensch *et al.* hypothesised that for certain combinations of expansionary and rationalising investment the economy would be characterised by two short-run equilibria representing full and underemployment. Under this assumption the simplist realisation is a cusp catastrophe with the levels of expansionary and rationalising investment (suitably normalised) as input parameters and the level of activity of the economy as state variable (assumed in short-run equilibrium). As the ratio of rationalising R to expansionary E investment increases, the (approximately) linear relationship between activity X and E becomes two-sheeted over a certain range. An important implication of such a model is related to the phenomenon of hysteresis mentioned above. In the bi-equilibrium region, once the economy has switched from the high to the low activity sheet, expansionary investment will have to be raised to a much higher level to trigger a spontaneous return to high activity than was necessary to keep the economy on the upper sheet. This may be the key to explaining why employment programmes often generate disappointing and only temporary increases in employment unless they exceed certain threshold levels.

The 1985 reformulation of the model differs from the original version in that (a) the procedure for identifying and incorporating the relevant input variables has been enlarged, and (b) short-period dynamics are also taken into consideration. The basic idea of a possible bi-stability in the system is retained, however. This leads to the construction of a fourth-order polynomial potential function with two time-dependent parameters. The potential function is estimated by least squares after filtering out fluctuations with an averaging process. This yields a time series for the two input variables, as yet unidentified. The relevant economic inputs are identified by assuming that the input variables in the potential function are linear combinations of variables selected from a set of possible candidates (including lags). The authors performed a correlation analysis on combinations of total investment, expansionary and rationalising investment, an 'investment structure index', open positions in industry, working hours in industry, and the rate of price increase. The best fit to the empirically estimated input variables for West Germany was obtained for linear combinations of expansionary investment lagged one year and rationalising investment lagged three years. For a thorough discussion of problems of estimation in catastrophe-theoretic models (in contrast to standard econometrics, bi- or multi-modal error distributions have to be assumed) in the context of a model of inflation by Woodcock and Davis (1979), see Fischer and Jammernegg (1986).

One drawback of much of the modelling inspired by catastrophe theory is the distinction between state variables and parameters. For example, in the two versions of Mensch's bi-equilibrium model, the components of investment are regarded as exogenous variables. In a complete dynamic description, however, it is clear that a feedback of some form exists between economic activity and investment. This is acknowledged in Zeeman's model by the introduction of the slow, second level of dynamic interaction between all the variables. The assumption that the motion can be clearly divided between fast and low responses permits the state variable/parameter distinction to be imposed mathematically, however, at least as an approximation. This procedure, known in physics as the adiabatic approximation, is the basis for Haken's so-called slaving principle, which establishes a hierarchy of causation between order parameters and 'slaved variables' near an instability in complex interdependent systems (cf. Haken, 1983a and b). Needless to say, the bifurcations involved can be of a more general type than elementary catastrophes. The distinction between slow and fast variables is implicit in most comparative statics exercises in economics. It is often assumed that some set of variables is in equilibrium while another set of parameters can be freely varied to represent economic change. The dangers of this kind of implicit dynamic reduction have been pointed out by Gandolfo and Padoan (1984). If one makes no *a priori* assumptions about the adjustment speeds of the various dynamic interactions and actually estimates them against the data, it turns out that the equilibrium assumptions of, for example, capital market clearing models are revealed to be untenable.

Selection models and Schumpeterian dynamics

Inspired by the original contributions of Schumpeter (1919, 1947) and Alchian (1951), a rapidly growing number of authors have attempted to model formally economic competition and growth, technical choice and diffusion, and technologically induced fluctuations as an *evolutionary* process. A glance at the biological literature shows that evolution is characterised by (a) selection of superior types from a heterogeneous population (the almost meaningless tautological phrase 'survival of the fitness' is replaced by the observation that environmental pressure does in general compel selection (cf. Eigen, 1971)), and (b) being open-ended and driven by the continual creation of variety originating in a primarily stochastic mechanism.

The economic models to be discussed in the following share a very similar methodological point of view and employ variants of the same basic mathematical structure. This mathematical structure has been termed *replicator dynamics* (Schuster and Sigmund, 1983) and has been at the centre of research in such seemingly diverse fields as sociobiology, prebiotic, macromolecular evolution, population ecology, and recently game theory as well. The basic equation was first introduced by R.A. Fisher in his mathematical formulation of natural selection:

$$\dot{x}_i = Ax_i[E_i - \langle E \rangle], \quad i = 1, n,$$

where

$$\langle E \rangle = \Sigma \, x_i E_i.$$

x_i represents the proportion of species i in some population of interacting species and E_i its related 'reproductive fitness'. $\langle E \rangle$ is the reference average fitness level of the population. The frequency of a species grows differentially according to whether it is characterised by above- or below-average 'fitness', while average fitness itself varies in response to changes in species frequencies.

The case originally investigated by Fisher was for constant E_i's. He showed that the system monotonically converges to a pure population consisting of the species with highest fitness. In the last few years considerable attention has been devoted to systems with quadratic or cubic dependence of the E_i's on the frequency vector $\mathbf{x}$ (and thus incorporating more complex feedbacks between the species such as the interesting case of cyclic interaction). Recent results are surveyed in Hofbauer and Sigmund (1984), Sigmund (1986), and Ebeling and Feistel (1982). The level of interactive complexity can be taken a step further by introducing additional dynamic variables $\mathbf{y}$ and lagged values of some of them $z_i(t) = y_i(t-\Delta)$, $i = 1, q$:

$$E_i = E_i(x, y, z)$$
$$\dot{y}_i = f_i(x, y, z), \, i = 1, p.$$

This type of system is necessary to model the vintage structure of capital stocks in disequilibrium and with possibly fluctuating rates of best practice technical change.

The models developed along these lines differ in a number of important respects, however, which can be roughly summarised under the following headings.

Unit of selection: Whereas the gene has come to be recognised as the fundamental unit of selection in biology, it is still unclear at what level evolutionary selection and innovation operate in socio-economic systems. In terms of the Schumpeterian model of creative destruction, for example, it is not obvious whether the basic unit should be the firm, or the innovation or technology itself. In addition, one may attempt to model behavioural strategies, rules of thumb, etc., as subject to an evolutionary process. All of these approaches are represented in the literature. It remains to be seen to what extent they can be reconciled, or whether they introduce an implicit bias into a model.

Behavioural assumptions and the role of anticipation, planning and 'rationality': Almost without exception, workers in the field of social evolution acknowledge that human societies are characterised by an emergent property almost totally absent from the biological domain—the presence of conscious goal-seeking behaviour partly guided by mental models of the world which attempt to anticipate the future course of the individual's environment. An extreme position might regard this fact as irrelevant to the ultimate outcome of the evolutionary process and therefore would dispense altogether with a detailed treatment of the behavioural level (Alchian, 1951, at times argues in this vein, and it seems to be implicit in the work of Marchetti, 1983). However, even under this assumption it would not be without interest to investigate the behavioural level as experienced by the actors themselves, if only as a problem in social psychology. Moreover, even if the outcome remained the same, the fact that the search process is not wholly random but directed, i.e. *orthogenetic* (cf. Lotka, 1956, p. 379), implies that it may be advancing much more rapidly than blind biological evolution. However, it is generally accepted that the behavioural level plays an essential role in the socio-economic process. One need only point to the importance of *imitation* in human affairs, which implies that successful strategies can be transferred between living agents and do not necessarily have to drive the carriers of other strategies physically out of existence. (As far as I am aware, only bacteria practise an analogous direct transfer of genetic information without reproduction.) And this example makes clear that the prevailing conception in economics of behaviour as 'rational' is woefully inadequate as a description of human beings interacting in a social and historical setting.

Unfortunately, it must be admitted that the behavioural level has been relegated to a mostly *ad hoc* part in most of the economic models, with the exception of some of the work of Nelson and Winter on the selection of decision rules. Particularly in the models based on evolution in technology as opposed to firm space, behavioural assumptions about, for example, the distribution of investment are often based neither on genuine profitability calculations of some kind nor on the sort of concrete decision procedures which have in fact been uncovered in the survey literature. Indeed, one of the strengths of economics over sociobiology, for example, is that the investigator can actually ask agents what influenced their decisions and in many cases expect a reasonably revealing reply, whereas even today the biochemical connection between genes and manifested behaviour in animals is little more than a fruitful heuristic hypothesis.

Phenotype vs. genotype: Although I have argued that reasoning by analogy is a less promising approach than the search for structural isomorphism, it is illuminating to try to apply for a moment this fundamental biological distinction to economics. It is not enough to locate units of competition such as technologies, firms' pricing, investment, or R & D policies. It is also necessary to specify in detail the *economic mechanism* governing their competitive interaction, which may be located at a somewhat different level of the system (the phenotypic level, so to speak). Thus it is a somewhat surprising fact that many of the selection models purporting to be descriptions of market competition do not have any but a rudimentary economic means of translating the underlying diversity of techniques or behaviour into the competitively relevant variables such as prices, production levels, delivery delays, product quality, etc. The evolutionary process does not simply work straightforwardly in both directions between the genotype and the phenotype, as the example of sexual reproduction and dominance makes clear. Too few of the models presented until now devote enough attention to the intervening variables mediating the process of economic competition.

Explanatory power of evolutionary modelling: Quite aside from such questions as superior correlative fit or predictive ability, it is important to ask what one hopes to achieve with this approach that is not attainable within the prevailing equilibrium/optimisation paradigm or with the use of specific *ad hoc* models. Simply to use evolutionary modelling to reproduce the common currency of orthodox theory strikes one as too modest a programme to justify the theoretical detours involved, even if the evolutionary approach may claim to be in some sense more realistic or plausible. One answer may lie in simpler and more robust solutions to such outstanding economic problems as oligopolistic pricing, which has not yielded up its secrets in the form of a usable dynamic description despite having been subject to an impressive assault with the sophisticated methods of game theory over the years. And this although the number of possible solutions in reality appears to be quite restricted and certainly smaller than the number of theoretical solution concepts proposed thus far. Problems such as these fall under the general heading of the origin and stability of cooperative behaviour, a subject which only recently has begun to be the focus of analytical investigation along evolutionary lines (cf. Axelrod, 1984).

Another goal to which many of the evolutionary models about to be discussed have addressed themselves is to uncover long-term patterns of technical change and economic development. One such result is the familiar logistic substitution curve of technological diffusion, but the question remains of how to embed it in a more general theory of economic dynamics. Another is the possible existence of long-term macroeconomic fluctuations and patterns of structural change, and the still highly contested long-wave hypothesis. Still another is the origin and persistence of patterns of unequal development in the world economy. One of the most promising questions, however, which has hardly been brought out in the literature, is the relationship between the process of technical change and the disequilibrium structures it engenders on the one hand, and short-period instabilities and the problem of effective demand on the other. This is one of the missing links (between Schumpeter and Keynes, so to speak) in economic theory which the equilibrium paradigm is singularly unsuited to deal with. On this more later.

To illustrate the basic form of the evolutionary argument let us start with the model in Nelson (1968) and Nelson and Winter (1982, pp. 235–40). While it is conceived to deal with underdeveloped economies characterised by a modern and a traditional industrial sector, in principle it is equally applicable to any closed economy which admits such a bipartite representation of capital-embodied technology. The technologies, assumed to be linear production functions, differ only with respect to their labour productivities. Each sector is wedded to its technology and reinvests its profits in capacity expansion (the rate of capacity utilisation is always one, output sells for a constant common price, and the wage rate is determined by a static labour supply curve), which results in differential growth rates of the two sectors. The more productive technique gradually replaces the less productive one in an approximately logistic fashion, depending on the form of the wage function. The rate of replacement is proportional to the difference in labour productivity.

A generalisation of this approach is presented in Silverberg (1984) based on Goodwin's growth cycle model (Goodwin, 1967). The argument consists of two parts: a hypothetical Gedankenexperiment and a descriptive dynamic analysis. The first part proceeds from the single linear technology Goodwin model and asks how the choice of technique problem can be answered dynamically in a Schumpeterian sense. That is, it asks under what circumstances an entrepreneur investing in a new technology of general linear form will eventually realise differential profits and establish himself in the economy. Using a method of analysis first applied by Allen (1975, 1976) to biological evolution in ecological systems, it is possible to derive an unambiguous selection criterion which is independent of factor prices prevailing at any given time. The well-known stylised facts of economic growth—approximate constancy of the capital/output ratio and the progressive increase of labour productivity—are shown to be necessary consequences of the assumptions underlying Schumpeterian competition, even if innovating entrepreneurs search for new technologies in a completely arbitrary manner. Thus the directed search for primarily labour-saving technologies is a logical and self-consistent consequence of this result.

The second stage of the analysis goes on to make the heroic assumption that the further evolution of the economy can actually be described by strict reinvestment of the respective retained earnings of the technologies. There is obviously a certain irrationality to an entrepreneur's continuing to invest in a demonstrably inferior technology over a considerable period of time, but it is not an entirely unknown phenomenon in business history. Under this assumption it is possible to derive an analytical expression for the substitution process of logistic type whose speed is proportional to the difference between the values of the technical choice function of the two techniques. Furthermore, the time paths of such macroeconomic variables as the rates of unemployment and average profits and the rates of growth of real wages and product result from a superposition of long- and short-period fluctuations.

A number of models have continued in a similar vein and examined the case of an arbitrary number of competing techniques under similar behavioural assumptions. Closely related are Gibbons and Metcalfe (1988) and Nelson and Winter (1982, pp. 240–5). In essence these are industry-level analyses because wages and other factor prices are taken as exogenous. The strict technology reinvestment assumption is retained. One may then demonstrate that for given factor prices and constant technology sets a best technology exists and the industry progressively converges to it. The rate of convergence of average industry unit costs to best practice is proportional to the variance of unit costs of the technologies present in the industry (using market shares as weights). If factor prices change exogenously, the best technique (in the sense of lowest unit costs) changes accordingly, and, depending on whether sufficient variety remains in the industry, the system now converges to that technique. This result is known in population genetics as Fisher's 'fundamental theorem of natural selection' (Fisher, 1930). For a good discussion of the underlying mathematics, see Ewens (1979), Hofbauer and Sigmund (1984), and Losert and Akin (1983).

The restrictive assumption of strict reinvestment in each technology can be relaxed by allowing investment to 'climb the ladder' of available technologies gradually over time, preferably in the direction of the techniques which are being selected for anyway. Examples of this sort of model are Soete and Turner (1984) and Iwai (1984a). The underlying assumption revolves around the idea that information about best practice diffuses only slowly, so that firms have to work their way up the production possibility set in a somewhat random fashion. This sort of process can be generated by positing that the rate at which profits earned on technique i are shifted to investment in technique j is proportional to the percentual difference in current rates of profit of the two techniques times the share of technique j in industry capacity (an imitation effect). This relationship is definitely situated in technology rather than firm space and is not clearly connected to any firm-level behavioural decision rule. (Thus two firms using identical technologies are completely free to pursue totally different investment strategies, a fact which is aggregated out of this kind of model.) The net effect of this assumption is simply to introduce a constant factor accelerating the rate of selection in the restrictive selection models discussed above.

Before going on to the more sophisticated evolutionary models in the literature, it may be useful to raise a number of questions about the proper representation of technology in such models. To begin with, the pure selection models deal with the adjustment of a disequilibrium industry state to a fixed best-practice technique. In contrast to most neo-classical models, this adjustment does take place in historical time. However, this phenomenon is not what one ordinarily considers to be technical change, which involves the continuous but perhaps uneven advance of best practice(s) themself(ves), as well as its (their) diffusion throughout the capital stock or product space of the economy. The frontier does not stand still and wait for average practice to catch up, but is rather the carrot dangling in front of the donkey (the stick presumably being backruptcy). Biological models of evolution are more justified in abstracting from this fact because mutation rates in general are considerably smaller than selection rates. This does not appear to be true for technological evolution in the present age. The neglect of this dimension is probably responsible for another widespread misconception: that disparities in average unit costs correspond to different *techniques* of production. This confusion can be dispelled somewhat by reexamining the vintage models which experienced a brief vogue in the 1960s (the original sources are Kaldor and Mirrlees, 1962, Salter, 1962, and Solow, 1960). These models had the virtue of recognising that (a) best practice is subject to continuous change, and (b) under the embodiment hypothesis the capital stock will always be a composite of investment slices acquired in the past (the vintages) and unit costs will reflect this fact in some way (most simply as an average over the vintages). Thus differences in unit costs need not correspond to differences in choice of technique. They could also be due to different time profiles of vintages of the 'same' technology. Thus a better distinction than that between a static best-practice frontier on the one hand and static techniques on the other is between vintages of a given technology or *technological trajectory* (cf. Dosi, 1982, 1984; Nelson and Winter, 1982, pp. 258–62; Silverberg, 1984) and changes of trajectory. A perusal of the management literature reveals that businessmen are well aware that capital equipment is continually being improved, so that, given that they are already established on a technological trajectory, it is very unlikely that they will be investing very far behind best practice (the problem of technologies with pronounced dynamic returns to scale is perhaps an exception here). The problem of diffusion becomes significant when a real choice of technique opens up. The vintage perspective also makes clear that there is an important distinction between diffusion in current investment and diffusion in the capital stock. Sahal (1981) is one of the few authors to present data substantiating this point. The former is necessarily more rapid than the latter. Moreover, the rate of diffusion through the capital stock is only partly determined by the speed with which entrepreneurs embrace a new technology; it will remain limited even if all entrepreneurs instantaneously shift their investment to the new technology, and it is not a sign in itself of some kind of technological inertia or irrationality. Finally, the embodiment hypothesis has the advantage of establishing a connection between the rate of change of average productivity and the composition and level of investment. In contrast to the steady-state vintage models extensively analysed in the 1960s and 1970s in which the rates of growth of best-practice and average-practice productivities are identical and independent of the rate of investment, this is no longer true with disequilibrium dynamics, as has been pointed out by Clark (1980).

The fact that best-practice technology cannot be taken as fixed during the selection process requires an extension of the basic model to include the mechanism by which this frontier is expanded and explored (not to mention how expectations about this frontier influence the scrapping decision). The simplest assumption is that the frontier moves at an exogenously given growth rate which is more or less correctly anticipated by firms. The task becomes considerably more difficult when this rate is made partly endogenous, and when switch points arise between technological trajectories. Although it is clear that both (costly) search and imitation effects are at work here, there is still no definitive agreement about how they should be incorporated into a model, and this will undoubtedly remain one of the most difficult aspects of evolutionary modelling. The approach adopted by neo-classical theory—optimal innovation as a problem of maximisation or a two-period game—is certainly very much at odds with the perspective inherent in the evolutionary framework, which, as we shall see, hinges in an essential way on the stochastic nature of search processes, the problem of decision-making under irreducible uncertainty, and collective effects.

The most ambitious attempt to incorporate these features is Nelson and Winter's evolutionary model of economic growth (Nelson and Winter 1974, 1982, Chapter 9; Nelson, Winter and Schuette 1976). Here we will restrict our discussion to the salient mathematical and economic features of the basic model to the exclusion of its extensions dealing with such questions as the so-called Schumpeterian hypothesis on industrial concentration and innovation. The model is formulated in firm space, which allows the explicit treatment of diverse firm strategies with respect to technological innovation and imitation. In contrast to the previous models, however, a deterministic mathematical formulation must give place to a stochastic computer implementation. Technologies are once again identified with the technical coefficients of linear production functions. Technical change is disembodied, however, so that, although firms may select new techniques either by copying competitors or exploring technology space around their current technique through R & D themselves, the changeover of their entire capital stock once a new technique is found is both instantaneous and costless. Investment serves to expand capacity of whatever technique is currently in use, scrapping is a stochastically varied percentage (with mean of 4 per cent) of capacity and is thus independent of technical change. The sophistication of the model resides in the stochastic rules for search and imitation, which, however, somewhat arbitrarily are only invoked if the firm falls below a threshold rate of return on capital. Thus technical change does not constitute a routine part of a firm's strategy but rather reflects dissatisfaction with its performance. Given that a firm is looking for a new technique, it will attempt to find one via either search or imitation with probabilities that can be varied between runs. Potential technologies are represented by a random array of points in the space of the logs of the capital and labour coefficients. A metric can be imposed on this space with directional weights representing possible capital or labour-savings biases. The probability of discovering a technique via local search is then inversely proportional to this distance. The probability of uncovering a technique via imitation, as in most of the diffusion theories, is proportional to the share of that technique in total capacity. Once a new technique is found via either procedure it is subject to a profitability test at current factor prices (subject to an additional stochastic error) before adaptation. A uniform price level is assumed so that profits are a function of unit costs. Wages are determined by a labour supply curve with a possible exponential time shift. Firms reinvest their profits in capacity expansion (after deducting a rate of required dividend payment). Production is always at full capacity utilisation. This results in the familiar selection structure via differential firm growth rates. Entry of new firms is also provided for using a stochastic criterion, but appears to play a secondary role in the runs actually explored.

Thus the basic structure of the model is that of a Markov process (with time-dependent transition probabilities in the event of a shift parameter in the labour supply function). Each particular computer run (for given values of the variable parameters) is a realisation of a possible economic history. Generalisations are possible by a Monte Carlo method: data from a sufficiently large number of runs can be accumulated and evaluated to see what relatively stable properties can be identified. Patterns similar to the aggregate time series data for the American economy which Solow employed in his original growth model can be produced. If the data generated by the model are subjected to a Cobb–Douglas production-function-fitting exercise, typical R^2s of 0.99 result (a fact which is less a characteristic of the model than of the mathematical vacuity of the Cobb–Douglas procedure).

The fact that the model is formulated as a Markov process does not rule out an analytical treatment, however. In an insufficiently known article by Jimenez Montaño and Ebeling (1980), the Nelson and Winter model is recast in technology instead of firm space. A differential equation for the probability distribution (representing the probability of finding any particular distribution of technologies at a given time) can then be formulated, the so-called master equation, from the individual transition probabilities for self-reproduction of a technology (reinvestment), depreciation, and adoption of a new technology due to R & D or imitation. Although the economic interpretation of the coefficients entering into some of the transition probabilities in the paper is not always entirely clear, a formula for the mean values of the frequencies of the different technologies can be derived which closely resembles the Fisher–Eigen equation for mutation/selection in biology, modified by the addition of an imitation term. A key role is played by threshold viability values governing the rise and decline of technologies. Although this review has not emphasised explicit stochastic modelling, the first part of Jimenez Montaño and Ebeling's paper also provides a good example of the kind of insight obtainable with these methods. There they formulate a pure selection/diffusion model as a Markov process. Going to mean values the well-known logistic substitution curves can be derived. One can also ask what will be the probability that a new technique initially present as a very small proportion of total capacity will become extinct after a certain period due to stochastic fluctuations, even if it is technologically superior. They demonstrate that a technique must be superior by at least a certain factor to have a good chance of avoiding this fate.

Iwai (1984b) is also an attempt to combine a selection model with a continually advancing technological frontier. Firms experience differential growth in their share of total capacity depending on whether their unit costs are above or below the industry average (the assumed relationship is that growth rates of capacity shares are proportional to the difference between the logs of costs). The first version of the model assumes a uniform price level. If oligopolistic mark-up pricing is used, Iwai makes additional assumptions about growth rates that allow the formulation to go through. Best-practice productivity is assumed to be growing at an exponential rate. Technical progress is disembodied, so that firms can jump between the unit costs associated with different techniques without any investment. Per unit time each firm has a certain probability of innovating and adopting the unique best-practice technique. Imitation is modelled as a probability per unit time of adopting a currently employed, lower-cost technique proportional to the share of that technique in total capacity. Iwai then proceeds to examine the long-run stationary distribution of firm size resulting from the combined action of these mechanisms. The main conclusion is that a plot of firm size vs. efficiency derived from this stationary distribution misleadingly suggests that over certain ranges decreasing and increasing economies of scale are operating.

Silverberg's study (1987) is an attempt to establish a basic dynamic structure governing prices and quantities in an industry driven by Schumpeterian competition, embodied and ongoing technical progress, decision rules modelled on actual business practice and reflecting the crucial role of forward-looking expectations, and taking into account certain stylised facts of industrial development. Kaldor (1983, 1985) in particular has singled out the following observations as being in basic contradiction to received wisdom and demanding a fundamental reinterpretation of the process of industrial competition and evolution:

1. Markets do not always clear in the Walrasian sense. Businessmen take this into account by carrying inventories and order books and responding to quantity signals.
2. The presence of business goodwill, differentiated products and market inertia excludes the existence of market-clearing equilibrium (and uniform) prices and mandates an oligopolistic and dynamic reformulation of the price/quantity relationship.
3. Mark-up pricing seems to be the pervasive rule of thumb in industry and trade. However, the existence of considerable variance in unit costs of firms in the same industry indicates that either there is no *tendency* to a uniform price or that competition enforces some pattern of deviation from strict mark-up pricing. Evidently some mechanism in between these two extremes must be in operation.
4. Okun's law—that the short-run elasticity of product with respect to employment is greater than one—was interpreted by Okun to imply that the short-run average cost curves of firms were declining due to the existence of overhead labour. While this is undoubtedly true, the other half of the story implies that short-run changes in demand cannot preferentially affect only marginal firms but must be more or less equally distributed over the entire industry. This is consistent with stylised facts 1–3 above about imperfect competition. Moreover, it necessitates enlarging the disequilibrium industry concept to variations in the rate of capacity utilisation of all firms instead of just the technologically marginal ones if short-period effective demand dynamics are to be integrated into a theory of economic evolution. (This connection was first pointed out by the German economist Rüstow as early as 1926; cf. Rüstow, 1951, 1984). The presence of static economies of scale also has implications for the investment decisions of firms.
5. Dynamic models are characterised by cumulative causation, i.e. negative and positive feedback loops. If competitive economies, at the industry, national and international levels, are characterised by diverse strategies and capacities, then virtuous and vicious cycles, i.e. cumulative winners and losers, should also be possible under certain circumstances.

To combine these features into a single industry-level model, a separation is introduced between the evolutionary process at the market and at the firm level. Firms' market shares in real orders are subject to a selection mechanism based on disparities in competitiveness as they are perceived at the market level, i.e. in terms of relative prices, delivery delays, possible quality factors and advertising (only the first two are explicitly incorporated in the model at this stage). In essence this is a dynamical description of the kind of 'imperfect' competition connecting price and other signals to quantity variations outlined above. The value of a single parameter encompasses the gamut from 'pure', i.e. instantaneous, competition to pure monopoly.

The cost, price, production, capacity and delivery delay variables for the individual firm change over time in response to its investment strategy, routine behavioural rules of thumb, and its success in the market. Embodied technical progress is represented as a vintage structure of each firm's capital stock. At each point in time firms have to decide how much new equipment to acquire (gross investment) and how much oldest vintage equipment to scrap, or, equivalently, the levels of net expansion of capacity (net investment) and replacement/modernisation investment. Unit prime cost is then an average over all vintages (as are overhead costs). It can be shown that it changes over time as a function of gross investment, scrapping and the differences between best practice and marginal vintage and best practice and average unit costs. The strategic parameters determining these components of investment are the desired payback period for replacement (which itself reflects expectations about the long-term rate of technical progress) and the firm's expected rate of growth of orders for capacity expansion (modified by its rate of capacity utilisation).

The routine decision rules are similar to those employed in the systems dynamics modelling tradition. Firms adjust their production level to maintain a desired delivery delay. Prices are adjusted to costs via a mark-up, but a concession must be made to the firm's competitiveness relative to the industry average (another example of a self-organisational relationship). Given a time path for the growth of best-practice productivity (which may but need not be taken as exponential), it is possible to test different investment strategies against each other under different financial regimes (e.g. internal financing from cashflow and liquid reserves vs. unlimited borrowing). In particular, an optimal payback rule can be established; firms which deviate from it are progressively driven off the market.

Silverberg, Dosi and Orsenigo (1988) extend this basic model by considering a change of technological trajectory: at a certain point in time firms are able to choose between two qualitatively different technologies, which themselves continue to evolve over time (in the standard vintage formulation investment is always in a unique best practice). In contrast to standard diffusion models, however, the adoption decision is not modelled as one of information dissemination or involving a distribution of unvarying firm characteristics. Rather, a specific skill level internal to the firm is associated with each technological trajectory which grows according to a learning-by-using rule as a function of the firm's cumulative production on the trajectory and eventually saturates. This introduces a strong non-linear positive feedback into firm productivity dynamics. In addition, the model includes an externality in the form of a public skill level available to all firms which lags behind the growth of the average internal skill level present in the industry. Realised productivity on a trajectory is the product of the underlying embodied productivity of the vintage in question and the skill level internal to the firm specific to it. This particular combination of exogenous embodied technical progress and disembodied learning makes the actual course of productivity growth even more a function of endogenous and costly investment and production effort, but also introduces a strong element of cumulativeness.

Firms' strategies are now parameterised by an anticipation factor reflecting their optimism about the development potential of the new trajectory and their ability to pre-empt their competitors by adopting earlier than their normal payback period investment criterion would allow. The other side of the coin is the real possibility of free-rider effects due to the externality. In fact, simulation runs show that, depending on the *dynamic appropriability* of the trajectory (the ratio of the rates of internal to public learning), the same configuration of anticipation factors over firms can lead to either first or middle adopters being the major net benefitors of the diffusion process. Very late laggards run the danger of being pushed on to a downward spiral and driven out of the market altogether. On the other hand, if insufficient variance is present in firms' strategies, a socially non-optimal outcome is possible. No adoption of the superior trajectory occurs because no firm is willing to incur the costs necessary to bring the technology to commercial maturity. This kind of model demonstrates that a complex tension can exist between individual behaviours and aggregate outcomes, which may indeed be the most interesting feature of social systems. In economics this may take the form of relational pay-offs to strategies (e.g. whether first or second adopters reap the profits of an innovation, or whether it is advantageous to bet with or against the majority).

The fact that an evolutionary system may lead to completely different but self-consistent long-run outcomes depending on initial conditions and/or small random disturbances has been termed 'hyperselection' (see Ebeling and Feistel, 1982, Chapter 7) in deterministic models and 'path-dependency' in stochastic models (see Arthur's chapter in this book). Hyperselection can occur if growth rates of species or strategies are non-linearly coupled. In biology hyperselection is believed to be responsible for the almost exclusive predominance of 'left-handed' organic molecules, although *a priori* both 'handednesses' are equally viable, as well as the uniqueness of the genetic code (in a more physical context this phenomenon is also referred to as symmetry-breaking). This is an example of a 'once-and-for-all' selection process which does not admit subsequent evolutionary change and locks the system into a particular structure. David (1985) has argued that the adoption of the QWERTY typewriter keyboard is an example of this kind of lock-in process in the technological realm (mostly due to learning externalities). Hyperselective/path-dependent behaviour need not rule out all further evolutionary progress, however, and can also result in the coexistence of species which have specialised and occupy different ecological niches, in each of which further evolution is possible (cf. Ebeling and Feistel, 1982, pp. 235–8). In the following section on the self-organisation of behaviour we will come back to the question of hyperselection and collective effects and their implications for political economy and economic theory.

The self-organisation of economic behaviour

The behaviour of human beings, to the extent that it is not genetically fixed for all times, is distinguished by the fact that it is *social* and subject to learning. Thus both socially inherited norms, behavioural patterns, institutions and values, as well as the ongoing interaction with other agents and the struggle for differential advantages, must be taken into account. Economic theory for the most part has detoured around this crucial fact by reducing the problem to one of static choice of the individual who is either assumed to be so small that his actions have no effect on others and their actions can be taken as given, or so overwhelmingly large that for all purposes he is the only actor. In both cases the problem reduces to one of simple maximisation in a game against nature which the 'rational' individual is at no computational loss to solve. Although the peculiar features of the intermediate case have been recognised since Cournot, von Neumann and Morgenstern, not very much of economic theory is actually based on them. Yet the intermediate case, especially once formulated dynamically, is indeed probably the only relevant one, with the other two being limiting cases of little practical interest. (In fact, even 'pure' competition, in a dynamic environment with uncertainty, ceases to be a game against nature, as the extreme instability of primary goods and spot markets and the disproportionate role of speculation in them show.)

This is especially so in non-zero-sum settings in which both competition and cooperation are potentially possible. The best-known example and the 'ideal type' to which much research has been addressed is Prisoner's Dilemma. A wide range of economic and social phenomena seem to be related to Prisoner's Dilemma, such as oligopolistic behaviour, protection vs. free trade, arms races, etc. The most widely employed static equilibrium concept—Nash equilibrium—is not Pareto optimal in this case. Other non-zero-sum games admit multiple Nash equilibria, some of which may be suboptimal. Thus the 'rationality' of a decision may depend on the predominant strategy of the other agents; the social system decides collectively. Hence the analysis of the representative agent is misplaced here. The crucial question revolves around the interaction of the collective and the individual, and individually 'rational' decisions may lead to system-level failures. This point has been illustrated in different contexts by, among others, Keynes (1936, pp. 156–7), Schwartz (1961), Schelling (1978), G. Hardin (1968), and R. Hardin (1982). It is also at the centre of the discussion of the theoretical consistency of the so-called rational expectations hypothesis (cf., for example, the contributions in Frydman and Phelps, 1983).

The key to overcoming the pessimistic implications of Prisoner's Dilemma seems to reside in going over to a dynamic context (i.e. iterated Prisoner's Dilemma) and allowing strategies to acquire a memory of their previous encounters with specific individuals. This radically changes the context of the game and permits stable cooperative strategies to emerge (cf. Axelrod, 1984). Before discussing the implications of these finding for social science modelling, we will briefly sketch some of the main ideas of what is coming to be known as evolutionary game theory, and compare it with other behavioural approaches in economics and with other possible self-organisational processes.

The idea of applying game theory to problems of evolutionary biology goes back to Maynard Smith (see Maynard Smith, 1982, for a survey of the biological literature). The argument in a sense is the reverse of that applied in Silverberg (1984). One asks under what circumstances a given distribution of genetically transmitted behavioural strategies in an animal population cannot be invaded by a mutant. The underlying evolutionary framework presupposes that animals interact pairwise and randomly and that the pay-offs of their interactions (e.g. in mating or territoriality contests) are reflected in their reproductive fitnesses. Such a distribution of strategies in the population (which can also be interpreted as a single mixed strategy with corresponding probabilities of being played) is called an *Evolutionary Stable Strategy* (ESS), and a simple, static criterion can be specified for the existence of an ESS. An ESS is a Nash equilibrium, but the converse need not be true. An evolutionary game may possess several ESSs or none at all. Thomas (1984, Chapter 8) presents a good textbook-level introduction to the subject. The ESS concept can be used to demonstrate why stags rarely injure each other in mating contests, for example, although myopically it might seem in the interests of an individual animal to be prepared to fight to the death. In iterated Prisoner's Dilemma the pay-off of an encounter of two strategies is a discounted sum of the pay-offs of the (potentially) infinite number of plays, the discount factor representing the probability of a further play (see Axelrod, 1984, Appendix B, for details on what follows). A strategy is a (possibly stochastic) rule for deciding whether to cooperate or defect on the next play given the history of the encounter until that time. There is no universally superior strategy, and a large number of pure strategy ESSs can exist depending on the value of the discount parameter. Thus constant defection is an ESS, i.e. if it is practised by all members of a population, a small number of deviants cannot invade it. But TIT FOR TAT (cooperate on the first move, do what your opponent did on the last move) is also an ESS for a sufficiently high probability of renewed encounters in the future. Thus being an ESS is a collective property, and a system may admit many mutually exclusive regimes. The question then arises of how a transition between ESSs could come about, for example, from a world of pure defection to a world of first and faithful cooperators (but quick yet forgiving retaliators) employing TIT FOR TAT. Axelrod demonstrates that if deviants enter the system in clusters instead of individually and thus have a higher probability of internal interaction than otherwise, a cooperative strategy can establish itself. This transition between high and low levels of cooperation is also reminiscent of Williamson's model of the dynamic bi-stability of oligopolistic markets (Williamson, 1965).

An Evolutionary Stable Strategy is a static concept, however. The evolutionary problem can be cast in a dynamic setting by making the reproduction rate of the frequency of a strategy in a population proportional to the difference between its average pay-off against the population and the average pay-off of all strategies against each other. This formulation, first introduced by Taylor and Jonker (1978), returns us to our basic evolutionary equation with a particular quadratic specification of fitness derived from the pay-off matrix. The concept of an ESS is now replaced by that of an attractor, and the methods of dynamical system theory become applicable. The main results in the literature are reviewed in Hofbauer and Sigmund (1984). Of particular interest here is Zeeman (1979), in which it is shown that point attractors exist which are not ESSs. If an ESS exists representing a mix of all strategies, then it is a global attractor in the interior of the population space. A non-ESS attractor in the interior need not be global, however: the interior may also contain a basin of attraction of another point attractor on the boundary. This is analogous to the phenomenon of hyperselection referred to before. The system may converge to either a coexistence of strategies or the complete elimination of some of them depending on initial conditions. Zeeman also examines the question of the structural stability of the game dynamics, i.e. whether the qualitative properties of the flow are robust with respect to small changes in the pay-off matrix. In another paper (Zeeman, 1981) he shows that the conclusions of a model may change when it is reformulated to make it stable. Finally, periodic solutions can also occur in evolutionary games.

As a model of the formation of patterns of social behaviour, evolutionary theory represents a considerable advance over the static individual maximisation paradigm by clearly underscoring the focusing effects mediating the interaction of individuals with the collective as a process in historical time. The representative agent can be dispensed with, and indeed equilibria may correspond to heterogeneous behavioural distributions. Moreover, the rationality postulate in its strong form need not be invoked. In its strong form this assumes not only that agents prefer higher pay-offs to lower ones, but that they are able to explore completely the pay-off matrix and coordinate their behaviours in a mutually consistent way *before* any interaction actually takes place (no out-of-equilibrium trading). This is indeed a rather superhuman assumption, since it not only places extraordinary informational and computational burdens on the individual agents but neatly abstracts from any realistic coordination mechanism (Walras' *tâtonnement* process obviously does not fit this bill). The various search and reaction mechanisms that have been modelled do not necessarily converge to the game-theoretic equilibria. The basic mechanism of evolutionary theory only requires that success differentially breeds more of the same strategy, whether this be due to market expansion via a profitability/growth feedback or additionally due to imitation and adoption of *ex post* successful strategies by less successful agents (which is a first step towards an economic rationality in real time). At the first level this provides a robust approach to the explanation of patterns of behaviour, norms, implicit forms of cooperation and the focusing value of institutions and regimes when behaviour involves frequently repeated interactions between agents committed to indefinite further play. The stability of the resulting industry patterns can be probed by introducing new strategies (representing Keynes's 'animal spirits' or Schumpeter's innovating entrepreneurs) and/or by varying parameters of the interaction.

The situation is somewhat different when an evolutionary game represents a less frequent kind of interaction and the parameters may be changing in a crucial but unpredictable way between interactions. This seems to be the case, for example, in the model analysed by Silverberg, Dosi and Orsenigo (1988). Changes of technological regime occur only intermittently and crucial parameters such as dynamic appropriability may vary between plays in unforeseeable ways. The asymptotic pay-off matrix depends in a very complicated way on the configuration of the anticipation parameters of all the other firms and is relational. Thus a firm cannot really decide to be second in because it cannot know the positions taken by others in advance. And because the same experiment will not exactly be repeated in the near future, little learning or convergence to an ESS, should one exist, can be expected. What can be learned from the past, however, is that an anticipatory position must be taken if someone else takes one. The resulting uncertainty about how best to do this makes a diversity of strategies with corresponding losses and gains almost inevitable and is what drives the process as a whole.

As we have indicated, the evolutionary paradigm differs in several fundamental ways from more classical approaches to the explanation of structure and change based on the concepts of optimisation and equilibrium. But it also sheds new light on the traditional question of system optimisation, both as a realisable process in natural systems and as a planning tool.

The evolutionary process differs from classical concepts of optimisation by mandating system *diversity* in order to work at all. Moreover, this diversity must be maintained over time if the system is to avoid stagnation and display sufficient resiliency. This diversity appears to be bought at the cost of lower overall efficiency compared to a uniformly 'optimal' structure.

However, the evolutionary procedure generally displays greater robustness, i.e. lower sensitivity to mis-specification of the optimisation problem and to fluctuations in the environment. It is often also computationally more efficient than traditional methods of numerical optimisation when implemented as a search procedure on an electronic computer (it should also be pointed out that evolution is an intrinsically parallel process and thus could be considerably accelerated numerically if it could be liberated from the serial architecture of present-day computers). The question of designing search procedures along evolutionary lines has been taken up by Holland (1975), Schwefel (1981), and Brady (1985), as well as in a number of contributions in Farmer (1986). Axelrod (1985) has applied Holland's approach to a genetic coding of iterated Prisoner's Dilemma strategies with play memory three moves deep to generate evolutionary solutions of considerable complexity and effectiveness. One of the strengths of evolutionary algorithms is their much higher probability of avoiding entrapment in local maxima.

The relationship between optimisation and evolution can also be looked at in the other direction: what if anything is being optimised by the evolutionary process occurring in natural systems? The answer is not always clear-cut and depends on the exact nature of the interactions between species in the system. Ebeling and Feistel (1982) provide a thorough discussion of this point. In some evolutionary models it can be shown that a function does indeed exist which monotonically increases over time as a result of the selection process. In other cases a function may only exist which is maximised at the asymptotic steady state but fluctuates before it gets there (i.e. overall system performance may decline before it finally improves). Notice that these 'extremal functions' are open-ended: they may be capable of even further increases if new species enter the system. In some cases, however, no such function can be defined. In physical and biological systems extremal functions may correspond to such key concepts as energy efficiency or reproductive fitness. In Silverberg (1984) a 'technological potential function' is derived which unambiguously separates superior from inferior techniques (not surprisingly, this function is primarily dependent on labour productivity). The question of the existence of extremal functions characterising the evolutionary process both at the system and at the agent level is of direct relevance to the validity of one of the standard procedures of orthodox economic modelling. It is usual to assume that the behaviour of individual agents can be described by a target function which they attempt to maximise. To the extent that they are interacting in a competitive environment which decides on their fortunes in terms of survivorship, growth and rates of return, it is not at all clear *a priori* which, if any, target function will be consistent with the resulting selection process. In fact such target functions should be derivable from the competitive process, and not the other way around. Thus the long-standing discussion of whether firms maximise profits or growth rates (whatever this may actually mean) is probably not resolvable at this level of analysis. It may ultimately turn out that the success of firms is not describable in terms of target functions at all.

The self-organisation of social structures can also be analysed without an explicit consideration of pay-offs. Weidlich and Haag (1983) develop a basic model of interacting populations on the assumption that attitudes or decisions have an objective and a socially conformist component. Thus the probability of someone changing his opinion is posited to be a function of the opinions held by others in society. In a limited economic sense this need not be at odds with individual egoism, since, as Keynes argued, the pay-off to speculative investment may depend on the ability to anticipate average opinion. Equally, it may be justified as a basic human instinct (herd tendency) or derived from an interpersonal utility function. On the basis of this assumption they formulate a continuous Markov process and show that qualitative collective changes in the stationary probability distribution can take place when fundamental parameters such as the strength of coupling between individuals are varied. The addition of feedbacks allows the model to be applied to the division of investment between expansion and rationalisation as a function of underlying technological trends and the dynamics of the investment climate. The particular specification chosen, based on a Schumpeterian alternation between an expansionary and a rationalising bias of pioneering investors, is shown to lead to a limit cycle under some parameter constellations, to a number of fixed points under others.

What are the implications of these admittedly very preliminary investigations of self-organisational dynamics in social systems? On the basis of a related modelling approach to regional economic development, Allen (1982, p. 110) concludes that:

This changes the whole concept of modelling and of prediction. It moves away from the idea of building very precise descriptive models of the momentary state of a particular system towards that of exploring how the interacting elements of such a system may 'fold' over time, and give rise to various possible 'types' corresponding to the branches of an evolutionary tree.

There are a number of qualitative features of this kind of process which deserve to be recalled in connection with policy issues. One is that non-linear systems may display hysteresis and threshold phenomena, so that it is not always possible to generalise from the effects of small policy actions to larger ones. The existence of collective phenomena and hyperselection also implies that we are not always free to do what we want, because the rest of the system may react in a very conservative, identity-preserving way, or in counter-intuitively disastrous ones. On the other hand, very astutely applied changes by an appropriately situated agent such as governments, social movements, etc. may be able to trigger a complete and self-propagating reorganisation of the system to an unequivocally more favourable state which may not be attainable by the agents acting routinely on their own. Thus while man is ultimately condemned to discover his own history in the process of making it, with the aid of the kind of reasoning we have tried to outline here, he may be able to catch a glimpse of the labyrinthine path he is treading between freedom and necessity and possibly avoid some of the more hopeless dead ends.

References

Alchian, A.A. (1951), 'Uncertainty, evolution and economic theory', *Journal of Political Economy*, vol. 58, pp. 211–22.
Allen, P.M. (1975), 'Darwinian evolution and a predator–prey ecology', *Bulletin of Mathematical Biology*, vol. 37, pp. 389–405.
—— (1976), 'Evolution, population dynamics and stability', *Proceedings of the National Academy of Sciences USA*, vol. 73, pp. 665–9.
—— (1982), 'Evolution, modelling and design in a complex world', *Environment and Planning B*, vol. 9, pp. 95–111.
Allen, P.M., Engelen, G. and Sanglier, M. (1984), 'Self-organising dynamic models of human systems', in E. Frehland (ed.), *Synergetics: From Microscopic to Macroscopic Order*, Berlin, Heidelberg, New York, Tokyo, Springer-Verlag.
Allen, P.M. and Sanglier, M. (1981), 'Urban evolution, self-organization and decisionmaking', *Environment and Planning A*, vol. 13, pp. 167–83.
Axelrod, R. (1984), *The Evolution of Cooperation*, New York, Basic Books.
—— (1985), 'The simulation of genetics and evolution', paper presented at the conference Evolutionary Theory in Biology and Economics, University of Bielefeld, 19–21 November 1985.
Boulding, K.E. (1978), *Ecodynamics: A New Theory of Societal Evolution*, Beverly Hills, London, Sage.
—— (1981), *Evolutionary Economics*, Beverly Hills, London, Sage.
Brady, R.M. (1985), 'Optimization strategies gleaned from biological evolution', *Nature*, vol. 317, pp. 804–6.
Clark, J.A. (1980), 'A model of embodied technical change and employment', *Technological Forecasting and Social Change*, vol. 16, pp. 47–65.
David, P.A. (1985), 'Clio and the economics of QWERTY', *American Economic Review*, vol. 75, pp. 332–7.
Dosi, G. (1982), 'Technological paradigms and technological trajectories', *Research Policy*, vol. 11, pp. 147–62.
—— (1984), *Technological Change and Industrial Transformation*, London, Macmillan.
Ebeling, W. and Feistel, R. (1982), *Physik der Selbstorganisation und Evolution*, Berlin (GDR), Akademie-Verlag.
Eigen, M. (1971), 'Self-organization of matter and the evolution of biological macromolecules', *Naturwissenschaften*, vol. 58, pp. 465–523.
Ewens, W.J. (1979), *Mathematical Population Genetics*, Berlin, Heidelberg, New York, Springer-Verlag.
Farmer, D. *et al.* (1986), *Evolution, Games and Learning: Models of Adaptation in Machines and Nature*, Proceedings of the Fifth Annual International Conference of the Center for Nonlinear Studies, *Physica 22D/1–3*, Amsterdam, North-Holland.

Fischer, E.O. and Jammernegg, W. (1986), 'Empirical investigation of a catastrophe theory extension of the Phillips curve', *Review of Economics and Statistics*, vol. 68, pp. 9–17.

Fisher, R.A. (1930), *The Genetical Theory of Natural Selection*, Oxford, Clarendon Press.

Frydman, R. and Phelps, E.S. (eds) (1983), *Individual Forecasting and Aggregate Outcomes: 'Rational Expectations' Examined*, Cambridge, Cambridge University Press.

Gandolfo, G. and Padoan, P.C. (1984), *A Disequilibrium Model of Real and Financial Accumulation in an Open Economy*, Berlin, Heidelberg, New York, Tokyo, Springer-Verlag.

Georgescu-Roegen, N. (1971), *The Entropy Law and the Economic Process*, Cambridge, Mass., Harvard University Press.

—— (1976), *Energy and Economic Myths*, New York, Pergamon.

Gibbons, M. and Metcalfe, J.S. (1988), 'Technological variety and the process of competition', in F. Arcangeli, P. David and G. Dosi (eds.), *Innovation Diffusion*, Oxford, Oxford University Press, forthcoming

Goodwin, R.M. (1951), 'The nonlinear accelerator and the persistence of business cycles', *Econometrica*, vol. 19, pp. 1–17.

—— (1967), 'A growth cycle', in C.H. Feinstein (ed.), *Socialism, Capitalism and Economic Growth*, London, Macmillan.

Haag, G., Weidlich, W. and Mensch, G.O. (1985), 'A macroeconomic potential describing structural change of the economy', *Theory and Decision*, vol. 19, pp. 279–99.

Haken, H. (1983a), *Synergetics: An Introduction*, 3rd edn., Berlin, Heidelberg, New York, Tokyo, Springer-Verlag.

—— (1983b), *Advanced Synergetics*, Berlin, Heidelberg, New York, Tokyo, Springer-Verlag.

Hardin, G. (1968), 'The tragedy of the commons', *Science*, vol. 162, pp. 1243–8.

Hardin, R. (1982), *Collective Action*, Baltimore, Johns Hopkins University Press.

Hirsch, M.W. and Smale, S. (1974), *Differential Equations, Dynamical Systems and Linear Algebra*, New York, Academic Press.

Hofbauer, J. and Sigmund, K. (1984), *Evolutionstheorie und dynamische Systeme*, Berlin, Hamburg, Verlag Paul Parey.

Holland, J.H. (1975), *Adaptation in Natural and Artificial Systems*, Ann Arbor, University of Michigan Press.

Iwai, K. (1984a), 'Schumpeterian dynamics: an evolutionary model of innovation and imitation', *Journal of Economic Behavior and Organization*, vol. 5, pp. 159–90.

—— (1984b), 'Schumpeterian dynamics, Part II: technological progress, firm growth and "economic selection"', *Journal of Economic Behavior and Organization*, vol. 5, pp. 321–51.

Jimenez Montaño, M.A. and Ebeling, W. (1980), 'A stochastic evolutionary model of technological change', *Collective Phenomena*, vol. 3, pp. 107–114.

Kaldor, N. (1983), 'Gemeinsamkeiten und Unterschiede in den Theorien von Keynes, Kalecki und Rüstow', *IFO-Studien*, vol. 29, pp. 1–10.

—— (1985), *Economics without Equilibrium*, Armonk, NY, M.E. Sharpe Inc.

Kaldor, N. and Mirrlees, J.A. (1962), 'A new model of economic growth', *Review of Economic Studies*, vol. 29, pp. 174–92.

Keynes, J.M. (1936), *The General Theory of Employment, Interest and Money*, London, Macmillan.

Losert, V. and Akin, E. (1983), 'Dynamics of games and genes: discrete versus continuous time', *Journal of Mathematical Biology*, vol. 17, pp. 241–51.

Lotka, A.J. (1924/1956), *Elements of Mathematical Biology*, New York, Dover.

Marchetti, C. (1983), 'Recession: ten more years to go?', *Technological Forecasting and Social Change*, vol. 24, pp. 331–42.

Marshall, A. (1890/1927), *Principles of Economics*, 8th edn., London, Macmillan.

Maynard Smith, J. (1982), *Evolutionary Game Theory*, Cambridge, Cambridge University Press.

Mensch, G., Kaasch, K. Kleinknecht, A. Schnopp, R. (1980), 'Innovation trends, and switching between full- and under-employment equilibria, 1950–1978', discussion paper IIM/dp 80–5, Berlin, International Institute of Management.

Monod, J. (1970), *Le Hassard et la Nécessité*, Paris, Seuil.

Nelson, R.R. (1968), 'A "diffusion" model of international productivity differences in manufacturing industry', *American Economic Review*, vol. 58, pp. 1218–48.

Nelson, R.R. and Winter. S.G. (1974), 'Neoclassical vs. evolutionary theories of economic growth', *Economic Journal*, vol. 84, pp. 886–905.

—— (1982), *An Evolutionary Theory of Economic Change*, Cambridge, Mass., The Belknap Press of Harvard University Press.

Nelson, R.R., Winter. S.G. and Schuette, H.L. (1976), 'Technical change in an evolutionary model', *Quarterly Journal of Economics*, vol. 90, pp. 90–118.

Nicolis, G. and Progogine, I. (1977), *Self-Organization in Non-Equilibrium Systems*, New York, Wiley-Interscience.

Poston, T. and Stewart, I. (1978), *Catastrophe Theory and Its Applications*, London, Pitman.

Prigogine, I. (1976), 'Order through fluctuation: self-organization and social system', in E. Jantsch and C.H. Waddington (eds.), *Evolution and Consciousness*, Reading, Mass., Addison-Wesley.

Prigogine, I., Allen, P.M. and Hermann, R. (1977), 'Long term trends and the evolution of complexity', in E. Laszlo and J. Bierman (eds.), *Goals in a Global Community*, vol. 1, New York, Pergamon.

Rüstow, H-J. (1951), *Theorie der Vollbeschäftigung in der freien Marktwirtschaft*, Tübingen, J.C.B. Mohr (Paul Siebeck).

Rüstow, H-J. (1984), *Neue Wege zur Vollbeschäftigung. Das Versagen der ökonomischen Theorie*, Berlin, Duncker & Humblot.

Sahal, D. (1981), *Patterns of Technological Innovation*, New York, Addison-Wesley.

Salter, W. (1962), *Productivity and Technical Change*, Cambridge, Cambridge University Press.

Saunders, P.T. (1980), *An Introduction to Catastrophe Theory*, Cambridge, Cambridge University Press.

Schelling, T.C. (1978), *Micromotives and Macrobehavior*, Cambridge, Mass., Harvard University Press.

Schumpeter, J. (1919), *Theorie der wirtschaftlichen Entwicklung*, English translation, *The Theory of Economic Development*, Cambridge, Mass., Harvard University Press, 1934.

—— (1947), *Capitalism, Socialism and Democracy*, New York, Harper & Row.

Schuster, P. and Sigmund, K. (1983), 'Replicator dynamics', *Journal of Theoretical Biology*, vol. 100, pp. 535–8.

Schwartz, J.T. (1961), *Theory of Money*, New York, Gordon & Breach.

Schwefel, H.P. (1981), *Numerical Optimization of Computer Models*, Chichester, John Wiley.

Sigmund, K. (1986), 'A survey of replicator equations', in J.L. Casti and A. Karlqvist (eds.), *Complexity, Language and Life: Mathematical Approaches*, Berlin, Heidelberg, New York, Tokyo, Springer-Verlag.

Silverberg, G. (1984), 'Embodied technical progress in a dynamic economic model: the self-organization paradigm', in R.M. Goodwin, M. Krüger and A. Vercelli (eds.), *Nonlinear Models of Fluctuating Growth*, Berlin, Heidelberg, New York, Tokyo, Springer-Verlag.

—— (1987), 'Technical progress, capital accumulation and effective demand: a self-organization model', paper presented at the Fifth International Conference on Mathematical Modelling, Berkeley, June 1985, in D. Batten, J. Casti and B. Johansson (eds.), *Economic Evolution and Structural Adjustment*, Berlin, Heidelberg, New York, Tokyo, Springer-Verlag.

Silverberg, G., Dosi, G. and Orsenigo, L. (1988), 'Innovation, diversity and diffusion: a self-organisation model', *Economic Journal*, vol. 98, forthcoming.

Soete, L. and Turner, R. (1984), 'Technology diffusion and the rate of technical change', *Economic Journal*, vol. 94, pp. 612–23.

Solow, R. (1960), 'Investment and technical progress', in K.J. Arrow, S. Karlin and P. Suppes (eds.), *Mathematical Methods in the Social Sciences*, Stanford, Stanford University Press.

Taylor, P. and Jonker, L. (1978), 'Evolutionary stable strategies and game dynamics', *Mathematical Biosciences*, vol. 40, pp. 145–56.

Thom, R. (1975), *Structural Stability and Morphogenesis*, Reading, Mass., Benjamin/Cummings.

Thomas, L.C. (1984), *Games, Theory and Application*, Chichester, Ellis Harwood Ltd.

Weidlich, W. and Haag, G. (1983), *Concepts and Methods of a Quantitative Sociology*, Berlin, Heidelberg, New York, Tokyo, Springer-Verlag.

Williamson, O.E. (1965), 'A dynamic theory of interfirm behavior', *Quarterly Journal of Economics*, vol. 79, pp. 579–607.

Woodcock, A.E.R. and Davis, M. (1979), *Catastrophe Theory*, London, Penguin.

Zeeman, E.C. (1974), 'On the unstable behavior of stock exchanges', *Journal of Mathematical Economics*, vol. 1, pp. 34–49.

—— (1979), 'Population dynamics from game theory', in Z. Neticki (ed.), *Global Theory of Dynamical Systems*, Berlin, Heidelberg, New York, Tokyo, Springer-Verlag.

—— (1981), 'Dynamics of the evolution of animal conflicts', *Journal of Theoretical Biology*, vol. 89, pp. 249–70.

25 The diffusion of innovation: an interpretative survey*

J. S. Metcalfe

PREST and Department of Economics, University of Manchester, Manchester

Introduction

The purpose of this chapter is to consider the diffusion of innovation from a number of different theoretical perspectives. In the process I will discuss the respective roles of equilibrium and disequilibrium methods of analysis, profitability and 'fashion' supply-side factors, and the interaction between changing technology and changing market environments. I shall not give equal weight to the topics, nor shall I attempt other than the briefest reference to the literature on the subject. My purpose is to highlight some alternative methods of analysis. Davies (1979), Stoneman (1983), and Thirtle and Ruttan (1987) provide valuable surveys of the (by now) immense literature on this topic.

For the purposes of this chapter, diffusion and structural economic change are treated as synonyms. In any study of innovation diffusion, we are concerned with the process by which new technological forms are integrated into the economy to impose changes upon its structure. Diffusion-related structural change may be considered at a number of analytical levels, from the macro development of an entire industry, to the micro level at which a new machine, or consumer good, is diffused to generate corresponding marginal changes in the behaviour of firms and individuals. Most diffusion research is conducted at the micro level, but the importance of the diffusion theme spreads far beyond any detailed concern with individual innovations. In terms of fundamentals, we are interested in diffusion phenomena as examples of economic change and development in how new technologies come to acquire economic significance, and, in the process, displace existing technologies either partially or totally.

Whatever the level at which diffusion phenomena are studied there are a number of basic issues which must be clarified. The first centres on whether diffusion is to be viewed in terms of an equilibrium or a disequilibrium process (Griliches, 1957), whether diffusion patterns reflect a sequence of shifting equilibria in which agents are fully adjusted and

---

*Collaboration over a number of years with M. Gibbons is gratefully acknowledged, as is collaboration with colleagues in PREST, in particular, Hugh Cameron. Work reported here has been funded within the ESRC programme on competitive performance. In preparing the final draft I have benefited greatly from comments and discussion at the Maastricht conference, and, in particular, from the incisive comments of the editor of this section, Gerald Silverberg.

informed, or whether, by contrast, they reflect a sequence of imperfectly perceived disequilibria lagging behind the development of a 'final' equilibrium position. Closely related to this dichotomy is the distinction between diffusion processes which are driven by changes in external events, and those which are driven by endogenous change from within. These are not as sharp a set of distinctions as might at first appear, since one can turn any disequilibrium model into an equilibrium equivalent and vice versa by a suitable definition of the information sets and perceptions of adopting agents. However, the distinction is critical to any understanding of the diffusion literature. A second, more fundamental issue concerns the decision-making procedures which are assumed to drive the diffusion process. Here the relevant distinction is between models which assume full information, classical rationality on the behalf of adopting agents, and models which postulate limited information, bounded rationality as the basis for decision-making. From these distinctions four classes of diffusion model can be constructed. Neo-classical theorists naturally find the matching of fully rational action with equilibrium models of analysis highly congenial. Others, this author included, find the conjunction of limited–information disequilibrium methods of analysis appealing, not least because of their more open treatment of human decision-making processes. Naturally, since I believe in the appropriateness of bounded rationality as a mode of behaviour, I also welcome diversity in our approaches to understanding diffusion. Boundaries are always interesting places to be, but boundary disputes are only occasionally illuminating, and are normally tedious and unproductive.

A third issue to be clarified involves the distinction between adoption and diffusion. Adoption analysis considers the decisions taken by agents, typically organizations such as firms, to incorporate a new technology into their activities. It is concerned with the process of decision-making, and leads to propositions linking the nature and timing of adoption decisions to specified characteristics of adopters, e.g. the size of firms, or their sociometric position within a communication network. By contrast, diffusion analysis is concerned with how the economic significance of a new technology changes over time. Economic significance may be measured in a number of ways, e.g. by the share of the market held by a product innovation or by the fraction of industry output produced with a process innovation. In this sense the analysis of diffusion is closely related to the analysis of technological substitution in which a 'new' technology displaces an 'old' technology (Linstone and Sahal, 1976; Nelson, 1968). The relation between the adoption pattern and the diffusion pattern depends upon a complex of factors, including differences in intra-firm rates of adoption, and time lags between the decision to adopt and the implementation of that decision.

The fourth issue relates to the specification of an innovation, and the environment within which adoption and diffusion take place. For it is frequently assumed that the innovation embodies a technology which does not change over time, and, less frequently, that adoption and diffusion occur in an unchanging environment. Neither of these assumptions is helpful except in special cases of 'minor' innovations. More typically, an innovation is one step in a sequence of innovations, within a particular technological regime. These post-innovative improvements play a vital role in increasing the rate of diffusion within existing applications, and extending the technology to new applications (Georghiou *et al.*, 1986; Hunter, 1949; Rosenberg, 1982). While some post-innovative improvements may be traced back to exogenous changes in knowledge, many arise from the experiences, incentives and bottlenecks which arise endogenously during the diffusion process. Furthermore, significant improvements are often induced in technologies under competitive threat from the new technology, so that the diffusion curve is shaped by the evolving pattern of competitive advantage between rival technologies — a phenomenon which is aptly named the 'sailing ship' effect (Graham, 1956). Endogenously driven changes apply not only to technology but also to its diffusion environment. When first introduced, a new technology is evaluated in terms of a price structure which is shaped by the prevailing technology. However, the increasing economic weight of the innovation reshapes this price structure in a way which may be favourable or unfavourable to the new technology. Indeed, whenever the existing technology is eliminated, the price structure will end up being conditioned entirely upon the characteristics of the new technology. In short, the environment in which competing technologies are evaluated evolves endogenously under the pressures of technological competition. This is not to deny that it may also change for exogenous reasons unrelated to the diffusion process, or that such changes (e.g. shifts in demand structures or the supply of inputs) may profoundly affect the evaluation of competing technologies.

The fifth issue relates to the relative importance of demand and supply phenomena in the diffusion process. This is brought out most sharply when one considers the question of profitability as the incentive to the adoption and diffusion of a new technology (Mansfield, 1961; Oster, 1982). But profitability to whom, the potential adopter or the potential producer, for innovations cannot be adopted unless they can be profitably produced? Indeed, any diffusion curve is the outcome of two processes: the one relating to the development of the market for the technology, and the other relating to the creation of the capacity to supply that market. Moreover, it is the relative profitability of competing technologies, not their absolute profitability, which is important: and this will change during the diffusion process under the influence of changes in the competing technologies and in their diffusion environment. Even in that special case where sufficient capacity already exists to meet the maximum rate of demand for an innovation, supply factors expressed in terms of pricing policy and rate of output decisions cannot be ignored (Stoneman and Ireland, 1983).

The final issue to be raised in this introductory section is perhaps the most difficult of all to treat. It is the distinction between technology as knowledge and technology as artefact (Layton, 1974). The studies of diffusion and adoption on which this survey is based are almost entirely about artefacts which, although they may be improving over time, are nonetheless readily identifiable. The study of the diffusion and adoption of technological knowledge raises quite different issues, many of which are identical to those faced in the technology transfer literature: issues relating to the cognitive and assimilative capacities of different organizations, of distinguishing organizational knowledge from technological knowledge, of imperfect property rights and the appropriability of knowledge, of the balance between codifiable, public knowledge and tacit, firm specific knowledge, and of the structure of learning activity in a given technological area. Suffice to say that these issues demand a survey of their own and will not be treated further here.

In the rest of the chapter I propose to explore some of these issues in the context of three principal themes: equilibrium models of diffusion; selection dynamics and diffusion; and a density-dependent model of diffusion and technological substitution.

The section on selection and diffusion also reflects a concern with new frameworks for analysing the process of economic change. For here we are exploring the link between variety and economic change and the role of mechanisms which enhance or diminish economic variety. There are important links here with the literature on biological and ecological change (Monod, 1963) and with the literature on evolutionary economics explored elsewhere in the volume (Silverberg). These last two sections have perhaps a modest claim to follow Marshall's dictum that 'biology is the mecca of the economist'.

Equilibrium approaches to adoption and diffusion

We begin with the equilibrium approach to adoption behaviour and diffusion, in which rational adopters possess full information about an innovation at all points along the diffusion path. The approach leads to diffusion paths, in which the timing of adoption is entirely explained by objective changes in the profitability of using a new technology. Lack of information or understanding does not constrain diffusion, and contagion effects and bandwagon effects are ruled out, *a priori*, as sources of information and influence upon adopter perceptions. The essential features of this approach are: (i) the dependence of diffusion patterns upon heterogeneity of adopter characteristics; and (ii) the identity between the objective benefits of adoption and the perceived benefits of adoption.

The general structure of an equilibrium model for the adoption of a capital-good innovation may be set out as follows. There is a given population of firms for which the capital-good innovation is technologically relevant. The size of this population may or may not be changing over time. Firms differ with respect to at least one characteristic which influences the profitability (benefit) of adoption, and the profitability of investing in the innovation is consequently distributed across the relevant population according to a density function such as B–B in Figure 25.1. For our purposes, benefits can be defined as the expected present value of profits arising from the adoption of the new technology. Obviously the shape of the benefit distribution also depends upon economic characteristics of the adoption environment, such as relative factor prices and the degree of competition faced by adopters.

Immediately one can divide the population of firms into two categories; non-adopters for whom $b_i < 0$, those firms to the left of the origin who will never rationally adopt unless subsidized to do so, and potential adopters for whom $b_i > 0$. In addition to the benefit function there is a distribution across firms of the costs of adopting the innovation. For ease of exposition, we shall assume that the present value of adoption costs is the same for all firms, at the level indicated by C–C.

The proportion of actual adopter firms follows immediately as the shaded area to the right of C–C. No rational profit-maximizing firm in this section of the distribution will fail to adopt. It follows that, to generate an adoption path over time, one or both of two events must happen: either the cost of adoption falls and C–C shifts to the left; or the benefit distribution shifts to the right in a more or less uniform manner. Either way, the outcome is to increase the size of the shaded adoption area to the right of C–C. Factors determining these rates of change would include: exogenous variations in the economic environment, e.g. a change in wage levels or in the price of primary material inputs; technical improvements to the innovation in question; and developments in complementary and competing technologies. The crucial point here is that the information sets of the

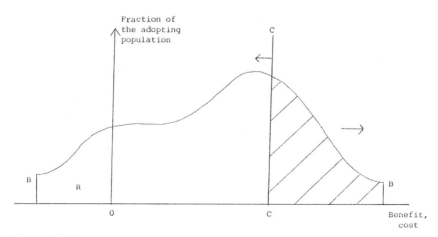

Figure 25.1

population of potential adopters are independent of the number of actual adopters of the innovation. They may well change for other reasons but these are unrelated to the adoption process *per se.*

To link the adoption curve with the diffusion curve (fraction of output produced with the innovation) is not difficult in principle but obviously the shape of this latter curve will depend upon the shape of the benefit distribution, the movements over time in it and the cost distribution, and the distribution of industry output across the adopting firms. In some cases, e.g. with economies of scale in adoption, there will be an obvious correlation between the benefit distribution and the distribution of output among adopters. Unfortunately, there appears to be no research on the way in which various relevant factors influence the entire benefit distribution, a matter crucial to the shape of the diffusion curve. We do, however, have some useful insights and empirical evidence on the general sorts of issues involved. Three may be mentioned here.

The first concerns the question of interrelatedness, the dependence of the benefits from adoption upon the firm-specific environment in which the innovation is to operate. A new capital good typically has to be operated in conjunction with the existing equipment of the firm, and if the latter must be altered in any way to accommodate the innovation, the additional costs of adjustment must be added to the capital cost of the innovation (Frankel, 1955; Rosseger, 1979; Lazonick, 1985). In this way interrelatedness limits the scope for adoption. Interrelatedness factors should not, however, be limited to physical effects alone. Account should also be taken of interrelatedness between an innovation and existing labour and management skills and their organizational context, and between an innovation and the composition of the adopter's output (Feller, 1966; Rosseger, 1974).

The second point to be emphasized is the distinction between investment decisions which expand the firm's capacity and those which replace existing capacity. As far as capacity expansion is concerned, the adoption decision should be based on a comparison of the net advantages of investing in competing, newly produced capital goods, of which the innovation is only one. If the innovation offers the highest net present value it would be chosen. Old and new compete in this context on equal terms. For the replacement decision this is not the case. The definition of capital costs relevant to the existing installed technique is based not on its current reproduction cost but on actual present value in the next best alternative use. This may be as low as scrap value, net of dismantling costs, and may even be a negative sum. Hence, the old and the new do not compete on equal terms. The existing technique has costs which have been to some degree sunk. As Marshall emphasized, the nature of capital costs *ex ante* is quite different from their nature *ex post.* Indeed, this is precisely the meaning of the oft-quoted phase, 'bygones are bygones'. When the alternative capital value of the existing technique is zero, an innovation will only replace it when the savings it generates in prime costs are less than the capital charges incurred by adopting the new capital good (Salter, 1960; Lutz and Lutz, 1951). It follows from this that where replacement decisions are important (e.g. when innovations are to be adopted in a static or declining industry) then the adopter benefit distribution will reflect a number of factors including: the coexistence of different vintages of equipment in different firms; echo effects from the past history of investment decisions; and the existence of institutional factors such as second-hand markets for durable equipment.

The third and final topic to raise here concerns the optimal timing of investment (Barzel, 1968; Lutz and Lutz, 1951). Put simply, when a potential adopter is choosing between alternative, mutually exclusive investment projects it cannot be assumed that investment today is the optimal strategy. The rational investment strategy is to adopt at that date which generates the greatest net present value for the firm, and in the presence of anticipated market growth or anticipated reductions in the cost of adoption this optimal date will often lie in the future. Rational behaviour may then involve a delay in adoption, such that for all firms finding it profitable to adopt (in the shaded area in Figure 25.1) we have a corresponding distribution of their optimal adoption dates.

A number of authors have made important contributions to the equilibrium diffusion literature. Davies (1979) builds his diffusion model around the concept of adopter heterogeneity and links the shifts over time in the benefit distribution to the growth in the size of adopters and to exogenously imposed patterns of post-innovation improvement in technology. David (1975) explains the slow initial diffusion of the McCormick reaper in the American Midwest in terms of shifts in the farm size (grain acreage), distribution and economies of scale associated with mechanical reaper technology. More recently, David and Olsen (1984) have applied arguments based on the optimal timing of investment to develop a diffusion path for a durable capital good. By linking the equilibrium patterns of the diffusion to learning economies in the capital goods industry, they are able explicitly to incorporate technological expectations (Rosenberg, 1976) into the derivation of the diffusion path. Stoneman and Ireland's (1983) paper applies a similar logic to the problem but also takes account of the effects of different market structures in the supply industry upon the diffusion path.

However, our chief concern here is with the general nature of the equilibrium approach to diffusion. The key problem is not that adopters have full *a priori* information, although this is problematic enough. Rather, the problem is the assumption of information sets which are given and interpreted independently from the process of diffusion. It is this which rules out any elements of fashion or bandwagon effects as an explanation of adoption. The appraisal by firms of an innovation is complete the moment the innovation is announced. Delay in adoption can only be the result of objective circumstances, not a failure to comprehend the significance of events. In this postulated world of change entrepreneurs never fail (Sandberg, 1984).

It would appear that the central difference between equilibrium and disequilibrium models of diffusion concerns the way in which agents acquire the information relevant to their adoption decisions. In the equilibrium approach this information is given *a priori*, and if it changes it does so for reasons exogenous to the diffusion process. In the disequilibrium approach this is not so: information changes because of the diffusion of a technology, and the ways in which knowledge is acquired and the relative costs of different sources of information become crucial, if implicit, elements in the analysis. The key question in a world of costly information and limited cognitive capacity is, 'How do firms come to know the *economic* properties of a new technology?' By this is meant not simply a knowledge of the existence of the innovation in question but rather knowledge of the precise relevance of the innovation to the adopter's own particular circumstances. Broadly speaking, two types of mechanisms can generate the relevant data, remembering here that data should not be equated *simpliciter* with knowledge. The first is internal experiment, learning, appraisal and evaluation of the technology which may or may not have a formal R & D component. The second is observation of the experience of others. It is this latter which is the basis for the density-dependent diffusion process found in the disequilibrium literature. From this follows a great deal in terms of managerial and organizational behaviour, the technological sophistication of adopters, and informal and formal communication links between the population of potential adopters and between them and suppliers of the innovation (Carter and Williams, 1957; Rogers, 1983; Czepiel 1985).

Summarizing these various contributions, it is clear that they are complementary with disequilibrium models of the adoption process. It would be an error to consider them to be incompatible. The key insight they contain is not the way in which information is acquired but rather the assumed heterogeneity of adopter benefits. Introducing arguments for delayed adjustment enriches this insight; it does not diminish it (cf. Heiner's chapter in this volume).

Diffusion of innovation as a process of selection

In this section we explore some simple dynamic models of an evolutionary kind, which treat the diffusion of technology as the outcome of a process of selective competition between rival technologies. The general structure of these models is treated in the introductory chapter by Silverberg. Our concern is with the mechanisms by which a technology acquires significance, mechanisms which are based upon a sharp distinction between firm and environment. At root the argument is extremely simple. Technological variety across firms is the basis for competitive advantage. The competitive advantages of different technologies, in conjunction with certain strategic attributes of firm behaviour, determine how the rival technologies diffuse relative to one another. By following this approach one can more readily relate the study of diffusion to the study of the more general issue of competition and structural change.

Firm and environment

Technologies do not compare in the literal sense. Only firms compete, and they do so as decision-making organizations articulating a technology to achieve specific objectives within a specific environment. The outcome of their decisions is precisely what determines the economic significance of rival technologies and how this changes over time. For our purposes the firm is an organizational unit, possessing a knowledge base and a design capacity to translate that base into products and processes of production. Such a firm may be represented in terms of three attributes. First is its *efficiency*, as measured by the quality of its products and the productivity of the methods of production it employs. Efficiency depends on two interwoven aspects of the firm's knowledge base: its technological knowledge of how materials and energy are to be transformed into the desired products, and its organizational knowledge base which determines the firm's managerial capacity to plan, coordinate, control and monitor its productive activities. The second attribute is the firm's *propensity to accumulate* the ability to translate profits into the expansion of the capacity to produce its current range of products. Accumulation is a question of the perception of growth opportunities, the ability to command internal and external capital funds, the investment requirements to expand capacity, the ability to manage growth without sacrificing efficiency, and, last but not least, the willingness to expand. A firm which does not wish to grow will, by definition, have a zero propensity to accumulate. Finally, we have the *creativity* of the firm: the ability to advance product and process technology either through improvements within existing design configurations, or by the addition of new design configurations to the technological portfolio. As with the other attributes, the creativity of a firm will depend on a number of considerations including: the richness of the firm's technological environment; the resources which the firm can marshall for research design and development activities; the incentives to advance technology, influenced in part by the scale of potential application and by the threat of competitive imitation; the ability of the firm to manage the process of acquiring new knowledge (from internal or external sources); and its ability to move from knowledge to artefact, by coordinating design and development with its production and marketing activities. In a world of bounded rationality, it is hardly surprising to find inter-firm differences in creativity. Much technological knowledge is specific to the firm and not codifiable in any ready fashion. The knowledge base builds cumulatively, in part as productive and marketing experience is acquired; and what the firm perceives as a possible development in technology is contingent upon an organizational memory which reflects the history of the firm (Pavitt, 1983). Three important points need to be stressed here concerning the relationship between creativity, knowledge base and revealed performance. Firstly, it is quite inappropriate either to depict the process of creativity as one in which the organization fishes without restriction in a common pool of public knowledge, or to equate data with knowledge. Data are fragmentary, knowledge is holistic, and two firms will often interpret the same data in quite different ways. Bounded rationality will see to that. Secondly, the knowledge base of the firm is structured within the organization and develops an inertia of its own. Creativity is canalized along trajectories of advance which are self-reinforcing and become embodied in the memory and decision-making style of the organization. An established pattern of advance often degenerates with time into the only possible line of advance. The knowledge base is not infinitely malleable. It will develop in certain directions but the firm will face great difficulty in moving into non-complementary lines of production which do not draw upon established knowledge (Richardson, 1972): hence the well-documented difficulties of technology transfer between organizations. Thirdly, because firms differ in their creativity they necessarily come to differ in one or more dimensions of their efficiency. It is these differences in creativity which ultimately underpin the competitive process. They generate and regenerate the variety without which competition cannot operate.

It is appropriate to say a little more about the boundaries of the firm. For in modern conditions, the firm is typically a multi-product, multi-process operation, commanding several different technologies. We shall define the 'firm' more narrowly, as that organizational sub-unit charged with articulating a distinct knowledge base and the related design configurations, accepting that this may involve the production of several products. It follows that part of the organizational environment of the firm is formed by the umbrella organization of which it is a part. How the firm competes for capital and other resources with other sub-units and how R&D activity is distributed between the umbrella organization and firm are important determinants of accumulation and creativity.

With this clarification of the boundaries of the firm, let us turn to the question of the environment. Again, this is not a simple concept. For the moment, concentrate on the notion of the market environment to which the firm sells its products and from which it acquires productive inputs. The central point about the environment is that it is an operator, evaluating the firm's current efficiency by translating product quality into a price premium, and resource productivity into unit costs of production. This economic evaluation forms the basis of a process of competitive selection across technologies. Here one must make a number of important distinctions. First, the market selection environment may be tranquil or turbulent. A tranquil environment grows steadily with gradually evolving patterns of relative input costs and product price premium. A turbulent environment experiences discrete shocks, e.g. non-trivial, unanticipated shifts in the scale of demand and in the supply conditions of productive inputs. Important contributions to the organizational literature are concerned with how the firm should be structured to deal with tranquil and turbulent environments (Burns and Stalker, 1961; Lawrence and Lorsch, 1967). Secondly, the market environment will have a particular frequency with which the process of selection operates. A firm which sells its products or buys inputs through long-term contracts will be in quite a different position from the firm which must trade on a daily basis. Moreover, the market may operate continuously, or at discrete intervals (as it does, for example, for major civil engineering or defence contracts). Thirdly, one can distinguish market environments according to their selective force, the degree to which they punish deviations in a firm's performance from the appropriate industry average. The classic competitive market is, in these terms, one of maximum selective ferocity. By contrast, a monopolist operates in an environment of zero selective ferocity. Finally, one can distinguish market environments according to the uniformity with which they select across different firms. In part, this is a question of the segmentation of the market into non-competing groups of buyers, but it also reflects factors, such as goodwill, which imply that selection is focused more upon some firms than upon others. Stinchcombe's (1965) concept of the 'liability of newness' is a relevant example of non-uniformity in the selection environment. Now the implication of these environmental attributes is that, in conjunction with variety in the attributes of firms, they determine the differential rates of diffusion of competing technologies. To explore this more fully we need first to present a distributional view of technology.

Technology as a distribution

It is commonplace to observe that in any industry one finds not uniformity but variety of economic performance. Take, for example, unit costs of production. Instead of one common cost level, one typically finds firms with a wide variation of unit costs of producing more or less identical commodities; from best practice through average practice to worst practice. Indeed, it was precisely such an observation which prompted Salter's (1960) pathbreaking analysis of the coexistence of competing production methods in terms of vintage investment and replacement decisions. As Silverberg (1985) has shown, the efficiency of a firm will be a function of the mix of capital vintages that it operates, with this mix being changed continually under the pressure of scrapping and investment decisions. Exactly the same observation underspins studies of the frontier production function (Farrell, 1957).

Consider an industry producing a more or less homogeneous product. At any one time, the variety within it can be expressed (as in Figure 25.2) in terms of a density function showing the fraction of production, s_i,

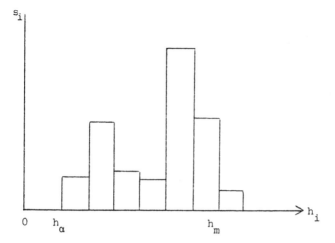

Figure 25.2

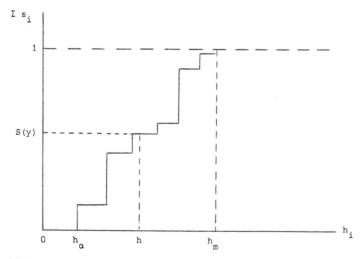

Figure 25.3

accounted for by each different unit cost level, or equivalently by the cumulative distribution function (Figure 25.3). The explanation of this variety may be found in one or more of the following factors: the environment is not uniform so that different firms pay different prices for identical productive services; the firms differ in their ability to organize the process of production; or the firms are employing technologically distinct methods of production or different combinations of the alternative technological vintages. Since our primary concern is with the diffusion of technologies, we shall equate, for pedagogic purposes only, differences in unit costs entirely with technological differences in the methods of production.

Variety is then defined in terms of the technology set with range $h_\alpha - h_m$. It helps exposition further if we assume that all firms operating the same process technology do so with the same unit costs. Then the fractions of production accounted for by each different technology, their market shares, accurately measure the different degrees to which they are currently diffused. Over time this distribution changes under the influence of three sets of forces, process innovations and related post-innovation improvements, process imitations, and market selection. The first two redefine the elements of the technology set and are properly related to matters of creativity. The third changes the economic weight of the rival technologies and depends on the environmentally contingent interaction between efficiency and fitness. It is this selection-induced repositioning of the elements in the technology set which traces out the diffusion curves of the different technologies.

This argument applies equally to questions of variety in product qualities. Each product may be considered as a bundle of characteristics. Depending on the (implicit) market valuations of these characteristics, the different products will command different market prices. In a uniform environment, the pressure of selection continuously changes the economic weight of the competing products exactly as it does with respect to the production methods. Product innovation and imitation similarly redefine this dimension of the technology set.

The above account leads us to a multi-technology picture of the diffusion process. The traditional bilateral model (new vs. old technology) is not always appropriate as a basis for analysing diffusion phenomena. Moreover, we see the direct link between diffusion and competitive selection. Rather than being on the fringes of competitive analysis, diffusion is quite central to it. Diffusion and competition are based upon rivalry and variety, and no dimension of variety is more telling in the long run than that which is based upon efficiency differences and canalized patterns of technological change.

A review of simple selection models

We can now put these general arguments to work in a sequence of illustrative but simple selection models which build upon the ideas of Steindl (1952), Downie (1955), Nelson and Winter (1982), and Iwai (1984). We consider first selection by differential accumulation in uniform environments of maximum selective ferocity. We then extend this formulation to cover imperfect customer selection, increasing returns and barriers to exit. The common theme running throughout these cameo studies is of firms earning differential quasi-rents which are then deployed to finance market expansion and creativity.

Selection by differential accumulation

Consider first a technology set comprising a given variety of process technologies for producing a homogeneous commodity. The market is tranquil, growing at a constant compound rate g_d. It is uniform and of maximum selective ferocity, so that every firm is forced to sell its output at the common market price, p. At each point in time, the market clearing value of p depends on the market demand curve and the schedule of supply, itself dependent on the cumulative total of capacity currently invested in each competing process technology. All firms pay the same price for productive inputs (uniformity), and this structure of input costs does not vary during the selection process (tranquility).

Each technology is of the constant returns kind with capital: output ratio, v_i. Unit costs with each technology u_i, are the sum of a fixed component, h_i, and a further component, $\rho_i g_i$; this latter reflecting the link between the rate of growth of the firm and its ability to avoid consequential current cost penalties. For expositional purposes we will term h_i, unit costs for the ith technology. Unit cost in this sense includes the element of normal return on capital invested in that technology.

At any point in time, the ith profitable technology has market share s_i, and this is our measure of its relative degree of diffusion. Consider now how these market shares change over time. Given the product price, firms with different technologies earn differential profits (rents) which they invest in further capacity expansion. The faster growing firms increase the relative diffusion of their technologies at the expense of the remaining firms. However, how quickly a firm grows depends not only upon its efficiency but also upon its propensity to accumulate. Let each firm acquire investible funds from internal and external sources, and let the ratio of the growth rate to rate of profit for a given firm be π_i. This is also the coefficient of investment in the particular technology articulated by that firm. Combining these hypotheses we can write

$$g_i = \left(\frac{\pi_i}{v_i}\right)[p - h_i - \rho_i g_i]$$

which gives

$$g_i = f_i(p - h_i), \tag{1}$$

with

$$f_i = \frac{\pi_i}{v_i + \pi_i \rho_i} \tag{2}$$

being the firm's accumulation coefficient. The firm has a higher propensity to accumulate, the smaller is its capital:output ratio, the more effectively it manages growth (smaller is ρ_i), and the larger is its investment ratio π_i. A firm which did not wish to grow or could not manage growth would have a zero value of f_i.

We can now divide the technology set into two groups. Profitable technologies in which investment is occurring, $p > h_i$, and bankrupt technologies for which output is zero, $p < h_i$. On the borderline of survival between these groups are the marginal technologies, in which output is positive although investment has ceased, $p = h_m$. Implicit in this partition is the assumption that bankruptcy results in immediate withdrawal from the market (on this see below).

Under conditions of uniform accumulation, $f_i = f$, the multi-technology diffusion process will operate in the following way. The aggregate growth rate of the profitable firms is $g = \Sigma s_i g_i$, from which we derive

$$g = f[p - \bar{h}] \tag{3}$$

with $\bar{h} = \Sigma s_i h_i$, the level of average practice cost units. Two types of selective situation may then apply, depending on whether there exists a marginal technology. If there is, then the market price will be fixed at the level of $p = h_m$, and any discrepancies between g and g_d will be reflected in a changing degree of capacity utilization in this marginal technology. Either $g > g_d$, in which case the utilization of the marginal technology is declining, or $g < g_d$, in which case its degree of utilization is increasing. In each case the marginal technology must eventually cease to be marginal (it moves into either bankruptcy or profitability). When this happens we find that p is no longer technologically determined and rises or falls over time as $g \gtrless g_d$ until g converges on g_d to give

$$p = \frac{g_d}{f} + \bar{h} \tag{4}$$

In what follows we can, with minimal loss of content, focus solely on a situation where marginal technologies have been eliminated.

To depict diffusion phenomena in a multi-technology context we have a number of options. The first is to consider directly the market share of the ith technology, which evolves according to the relation

$$\frac{ds_i}{dt} = s_i(g_i - g) = f[\bar{h} - h_i] \tag{5}$$

It follows that the rate of diffusion is linked directly to that technology's distance from average-practice technology. Provided the technology has unit costs below the average level, its level of diffusion increases; otherwise it declines in relative significance, surviving as long as it remains profitable. It can be shown that this process brings to economic dominance the lowest-cost, best-practice technology, the diffusion of all other technologies dropping in relative terms to zero. Crucial to this process is the fact that this multi-technology diffusion process continually defines the value of $\bar{h}$, since the more efficient technologies are always increasing in relative weight. Thus any technology which is not best practice but which starts with lower costs than average will first experience increased diffusion until such time as $\bar{h}$ falls sufficiently to make it above average in terms of unit costs, when its level of diffusion declines. Ultimately, $\bar{h}$ will tend to the best-practice unit cost level, h_a.

A second way to depict the diffusion process is in terms of the evolution of the statistical moments of the technology disltribution. An obvious candidate is the evolution of average-practice unit costs, according to the zero order replicator equation (Schuster and Sigmund, 1983, and Silverberg in this volume).

$$\frac{d\bar{h}}{dt} = \sum_i \frac{ds_i}{dt} hi = \sum_i s_i(g_i - g)h_i = C(g, h) \tag{6}$$

The rate of change of average-practice costs is equal to the covariance between growth rates and unit cost levels in the technology set. This is a fundamental and typical result in a selection framework (Price, 1972). The evolution of any statistical movement of the technology distribution depends on some measure of variety of performance across the distribution. However, we can go further, for $[g_i - g] = f[\bar{h} - h_i]$, which gives

$$\frac{d\bar{h}}{dt} = -fV(h) \tag{7}$$

where $V(h)$ is the variance of unit costs across the profitable firms. This result is directly analogous to Fisher's fundamental law of natural selection in genetic biology (Nelson and Winter, 1982, p. 243). Here we also see the accumulation coefficient as a measure of the ferocity of the selection process. Competition is fiercer, and average practice falls faster, the greater the propensity to accumulate of the firms in this industry. By an exactly similar argument, one can show that the variance of unit costs evolves in proportion to the third movement around the mean of the technology distribution.

Yet a third method of depicting the diffusion process, is to consider the evolution of the cumulative distribution function of the technology set (Iwai, 1984). Choose a unit cost level, y, $h_a \leq y < h_m$) and define $S(y)$ as the cumulative fraction of industry output produced by technologies with costs less than or equal to y (Figure 25.3). This choice of y divides the distribution of profitable technologies into two parts. Let $\bar{h}_1$ be average unit cost for all technologies with $h_1 \leq y$, and let h_2 be average unit cost for the remaining technologies, with $h_2 > y$. Then it can be shown that $S(y)$ evolves with time according to

$$\frac{dS(y)}{dt} = f[\bar{h}_2 - \bar{h}_1]S(y)(1 - S(y)) \tag{8}$$

that is, logistically, at a rate determined by the propensity to accumulate and the cost gap $\bar{h}_2 - \bar{h}_1$. Of course, $S(y)$ will not follow a logistic curve through time, since this cost gap is itself changing as selection proceeds.

Each of these methods provides a valid way of describing the multi-technology diffusion process, and each requires some minor modification once we admit the existence of marginal technologies and the transition into bankruptcy. The point here is that with the growth of capacity, the price of the product follows a halting downward trend, so squeezing progressively more technologies into bankruptcy. Ultimately, best practice dominates the production of the industry. While those technologies which can satisfy the condition $f[h_i - h_a] < g_d$ survive, they will all ultimately acquire a zero measure in terms of relative diffusion. This leads directly to some crucial distinctions. Absolute growth in the output from a technology should not be confused with its diffusion, which is a relative matter: a technology can grow in terms of absolute measures but still be declining in economic significance. Similarly, one must distinguish significance from survival. To survive, all that is required is that a technology's unit costs permit profitable production, $p > h_i$. To have lasting significance a technology must be best practice. Notice that the margin for the survival of non-best-practice technologies is greater the greater is the growth rate of the market environment. It is static conditions that impose the 'survival of the most efficient' as an equilibrium requirement.

Customer selection

We maintain the assumption of a uniform propensity to accumulate and analyse the effects of alternative specifications of the diffusion environment. We consider first the consequences of weakening the force of market selection, so that a firm with a 'high' price is not immediately punished by finding its sales drop to zero. In effect, this introduces elements of dynamic imperfect competition into the selection process. To fix ideas, imagine that customers in the market at any time are divided between the firms in a particular pattern but allow the firms to set different prices for the same product. Each firm has a different customer base but interaction between the customers of different firms spreads knowledge about the price distribution, so that customers switch gradually from high-priced to lower-priced firms. Let the customer learning mechanism reflect random mixing between the customers of different firms and follow the rule

$$\frac{ds_i}{dt} = \delta \sum_j s_i s_j (p_j - p_i)$$

When customers from two firms interact, the one paying the higher price switch to the lower price firm at a rate proportional to the coefficient δ. In so doing they redistribute the derived demand for the different process technologies. This particular adjustment process generates a growth rate of demand for each firm.

$$g_i = g_d + \delta(\bar{p} - p_i) \tag{8}$$

where $\bar{p} = \Sigma s_i p_i$, is the industry average price, and δ is the coefficient of customer selection. Equation (8) satisfies the necessary aggregation condition that $\Sigma s_i g_i' = g_d$. When $\delta = \infty$ we have the case already considered, effective perfect competition, with each firm forced to charge the same price. When $\delta = 0$, we have a world of independent monopolies since the customer base of each firm is quite independent of the price that it charges relative to other firms. Customers are completely loyal to their existing supplies. In between we have a world of dynamic imperfect competition — dynamic because the demand curve for each firm shifts over time in proportion to its average price differential. Combining this customer selective mechanism with the differential accumulative mechanism, and imposing the balance condition that $g_i = g_i'$, we find that

$$g_i = \frac{fg_d + \delta g}{f + \delta} + \frac{\delta f}{f + \delta} (\bar{h} - h_i)$$

If we again ignore the existence of marginal firms, and focus on those tranquil situations in which market demand and aggregate capacity grow in step, we find

$$g_i = g_d + \frac{\delta f}{f + \delta} (\bar{h} - hi) \tag{9}$$

Now (9) is a selective mechanism of identical form to (1), except that imperfect market selection interacts with accumulative propensity to slow down the rate at which selection operates. At the extremes, when $\delta = \infty$, we have market selection at its maximal rate; when $\delta = 0$, selection is ruled out. In this latter case $g_i = g_d$ for all the technologies, and the diffusion process has its structure frozen into a pattern determined by initial market shares.

Turning now to the evolution of the technology distribution, we find that

$$\frac{d\bar{h}}{dt} = -\frac{f\delta}{f + \delta} V(h), \tag{10}$$

which reduces to (8) when customer selection is of maximal ferocity. When $\delta = 0$, we naturally find that the technology distribution ceases to evolve. The one line of argument which cannot be carried over to these conditions of imperfect customer selection is that relating the market demand curve to a uniform price. For now we have a distribution of prices and cannot define a market demand curve. It is easily shown that $(\bar{p} - p_i)$ is proportional to $(\bar{h} - h_i)$, and hence the variance of prices is given by

$$V(p) = \left[\frac{f}{f + \delta}\right]^2 V(h) = \frac{f}{f + \delta} C(p, h) \tag{11}$$

while

$$\frac{d\bar{p}}{dt} = \delta^2 V(h) \tag{12}$$

so that selection generates lower average prices as well as lower average unit costs. The survival condition also requires some modification. A firm remains viable as long as it covers unit costs but the permissible lag behind average-practice costs is greater the greater is the growth rate of demand, and the lower is the ferocity of customer selection. Once again we find that rapid market growth is conducive to the survival of inefficient techno-logies. From this we conclude that the ferocity of the market selection environment is a key determinant of patterns of technology diffusion. The more benign the environment, the smaller is δ, and the less quickly does the best-practice technology establish its dominance. More generally, one can allow the ferocity of customer selection to be uneven across the tech-nologies (specifying δ_{ij} different for any pair of firms) with effects similar to those generated by non-uniform fitness. A firm whose customer base is relatively 'sticky' can tolerate greater inefficiency and thus survive longer than in a world of uniformity in the market selection process.

A digression: increasing returns and the Verdoorn Law

We return again to the basic selection model but allow for increasing returns to scale as firms expand their productive capacity. Again, to see the essentials, imagine that scale effects are Harrod neutral (leave the capital:output ratio of each technology unchanged), and that the scale elasticity, ε, is the same for each technology. Then, along familiar lines, average-practice unit cost evolves according to

$$\frac{d\bar{h}}{dt} = \sum_i \frac{ds_i}{dt} h_i + \sum_i s_i \frac{dh_i}{dt}$$

$$= -fV(h) - \varepsilon \Sigma s_i h_i g_i$$

Simplifying this expression further we can write

$$\frac{d\log(\bar{h})}{dt} = -\left[f(1-\varepsilon) \frac{V(h)}{\bar{h}} + \varepsilon g_d \right], \tag{13}$$

which is precisely the 'form' of relationship postulated by the Verdoorn Law, with empirical values of the scale elasticity typically found in the range $0 \le \varepsilon < 1$.

Barriers to exit

It is natural for the study of technical change to focus upon the frequency and character of innovation events. We cannot, however, forget the con-verse phenomena, the elimination of once economic technologies and the bankruptcy mechanisms which bring this about. In fact, the processes of selection we have described depend upon two rules of behaviour: the accumulation rule, which relates capacity growth rate to profit margin; and the survival rule, which states that non-profitable technologies exit the industry.

There are, however, good reasons to expect the survival rule to be violated in many situations. Even though a firm cannot cover its costs, it may still draw upon accumulated capital resources in the hope of better times to come. If it is part of a larger multi-product organization, the profits generated elsewhere may be used to shore up the bankrupt technology. Finally, public subsidy may and often does keep 'bankrupt' technologies in operation. Now whatever the other implications of these violations they do have one obvious consequence: they slow down the selection process because the capacity invested in the bankrupt technologies remains in production and depresses the market price. Consequently, the profitable technologies are less profitable and their collective rate of diffusion is correspondingly reduced. Certainly, in any study of diffusion and the competitive process the conditions and timing of technology exit should be given due consideration.

Some extensions

It is possible to develop this simple selection model in a number of ways. Differences in product quality which generate different product prices may be combined with cost differences to give two sources of differential profitability. Similarly, different propensities to accumulate can be introduced, so that the simple link between efficiency and capacity growth rate is broken. Then it no longer follows that it is the best-practice technology which rises to relative market dominance (Metcalfe, 1984). One may also introduce the effects of turbulence in the environment, with demand curve or factor price shocks displacing the selection process from its initial path. But in each case the central logic of the multi-technology diffusion process remains unaltered. Selection works on economic variety at a pace which is greater, the greater is the economic variety at any point in time.

A Marshallian diffusion process

While the approach to multi-technology diffusion in the previous section has the advantage of generality, it has the consequential disadvantage that explicit diffusion curves cannot be derived. In this final section we outline a process of competition between an old and a new technology which permits the derivation of a solution for both the traditional diffusion curve and for the relative diffusion or substitution curve. The approach is Marshallian, both in terms of the use of partial equilibrium methods, and in illustrating the fundamental distinction between expanding and contracting industries. The latter are in a long-period situation of capacity expansion, while the former are necessarily in a short-period situation with given productive capacity. The approach also allows an explicit analysis of the role of profitability and fashion, as incentives to adoption and as stimuli to capacity expansion. Demand and supply sides of the diffusion process are brought together to determine simultaneously patterns of output, prices, unit costs and profitability for the two technologies. The approach also permits an integration of equilibrium and disequilibrium approaches to diffusion, precisely to emphasize their complementarity. This integration, however, is bought at a price, namely the reliance on path-independent methods of analysis. For we construct positions of equilibrium which are quite independent of the paths towards those long-period positions. While this method has an honourable history in both classical and neo-classical economic thought, it seems to be peculiarly inappropriate for the analysis of the process of competition and techno-logical change (see the chapters by Dosi and Orsenigo and by Arthur). It is worth noting that the type of process outlined below has direct parallels in the ecological literature on inter-species competition. It is in fact an example of a density-dependent selection process, in which competition settles the two technologies into their respective niches.

The problem

The process of competition is between two technologies which supply the same productive service to users. We choose units such that one unit of the old commodity provides one unit of productive service, while α units of the new commodity $(\alpha < 1)$ provide one unit of the productive service. The coefficient α measures the qualitative superiority of the new technology and thus its equilibrium price premium. In equilibrium the price of the old, p_o, and new, p_n, commodities must satisfy the condition $p_n/p_o = \alpha$. The two commodities also have different, constant returns technologies of production, and correspondingly different equilibrium supply curves. Within each technology, all firms produce under the same cost conditions. The market environment is uniform, and there is a given, static demand curve for the productive service. The two technologies draw upon dif-ferent markets for their productive inputs, and as the output of each expands external diseconomies are encountered which increase the equilibrium supply price.

The equilibrium niche

At the date of innovation of the new technology, the old technology supplies the entire market for the productive service. This market is in long-run equilibrium with price p_o^* and output level C_o^*. The entry of the new technology redefines this position and creates a new set of niches for the two technologies. Either the old is completely eliminated, or the two

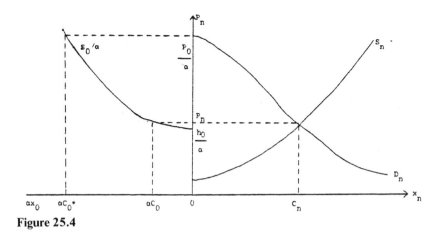

Figure 25.4

technologies share the market for the productive service. The outcome depends on the demand curve for the productive service, the two supply curves, and the qualitative superiority of the new technology (α). By comparing prices and quantities in terms of units of the new material we can depict the possible outcomes in Figure 25.4.

D_n is the excess demand curve for the new material, which is derived by subtracting, at each price, the supply of productive service from the old technology from the corresponding market demand for the productive service. Hence the intercept of this curve with the vertical axis has the value p_o^*/α. With S_n as the equilibrium supply curve for the new technology, its equilibrium niche is C_n and corresponding price p_n. Prior to the innovation date the old technology has output αC_o^*. In the new niche the output from the old technology has contracted to αC_o on its supply curve. The long-run demand is shared between the two technologies in the proportion s_1 given by

$$s_1 = \frac{C_n}{\alpha C_o + C_n} \tag{14}$$

In Figure 25.4, the two technologies coexist. This need not be so. If $h_n > p_o^*/\alpha$, then the new technology cannot be established, which, if $h_o/\alpha > p_n$, then the old technology certainly cannot survive. Some supply inelasticity is crucial to its survival (Harley, 1975). It readily follows that s_1 is greater, the smaller is α, and the greater is the cost superiority of the new technology.

Transition to the equilibrium niche

Consider now the process by which the long-run equilibrium position is attained. For the new technology to displace the old, its productive capacity must be built up and users must be induced to switch their demand away from the old technology. Neither effect can take place instantaneously.

On the capacity growth side, we can employ the argument of the second section of this chapter. Growth is proportional to the profitability of the new technology, with the added constraint that unit cost now depends on the scale of production from the new technology. We can write this as

$$\frac{\mathrm{d}x_n}{\mathrm{d}t} = fx_n[p_n - S(x_n)] \tag{15}$$

where $S(x_n)$ is the long-period supply curve of the new commodity. For given p_n this gives a determinate growth path of productive capacity.

The old technology is, of course, in a quite different situation. It is marginal, with firms just earning the normal return required to keep them in production. Investment decisions are no longer relevant, and the only decisions to be made concern the rate of contraction down the long-period supply curve.

On the demand side, users have to learn of the attributes of the new technology before they will adopt it. Following the argument in the first section, this leads to a learning process in which non-adopters learn by observing the experience of existing adopters, so creating a 'fashion' element in the diffusion process. Under conditions of random interaction, and no external influences in the learning process, this leads to the following differential equation for the growth of demand for the new commodity.

$$\frac{\mathrm{d}x_n}{\mathrm{d}t} = \beta x_n[D_n(p_n) - x_n] \tag{16}$$

where β is the constant, adoption coefficient and $D_n(p_n)$ is the long-run demand curve for the new commodity.

Now for a given value of p_n we have two fully determined growth paths for the new commodity. Moreover, if $D_n(p_n)$ and $S_n(x_n)$ are linear functions, then (15) and (16) reduce to a pair of logistic differential equations. But for arbitrary p_n they also generate different time paths for capacity and demand. In a closed economy this cannot be so. Capacity and demand cannot grow in an inconsistent fashion, for entrepreneurs will neither tolerate capacity shortages nor excess capacity. In the short term such deviations are probable but not in the long term. So we seek balanced paths of diffusion to generate the secular trend of the diffusion process (Kuznets, 1929; Burns, 1934), along which p_n varies to maintain the growth rate of capacity equal to the growth rate of demand.

In the particular case where $D_n(p_n)$ and $S_n(x_n)$ are replaced by first-order approximations then the balanced diffusion curve of the new technology can be derived explicitly. Along the balanced path we find that

$$\frac{\mathrm{d}x_n}{\mathrm{d}t} = Bx_n[C_n - x_n] \tag{17}$$

where C_n is the niche defined in Figure 25.4, and B is the diffusion coefficient which depends on β, f and the slopes of all the equilibrium curves in Figure 25.4. A higher value of f or of β increases the magnitude of β. C_n, is independent of both these dynamic coefficients (Cameron and Metcalfe, 1987).

Solving (17) leads to the familiar logistic equation

$$x_n(t) = C_n[1 + A \exp(-BC_n t)]^{-1} \qquad (18)$$

where A is a constant depending on the scale of output of the new technology at the innovation date. Despite the complexities of this competitive process, with endogenous changes in price, profitability, and unit costs, the output of the new technology follows a logistic curve towards its equilibrium niche. The properties of this process are more readily seen in Figure 25.5. In Figure 25.5(a) we have the curve of balanced logistic growth for X_n, and in 25.5(b) the curve of the growth rate in output of the new technology showing the familiar pattern of retardation. In Figure 25.5(c) is the path of decline in the output of the old technology, while 25.5(d) shows the path of price and output for the new technology. Given that f and β are both finite, the path starts from point a and reaches the long-period

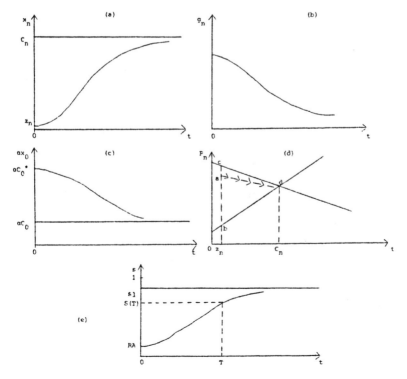

Figure 25.5

position at d. Two special cases then fall into place. With $\beta = \infty$, there is no customer learning and $p_n(t)/p_o(t) = \alpha$ throughout the diffusion process. The path followed is then along the demand curve from c to d. With $f = \infty$ we have the corresponding case of no accumulation constraints on the diffusion process, and the path followed is along the supply curve from b to d.

From this we draw an important implication. Along any balanced path with $\beta < \infty$, we find that $p_n(t)/p_o(t) < \alpha$. This means that during the diffusion process the new technology is always more profitable to adopt than the old technology, and it is only the lack of familiarity with its attributes that holds back adoption. Any adopter switching to the new commodity will lower the cost of acquiring the productive service, although this cost advantage declines over time. In the long-run position the new commodity will sell at its full premium, and only then will the marginal user be economically indifferent between the two technologies. Thus the diffusion process has built into it a clear incentive to switch to the new technology once its attributes are properly understood. Indeed, without this economic incentive, the market for the new technology could not begin to grow.

The substitution curve

Having determined the outputs of the old and new materials we may now derive the substitution curve for the new technology. An extensive literature exists on technological substitution (Linstone and Sahal, 1976; Mahajan and Peterson, 1985), but no adequate theory exists on the determinants, as distinct from the empirical properties, of substitution curves. Within this two-technology diffusion framework, the substitution curve corresponding to a balanced path can be derived as follows, although one must first decide how market shares are to be measured. The obvious method is to employ current prices and to measure shares in total expenditure, but this is unnecessarily complex and permits no easy solution since the prices are changing over time. However, since the materials are physical substitutes, we can justifiably use their relative efficiency in supplying production services to compare them on a common basis. Thus the market share of the new material at time t can be computed as

$$s(t) = \frac{x_n(t)}{\alpha x_o(t) + x_n(t)} \tag{19}$$

This is equivalent to combining the old and new commodities at their long-run relative prices.

On differentiating (19) we have

$$\frac{ds(t)}{dt} = s(t)(1 - s(t))(g_n(t) - g_0(t)) \tag{20}$$

Provided the growth rate of output of the new material, $g_n(t)$, exceeds the corresponding growth rate of the old, $g_o(t)$, then $s(t)$ increases over time. At what rate it increases is not transparent, since the two output growth rates are themselves varying over the substitution process. However, these growth rates are also determined once we know the balanced diffusion path. Taking account of this we find that the substitution curve is given by

$$s(t) = s_1[1 + RA \exp(-BC_nt)]^{-1} \tag{21}$$

where s_1 is as determined in (14), and R is the ratio of sizes of the equilibrium markets for the productive service in the old and new equilibrium positions. $[R = \alpha C_o^*/(\alpha C_0 + C_n) < 1]$ R is a measure of the long-run impact of the new technology upon the market for the productive service. All the remaining coefficients in (21) are as defined in (18).

Figure 25.5(e) shows the typical path of substitution, which follows a logistic curve from a value $s(0) = RA$, towards the upper asymptote s_1. It is not surprising that the coefficient BC_n determines simultaneously the rate of diffusion and the rate of substitution, since the output of the old technology is simply responding passively to the growth of the new commodity. It is the dynamics of the new technology which is driving the process.

As an index of the rate of substitution we can derive the time, T, taken to reach some target substitution level $s(T)$. Simple manipulation gives this as

$$T = \frac{1}{BC_n} \left(\log RA + \log\left[\frac{s(T)}{s_1 - s(T))} \right] \right) \tag{22}$$

This time is greater the smaller is BC_n and the greater is R. The more significant the new technology, the longer, *ceteris paribus*, will it take to reach a given level of substitution.

Thus the substitution curve is akin to the hands of a clock, tracing out the surface phenomena of substitution, while, hidden from view, a complex dynamic of prices, production and profitability drives the process of technological competition. For our purposes the significance of (21) lies in its non-arbitrary nature. The substitution curve is an explicit reflection of the process of competition between the old and the new materials as reflected in the relative profitability of using and producing them.

One advantage of this approach is that it enables us to enquire into the factors hidden behind the substitution curve and thus to investigate the effect of parameter changes upon the substitution process. Any such change can be assessed in terms of its impact on s_1, R, BC_n and A. One possibility is to compare substitution processes identical in all respects except one, and to infer the effects of the specified difference upon the substitution curve. Two examples will suffice to illustrate the method. Consider first the effects of an improved process for producing the new material, corresponding to a rightward shift in the supply curve $S_n(x_n)$.

Taking first the effects on the long-run position we see that C_n is increased and p_n reduced with the consequence that C_0 is also smaller. Together these changes mean that an improved process is associated with a higher value of s_1. With respect to the dynamics of adjustment it follows immediately that the improved process is associated with a higher value of BC_n, the substitution rate coefficient, and a higher value of product RA. Thus improved methods for producing the new material work to expand its equilibrium market share and ensure it is diffused more rapidly, so that any given substitution level is reached sooner. By symmetry, inferior methods for producing the old material have exactly the same effect.

As a second example, consider the impact of a greater willingness on the part of users to switch to the new commodity, as reflected in a higher value for β. Such a change has no effect on the equilibrium niches, nor the values of RA and s_1. But it does increase BC_n and hence the rapidity with which diffusion and substitution take place. Exactly similar implications follow from an increase in the accumulation coefficient f.

Using this method, all manner of factors affecting the substitution process may be made explicit and precise in terms of a comparison between different substitution curves. Moreover, such exercises provide a basis not simply for comparing different substitution processes but for discussing the more complex consequences of changes in parameters during the substitution process. Taking account of such changes, we can generate a family of logistic substitution curves which typically form a non-logistic substitution envelope. The precise shape of this envelope depends on the nature and magnitude of the parameter changes and their temporal incidence. The cautionary implication is clear. Without a knowledge of the changes in determining conditions during the diffusion process, it is not possible to infer the dynamics of substitution from an empirical knowledge of the substitution envelope. Even simple logistic substitution, processes of the kind discussed above, may be associated with markedly non-logistic diffusion and substitution envelopes.

The framework of our Marshallian model is perhaps too simplistic. We have not allowed for foreign trade (Metcalfe and Soete, 1984) or for situations in which the old technology is not in its long-run niche when the innovation occurs (Metcalfe and Gibbons, 1987). Nonetheless, this simple model does make explicit the factors shaping the diffusion and substitution process within the competitive context.

Conclusions

In this chapter we have outlined alternative approaches to the study of innovation diffusion, and suggested that diffusion phenomena should be treated as part of the broader picture of competition and structural change in capitalist economies. At the root of our review is the notion that competition is driven by technological variety, variety which is evaluated in economic terms by the prevailing market environment. Both equilibrium and disequilibrium methods for analysing diffusion play a role in defining niches for technologies, and the paths of adjustment towards these niches.

We have not treated adequately the complex question of the link between the diffusion process and the mechanisms which generate technological variety. Possibly the ideas presented here will provide one foundation for such a study but this task remains unaccomplished.

References

Barzel, Y. (1968), 'The optimum timing of innovations', *Review of Economics and Statistics*, vol. 50.

Binswanger, H. and Ruttan, V. (1978), *Induced Innovation*, Baltimore, Johns Hopkins University Press.

Burns, A. F. (1934), *Production Trends in the United States Since 1870*, NBER.

Burns, T. and Stalker, G. (1961), *The Management of Innovation*, London, Tavistock.

Cameron, H. and Metcalfe, J. S. (1987), 'On the economics of technological substitution', *Technological Forecasting and Social Change*, vol. 31.

Carter, C. and Williams, B. (1957), *Industry and Technical Progress*, Oxford University Press, Oxford.

Czepiel, Z. (1975), 'Patterns of interorganizational communication and the diffusion of a major technological innovation in a competitive industrial community', *Academy of Management Journal*, vol. 18.

David, P. (1975), 'The mechanization of reaping in the anti-bellum Midwest', in *Technical Innovation and Economic Growth*, Cambridge, Cambridge University Press.

David, P. and Olsen, T. (1984), 'Anticipated automation: a rational expectations model of technology diffusion', Stanford, mimeo.

Davies, S. (1979), *The Diffusion of Process Innovations*, Cambridge, Cambridge University Press.

Dosi, G. (1986), 'Institutions and markets in a dynamic world', SPRU, University of Sussex, mimeo.

Downie, J. (1955), *The Competitive Process*, London, Duckworth.

Farrell, M. (1957), 'The measurement of productive efficiency', *Journal of Royal Statistical Society*, (A), vol. 120.

Frankel, M. (1955), 'Obsolescence and technological change', *American Economic Review*, vol. 45.

Feller, I. (1966), 'The draper loom in New England Textiles, 1894–1914: a study of diffusion of an innovation', *Journal of Economic History*, vol. 26.

Georghiou, L. *et al.* (1986), *Post Innovative Performance*, London, Macmillan.

Gold, B. (1981), 'Technological diffusion in industry: research needs and shortcomings', *Journal of Industrial Economics*, vol. 30.

Graham, G. S. (1956), 'The ascendancy of the sailing ship', *Economic History Review*, vol. 9.

Griliches, Z. (1957), 'Hybrid corn: an exploration in the economics of technological change', *Econometrica*, vol. 25.

Hannan, M. and Freeman, J. (1977), 'The population ecology of organizations', *American Journal of Sociology*, vol. 82.

Harley, C. K. (1975), 'On the persistence of old technologies', *Journal of Economic History*, vol. 33.

Hunter, L. (1949), *Steamboats on the Western Rivers,* Cambridge, Harvard University Press.

Iwai, K. (1984), 'Schumpeterian dynamics, Parts I and II', *Journal of Economic Behaviour and Organization*, vol. 6.

Kuznets, S. (1929), *Secular Movements in Prices and Production,* Boston, Houghton Mifflin.

Lawrence, P. and Lorsch, J. (1967), *Organization and Environment,* Cambridge, Mass., Harvard University Press.

Layton, E. (1974), 'Technology as knowledge', *Technology and Culture*, vol. 15.

Lazonick, W. (1983), 'Industrial organization and technological change: the decline of the British cotton industry', *Business History Review*, vol. 57.

Linstone, D. and Sahal, D. (1976), *Technological Substitution: Forecasting Technologies and Applications,* New York, Elsevier.

Lutz, F. and Lutz, V. (1951), *The Theory of Investment of the Firm,* Princeton, Princeton University Press.

Mahajan, V. and Peterson, R. A. (1985), *'Models for Innovation Diffusion',* New York, Sage.

Mansfield, E. (1961), 'Technical change and the rate of imitation, *Econometrica*, vol. 29.

Metcalfe, J. S. (1981), 'Impulse and diffusion in the study of technological change, *Futures*, vol. 13.

—— (1984), 'Technological innovation and the competitive process', in P. Hall (ed.), *Technology, Innovation and Economic Policy,* London, P. Allen.

Metcalfe, J. S. and Gibbons, M. (1987), 'On the economics of structural change and the evolution of technology', in L. Pasinetti (ed.), *Growth and Structural Change*, London, Macmillan.

Metcalfe, J. S. and Soete, L. (1984), 'Notes on the evolution of technology and international competition', in M. Gibbons *et al.* (eds), *Science and Technology Policy in the 1980s and Beyond,* London, Longman.

Monod, J. (1983), *Chance and Necessity,* Hammondsworth, Penguin Books.

Nelson, R. (1968), 'A diffusion model of international productivity differences in manufacturing industry', *American Economic Review*, vol. 58.

Nelson, R. and Winter, S. (1982), *An Evolutionary Theory of Economic Change,* Cambridge, Mass., The Belknap Press of Harvard University Press.

Pavitt, K. (1983), 'Patterns of technical change: evidence, theory and policy implications', *Papers in Science Technology and Public Policy*, SPRU.

Price, G. R. (1972), 'Extension of covariance selection mathematics', *Annals of Human Genetics*, vol. 35.

Oster, S. (1982), 'The diffusion of innovation among steel firms: the basic oxygen process', *Bell Journal of Economics*, vol. 13.

Ray, G. (1984), *The Diffusion of Mature Technologies,* Cambridge, Cambridge University Press.

Richardson, G. B. (1972), 'The organization of industry', *Economic Journal*, vol. 82.

Rogers, E. M. (1983), *Diffusion of Innovations*, 3rd edn., New York, Free Press.

Rosenberg, N. (1976), 'On technological expectations', *Economic Journal*, vol. 86.

—— (1982), *Inside the Black Box,* Cambridge, Cambridge University Press.

Rosseger, G. (1979), 'Diffusion and technological specificity', *Journal of Industrial Economics*, vol. 28.

Salter, W. E. G. (1960), *Productivity and Technical Change*, Cambridge, Cambridge University Press.

Sandberg, L. (1984), 'The entrepreneur and technological change', in R. Floud and D. McCloskey (eds), *The Economic History of Britain Since 1700*, vol. 2, Cambridge, Cambridge University Press.

Schmookler, J. (1966), *Invention and Economic Growth*, Cambridge, Mass., Harvard University Press.

Schuster, P. and Sigmund, K. (1983), 'Replicator dynamics', *Journal of Theoretical Biology*, vol. 100.

Silverberg, G. (1987), 'Technical progress, capital accumulation and effective demand: a self-organizational model', in D. Batten, J. Costi and B. Johansson (eds), *Economic Evolution and Structural Adjustment,* Berlin, Heidelberg, New York, Tokyo, Springer-Verlag.

Soete, L. and Turner, R. (1984), 'Technology diffusion and the rate of technological change', *Economic Journal*, vol. 94.

Steindl, J. (1952), *Maturity and Stagnation in American Capitalism*, Monthly Review Press. New York.

Stinchcombe, L. (1965), 'Social structure and organizations', in J. G. March (ed.), *Handbook of Organizations*, New York, Rand McNally.

Stoneman, P. (1983), *The Economic Analysis of Technological Change*, Oxford, Oxford University Press.

Stoneman, P. and Ireland, N. (1983), 'The role of supply factors in the diffusion of new process technology', *Economic Journal*, vol. 93.

Thirtle, C. and Ruttan, V. (1987), *The Role of Demand and Supply in the Generation and Diffusion of Technological Change*, vol. 21, Fundamentals of Pure and Applied Economics, New York, Harwood.

Vincenti, W. de (1985), 'Technological knowledge without science: the innovation of flush riveting in American airplanes', *Technology and Culture*, vol. 25.

26 Competing technologies: an overview*

W. Brian Arthur

Food Research Institute, Stanford University, Stanford, California

Every steam carriage which passes along the street justifies the confidence placed in it; and unless the objectionable feature of the petrol carriage can be removed, it is bound to be driven from the road, to give place to its less objectionable rival, the steam-driven vehicle of the day.

William Fletcher (1904), *Steam Carriages and Traction Engines*, p. xi.

Introduction

When a new engineering or economic possibility comes along, usually there are several ways to carry it through. In the 1890s the motor carriage could be powered by steam, or by gasoline, or by electric batteries. In more modern times nuclear power can be generated by light-water, or gas-cooled, or heavy-water, or sodium-cooled reactors. Solar energy can be generated by crystalline-silicon or amorphous-silicon technologies. An AIDS vaccine may eventually become possible by cell-type modification methods, or by chemical synthesis, or by anti-idiotype methods. Video recording can be carried out by Sony Betamax® or by VHS technologies.

In each case we can think of these methods or technologies as 'competing' for a 'market' of adopters (Arthur, 1983). They may 'compete' unconsciously and *passively*, like species compete biologically, if adoptions of one technology displace or preclude adoptions of its rivals. Or they may compete consciously and *strategically*, if they are products that can be priced and manipulated. (In this latter case, following nomenclature introduced in Arthur (1985), we will say they are *sponsored*).

What makes competition between technologies interesting is that usually technologies become more attractive — more developed, more widespread, more useful — the more they are adopted. Thus competition between technologies usually becomes competition between bandwagons, and adoption markets display both a corresponding instability and a high degree of unpredictability.

Increased attractiveness caused by adoption, or what I will call 'increasing returns to adoption', can arise from several sources; but five are particularly important:

---

* I am grateful to Paul David, Giovanni Dosi, Frank Englmann, Christopher Freeman, Richard Nelson, Nathan Rosenberg, Gerald Silverberg and Luc Soete for comments on this chapter, and to participants at the May 1987 IFIAS meeting on Technical Change and Economic Theory, Maastricht, The Netherlands.

(i) *Learning by using* (Rosenberg, 1982). Often the more a technology is adopted, the more it is used and the more is learned about it; therefore the more it is developed and improved. A new airliner design, like the DC-8, for example, gains considerably in payload, passenger capacity, engine efficiency and aerodynamics, as it achieves actual airline adoption and use.

(ii) *Network externalities* (Katz and Shapiro, 1985). Often a technology offers advantages to 'going along' with other adopters of it—to belonging to a network of users. The video technology VHS is an example. The more other users there are, the more likely it is that the VHS adopter benefits from a greater availability and variety of VHS-recorded products.

(iii) *Scale economies in production.* Often, where a technology is embodied in a product, like the polaroid technology, the cost of the product falls as increased numbers of units of it are produced. Thus the technology can become more attractive in price as adoption increases.

(iv) *Informational increasing returns.* Often a technology that is more adopted enjoys the advantage of being better known and better understood. For the risk-averse, adopting it becomes more attractive if it is more widespread.

(v) *Technological interrelatedness* (Frankel, 1955). Often, as a technology becomes more adopted, a number of other sub-technologies and products become part of its infrastructure. For example, the gasoline technology has a huge infrastructure of refineries, filling stations, and auto parts that rely on it. This puts it at an advantage in the sense that other technologies, if less adopted, may lack the requisite infrastructure or may require a partial dismantling of the more widespread technology's in-place infrastructure.

Of course, with any particular technology, several of these benefits to increased adoption may be mixed in and present together. Rarely do we have a pure source of increasing returns to adoption.

Whatever the source, if increasing returns to adoption are indeed present, they determine the character of competition between technologies. If one technology gets ahead by good fortune, it gains an advantage. It can then attract further adopters who might otherwise have gone along with one of its rivals, with the result that the adoption market may 'tip' in its favor and may end up dominated by it (Arthur, 1983). Given other circumstances, of course, a different technology might have been favored early on, and *it* might have come to dominate the market. Thus in competitions between technologies with increasing returns, ordinarily there is more than one possible outcome. In economic terms there are multiple equilibria. To ascertain how the *actual* outcome is 'selected' from these multiple candidate outcomes, we need to keep track of how adoptions of rival technologies build up (together with the small events that might influence these) and how they eventually sway and tip the market. We need, in other words, to follow the dynamics of adoption.

Where competing technologies possess increasing returns, a number of very natural questions arise:

1. How can we model the adoption process when there is competition between increasing-return technologies and hence indeterminacy in the outcome?
2. What analytical techniques can be brought to bear on this increasing-return allocation problem? In particular, what techniques can help us determine the possible outcomes of the adoption process?
3. When technologies compete, under what circumstances *must* one technology—albeit an indeterminate one at the outset—achieve a monopoly and eventually take 100 per cent of the adoption market? Under what circumstances will the market eventually be shared?
4. How does the 'competing standards' case differ from the competing technologies one?
5. What difference does it make to have different sources of increasing returns: network externalities rather than learning effects, for example?
6. What policy issues arise in the competing technology case?
7. What major research questions remain to be answered?

In this chapter I have been asked to provide an overview of my work on the competing technology problem, highlighting in particular the dynamic approach. Where possible I will connect my approach and results with those of others and I will mention open research problems. I begin with a review of the basic competing technologies model and then go on to discuss some of the questions raised above.

Lock-in by small events: a review of the basic model

As one possible, simple model of competition between technologies with increasing returns (Arthur, 1983), imagine two unsponsored technologies, A and B, competing passively for a market of potential adopters who are replacing an old, inferior technology. As adoptions of A (or B) increase, learning-by-using takes place and improved versions of A (or B) become available, with correspondingly higher payoffs or returns to those adopting them. Each agent—each potential adopter—must choose either A or B when his time comes to replace the old technology. Once an agent chooses he sticks to his choice. The versions of A or B are fixed when adopted, so that agents are not affected by the choices of future adopters.

Suppose for a moment, in a preliminary version of this model, all agents are alike. And suppose that returns to adopting A or B rise with prior adoptions as in Table 26.1. The dynamics of this preliminary model are trivial but instructive. The first agent chooses the higher payoff technology —A in this table. This bids the payoff of A upward, so that the next agent

Table 26.1   Returns to adopting A or B, given previous adoptions

Previous adoptions	0	10	20	30	40	50	60	70	80	90	100
Technology A	10	11	12	13	14	15	16	17	18	19	20
Technology B	4	7	10	13	16	19	22	25	28	31	34

a fortiori chooses A. A continues to be chosen, with the result that the adoption process is locked in to A from the start. Notice that B cannot get a footing, even though if adopted it would eventually prove superior.

Already in this simple preliminary model, we see two properties that constantly recur with competing technologies: *potential inefficiency* in the sense that the technology that 'takes the market' need not be the one with the longer-term higher payoff to adopters; and *inflexibility*, or lock-in, in the sense that the left-behind technology would need to bridge a widening gap if it is to be chosen by adopters at all.

Although there are examples of technologies that lock out all rivals from the start, this preliminary model is still not very satisfactory. The outcome is either predetermined by whichever technology is initially superior or, if both are evenly matched the outcome is razor-edged. In reality, adopters are not all alike and, at the outset of most competitions, some would naturally prefer technology A, and some technology B. If this were the case, the order in which early adopter types arrived would then become crucial, for it would decide how the market might 'tip'.

Consider now a full model that shows this. We now allow two types of adopters, R and S, with 'natural' preferences for A and B respectively, and with payoffs as in Table 26.2. Suppose each potential-adopter type is equally prevalent, but that the actual 'arrivals' of R and S agents are subject to 'small unknown events' outside the model, so to speak. Then all we can say is that it is equally likely that an R or an S will arrive next to make their choice. Initially at least, if an R-agent arrives at the 'adoption window' to make his choice, he will adopt A; if an S-agent arrives, he will adopt B. Thus the difference in adoptions between A and B moves up or down by one unit depending on whether the next adopter is an R or an S, that is, it moves up or down with probability one-half. This process is a simple gambler's coin-toss random walk. There is only one complication. If by 'chance' a large number of R-types cumulates in the line of choosers, A will then be heavily adopted and hence improved in payoff. In fact, if A gains a sufficient lead over B in adoptions, it will pay S-types choosing to switch to A. Then both R- and S-types will be adopting A, and only A, from then on. The adoption process will then become locked in to technology A. Similarly, if a sufficient number of S-types had by 'chance' arrived to adopt B

Table 26.2 Returns to adopting A or B, given n_A and n_B previous adopters of A and B^a

	Technology A	Technology B
R-agent	$a_R + rn_A$	$b_R + rn_B$
S-agent	$a_S + sn_A$	$b_S + sn_B$

^{a} The model assumes that $a_R > b_R$ and that $b_S > a_S$. Both r and s are positive.

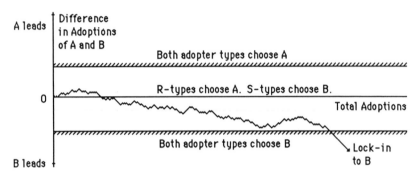

Figure 26.1 Difference in adoptions: random walk with absorbing barriers

over A, B would improve sufficiently to cause R-types to switch to B. The process would instead lock in to B (see Figure 26.1). Our random walk is really a random walk with absorbing barriers on each side, the barriers corresponding to the lead in adoption it takes for each agent-type to switch its choice.

All this is fine. We can now use the well-worked-out theory of random walks to find out what happens to the adoption process in the long run. The important fact about a random walk with absorbing barriers is that absorption occurs eventually with certainty. Thus in the model I have described, the economy *must* lock in to monopoly of one of the two technologies, A or B, but *which* technology is not predictable in advance. Also, the order of choice of agent is not 'averaged away'. On the contrary, it decides the eventual market outcome. Thus, the process is *non-ergodic*—or more informally we can say that it is *path-dependent* in the sense that the outcome depends on the way in which adoptions build up, that is, on the path the process takes. As before, the process becomes inflexible: once lock in occurs the dominant technology continues to be chosen; hence it continues to improve, so that an ever larger boost to the payoff of the excluded technology would be needed to resuscitate it. Further, it is easy to construct examples in which this 'greedy algorithm' of each agent taking the technology that pays off best at his time of choice may miss higher

rewards to the future adoption and development of the excluded technology. As in the preliminary model, economic efficiency is not guaranteed.

This model, like all theoretical models, is obviously stylized. But it does
capture an important general characteristic of competition between
technologies with increasing returns. Where the competition is not dead at
the outset, with a single technology dominating from the start, the
adoption process is inherently unstable, and it can be swayed by the
cumulation of small 'historical' events, or small heterogeneities, or small
differences in timing. Thus low-level events, stemming from the inevitable
graininess present in the economy, can act to drive the process into the
'gravitational orbit' of one of the two (or, with several technologies competing, many) possible outcomes. What we have in this simple model is
'order' (the eventual adoption-share outcome) emerging from 'fluctuation'
(the inherent randomness in the arrival sequence). In modern terminology,
our competing-technologies adoption process is therefore a *self-organising
process* (Prigogine, 1976). (For further details on self-organisation, see the
chapters of Silverberg, Corncelli and Dosi, and Dosi and Orsenigo in this
volume).

Of course, it could be objected that at some level—in some all-knowing
Laplacian world—the arrival sequence in our model is fore-ordained, and
that therefore the outcome that this sequence implies is fore-ordained, and
that therefore our technology competition is determinate and predictable.
Ultimately this comes down to a question of modelling strategy. Where
increasing returns are present, different patterns of small events—whether
known or not—can lead to very different outcomes. If they are unknown at
the outset, if for practical purposes they lie beneath the resolution of our
model, we must treat them as random; so that unless we believe we know
all events that can affect the build-up of adoptions and can therefore
include them explicitly, models of technological competition must typically
include a random component. In the model above, randomness was introduced by lack of knowledge of the arrival sequence of the adopters. But in
other models it could have different sources. Randomness might, for
example, enter in a homogeneous adopter-type model because technological improvements occur in part by unpredictable breakthroughs. The
subject is new enough that even obvious extensions like this have not yet
been studied. There may be a wide class of competing-technology models,
but we would expect to see much the same properties as we found above
upheld: inflexibility or lock-in of outcome; non-predictability; possible
inefficiency; and non-ergodicity or path-dependence.

Do real-world competitions between technologies show these properties? Does the economy sometimes lock in to an inferior technology because
of small, historical events? It appears that it does. Light-water reactors at
present account for close to 100 per cent of all US nuclear power installa-
tions and about 80 per cent of the world market. They were originally
adapted from a highly compact unit designed to propel the first American
nuclear submarine, the USS *Nautilus*, launched in 1954 (Weinberg, 1954).

A series of circumstances—among them the US Navy's role in early construction contracts, political expediency within the National Security Council, the behavior of key personages like Admiral Rickover, and the Euratom Program—acted to favor light water, so that learning and construction experience gained with light water early on locked the market in by the mid-1960s (Cowan, 1987). And yet the engineering literature consistently argues that, given equal development, the gas-cooled design would have been superior (Agnew, 1981).

Similarly, gasoline now dominates as the power source for automobiles. It may well be the superior alternative, but certainly in 1895 it was held to be the least promising option. It was hard to obtain in the right grade; it was dangerous; and it required more numerous and more sophisticated moving parts than steam. Throughout the period 1890–1920, developers, with predilections depending on their previous engineering experience, produced constantly improving versions of the steam, gasoline and electric automobiles. But a series of circumstances—among them, in the North American case, unlikely ones like a 1895 horseless carriage competition which appears to have influenced Ransom Olds in his decision to switch from steam to gasoline, and an outbreak in 1914 of hoof-and-mouth disease that shut down horse troughs where steam cars drew water (McLaughlin, 1954; Arthur, 1984)—gave gasoline enough of a lead that it subsequently proved unassailable. Whether steam and electric cars, given equal development, could have been superior is not clear; but this question remains under constant debate in the engineering literature (Burton, 1976; Strack, 1970).

Is lock-in to a possibly inferior technology permanent? Theoretically it is, where the source of increasing returns is learning-by-using, at least until yet newer technologies come along to render the dominant one obsolete. But lock-in need not be permanent if network externalities are the source. Here, if a technology's advantage is mainly that most adopters are 'going along' with it, a coordinated changeover to a superior collective choice can provide escape. In an important paper, Farrell and Saloner (1985) showed that as long as agents know other agents' preferences, each will decide independently to 'switch' if a superior alternative is available. But where they are uncertain of others' preferences and intentions, there can be 'excess inertia': each agent would benefit from holding the other technology but individually none dares change in case others do not follow.

Whatever the source of increasing returns in competitions between technologies, the presence of lock-in and sudden release causes the economy to lose a certain smoothness of motion.

Technology structure: the path-dependent Strong Law of Large Numbers

In the discussion so far, we have derived some basic ideas and properties of technology competition from a dynamic model with a very particular linear-returns-from-learning mechanism. We would like to be able to handle competing-technology problems with more general assumptions and returns-to-adoption mechanisms. In particular we are interested in qualitative questions such as whether, and under what circumstances, an adoption market must end up dominated by a single technology.

In thinking about the type of analytical framework we would need for more general versions of the problem, it seems important to preserve two properties: (i) that choices between alternative technologies are affected by the numbers of each alternative present in the adoption market at the time of choice; equivalently, that choices are affected by current market shares; (ii) that small events outside the model may influence the process, so that a certain amount of randomness must be allowed for. Thus the 'state' of the market may not determine the next choice, but rather the probability of each alternative being chosen.

Consider a dynamical system that abstracts and allows for these two properties. I will call it an *allocation process*. At each time that a choice occurs, a unit addition or allocation is made to one of K categories, with probabilities $p_1(x)$, $p_2(x)$ . . ., $p_K(x)$, respectively, where this vector of probabilities p is a function of x, the vector giving the proportion of units currently in categories 1 to K (out of the total number n so far in all categories). In our competing technologies problem, this corresponds to a choice of one technology from K competing alternatives, each 'time' of choice, with probabilities that depend upon the numbers of each alternative already adopted and therefore upon current adoption shares.[1] (For a given problem, if we know the source of randomness and the payoff-returns at each state of the market, we can, in principle at least, derive these probabilities as a function of adoption shares.)

Our question is: what happens to the long–run proportions (or adoption shares) in such a dynamical system? What long-run technological structures can emerge? The standard probability-theory tool for this type of problem is the Strong Law of Large Numbers which makes statements about long-run proportions in processes where increments are added at successive times. For example, if we successively add a unit to the 'category' Heads with probability 1/2 in tossing a coin, the standard Strong Law tells us that the proportion of Heads must settle to 0.5. But we cannot use the standard Strong Law in our process. We do not have the required *independent* increments. Instead we have increments—unit adoptions or allocations to technologies 1 through K—which occur with probabilities influenced by past increments. We have a 'coin' whose probability of Heads changes with the proportion of Heads tossed previously.

We can still generate a Strong Law for our dependent-increment process. Suppose we consider the mapping from present proportions, or adoption shares, to the probability of adoption, as with the two examples in Figure 26.2, where $K = 2$. We can see that where the probability of adoption A is higher than its market share, there would be a tendency in the allocation (or adoption) process for A to increase in proportion; and

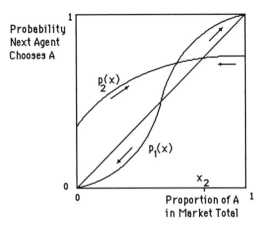

Figure 26.2   Probability of adoption as a function of adoption share

where it is lower, there would be a tendency for it to decrease. If the proportions or shares in each category settle down as total allocations increase, then they should settle down at a fixed point of this mapping. In 1983 Arthur, Ermoliev and Kaniovski proved that (under certain technical conditions) indeed this conjecture is true.[2] Allocation processes indeed settle down in the long run, with probability one, to an unchanging vector of proportions (adoption shares) represented by one of the fixed points of the mapping from proportions (or adoption shares) to the probability of adoption. They converge to a vector of adoption shares x where $x = p(x)$. Not all fixed points are eligible. Only 'attracting' or stable fixed points (ones that expected motions lead toward) can emerge as the long-run outcomes. (Thus in Figure 26.2 the possible long-run shares are 0 and 1 for the function p_1 and x_2 for the function p_2.) Of course, where there are multiple fixed points, *which* one is chosen depends on the path taken by the process: it depends upon the cumulation of the random events that occur along the way. This very general Strong Law for dependent-increment processes (which, following convention, I shall label 'AEK') generalizes the conventional Strong Law of Large Numbers.

The *allocation process* framework, with its corresponding Strong Law, applies to a wide variety of self-organizing or autocatalytic problems in economics and physics (Arthur, Ermoliev and Kaniovski, 1984, 1987; Arthur, 1986, 1987). For our competing-technology purposes, however, we now have a powerful piece of machinery that enables us to investigate the possible long-run adoption outcomes under different adoption-market mechanisms. For a particular problem we would proceed in three steps:

1. Detail the particular mechanisms at work in the adoption process, paying special attention to returns functions, heterogeneities, and sources of randomness.

2. Use this knowledge to derive the probabilities of choice of each technology explicitly as a function of current adoption shares.
3. Use the AEK Strong Law to derive actual long-run possible adoption shares as the stable fixed points of the adoption-share-to-probability mapping.

A number of studies now use this technique (see, for example, David, 1986). The 'informational increasing returns' model of Arthur (1985b) is an example. In this model risk-adverse potential adopters are uncertain about the actual payoff of two fixed payoff technologies they can choose from. They gather information by 'polling' some random sample of previous adopters. (Neither learning-by-using nor network effects are present.) Increasing returns come about because, if adopters of A are more numerous, the next chooser will likely sample more A's than B's, and will therefore be better informed on A. Being risk-averse, he will therefore choose A with a probability that increases with A's proportion of x of the market. Application of the AEK Strong Law to a rigorous model of this mechanism yields precise circumstances under which 'informational increasing returns' allow stable fixed points only at the points $x = 0$ and $x = 1$. That is, it yields circumstances under which informational increasing returns alone cause eventual monopoly of A or of B with probability 1.

When is technological monopoly inevitable?

Is it inevitable that one technology must eventually shut out the others when there are increasing returns to adoption? The answer is no. Consider a more general version of the heterogeneous-adopter-unknown-arrival-sequence model, in which there is now a continuum of agent types rather than just two. We can now think of agents—potential adopters—as distributed over adoption payoffs as in Figure 26.3. An adopter is chosen at random from this probability distribution each time a choice is to be made; and the distribution itself shifts either to the right or upward as returns to A or B increase with an adoption of either A or B respectively. Monopoly—lock-in to a single technology—corresponds to the distribution of payoffs getting 'driven' over the 45° line in this two-technology case. (We assume the distribution of adopter payoffs has 'bounded support'—that is, it does not tail off to infinity in any direction.) Where K technologies compete, we can use the AEK Strong Law to show that where there is no ceiling to the increasing returns (so that returns increase without bound as adoptions increase) then sooner or later one technology *must* by the cumulation of chance achieve sufficient adoption advantage to drive the distribution of adopters 'over the line'. With unbounded increasing returns eventual monopoly by a single technology is indeed inevitable (Arthur, 1986).

But where returns to adoption increase but are bounded, as when learning effects eventually become exhausted, monopoly is no longer

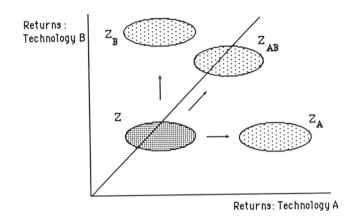

Figure 26.3 Payoffs to adoption of A and B under a continuum of adopter types[a]

[a] At the outset adopter payoffs lie in set Z. Adoptions of technology A only shift this set horizontally to the right as in Z_A. Adoptions of B only shift it vertically as in Z_B. Adoptions of A and B shift it diagonally as in Z_{AB}.

inevitable. The reason is interesting. In this case, certain sequences of adopter types could bid the returns to both technologies upward more or less in concert. These technologies could then reach their 'increasing returns ceilings' together, with adopter-type-payoffs still straddled across the 45° line (as with Z_{AB} in Figure 26.3), and thus with the adoption market shared from then on. But other adopter-arrival sequences may push the payoff distribution across the line early on. Thus with increasing returns to adoption that are bounded, the general finding is that some 'event histories' dynamically will lead to a shared market; other event histories lead to monopoly (Arthur, 1986).

Exact conditions for monopoly in the strategic-competition case where technologies exist as 'sponsored' products are not yet known. Hanson (1985) explored a version of this IBM-versus-Apple problem, building on the basic linear-increasing-returns model above. He assumed that firms could price technologies and thereby manipulate adoption payoffs in a market where heterogeneous adopters arrived at random. Hanson was able to show in this stochastic-duopoly problem that firms would price low early on to gain adoptions, possibly even taking losses in an arm-wrestling match for market share. If both firms were evenly matched enough to stay in the market under these circumstances, then sooner or later the cumulation of 'chance events' might allow one firm sufficient adoption advantage to tip the market in its favor. It would then have sufficient advantage to be able to raise its price and take monopoly profits, while keeping the other firm on the contestable margin of the market. Using AEK, Hanson was able to detail certain conditions under which monopoly by a single-technology-product would be inevitable. It is clear, however, that conditions can be constructed where the markets can also end up shared. For example, when increasing returns are bounded, and firms discount future income heavily so that they are mainly interested in present sales, neither firm may wish to price low early on. Neither might then eventually win the 'natural customers' of the other and the result would be a shared market.

Competing standards and the role of expectations

The term 'standard' has two meanings in the technology literature: that of a convention or code of practice, such as distributing alternating current at 110 volts or transmitting it at 60 hertz; and that of the technology or method or code that comes to dominate—that becomes 'standard'. Standards in the first sense—conventions—can compete much the same as method-technologies do, for a market of adherents, or users, or adopters. Competing standards raise somewhat different issues from competing technologies (see David, 1986, and the papers of Katz and Shapiro, and Farrell and Saloner). I will treat standards here only in so far as they overlap with our dynamics-of-adoption problem.

With standards, learning, information and production externalities are less important and the main sources of increasing returns are network externalities and possibly technological interrelatedness. Both sources confer benefits if *future* adopters go along with one's choice. This introduces something not yet considered in our discussion—*expectations*.

Katz and Shapiro, in an important paper (1985), consider a static version of the problem of competing 'networks' of different standards, in which 'network externalities' accrue to increased network size. The networks are provided by firms which must determine network size in advance. It pays firms to provide large networks if potential adopters expect these networks to be large and thereby commit their choice to them. Therefore if, prior to adoption, sufficient numbers of agents believe that network A will have a large share of adopters, it will; but if sufficient believe B will have a large share, *it* will. Katz and Shapiro showed that there could be multiple 'fulfilled-expectation equilibria' that is, multiple sets of eventual network adoption shares that fulfil prior expectations.

In this simple but important model, expectations are given and fixed before the adoption process takes place. More realistically, if adoption were not instantaneous, potential adopters might change or modify their expectations as the fortunes of alternatives changed during the adoption process itself. One possible formulation (Arthur, 1985a) is to assume that agents form expectations in the shape of beliefs about the adoption process they are in. That is, they form probabilities on the future states of the adoption process—probabilities that are conditioned on the numbers of current adoptions of the competing alternatives. Thus these probabilities, or beliefs, change and respond as the adoption market changes. (We would have a *fulfilled-equilibrium-stochastic-process* if the *actual* adoption process that results from agents acting on these beliefs turns out to have conditional probabilities that are identical to the *believed* process.) In this model, if one standard, or technology, gets ahead by 'chance' adoptions, its increased probability of doing well in the adoption market will further enhance expectations of its success. Analysis here confirms the basic Katz and Shapiro finding. Adaptive or dynamic expectations act to destabilize further an already unstable situation: lock-in to monopoly positions now occurs more easily.

Policy issues

We have seen that in uncontrolled competitions between technologies with learning effects, or network externalities, or other sources of increasing returns to adoption, there is no guarantee that the 'fittest' technology—the one with superior, long-run potential—will survive. There are therefore grounds for intervention.

Where a central authority with full information on future returns to alternative adoption paths knows which technology has superior long-run potential, it can of course attempt to 'tilt' the market in favor of this technology. Timing is, of course, crucial here (Arthur, 1983): in Paul David's phrase (1986) there are only 'narrow windows' in which policy would be effective.

More often, though, it will not be clear in advance which technologies have most potential promise. The authorities then face the difficult problem of choosing which infant technologies to subsidize or bet on. This yields a version of the multi-arm bandit problem (in which a gambler plays several arms of a multi-arm bandit slot machine, trying to ascertain which has the highest probability of producing jackpots). Cowan (1987) has shown that, where central authorities subsidize increasing-return technologies on the basis of their current estimates of future potential, locking into inferior technologies is less likely than in the uncontrolled adoption case. But it is still possible. An early run of bad luck with a potentially superior technology may cause the central authority, perfectly rationally, to abandon it. Even with central control, escape from inferior technological paths is not guaranteed. This finding is important for projects like the US Strategic Defense Initiative, where ground-based excimer lasers, particle-beam weapons, X-ray lasers, homing vehicles and other devices compete for government subsidy on the basis of expected long-run promise. Where each of these improves with development, it is likely that lock-in to one will occur; however it may not be lock-in to the one with superior long-run potential.

It may sometimes be desirable as a policy option to keep more than one technology 'alive', to avoid monopoly problems (if the technology is marketed), or to retain 'requisite variety' as a hedge against shifts in the economic environment or against future 'Chernobyl' revelations that the technology is unsafe. The question of using well-timed subsidies to prevent the adoption process 'tipping' and shutting out technologies has not yet been looked at. But its structure—that of artificially stabilising a naturally unstable dynamical process—is a standard one in stochastic feedback control theory.

Some research questions

Several open or only partially resolved research questions have already been mentioned. Besides these, there are at least three major classes of problems that I believe would benefit from future study:

1. *Recontracting models*. Where the sources of increasing returns is learning-by-using, results would change little if adopters could re-enter the 'queue' and change their choice at a future date. What counts with learning is the previous number of adoptions of a technology, not the fact that an agent is choosing a second time.[3] Where the source is network externalities, results *would* change substantially. In this case, with agents changing their preferences occasionally as well as striving to go along with the more prevalent alternative, recontracting or changing choice would take place as adoptions built up and might continue even when the market was at its full, saturated size. We would then have something akin to a stochastic version of the Farrell and Saloner (1985) model. The important difference from our earlier models is that with 'deaths' as well as 'births' of adoptions allowed, increments to market-share position would tend to be of constant order of magnitude. Adoption processes with recontracting would therefore tend to show convergence in distribution rather than strong convergence, with 'punctuated equilibria' possible in the shape of long sojourns near or at monopoly of one technology coupled with inter-mittent changeover to monopoly by a different technology. This type of structure has counterparts in genetics, sociology and in far-from-equilibrium thermodynamics (see Haken, 1978; Weidlich and Haag, 1983). But it has not yet been studied in the technology context.

2. *Empirical studies*. So far we have two excellent historical studies on the set of events and varied sources of increasing returns that led to dominance of the QWERTY typewriter keyboard (David, 1985) and the dominance of alternating current (David and Bunn, 1987). For most present-day uses, alternating current indeed appears to be superior to the alternative, direct current. The QWERTY keyboard, however, may be slightly inferior to the alternative Dvorak keyboard. Norman and Rumelhard (1983) find Dvorak faster by 5 per cent. Missing as yet, however, are detailed empirical studies of the actual

choice-by-choice dynamics of technological competitions. For prominent competitions such as that between nuclear reactors it might be possible to put together a complete account of the adoption sequence and the events that accompanied it. This would allow identification and parameter estimation of the stochastic dynamics of an *actual* rather than a theoretical case.

3. *Spatial technological competition*. One of the striking features of the classical technology diffusion literature (Griliches, 1957; David, 1969) is its concern with the spatial dimension—with the fact that a technology diffuses geographically as well as temporally. In the *competing* technologies problem, geographical diffusion would of course also be present. The spatial dimension would become particularly important if returns to adoption were affected by neighbors' choices. This was the case historically in competitions between railroad gauges (Puffert, 1988) where it was advantageous to adopt a gauge that neighboring railroads were using. The dynamics of spatial-technology competitions have not been explored yet. But they would resemble those of the well-known Ising model in physics and voter models in probability theory, where dipoles and voters respectively are influenced by the states of their nearest neighbors (Liggett, 1979). Here geographical clusters of localities locked in to different technologies might emerge, with long-run adoption structure depending crucially on the particular spatial increasing-returns mechanism at work.

Conclusion

In the classical literature on the economics of technology, a new and superior technology competes to replace an old and inferior one. In this new literature, two or more superior technologies compete with *each other*, possibly to replace an outmoded one. Competition assumes a stronger form. In the competing technologies problem, the theory that emerges is a theory of non-convex allocation. There are multiple equilibria—multiple possible long-run adoption-share outcomes. The cumulation of small 'random' events drives the adoption process into the domain of one of these outcomes, not necessarily the most desirable one. And the increasing-returns advantage that accrues to the technology that achieves dominance keeps it locked in to its dominant position.

I have indicated that competing technologies are examples of self-organising, order-through-fluctuation systems. They are also examples of evolutionary systems, although the mechanisms are quite different from the ones in Nelson and Winter (1982). Where competing technologies possess increasing returns to adoption, one technology can exercise 'competitive exclusion' on the others; if it has a large proportion of natural adopters it will have a 'selectional advantage'; and the importance of early events results in a 'founder effect' mechanism akin to that in genetics.

The dynamical picture of the long-term economy that results is less like that of a sphere smoothly rolling on a flat surface, with its point of contact with the ground unique and ever changing, and more like that of a polytope lurching down a slope. Where technologies compete, patterns—technology adoption structures—lock in. But as time passes and new technological competitions come about the old patterns are changed, shaken up and re-formed, and in due course a new one is locked in.

To the extent that this happens, there may be theoretical limits as well as practical ones to the predictability of the economic future.

Notes

1. If these probabilities depend on *numbers adopted* rather than directly on market shares we can write them as $(p_1(nx), p_2(nx), p_K(nx))$. This becomes equivalent to a probability function p_n that depends on 'time' n as well as adoption share x.
2. Hill, Lane and Sudderth proved a version of this theorem in 1980 for the case $K = 2$ and p unchanging with time n. The informally stated version in the text holds for $K \geqslant 2$ and for time-varying functions p_n provided they converge to a limiting function p (Arthur, Ermoliev and Kaniovski, 1983, 1984, 1986). Technically, the sequence of Borel functions p_n needs to converge to p at a rate faster than $1/n$ converges to zero; the set of fixed points of p needs to have a finite number of connected components, and for $K > 2$ convergence to a point rather than to a cycle or more complex attractor requires the deterministic dynamics formed by the expected motion of the process to be a gradient system. The 1986 paper is perhaps the best introduction to this theorem.
3. Agent arrivals, if second-time choosers, might, however, be dependent on the previous arrival sequence

References

Agnew, H.M. (1981), 'Gas-cooled nuclear power reactors', *Scientific American*, vol. 244, pp. 55–63.

Arthur, W.B. (1983), 'Competing technologies and lock-in by historical events: the dynamics of allocation under increasing returns', International Institute for Applied Systems Analysis, Paper WP-83-90, Laxenburg, Austria.

-— (1984), 'Competing technologies and economic prediction', *Options*, International Institute for Applied Systems Analysis, Laxenburg, Austria.

—— (1985a), 'Competing technologies and lock-in by historical events: the dynamics of allocation under increasing returns', revised from 1983 paper as Center for Economic Policy Research, Paper 43, Stanford, *Economic Journal*, 99 March 1989.

—— (1985b), 'Information, imitation and the emergence of technological structures', Stanford, mimeo.

—— (1986), 'Industry location and the importance of history', Center for Economic Policy Research, Paper 84, Stanford.

—— (1987), 'Urban systems and historical path-dependence', Chapter 4 in R.

Herman and J. Ausubel (eds.) *Cities and Their Vital Systems*, National Academy Press, Washington, D.C.

Arthur, W.B., Ermoliev, Yu. M., and Kaniovski, Yu. M. (1983), 'On generalized urn schemes of the polya kind' (in Russian), *Kibernetika*, vol. 19, pp. 49–56; English trans. in *Cybernetics*, vol. 19, pp. 61–71.

—— (1984), 'Strong Laws for a class of path-dependent urn processes', in Arkin, Shiryayev and Wets (eds.), *Proceedings of the International Conference on Stochastic Optimization, Kiev 1984*, Berlin, Heidelberg, New York, Tokyo, Springer.

—— (1987), 'Path-dependent processes and the emergence of macro-structure', *European Journal of Operational Research*, vol. 30, pp. 294–303.

Burton, Rodney L. (1976), 'Recent advanced in vehicular steam engine efficiency', Society of Automotive Engineers, Preprint 760340.

Cowan, R. (1987), 'Backing the wrong horse: sequential technology choice under increasing returns,' Ph.D.diss., Stanford.

David, P. (1985), 'Clio and the economics of QWERTY', *American Economic Review, Proceedings*, vol. 75, pp. 332–7.

—— (1969), 'A contribution to the theory of diffusion', Memo 71, Stanford Center for Economic Growth, Stanford.

—— (1986), 'Some new standards for the economics of standardization in the information age', Paper 79, Center for Economic Policy Research, Stanford.

David, P. and Bunn, J. (1987), 'The battle of the systems and the evolutionary dynamics of network technology rivalries', Stanford, mimeo.

Farrell, J. and Saloner, G. (1985), 'Standardization, compatibility and innovation', *Rand Journal of Economics*, vol. 16, pp. 70–83.

—— (1986), 'Installed base and compatibility', *American Economics Review*, vol. 76, pp. 940–55.

—— (1986), 'Standardization and variety', *Economic Letters*, vol. 20, pp. 71–4.

Fletcher, W. (1904), *English and American Steam Carriages and Traction Engines*, reprinted, Devon, David & Charles, 1973.

Frankel, M. (1955), 'Obsolescence and technological change in a maturing economy', *American Economic Review*, vol. 45, pp. 296–319.

Griliches, Z. (1957), 'Hybrid corn: an exploration in the economics of technological change', *Econometrica*, vol. 25, pp. 501–22.

Hanson, W. (1985), 'Bandwagons and orphans: dynamic pricing of competing systems subject to decreasing costs', Ph.D.Diss., Stanford.

Haken, H. (1978), *Synergetics*, Berlin, Heidelberg, New York, Tokyo, Springer.

Katz, M. (1986), 'The economics of standardization in networks industries', Princeton, mimeo.

Katz. M. and Shapiro, C. (1985), 'Network externalities, competition and compatibility', *American Economic Review*, vol. 75, pp. 424–40.

—— (1986), 'Technology adoption in the presence of network externalities', *Journal of Political Economy*, vol. 94, pp. 822–41.

Liggett, T. (1979), 'Interacting Markov processes', in Lect. Notes in Biomath 38, Berlin, Heidelberg, New York, Tokyo, Springer.

McLaughlin, C. (1954), 'The Stanley steamer: a study in unsuccessful innovation', *Explorations in Entrepreneurial Hist.*, vol. 7, pp. 37–47.

Nelson, R. and Winter, S. (1982), *An Evolutionary Theory of Economic Change*, Harvard, Mass., The Belknap Press of Harvard University Press.

Norman, D. and Rumelhart, D. (1983), 'Studies of typing from the LNR Research

Group', in W. Cooper (ed.), *Cognitive Aspects of Skilled Typewriting*, Berlin, Heidelberg, New York, Tokyo, Springer.

Prigogine, I. (1976), 'Order through fluctuation: self-organization and social system', in E. Jantsch and C.H. Waddington (eds.), *Evolution and Consciousness*, New York, Addison-Wesley.

Puffert, D. (1988), 'Network externalities and technological preference in the selection of railway gauges', Ph.D.dissertation, Stanford, forthcoming.

Rosenberg, N. (1982), *Inside the Black Box: Technology and Economics*, Cambridge, Cambridge University Press.

Strack, W.C. (1970), 'Condensers and boilers for steam-powered cars', NASA Technical Note, TN D-5813, Washington, DC.

Weidlich, W. and Haag, G. (1983), *Concepts and Models of a Quantitative Sociology*, Berlin, Heidelberg, New York, Tokyo, Springer.

Weinberg, A.M. (1954), 'Power reactors', *Scientific American*, vol. 191, pp. 33–9.

27 Formalizing growth regimes

Robert Boyer

Centre d'Etudes Prospectives d'Economie Mathematique Appliquees a la Planification,
Centre National de la Recherche Scientifique, ecole des hautes etudes en Sciences Sociales,
Paris

Technological change and macroeconomics

This chapter deals with some methods for embodying technical change in macroeconomic models, however simple. In a sense it is a follow-up to Chapters 2 and 4. Both of them discuss the need for an analysis of the conditions which must hold between the technological regime and institutional structures in order to make sustained and relatively stable growth possible, or, conversely, the possible mismatchings at the root of unstable and/or slow growth.

The 'régulation' approach has already tried to elaborate such models, even if they are not totally suitable for the present purpose. In the very beginning of the regulation approach, two sectoral models were built (Aglietta, 1974; Billaudot, 1976). They show the necessity of a connection between the consumption and production goods sectors if accumulation is to be a permanent and relatively stable process. Along the same lines, subsequent works have investigated the specificities of the long post-1945 boom in France (Bertrand, 1978, 1983). In this context, Fordism results from a specific growth regime in which intensive technological change and new forms of social organization promote a complementarity between mass production and consumption, modernization and capital deepening. Furthermore, three theoretical models, corresponding to extensive accumulation, Taylorism and Fordism, have been investigated (Fagerberg, 1984). Similarly, a simple growth model of Kaldorian spirit has been compared with stylized historical facts (Boyer and Coriat, 1987) and then used to analyse the viability of flexible specialization or, alternatively, flexible automation.

In a sense, the model presented here benefits from all these formalizations, but tries to go a little beyond them. On the one hand, the model is simplified and keeps only the core of the relevant mechanisms. It has been suggested (Bertrand, 1983) that an aggregate model can retain a large number of the properties of sectoral/disaggregated analysis. On the other hand, the model is nevertheless more general since it investigates not only Fordist but also a large number of other regimes.

The argument consists of five steps. First, the general hypotheses about technological change and productivity, income distribution and demand formation are presented and lead to a simplified growth model. Second, it is shown that according to the precise features of the productive systems and economic mechanisms, very different growth or crisis regime may exist. Then the predictions of the model are compared to some stylized facts concerning capitalist economies over one or two centuries, the test of these hypotheses being left to future econometric work. Finally, this framework helps us analyse the present economic and technological transition: are the present transformations promoting growth or, on the contrary, deepening unemployment and/or instability? Brief concluding remarks summarize the major findings and propose some areas for future research.

Formalizing the sources of productivity gains and their sharing: back to growth theories

Ideally, the model should distinguish at least between two sectors producing consumption and investment goods. Nevertheless, previous attempts by Boyer (1975), Bertrand (1983) and Fagerberg (1984) do suggest that most of the arguments can be captured within a one-sector model. Thus an aggregate approach is adopted here. The starting point will be a generalization of a previous formalization (Boyer and Coriat, 1987). We want to study a larger variety of accumulation regimes, intensive as well as extensive, with or without mass consumption.

The main hypotheses in a nutshell

The economy is assumed to be closed — thus applicable at the world level or to a national economy not open to external trade. The model could easily be extended to an open economy, as has already been done in, for example, Boyer and Petit (1981a, 1984). We basically want to formalize both productivity gains and their division between wages and profits, i.e. the simultaneous dynamics of production and consumption. Our model will consist of seven endogenous variables, entering into seven behavioural or accounting equations.

Productivity trends plays a prominent role in the system. They are related to three factors. The first is the intensity of innovation as measured by R & D expenditures, number of patents, or the orientation of technical progress towards labour-saving equipment (variable *INNO*). This is supposed to represent a Schumpeterian explanation of productivity. The second is capital deepening, expressed by the investment/output ratio (variable I/Q). This effect could be termed Salterian, since this variable captures the renewal of capital in a vintage model. Third is a Kaldor–Verdoorn effect, linking productivity to output growth via dynamic increasing returns to scale (variable $\overset{\circ}{Q}$). One might imagine learning-by-doing effects, or long-run properties linking the division of labour, productivity and the size of the market. Hence we propose the following productivity equation:

$$P\overset{\circ}{R} = a' + b' . \frac{I}{Q} + d' . \overset{\circ}{Q} + e' \overline{INNO} \quad b', d', e' > 0 \tag{1'}$$

Investment reacts to the dynamism of household consumption (C), according to a traditional Keynesian accelerator effect. But in order to contrast different accumulation regimes, one must add another determinant usually introduced by classical theory: the profit share (PRO/Q). Contemporary research usually combines these two factors: investment is either limited by demand — here restricted to consumption — or by profitability. Furthermore, another Schumpeterian effect might also be of some interest in dealing with technical innovation: if innovations are available, firms will be induced to invest more in new products (variable $INNO$). This leads to the formulation:

$$\frac{I}{Q} = f' + v' . \overset{\circ}{C} + u' . \left[\frac{PRO}{Q} \right] + e'' . \overline{INNO} \quad v', u', e'' > 0 \qquad (2')$$

Households' consumption is modelled in a very traditional way. The marginal propensity to consume is supposed to be different for wages and profits (c_1 and c_2 respectively). Since the other mechanisms are related to medium-term trends, no lags are introduced in the equation. Hence we have the following equation:

$$\overset{\circ}{C} = c_1 . (N \overset{\circ}{.} RW) + c_2 . (\overline{Q - N} \overset{\circ}{.} \overline{RW}) + g \quad c_1 > c_2 > 0 \qquad (3')$$

Wage formation has to be richer in order to deal with at least two polar cases: purely competitive determination of real wages and productivity increases shared with wage earners more or less according to what has been called the Fordist capital–labour compromise. The first mechanism is captured by a linear elasticity of real wages with respect to employment variations (parameter l). The logic of a Phillips curve is therefore extended to real wages analysed in the medium term. The second one is described by a second elasticity with respect to productivity trends (parameter k). As usual, a constant term is added to capture any other factor. This leads to the following equation:

$$R\overset{\circ}{W} = k' . \overset{\circ}{PR} + l' . (\overset{\circ}{N} - \overline{LF}) + h \quad k \geq 0, l \geq 0 \qquad (4')$$

$\overline{LF}$: exogenous evolution of total labour force

Three accounting identities close the model. The first one describes the national accounts identity about resources and uses of total production. The only difficulty is in converting levels into rates of change, α being the share of consumption in total net output for the previous period. The second relation defines changes in employment as the difference between the rate of output growth and productivity increase. Finally, the last equation says that net output is equal to the sum of profit and wages. Thus we have:

$$\overset{\circ}{Q} = \alpha . \overset{\circ}{C} + (1 - \alpha) . \overset{\circ}{I} \quad 0 \leq \alpha \leq 1 \qquad (5')$$

$$\overset{\circ}{N} \approx \overset{\circ}{Q} - \overset{\circ}{PR} \qquad (6')$$

$$\frac{PRO}{Q} = 1 - \frac{RW}{PR} \tag{7'}$$

The basic economic ideas are fairly simple, but the analytics are a little bit more complex, as is usual when variables expressed in levels and rates of change are mixed. So the next step is to build an approximate version which can be completely solved and discussed mathematically without the need for simulations or the use of general fixed point theorems.

A simplified model

In order to do this, the first three equations are linearized and written in a less satisfactory form, but one which is easier to solve. Thus productivity trends in the medium run are assumed to be linearly linked to investment and output rates. Moreover, Schumpeterian variables related to technological change are estimated by incorporating them into the constant term *a*. Similarly, by modifying the traditional accelerator equation, the variation in investment is dependent on consumption and the so-called wage gap, i.e. the difference between productivity and real wages, a very crude proxy for the evolution of the profit share. This change would be detrimental if our aim were to study cycles and stability properties, but seems admissible as far as growth paths are concerned. The last change concerns consumption: profits are assumed to be totally saved, whereas the propensity to consume out of wages is *c*, not necessarily equal to 1. This is a Kaleckian hypothesis, which does not change too much the global properties of the model.

After making these simplifications, the model is now as follows:

THE BASIC MODEL

(1) $\overset{\circ}{PR} = a + b.\overset{\circ}{I} + d.\overset{\circ}{Q}$ Productivity equation

(2) $\overset{\circ}{I} = f + v.\overset{\circ}{C} + u.(\overset{\circ}{PR} - \overset{\circ}{RW})$ Investment equation

(3) $\overset{\circ}{C} = c.(N\overset{\circ}{.}RW) + g$ Consumption equation

(4) $\overset{\circ}{RW} = k.\overset{\circ}{PR} + l.\overset{\circ}{N} + h$ Real wage formation

(5) $\overset{\circ}{Q} = \alpha.\overset{\circ}{C} + (1 - \alpha).\overset{\circ}{I}$ Accounting identities

(6) $\overset{\circ}{N} \approx \overset{\circ}{Q} - \overset{\circ}{PR}$ Accounting identities

ENDOGENOUS VARIABLES: 6   *PR, I, Q, C, RW, N*.

EXOGENOUS VARIABLES: none, since exogenous factors are reflected by the constant terms *a, f* and *h*.

CONDITIONS ON PARAMETERS: $b \geq 0$, $d \geq 0$, $v \geq 0$, $u \geq 0$, $0 \leq c \leq 1$, $k \geq 0$, $l \geq 0$, $0 \leq \alpha \leq 1$.

However simplistic, this framework is rich enough to deal with most of the issues discussed in the previous section. Let us make a list of the various polar cases:

— Technical progress is not only defined by the exogenous trend a— which might be high or low according to long-run evolution—but by various mechanisms related to productivity formation. These could be due either to capital deepening (high b, possibly $d=0$) or to pure increasing returns to scale, without any link with investment ($b=0$, d important). The last case reflects a learning-by-doing effect 'à la Arrow/Wright'.

— Contemporary macroeconomic theory is highly concerned with the question of investment determination: is investment profit-, demand- or credit-led? The present model deals mainly with the two first alternatives. In the pure Keynesian case, only demand expectations play a role in investment decisions ($u=0$, v related to the capital–output ratio). At the opposite extreme, in the Classical Marxian case, the profit rate is the only factor determining investment ($v=0$, u important).

— Similarly, wage formation is at the core of many discussions about the links between economic policy and the rigidity or flexibility of labour markets. In this model, and contrary to the traditional presentation, the indexation of wages to productivity is seen as the outcome of a Fordist compromise, and not that much as due to pure market mechanisms (in that case, $l=0$, k is positive or even close to one, with $h\approx0$). In the other extreme case, wage formation is purely competitive, i.e. linked to the evolution of employment, for a given trend in total labour force ($k=0$, l positive and high).

The task then is to play with this small model by first studying in the next section its analytical properties, and then in the following section looking for interpretations of very stylized historical facts.

Very contrasted growth or crisis configurations may exist

For simplicity, the solution of the model can be organized around a very simple idea: where does the productivity growth trend come from? A subpart of the model can be solved in order to associate such a trend with any given level of growth (relation I). Second question: how are productivity gains shared between wages and profits? Another part of the model (of course, with some common equations) allows us to compute the growth in demand associated with each productivity rate (relation II). Let us briefly study these two parts.

The productivity regimes: the joint result of technology, demand and income distribution

Using equations (1), (2), (3) and (4), one gets the following 'sub-reduced form' for productivity:

$$\text{(I)} \quad P\mathring{R} = \frac{b[vc(1+l)-ul]+d}{1-b(vc-u).(k-1-l)} \cdot \mathring{Q} + \frac{a+bf+vg+b(vc-u).h}{1-b(vc-u)(k-1-l)}$$

i.e.

$$P\mathring{R} = B.\mathring{Q} + A$$

One recognizes the usual form of the so-called Kaldor–Verdoorn relations, but the matter is more complex than initially thought by these two authors.

First, such an equation is not purely a matter of technology, since demand formation and income distribution do play a role. The relation is a function of purely technical aspects if and only if investment has no influence upon productivity ($b = 0$), i.e. only in a very special case.

But even if the technical frontier is kept constant, the productivity-growth reduced form can shift or rotate when income distribution changes. For example, when wage earners benefit from more favourable shares (increase in k), the elasticity of productivity with respect to growth increases when investment is more sensitive to demand than to profit ($v/u > 1/c$), and decreases in the opposite case. This last situation might apply to the tendencies observed after 1973, which are characterized by a significant shift in income distribution. This is a possible explanation of the instability stressed by Rowthorn (1975), which seems to be confirmed by the breaking down of the formula since 1973 (Michl, 1984; Boyer and Ralle, 1986a).

Similarly, any change in the investment function shifts the Kaldor–Verdoorn relation in a rather complex manner, since it depends on the whole set of parameters. For low indexation to productivity (i.e. $k < 1 + l$), a strengthening of the profit motive in investment (rise of u) and milder accelerator effects reduce the apparent size of increasing returns to scale. This is the kind of evolution which seems to have been observed during the last decade.

Combining the factors characterizing technology, investment determination and income distribution gives a large set of configurations. Instead of presenting all of them, it is convenient to discuss only major cases (Figure 27.1). It turns out that four very contrasted cases might appear, according to the intensity of the various mechanisms. Let us stress only two major findings. First, in the pure Fordist case, the usual Kaldor–Verdoorn relation is observed only if wage indexing is not too high (case 3), since up to a certain threshold a perverse configuration may emerge (case 4). Second, the same *ex post* reduced form may result from very different mechanisms: purely competitive wage and exhilarationist effects of profit upon investment (case 2), whereas for more likely hypotheses productivity increases are lower, the higher the growth (case 1).

The previous discussion enables us to present a taxonomy of the various technological systems and/or accumulation regimes. The former can be distinguished according to the configuration of the whole set of parameters

Figure 27.1   The various productivity regimes

I.   The pure classical cases

They can be characterized by three principal hypotheses:

  (i)   No increasing returns to scale: $d = 0$
 (ii)   Investment is purely profit driven: $v = 0 \; u \gg 0$
(iii)   No *ex ante* productivity-sharing but competitive mechanism for wages: $k = 0$,
        $l \geq 0$

Then by (I): $P\overset{\circ}{R} = \dfrac{-b.u.l.}{1 - u(1 + l)} \cdot \overset{\circ}{Q} + \dfrac{a + b(f - uh)}{1 - u(1 + l)} = B.\overset{\circ}{Q} + A$

According to the relative size of the effect of profit upon investment and employment upon real wages, two polar cases can be observed.

Case 1: The profit effect is limited   Case 2: The profit effect is important

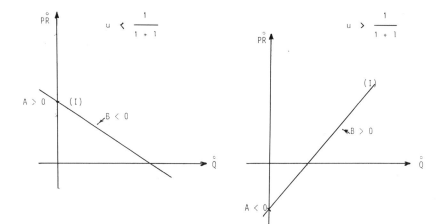

The productivity–growth relation is   The productivity–growth relation is
downward sloping   upward sloping

In both cases we assume that: $u < \dfrac{a + bf}{bh}$

Figure 27.1 The various productivity regimes

II. The pure Fordist cases

By contrast, they are defined by inverting the three hypotheses of the classical case:

(i) Significant increasing returns to scale: $d \gg 0$
(ii) Investment is totally demand driven: $v \gg 0 \ u = 0$
(iii) Productivity-sharing of wages, absence of competitive mechanism: $k \gg 0 \ l = 0$

$$\text{Then by (I): } \overset{\circ}{PR} = \frac{bvc + d}{1 - bvc(k-1)} \cdot \overset{\circ}{Q} + \frac{a + bf + vg + bvch}{1 - bvc(k-1)}$$

By hypothesis $bvc + d > 0$ and it may be assumed that $(a + bf + vg + bvch) > 0$. According to the relative size of the wage indexing and accelerator effects, two other polar cases can be observed:

Case 3: Wage indexing is limited   Case 4: Wage indexing is high

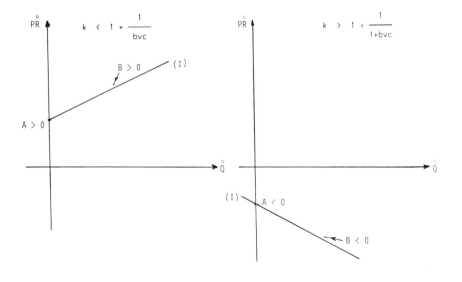

The usual upward-sloping Kaldor–Verdoorn relation appears as a reduced form   A perverse and negative relation between growth and productivity

$(a, b, d, f, v, ...)$. The latter would be defined as mainly extensive or intensive by looking at the reduced form for productivity. Intensive accumulation refers to spillover effects from growth to productivity, and not that much to the size of productivity increases *per se*. Thus extensive accumulation will prevail if B is fairly low, intensive accumulation when B is high.

Demand regimes defined by the wage formation and investment functions

Let us now assess the consequences of a given productivity rate upon the growth of demand, since in this model production is always fixed accordingly. Solving the system without using the productivity equation (1) leads to the following reduced form:

$$\text{(II)} \quad \mathring{Q} = \frac{[\alpha c + (1-\alpha)vc - (1-\alpha)u].(k-l-1)}{1-[\alpha+(1-\alpha)v].c(1+l)+l(1-\alpha).u} . \mathring{PR}$$

$$+ \frac{(1-\alpha)f + (ch+g)[\alpha+(1-\alpha).v] - h(1-\alpha)u}{1-[\alpha+(1-\alpha)v].c(1+l)+l(1-\alpha).u}$$

i.e.

$$\mathring{Q} = D.\mathring{PR} + C$$

We will denote by demand regimes the various configurations taken by this reduced form. Basically, whether the curve slopes upward or downward will depend upon two main factors: first, income distribution, i.e. productivity sharing between wages and profits, and, second, the sensitivity of investment to either profit or demand variations (Figure 27.2).

The complete discussion will not be given here. Instead we shall present four polar cases, combining two extreme hypotheses about investment and income distribution.

— A pure classical demand regime associates profit-led investment with mainly competitive wage formation (configuration 1). In this case, productivity increases promote profits, hence investment and effective demand, which enhance employment, therefore consumption, according to a classical virtuous cumulative growth model. As a consequence, demand increases with productivity. The functioning of this regime can be summarized by a very simple causation mechanism:

$$\text{Productivity} \xrightarrow{+} \text{Profit} \xrightarrow{+} \text{Investment} \xrightarrow{+} \text{Employment} \xrightarrow{+} \text{Consumption}$$

— A hybrid classical demand regime combines demand-led investment with the same competitive wage formation mechanism (configuration 2). The previous mechanisms are then reversed: more productivity induces lower wage increases, hence lower consumption, in such a manner that investment is also reduced via an accelerator based upon

Figure 27.2 The different demand regimes

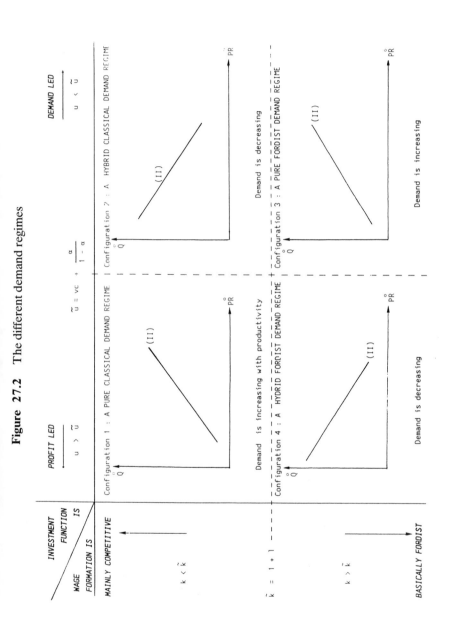

consumption. Therefore, demand is now declining with productivity, according to the following stylized analysis:

$$\text{Productivity} \overset{-}{\rightarrow} \text{Real wages} \overset{+}{\rightarrow} \text{Consumption} \overset{+}{\rightarrow} \text{Investment} \overset{+}{\rightarrow} \text{Employment}$$

— A pure Fordist demand regime associates the same demand-led investment with an explicit sharing of productivity between wages and profits (configuration 3). Now the growth of demand is wage-led: any improvement in productivity raises *ex ante* real wages, hence consumption, investment and effective demand. As in the pure classical case, the law is now increasing but according to a very different mechanism:

$$\text{Productivity} \overset{+}{\rightarrow} \text{Real wages} \overset{+}{\rightarrow} \text{Consumption} \overset{+}{\rightarrow} \text{Investment} \overset{+}{\rightarrow} \text{Employment}$$

But by comparison with the hybrid classical case, the only change relates to real wage formation.

— A hybrid Fordist demand regime can be observed when wage indexation to productivity is up to a certain threshold, whereas investment is now highly sensitive to profits (configuration 4). The rationale of the declining demand curve is clear enough: more productivity induces more consumption (via real wage increases) but less investment (due to declining profits), in such a manner that the second factor plays a dominant role. The causation now runs according to the following diagram:

$$\text{Productivity} \overset{-}{\rightarrow} \text{Profit} \overset{+}{\rightarrow} \text{Investment} \overset{+}{\rightarrow} \text{Employment} \overset{+}{\rightarrow} \text{Consumption}$$

Once again this configuration looks like the hybrid classical one, but the reasons are quite opposite, since the mechanisms of income distribution and demand generation are different indeed.

Finally, a growth (or accumulation) regime can be defined for each combination of productivity-growth relations and demand regimes. Instead of presenting a purely formal analysis, the macro-model will be confronted with the historical trends and periods already examined by the regulation approach, as presented in Chapter 4.

Historical stylized facts over a century: an interpretation

If one considers the evolution of capitalism since the first industrial revolution, the model suggests the possible succession of four stages, combining specific technological systems and forms of socio-economic tuning (Figure 27.3).

The nineteenth century: moderate increasing returns and investment-led growth

This period is basically characterized by the penetration of new methods of production, via rapid industrial investment promoting this new produc-

Figure 27.3 An interpretation of typical historical periods

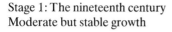

Stage 1: The nineteenth century
Moderate but stable growth

Stage 2: The inter-war period
Structural instability and crisis

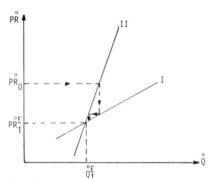

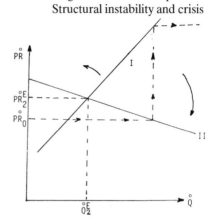

Hypotheses:

1. Moderately increasing returns of scale $(d \cong 0$, but $b > 0)$
2. Competitive wages $(k\ 0,\ l > 0)$
3. Profit-led investment $(v \cong 0,\ u > \tilde{u})$

Hypotheses:

1. Significant returns to scale due to Taylorism $(d > 0,\ b > 0)$
2. Still competitive wages $(k \cong 0,\ l > 0)$
3. Demand-led investment $(v > 0,\ u < \tilde{u})$

Stage 4: The Seventies
Slow and unstable growth: a structural crisis

Stage 3: The 'Roaring Sixties'
Unprecedented high and stable growth

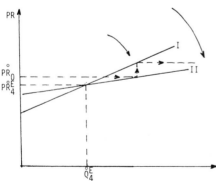

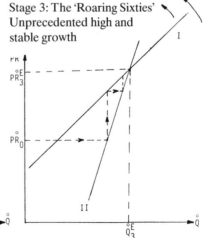

Hypotheses:

1. Exhaustion of increasing returns to scale $(d$ and b declining)
2. An over-indexing of wages to productivity $(k > 1 + l)$
3. The profit motive is back $(v$ is declining, u increasing)

Hypotheses:

1. Fordism brings significant returns to scale $(d > 0,\ b > 0)$
2. Capital–labour compromise over productivity sharing $(k \gtreqless 0\ l \gtreqless 0)$ but $k < 1 + l$
3. Consumption-led investment $(v \gg 0,\ u < \tilde{u})$

tive system. From the technological standpoint, the increasing returns to scale associated with the deepening of the division of labour are in line with the previous trends. Nevertheless, a high ratio of investment allows significant productivity increases. Thus the productivity regime corresponds roughly to a profit-led productivity–growth relationship (as shown by case 2 in Figure 27.5). As far as demand generation is concerned, investment again is the leading factors via an income distribution initially very favourable to entrepreneurs. Wage-earners only benefit from this industrialization process if employment is increasing, wage formation being mainly competitive (the demand regime is close to configuration 1 in Figure 27.2).

Consequently, one can imagine this first stage as associating an average elasticity of demand with a moderately upward-sloping productivity curve (Figure 27.3, stage 1). During this period, industrial crises are observed from time to time, but according to a process which is usually self-regulating, with the exception of the major crisis of 1848 or the Great Depression of 1873–96. It can then be assumed that the growth model is stable, i.e. that any disturbance affecting either productivity or demand levels off. A necessary condition for that property ($|BD| < 1$) is that *ex post* increasing returns and demand elasticity are not too high.

The equilibrium growth path is stable and depends on the accumulation regime. If, for example, innovation raises the exogenous trend of productivity, both productivity and growth rates will be higher. The outcome for employment is related to the elasticity of demand: a reduction if this elasticity is low, an increase if it is high. Similarly, an upward shift usually increases growth and productivity, but the precise results do vary if structural change has effects upon investment, consumption or income distribution.

The inter-war period: a surge of increasing returns and a shift towards demand-led investment

The model allows an interpretation of the contradictions associated with the transition from an extensive to an intensive accumulation regime. In some respects the mode of regulation shows continuities, especially as far as competitive wage formation is concerned. But in other respects two structural changes speed up after the First World War. First, Scientific Management leads to a strengthening of increasing returns, by deepening the division of labour and employing highly specialized equipment. This results in an upward shift of the productivity–growth function (Figure 27.3, stage 2). Second, mass production has to be complemented by mass consumption, so that investment is now linked not only to profits, but also to household consumption. Therefore the demand regime drastically changes, rotating from an upward- to a downward-sloping curve.

The new global regime is then quite new, at odds with the previous one. Of course, medium-term growth rates are logically higher, which explains the unprecedented Roaring Twenties. Potentially, the new technological system accelerates the industrial pace. But the opposite side of the coin has quite dramatic consequences: since the demand regime now declines with productivity, the new technological system ultimately spurs productivity growth but at the expense of employment. Furthermore, the excess of productive capacity over demand is such that the whole system finally becomes unstable. This is a possible theoretical explanation of the vicious spiral of intensive accumulation without explicit mass consumption stressed by previous analyses (Chapter 4 Figure 4.2).

Post-Second World War boom: a capital–labour accord consistent with the technological pattern

After the Second World War the technological paradigm remains more or less the same, but two major structural changes affect income distribution and demand. First, a new capital–labour accord about productivity-sharing induces a brand-new wage mechanism, hence a consumption function increasing with productivity. Second, investment is now more and more linked to demand, and not that much to profit rates, which are already very high. Consequently, aggregate demand becomes an increasing function of productivity, contrary to what was observed during the inter-war period.

The model confirms that there may be a stable and fast growth path within this general accumulation regime with which mass production and consumption are associated (Figure 27.3, Stage 3). The rate of growth is higher, since demand is much more dynamic and spills over to productivity via increasing returns to scale, while capital deepening associated with the accelerator mechanism strengthens even more the productivity–growth relation. The pattern of development is stable if the indexing of wages to productivity is sufficient but not too high, so that it guarantees that any discrepancy between productive capacity and demand is self-correcting (Boyer and Coriat, 1987).

Thus this analysis confirms the previous hypothesis about the shift from an unstable accumulation regime to a stable one during the 1950s. Consequently, the economic system reacts differently to the unfolding of the same technological path. During the inter-war period, more productivity ultimately meant less employment (compare, on Figure 27.3, stage 2 by shifting upwards relation 1). After the Second World War, within the new demand regime, the same movement simultaneously increases productivity, growth and possibly employment (imagine the same shift on Figure 27.3, stage 3).

The present crisis: the exhaustion of the technological path and contradictions over income distribution

The very implementation and diffusion of Fordism set into motion slow adverse trends which finally destroyed the structural stability of the system, and thus made it very vulnerable to external shocks, whether stemming from energy supply or financial markets. Among the three factors to be taken into account, the struggle for external competitiveness cannot be treated within a closed macroeconomic model, but the other two have consequences which are easier to analyse.

The fact that most economies operated at quasi-full-employment level largely benefited wage earners, who at the end of the 1960s won significant increases in real wages and a rise in the degree of indexing, explicitly in terms of consumer prices, implicitly in terms of medium-term productivity gains. Therefore demand becomes more sensitive to productivity, if investment is still buoyant, and even if profit trends might be deteriorating. Above a certain threshold the growth path becomes unstable (Figure 27.3, stage 4), which seems likely given the developments in OECD countries since the early 1970s.

The erratic character of demand aggravates the productivity problem, since markets are more and more difficult to forecast and do not allow the increasing returns associated with stable and growing markets to be realized. But the underlying difficulties of Fordism are much more severe: more capital is needed to get the same labour–productivity growth, and the maturing of the technological system makes it less efficient in improving industrial organization. This second change shifts downward the productivity–growth function (for example, in the United States) or even reduces drastically the significance of the Kaldor–Verdoorn hypothesis (Mitchl, 1984; Boyer and Ralle, 1986a). Consequently, the rate of growth is itself reduced, a second feature of the present crisis.

Of course, this sketch is more suggestive than really demonstrative. Many detailed statistical and econometric studies will be needed in order to support these hypotheses. Preliminary estimates for the United States (Caussat, 1981) or EEC countries (Boyer and Petit, 1986) seem rather promising as regards the general structure of the model, if not the precise timing of the stages (Boyer, 1986a). It is now time to derive some prospective views from this historical perspective.

The present economic and technological transition: is a new growth regime emerging?

It would take us too far afield to present the various and very contradictory transformations now affecting different institutional structures (nature of competition, wage–labour nexus, state interventions, international and monetary regimes). One can find such analyses in recent publications by the authors of the 'régulation school' (Aglietta and Orlean, 1982; Aglietta and Brender, 1984; Boyer, 1986c; Boyer et al., 1987). Here the emphasis will be upon both the technological system and the wage–labour nexus. Among many combinations of different evolutions, two typical scenarios will now be presented which serve as illustrations of the use of the model.

Wage austerity and traditional technical flexibility: towards stagnation?

It may not be an exaggeration to talk about a complete breakdown of the whole pattern of industrial relations typical of Fordism: decentralization of collective bargaining, general de-indexing, guidelines by governments implying stability of real wages, and significant changes in wage differentials. Thus the shift in income distribution observed after 1973 has been reversed during the 1980s, with productivity gains now accruing mainly to profits and far less to wage-earners.

If this change is assumed to be a structural and lasting phenomenon, its consequences can be analysed within the previous Fordist growth model. It would be interpreted as a de-indexing of wages with respect to productivity. If such a transformation were permanent, the consequences would be twofold (Figure 27.4, step 1). Up to some threshold for de-indexing, the growth pattern is again stable since demand is then kept in line with production, which is new by comparison with the 1970s (step 0). But this result has a major drawback: the equilibrium growth rate is lower since consumption and hence investment (via an accelerator mechanism) are less dynamic.

A second change concerns investment determinants. It seems that the econometric equations estimated before the 1980s usually overestimate the recovery of investment for a given increase in aggregate demand (for example, Artus and Muet, 1984). Two different factors might explain this new pattern. First, the atypical configuration of most key macroeconomic variables (level of demand, rate of return, real interest rate) makes firms more cautious before deciding upon investment. Second, the specialists in industrial organization are suggesting that the introduction of electronic devices into industrial processes and services has reduced the bottlenecks associated with earlier Fordist equipment, which was highly specialized. Since the same equipment can be shifted from one product to another of the same variety, the investment level will react slower and to a lesser extent to the same increase in demand (Bultel, 1983; Kundig, 1984).

Whatever the reasons (the macroeconomic ones might be dominant for the 1980s, the flexibility argument possibly more significant in the long run), this change weakens the accelerator mechanisms in the investment function (decrease in parameter v without any offsetting increase in u or f). It is easy to check that demand is now less sensitive to productivity, i.e. that its slope is steeper in the usual (growth–productivity) diagram (Figure 27.4, step 2). But simultaneously, lesser accelerator effects induce lower productivity increases via the traditional capital–labour substitution mechanism. As a consequence, these shifts reinforce the impact of wage de-indexing: the economic system is stabilized but at the cost of a reduction in medium-term growth.

One last hypothesis about the technological system has to be added. Among the very contradictory trends observed in the last one or two decades, some observers stress that the flexibility–productivity trade-off

Figure 27.4   A first scenario: wage austerity and technical flexibility

Step 0: The crisis of the Fordist regime
Low growth and instability

Step 1: A significant de-indexing of wages
Slower growth, but possibly stable

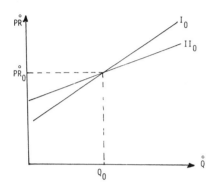

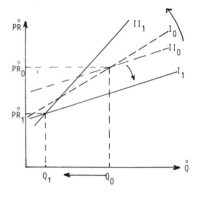

Hypotheses:

1. Low increasing returns and invest ment efficiency (d and b small)
2. Overindexing of wages to productivity ($k > 1 + l$)
3. A mix of profit and demand in investment (v and u average)

Changes:

2'. Subindexing of wages ($k < 1 + l$ and stability condition)

Step 3: Flexible specialization
Lower and stable growth

Step 2: More investment inertia
Still slower growth, but stable

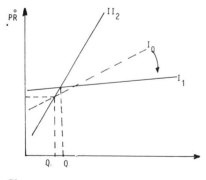

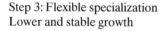

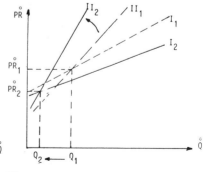

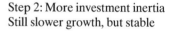

Changes:

2', 3' and 1': almost complete flattening of the law of return

Changes:

2' and 3': lesser accelerator effect (v is lower)

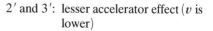

has been shifting towards methods to cope with variability, even at the cost of lower productivity increases. Hence, even if from a static point of view flexible equipment is superior to specialized machines, the cumulative improvement in technical efficiency is inferior. Impressed by Italian industrial organization, some authors have prognosticated a new industrial divide, far from Fordist mass production, towards a modernized and computerized variant of the Proudhonian logic (Piore and Sabel, 1985).

Taking into account that at an aggregate level and for mature industries the Kaldor–Verdoorn relation has broken down, one could expect the complete disappearance of increasing returns and a moderate exogenous increase in productivity near the trend observed in the 1980s. Consequently, the productivity relations would rotate clockwise and become horizontal. Here again, this shift has two opposite effects: lower, but stable growth (Figure 27.4, step 3).

This scenario roughly extrapolates some of the spontaneous developments of the present decade. The puzzling conclusion would be that a series of strategies of adaptation to the crisis might induce, at the macro-economic level, stability within stagnation, but without eliminating mass unemployment. This hint is linked indeed to a very specific model, and a crucial question remains open: what other mechanisms could counteract these disappointing tendencies?

A compromise about flexible automation and income distribution: difficult to reach, promising for employment and stability

At the core of this second scenario is a general hypothesis about the novelty of socio-technical trends observed during the last decade. The Fordist conception assumed a clear-cut distinction between productivity gains generation (originating in scientific management and specialized equipment) and their sharing via collective bargaining. Nowadays, in many instances, such a split is detrimental both to economic efficiency and workers' expectations, so that key bargaining—explicitly or more often implicitly—now revolves around know-how, motivations concerning productivity, and quality. Therefore a possible new compromise compatible with the present process of industrial restructuring would be more readily accepted if firms concentrated on defining new wage formation guidelines leading to a sharing of the benefits.

From the technological standpoint, the key issue is about the possible productivity regime associated with such a new New Deal. According to a rather widely accepted view, economies of scope would replace economies of scale and therefore increasing returns to scale would no longer be at the core of the competitive mechanism. Productivity trends would then be quite independent of growth, even if potentially large. Actually, a lot of evidence suggests a more balanced view. First, it can be shown that economies of scope might be complementary to economies of scale (Bailey and Friedlander, 1982), since the same inputs, equipment and know-how can be shared by various products. Second, a significant increase in final product variety can be obtained by combining different, highly standardized subparts; therefore differentiation and economies of scale can be jointly reaped. Third, detailed studies of experience curves show that the more recent goods (disc memory drives, digital watches, integrated circuits, MOS dynamic ram, etc.) are even more sensitive to such effects than typical Fordist goods (model-T Ford, steel production, etc.) (Ayres, 1985). Finally, such a diagnosis seems to be confirmed by a purely macroeconometric study of productivity regimes since 1973 (Boyer and Coriat, 1987). The industries in which demand is buoyant are experiencing very significant returns to scale (between 0.7 and 0.8).

Therefore a future upward shift of the productivity regime is likely to the extent that the new technological system is implemented in new industries and possibly some modern services. This would exert a positive influence upon medium-term rates of growth and productivity increase. Given an adequate elasticity of demand, this would promote a recovery of employment (Figure 27.5, step 1 compared with the initial equilibrium in step 0). It has to be noted that this tentative new virtuous circle presupposes that demand increases with productivity.

This feature is indeed crucial. Since demand characteristics matter even in the medium or long run, it is possible to design a capital–labour accords in order to satisfy two different objectives: speeding up growth, without generating structural instability. Given all other parameters of the economy and technology, productivity-sharing has to be bounded by two limits (Boyer and Coriat, 1987). In such a case, the configuration of the system is very favourable: industrial modernization and job creation might again be coherent (Figure 27.5, step 2). From a purely economic standpoint, the economic system is very close to the typical Fordist one (Figure 27.3, stage 3). Nevertheless, from a social and technological viewpoint, the outlook is quite different as regards work organization, the nature of products, and the structure of industrial relations and collective bargaining.

Concluding remarks

The present chapter has tentatively combined two lines of analysis: on the one hand, the 'régulation approach' which stresses the succession of various accumulation regimes, and, on the other, a renewal of a post-Keynesian theory of growth. In comparison to previous work, some steps have been made towards a better integration of macro modelling and historical analysis. First, a whole family of macro models has been proposed in order to substantiate the basic hints of Chapter 4. Second, the hypothesis of full employment, often made in the 1960s by post-Keynesians, is removed in order to deal with cases in which the labour force and employment are diverging. Third, the cumulative causation model proposed by

Figure 27.5 A second scenario: a cooperative approach to automation and income distribution

Step 0: The initial situation
Stability within stagnation

Step 1: A surge in increasing returns
More growth, and possibly employment

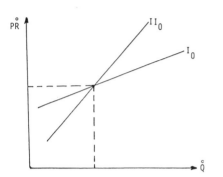

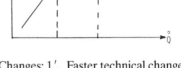

Hypotheses: same as Step 2, Scenario 1

Changes: 1'. Faster technical change (d higher, or a)

Step 2: An adequate productivity-sharing
A possible way out of the crisis

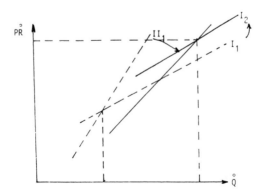

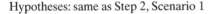

Changes: 2'. Higher share of productivity to wage earners (k high but such that $BD < 1$)

Kaldor (and especially the so-called Kaldor–Verdoorn equation) is analysed within a more detailed and precise framework, in order to explain possible structural shifts in the model. Fourth, special attention has been devoted to the consequences of the matching or mismatching between the technological regime and institutional conditions (Chapter 3).

Four major results emerge from the analysis:

1. One of the main features of the theory is its roots in the following question: how are productivity gains generated (via innovations, capital deepening, division of labour and extension of markets), and how are they shared between wages and profits, consumption and investment? The two major components of the model are thus productivity regimes and demand regimes.

2. Fordism, i.e. the simultaneous transformation of productive organization and lifestyle, appears as one very specific accumulation regime (intensive with mass consumption) within a whole family. At least eight regimes can be identified by varying structural parameters. The productivity regime can be intensive or extensive, according to the spillover effects between growth of the market, investment and productivity. Similarly, four demand regimes were found: pure classical, hybrid classical, Fordist, and hybrid Fordist, according to the relative importance of demand and profits in investment decisions and the nature of the wage formation process.

3. Further analysis shows that only some of these regimes are viable, i.e. they induce a stable growth path. The technological and industrial characteristics at the origin of the productivity regime have to be compatible with the income distribution mechanism (either competitive, 'monopolist' or 'Fordist') and demand generation (relative size of consumption and investment, profit or demand-led investment). Some subperiods of the nineteenth century and still more the post-Second World War long boom are examples of such a virtuous circle.

4. Conversely, structurally unstable systems might correspond to structural crises (for example, the 1929 crash) or depressions, sometimes called phase B in the Kondratiev waves literature. Therefore this is a possible reinterpretation of these findings. During the first period, the very success and deepening of a given accumulation regime induces a slow shift in structural parameters (upswing of phase A). But beyond some threshold (given by the condition of stability), the system becomes unstable, which leads to the crisis of the whole technological system and the institutional forms. According to this view, the way out of structural crisis would be neither automatic nor deterministic, but would depend upon innovations, social and political struggles, trials and errors, as well as chance.

Of course, all these findings are not definitive at all, since they rely upon a very specific macroeconomic model. Therefore further analysis is definitely needed. From an empirical standpoint, the stylized historical facts should be confronted with the results of very detailed studies. Similarly, the origins of the present crisis must be investigated again, in order to check whether this description fits the simulations of a full fledged macroeconomic model. From a theoretical point of view, the model of the economy should be opened to external trade and capital flows. Furthermore, a careful study of dynamic patterns (especially of long- and medium-term cycles) should be integrated into the analysis of growth trends.

References

Aglietta, M. (1974), 'Accumulation et régulation du capitalisme en longue période: exemple des États-Unis (1870–1970)', Thèse Paris I, Octobre.

Aglietta, M. and Brender, A. (1984), *Les Métamorphoses de la société salariale*, Paris, Calmann-Levy.

Aglietta, M. and Orléan, A. (1982), *La Violence de la monnaie*, Paris, P.U.F.

Artus, P. and Muet, P. A. (1984), 'Un panorama des développements récents de l'économétrie de l'investissement', *Revue Économique*, vol. 35, No. 5, Septembre.

Ayres, R. U. (1985), 'A Schumpeterian model of technological substitution', in *Technological Forecasting and Social Change*, vol. 27, Elsevier Science Publishing Company.

Bailey, E. and Friedlander, A. (1982), 'Market structure and multiproduct industries', *Journal of Economic Literature*, vol. XX, September, pp. 1024–48.

Bertrand, H. (1978), 'Une nouvelle approche de la croissance française de l'après-guerre: l'analyse en section productives', Statistiques et Études Financières, Série Orange, No. 35.

—— (1983), 'Accumulation, régulation, crise: un modèle sectionnel théorique et appliqué', *Revue Économique*, vol. 34, No. 6, Mars.

Billaudot, B. (1976), 'L'accumulation intensive du capital', Thèse Paris I.

Boyer R. (1975), 'Modalités de la régulation d'économies capitalistes dans la longue période: quelques formalisations simples', CEPREMAP, Juin, ronéo-typé.

—— (ed.) (1986a), *La Flexibilité du travail en Europe*, Paris, La Découverte.

—— (ed.) (1986b), *Capitalismes fin de siècle*, Paris, Presses Universitaires de France.

—— (1986c), *La Théorie de la régulation: une analyse critique*, Paris; La Découverte (American edition, Columbia University Press, 1988).

—— (1986d), 'Informatisation de la production et polyvalence...ou comment une flexibilité peut en cacher une autre', *Formation, Emploi*, No. 14, *La Documentation Française*, Avril–Juin.

—— (1987), 'Réflexions sur la crise actuelle', *Revue Française d'Économie*, No. 5, Mai.

Boyer, R. *et al.* (1987), 'Aspects de la crise', Rapport de Recherche CGP/ CEPREMAP No. 23–84, Réf, 4584/60-01, 3 Tomes, Février.

Boyer, R. and Coriat, B. (1987), 'Technical flexibility and macro stabilisation: some preliminary steps', *Ricerche Economiche*, No. 4, 1986.

Boyer, R. and Mistral, J. (1978), *Accumulation, inflation, crises*, Paris, P.U.F. (2ème edition, 1983).

Boyer, R. and Petit, P. (1981a), 'Employment and productivity in the EEC', *Cambridge Journal of Economics*, vol. 5.

—— (1981b), 'Forecasting the impact of technical change on employment: methodological reflections and proposals for research', in Diettrich and Morley (eds), *Relations Between Technology Capital and Labour*, Commission of European Communities EUR 8181 EN, pp. 49–69.

—— (1981c), 'Progrès technique, croissance et emploi: un modèle d'inspiration Kaldorienne pour six industries européenes', *Revue Économique*, vol. 32, pp. 1113–53.

—— (1984), 'Politiques industrielles et impact sur l'emploi: les pays européens face à la contrainte extériure', *Revue d'Économie Industrielle*, No. 27, Janvier.

Boyer, R. and Ralle, P. (1986a), 'Croissances nationales et contrainte extérieure avant et après 1973', *Economie et Société*, Cahiers de l'ISMEA, No. P29.

—— (1986b), 'L'insertion internationale conditionne-t-elle les formes nationales d'emploi? Convergences ou différenciations des pays européens', *Economie et Société*, Cahiers de l'ISMEA, No. P29, Janvier.

Bultel, J. (1983), 'Flexibilité de production et rentabilité des investissements: l'exemple de la robotisation de l'assemblage tôlerie en soudage par points', *Revue d'Économie Industrielle*, No. 26, 4ème trimestre.

Caussat, L. (1981), 'Croissance, emploi, productivité dans l'industrie américaine (1899–1976)', CEPREMAP, Septembre, mimeograph.

Fagerberg, J. (1984), 'The "régulation school" and the classics: modes of accumulation and modes of regulation in a classical model of economic growth', Couverture Orange CEPREMAP, No. 8426.

Kaldor, N. (1966), *Causes of the Slow Rate of Growth of the United Kingdom*, Cambridge, Cambridge University Press.

—— (1975), 'Economic growth and the Verdoorn law: a comment on R. Rowthorn's article, *Economic Journal*, vol. 85, pp. 891–6.

Kundig, B. (1984), 'Du taylorisme classique à la flexibilisation du système productif: l'impact macroéconomique des différents types d'organisation du travail', *Critiques de l'Économie Politique*, No. 26–27, Janvier–Juin.

Mitchl, Th. (1984), 'International comparison of productivity growth: Verdoorn's law revisited', Colgate University, Hamilton, NY, July, mimeograph.

Piore, M. and Sabel, Ch. (1985), *The Second Industrial Divide: Possibilities of Prosperity*, New York, Basic Books.

Rowthorn, R. (1975), 'What remains of Kaldor's law?', *Economic Journal*, vol. 85, pp. 10–15.

Part VIII Conclusion

28 Policy conclusions

Richard R. Nelson and Luc L. G. Soete

Columbia University, New York
MERIT, Faculty of Economics, State University of Limburg, Maastricht

This is a lengthy book, and a reprise should be kept very short. However, we feel it important to end with at least a few words regarding the implications of an evolutionary theory of technical advance for thinking about public policy. Not many, just a few.

From a traditional economic point of view science and technology policy will be guided by a set of relatively minimalistic questions such as: is there a case of market failure here or suboptimality in science or technological effort? Since Arrow's seminal contribution in this area some twenty-five years ago, there is general agreement that market failure is indeed one of the intrinsic characteristics in this area and that *under*investment in R & D will be the logical outcome of market allocation. The fact that technological advances can be readily copied will deter companies from investing in these, even though a significant advance would lead to enhanced efficiency or performance. Particularly, in cases where technological advances are not well protected by patents and easily copied, one can find plenty of examples of such R & D underinvestment. Before the advent of hybrid corn seeds, which cannot be reproduced by farmers, seed companies had little incentive to do R & D on new seeds, since the farmers, after buying a batch, simply could reproduce them themselves. The farmers themselves had little incentive to do such work since each was small and had limited opportunities to gain by having a better crop than a neighbour. Similarly, within an industry where scientists and engineers are mobile it is hard to keep secret for very long information about the broad operating characteristics of a particular generic design, or about the properties of certain materials. Such knowledge is not patentable and, if patentable, would be very hard to police.

On the other hand, and as the more recent contributions in the field of industrial economics (see e.g. Dasgupta and Stiglitz, 1980) have tended to emphasize imperfect market competition might also lead to *over* investment in R & D. There is virtually certain to be a clustering of effort verging on duplication, on alternatives widely regarded as promising, and often a neglect of long shots that from society's point of view ought to be explored as a hedge. The premium placed on achieving an invention first, so as to get a patent or at least a headstart, may lead to undue haste and waste and duplication of effort.

It is tempting to regard these kinds of 'market failures' as providing both justification and guidance for governmental actions to complement, substitute for or guide private initiatives. At the least their recognition guards against the simplistic position that the R & D allocation is in any sense 'optimal'. However, such propositions about where and how market forces work poorly will not carry the policy discussion very far.

Indeed, in practice these arguments have led to the justification for active government support policies in the science and technology field, with government support for R & D investment as the (only) central issue at stake. Big national and international R & D projects financed and planned directly by the state have thus become some of the most dramatic illustrations of 'government failure'. Elsewhere, one of us (Nelson, 1982, 1984 and 1987) has discussed in detail the conditions under which this is more or less likely to occur. The complexity and subtlety of the problems involved suggest that general principles and propositions about the appropriate roles and relative merits of governmental and private activity in the field of R & D policy will neither describe the experience accurately nor provide much normative guidance.

From these couple of comments it will be clear that in our view and in line with the other chapters in this book orthodox economic theory will be of little help in recommending reasonable policies in the field of science and technology. As Nelson and Winter put it: 'Orthodox theory cannot adequately provide that analysis and understanding because it is an ahistorical world in which genuine novelties do not arise.' (Nelson and Winter, 1982, p. 413.)

The 'anatomy of market failure' discussion in neo-classical economics is indeed focused on equilibrium conditions of stylised market systems. What the chapters in this book suggest, in line with evolutionary thinking, is that such a discussion should properly focus on problems of dealing with and adjusting to change. It involves in the first instance abandonment of the traditional normative goal of trying to define an 'optimum' and the institutional structure that will achieve it, and an acceptance of the more modest objectives of identifying problems and possible improvements. In part it also represents a more general acknowledgement that notions like 'market failure' cannot carry policy analysis very far, because market failure is ubiquitous.

Common to the theoretical approaches sketched out in the various chapters in this book is an understanding of the process of technical change, as being truly evolutionary in nature. Such evolutionary processes particularly with regard to technical change, will be inherently wasteful, at least with the vision of hindsight. There is, for example, as already mentioned in our previous discussion on 'market failure', bound to be duplication or near duplication of effort. Economies of scale and scope that might be achieved through coordination will be missed. Certain kinds of scientific or technological research that would have high social value simply may not be done because they would not yield proprietary advantage, or because no one is minding the overall portfolio. To the extent that technology is proprietary, many enterprises might be operating inefficiently, even failing at a considerable social cost, for want of access to best technology.

Within such an evolutionary approach, policies with regard to technological change encompass not just R & D, but the whole spectrum of scientific and technological activities from invention to diffusion, from basic research to technological mastery. As a paranthesis, and reiterating the point made in many of the chapters in this book, such a view of technological change rejects also the orthodox economics definition of technological capabilities in terms of 'knowledge' or 'information' with the connotation that industrial technology is like a recipe; understood by particular individuals and readily articulatable and communicable from one individual to another with the requisite background training. From our perspective, what is written down—the recipe, the textbook discussion, the patent—provides a start, but only in the sense that a recipe provides a start. Knowing how to produce a product, is as much experienced tacit skill as articulatable knowledge. And contrary to the implicit general theory the tacit skills of one 'skilled in the art' are not interchangeable: who works with the recipe makes a difference.

At a more general level, such a view points to the importance of the technical as well as social integration of technological change: within firms as much as within society at large. The implicit idea in the orthodox economics view of technology that what one firm can do, others firms can do too, if they had access to the relevant 'information', is not only rejected but replaced by the fundamental question about what determines the kinds of technological capabilities firms get under control and how these capabilities do evolve over time. Similar questions as illustrated in the chapters in Sections V and VI can be raised at the country level.

In other words, the recognition that the creation of technological capabilities involves an evolutionary, endogenous process of change, negotiated and 'mediated' with society at large, implies that policies in the area of science and technology will not, nor should be limited to questions about the economic 'integration' of technological change, but will include all aspects of the broader societal 'integration' of such change. Indeed it will be the broad societal context: including economic, but also social and ethical factors which will set the conditions within which technological change will be adapted, even selected.

From the dynamic, evolutionary perspective presented in this book, the long-term implications of technical change, the 'externalities' of orthodox economics, will not be susceptible to definitive once and for all categorisation and are intimately related to particular historical and institutional contexts. To a large extent, the problems involved are aspects of economic change. The processes of change are continually tossing up new 'externalities' that must be dealt with in some manner or other. In a regime in which technical advance is occurring and organizational structure is evolving in response to changing patterns of demand and supply, new nonmarket interactions that are not contained adequately by prevailing laws and policies are almost certain to appear, and old ones may disappear. Long-lasting chemical insecticides were not a problem eighty years ago. Horse manure polluted the cities but automotive emissions did not. The canonical 'externality' problem of evolutionary theory is the generation by new technologies of benefits and costs that old institutional structures ignore.

From such a perspective the concept of a 'social optimum' disappears. Occupying a central place in the policy analysis are now the notions that society ought to be engaging in experimentation and that the information and feedback from that experimentation will be of central concern in guiding the evolution of the economic system.

The array of present policy debates about some of the long-term, *inter-national* 'externalities' of change, and technological change in particular, in terms of impact on the physical global environment (air, land and water pollution), or even in terms of impact on society's future genetic capital (genetic manipulation, pre-embryo research), or on privacy, cry out for such a new technology 'assessment' and institutional experimentation in the field of science and technology. Confronted with rapid scientific and technological change, governments are today faced with a major challenge. How to assume the State's function as social 'regulator' of technical change in a period of deregulation 'destruction *tout-court*', aimed itself at stimulat-ing further innovation. As Jean-Jacques Salomon puts it: 'Si les moeurs précèdent la loi, comme disait Montesquieu, le changement technique précède les moeurs et la loi' (Salomon, 1987). In a period in urgent need of a new regulatory framework, it will be tempting to equate the need for 'less State', with the notion of 'technological laissez-faire'.

But, in our view, that would be a serious mistake. The argument that it is important to keep on experimenting, and that private enterprise is a powerful mechanism for doing that, by no means implies that what private parties find profitable to do necessarily should be accepted by society. There is an essential governmental role in monitoring as well as encourag-ing innovation. While fears of an Andromeda strain perhaps are exag-gerated, experience with nuclear power should warn that new technology is not always benign. It is not yet clear what is happening to the world's ozone, but it is clear that it is important to be attending to that matter and to be prepared to marshall the forces that only governments can to deal with the problem.

The ozone problem signals that the issues raised by new technology not only require government regulation, but challenge the current system of national governments and only limited means of world governance. The ozone issue, may, or may not, come to equal or dwarf the problems of arms control. At a less dramatic but more insidious level, there are the world-wide issues created by the new information systems. It is not clear that humankind currently has the governing strategies to deal with these adequately.

In this volume several authors, but especially Carlota Perez and Chris-topher Freeman, have proposed that we are entering a new era with a drastically different operative economic-technological paradigm. Not all of the authors of this book would put the matter as sharply. But all would agree that there are important new things going on and to be monitoring. Let the exploration go on. Let it be urged and supported. But new government structures and public laws will be needed to support the valuable of the new, and to constrain the pernicious.

References

Dasgupta, P. and Stiglitz, J. (1980), 'Industrial structure and the nature of innovative activity', *Economic Journal*, vol. 90, pp. 266–93.

Nelson, R.R. (ed.), (1982), *Government and Technical Progress: A Cross Industry Analysis*, New York, Pergamon Press.

Nelson, R.R. (1984), *High Technology Policies: A Five Nation Comparison*, Washington, DC. American Enterprise Institute.

Nelson, R.R. (1987), *Understanding Technical Change as an Evolutionary Process* (de Vries Lectures in Economics, Vol. 8), Amsterdam, North Holland.

Nelson, R.R. and Winter, S.G. (1982), *An Evolutionary Theory of Economic Change*, Boston, Mass., The Belknap Press of Harvard University Press.

Salomon, J.-J. (1987), 'Implications sociales des nouvelles technologies', OECD, SME, Paris, mimeo.

Index